The Official History of North Sea Oil and Gas

Written by the leading expert in UK petroleum economics, Volume I of this UK Government Official History provides a new, unique, in-depth analysis of the development of British policies towards the North Sea oil and gas industry from the early 1960s to the early 1980s.

Drawing on full access to the UK Government's relevant archives, Alex Kemp examines the thinking behind the initial legislation in 1964, the early licensing arrangements, and the events leading up to the boundary delimitation agreements with Norway and other adjacent North Sea countries. He explains the debate in the later 1960s about the appropriate role of the state in the exploitation of the gas and oil resources, the prolonged negotiations resulting in the early long-term gas contracts, and the continuing debate on the role of the state following the large oil discoveries in the first half of the 1970s, resulting in the formation of the BNOC (British National Oil Corporation). The debate leading up to the introduction of, and subsequent increase in, the Petroleum Revenue Tax is fully explained, as is the introduction of Supplementary Petroleum Duty. The author also outlines the debates around interventionist depletion policies and how the oil revenues should best be utilised.

The Official History of North Sea Oil and Gas will be of much interest to students of North Sea oil and gas, energy economics, business history and British politics, as well as to petroleum professionals and policy-makers.

Alex Kemp is Professor of Petroleum Economics and Director, Aberdeen Centre for Research in Energy Economics and Finance (ACREEF) at the University of Aberdeen. He has published widely on the licensing and taxation aspects of the relationship between the oil companies and Governments, with particular reference to the North Sea. From 1993 to 2003 Professor Kemp was a member of the Energy Advisory Panel to the DTI. He has also advised many other Governments, companies, and the World Bank on petroleum licensing and taxation. In 2006 he was awarded the OBE for services to the oil and gas sector.

Whitehall histories: government official history series
ISSN: 1474-8398

The Government Official History series began in 1919 with wartime histories, and the peacetime series was inaugurated in 1966 by Harold Wilson. The aim of the series is to produce major histories in their own right, compiled by historians eminent in the field, who are afforded free access to all relevant material in the official archives. The Histories also provide a trusted secondary source for other historians and researchers while the official records are not in the public domain. The main criteria for selection of topics are that the histories should record important episodes or themes of British history while the official records can still be supplemented by the recollections of key players; and that they should be of general interest, and, preferably, involve the records of more than one government department.

The United Kingdom and the European Community:
Vol. I: The Rise and Fall of a National Strategy, 1945–1963
Alan S. Milward

Secret Flotillas
Vol. I: Clandestine Sea Operations to Brittany, 1940–1944
Vol. II: Clandestine Sea Operations in the Mediterranean,
North Africa and the Adriatic, 1940–1944
Sir Brooks Richards

SOE in France
M. R. D. Foot

The Official History of the Falklands Campaign:
Vol. I: The Origins of the Falklands War
Vol. II: War and Diplomacy
Sir Lawrence Freedman

The Official History of Britain and the Channel Tunnel
Terry Gourvish

Churchill's Mystery Man: Desmond Morton and the World of Intelligence
Gill Bennett

The Official History of Privatisation
Vol. I: The Formative Years 1970–1987
David Parker

Secrecy and the Media: The Official History of the D-Notice System
Nicholas Wilkinson

The Official History of the Civil Service: Reforming the Civil Service
Vol. I: The Fulton Years, 1966–1981
Rodney Lowe

The Official History of North Sea Oil and Gas
Vol. I: The Growing Dominance of the State
Vol. II: Moderating the State's Role
Alex Kemp

The Official History of North Sea Oil and Gas

Vol. I: The Growing Dominance of the State

Alex Kemp

Routledge
Taylor & Francis Group

LONDON AND NEW YORK

First published 2012
by Routledge
2 Park Square, Milton Park, Abingdon, Oxon OX14 4RN

Simultaneously published in the USA and Canada
by Routledge
711 Third Avenue, New York, NY 10017

Routledge is an imprint of the Taylor & Francis Group, an informa business

British Library Cataloguing in Publication Data
A catalogue record for this book is available from the British Library

Library of Congress Cataloging in Publication Data
A catalog record has been requested for this book

ISBN: 978-0-415-44754-6 (hbk)
ISBN: 978-0-203-80624-1 (ebk)

Typeset in Baskerville
by RefineCatch Limited, Bungay, Suffolk

Printed and bound in Great Britain by
TJ International Ltd, Padstow, Cornwall

Contents

Abbreviations and acronyms

ACAS	Advisory, Conciliation and Arbitration Service
AFRA	Average Freight Rate Assessment
AMA	Amalgamated Engineering Union
API	American Petroleum Institute
APRT	Advance Petroleum Revenue Tax
ASTMS	Association of Scientific, Technology and Managerial Staff
bcf/d	billion cubic feet per day
b/d	barrels a day
BGC	British Gas Corporation
BGS	British Geological Survey
BET	Blow-out Emergency Team
BMP	British Marine Pipelines Ltd (subsidiary of GGP)
BODL	Burmah Oil Development Ltd
BONSL	Burmah Oil North Sea Ltd
BOSVA	British Support Vessels Association
BP	British Petroleum
BPEO	Best Practicable Environmental Option
BRINDEX	Association of British Independent Oil Companies
BRIT	British Indigenous Technology Group
BSC	British Steel Corporation
BSJC	British Seafarers Joint Council
CAA	Civil Aviation Authority
CATS	Central Area Transmission System
CBI	Confederation of British Industry
CEGB	Central Electricity Generating Board
c.i.f.	cost, insurance and freight
COFACE	Compagnie Francaise d'Assurance pour le Commerce Exterieur
COP	Cessation of Production
COSLA	Convention of Scottish Local Authorities
CPCG	Central Pollution Control Group
CPRS	Central Policy Review Staff
CRINE	Cost Reduction Initiative for the New Era
CRISTAL	Contract Regarding an Interim Supplement to Tanker Liability for Oil Pollution

CSO	Central Statistical Office
DAFS	Department of Agriculture and Fisheries for Scotland
DGIV	Competition Directorate of European Commission
DEN	Department of Energy
DOE	Department of Employment
DOI	Department of Industry
DTI	Department of Trade and Industry
dwt	deadweight tonnage
EADU	Exploration, Appraisal and Development Unit (DEN)
EC	European Community
ECGD	Export Credit Guarantee Department
EEC	European Economic Community
EEPTU	Electrical, Electronic, Telecommunications and Plumbing Union
EFL	External Financing Limit
EIA	Environmental Impact Assessment
EOR	Enhanced Oil Recovery
E & P Forum	Oil Industry International Exploration and Production Forum
EPC	Economic Policy Committee
EQO	Environmental Quality Objectives
ESDs	energy shut down valves
ETUC	The European Trade Union Confederation
FAA	Federal Aviation Administration
FCO	Foreign and Commonwealth Office
f.o.b.	free on board
FFO	Full and Fair Opportunity
FRC	Fast Rescue Craft
GDP	Gross Domestic Product
GGP	Gas Gathering Pipeline
GMB	General, Municipal and Boilermakers Union
GNP	Gross National Product
GRT	Gross Register Tonnage
GVA	gross value added
HSC	Health and Safety Commission
HSE	Health and Safety Executive
ICMS	Inter-Departmental Committee on Marine Safety
ICTA	Income and Corporation Taxes Act
IDE	Industrial Development Executive
IDS	Industry Department for Scotland
IEA	International Energy Agency
IGS	Institute of Geological Sciences
IMCO	Intergovernmental Maritime Consultative Organisation (later IMO)
IMO	International Maritime Organisation
IRGS	Interest Relief Grant Scheme

IMEG	International Management and Engineering Group of Great Britain
IP	Institute of Petroleum
IPE	International Petroleum Exchange
IR	Inland Revenue
IRR	Internal Rate of Return
IRS	(US) Internal Revenue Service
IUOOC	Inter-Union Offshore Oil Committee
JOA	Joint Operation Agreement
LNG	Liquified Natural Gas
LPG	Liquified Petroleum Gas
MAFF	Ministry of Agriculture, Fisheries and Food
MMC	Monopolies and Mergers Commission
mmboe	million barrels of oil equivalent
mmcf/d	million cubic feet per day
mw	megawatts
MOD	Ministry of Defence
MPCU	Marine Pollution Control Unit
MTFS	Medium Term Financial Strategy
NCB	National Coal Board
NCC	Nature Conservancy Council
NEC	(Labour Party) National Executive Committee
NERC	National Environment Research Council
NESDA	North East of Scotland Development Authority
NGLs	Natural Gas Liquids
NHC	National Hydrocarbons Corporation
NLF	National Loans Fund
NOA	National Oil Account
NEB	National Enterprise Board
NEDO	National Economic Development Office
NOSHEB	North of Scotland Hydro Electric Board
NSRC	North Sea Oil Renegotiation Committee
NTS	National Transmission System
NPV	Net Present Value
NSOCN	North Sea Operators Committee Norway
NUS	National Union of Seamen
OCC	Offshore Contractors' Council
OETB	Offshore Energy Technology Board
OFGAS	Office of Gas Supply
OFGEM	Office of Gas and Electricity Markets
OFT	Office of Fair Trading
OIAC	Oil Industry Advisory Committee
OILCO	Oil Industry Liaison Committee
OIM	Offshore Installation Manager
OPA	Oil and Pipelines Agency

OPOL	Offshore Pollution Liability Association
OSCP	Oil Spill Contingency Plan
OSO	Offshore Supplies Office
OTO	Oil Taxation Office
OVB	Oil Valuation Board
PCBs	polychlorinated biphenyls
PED	Petroleum Engineering Division (of DEN)
PESC	Public Expenditure Survey Committee
PIDs	Perimeter Detection Systems
PPI	Producer Price Index
ppm	milligrammes of oil per litre of discharged water
PRT	Petroleum Revenue Tax
PSA	Property Services Agency
PSBR	Public Sector Borrowing Requirement
PSIB	Petroleum Supplies Industry Board
PSP (Act)	Petroleum and Submarine Pipelines (Act)
RGC	Redpath, Dorman Long and de Groof (joint venture)
RSPB	Royal Society for the Protection of Birds
SAGE	Scottish Area Gas Evacuation Scheme
SDD	Scottish Development Department
SEPD	Scottish Economic Planning Department
SMRE	Safety in Mines Research Establishment
SMTRB	The Ship and Marine Technology Requirements Board
SOAFD	Scottish Office Agriculture and Fisheries Department
SPD	Supplementary Petroleum Duty
SPEKPs	Super Priority Economic Key points
tcf	trillion cubic feet (of gas)
TGWU	Transport and General Workers' Union
TLP	Tension Leg Platform
TOVALOP	Tanker Owners Voluntary Agreement Concerning Liability for Oil Pollution
TRA	Tariff Receipts Allowance (PRT)
TUC	Trades Union Congress
UCS	Upper Clyde Shipbuilders
UES	Uniform Emissions Standards
UIE	L'Union Industrielle et d'Enterprise
UKOOA	United Kingdom Offshore Operators Association
UKCS	United Kingdom Continental Shelf
UKOITC	United Kingdom Oil Industry Taxation Committee
WGDP	Inter-departmental Working Group on Depletion Policy

Preface

The discovery and exploitation of North Sea oil and gas has arguably been one of the most important episodes in the post-Second World War economic history of the UK. It produced major national direct and indirect benefits, involving at its peak in 1984 a direct contribution of nearly 7% to UK gross value-added. The benefits to the balance of payments and the national budget were also very large, with the contribution to the UK Exchequer being £12 billion at its peak in 1984[1] (£28 billion at 2008 prices). The contribution to the nation's investment has also been remarkable. Thus in 1976 investment in the UKCS was the equivalent of 33% of all UK investment in the manufacturing sector. In that year expenditure on exploration, appraisal and field developments amounted to £13 billion at 2008 prices. In 1991 total expenditure in the UK Continental Shelf (UKCS) reached an all-time peak of £16 billion at 2008 prices.

The fruits of the investment were a remarkable increase in oil production from a tiny base in 1975 to around 2.6 million barrels per day in 1985. This was a remarkable achievement in any circumstances but in the challenging operating environment of the North Sea it was doubly remarkable. New technologies had to be developed to facilitate production in the Central and Northern Waters, and, while at the time frustrations were sometimes expressed at the delays in achieving first production in a field, the more mature assessment is to highlight and acknowledge the technological achievements.

The subject matter of this Official History is primarily a detailed discussion of British Government oil and gas policies relating to the UKCS from the early 1960s to the early 1990s. Thus it does not cover in any detail the many other facets of the discovery and exploitation of the oil and gas, including the technological and human achievements which have clearly been memorable. Rather, the study seeks to explain the evolution of and debates surrounding all the relevant Government policies and to assess them. Thus detailed attention is given to the debates within Government and with outside bodies which generally preceded decisions across a range of policies. To undertake the study, full access was given to the files of all the relevant Government Departments covering the period. These proved to be very voluminous, but, in spite of this, occasional gaps were found which put constraints on the comprehensive coverage of the study.[2]

The specific subject areas covered are all those felt to be important from a policy viewpoint. Thus attention is given to the development of the initial primary legislation in 1964, the boundary delimitation agreements with the neighbouring North Sea countries, and all the licensing rounds up to the Fourteenth Round. The early gas contracts in the 1960s are examined in depth because of their importance to UK gas supplies for many subsequent years. The North Sea taxation system had major consequences for licensees, Government, and the nation at large, and thus detailed attention is given to the thinking behind the initial 1975 package and the many subsequent changes. Direct state involvement in oil and gas exploitation has been both common and controversial in many countries around the world, and the experience of the UK exhibits strong support for and against the notion of a state oil company. The history highlights the thinking behind the decisions to introduce a state oil company and the subsequent decision to privatise both state oil and gas companies.

Depletion policy occupied much attention of policy-makers in the 1970s in particular, but, despite the development of detailed instruments for implementing an interventionist policy, little intervention actually occurred. The development of thinking on oil and gas depletion including the role of British Gas Corporation (BGC), is examined in some detail. This subject also relates to the question of the utilisation of the benefits from hydrocarbon depletion. While the eventual decision was essentially to employ the revenues as part of general macroeconomic policy and to treat oil revenues as being conceptually no different from those from income tax or VAT, consideration was given to the idea of an Oil Fund to regenerate the less developed areas of the UK where unemployment was high. The role of an Oil Fund as an instrument to produce sustainable income and inter-generational equity from the depletion of the reserves as part of the nation's capital stock deserved more attention than it received.

The response of British industry to the North Sea oil opportunity has generally been recognised as mixed. The Government through the Offshore Supplies Office (OSO) devoted substantial resources to cajole the operators to give every opportunity to British suppliers, and the OSO also directly made British industry aware of these opportunities. While their efforts increased the UK content, the response could have been stronger. Health, safety, and environmental policies probably did not receive the priority they deserved in early legislation and regulations, and some of the later effort in these areas had to deal with problems which had already arisen. In the safety area in particular the design of appropriate policies has tended to be reactive and insufficiently proactive.

In writing this history I have had the benefit of discussions with many who have played substantial personal roles in the development of North Sea oil and gas. These include several former Ministers with responsibilities for the sector and many retired senior civil servants who were intimately involved in the policy-making process. I have also benefited from discussions with many retired senior oil industry executives who had close involvement with the development of the North Sea industry. The list is long and I hope that they will be content with my private thanks. The history project was sponsored by the Cabinet Office and I would like to thank Mrs Tessa Stirling, then Head of the Histories, Openness and Records Unit for her continuous support and encouragement throughout the long life of this project. Miss Sally Falk, Mr Chris Grindall and Mr Richard Ponman, also of the Cabinet Office, were all extremely helpful in the practicalities of facilitating access to the many files necessary for the study. Dr John Jenkins was for some time my researcher on the project, and I am very grateful for his diligence, and in particular his extensive contributions to the chapters on the onshore impact and safety. Mr David Tookey, retired archivist of the Department of Trade and Industry (DTI), was very helpful in (successfully) searching for many elusive files in the Department of Energy (DEN)/DTI archives. I am also grateful to the members of the Project Board for their constructive comments on an early draft of the study. I owe a particular debt to Mr John Evans, formerly of the Inland Revenue, for most meticulously undertaking the work of copy editor. In addition to performing those duties he gave me insights into a number of complex topics which resulted in a distinct improvement to the text.

Alex Kemp
University of Aberdeen

1 Initial legislation and licensing

Interest in the possibility that the North Sea might contain oil and gas was triggered by the discovery of the huge Groningen gas field in the Netherlands at the end of May 1959. This turned out to be one of the world's largest gas fields. It led to consideration of the possibility that gas deposits could extend into the North Sea. Several oil companies started seismic work in the North Sea soon after the Groningen discovery. Shell commenced seismic work off the British coast in 1961. Outside territorial waters no rights regarding petroleum were then available to the littoral states. They had no powers to regulate the activities of oil companies in what constituted the high seas.

Law of the Sea Conference, 1958

Steps had already been taken towards the designation of mineral rights to individual states with respect to their continental shelves. The International Conference on the Law of the Sea was held in Geneva from 24th February to 27th April 1958 under the auspices of the United Nations. At this major event five main committees were created dealing with (1) the Territorial Sea and the Contiguous Zone, (2) The General Régime of the High Seas, (3) The High Seas Fisheries and Conservation of the Living Resources of the High Seas, (4) The Continental Shelf, and (5) The Question of Access to the Sea by Land-Locked States.

The general purpose of the Conference was to examine all main issues relating to the Law of the Sea. Agreement was reached on the first four of the subjects noted above.[1] The results were incorporated in four Conventions. The Convention on the Continental Shelf is central to the present study.

The Convention contains 15 Articles. Article 1 defines the term continental shelf to refer "(a) to the seabed and subsoil of the submarine areas adjacent to the coast but outside the area of the territorial sea, to a depth of 200 metres or, beyond that limit, to where the depth of the superjacent waters admits of the exploitation of the natural resources of the said areas; (b) to the seabed and subsoil of similar submarine areas adjacent to the coasts of islands".[2] This article contains ambiguities which turned out later to be very important. Interestingly, the UK Government was well aware of the important ones at the time. In its Report to Parliament the Foreign Office pointed out that "it is uncertain whether all submarine areas adjacent to the coast which are capable of exploitation are covered by the definition, e.g. where there is, adjacent to the coast, a length of water of a depth greater than 200 metres before a shallower depth is reached".[3] This issue is directly relevant to the question of the delimitation of the boundary between the UK and Norway, a subject which achieved major importance when discoveries were later made.

Article 2(1) of the Convention states that "the coast State exercises over the continental shelf sovereign rights for the purpose of exploring and exploiting its natural resources".[4] In its Report to Parliament at the time the Foreign Office stated that "the Convention does not state that the coastal State has "sovereignty" over the continental shelf: the concept of full sovereignty over the continental shelf outside territorial waters was considered to be inconsistent with the concept of the legal status of the superjacent waters as high seas and that of the air space above these waters".[5]

This subject also subsequently became important when the question of ownership of the petroleum became a live issue. In 1958 the UK Government was clear that the Convention on the Continental Shelf did not confer full sovereignty over its designated areas. Its powers were limited to those provided for in the Convention.

Article 6(1) and 6(2) state that "where the same continental shelf is adjacent to the territories of two or more States whose coasts are opposite each other, the boundary shall be determined by agreement between them. In the absence of agreement, and unless another boundary line is justified by special circumstances, the boundary is the median line, every point of which is equidistant from the nearest points of the baselines from which the breadth of the territorial sea of each state is increased".[6] In commenting on this article at the time the Foreign Office reported that the UK delegation attempted to ensure that more prominence was given to the principle of the median line as the starting point for any delimitation of the boundary of the Continental Shelf.[7] The thinking of the Government on this issue which was later to assume so much importance was clearly revealed in 1958.

In exercising its rights regarding the exploitation of minerals the coastal states were constrained by other provisions under the Convention. Article 5 declares that such exploitation must not result in any unjustifiable interference with navigation, fishing or the conservation of the living resources of the sea or other scientific research being carried out. Coastal states were given powers to construct and maintain installations for exploration and production purposes, but they had to take steps to establish safety zones around these installations. These could extend to a distance of 500 metres around each installation. There was an obligation to provide permanent warning of the presence of the installation to other mariners. Within the safety zones the coastal state had to take measures to protect the living resources of the sea from harmful agents associated with the exploitation of the natural resources. Article 5 also provided that installations should not be installed where they would cause interference with recognised sea-lanes essential to international navigation. A further obligation was to remove (in their entirety) installations which became abandoned or disused. All of these provisions subsequently became highly important as exploration and exploitation proceeded.

The Convention on Fishing and Conservation of the Living Resources of the High Seas also contained measures which became important as the prospect of natural resource exploitation turned to reality. States which became parties to the Convention were required to introduce legislation covering several issues of direct relevance to oil and gas exploitation. Thus measures were required which prevented pollution of the seas by the discharge of oil from ships or pipelines or resulting directly from exploitation of the seabed and subsoil. Measures were also required to prevent pollution arising from the dumping of radioactive waste. Yet further requirements were measures to penalise wilful or negligent damage by national flagships to submarine cables and pipelines. Measures were also required to ensure that owners of ships who sacrificed their gear in order to avoid damaging a submarine cable or pipeline would be indemnified by the owners of these cables or pipelines.

Response to UK Government

It was incumbent on individual governments to enact legislation to give effect to the Conventions. The UK Government was under some pressure to do this. Following the Groningen discovery in 1959 oil companies had expressed interest in exploration in the North Sea. In that year Shell inquired about the possibility of obtaining an exploration licence from the Ministry of Power. In the absence of legislation it was not possible to award any licences outside territorial waters. The company asked whether, in the absence of comprehensive legislation, including boundary agreements with neighbouring countries, it would be possible to extend the Petroleum (Production) Act, 1934 to areas of the North Sea which would clearly fall within the jurisdiction of the British Government. The company was disappointed on being told that there was a prospect of a two-year delay before comprehensive legislation could be introduced. The view of Legal Branch of the Ministry of Power was that licences could not be issued before general legislation was enacted. Legal Branch acknowledged that it was arguable that a company could engage in exploration drilling in the Continental Shelf so long as international legal requirements to comply with safety of navigation and related subjects were observed.

The Ministry certainly did not wish to encourage such activities in the absence of legislation, and other companies including BP and Esso were so informed. The latter company submitted a formal request for a prospecting licence in August 1961. Another company expressing interest was the Natural Gas Development and Transportation Company which inquired about the possibility of obtaining a licence covering the Dogger Bank area. The request was accompanied by a legal opinion prepared by Professor C. H. M. Waldoch of All Souls College, Oxford. This indicated that the Dogger Bank (and the Goodwin Sands in which interest was also expressed) would fall within the UK Continental Shelf (UKCS). The opinion further stated that, if measures were taken to ensure safety of navigation and the protection of living resources, there did not appear to be a bar to the exploitation of mineral resources.

Following consultation with the Foreign Office, the Ministry of Power replied to the Natural Gas Development and Transportation Company emphasising that, in the absence of legislation, the UK Government had no power to grant licences for areas which would fall within the British side of the median line. The company was also informed that the UK Government would be embarrassed if one of their nationals began operations in such an area in anticipation of legislation, and that the operator in question could have no assurance that the work which he had undertaken in advance of legislation would give him any preferential right to a concession when such legislation had been enacted.

Preparation of Continental Shelf Bill

In early 1961 the Foreign Office included in its list of proposed legislation for 1961/62 a Bill to give effect to the 1958 Convention. Meetings were arranged between the interested Departments. Following these it was agreed that, as the Ministry of Power had the dominant interest, it should coordinate the work and promote a Bill. At that time the Petroleum Division was heavily engaged in the preparation of the Pipelines Bill, but there was felt to be no immediate urgency for legislation. This was because the Convention required ratification or accession by 22 of the signatory states. In 1961 only 5 signatories had ratified.

In April 1962, the Future Legislation Committee asked the Minister of Power to examine the possibility of combining within a single Bill the proposed separate Bills on the Conventions of the Continental Shelf and High Seas. The Minister replied that this could be done expeditiously if the perceived difficult issues of the extension to the UKCS of a system of civil and criminal law could be left out and dealt with at a later date. The Leader of the House then indicated that there was no prospect of including a combined Bill in the 1962/63 session. He also argued that the law and order issues should be included in a combined Bill. Other Ministers, including the Lord Chancellor and Foreign Secretary, supported the view that the Bill should be comprehensive in character.

At June 1962, 13 signatories to the Continental Shelf Convention had ratified it. The Foreign Office was now pressing for legislation to be introduced. By this time four oil companies and the Gas Council were conducting seismic operations outside territorial waters. They were keen to obtain exclusive licences which would enable them to undertake the more expensive exploration drilling work, and, in the event of success, the vastly more expensive field development. The Minister of Power asked his officials to consider whether it would be possible to issue licences in the absence of legislation ratifying the conventions. The advice was that this was not possible. The Leader of the House remained opposed to the introduction of a short Bill which excluded provision for law and order. The Ministry then prepared a paper setting out the policy issues, and in the autumn of 1962 sent it to the Home Affairs Committee with the request that approval be given for the preparation of a Bill to give effect to the relevant articles of the Conventions. The Home Affairs Committee approved the proposals in November 1962. The Minister then obtained authority to employ Parliamentary Counsel with a view to introducing a Bill in the early part of the 1963/64 Session.

Detailed preparatory work

While the pressures on Parliamentary time delayed the introduction of legislation serious preparatory work had actually started in 1961. The Ministry of Power managed and coordinated work on the detailed provisions of the Bill which involved over 20 Government Departments. While the legislation had to cover a very wide range of detailed issues there were essentially only 3 key policy objectives. These were (1) the provision of the legal framework for the exploration and exploitation of natural resources in the UKCS as defined in the Convention, (2) the provision in law for obligations and prohibitions as stipulated in the Convention, and (3) the provision of law and order on the UKCS in relation to the exercise of the rights conferred by the Convention. The Ministry of Power was involved in all the issues to a greater or less extent.

At an early stage in discussions on the Bill a basic legal problem was encountered, the resolution of which required the opinion of the Law Officers. The subject was the extent to which the UK could exercise control outside territorial waters, with the key question being the interpretation of the term "sovereign rights" employed in the Convention on the Continental Shelf. Both the Ministry of Power and the Foreign Office interpreted the Convention as limiting the exercise of sovereignty to those areas specifically discussed in the Convention. Other bodies which were consulted (such as the National Coal Board and the Crown Estates Office) thought that there was nothing in the Convention which prevented the UK from exercising full sovereignty over the continental shelf relating to the UK.

The issue was thus referred to the Law Officers. Their legal advice was that the UK Government should enact legislation on the assumption that the Convention did not confer the right to exercise full sovereignty over its Continental Shelf. This meant that the Bill would have to incorporate provisions for the extension of the relevant elements of statute and common law to the Continental Shelf over which the UK was proposing to exercise sovereign rights.

The Law Officers were also asked to give their legal advice on the question of whether the limited rights to explore for and exploit natural resources emanated from the Convention, or whether the Convention was merely making a declaration of rights which already existed, and which could have been proclaimed and exercised by the UK Government at any time. Legal advice was that the rights were not necessarily dependent on the Convention. The drafters of the Bill reflected this view by not referring to the Convention either in the Long Title or within the actual content of the Bill.

The Law Officers were also asked to give legal advice on the question of whether, if the UK became entitled to exercise sovereign rights under the Convention, the relevant Continental Shelf would become part of Great Britain for purposes of the Coal Industry Nationalisation Act, 1946 and the Petroleum (Production) Act 1934. The advice was that the provisions of these Acts were not automatically extended, and that special legislation would be necessary to extend these laws to the Continental Shelf.

The opinion of the Scottish Law Officers was also sought. On most issues they agreed with the English Law Officers. They thought that the term "Great Britain" appeared to be employed in a geographic sense, but when it was used in an Act the term became a statutory one as defined in 1707 to mean the Kingdom formed by the Union of England and Scotland. The Scottish Law Officers did express one view which differed from that of their English counterparts. They thought that it would be safe to assume that under international law the United Kingdom would be entitled to enforce the rights offered by the Convention against other states. The English Law Officers felt that it would not be safe to assume that the rights so provided could be enforced against States not party to the Convention.

Which laws to apply to UK Continental Shelf (UKCS)

The question of which law should apply to the Continental Shelf was not addressed by the Law Officers. Their opinions had not been sought on this particular occasion. The issue had been recognised for some time, however. In an earlier paper prepared for the Home Affairs Committee the Minister of Power had stated that with respect to criminal and civil law, it might become necessary to determine the limits of applicability on the Shelf of English Law, Scots Law, and other local systems of law. The Continental Shelf Act 1964 itself did not elaborate on which specific laws would be applicable when offences under the Act took place, merely stating that such offences would be treated as having been committed in any place in the United Kingdom, thus leaving open the question of the specific legal system for later clarification.

Position of Northern Ireland, Isle of Man and Channel Islands

A further constitutional issue also had to be faced, namely the applicability of the Bill to Northern Ireland, the Isle of Man, and the Channel Islands. The Northern Ireland Government had been consulted on the provisions of the Bill. Their view was that the Bill should enable them to control the exploitation of the continental shelf adjacent to their territorial waters. The UK Government felt that, because the Government of Ireland Act 1920 prohibited the Northern Ireland Parliament from making laws with respect to international relations, defence, and shipping matters with which exploitation is inter-woven, the UK Government should have control. Thus the Minister of Power would have control over activities in any parts of the Continental Shelf specified in Orders in Council. The Act acknowledged that the Parliament of Northern Ireland could make laws with respect to any matter over which it had powers without discussing the details. The Northern Ireland Government had agreed that specific mention of Northern Ireland was not necessary in the Bill, subject to the UK Government investigating the possibilities of some kind of pooling arrangements by which the profits from any exploitation of resources of the UKCS could be divided between the two Governments.

So far as the application of the Bill to the Isle of Man and the Channel Islands was concerned the Minister of Power was advised that, while these islands were not part of the United Kingdom, any exploitation of the resources of the shelf raised questions of international relations that, in respect of the islands, were the responsibility of HMG. Thus the Bill enabled areas to be designated offshore of any of these islands. The Insular Governments were so informed, and the UK Government was prepared to examine with them what arrangements should be made for recognising their claims to a share in the benefits of exploiting any part of the Shelf. The Minister was also advised that there was no likelihood of exploitable resources being found offshore of any of the islands in the foreseeable future, but that pooling arrangements as for Northern Ireland could be made if the need arose.

Legal basis for licensing of UKCS

The most obvious requirement of legislation was to provide a legal basis for the UK Government to award licences to companies wishing to explore for and exploit the natural resources of the seabed. Investors required some security of tenure before committing large sums of money on risky ventures. On land and in the territorial waters of Great Britain the mineral rights with respect to oil and gas had been vested in the Crown since the Petroleum (Production) Act, 1934. The Ministry of Power administered their exploitation by private companies. The rights to coal for onshore and territorial waters had been vested in the National Coal Board since 1946. It thus appeared fairly obvious to all Departments that similar arrangements should apply to the Continental Shelf. With respect to (non-living) natural resources other than oil, gas, and coal, the Crown Estate Office proposed that the Crown Estates Commissioners should have the rights and responsibilities. It was agreed that the Commissioners already had such rights within territorial waters with respect to minerals such as sand and gravel, and that the provision of similar rights on the Continental Shelf was a natural extension of these. There was no disagreement among Departments to this view.

Pre-1964 legislation and regulations

There already existed both primary legislation and subordinate regulations for oil and gas exploitation on land and in territorial waters.[8] First oil production in Britain started in 1850 in the form of shale oil. Output remained very small, with peak supply reaching around 6,000 barrels per day (b/d) in 1913. Because the scale was very limited there was no need for special legislation, and so common law was applied to the activity. Under this the accession system gave to the land-owner not only ownership of the land but of the subsurface as well. Common law also gave the owner the right to exploit the subsurface. He could do so directly, or sell or lease his interests.

When the First World War broke out the demand for oil shot up. The purchase of a majority shareholding in the Anglo-Persian oil company by the British

Government was a well-known response to the need for oil for use in warships. Another response was to encourage exploration for petroleum at home. A Bill for this purpose was introduced in 1917. It was dropped because of opposition, and a Regulation was introduced under the Defence of the Realm Act, 1914. The key provision gave the Government the exclusive right to enter property to explore for and exploit petroleum. Soon after the Petroleum (Production) Act, 1918 was passed. The industry had requested a clear legislative framework including measures to counter the problem of "wasteful" drilling which had become a major phenomenon in the United States.

The problem related to property rights in the circumstance where, as a consequence of drilling, the petroleum migrated from one geographic area to another, with no account being taken of different ownership of surface rights. The regulatory system in the United States recognised the issue by making the surface owner's rights subject to the rule of capture. This meant that a surface owner would actually lose title to oil beneath his land if it were produced through drilling in another property, so long as such drilling did not extend into the first owner's land. It followed that full title to the oil was obtained only when it was produced. This solution to the subject of property rights led to much competitive and "wasteful" drilling.

The 1918 Act approached these issues differently by prohibiting petroleum exploitation except by the Crown or by others licensed by the Crown at its discretion. Surface owners still controlled rights of access to land. The issue of property rights was not resolved by the 1918 Act. In 1919 the first conventional oil discovery was made by S. Pearson and Sons in Derbyshire, but the quantities were too small for commercial exploitation. Little activity ensued, and in the early 1930s further initiatives were made. The property rights issue was perceived to be a disincentive to exploration, as discoveries were quite likely to extend across the land of more than one landowner.

The Government's response to these perceived problems was to pass the Petroleum (Production) Act, 1934. The key provision of the Act was to nationalise the petroleum rights in situ in Great Britain, with the exception of those currently under licence. Interestingly, no compensation was given on the grounds that "a landowner could not reasonably expect compensation for petroleum of which he had no knowledge".[9] A further provision removed the right of the landowner to prevent access to his land. The 1934 Act gave the Minister for Mines the authority to make detailed regulations and to issue Model Clauses which were incorporated into licences. These Petroleum (Production) Regulations were issued in 1935. The net result was a system whereby the licences were both a commercial contract and a key element of Government regulation. An important ingredient of the Regulations was the ability of Government to change them at its discretion, a feature which was later to cause much controversy.

Following the 1934 Act a number of discoveries were made in various parts of the country, but they were all quite small. During the Second World War the search for petroleum was increased, but again with only modest success.[10] There is no evidence that the onshore discoveries encouraged interest in exploration offshore. The discovery of the giant Groningen field in the Netherlands did encourage such interest because the sedimentary basin in the Netherlands extended into the North Sea.

Decision to extend onshore legislation

The Ministry of Power did not give serious consideration to any method of designing the legal arrangements other than extending the onshore primary and secondary legislation which was seen as the obvious, natural, and perhaps easiest approach. While it was understood that the operating environment offshore would be different from that onshore, little attempt was made to reflect this in the primary legislation, though more recognition of this was given in some of the secondary Regulations.

Other approaches were possible. In a comparative study of offshore legislation in the USA and UK[11] Vass refers to the "skeletal statutory framework" in the UK, and found that the whole body of the Petroleum (Production) Act, 1934 was smaller than many individual sections of the comparable US legislation, namely the Outer Continental Shelf Lands Act, 1953. He concluded that, in contrast to the USA, "United Kingdom oil and gas law [has been] almost wholly the product of regulations".[12]

Detailed provisions on natural gas

While the Continental Shelf Act, 1964 for the most part confined itself to high level issues there were exceptions. The lengthy Section 9 dealt with the use and supply of natural gas. This subject involved very lengthy discussion within the Ministry of Power, and with other Departments and external organisations, particularly the Gas Council and prospective licensees. The policy and legal issues were recognised in a paper prepared by Gas Division in the Ministry of Power in late 1962. It was argued that, in contrast to the 19th century, the monopoly positions held by the Area Gas Boards in the supply of piped gas to the residential sector were such that competition from other piped gas suppliers was no longer commercially feasible, even if it were to become statutorily permissible. The authors had in mind the possibility of competition from supplies through pipelines other than those owned by the Area Gas Boards.

The paper recognised, however, that there was scope for a limited but important area of possible competition, namely the distribution of natural or by-product gases to factories or to industrial estates. Again the authors had in mind the use of pipelines other than those of the Area Gas Boards. The issue raised complex legal as well as policy issues. Under Section 52 of the Gas Act, 1948 if any potential gas suppliers other than a Gas Board wanted to supply pipeline gas other than for his own use or to a subsidiary company, he had to obtain the consent of the relevant Area Gas Board. The 1948 Act did not contain a definition of gas. When the Government spokesman was queried on this matter during the debate on the Bill he replied that it was sufficiently clear from the general tenor of the Bill that it applied to coal gas and not to the various types of industrial gases.

Since the passing of the 1948 Act different interpretations of the definition of gas had been proposed. Thus Shell argued in 1957 that refinery gas was outside the scope of the Act, a view supported by legal opinion (Mr Colin Pearson) who argued that Section 52 referred only to gas used as a fuel. On the other hand the Gas Council, supported by a legal opinion of Sir Frank Soskice in 1957, argued that Section 52 gave the Area Boards the exclusive right to supply gas in pipes. This latter legal opinion also stated that Section 52 applied to natural gas. If this opinion were confirmed it would have been in conflict with Section 4 of the Petroleum (Production) Act, 1934. This allowed the Minister of Power to authorise suppliers other than an Area Gas Board to supply natural gas to industrial users so long as he was satisfied that it had been offered to the appropriate Gas Board at a reasonable price. Thus the situation could arise whereby an authorisation given by the Minister of Power could be overruled by a Gas Board.

The same Gas Division paper also noted that Sir Hartley Shawcross in his capacity as legal adviser to Shell had given an opinion favourable to suppliers other than the Gas Boards. A recent development had been the development of a Draft Agreement between the Gas Boards and the oil companies (as the most likely alternative suppliers) to provide a way forward. There were two key features of this Draft Agreement, namely (1) that the oil companies would regard both refinery gas and natural gas as being within the scope of Section 52 of the 1948 Act, and (2) the Gas Boards would permit the oil companies to distribute these gases so long as they were only used as petrochemical feedstocks.

The Gas Division paper expressed surprise that the oil companies were contemplating such an agreement as they appeared to be giving away a major disputed point in return for a benefit which they would probably have received in any case in a court of law. While the Draft Agreement appeared at first sight to reduce the potential problems the Ministry was concerned that other potential distributors (non-oil companies such as ICI) could cause problems. They would be caught by Section 52 of the 1948 Act on manufactured gases and by Section 4 of the 1934 Act on indigenous natural gas. There was a concern that a strong company in this position could import natural gas and/or challenge Section 52 through the courts. There was a concern that a chaotic and awkward position might develop.

Wider policy issues

The wider policy issues had to be considered before legislative decisions could be finalised. The Gas Division paper raised the question of whether suppliers other than the Gas Boards should be allowed to compete to supply industrial premises. If natural gas were to become a commodity like oil should not this market be opened to competition? The alternative view was that the nationalised gas industry had obligations, statutory and otherwise. It had to take the rough with the smooth, peak loads as well as base loads, and less profitable business as well as more profitable. Further, it was questioned whether it was fair to allow others, who had no such obligations, to skim the cream off the industrial market, picking and choosing their points of entry.

The final judgement of the paper was that, while there were strong arguments on both sides, the damage done to the gas industry by a breach in the monopoly of piped supply would probably be greater than the benefits which would accrue to the competing suppliers and to industrial customers. The paper proposed that Section 52 of the 1948 Act be amended to exclude gas used for petrochemical purposes from the consent procedure. The specific proposal was to make the consent of the Gas Board refer only to the supply of premises for use wholly or mainly as a fuel. A further proposed modification was to exclude from the consent procedure gas supplied with the authority of the Minister under Section 4 of the Petroleum (Production) Act, 1934. The effects of these proposals would (1) ensure that Area Gas Boards could not interfere with the supply of gas as a petrochemical feedstock, and (2) that, while imported natural gas would come under the consent procedure involving the Gas Board, indigenous natural gas would be disposed of under the Petroleum (Production) Act, 1934. Interestingly, the paper added that consideration had been given to the exemption of gas supplied to the Central Electricity Generating Board (CEGB) power stations, but the conclusion was that such an exemption could not be defended in logic without admitting the case for similar concessions to big industry which would undermine the preferred policy towards the latter. The only exception which the authors envisaged was a fairly limited one, however, namely a power station located close to an oil refinery which had surplus refinery gas.

Legislation problems

As work proceeded on the Continental Shelf Bill legislative difficulties relating to the proposals outlined above became apparent. In a note agreed by Petroleum Division and Gas Division it was acknowledged that the Continental Shelf Bill could not deal with refinery gas, gas from abroad or ordinary manufactured gas, but only indigenous natural gas. The two Divisions proposed that the Bill include provisions stating that Section 52 of the Gas Act, 1948 would not apply to the supply of natural gas obtained as a consequence of a licence issued under the Petroleum (Production) Act 1934, so long as the gas in question was supplied wholly or mainly for use otherwise than as a fuel, or if the person to whom the licence was granted was authorised to supply gas under Section 4 of the Petroleum (Production) Act 1934. The effects of these proposals would have been to ensure that gas producers could sell gas for use as a petrochemical feedstock without the involvement of a Gas Board. Further the Gas Boards would not be able to veto the supply of indigenous natural gas, for industrial use wholly or mainly as a fuel, which they had earlier refused to purchase.

Discussion with Gas Council and oil companies

The Ministry was much engaged in consultations with the Gas Council and the oil companies on the gas provisions in the Bill. At November 1963, the Gas Council had not formally agreed to the proposals noted above. At this time a small group of major oil companies had urged that Section 4 of the Petroleum (Production) Act 1934, should not be extended to the Continental Shelf, but had suggested that gas emanating from the UKCS should be governed by Section 52 of the Gas Act 1934. The Ministry interpreted this rather surprising suggestion as emanating from the agreement which this group of companies had made with the Gas Council earlier in 1963 whereby the members of the group obtained assurances that the Gas Boards would not withhold consent to the sale of gas for petrochemical feedstock purposes by integrated oil companies. Such advantages would accrue only to the members of this group. Others would not benefit, but they would if Section 52 was amended in the manner the Ministry had in mind.

A further issue related to the position of potential independent purchasers of gas such as ICI. This company had approached the Board of Trade and the Ministry of Power with a request that it be allowed to bid for gas directly from producers, particularly when the gas was to be used as a feedstock rather than as a fuel. The Gas Council had also been making its views known on this subject. The Chairman, Sir Henry Jones, informed Sir Dennis Proctor, Permanent Secretary at the Ministry of Power, of his views in December 1963. He argued that, if gas for chemical purposes had a higher value than gas to be used as a fuel then the freedom of companies (such as ICI) to bid for gas directly from the producers might raise the price to the gas industry. He also argued that, if the chemical industry obtained new gas supplies on specially favourable terms, others such as the steel industry, the glass and pottery industry, the cement industry and the motor industry, would all claim that they were just as important and should have equivalent benefits. Sir Henry subsequently reiterated his views to Sir Dennis Proctor stating that it would be most undesirable if the Continental Shelf Bill included any modification of the existing statutory position as it existed under Section 4 of the 1934 Act and Section 52 of the 1948 Act.

In the elaboration of his position he expressed sympathy with the position of ICI and agreed that they would be handicapped if their competitors (oil companies) obtained natural gas as a feedstock on better terms than ICI could buy it. He thought that with respect to feedstocks the Gas Council would be able to reach a satisfactory negotiated agreement with chemical manufacturers under the umbrella of Section 52 just as had been done with the group of oil companies discussed above.

Sir Henry reinforced his position by arguing that the Gas Act 1948 was designed to give the nationalised gas industry responsibility for coordinating supplies of gas arising in this country, and it was clear that the provisions of Section 52 of that Act were not limited to gas supplied at gasworks. If the special position of the chemical industry was prescribed by legislation, it would only be a matter of time before other industries made equally justifiable claims for special treatment, such as ore smelters, cement manufacturers, the ceramic industry, the motor car industry and glass manufacturers. He again reiterated his willingness to enter into an agreement with ICI similar to that already made with the group of oil companies. He further argued that, if gas discoveries were made on the scale envisaged by those presently engaged in exploration, the result would alter radically the whole energy

situation in the United Kingdom. In such circumstances it would be more important than ever for the Minister to retain, through the nationalised gas industry,
effective powers for the coordination of this new source of energy.

The debate continues

The evolving views of Petroleum Division and Gas Division did not always coincide. At December 1963 both agreed that the Gas Boards should not have the
power to block a ministerial consent under the Petroleum (Production) Act, 1934.
They also agreed that any danger of gas being locked up in the event of a price
dispute between a producer and a Gas Board should be removed. Petroleum
Division also wanted to modernise the legislation by permitting sales by a producer
to a consumer for non-fuel use without the gas first being offered to a Gas Board.
They argued that it should be the Minister who should consent to the use of gas
for a producer's own purposes. They envisaged the possibility that it might be
desirable for some natural gas to be used as a chemical raw material rather than
as a fuel. The Minister rather than a Gas Board should be responsible for such a
decision.

Petroleum Division's view prevailed on the issue of first refusal of the Gas
Boards for non-fuel uses of gas. Proposals were also made that producers from the
UKCS should be able to use gas for their own purposes without involvement of
the Gas Boards. More generally they should also be able to supply natural gas for
use wholly or mainly otherwise than as a fuel. The market place would decide
whether any particular gas volumes should best be used for petrochemical or
burning purposes. Producers from the UKCS would also be allowed to sell natural
gas for use as an industrial fuel provided that the Minister was satisfied that the
Gas Boards had been given an opportunity of buying the gas at a reasonable price.
This clause was designed to protect the position of the Gas Boards. There was
sympathy with the view that, given the special status of the Boards it was unfair to
allow others, who did not have the same statutory obligations, to cream off trade
which the Boards were able and willing to do on "reasonable" terms. It was also
proposed that, as in the Regulations made under the Petroleum (Production) Act
1934, the right to export gas from the UKCS could only be made with the consent
of the Minister. The justification for continuing this power was to ensure that the
Minister was in a position properly to fulfil his functions of coordinating fuel
supplies in the United Kingdom. Interestingly, it was suggested that, if the
proposals were endorsed by the Minister, the Gas Council should be informed,
and if strong objections were made, the Minister would be informed before matters
were taken further.

The Permanent Secretary endorsed the above proposals, as did the Minister on
18th December 1963. This led to further discussions with the Gas Council. At a
meeting on 21st January 1964, the Gas Council argued that if a gas producer from
the UKCS was allowed to supply gas for his own use he could establish a subsidiary
and supply it with gas which would enable it to compete unfairly with a company
(such as ICI) which did not have access to its own gas. The Council also argued that

if a gas producer from the UKCS was allowed to supply gas to another company for use wholly or mainly otherwise than as a fuel (the term then proposed by the Ministry of Power), a situation could still emerge whereby a chemical company, legitimately requiring gas to, say, 9 therms for feedstock and 1 therm for fuel, could profess to need, say, 9 therms and 5 therms respectively and sell the surplus 4 therms to another concern for fuel, thus becoming a gas supplier competing with the Gas Board.

In a further letter to the Permanent Secretary Sir Henry Jones reiterated his views. He argued that if gas producers from the UKCS were allowed to supply their gas for their own use (including use by associated companies irrespective of the end use), it would have far reaching consequences, would infringe seriously on the Gas Council's monopoly, and interfere with their duty of providing an efficient, coordinated and economical system of gas supply. He also suggested that it would impair the Minister's powers of coordination.

The Ministry took the view that Sir Henry was claiming too much, and that his fears were exaggerated. They noted that at that time manufacturers of gas (i.e. town gas) were entitled to supply themselves and their associates. It was noteworthy that, in spite of this, large quantities of gas made in steelworks had been sold at low prices to Gas Boards, and there was no rush by the manufacturers to send supplies to their subsidiaries. The Ministry concluded that there was no good reason to distinguish between natural gas and manufactured gas from this perspective. They also considered that it would be discouraging to producers in the North Sea to be obligated to deal with the Gas Board in any proposed sale of gas to their own associates. With respect to the issue of coordination the Ministry felt that the Minister had adequate powers under the existing Pipelines Act to prevent unnecessary multiplication of pipelines, and he should not be embarrassed to use these powers. (There was, of course, no thought of third party access at this time.)

Sir Henry Jones also objected to the proposal to give the right of gas producers from the UKCS to supply natural gas for use wholly or mainly otherwise than as a fuel. The Ministry accepted that the phrase "wholly or mainly" might be too loose, and permit too free a use of natural gas for burning purposes in chemical and similar industries, and re-examined this part of the proposed legislation. They enlisted the Chief Scientist's Division for advice on the technical aspects of the issue. The response highlighted the difficulties in designing rules which would meet the policy objectives while still being economically and operationally sensible. It was pointed out that in many important chemical processes for which natural gas was a highly suitable feedstock, the chemical transformation which the feedstock underwent took place only at high temperatures, and in such processes there was an economic advantage to be had from using the same raw material as feedstock and a source of heat to raise the reactants to the required temperature. There were even some processes where these two usages of the raw material occurred simultaneously and were inseparable. The conclusion was that to restrict removal of the gas industry's prerogative literally to cases where the gas would be used for non-fuel purposes would place serious and undesirable restrictions on its use as a chemical.

The Minute from Chief Scientist's Division then considered the question of the *degree* of fuel use which might be permitted along with non-fuel use. It pointed out that the transformation of a chemical feedstock was often carried out in a number of stages, with the chemicals made at one stage being passed on to succeeding stages for further treatment. Surplus energy, such as in the form of waste gases, from a given stage could be used to provide the energy required for other stages, producing a situation in which the use of natural gas as a fuel, in association with its use as a chemical, would inevitably provide energy for a further process in which natural gas was not one of the chemicals being processed. This was felt to be a legitimate fuel use, and it was felt that the Gas Council would also regard it in that light.

The Minute also considered the issue of claims for special treatment from industries other than the chemical industry, and expressed the view that it would be very difficult to resist such claims. Thus in the iron making industry natural gas was highly suitable as a chemical for partial or even complete replacement of coke as a chemical to transform iron ore into iron. It could be contested that this was largely non-fuel in nature.

The views of the Chief Scientist's Division were taken seriously. In a Minute to the Minister it was stated that Parliamentary Counsel should be informed of the intention and asked to find the appropriate legal language. The intention was that the gas industry's right of first refusal should not operate in cases where the gas would be used primarily for non-fuel purposes, and when its use for fuel purposes was restricted to the provision of the heat or other energy necessary for the non-fuel usage, and, if such non-fuel usage was (broadly) for a stage in a connected and progressive series of processes.

Major decisions made

On 31st January 1964 the Minister approved the proposals. He had also seen Sir Henry Jones and informed him that he hoped it might be possible to meet the Gas Council's points at least in part. In response Sir Henry Jones expressed his gratitude, indicating that he had made his representations and would now rest content.

The end result of these deliberations was Section 9 of the Continental Shelf Act. The great complexity of this section reflects a combination of the policy objectives and the technical difficulties of providing for them in legislation. The provisions had momentous repercussions when gas discoveries were subsequently made in the North Sea. They provided the basic framework for the negotiations of the gas contracts for many years, and ensured the prominence of the Gas Council in both the pattern of gas exploitation and its use.

Reflections on policy debate

The debate on the policy alternatives reflected both the historic background and the conventional thinking of the times. Historically, competition in the supply of gas to households involving different companies with separate pipelines had not been regarded as an economically efficient arrangement. The notion that there might be virtue in permitting competition to supply large industrial consumers was acknowledged within Government, but the benefits were not perceived to be sufficient to exceed those obtained from the monopolistic coordination of the gas market by the Gas Council and Area Boards, including the provision of gas under peak and non-peak conditions in profitable and less profitable conditions.

The oil companies as prospective producers did not make very strong efforts to persuade the Government that they should be allowed to market gas independently. There was no coordinated campaign to procure such rights. No detailed studies were produced at this time to show the advantages of competition in this area. An underlying assumption was that suppliers other than the Gas Council and Area Boards would have to build their own onshore pipelines which would have reduced the profitability of such activities.

The main campaign of the oil companies was to ensure that they had unrestricted access to gas produced from the North Sea for their own use, particularly as a petrochemical feedstock. This industry was growing rapidly at the time, and the attractions of continuing growth were seen as a priority area for the vertically integrated companies. It is thus understandable that they concentrated their efforts on this limited area. The evidence is that substantial efforts were required to procure rights to North Sea gas for their own use. The Gas Council argued strongly that it should have first refusal on such gas, even though it had general sympathy with the position of the oil companies on the issue. It is clear that the Gas Council lobbied quite strongly, and that the Ministry of Power listened very carefully to arguments presented to it. While the oil companies won their main argument the Ministry went out of its way to minimise the extent of the perceived reduction in the Gas Council's role and powers. This is the background to the complex Section 9 of the Continental Shelf Act.

The continuing dominant role for the Gas Council and Area Boards in the event of the discovery of gas in the North Sea was essentially taken for granted. At the time much of the energy sector in the UK was in public ownership. Politically there was no significant pressure to reduce the role of the Gas Council despite the fact that the debate took place under a Conservative Government.

Much attention was paid to the coordinating role of the Gas Council in the gas market. The Council itself emphasised the importance of this activity. There is, however, little or no evidence of systematic examination of the national benefits of reliance on the nationalised gas industry for this purpose compared to other market structures and regulatory arrangements. The word "coordination" appears frequently in this context, but its precise meaning is generally not fully clarified, nor is the importance of it given detailed examination. Other possible forms of regulation/coordination were generally not discussed.

What is more surprising is the near absence of any discussion of the concept of "reasonable price". This phrase appeared in the 1934 Act and is repeated in Section 9 of the Continental Shelf Act. There is no definition of the term in the Act. Further, there is no evidence of detailed deliberations having taken place on the subject within Government. The general understanding was that the concept was designed to give comfort to the relevant Gas Board as prospective buyer of gas which the producer might wish to sell into the industrial market.

The gas price issue was raised by the oil companies in their discussions with the Ministry to only a minor extent prior to the passing of the Act. One occasion was the meeting between the Minister and the chairman of BP Sir Maurice Bridgeman on 21st January 1964. At the meeting BP noted that Gas Boards had in the past been prepared to pay only a very low sum for natural gas found in the UK – about 4d per thousand cubic feet. Because offshore operations were much more expensive than land-based operations, it was possible that gas found on the UKCS could be made available commercially at only a much higher figure – perhaps 7d per thousand cubic feet. Sir Maurice pointed out that it would be a pity if the gas industry's expectation that natural gas could always be bought very cheaply were to prevent the commercial exploitation of useful quantities of gas. He added that this consideration would apply particularly to marginal discoveries, while if very big discoveries were made it might be commercially attractive to make it available at a much lower figure than 7d per thousand cubic feet.

At this time there was little serious discussion on the possibilities of producers from the UKCS selling to industrial consumers. There were several reasons for this. One is that among the companies it was felt that there were no serious prospects of being allowed to sell directly into the industrial market. On 14th February 1964, a letter was sent to the Ministry of Power on behalf of the committee of lawyers representing various oil companies stating that the Bill as it stood then was ambiguous regarding the rights that producing companies had to use natural gas for purposes other than in their own plants or the plants of subsidiaries. It was requested that the clause be clarified to indicate clearly that the Minister had the power to consent to such other uses. The Minister's continued discretionary powers in the matter were still unfettered by this request. The strongly entrenched position of the Gas Council/Area Boards, the vigour with which they defended their perceived rights, plus the lack of any obvious political encouragement, certainly lend support to the view that it was unlikely that uninhibited sales to the industrial market would have been permitted. The oil companies may also have felt that selling gas to the Gas Council was an acceptable marketing arrangement, and that the price issue could be dealt with in a satisfactory manner as part of a range of contractual issues which would be dealt with much later after discoveries had been made.

Legal issues relating to status of UKCS

Because of the unique position of the UKCS, with full sovereignty not being applicable, consideration had to be given regarding how various UK laws and regulations could be applied. On some substantive subjects deliberations did not result in any legislation in the Continental Shelf Bill. An example was Customs and Excise issues. The Board of Trade, Customs and Excise, Foreign Office, and Ministry of Power were all involved in intensive discussions on these matters, particularly in early 1964 when the Bill was being debated in the House of Commons.

With respect to products produced from the UKCS, under the law in force at the time, when they were shipped or piped to the UK mainland, they would be regarded as imported goods and thus liable to customs duties. There was unanimity across Departments that protective duties should not apply to products from the UKCS. Accordingly, it was proposed that amendments would be made either in the Continental Shelf Bill or in a Finance Bill to ensure that products from the North Sea would be deemed not to be imported for purposes of protective duty. In practice this would mean that petroleum gases would not be liable for the 10% duty then in force (though no duty was charged on methane).

Import duties and UKCS

The issue of duties on equipment and other supplies for use in the exploration and production operations caused much more debate. As part of a wider policy on protective tariffs the Board of Trade view was that duties on equipment applied to foreign goods imported into the UK should also apply to such equipment taken to the UKCS. Execution of this policy meant that equipment imported into the UK mainland would not be eligible for drawbacks or other reliefs from protective duties which would normally apply to re-exports from the UK. Further, arrangements would have to be made to ensure that such import duties were paid on equipment taken directly to North Sea installations from foreign sources. In essence the Board of Trade policy meant that offshore installations would be treated for protective duty purposes as if they were part of the UK. The tax treatment of goods used in the UKCS but subject to revenue duties in the UK also had to be considered. While revenue duties would be dealt with on the same basis as protective duties it was understood that different considerations arose, and the same treatment need not be followed.

The resolution of these issues proved troublesome. There were both practical complexities and issues of international law. On the latter aspect Customs and Excise sought the views of the Foreign Office. The most thorny issue concerned the ability of the Government to levy customs duties on items used outside territorial waters, given that the Convention of the Continental Shelf had given only limited sovereign rights to the states in question. Thus it was unclear whether the UK government could charge customs duties on goods destined for the UKCS and whether it had the right to board installations and ships (including foreign ones) to enforce any duties levied, including the right to take legal action against offenders.

The response from the Foreign Office admitted the complexities of the issue and suggested that distinctions might have to be made between (a) exploration, (b) erection of fixed installations, and (c) operation of these installations. Exploration could perhaps be treated for customs purposes in the same way as shipping. The other phases of offshore activity raised more intractable problems. Customs and Excise pursued the policy issues with the Board of Trade who doubted whether it was necessary to subject consumer goods used on installations to protective duty, and that the major policy issue was to ensure that the equipment used in petroleum exploitation should not escape duty.

Parliamentary Counsel informed Customs and Excise of the novelty of the concept that goods should come within Customs control, not because the geographic area to which they were brought was within the Customs territory, but only because they were brought by a certain specified class of people for a specific purpose to a point in that area which was determined only by the fact that certain people were licensed to pursue a specified form of activity there. Customs and Excise were concerned that these areas would have to be treated as in effect foreign parts, to which the Customs laws were not exportable, whereas for the purposes of the Board of Trade's protective policies these areas would be treated as if they were part of the UK. It was difficult to see how this differential treatment could be convincingly defended. Customs and Excise also pointed out that under existing law a complete floating installation would be exempt from duty. There was the prospect of an odd situation emerging whereby complete installations could be brought from abroad to the UKCS free of duty, while parts of, or equipment for, such installations would be subject to duty.

The Board of Trade still felt that protective tariffs should apply to equipment and machinery used in the UKCS emanating from any source. In response to Customs and Excise they agreed that revenue duties (levied on consumption goods) would be excluded as their purpose was different from protective duties, noting that the ability to buy tobacco and alcoholic drinks free of duty might be some small compensation for the hardy individuals "marooned" on the Shelf, and that it was unreasonable to deny them this when the crews of ships sailing around them were able to get their supplies duty free.

With respect to the possibility that an entire structure imported for use in the UKCS might attract no duty while equipment used on such a structure might attract duties, the Board of Trade raised the issue of whether complete structures would be classified along with ships (attracting no duty) or structures "other than vessels" (attracting duty at 16%). In any case the Board of Trade saw no inconsistency between allowing duty free use of a complete structure (if it were to be classified along with ships), while imports of equipment were subject to duty. This was perfectly consistent with policy regarding imports into the UK mainland.

The Board of Trade doubted whether the distinction between exploration and exploitation was appropriate for policy purposes. Their concept was that goods should be dutiable if they were required to form part of a fixed installation. Thus goods sent to a secure base either to form part of it or to be used on it should be dutiable, while others (i.e. goods that remain on a survey ship) should not. The real distinction was between making surveys from vessels to determine a likely spot, and, having determined it, carrying out subsequent operations from a fixed base, whether these were still exploratory or exploitative. Customs and Excise felt that this suggestion made an inappropriate distinction between fixed installations and vessels, and that the consequences would be incongruous. Thus goods brought direct from abroad for use in exploration or exploitation would become liable to duty, not because they had been brought for that purpose, nor because they had been brought to a given spot, but because, having been brought for that purpose to a given spot, it happened to be one where there was a fixed installation as opposed to a floating one. Their view was that the Customs law could not be amended in such a fundamental respect for the purpose of seeking to bring licensed activities in the UKCS within the scope of the protective duty system without in fact effectively doing so. They therefore concluded that while no difficulty was foreseen in executing whatever policy was deemed appropriate regarding foreign goods taken to the UKCS from the UK mainland it was not practical to apply Customs control to goods brought direct to the Shelf from abroad.

Further to this the legal advisers of both the Customs and Excise and the Foreign Office indicated that it was doubtful whether adequate powers could be taken to control goods brought direct from abroad to the so-called fixed installations. Faced with these arguments the Board of Trade agreed that it should abandon the idea that foreign goods sent direct to offshore installations should be subject to protective duty. They did suggest, however, that further consideration should be given to an alternative method of achieving the same objective. This was to amend existing laws to require that foreign goods required for use in the UKCS should be taken there from a UK port, unless HM Customs were to grant a dispensation which would require the payment of a sum equivalent to the duty which would have been chargeable if the goods had come from a UK port.

In reply to this suggestion Customs and Excise stated that it could not be enforced as a Customs provision and they could not undertake responsibilities that they could not enforce. They also expressed doubts about the political propriety, and the apprehensions about the implications in the international and shipping fields, of requiring all dutiable goods to be taken via the United Kingdom. The Ministry of Power also supported this view.

The end result of this debate was that no legislation on this subject was contained in the Continental Shelf Bill. Thus customs duties were not applied to goods supplied directly from foreign sources to the UKCS. Reliefs from customs duties for goods supplied to the UKCS from the UK mainland was made available under Section 7 of the Import Duties Act, 1958. The precise Regulations were quite complex and were designed to ensure that the reliefs were clearly targeted only on the intended beneficiaries.

The Board of Trade, while accepting the practical difficulties of providing protection for British industry, had some misgivings about the outcome. In a letter to Maurice MacMillan, Economic Secretary to the Treasury, Edward du Cann pointed out that other countries would be able to exercise mineral rights in the North Sea. He was concerned that these neighbouring countries might contrive to make foreign goods (including British goods) liable to their protective duties, even if sent direct to their installations. There would be strong and justifiable criticism from the United Kingdom equipment industry if the absence of tariff protection in the UKCS were not matched by opportunities to compete freely for business in the areas allotted to other countries.

Health and safety laws

Because the Convention did not confer full sovereignty to a state with respect to its Continental Shelf, consideration had to be given to the question of how various UK laws, not dealing exclusively with petroleum issues, could be applied to the UKCS. In several instances the approach taken was to apply selected provisions of these laws to North Sea activities. Judgements had to be made about the specific provisions which inevitably required considerable inter-departmental consultations. With respect to health and safety issues, the Ministry of Labour felt that the provisions of the Offices, Shops and Railway Premises Acts which required employers to take steps to protect the health and safety of their employees should apply to the UKCS. It was recognised that these Acts would apply only to a limited range of operations. Thus there were doubts about whether a workshop on a drilling platform might be regarded as a factory under the Factories Act, 1961. Similarly, while the setting up of a fixed platform would probably qualify as a work of engineering construction to which the Factories Act would apply, it was doubtful if these provisions would apply to a floating platform.

In general the Ministry of Labour supported the view that, to the extent that the offshore installations fell within the scope of the Factories Act, all the related safety requirements would apply. These included the provisions relating to claims for damages based on breaches of the Act. It was recognised, however, that the scope of the Act did not extend to the main activity, namely the exploitation of oil and gas. The Ministry of Labour took the view that, just as safety in mines and quarries rested with the Ministry of Power, so should such issues relating to oil and gas exploitation. This was because the Factory Inspectorate had no expertise in this area. The Ministry of Labour thus favoured the extension of the safety regulations including inspection rights then applicable to onshore oil and gas production under the 1934 Act to activities on the UKCS.

While the Ministry of Power generally agreed with these propositions the issue was raised of the applicability of the Mines and Quarries Act to offshore activities. This came within the responsibilities of the Ministry, and was at first blush fairly close to oil and gas operations. On detailed examination, however, it was concluded that this Act had been drafted very precisely to the particular circumstances of mines and quarries and it could not readily be adapted to oil and gas operations. The preferred option was thus to provide that in the Regulations which would accompany the Continental Shelf Act, the Minister would be able to give instructions for securing the health and safety of employees. A suggestion had been made that these Regulations should require licensees to observe the Institute of Petroleum's Code of Safe Practice. This proposal was objected to by the Ministry's Legal Branch which pointed out that this would in effect delegate the Minister's duty to another body which might revise its code without reference to the Minister. The conclusion was that the Regulations should provide that the Minister could make additional instructions as the need arose. This view prevailed. It was recognised that, while this gave much flexibility to the Government, by the same token Parliament would not know the full consequences of the Act.

National Insurance and UKCS

The UK National Insurance legislation applied only to employment on the mainland or on board ships and aircraft. Accordingly, the Continental Shelf Bill proposed legislation to extend the Acts to employment on the UKCS. Thus the Ministry proposed that the Minister be given powers to enable benefits under the National Insurance (Industrial Injuries) Act, 1946 to be paid for accidents occurring to insured persons employed in petroleum activities in the UKCS or while travelling to or from such employment. It was also proposed that the Minister be given power to modify the application of the National Insurance Act for people employed in the UKCS. In particular it was proposed to extend the power to provide insurance to people employed in the UKCS even though they had never been employed or resident in Great Britain.

An issue arose as to whether the British scheme of industrial injuries insurance would unambiguously cover *all* people employed in the UKCS. It was clear that all British workers should be covered. It was less clear to the Ministry that the British scheme should be extended to people such as foreign workers employed by foreign companies. Until the circumstances of employment in the UKCS became clearer the Ministry preferred to reserve judgement on this point. It was for this reason that the Minister rejected a proposed amendment to make the benefits clearly available to all employees in the UKCS.

Application of Emergency Powers Act

Consideration was also given by the Ministry of Power to apply the Emergency Powers Act, 1920 (being amended by the Emergency Powers Bill, 1964) to the UKCS. The circumstances in which the powers under this Act might be employed were a shortage of oil owing to a boycott by the oil producing countries, when it might be desirable that the Minister of Power should be enabled to require a company to continue or resume production of oil from an installation on the Shelf.

The Home Office was unconvinced. They thought that the situation contemplated was hardly likely to justify the extension of the 1920 Act. The circumstances required a combination of (1) a perceived shortage of oil in Great Britain, (2) the difference between the amount of oil actually being produced from the UKCS and the amount which could be produced being enough to increase the shortage substantially, and (3) the unwillingness of the companies to increase production to full capacity being such that the Government had to force them to do so by law. The Home Office also pointed out that under the 1920 Act the shortage had to be such as to deprive the community, or any substantial part of it, of the essentials of life. It was thus felt that requiring oil companies to produce oil against their wishes would seem a surprising and drastic step to take under the 1920 Act and other solutions to the problem were preferable. They suggested that the companies should comply with any direction of the Minister of Power to produce oil to their full capacity. The Minister might also be empowered, instead of giving directions to the company which owned an installation, to authorise other persons to occupy the installations and themselves to produce the oil.

The subject was discussed with Parliamentary Counsel who expressed the view that the scope of the 1920 Act and Regulations which might be made, would be so wide that no guarantee could be made that the action taken under Regulations for the offences created thereby would be "exportable" to the UKCS. The view of Parliamentary Counsel was that the only way to secure full application of the 1920 Act would be to make specific provisions that for the purpose of that Act installations should be deemed to be within Great Britain. As discussed above it was the clear view both of the Law Officers and the Foreign Office that the UK Government did not have full sovereignty over its Continental Shelf. Thus the extension of criminal law to installations in the UKCS could be justified only on the grounds that it was necessary for the protection of these installations. This was allowable under Article 5 of the Convention on the Continental Shelf. Legal Branch of the Ministry felt that to apply the Emergency Powers Act to the UKCS meant that Regulations of such scope would have to be made that they approached complete sovereignty.

Legal Branch thus suggested that an alternative solution might be found in the licence Regulations, pointing out that Section 2 of the 1934 Petroleum Act gave the Minister wide powers to grant licences "upon such other terms and conditions as the Minister thinks fit". This would include suspension or even termination, or powers for the Minister to direct production in specified quantities, assuming that the capacity was there.

But Legal Branch also felt that there were difficulties associated with the general licence Regulation approach. Thus the precise action which might be required could not now be foreseen, and it would therefore be almost impossible to draft an appropriate clause. If the clause were very widely drawn it would, in a contractual document, be liable to fail for uncertainty, and would be unlikely to be acceptable to the licensees. It might also be unacceptable to Parliament. In the event of an emergency it would be possible to introduce Regulations which were appropriate to the circumstances. Legal Branch was also aware that, if licences were granted with a particular Model Clause included, it would be impossible to revise that clause except with the agreement of both parties to the contract.

Petroleum Division in the Ministry of Power felt that the objections of the Home Office to the extension of the 1920 Act to the UKCS were formidable in number but not in substance. What had to be considered was what the Government's powers ought to be if a serious problem arose. With respect to the rights of the UK Government under international law it was arguable that, as these were for the purposes of exploring and exploiting oil and gas, this meant the right to compel exploitation. The view was reaffirmed that it would be undesirable to risk leaving the Minister in the position that, if an emergency was proclaimed, his powers stopped short of oil and gas on the Shelf. It was logical and not unreasonable that he should have the same powers over oil and gas from the Shelf as he had from production on the mainland.

In a further Minute on the subject the Under Secretary at the Ministry of Power, Mr Angus Beckett, acknowledged the strength of these arguments, but concluded that the legal and Parliamentary problems which would be involved if these powers were sought in the Continental Shelf Bill were excessive, and he stressed that the Minister would have powers under the Bill to withhold consent to export oil and gas, and when they reached territorial waters they would automatically become subject to the Emergency Powers Act. He also argued that to direct companies to increase production was a drastic step. There was even some doubt about whether such an order was consistent with Section 2 of the 1920 Act, which prohibited the imposition of any form of industrial conscription. If a serious emergency arose he anticipated cooperation with the oil industry as had occurred during the Suez crisis. He questioned the need for powers to direct production. In support of this view he added that he knew of no instance when powers to direct production of any basic commodity had been used under the 1920 Act. He concluded that an amendment to the Continental Shelf Bill to deal with the problem should not be pursued because of the serious problems involved in permitting powers which for practical purposes were most unlikely to be required. He added that attempts should continue to persuade the Home Office that the then current Emergency Powers Bill should be extended to the UKCS. The Minister accepted these recommendations.

The Home Office was not persuaded by the arguments of the Ministry of Power and expressed doubts as to whether the emergency powers which had been taken in the past would be wide enough for the purpose in mind. Thus they felt that the Regulation relating to the requisitioning of chattels could probably not be applied to directions requiring the production of additional oil. They also doubted whether Section 2 of the 1920 Act which contained the words "for securing and regulating the supply and distribution of . . . fuel" were appropriate to direct oil producers to increase their production.

Legal Branch of the Ministry of Power considered that the Regulation relating to the supply of fuel should include provisions for production as well as distribution, since otherwise the word "supply" would have little or no meaning. They also questioned whether action in response to an emergency would involve industrial conscription. They felt that oil companies could very easily increase production without having to compel existing or additional labour. On the question of whether the Emergency Powers Bill could be amended to apply to the UKCS, Legal Branch found it difficult to see exactly what was thought to be controversial in the current proposals given that it was agreed that the Emergency Powers Act should be available in slightly wider circumstances than at present, provided that the existing safeguards and the prohibition on industrial conscription were retained. But the Home Office was still unwilling to extend the Emergency Powers Bill to the UKCS. The matter rested there with the Ministry of Power noting that the Home Office arguments would afford no worthwhile defence if in an emergency the Minister had to admit to having inadequate powers.

Landing obligation

The Ministry of Power was anxious to ensure that any oil or gas produced from the UKCS would be brought to the UK unless the Minister authorised exports. To effect this the original method contemplated was to utilise Regulations currently existing under the 1934 Petroleum (Production) Act. The relevant clause in these Regulations stipulated that the licensee should, if so required, ensure that crude oil or products would be sold only for consumption in Great Britain or Northern Ireland. Doubts emerged within the Ministry regarding the adequacy of this provision on the grounds that (1) it did not cover natural gas, (2) the place of consumption was not the essential concern, and (3) the effect of the word "ensure" in law was problematic. It was argued that when crude oil entered the UK it could be refined into products, consumed, or exported. It was, however, impracticable and unnecessary to trace these commodities through those various stages. The concern was about the total quantity of petroleum available in the country. If it was desired to prohibit exports, the Government could use existing Board of Trade powers, and there would be no particular point in prohibiting the export of substances originating on the UKCS rather than similar substances originating elsewhere. Thus to provide for consumption in the country was unnecessary. It was sufficient that the substance should, except with the Minister's permission, be brought to the UK mainland.

Doubts about the word "ensure" related to whether the licensee could in practice ensure the desired result. In turn this was because the licensee would normally seek to sell the oil or gas to a company able to use it or process it in the UK or elsewhere. In some cases the purchaser might re-sell to a third party without ever having taken physical possession at all. There could be a whole series of sales and purchases more or less divorced from the physical movement of the commodity. The problem was compounded because the law of contract normally gave no rights to anyone other than the parties to the contract. If a company second or third in line from the licensee sold crude oil obtained under the licence to an overseas customer it was not clear what the Minister could do about it.

In recognition of these realities further consideration had to be given to possible legal remedies. Although there was a preference for dealing with the issue in Regulations rather than in primary legislation, clarification was required on how the policy objectives could best be met. The response from Legal Branch of the Ministry of Power was to provide reassurance that Regulations accompanying a licence were adequate for the purposes in mind. It was admitted, however, that it was doubtful whether a licence could ensure that crude oil from the UKCS would ultimately be consumed in Great Britain because any Model Clause could only cover sales by the licensee. If the buyer from the licensee were later, contrary to his agreement with the licensee, to sell crude oil for consumption outside Great Britain or Northern Ireland, then the Ministry could do nothing. This was inherent in the system of licences.

Legal Branch also agreed that it would be difficult to identify crude oil from the UKCS after it had gone into storage or a refinery. They pointed out, however, that another clause in the existing Regulations required the licensee to keep records of the oil produced, and thus it would be possible to ascertain the amounts of oil so obtained and if necessary where it went. If it went into general storage or into a refinery, provided that a similar amount was sold within Great Britain or Northern Ireland, the Ministry would not have anything to complain about.

The result of these deliberations was that no provisions regarding landing obligations or exports were included in the Continental Shelf Bill but a landing obligation was incorporated into the licence Regulations. The issues raised were to return with a vengeance.

Consultation with oil companies – freedom of establishment

The Ministry of Power engaged in a considerable amount of consultation with the oil industry during the preparatory stages of the Continental Shelf Bill. The US oil companies presented a memorandum which dealt with an issue of much importance to them, namely freedom of establishment. Their purpose was to demonstrate that a discontinuance of the present restriction requiring local incorporation contained in the Petroleum (Production) Regulations 1935, and the granting of full flexibility to each oil company in its choice of corporate organisation would have a beneficial influence on the development of the UKCS, whilst in no way diminishing the United Kingdom tax yield from the activities or impairing control of the United Kingdom authorities over the companies operating there.

In essence the request for freedom of establishment meant that the investor sought the right to operate in the UKCS using a branch of a foreign company if he so chose, rather than via an incorporated UK subsidiary. If a branch of a US company was employed to conduct exploration in the UKCS the investor would be able to claim deductions for Federal income tax relating to operating expenses, intangible drilling costs, and some development costs during the exploration phase. Such deductions were available irrespective of the success of the venture. The group argued that, if the same activities were undertaken by the UK subsidiary of the US investor the tax treatment in the US would be quite different. In essence it would be necessary to accumulate all capital advances made to the subsidiary for financing the exploration, and the parent company would only be allowed a tax deduction if the project were eventually abandoned. The subsidiary would be unable to obtain tax relief in the UK unless and until it had other UK income against which to get its deductions from its UK operations.

The group argued that the tax reliefs available to US companies were instruments of policy designed to foster and encourage the active exploration for and development of available petroleum resources. If the effect of such reliefs was nullified by local restrictions the inducement to invest risk capital in such an area was reduced in comparison to areas where their benefit was not denied by local law. The group emphasised that whichever form of corporate organisation was adopted the UK tax yield was not affected since this liability is paid first and the amount so paid was allowed as a credit against US taxes. They argued further that UK tax laws were sufficiently comprehensive to ensure that no tax avoidance could take place, and the provisions of the Exchange Control Act, 1947 would prevent any erosion of the UK foreign exchange reserves. It was suggested that the present restriction requiring local incorporation contained in the Petroleum (Production) Regulations 1935 for operations on the Continental Shelf could be replaced by a minimum requirement of registration as an overseas company under the Companies Act, 1948 and the vesting of a discretion in the Minister of Power.

The Ministry of Power considered these proposals. Historically, as a safeguard, it had been the normal practice, as far as foreign companies were concerned, to award (onshore) licences only to subsidiaries incorporated in the UK. A UK company was more amenable to legal process than a foreign one, and obligations could be imposed regarding the nationality of at least some of the operating and administrative staff. Since the 1934 Act issues relating to the balance of payments and taxation had become very important and increased the need for safeguards. The views of the Treasury on these issues were thus sought.

The response was that in principle there was no need to insist that licences should be granted to companies incorporated in the UK. The main concern of the Treasury was to ensure that foreign companies operating in the UKCS came under UK control, particularly so far as concerned earnings, profits and eventual repatriation of capital. From an exchange control viewpoint local incorporation was not essential. An approved UK branch could be designated as resident in the UK for exchange control purposes. It would then follow that normal exchange control procedures would ensure that there would be a proper control over the operations of the branch.

The Inland Revenue's perspective obviously centred on the taxation conse-quences of different corporate structures. While agreeing that the place of incor-poration of the company would not normally affect the tax yield the point could be material, and in the interests of equity and of simplicity they favoured making incorporation of a UK subsidiary a condition of operating in the UKCS. More-over, the UK subsidiary should have its central management and control in the UK. The key point as far as income tax was concerned was that a company should be resident in the UK for tax purposes. This in practice required that central management and control of its operations was in the UK. If a licence were given to a company not resident in the UK tax would be chargeable on its profits arising from trading in the UK. There was some doubt as to whether such profits would include those derived from operations in the UKCS.

The Ministry of Power concluded from the above that it should aim to ensure that all licensees had their central management and control in the UK *and* that they should be incorporated in the UK. They had then to consider whether there was a need to incorporate such requirements in the Continental Shelf Bill or whether they had adequate powers under the Regulations. In the event it was decided that provisions in the Bill were not required. The issue of allowing opera-tions on the UKCS via the branch of a foreign company was subsequently to re-emerge as a substantial issue.

The policy issues were discussed at the Economic Policy Committee (EPC). The Foreign Office expressed disquiet at the proposal to ensure that licensees would be subject to UK exchange control. They were concerned that restrictions on the ability of companies to make remittances out of a producing country could create a dangerous precedent which might be seized on by Middle East or other producing countries. The Minister's paper to the Economic Policy Committee had acknowledged that arrangements made for operations in the UKCS should not form an embarrassing precedent for the UK's large and proven overseas investments. The Foreign Office felt that the proposal with respect to exchange control did precisely that. As a result it was decided that the issue of exchange control would be considered further. But such consideration took place after the Bill was enacted.

Criminal and civil law

As early as April 1962, it was recognised by an inter-departmental group that some system of criminal and civil law would have to apply to activities in the UKCS. The group thought that it was more than doubtful if criminal law in its existing form could be applied to installations in the North Sea. The group was aware, however, that the International Law Commission had stated that even limited sovereignty could in certain circumstances be taken to include criminal law. Further, an extension of existing law to the installations appeared to be permissive, and this could in turn be extended to the seabed, even if foreign nationals were involved. With respect to civil law the group felt that there were no great difficulties. To the extent that the parties concerned were within the jurisdiction of British law actions could proceed for torts and breach of contract. Further, a ship could be dealt with by the Admiralty Court if it came within its jurisdiction. It was recognised that in some circumstances an individual would have to be brought within UK jurisdiction, and civil actions could be brought against persons who were abroad provided that the tort was committed in the UK. It was recognised that the UKCS would have to be divided into sections to be covered respectively by English, Scots and other law. The group's conclusions were that both criminal and civil law should be extended to the UKCS. This could best be achieved through a general law with delegated powers to deal with minor details.

The general extension of civil law to the UKCS was widely supported among Departments. With respect to criminal law Parliamentary Counsel felt that it should extend only to the specific areas contained within the safety zones surrounding offshore installations. These had been defined in Article 5 of the Convention on the Continental Shelf as areas extending to a distance of 500 metres around installations employed to exploit oil and gas. This view eventually prevailed and was reflected in the Bill and subsequently the Act. Thus criminal law does not automatically apply to all parts of the UKCS, but only within the safety zones. In general the effect of the legislation was to "assimilate acts on and around installations over the Continental Shelf to acts anywhere in the UK".[13] While the division of the UKCS into sectors where different legal systems prevail applies to civil law this does not operate with respect to criminal law.

Pipelines

A particular issue arose with respect to pipelines in the UKCS. The Ministry of Power view in late 1963 was that the Pipelines Act, 1962 being largely concerned with the regulation of onshore pipelines was substantially irrelevant. It included sections dealing with subjects such as compulsory acquisition of land and pipelines in streets. Interestingly, the Ministry also felt that the sections of the Act dealing with sharing of pipelines appeared to be unnecessary since their primary purpose was to avoid the construction of superfluous pipelines. Further, it was thought that pipelines laid on the seabed would not give rise to any risk of fire, explosion or pollution of drinking water, and safety controls would therefore also be unnecessary. The key objective was to ensure that pipelines did not interfere with one another or with other things laid on the seabed. This could readily be achieved by Regulations, and there did not seem to be a need for special provisions on pipelines in the Bill. It was acknowledged that such Regulations would not capture international pipelines laid right across the UKCS, but these would come within the scope of the 1962 Pipelines Act as soon as they entered territorial waters. The Government would thereby be able to exercise control over such pipelines.

After further deliberation it was decided that, as far as licensees in the UKCS were concerned, it was more appropriate that the rights to build pipelines be given through the applications of Section 3 of the 1934 Act. Such pipelines would, of course, extend outside licensed blocks. This gave rise to another issue generally termed ancillary rights. The oil companies had raised this subject. Their legal group made a submission to the Ministry of Power which distinguished sharply between rights within the licensed area and rights outside it. The latter included rights onshore relating, for example, to pipeline landing points and terminals. Their main proposal was that the Minister, when persuaded that an application by a licensee was necessary for the efficient exploitation of the petroleum, should compulsorily acquire the necessary land or other ancillary rights. It was recognised that compensation for the acquisition of such rights would be appropriate. The industry group proposed that the Minister be liable for such compensation, but that the relevant licensee would indemnify and hold harmless the Minister for all costs relating to the acquisition of the rights and pay the compensation. Before exercising his rights of compulsory acquisition the Minister had to be satisfied that the licensee, acting in good faith, had failed to acquire the rights by negotiation with the relevant parties.

The Ministry of Power considered these proposals. Their conclusion, noted above, was that Section 3 of the 1934 Act which applied onshore should be applied to the UKCS. This Act in turn attracted Part 1 of the Mines (Working Facilities and Support Act, 1923). The effect was that a licensee, having failed to acquire the ancillary rights he desired by negotiation, could apply to the Minister for a grant of that right. If the Minister felt that a *prima facie* case had been made the matter would be referred to the High Court. In turn if the High Court was satisfied that the statutory requirements were complied with, and that it was expedient in the national interest, it could grant the applicant the right he sought, subject to his paying compensation. The Ministry felt that the requests from the oil industry group for compulsory purchase powers would be going too far for private industry. For activities relating to onshore petroleum the companies required a Private Bill to obtain compulsory powers. If their proposals were enacted there would be a large and odd distinction between, say, storage tanks required to hold offshore and onshore oil. The Ministry's proposal was a compromise which did offer some help to a licensee in the UKCS. In the event that the required rights were not forthcoming through voluntary negotiation the Ministry's proposals offered a facility which would be useful, and perhaps preferable to the elaborate and expensive procedure of a Private Bill. The legal and policy issues relating to ancillary rights and the construction and use of offshore pipelines were by no means settled by the 1964 Act and associated Regulations, and were to be the subject of much further debate at a later date.

Fishing industry interests

North Sea oil exploration and the prospective presence of pipelines and other installations had already attracted the attention of the fishing industry. In the early 1960s a significant amount of (unlicensed but legal) seismic work was undertaken. Complaints were made by the fishing industry, to the effect that (a) charges in excess of the agreed maximum were being exploded, (b) that they had been exploded well within the agreed minimum distance of half-a-mile from any ship, (c) that they had been exploded at depth, and that quantities of fish had either been killed or frightened away, and (d) that there was inadequate consultation with local representatives of the Ministry of Agriculture, Fisheries, and Food (MAFF).

A meeting comprising representatives of the Ministry of Power, MAFF, Ministry of Transport, 3 geophysical companies and 2 oil companies was held in July 1963 to discuss these claims. In discussion the Departmental representatives pointed out that when the 50lbs maximum weight, ½ mile distance rules were introduced it was anticipated that the normal charge would be one of 16⅔lbs with charges of 33⅓lbs and 50lbs being used only as absolutely necessary. Officials suggested that consideration might be given to the use of black powder in place of ammonium nitrate, and reference was made to experiments carried out off the Californian coast, as a result of which 50lbs of black powder was considered to be the maximum necessary. Charges should be kept as small as possible and exploded at as great a distance from shipping as possible.

The contractors responded by stating that black powder was not as effective as ammonium nitrate. Further, a charge of 16⅔lbs of the latter was often inadequate as the noise of the explosion frequently did not exceed that of water turbulence. It was also of universal interest to use the minimum charge possible, but in about 50% – 75% of cases it was necessary to use 33⅓lbs. charges. With respect to the USA, the contractors stated that the Californian laws were introduced under pressure from sporting as distinct from commercial fishermen. Among other states, when fishing conditions were comparable to those of the North Sea, Mississippi and Louisiana had maximum limits of 50lbs of any kind of explosive and in Texas the limit was 40lbs. The charges were never deliberately exploded at depths of more than 6 feet, though on occasion the flotation device failed. It was inevitable that some fish would be killed, but experience in other parts of the world showed that fish were attracted by seismic survey operations.

Following discussion the company representatives gave assurances that all charges would be kept to a minimum, that no charges would be exploded within a minimum distance of ½ mile from any ship, that no charge would be deliberately exploded at a depth greater than 6 feet, that regular contact would be made with representatives of MAFF, and that instructions on these lines would be given to captains of all survey vessels. At this time the Government had limited powers in this area. Officials reminded the contractors that within territorial waters their activities were controlled by the terms of licences awarded under the 1934 Act. In waters outside these limits such Regulations did not apply.

Safety zones

The fishing industry had other concerns. The Ministry of Power had proposed that no ships be allowed to enter safety zones around installations (500 metres). The Department of Agriculture and Fisheries for Scotland (DAFS) argued that the installations in the North Sea and the associated proposed safety zones would cause much more inconvenience to fishing vessels than to other ships such as cargo vessels. In particular there were problems for a vessel engaged in drift net fishing which might have hundreds of yards of net paid out on the beam of the vessel. So far as the trawlers were concerned it was probably not so much the exist-ence of artificial islands with their navigational hazards and possible zones of protection around them which might impede fishing, as the pipelines which might be strung across the seabed. Upon further inquiries by the Ministry of Power it was confirmed that the yardage of nets from drifters could be as much as 3,500.

The Ministry responded by expressing the view that, while there were reason-able hopes that the North Sea would yield commercially exploitable reserves, it was unlikely that this would result in a proliferation of pipelines in the area. When the exact location of these pipelines became known administrative arrangements could be made to advise the trawling interests of their existence. The Ministry did not envisage the creation of what the Chancellor of the Exchequer described as a "network of spaghetti" in the North Sea.

The Ministry also offered some comfort to the drifter interest by pointing out that, provided a drifter kept outside the safety area, irrespective of where his nets happened to be in relation to the installation, no offence would have been committed in law. The Ministry acknowledged that this would be of little consola-tion to the owner master of the drifter and the owner of the installation if the former's nets become entangled in the installation.

The Ministry had already considered that, in such circumstances, the principle of compensation for sacrifice of fishing equipment was worthy, and this was planned for inclusion in the Continental Shelf Bill. One of the oil industry consult-ative groups had suggested that such compensation should be extended to those cases where equipment was sacrificed for the protection of installations and devices other than submarine cables and pipelines. The Ministry was considering whether such an extension was appropriate. The DAFS was in no doubt that fishing inter-ests would feel more secure if there were a statutory requirement that the owners of Continental Shelf installations should pay compensation in cases where fishermen had to sacrifice their gear as a consequence of entanglement with the installations. In the event while the principle of compensation was established in the 1964 Act the details of the mechanism had to be worked out at a later date.

Pollution of seas

In the Continental Shelf Bill the Government responded to the requirement under Article 24 of the High Seas Convention to legislate to prevent pollution of the seas arising from petroleum exploitation in the UKCS. Pollution from shippers was already dealt with by the Oil in Navigable Waters Acts (1955 and 1963), but new legislation was required to deal with discharges of oil from pipelines and installations. While there was widespread agreement on the principles debate arose over how offenders would be dealt with under the law. The draft Bill did not specify any Department as being responsible for bringing prosecutions. This was because the Ministry of Power had been advised that this was not necessary as it was open to any person in England and Wales to initiate proceedings against an offender, while in Scotland only the Procurator Fiscal could take action. Any attempt to depart from this position and to limit the right to prosecute would meet with strong opposition from the Lord Chancellor. It was understood that this procedure left doubts about the identity of the Minister who could be questioned in the event of any pollution.

There were also unresolved problems regarding how the provision would be administered. The Minister was advised that enforcement of the similar provisions in the Oil in Navigable Waters Acts, in regard to the discharge of oily mixtures from ships, had proved so far to be virtually impossible. The advice to the Minister was to proceed with the subject in the Bill in general terms and consider the detailed administrative procedures at a later date with the Ministry of Transport.

In debate at Committee Stage the Opposition wanted to impose more severe penalties on offenders than were contemplated by the Ministry, and in particular proposed the possibility of a prison sentence as well as much higher fines than the Ministry was contemplating. The Government resisted this on the grounds that penalties in the Bill had to be consistent with the penalties for those offences; it was inappropriate to provide higher penalties for the limited aspect of oil pollution within the clause. The result in the Act was a maximum fine of £1,000 on summary conviction, and on indictment a fine at the discretion of the courts. All the issues noted above re-emerged for further consideration as North Sea activity developed.

Article 25 of the High Seas Convention required states to prevent the pollution of the seas by the dumping of radioactive wastes. Legislation had to take account of standards formulated by appropriate international organisations. When the Continental Shelf Bill was being prepared such standards had not yet been determined. The Ministry's approach was thus to apply the relevant sections of the Radioactive Substances Act, 1960 to offshore installations, and to make provision for modifications to be made. Further, some new legislation was required, because licensees would employ radioactive substances to obtain information on the characteristics of the subsoil through which they drilled in order to ascertain the presence of petroleum. Thus the radiations penetrated the surrounding strata and were reflected to recording devices which provided information on the porosity and permeability of the strata. The Ministry required powers to control the disposal of radioactive wastes emanating from the drilling activities. Thus disposal into the sea would not be authorised until the Fisheries Minister had been consulted. The issue was later to emerge in a substantial way with respect to drill cuttings.

The Ministry recognised that there could be problems of exercising control over harmful substances. The main purpose of the 1960 Act was to prevent the unnecessary production of radioactive wastes, but it did not provide the means for safeguarding people who had to handle the radioactive materials. In most circumstances where they were used control was via Codes of Practice. The Ministry was aware that the Institute of Petroleum was planning to include this subject in its Code of Safe Practice which was to be applied to the North Sea, but felt that it should make its own further investigations into the subject. Thus in the Bill provision was made to make modifications to the 1960 Act.

Reflections on general approach to primary legislation for UKCS

It is clear from the above discussion of how the 1964 Act evolved that very heavy reliance was placed on amending and extending existing legislation. (This was to apply to the detailed Regulations as well.) While this is both understandable and consistent with the tradition of law-making in the UK, it remains surprising that the notion that petroleum exploitation offshore was fundamentally different in character from onshore activity was not considered to be strong enough to warrant a different legal framework. There is little evidence of an examination of the primary petroleum legislation of other countries (though the detailed regulations of other countries were examined).

The oil industry legal group did raise this issue. In a memorandum to the Ministry of Power their opening statement strongly recommended that, instead of using the UK 1934 Petroleum Act as a model, a modern, comprehensive and all-inclusive Act be considered. The group argued that the petroleum law should be inclusive and comprehensive, because any attempt to use licensing and regulations applicable to hard rock minerals created problems. All modern petroleum laws recognised that exploration, drilling, development and production of petroleum were not similar to the licensing and regulations applicable to hard minerals.

The emphasis on the need to distinguish between legislation appropriate for petroleum and for hard rock minerals is certainly correct, but the lawmakers of 1964 were aware of the differences and did take cognisance of the characteristics of petroleum exploitation. Whether they fully recognised the differences in the nature of offshore petroleum activity compared to onshore is much more open to debate. Whether petroleum laws should be comprehensive and all-inclusive is also open to debate. In many countries in primary legislation petroleum laws are brief and deal only with high-level principles. Detailed issues are dealt with in subsidiary Regulations. As noted above the latter may be changed relatively easily. From the Government's viewpoint this gives flexibility to deal with evolving issues. From the oil company's viewpoint, however, it could introduce an element of uncertainty into the investment climate. It is certainly the case that the Government did not foresee many of the issues requiring legal or regulatory action on its part as North Sea activity evolved. But such foresight was not generally noticeable among other interested parties either. The lack of acknowledgement of the fundamental differences in offshore activities compared to onshore remains a valid criticism. Some important subjects were either not dealt with comprehensively or were omitted altogether as is discussed later in this history.

The Bill completed its passage through Parliament on 13th April 1964, and received the Royal Assent on 15th April. Following enactment the Government could proceed to ratify the Convention on the Continental Shelf. This was undertaken on 11th May 1964. The UK's instrument of ratification was the twenty-second such instrument. This was the number required for bringing the whole Convention into force which occurred thirty days later.

Ministry's approach to Regulations

Preparatory work for the first Licence Round proceeded in parallel with that on the primary legislation. In its approach to the design of Regulations the Ministry of Power felt that two distinct aspects had to be addressed. Thus the Government was the guardian of the country's economic well being, and at the same time it was effectively the proprietor of the assets and was making a bargain with private concerns. In recognition of the first aspect the Ministry felt that the objectives should be (1) to encourage the earliest possible discovery of maximum quantities of fuels to provide a new indigenous source of energy, (2) to require that they be exploited in the manner which was most economical in the long term, and (3) to require that they be exploited at a rate commensurate with the country's energy requirements.

With respect to the second aspect, the Ministry considered that the Government should attempt (1) to obtain the maximum revenue for the Exchequer, (2) to ensure that competition between the companies was, and was seen to be, free, (3) to award licences in a way which was, and was seen to be, fair, (4) to respect the Government's contractual obligations towards licensees, and (5) to avoid treating foreign oil interests in a way which foreign Governments could cite in justification of measures taken against UK oil interests abroad.

The Government's objectives would be pursued through the use of the licence system. It was recognised that there was no reason to suppose that any particular company's interests would coincide with those of the Government. An oil company would typically have operations in several countries and its actions would be primarily concerned with its overall profits including the minimisation of taxation. Thus the system of issuing licences and the terms of these would have to represent a compromise between the interests of the two parties.

The Ministry felt that several main problems had to be resolved in framing the Regulations to accompany the licences. The first was the appropriate system for dealing with competing applications for the same area of the UKCS. The Ministry recognised that there were two main methods, namely formal competitive tenders or the exercise of Ministerial discretion. Under the first method applicants would submit competitive sealed tenders which could be related to (1) a stated quantity of work, or (2) a stated value of work, or (3) a stated cash bonus payment, or (4) a stated royalty above the minimum. A possible variation would be a combination of these. An implication of this method was that the Minister would have to accept the most favourable tender, though he might be able to reserve the right to do otherwise for publicly stated reasons. It was recognised that under this system potential applicants would have to provide satisfactory evidence about their competence to carry out their obligations.

Under the discretionary system the Minister would reserve full powers to reject any application. To inform decision-making, applicants would be invited to submit information either (a) about their intended work programme and other relevant matters or (b) any relevant information they might care to volunteer in support of their application.

The next main issue identified by the Ministry related to the system of royalties. There were choices to be made (for oil and gas separately) on several matters, namely (1) whether the royalty should be specific or *ad valorem*, (2) if *ad valorem* the basis of valuation, (3) whether there should be a sliding scale based on production, (4) what provision should be made for positive revisions to obligations, and (5) what scope there should be for arbitration.

The third main issue identified by the Ministry was the appropriate size of area (block) for the licences. The considerations involved in determining these were that they should be (1) large enough to form an area to be economically workable without recourse to unit development schemes, (2) large enough to relieve the Ministry of dealing with unnecessary numbers of separate applications, and (3) small enough to encourage competition for licenses and to discourage sterilisation.

The next major issue was whether to allow US companies to apply without incorporating a UK subsidiary. They would thereby have a competitive advantage over British and other foreign companies because of the generous US tax laws relating to tax deductions and allowances.

A further perceived major issue was whether there should be some safeguards against the contingency of oil or natural gas from the UKCS being exported with the result that more oil or gas was imported, at higher cost in sterling or foreign exchange. As discussed above it was recognised that there were technical limitations on the Government's powers in this area. Thus any prohibition on export under the licence would bind only the licensee. He could be required to stipulate, on selling the oil or gas, that the purchaser would not export it, but the Minister would have no direct rights against the purchasers, and the object could easily be defeated in practice by a series of sales. It was recognised that a more effective safeguard would be a statutory prohibition on export effective against all persons whatsoever, but in view of the possibilities of substitution and processing this prohibition might have to extend to petroleum in all its forms.

While the above were considered to be the major policy issues the Ministry recognised that other matters would also give rise to controversy. These related to (1) assignment of licences, (2) duration of licences, (3) work obligations, (4) minimum annual payments, and (5) non-exclusive licences for exploration only.

Views of oil companies

By this time the Ministry had already been appraised of the views of the oil companies. As early as November 1962, Shell had indicated their views. With respect to
the appropriate size of licence area the company thought that for a prospecting
licence it should be 1,000 square miles and that the maximum permitted area for
a mining licence should be 500 square miles. These areas compared with 200 and
100 square miles respectively under the existing Regulations for onshore prospecting and mining. Shell argued that in an area virtually unknown geologically
such as the North Sea, where the information on which area to choose with much
precision was lacking, a very large number of licences of this size [200 square
miles] would be needed by an intending prospector, which would create difficulties for the carrying out of a logical and progressive exploration programme.

With respect to the duration of the prospecting licence Shell again argued that,
because the North Sea area was so little known geologically, plus the fact that
seismic work could not be carried out during the winter, a fixed six-year period
was appropriate, plus a two-year renewal period at the investor's option. Within
this period the company would have the right to proceed to a mining licence. As
noted above the maximum permitted area for this would generally be 500 square
miles. A further reason for preferring this large size was because it would enable a
successful licensee to hold a larger area with offset of the very high rates of surface
rental payments which was reasonable in view of the considerably greater expenditure involved in operations over areas covered by the sea. The company suggested
that, as an alternative, the surface rentals for mining licences should, for marine
areas, be very considerably reduced. On the question of royalties on natural gas,
Shell felt that the current scheme involving a rate of 5% of the selling price less the
cost of getting the gas from wellhead to the point of sale was appropriate for
licences in the UKCS.

Subsequently, the oil industry formed a committee to consider licensing terms
for the UKCS. There were 17 company members of this group, including both
large and medium sized ones. They met on 6 occasions in the last quarter of 1963
and submitted a report to the Ministry of Power on 12th December 1963.

The Committee proposed that a new form of licence, with the suggested title of
Exploration Licence, be introduced. This would permit geophysical work and
core drilling but not the drilling of test wells. The licence would carry no other
rights, would be non-exclusive, and would apply only to areas not covered by
mining licences. There would be no limit to the size of area covered by such
licences. The licence period should be 3 years. An application fee of £1,000 should
be payable.

The Committee recognised that it was quite likely that, with respect to exclusive
licences to explore and exploit, there would be applications for areas which would
overlap one another very extensively. To reduce such overlapping to a relatively
simple pattern, the Committee recommended that the Minister should determine
and announce a series of numbered blocks over which he was willing to accept
applications. These areas would be bounded by lines of latitude and longitude

representing equal subdivisions of a degree, and would each be of a size equal to the maximum size permissible for an exclusive licence. The Committee termed this procedure the predesignation of licence areas. All applications for licences would have to conform to this predesignated pattern. A minority of the Committee (3 companies) did not favour advance predesignation by the Ministry on the grounds that choice of area should nowhere be restricted in advance. This view was based on a wish, in the interest of economy and efficiency, to avoid as far as possible restrictions on freedom of choice by the investor.

Among the membership of the Committee there was no unanimity regarding the maximum size of exclusive licence. Some favoured areas of the order of 900-1,000 square miles to secure maximum freedom of operation both in the exploration and development stages, and because they felt that materially smaller areas, particularly if these were awarded in accordance with the predesignated pattern, would tend unnecessarily to subdivide individual geological structures capable of containing petroleum among several companies which was not conducive to the best methods of appraisal and exploitation. This argument was not developed further, but attention could have been drawn to the possibility that petroleum discoveries might be made which straddled separate blocks in the hands of different licensees. In the event this was not uncommon, and gave rise to quite troublesome problems of unitisation and delays in the whole field development process.

A number of members of the Committee preferred smaller sizes of licence areas by which they meant around 500 square miles. This group felt that there was likely to be intense competition in some parts of the North Sea where preliminary seismic surveys had already been made and where prospects were regarded as favourable. Thus if the blocks were around 1,000 square miles there would be much overlapping or multiple applications for one block. The group felt that in these circumstances if would be a difficult task for the Minister to allocate the licences. If, however, the size of blocks were smaller, overlapping applications for any block would be less likely. Further, if the blocks were as large as 1,000 square miles only a few applicants would have the chance to obtain licences in the best areas, but if the blocks were smaller more companies would be able to obtain licences. This group concluded that a system with smaller blocks was more equitable and would encourage more intensive exploratory activity. For these reasons two member companies preferred still smaller areas of around 200 square miles.

The Committee also considered how overlapping or competing applications for the same blocks should be handled. It felt that when overlapping applications were received the Minister should notify all those concerned. Subsequently they should endeavour to reach agreement amongst themselves within a stated period. If they were to do so, and if the Minister agreed with the arrangements made, he might grant the licence on the standard terms.

In the event that the competing applicants for a block were unable to agree among themselves the Committee considered two main possibilities. The first was a form of competitive tender, based upon applicants' comparative willingness to submit to certain obligations. These obligations could sometimes take the form of bids of money payable as a premium on grant of licence, sometimes of commitments to do stated amounts of work, or work to a related cost. The Committee, with only one dissentient, felt that cash premia were not an appropriate consideration in the UK, and that the tender price, as it were, should take the form of an offer of work; the dissenting company thought that cash bids were appropriate as producing a useful source of revenue for the Government.

The second method considered by the Committee was to leave the decision to the unqualified discretion of the Minister. Applicants would be free to indicate to the Ministry what programme of work they intended to undertake, so that the Minister would be able to take into account, and pay due regard to, this as well as other factors which were considered relevant.

The argument of the members who favoured the full Ministerial discretion method was that apart from basic criteria of eligibility such as were already in the Regulations, there were many matters which a Minister in the UK might have to take into account in exercising a discretion entrusted to him to grant licences, including varying considerations stemming from Parliamentary and public feeling and many fine shades of individual circumstances! This group thought it reasonable that investors should rely entirely on the discretion of the Minister after he had made himself aware of all the relevant circumstances. The group noted that this was the situation onshore in the UK and it had operated perfectly satisfactorily without impeding the discovery of oil and gas. A further argument presented by this group was that exploration of unproven areas proceeded step by step, and was most efficiently carried out free from heavy work commitments extending over a long term, in excess of the minimum necessary to ensure adequate diligence.

The group of companies which favoured the tender system argued that there might well be intense competition for some blocks. In these circumstances the Minister would be substantially assisted in reaching a decision by obtaining comparable information from all interested applicants on a uniform set of relevant factors, or, alternatively, on a single factor in a competitive tender. This group was not opposing exercise of Ministerial discretion in dealing with overlapping applications. They felt, however, that the use of objective criteria would ensure that all applicants would have an equal opportunity to present their proposals on a comparative basis, and an objective decision by the Ministry on that basis would be facilitated. The group proposed two possible courses of action. Under the first the Minister would request each applicant to submit further information on those factors which he then determined to be relevant, and which would include a description of the exploration and drilling programme that they were willing to undertake, and a statement of the amount of money to be spent each year on this programme. On the basis of this further information the Minister would make his decision.

The alternative possible procedure would require applicants to submit their proposed work programmes for the block in question, expressed in money terms on an annual basis, on the understanding that the block would be granted to the applicant submitting the most advantageous proposed work programme. Under both of these proposals the winning applicant would have to provide a guarantee for the performance of the obligations incorporated in his bid.

The Committee informed the Ministry that approximately 50% of their members favoured the full discretionary approach and 50% the competitive tender route. As noted above, only one member of the Committee favoured the cash bonus bid method of allocating blocks. The company in question was Superior Oil, and in a letter to the Ministry the company argued that cash bonuses should not be looked upon lightly considering the hundreds of millions of dollars received by the United States in this manner on blocks in the Gulf of Mexico, and by Venezuela and certain of the Canadian provinces for leases. The company added that the benefit to the Crown from this type of bidding was far greater than the benefit of a work commitment. Such work would be performed in any event because it was essential for the proper exploration and exploitation of the licensed area. There were further possible secondary benefits from the bonus bid method. It would preclude speculative acquisition of areas by anyone not interested in their development, and would obviate the necessity of systematic and detailed bookkeeping and auditing to verify work commitments and the justification of including expenses that would be necessary in order to substantiate a work-obligation type bid.

In the same letter Superior Oil also expressed its views on the subject of the appropriate size of blocks. They stated that for an exclusive prospecting licence the area should cover one unit of the proposed five-minute grid or approximately 33.33 square miles. In amplification of their case they added that such an area of 21,000 plus acres was large in comparison to the 5,000 acre blocks awarded as leases in the Gulf Coast waters by the states of Louisiana and Texas and by the United States Federal Government. A prospecting block of this size appeared small in comparison to the very large blocks (1,000 square miles) that had been proposed by several companies in the industry committee. Superior noted that practically all these companies were highly competitive in seeking the 5,000 acre blocks in the Gulf Coast waters. The company felt that if an investor desired to acquire a large amount of acreage then he should apply for a large number of blocks. With respect to what were then termed mining licences (for exploitation) the company stated that an area of 16.66 square miles was large enough, claiming that oil and gas fields of 10,600 + acres and 21,600 + acres were of good size and, depending upon subsurface conditions and petroleum practice, could be very economic and profitable to both the Crown and the company.

Other companies also made individual representations on the method of allocating blocks. At a meeting with the Minister of Power, the Chairman of BP, Sir Maurice Bridgeman, indicated his understanding that the Government's intention was to allocate blocks impartially. He was anxious that the Government should not lean over backwards in its impartiality, pointing out that in no countries where BP operated was it permitted to do so on equal terms with local companies. In the North Sea he felt that the Germans, Danish and French were showing strong preference for companies owned by their respective nationals. Even in the Netherlands, where impartiality was carried further than in most other countries, preference was given in effect to Shell, which was regarded in many ways as a wholly Dutch company. He also argued that, because BP was more dependent on

Middle East supplies than any other, it followed that diversification of sources of supply was more valuable to BP, and hence to the British national interest, than to other companies.

The Committee of oil companies expressed their views on several other licence issues. All members believed that there should be no absolute limitation on the number of licences granted to one company. Several companies felt, however, that some restrictions should apply. One member felt that there should be a limitation on the number of contiguous blocks held by any one licensee, even of 500 square miles. (This was felt to be a comparatively small size.) Further, this member felt that not more than three adjacent licence blocks should be granted to any one applicant in "overlap" areas. Four companies felt that to limit the number of blocks that any company could apply for would help to reduce the scale of any problem of overlapping applications, and suggested that this might be effected in an indirect manner by requiring an applicant to undertake to spend on exploration a minimum sum which should be substantial. However, in order not to make the obligation too rigid to be practical, the applicant should be free to aggregate licences for the purpose of fulfilling this undertaking.

The Committee gave its views on another important issue, namely the disposal of oil and gas. Under the existing (1935) Regulations the Minister could require a licensee to sell his petroleum for consumption in the UK up to the amount of the total domestic requirements. The Committee suggested that this requirement be limited to a proportion of a licensee's production equal to that which his production had to the total production of all licensees within the United Kingdom and the UK Continental Shelf. Subject to this provision the Committee thought that there should be freedom to export.

Debate within Ministry

The Ministry decided that changes in the types of licences were necessary for the UKCS. They favoured the introduction of a non-exclusive Exploration Licence which would permit exploration, up to but excluding the drilling of test wells. They also felt that the distinction between (exclusive) prospecting and mining licences issued under the 1935 Regulations had caused misunderstandings. They thus proposed to replace both with one type of licence which would permit exploration for an initial period followed by relinquishment of at least part of the acreage, with retention of the remainder for a further period. This licence would be called a Production Licence. This issue was resolved without significant debate.

The Ministry prepared a paper on important licensing issues for discussion with the Minister and for submission to the Economic Policy Committee (EPC). The paper highlighted the background against which licensing regulations had to be determined. There were now around 20 companies involved in initial surveying and it was clear that there was encouraging information. Of the 20 companies around 25% were British, with the great majority of the remainder being American. It was acknowledged that US companies were more numerous and that they had more experience of offshore operations. Their expertise and financial resources would be of great assistance in exploring and exploiting the North Sea area, and the UK must welcome their participation in these operations which were expensive and speculative. There should be special regard for those who had already made major contributions to the British economy – e.g. through building refineries here. The memorandum added that the Government would also be open to criticism if the arrangements were not of a kind which would give full opportunities for British-controlled companies up to the limits of their capacity. It was noteworthy that in the debate on the Continental Shelf Bill the case for a special position for British companies was mentioned by one or two speakers. It was acknowledged, however, that even if British participation were favoured in aggregate it was likely to be less than American.

The main objective in the licensing arrangements was seen to be to secure rapid and thorough exploration, and the economical exploitation, of the UKCS. The Regulations should be designed to harness competition among the operators to this end. The prime concern was the economic advantages to the wider community but there were also possibilities of substantial benefits to the Exchequer in the form of royalties and similar payments. But it was also recognised that there were limitations in this area. Thus the UK had very important oil concessions overseas and UK companies were under pressures in relation to these. It followed that care had to be taken to ensure that any arrangements taken in regard to the UKCS did not form an embarrassing precedent for the UK's large and proven overseas investments.

Several conclusions were made from the above reasoning. There should be a requirement that licensees should be registered in the UK. This was common practice and it ensured reasonable equality of financial treatment among the licensees. Moreover it would reduce the prospects of remittances of foreign exchange by operating companies which were foreign controlled. Such remittances could become a substantial foreign exchange drain in the event of a large and fortunate strike. In considering the award of licences to foreign companies there would also be regard to the question of how far British controlled companies received equitable treatment in the foreign country in question.

Method of award of licences

The memorandum then discussed the method of award of licences. It noted that in some countries, particularly the USA, concession areas were put up to auction. It was acknowledged that this had advantages, namely administrative simplicity, impartiality and financial return to the Exchequer, whether oil was found or not. The memorandum continued, however, that the Minister could not regard a system of that kind as appropriate at the present time. Because there could be no assurance of British shareholdings, a situation where, as a result of the auctioning of licences, there was little or no British ownership and participation was not tolerable. The memorandum also noted that the potential in the UKCS was still unproven, and it would not be right to impose into these matters a strong element of financial speculation. Further, there were other considerations which made it inevitable that the granting of licences should be at Ministerial discretion. It was clearly undesirable that these assets should be in the ownership, direct or indirect, of unfriendly foreigners!

Views from USA

In arriving at the views noted above the Ministry had available to it not only the recommendations of the oil industry but also those of the British Embassy in Washington of whom inquiries had been made. The Embassy had consulted with the Geological Survey Department of the Interior, particularly the Conservation Division. The latter strongly favoured the US system of bidding to decide between applicants competing for the same block. This was seen as avoiding all accusation of favouritism in the award of leases, and ruling out fly-by-night speculators. Moreover, the comparison and supervision of work programmes under the alternative method would be difficult and expensive, and there would always be plenty of excuses if, after an award on such a basis, licence holders were laggard in their work programmes. The Deputy Assistant Secretary in the Department of the Interior was also consulted. He favoured competitive bidding and added the view that, under the US variant involving sealed bids, while rigging of the bids was always possible, the system forced a company which strongly favoured a particular block to bid very much higher for the licence than would be the case in open auction.

Views of British Embassy in Washington

The British Embassy also expressed their views on the subject. How the UK Government chose to decide between competing applicants need not be determined or even influenced by the experience of other countries. In a subsequent letter it was noted that most of those talked to in the USA saw no alternative to competitive bidding as the means of settling which company should have what area. The Geological Survey were horrified at the concentration of power in one hand that a discretionary judgement by a UK Minister would confer. They pointed out that there would be a lot of misunderstanding on why some companies were turned down and some were successful. The letter concluded, however, by stating that it would be better to eschew bidding. The UK was not after the revenue, and the money might frighten off smaller but useful companies and ought to be reserved for exploration.

Further thinking within Ministry on financial aspects

Meanwhile the Ministry was developing its own thinking with respect to the financial aspects of licensing. On the assumption that the discretionary system of awarding licences would prevail, the view was that the financial terms should be the same for all applicants. There was concern that the perceived generous deductions available to US companies might give these companies a competitive advantage over others, and for this reason the Ministry still felt it desirable that all licensees should be registered companies in the UK.

At this time various fees were payable by holders of exclusive licences onshore. The first was the application fee the value of which was £20 or £40 according to the type of licence. Its purpose was simply to make a contribution to the Government's costs of handling applications. The Ministry now proposed a figure of £200 for offshore licences.

Initial fees were also payable. These were designed to test whether an application was serious, to act as a disincentive to tie up acreage, and to provide some useful revenue to the Exchequer. The tentative views of the Ministry were that up to £50 per square mile was justified. There were also annual payments. For onshore activities these had been kept at very low levels for all but three of the 328 licences, with the amounts varying from 5s to 15s per square mile according to the date of issue of the licence. The low rates had remained unchanged since 1935 in view of the meagre results obtained! The Ministry felt that the initial fee noted above would suffice over the first three or five years as a financial disincentive to leaving the acreage unworked. After that the annual fee could be increased yearly from perhaps £100 per square mile to £700 per square mile over a period of 10 years.

Royalties

With respect to royalties the Ministry now felt that they should be related to the value of the oil and gas rather than the quantity produced. It was noted that this was now the most common method around the world. Consideration had been given to the idea of a sliding scale where the rate of royalty varied with annual output, but the view was taken that without any information about the amounts that might be produced it would not be possible to determine the steps of such a scale in any way that would bear examination. A flat rate of 12.5% for both oil and gas was suggested as being in line with practice in other countries. The scheme of licence payments suggested permitted the fees paid to be fully offset against liability to royalty.

Discussions with Treasury

The views of the Treasury were sought on all the financial aspects relating to offshore licensing. A meeting was held on 3rd March 1964, at which the Ministry presented the suggestions discussed above. With respect to the proposed method of awarding licences Treasury representatives wondered whether there was a danger that a discretionary system (as opposed, for example, to an auction system) would lead to the Exchequer getting less than market value for the licences. Further, Treasury representatives wondered whether a discretionary system would be publicly defensible. The Ministry representatives had concluded that there was no alternative to a discretionary system unless the Government were prepared to accept the consequences of an automatic system, such as an auction.

For the reasons discussed in the draft EPC paper, the Ministry believed that the consequences of an automatic system would not be acceptable to the Government. The Ministry representatives further argued that, apart from broader political considerations, the financial and practical considerations did not necessarily favour an auction system. The existence of oil or gas on the UKCS was entirely speculative, and in these circumstances an auction might not be easily defensible in principle, and would be uncertain in its results. It could by no means be assumed that such a system would be financially to the advantage of the Exchequer.

The Ministry officials recognised that any discretionary system was bound to remain a potentially explosive question for Ministers especially when there was likely to be keen competition for certain sectors, and there would be obvious difficulties in deciding between competing and overlapping applications. There was some reassurance, however, in the fact that the overwhelming majority of the companies who had been consulted informally, accepted the need for a discretionary system.

Following discussion there was general agreement with the Ministry's view that the discretionary system should be employed. The Ministry was asked to redraft the paper to explain more fully and stress the importance of the issues involved in choosing between the auction and discretionary schemes.

In the discussions on the licence fees the Ministry acknowledged that there was necessarily an element of arbitrariness in the choice of the application and initial licence fees. With regard to those for the second phase of the licences it was felt that the incentive effect of payments of a scale of £100 per square mile rising to £700 (compared to £80 suggested by the oil companies) was unlikely to be significant. The Ministry in fact felt that the only effective weapon against "locking up" of acreage would be the provisions of the licence agreement for a work programme.

The Treasury representatives generally agreed with the levels of fees and royalty proposed by the Ministry. It accepted the need to avoid embarrassing UK companies' operations abroad by fixing the royalty rate too high. From this point of view 12.5% seemed right. The Ministry expressed concern that oil or gas might be found which could not be profitably exploited with a royalty rate of 12.5% and a discussion ensued on possible solutions to this problem. One was to provide in the Regulations for variations in royalty rates below 12.5%. There was a concern that this procedure would leave the Minister open to heavy pressure from companies for reductions which were not justified by the circumstances. An alternative procedure would be for the Minister to make variations in individual cases with the agreement of the Treasury. A Treasury representative suggested that the Regulations might provide that the Minister had reserve powers to waive royalties, but it would be clear that the concession would only be available in exceptional cases. The issue was left for further deliberation.

Exchange control

At this meeting the Treasury also raised the exchange control issues. If foreign investors had to incorporate subsidiaries in the UK this would mean that they were automatically resident for exchange control purposes. Under the exchange control rules non-sterling companies establishing in the UK were required to bring a reasonable proportion (such as 75%) of external capital with them, but would also have freedom to remit profits and repatriate capital. The Treasury would also wish to ensure that oil shipped abroad from the UKCS was paid for as an export. The Ministry acknowledged that a solution had not yet been found to the latter issue with respect to enforcement. Customs and Excise had been opposed to any form of policing of the Shelf for this purpose. This subject, therefore, needed to be examined further.

Detailed licensing Regulations

The Ministry's further deliberations on licence Regulations produced instructions to Legal Branch. These dealt with variations from the existing 1935 Regulations which applied onshore. On the larger subjects the Ministry felt that the initial term of the proposed Production Licence should be three years, after which time at least 50% of the area should be relinquished. Further, with respect to that part of the block, in formal language it was suggested that any section of the boundary of the part(s) which were not coincident with a boundary of a block should follow a line of latitude or longitude, and any such line should divide a block only so that the abandoned part of the block was not less in area than 60 square kilometres. This constrained the freedom of the investor in relinquishing acreage. It was also suggested that the term of the second part of the licence should be 25 years from the notification of the first relinquishment details.

With respect to the licence fees and royalties the amounts suggested at this time were in line with those discussed above, but it was proposed that the fees should be expressed in terms of square kilometres rather than square miles. It was also proposed that the accounting period for royalties be the calendar year, with payment to be made within two months of the end of the period. However, the Minister should have power to require reasonable payments on account, not more frequently than every three months.

On royalty matters it was proposed that valuation should be on the basis of an arm's length sale at wellhead. In a prophetic statement it was added that the task of making this more precise was not easy. As a basis for such a calculation it was suggested that it could be assumed that the petroleum was intended for transport to the nearest landing point in the UK, that all transport expenses were paid by the buyer, and that there was no commercial relationship between the buyer and seller. It was proposed that disagreement over the value should be made subject to arbitration. Confirming earlier views licence fees should be deductible from royalties payable but for the same period only.

Assignment

The Ministry now wanted a Regulation that a licensee could not assign his rights without the express permission of the Minister. Great emphasis was to be placed on the Minister's discretion in choosing licensees. Consistent with this, on a proposal for assignment the Minister should be free to consider all circumstances. Reflecting considerations raised by the Inland Revenue the Ministry also desired that the licence would determine when a licensee ceased to have its central management and control in the United Kingdom, and also when he ceased to be registered in the United Kingdom.

Landing obligation

The Ministry now proposed that there be a Regulation stipulating that any petro-leum obtained from the UKCS should be landed in the UK except with the prior consent of the Minister. The Regulations should also ensure that it would not be possible to avoid the Government's intention by routing a tanker containing petroleum through territorial waters on its way to an overseas destination.

Health and safety

With respect to health and safety issues the Ministry's proposals for Regulations at this stage were very general. The licensee should be obliged to comply with any requirements contained in the Code of Safe Practice of the Institute of Petroleum. The Minister would expect normally to be content with the Code, but in order that he should not be bound by the actions of a private body, he should be free if necessary to issue supplementary instructions.

Views of Legal Branch

Legal Branch expressed concern regarding some of these suggestions, and about the suggestion, emanating in a proposed amendment to the Continental Shelf Bill from the Opposition, to make specific provision for health, safety and welfare in the Model Clauses to the licences. Legal Branch pointed out that once a licence had been granted under any Regulations, the provisions were contractually binding and did not change when new Regulations came into force, as those would only prescribe clauses for licences granted later. Thus specific safety provi-sions should not be made in the Model Clauses accompanying licences. Legal Branch further reiterated its view that Regulations and Model Clauses could not refer directly to bodies such as the Institute of Petroleum. It was pointed out that the Select Committee on Statutory Instruments had recently taken strong objec-tion to Instruments which purported to incorporate the provisions of documents which were prepared by outside bodies.

With respect to the exchange control issues the Ministry had now learned from Customs and Excise that there should be no undue difficulty arranging adminis-trative procedures such as to ensure that the licensee obtained foreign currency for exports for which the Minister's prior consent had been obtained. Currently, every exporter lodged documents on export statistics with Customs and Excise, and once it was known how much oil and gas had been exported it was a relatively simple matter by referring to the licensees' books, to ensure that the proper currency had been obtained for it.

Views of Oil Industry Consultative Committee

At this stage in the debate on licensing terms the Oil Industry Consultative Committee submitted a detailed statement of their views on the above proposals which had been presented to them by the Ministry on 25th March 1964. The accompanying letter from the chairman indicated the very deep concern and anxiety which all the companies' representatives expressed at the overall effect of the provisions on the attractiveness of the UK offshore areas. They were of the unanimous provisional opinion that a régime incorporating the proposals would be of a severity, from the investor's point of view, unequalled in any comparable prospective environment elsewhere. They had fully expected that the speculative and operationally hazardous character of the UKCS would be recognised by the grant of terms likely to afford positive encouragement to prospective investors.

The Annexures to the letter amplified the Committee's views. With respect to the proposal that 50% of a licence area be surrendered after 3 years they were concerned that a company which had expended much effort and money might have to return to the Government petroleum bearing areas which could then be taken up by others. In arriving at this view the Committee pointed out that considerable geological and geophysical work was required. This could only be carried out in the summer months. Considerable time for interpretation was also required. Thus to select an area or areas for surrender needed precise calculations based on a very large amount of technical knowledge which could not be accumulated in the time period. For a company which had a number of blocks this problem would be more serious because it would have to carry out sufficient work, including drilling, practically simultaneously, so that it could be in a position at the end of the three year period to select the half of each block that it wanted to retain. The Committee then reiterated its recommendation that the initial period should be seven years. It also argued that the relinquishment obligation should not be such as to reduce the remaining area to less than 250 square kilometres (c. 100 square miles).

The group then argued that the proposal of the Ministry to make the original size of the blocks equal to 250 square kilometres was not understood. They argued that so small an area was rarely prescribed in comparable marine areas, and then only in regions which had been proved prolific in petroleum. The Committee was concerned that with such small licence areas, many, if not a majority of the structures that might be found, would, no doubt, be cut by the licence boundaries, a situation aggravated still further by the need to surrender half of the initial area of each licence.

The companies were also unhappy about the proposed duration of the licences, namely an initial period of three years plus a second period of twenty-five years. They pointed out that, in the event of a discovery, appraisal was required followed by the construction of the necessary installations for production and transportation. Then, after commencement of production some considerable time, several years at least, was still required before the level of optimum production could be achieved. The remaining period of, say, fifteen years might well be insufficient to recover investment and adequately reward the investor, when it was considered that the cost of offshore development was very much greater than development on land. The Committee asserted that the total proposed twenty-eight year period for exploration and production was believed to be the shortest period anywhere in the world. The group maintained that the total period of the licence should be not less than fifty years.

The Committee felt that the proposed royalty rate of 12.5% was unduly onerous in the existing circumstances. It was acknowledged that such a figure was not unusual, but in countries where it existed it was accompanied by taxation benefits not available in the UK. Thus in the main producing countries where 50/50 profit-sharing arrangements prevailed the royalty was fully incorporated into the Government's 50% share. (In other words the royalty was a credit for purposes of the profits tax calculation.) It was acknowledged that in the United States royalty was not a credit for profits tax but a deduction. However, in the United States the rate of profits tax at 48% was lower than in the UK and in addition there was a generous depletion allowance resulting in a substantially lower total government take than would be the case in the UK. In the UK the investor would have to pay the royalty plus tax in the neighbourhood of 54%. The Committee cited the case of Denmark which had a royalty rate of 5% for the first five years of production followed by a rate of 8.5%, even though the effective tax rate was 38%.

With respect to some of the detailed proposals of the Ministry the Committee was able to express agreement. This applied to the concept of valuation for royalty purposes being based on the arm's length sales method netted back to the well-head, and to the time period for rendering royalty accounts. With respect to ancillary rights the Committee recommended that the right of licensees to lay pipelines on the seabed for connection to the shore or to other pipelines should be explicitly recognised. Where such rights were exercised over concession areas of other licensees no unreasonable interference with the operations of the latter should take place. With respect to the power given to the Minister to revoke a licence in the event of a breach of licence conditions the Committee proposed that this be exercised only in the event of a serious breach. The licensee should also have the ability to invoke the arbitration procedure if he disputed the occurrence of the alleged breach.

Ministry/industry discussions

Following receipt of this document from the Committee a meeting was held in April 1964 between Ministry officials, including Mr Angus Beckett, Under Secretary, and oil company representatives. With respect to licence areas the Ministry clarified an apparent misunderstanding on the part of the companies. Thus the licensed area of an investor could cover more than one block. The small block was devised for administrative convenience and for reasons of fairness to the companies. With respect to the duration of the licence, the Ministry had taken into account the fact that oil companies had already undertaken some preliminary work in the North Sea. The Ministry did want to align the initial period with the time needed to undertake exploration, and recognised that shortage of equipment might hold up operations at the start of licence periods. On many other technical and minor issues views were exchanged and clarified. With respect to revocation of licences the proposals of the companies would cause great complications. They could require the preparation of lists of obligations categorised as major and minor. There was no precedent for this, and, even if it could be done, there would still be the position that there could be litigation and that the Minister might have no effective way of dealing with minor breaches. Present contract law did not permit the writing in of penalties; damages could not be claimed or assessed. The view of the Ministry was that the licensees would have to rely on the good sense of the Minister.

The Ministry made it clear that they were not enamoured with the principle of imposing work obligations, but they would consider this suggestion. They were not proposing to have an internal auction of work obligations nor to prescribe a minimum. There would have to be extensive "coming and going" between the Department and the various companies before licences would be issued for areas covered by two or more applications.

A further meeting was held three days later between the same Ministry officials and a group of oil company representatives to further discuss licensing issues. With respect to the method of application it was eventually agreed that each company should include in one application details of all the blocks for which it sought licences. The Ministry would subsequently advise companies of the blocks for which licences might be granted. The companies in question would then submit their proposed work programmes for final Ministry decision.

The companies again pressed for a lengthening of both the initial and second periods of the licence. With respect to the initial period they cited difficulties in obtaining equipment, and the difficult weather conditions. With respect to the second period they felt that twenty-five years was not long enough to deplete discoveries. They cited the corresponding position in several other countries including France, Algeria and Denmark at 50 years each, Venezuela at 40 years, and Columbia at 40 + 10 years. After discussion the Ministry agreed to support 6 years for the initial period and agreed to reconsider the length of the second period.

Another meeting between Ministry officials and oil company representatives was held to discuss financial matters. There was agreement on the general principles to be followed in valuing petroleum for royalty purposes. The companies were, however, unanimously opposed to an *ad valorem* rate of 12.5%. They argued that this produced an entirely new situation compared to the position for onshore activities. (These were then 4 shillings per ton for crude oil and for natural gas 2d per thousand cubic feet or 5% of the selling price whichever was the greater.) The consequence was that the potential profitability of the Shelf was substantially lessened, and the chances of investment in exploration and exploitation reduced. The companies reiterated the position in other countries which they had stated in their written submission in support of their view that the proposals were too severe. They added that the effect of the proposed rates throughout the rest of the world would be serious.

The companies also argued that the licence fees proposed by the Ministry were excessive. They argued that they were the highest in the world, and suggested that a licensee be allowed to offset a percentage of the expenditure on actual operations in each licensed area against the charges concerned or be allowed to offset the total of the charges against the aggregate of the royalties due. The Ministry regarded the first possibility as impracticable. Adopting the second would probably have to mean one licence for the whole of a company's holdings in a designated area. This would run counter to other proposals made by the industry, namely that an individual licence should contain not more than six blocks. The companies promised to consider the issue further.

The number of blocks to be covered by a licence and related issues had been the subject of debate within the Ministry. One view was that there should be a separate licence for every block. This was overruled, and the debate centred on the number of blocks that could be held under a single licence. A related consideration was the maximum area which could be included in an individual application. One suggestion had been that a company should be permitted to include in one application *all* the blocks for which a licence was requested. Views were expressed that this could cause difficulties which would increase with the extent to which the number of blocks in an individual application exceeded the maximum which the Ministry felt should be included in one licence. One objection was that the chances of avoiding overlapping applications decreased with the maximum permitted area in an individual application. A second problem could arise because oil companies would regard the individual application as one basic unit and would not be disposed to agree to the issue of licences for part of the basic unit until a decision on the whole had been reached. The ability to issue licences for areas in which there was no competition would thus be seriously impaired. A third problem would be that there would be a far greater tendency for oil companies to include in an overall application blocks which they did not really want for use as a bargaining or negotiating factor. The precision and sense of reality attached to a small application would be entirely missing. These arguments pointed towards the need for a substantial restriction on the permitted number of blocks per licence application.

Resolving remaining issues

Following the flurry of meetings with the industry and further internal discussions a progress report was prepared by Mr J. A. Beckett, Under Secretary. This emphasised that the oil companies had now agreed to block sizes of around 250 square kilometres, and to the basis of valuation for royalty. There were four remaining substantial policy issues on which the companies had made representations and on which final decisions had now to be made. The first was the maximum area to be covered by one licence. This was important because it was from one licence area that the investor could choose the 50% which he had to surrender at the end of the initial period. Also, it was on the basis of the licence area that he could offset his annual payments against his royalty obligations. His work obligations were also based on the whole licence area. From all this it followed that if the area was large the licensee could concentrate his investment on a small section, and yet prevent others exploiting the large section he left fallow. If it were too small, there would be a disincentive to investment and difficulties both for the Ministry and the industry over the surrender provisions.

Following discussions the Ministry now felt that a reasonable compromise would be to set a maximum of ten blocks for any one licence. An applicant could still obtain more than ten blocks, but they would have to be spread over more than one licence.

The second policy issue concerned the duration of the production licences. The companies had argued that the earlier proposals of the Ministry were of too short duration, both for the initial and second periods. The Ministry was now persuaded that the arguments of the companies discussed above, relating to the inclement North Sea weather, shortage of equipment, and the time needed to develop and deplete a discovery, had real weight. Therefore, it was now proposed to have a time period of six years for the initial period and forty years for the second period.

The third unresolved issue related to the request by the companies that they be allowed to surrender part of a licensed area at any time. (This was a separate issue from the requirement to surrender 50% at the end of the initial period.) The Ministry now proposed that this suggestion be accepted. Conditions would be attached. Thus any portion relinquished voluntarily would have to be of a prescribed shape and minimum size so that it could be offered to other concerns. Further, early relinquishment would not reduce the work obligations for the licensed area.

The fourth main issue was the rate of royalty. The companies had objected to the 12.5% rate proposed on the grounds discussed above. The Ministry was not disputing the claim that the UK tax rate of 53.75% (38.75% income tax plus 15% profits tax) was among the highest anywhere, and that in other countries where 12.5% royalty was imposed there were either special tax reliefs or royalties paid with a full credit against tax liability. The conclusion of the Ministry, however, was that the complaint of the companies was really against the level of taxation and not against 12.5% as a proper amount for the Government to exact for its property, and for this reason the Ministry was not disposed to give weight to the companies' argument.

It was acknowledged that the companies had to make allowance for all payments which they had to make to Government. The view of the Ministry at this time was that it was very unlikely that at this early stage, when not a single well had been drilled in the North Sea, any of the companies could make a financial forecast accurate enough to show whether a particular rate of royalty would be crucial. Elaborating on this subject the Ministry felt that even if the company judged, from offshore experience elsewhere, the capital cost per foot drilled, they could have no idea how many dry holes they would have or the extent of the reserves when found. It was acknowledged that such few objective facts as the companies had they would obviously keep to themselves, and the Ministry certainly had no independent sources of information. The conclusion was thus that it was recognised that in selecting 12.5% an arbitrary decision was taken but one which could stand on precedent: the fear of inhibiting activity was probably not very real. Although no hints had been given to the companies the commitment to 12.5% rate was not for all time, and thus if in a few years the companies showed signs of withdrawing their interest from the North Sea, for financial reasons rather than geological, the Ministry could, with Treasury agreement, offer new licences at a lower rate and even reduce the royalty administratively on current licences. In discussion with the companies the Ministry had also tacitly accepted the fiction that all companies would pay UK tax at the full rate. It was known, however, that the largest British companies paid hardly any tax in the UK at the present time because of double taxation and other reliefs. Some of the American controlled companies could be in the same position.

Further inter-departmental debate on financial terms

The Ministry's royalty and tax proposals were agreed by the Treasury but were the subject of further discussions within Government. Internal Ministry correspondence raised the subject of international repercussions of perceived onerous financial terms. It was suggested that there could be problems for both the Government and British based oil companies. Thus it could well cause the companies embarrassment, for instance in their negotiations with OPEC, and could equally be embarrassing to HMG in support of the operations of the international oil companies. It was argued that, from the viewpoint of overseas oil policy, the UK ought not to miss a splendid opportunity for giving the lead in some positive encouragement towards development, rather than to supply some ammunition to those countries who were wanting to tighten up concessionary terms. The conclusion was that UK conditions ought to be clearly seen to be at least as good as those elsewhere and preferably better, otherwise comparisons were bound to be made which would be to the UK's disadvantage overseas.

This issue was also taken up by the Foreign Office. In correspondence with the Ministry of Power they registered their concern that the licence Regulations should not store up undesirable repercussions on the international oil scene. It was acknowledged that the proposed financial terms were not out of line with current international levels, but the Foreign Office requested assurances that the Ministry of Power did not intend to ask more than this from companies exploiting the UKCS.

Regulations finalised

The Regulations were finalised and came into operation on 15th May 1964. The main terms conform to those discussed above. They thus drew heavily on the 1935 Regulations, but also reflected the Ministry's experience since then and their views of the conditions likely to prevail in the North Sea. At the time of their promulgation the Ministry highlighted the major points of interest from their perspective.

The Regulations would apply to territorial waters as well as areas of the Continental Shelf designated as coming within the UK's rights with respect to petroleum. It had been decided that, to maximise interest among investors those designated areas would consist of almost all of the UK's part of the North Sea. Somewhat curiously the financial terms of the licence were not in the Regulations because the working of the 1934 Act did not permit this. They were thus published in the London and Edinburgh Gazettes, and contained in a Schedule to a licence when the latter was issued. A clause was included with the intention of restraining a licensee from draining petroleum from another licence area. No part of a well could be less than 125 metres from the boundary of the block in question unless with the permission of the Minister. A further, complex clause on unit development was designed in the first place to encourage, and later, if necessary to compel, cooperative working of contiguous licensed areas with a view to securing the maximum recovery of oil or gas. Another clause was designed to ensure that petroleum from the UKCS was landed in the UK unless the Minister consented to its going elsewhere. Power was taken to attach conditions to such consent. This was to ensure that any petroleum sent directly overseas should comply with exchange control rules applicable to payment for exports. Another clause gave the Minister power to prohibit assignments. This was to prevent licensees attempting to assign licences to persons who would not themselves be eligible to secure licences. The clause dealing with revocation included the important power to revoke if the licensee ceased to be eligible as regards nationality, residence or central management and control. With regard to default on licence terms generally, the Ministry acknowledged that, in view of the large sums of money which would be committed by the licensees, the Minister could not in practice use the power except to deal with a board of directors who deliberately and flagrantly defied him in major matters over a period of time.

The sensitivities of the Foreign Office to reaction abroad were reflected in the Guidance Notes provided to foreign representatives of the Government. They were made aware that press comment in the UK had indicated that the financial terms of the licenses involved a 60:40 sharing in favour of the Government. It was suggested to recipients that, if faced with the proposition that the UK Government might have "sold the pass" in proposing terms which were significantly more favourable to the Government than those operating at present in the Middle East, it should be pointed out that assuming full payment of Income Tax and Profits Tax on top of the 12.5% royalty the Government take would be of the same order as that of the governments of several of the main producing countries. The Note added that the so-called 50:50 split then common in the Middle East worked out in practice to about 57:43 in favour of the Government because the Government take was calculated on the basis of posted prices while the oil companies had to sell their oil at realised prices which were significantly below the posted prices. The Note also emphasised that it was now common practice for host Governments to insist on bonus payments for concessions. These often involved very considerable sums. However, the UK Government had decided against this method of allocating blocks, and the payments during the initial licence period were modest.

Reflections on licence terms for First Round

These then were the considerations which went into the design of the licence terms for the First Licensing Round. How well they have served the nation has been the subject of much debate, informed with the benefit of hindsight. The prospective outcome of the exploration was clearly highly uncertain. The fact that over twenty companies had already undertaken some seismic work and had shown very keen interest in the legal and licensing terms were positive but not infallible indicators. The Ministry was handicapped by the lack of data which would have enhanced their knowledge of the prospectivity. Several companies had an advantage because they had at least some such data which they were not obliged to share with the Ministry because the legal and licensing framework had not yet been enacted. The revenues which might have been raised by licence auctions were certainly highly uncertain. One advantage of their employment, apart from any revenues, would have been the increased knowledge of the perceived attractiveness of the blocks in different areas. This would have helped to inform plans for subsequent licensing. At the time of the First Round the bonus bids would have been based on very sparse information, however, and could have been seriously misleading with regard to the prospectivity. In virgin territory there is much to be said for putting the main emphasis on the exploration activity itself. This will maximise the amount of relevant knowledge and information, and the prospects of early discoveries and production. On these grounds the use of the discretionary method in the First Round was quite defensible.

With respect to some of the individual licence terms hindsight reveals a few problems which might have been foreseen. One concerns the second period of the licence. In the event the duration of this at forty years will not be unduly long for some of the fields discovered in the First Round. In fact, some will require licence extensions. The problem relates to the conditions for retention of the acreage after first relinquishment. The only obligation was to pay an annual fee which increased to a stated maximum. This was relatively modest and was not even indexed for inflation: in other words the holding costs were quite low. In later years this was to become a major issue under the heading of fallow blocks and fields. The possibility was recognised by the Ministry at the time of the First Round, but understandably was not pursued. The rather disappointing experience of onshore activities would have relegated this consideration to a low priority.

The high level principles to be employed for the valuation of petroleum for royalty purposes when stated in general terms appeared uncontroversial. When subsequently practical applications were required difficulties emerged. The process for the determination of the wellhead value from a given landed value was not given detailed attention and subsequently led to long-lasting disputes with licensees. Even the determination of fair market value for petroleum landed in the UK was later found to raise serious practical problems.

It was recognised that offshore production methods would be different from onshore, most obviously involving installations specifically designed for operating in water. The Regulations relating to this concentrated on the Minister's rights to approve the drilling of wells. This was borrowed from the onshore Regulations where the well was by far the most important element in the whole exploitation process. With respect to offshore, however, there were other important issues including the type of producing system (for example, fixed, floating or jack-up) and transportation (pipeline or tanker). The choice among these development options and the more detailed characteristics of the production facilities were of wide national interest. The choices made could have repercussions for other users of the sea and on the recovery achieved from the field. But no formal field development approval was specified in the Regulations, an omission which subsequently had to be rectified for later licence rounds. Similarly powers relating to pipeline developments had to be taken in later legislation.

In the field of health and safety the Regulations were specified in very general form. Sadly, as events were soon to demonstrate, they were found to be inadequate to deal with the serious accidents which could occur in the North Sea working environment, and stronger legislation had to be introduced.

In sum the 1964 Act and the accompanying Regulations maintained a strong investor interest. The large number of applications plus the rapid growth in exploration when licences were awarded indicated that a régime had been developed which resulted in high activity. The system was thus successful in its prime objective.

Criteria governing award of licences

The key factors governing the award of licences were announced by Mr Fred Erroll, the Minister of Power, in a statement in the House of Commons on 7th April 1964. He itemised five, namely, "First, the need to encourage the most rapid and thorough exploration and economical exploitation of petroleum resources on the Continental Shelf. Second, the requirement that the applicant for a licence shall be incorporated in the United Kingdom and the profits of the operations shall be taxable here. Thirdly, in cases where the applicant is a foreign-owned concern, how far British oil companies receive equitable treatment in that country. Fourthly, we shall look at the programme of work of the applicant and also at the ability and resources to implement it. Fifthly, we shall look at the contribution the applicant has already made or is making towards the development of resources of our Continental Shelf and the development of our fuel economy generally". The Ministry had also decided that there would be two other strands of policy namely that the British share of the principal untested area should not be less than one-third, and that awards should be made to as many companies as possible that matched up to the essential criteria.

The First Round is launched

Events moved very rapidly after this. On the same day on which the Regulations became effective (15th May) notices inviting applications for both exclusive production licences and non-exclusive exploration ones were published in the London and Edinburgh Gazettes. The closing date for receipt of applications was set at 20th July. A total area covering c. 86,000 square miles of the North Sea stretching from the Shetlands to the English Channel had been designated by Orders in Council on 12th May. The total area chosen reflected a desire to maximise the potential interest, but also to ensure that no acreage was designated which could reasonably be claimed by neighbouring countries. The total area offered for licensing was divided into 960 blocks, with each covering an area of around 250 square kilometres (c.100 square miles).

Very encouraging response

The response was very encouraging. Applications were received for nearly 400 blocks covering a total area of around 38,000 square miles. There was much over-lapping in the applications. On examination the Ministry found that competition was particularly keen in an area of about 10,000 square miles, lying east of a line between Middlesbrough and the Wash, where on average there were about 9 applicants for every block. In total there were 61 individual applicants. They were often organised in groups which resulted in 31 separate applications, many of which covered several blocks. The concentration of bids was such that 230 blocks were contested by 29 applicants. On the other hand for no less than 164 blocks there was only one applicant.

The well-known, major international oil companies had applied for large numbers of blocks. There was also a substantial number of applications from middle-sized oil companies, largely American and Canadian. There were also applications from non-oil companies, an example being the Domestic Detergent Supply Company. Finally, there were several applications from individuals.

The Ministry was under considerable pressure to assess the applications quickly. Mr Erroll was anxious to make fast progress. In June 1964 he had sent a Minute stating that "with the finds made off Germany and Holland we may be pressed to move quicker ourselves. Can we speed up the licensing process?" He added that "I have a feeling that our procedure is going to look too leisurely now that gas is bubbling up uncontrolled in the North Sea".

Mr Angus Beckett, the Under Secretary, felt that the Minister could not prop-erly be criticised for being too leisurely. In support of this view he argued that the UK was, in the words of companies, "right out ahead" of the other North Sea countries. The Dutch Government had just produced a first draft of an enabling act, but the general consensus was that their Regulations would not see the light of day in 1964. The Norwegians hoped to enact legislation in 1965 which would be based on the UK's. In Germany the tussle between the Federal Government and the Lander was still going on. The Federal Government issued a decree prohib-iting anybody from operating in the German North Sea without permission, but in granting a consortium permission to drill it was entirely without prejudice to future legislation.

In the period immediately after the invitations to apply for blocks was announced the Ministry had been busy answering queries from prospective applicants. They also had to face the fact that at least a substantial number of companies would put in their applications on the very last day because they saw no need to take their final decision a moment before it was necessary.

Views of Opposition

There were also some political pressures urging restraint. Mr Tom Fraser, the Opposition Spokesman, requested a meeting with the Parliamentary Secretary. He wondered whether the national interest would not be better served by reserving some blocks for disposal later. It might be argued, he thought, that the Government should retain freedom for manoeuvre if developments on the Shelf indicated the need to change, for example, the conditions of licences or the level of royalties. The Minister's perspective was very different. He accepted that a date of 20th August – one month after the closing date for receipt of applications – for the announcement of awards, would not be possible, but, to avoid clashing with the election campaign he thought it imperative that the announcement should be made not later than the middle of September.

Assessing the bids

When all the applications had been received the Ministry had much work to undertake, particularly with respect to the competing bids. Specifically, with respect to the 29 overlapping applications for 230 blocks they had to draw up a list of relative eligibility using such criteria as (1) extent of British interest, (2) contribution to the UK fuel economy, and (3) reciprocity in foreign countries. Next, using this list plus the knowledge of the applicants' own preferences a provisional allocation would be made of these 230 blocks. Following that, each of the applicants would be informed that he was in the running for certain blocks, subject to his offering an adequate work programme. The Ministry would not reveal which of the blocks was uncontested in case the applicant then offered a poor work programme for these.

The applicant would then have to prepare his work programme which could be in terms of money to be spent over a period, footage of wells to be drilled, or rigs to be constructed and kept employed. It had been established with the oil companies that work programmes could not be submitted with applications as they had to relate to specific areas, and at the time of application the applicant would have no idea what he was likely to be allocated. Following this the Ministry would examine the proposed work programmes. They would press for any poor offers to be improved, using the implied threat of altering the provisional allocation. Following that the provisional allocations would be confirmed or altered. The applicants would then be informed. This could not properly be done until negotiations with all applicants had been completed partly because the negotiations were inter-connected, and partly because a single announcement was preferable.

It followed from the above that the timetable was primarily governed by the speed at which negotiations on work programmes could be completed. The Ministry was clear that the work programmes were the competitive element in the whole process. Once settled they ran for the life of the licence, unless both parties agreed to a change. The Ministry also felt that if they gave any hint that the Government were in a hurry to settle, the applicants would be encouraged to think that they could get away with poor work programmes.

The Ministry proceeded with its assessment based on the above considerations. Three distinct areas were discerned in the applications. They found that the area of greatest interest (Southern North Sea) comprised a total of 97 blocks. Of these, 26 were contested by 10 or more applicants. The overall average of applications to blocks was as high as 8:1. The secondary contested area comprised 133 blocks for which there were 393 applications, resulting in a ratio of 3:1. There were 165 blocks in the third, uncontested area.

On the basis of the procedure outlined above provisional awards were made for each of the 3 areas of the North Sea. All the factors noted above were taken into account and an estimated value was worked out based on relative block values. These values reflected the intensity of competition and were set at 7.5 for the main contested area, 3 for the secondary contested area, and 1 for the uncontested area. Thus it was possible to compare in arithmetical terms the tentative grants proposed for all applicants.

At the next stage in the process the applicants' expressed preferences were taken into account, as was the question of contiguity of blocks to facilitate operations. The Ministry found this to be a very complex exercise, particularly because of the wide variety of methods used by the applicants in expressing their preferences. Following this the provisional awards were discussed with each applicant on a confidential basis. In cases where the preliminary allocations covered more than 10 blocks, agreement was sought on the grouping of blocks into individual licences. After that the work programmes of applicants were discussed on the basis that this was a firm stage in the negotiations and that the competitive element of work programmes might increase or decrease an area offered.

This particular stage lasted about 3 weeks, involving over 60 meetings with applicants. During the process it became clear what the work programme norms should be in terms of numbers of wells to be drilled. Thus it was found that in the main contested area, at least 3 exploration wells per average licence of 7 blocks came to be the norm. Of course, some applicants offered work programmes in excess of the norm and some below it. Companies in the latter case were invited to revise their programmes and did so. In making its assessment of whether a proposed work programme was appropriate for a particular block, the Ministry gave credit for any wells which the applicants proposed to drill in adjacent blocks.

Intervention of Mr Tom Fraser for Opposition

While all these activities were taking place the Ministry also had to deal with other issues. The Opposition Spokesman, Mr Tom Fraser, had written to the Minister on 29th July, proposing that the issue of licences should be delayed until after the General Election. The draft response prepared for the Parliamentary Secretary expressed surprise at this, stating that it was not in the national interest that these developments should become the subject of controversy in the Election. There was no reason why they should. The Continental Shelf legislation had been fully debated in Parliament: the Regulations, governing the terms and conditions of licences, had been laid before Parliament and were not prayed against. The financial terms and conditions of licences had been published in the London Gazette without evoking any serious criticisms.

Mr Fraser also suggested that under the Ministry's method of allocating licences there would be allegations that some companies had been favoured. The draft reply to Mr Fraser argued that such allegations could arise under any Government. The system was based on Ministerial discretion, the reasons for which had been explained to the House. General principles had been indicated which would guide the Minister in his decision-making. Thus insofar as preferences were given to particular concerns they would be preferences based on principles already announced in Parliament.

Mr Fraser also raised doubts about the adequacy of royalties. The draft reply indicted that the detailed licence terms including royalties had been announced nearly three months earlier. There had thus been ample opportunity for criticism but no substantial criticism had been raised either in the House or elsewhere. He might have added that what criticism the Ministry had received was to the effect that the proposed rates were too high rather than too low.

In favouring a delay in the award of licences until after the General Election Mr Fraser argued that, as the licences were likely to be awarded when Parliament was not sitting, the Minister would be unable to justify his decisions to Parliament. It was acknowledged within the Ministry that this was a more difficult point to answer. In normal circumstances the Minister would indeed have been questioned about the award of licences. Likely questions might have included the British share of the licences awarded. The issue was an awkward one because the Minister's action would be enshrined in contracts for forty-six years, which, unlike most administrative decisions, could not be upset by a successor.

Labour Party's plans

A further factor in the debate on licensing at the political level was an article in *The Guardian* of 5th August about the Labour Party's plans for North Sea licensing in the event that it won the election. According to this report "a Labour Government would divide its plots [blocks] into quarters and sell the rights in only two of them diagonally opposed. The rights in the other two quarters would be retained in public ownership. This, Labour believes, would ensure that the state would have a stake in any promising find, and that the Government could develop its own wells or sell its rights in productive areas".[14] The Ministry's views on this suggestion were that they would require the cancellation of all the applications recently made, and the making of a fresh offer in the London Gazette on a new basis. The Ministry also noted that if the purpose of the scheme was to preserve half the designated area for later disposal by the state this was substantially achieved by the present requirement that not less than half of the area of any licence had to be surrendered before the end of six years.

Finalising the awards

Meanwhile the work on finalising the awards continued. Proposals were submitted to the Minister for the grant of licences. When agreement was obtained letters of intent were sent to the successful applicants. When they replied indicating their willingness to accept the work commitments itemised in the letters preparations were made for licence signature and sealing. On 17th September 1964 the Minister announced the awards. Fifty-two production licences were issued to 22 applicants. Another was added at a later date. The total number of blocks licensed was 394 (compared to 960 offered). The total number of companies involved was 51. The well-known major oil companies were all represented with a substantial presence of middle-sized ones. Non-oil company applicants (such as the Domestic Detergent Supply Company) and individual, personal applicants had either withdrawn or been rejected. (The Ministry had considerable bother dealing with the application fees of some individuals.) The overall British content was around 30%. The Gas Council accounted for around 3% and BP for around 6.5%. In the main contested area (Southern Gas Basin) British participation was 42% with the Gas Council having 4% and BP 22.5%.

Labour Government's position

On 19th September the Opposition Spokesman announced that, in a future Labour Government, the Minister of Power would be obliged to examine all the information on which the licences had been granted, and if he were not satisfied, ask Parliament to change them. Soon after that a Labour Government was elected. The Ministry was anxious to ensure that the licence awards and their terms remained as agreed. In briefings to the new Minister, Mr Fred Lee, several points were made. Firstly, the work obligations agreed had a minimum value of £80 million. Most of the licensees had been pressing on with seismic work and over half planned to start drilling (which could cost £1 million per well) during the course of 1965. Orders for five offshore drilling platforms, costing roughly £2 million each, had already been placed with British firms. It followed that the Government would incur considerable criticism, and damage would be inflicted on the economy if this work were brought to a halt. Further, the licences were legally binding contracts and unilateral revocation by the Government would give rise to accusations of bad faith and raise problems of statutory powers and compensation. There would be serious loss of confidence among the prospectors.

In subsequent further briefing additional arguments were presented. Because Britain had passed legislation before the other coastal states it had cashed in on the present intense interest in the North Sea. But it would not be long before other countries were ready to invite applications, and if licence holders in the UK were disappointed they would no doubt turn their attention to the other parts of the Shelf. It might then be many years before the UK could get work started again in the UKCS.

In the event that the above arguments prevailed it was suggested that the Minister might clarify the position by an answer to a Parliamentary Question on the subject. This occurred on 1st December 1964 when Mr Lee stated that, as these licences had already been issued, the Government had concluded that it would not be in the public interest to disturb them. In response to supplementary questions the Minister said that he could not make commitments about the future at this stage. For the present the exploration could now proceed apace with major legislative uncertainties removed.

2 The early North Sea boundary issues

Lord Shackleton's question and Ministry's response

The First Licensing Round was completed before the boundaries of the UKCS with neighbouring countries had been determined. The Government's approach was to designate licensing areas which, consistent with the 1958 Convention, could not reasonably be claimed by other countries. Thus Statutory Instrument 1964, No. 697 designated a very large part of the North Sea for licensing, but carefully refrained from including acreage near the location of likely median lines with neighbouring countries.

The Foreign Office had the main departmental responsibility for dealing with boundary issues and had been working on the subject since the early 1960s. Because the Convention had not been ratified by at least 22 signatories the matter was not perceived to be urgent. However, when the Continental Shelf Bill was being prepared the subject had to receive much more attention. What became a major issue was highlighted during the debate on the Second Reading of the Bill in the House of Lords on 3rd December 1963. Lord Shackleton asked how the existence of the Norwegian Deep would affect the sharing of the North Sea lying between the UK and Norway. He expressed the view that the British area should extend to the westward limit of the Deep, leaving Norway with only a very small Continental Shelf. Lord Shackleton appeared to base his argument on a definition of the Continental Shelf extending to a water depth of 200 metres.

In response to this assertion the Ministry of Power emphasised that Article 1 of the Convention had an element additional to the 200 metre water depth namely "or, beyond that limit, to where the depth of the superjacent waters admits of the exploitation of the natural resources". The briefing for the Minister, Mr Richard Wood, stated that the Government was informed that even the greatest depth (about 349 metres) of that part of the Norwegian Deep of concern to the UK was capable of being exploited. The briefing added that the consequence was that, for purposes of negotiating with the Norwegian Government, the UK had to start from the principle of a theoretical pre-existing median line between the 2 coasts.

Foreign Office views

This was the Foreign Office view and had consistently been the case since the debate at the time of the Convention in 1958. In a report to the Secretary of State for Foreign Affairs the leader of the UK delegation, Mr G. G. Fitzmaurice, reported that they had felt there were defects in the provisions of Article 1. They were concerned about the uncertainties regarding whether all submarine areas adjacent to a coast were capable of exploitation. The introduction of the concept of exploitability gave rise to uncertainties which could in turn result in disputes. The UK Delegation had even considered the possibility of submitting a proposal based on an alternative definition based on a water depth of 550 metres which exceeded the deepest part of the Norwegian Deep.

The Foreign Office thus consistently felt that the median line was the appropriate starting point for negotiations with neighbouring countries. By the time of the debate on the Continental Shelf Bill the view had been formed that negotiations with neighbouring countries, including Norway would have little prospect of success unless the UK showed willingness at the outset to conduct them within the framework of the 1958 Continental Shelf Convention. The Foreign Office view was reinforced in a further briefing to the Minister during the Second Reading of the Bill in the House of Commons. Because it was felt that exploitation was possible in water depths of 340 metres the Government did not consider that that part of the Deep precluded Norwegian claims to the seabed and subsoil of the shallower waters beyond.

Further inter-departmental discussions

The Ministry of Power asked the Foreign Office to clarify its position, particularly in the light of Lord Shackleton's remarks. In a letter to the Ministry the Foreign Office stated that its interpretation of the stance taken by the UK Delegation at the Geneva Convention was that the North Sea Continental Shelf could be regarded as a whole, in the sense that the Norwegian Deep was a partial interruption of the North Sea Continental Shelf, rather than a complete break in it. The Norwegians would consequently be entitled to ignore it in calculating their median lines, an interpretation which was consistent with the view of the UK Delegation.

On 18th February 1964 a meeting took place of representatives of the Foreign Office, Ministry of Power, and the Admiralty's Hydrographic Section to progress matters. It was agreed that, for the purposes of licensing, areas of the UKCS should be designated up to a simplified median line which was most unlikely to vary more than 1.5 miles from any subsequently negotiated median line. A simplified median line was felt to be necessary because the true median line was likely to have numerous curves and be impossible or very difficult to define in practice. The simplification would reduce the curves to straight lines of not less than one mile in length. The group felt that this procedure would permit licences to be awarded up to around two miles inside the amended median line.

An alternative course was also considered. This was to designate up to a line representing at each point the minimum which might accrue to the UK under any of the various interpretations of median and methods of deciding the baseline used by the countries concerned. In practice this would produce a line up to around 1.5 miles inside what was thought to be the median line.

There were felt to be several advantages of this approach. Firstly, the Foreign Office preferred to make a limit bid since there would be a danger that in negotiation the UK would be unable to make up an underbid. Secondly, it was felt that designating up to the median line would avoid the difficulty of the interloper exploiting inside what the UK considered to be part of the UKCS but outside the designated area. Thirdly, the group felt that their approach gave them greater manoeuvrability in negotiations. It was recognised that an oil bearing structure might be discovered which extended a mile or so beyond the area of concession. If the UK conceded up to the line of designation, it would not be able to extend the concession. Thus the UK should concede up to a line within the line of designation. To maximise the area of concession, the line of designation should be as far out as possible (i.e. the median line). A last advantage of the preferred approach was that if the UK Government designated an area which another country felt was in their Continental Shelf that country would make more haste to open negotiations with the UK.

The group did recognise that there were some disadvantages of their preferred approach. Thus neighbouring countries might be irritated if they felt that the UK had designated part of their areas. The Foreign Office felt that this problem could be handled. A different issue would arise if an investor made a discovery in an area awarded in a concession given by the UK Government which subsequently had to be transferred to another country. This was not thought to be a major problem in practice. The most likely outcome would be that the development would proceed, but royalty and tax payments would be paid to the relevant other country.

Foreign Office opens discussions with neighbouring countries

During February 1964 the Foreign Office contacted the Governments of the neighbouring North Sea countries with suggestions that bilateral negotiations commence on the determination of boundaries. The Norwegian Ministry of Foreign Affairs in acknowledging receipt of the approach by the UK Government quoted approvingly the proposal that discussions should commence with a view to agreeing a boundary based on the median line principle. The Danish Government responded in similar vein, and the UK Embassy in Copenhagen reported to London that the Danes seemed acutely interested and relieved to know that the UK accepted the extension of Norwegian rights beyond the Norwegian Deep. Messages were also received from the Belgian Government indicating general support for the UK Government's approach.

The issue of the appropriate tactics to employ in designating areas for licensing in the First Round with respect to likely boundaries received further discussion.

The view of the Foreign Office that designation should be made right up to the median line was queried by some in the Ministry of Power who argued that the UK should use as the seaward boundary of the first designated area the easterly limit of the gridded up area, subject to there being a gap of at least 2 miles at all points between this limit and the true median line. Mr Angus Beckett, Under Secretary, Ministry of Power, argued that, as a matter of negotiating tactics, there was every advantage in designating right up to the true median line and covering this with a grid.

While this debate was proceeding meetings commenced between UK and Norwegian representatives with a view to establishing the general principles to be employed in arriving at a division. The UK Government wished to calculate the boundary starting from baselines drawn in accordance with the 1958 Geneva Convention on the Territorial Sea, and hoped that the Norwegian Government would accept this approach. The Norwegian representatives pointed out that Norway's base lines were not drawn on Geneva principles: they employed low water features in their definition. All agreed, however, that, in defining the boundary lines, base lines did not need to be a matter of principle. The important issue was to arrive at a line acceptable to both sides through negotiation. The Geneva Convention referred to the use of the median line only if agreement could not be reached by negotiation.

The Norwegian representatives accepted the proposal that the UK would prepare a chart for further discussion showing the calculation of both the exact boundary line drawn from their respective base lines and a straightened out compromise line to eliminate irregularities which it was hoped would be mutually acceptable. It was agreed that the boundary line to be established in the current negotiations should not extend further north than the 100 fathom line. Beyond that there were further complications because of the need to consider the claims of the Faroe Islands (Denmark), and Iceland.

Ministerial sanction was required before a chart could be submitted to the Norwegian Government. In late March 1964 the Minister of State, Foreign Office, circulated a draft map based on the considerations noted above to a large number of Ministers for their approval. The Law Officers comments were that, while continuous bay closing lines and straight base lines had been employed on the Norwegian side, they had not been shown on the UK side except for the Moray Firth and the Firth of Forth. They suggested that such lines should be shown for the Orkney and Shetland Islands in particular. In reply the Foreign Office pointed out that, because the UK had adopted the 1958 Geneva Convention baselines, the only alterations which could be made to the pre-existing lines were the bay closing lines across the Moray Firth and Firth of Forth. Further, as a result of discussions at the Law of the Sea Committee in September 1962, no straight base lines could be drawn round the Orkney and Shetland Islands.

The chart was duly submitted to the Norwegians. Their hydrographers pointed out that the proposal for the median line had been calculated on charts based on Mercator's projection which did not take the earth's curvature into account. It was acknowledged that this would make a difference to the position of the median line by as much as 1.5 miles. The Norwegians suggested that the chart should be redrawn based on the Gnomic projection.[1] In most cases this had the effect of moving the median line slightly further to the west. By this time the UK Government was finalising the coordinates for defining the designated areas for the First Licensing Round. Two of the coordinates had to be altered to comply with the agreed procedure that the designated areas were at least 2 miles to the west of the proposed median line.

Formalising agreement with Norway

The Norwegian Government readily accepted the revised charts showing the boundary line. Foreseeing that agreement could soon be reached the Foreign Office gave consideration as to how such agreement might be recorded. In a letter to the Ambassador in Norway the Foreign Office suggested that the easiest way would be by means of an Exchange of Notes, to which charts indicating the agreed line would be attached. The Norwegian Government replied that it had decided that its agreements with Denmark and Sweden would be recorded in a formal Protocol which would be subject to ratification by the Governments concerned. The Norwegians added that they were prepared to consider recording the agreement with the UK by means of an Exchange of Notes if this was preferred. The Foreign Office then decided that they would be prepared to consummate the agreement in an instrument more formal than an Exchange of Letters, and asked the Ambassador in Oslo to invite the Norwegians to submit a draft on the formal issues.

The submission received was rather skeletal. There were two particular issues of concern to the Ministry of Power at this time. The first related to the definition of the median line. The Ministry much preferred that the agreed line should be the simplified one. The accurately calculated line would require very many coordinates and would be administratively inconvenient for the Ministry and licensees. The second issue related to the consequences of a discovery which crossed the median line. In such an event there had to be provision for consultation regarding the most economical method of exploitation, and the apportionment of the proceeds from joint development.

There ensued some negotiations on precisely where the administrative boundary would be drawn, with some give and take on both sides. The Hydrographic Department of the Ministry of Defence advised that positions on the line should be expressed in seconds of arc rather than 10ths of a minute. Use of the former implies that the positions are meant to be precise which might be important in the event of a dispute. For the same reason the advice was given that the lines joining any two positions should be defined as the arc of a Great Circle passing through the two positions, which is a more precise definition than "straight line" which could be either a straight line on a chart or a straight line on the earth's surface. The difference between the two lines could be appreciable. A draft was then prepared based on arcs of Great Circles between the eight points defined by latitude and longitude on European Datum.

The Foreign Office then circulated the draft agreement on the lines outlined above to Ministers from a considerable number of Departments for their approval. On obtaining this arrangements were made to finalise the agreement with the Norwegians. It was signed on 10th March 1965 and presented to Parliament for ratification in April. It came into force on 29th June 1965.

Momentous consequences of agreement

The consequences of the agreement, the first made by the UK with its North Sea neighbours, were momentous. Thus the principles employed were used by the UK in its negotiations with other North Sea Governments. Of course, no one could have foreseen that many prolific fields would subsequently be discovered around the median line determined in 1965, a development which led to much retrospective attention being given to the agreement. The legal debate had been based not only on the 1958 UN Convention and its aftermath, but on practice based on customary international law. Daintith and Willoughby state that "there is now a permissive rule of international law authorising a state to take measures necessary to explore the shelf proximate to its coasts and exploit some of the resources thereof. This permissive rule derives from the relationship between the submarine areas and the adjacent – non-submerged land".[2] In support of this approach they note that both the International Law Commission and the International Court of Justice emphasised the importance of the connection between the Continental Shelf and land territory. The latter body in 1969 stated that "what confers the *ipso jure* title which international law attributes to the coastal state in respect of its Continental shelf, is the fact that the submarine areas concerned may be deemed to be actually part of the territory over which the coastal state already has dominion – in the sense that, although covered with water, they are a prolongation or continuation of that territory, an extension of it under the sea".[3] Further, the International Court stated that adjacency was not a "fundamental or inherent rule, and, insofar as it has some relevance, is to be understood as 'proximity in the general sense' ".[4]

These interpretations of the concept of Continental Shelf when set alongside those of the 1958 Convention permit quite different definitions of the outer limit to be made. Thus one interpretation of the Convention would be that the limit moves progressively outwards, apparently without limit, as the technological capability to exploit the seabed keeps advancing. A second view would be that "the exploitability criterion is governed by the overall conception of the shelf as a geological feature (that is a natural extension of a State's land territory) and by the principle of adjacency . . . [meaning that] the furthest that a state can lawfully claim beyond the 200 metres line by the utilisation of the exploitability test is to the foot of the continental margin".[5]

There is no evidence that the Foreign Office (or indeed any other Government department) gave serious consideration to this second interpretation at the time of negotiations with Norway. A consistent position was taken in favour of negotiations based on the median line, reflecting the earlier support for the median line at the 1958 Convention.

Subsequent inquest on agreement

When significant discoveries were made around the median line interest in the boundary issue increased. The Central Policy Review Staff (CPRS) took a keen interest in North Sea oil issues. In 1973 Lord Rothschild sent a note to the Prime Minister, Mr Edward Heath, on the implications of the acceptance of this boundary. The note had been prepared by Dr Eli Lauterpacht QC. He argued that the emphasis which the International Court for Justice had given to the Continental Shelf as a prolongation or continuation of a state's territory under the sea was stating nothing that was not known to lawyers in 1965. He then argued that the British Government could have argued that the Norwegian Continental Shelf stopped on the Norwegian side of the trough and that the British Continental Shelf extended to the outer edge of the Norwegian trough.

In support of his view Dr Lauterpacht cited the judgement of the International Court in 1969 in the case brought by Germany against Denmark and the Netherlands. Germany successfully challenged the application of the equidistance principle in a situation where there was not even a trough. Lauterpacht highlighted the statement by the Court that the shelf areas in the North Sea separated from the Norwegian coast by the 80–100 kilometres of the trough could not in any sense be said to be adjacent to it, nor to be its natural prolongation.

Lauterpacht pondered over the basis of the British Government's stance in 1964–65. He emphasised that if the Government had wanted to press its claim beyond the equidistance line it could have gone to the International Court, pointing out that both states were bound by the compulsory jurisdiction of the Court. The case was one in which the UK had nothing to lose, only something to gain. He pointed out that Germany's action in going to the Court in 1967–69 with the Netherlands and Denmark was essentially the same, and a positive result was achieved. Even a compromise judgement of the Court resulting in the line being moved a few miles eastward would have brought substantial benefits. He argued that while direct legal redress was difficult, given that a treaty had been signed, attempts should be made in negotiations on other issues now and in the future to prevent recurrences unless the UK was to conclude that the Government really wanted to make Norway perhaps the most generous present in English history.

In his covering note to the Prime Minister Lord Rothschild stated that it was hard to estimate the resource loss that had been caused but would put it at £500 million. The Prime Minister was anxious that the subject be investigated further, including the issue of whether the preparatory work had been done under the Conservative Government before October 1964, or whether the Labour Government was solely responsible.

The result of this was a request from Sir Burke Trend to the Foreign Office to provide background information. Defending the use of the median line principle the Foreign Office reply was that in the absence, at the time, of any indication that there was oil in substantial quantities under the North Sea, they had no reason to doubt that the median line best served our interests. In response the CPRS argued that no matter what view was taken of the possible resources it would be in the UK's best interests to have rights over as large an area as possible. There were no apparent disadvantages elsewhere in taking such a stance.

The subject was raised again much later in June 1974, when Lord Balogh, Minister of State at the Department of Energy, requested his officials to produce a note on boundary issues with several different countries. With respect to the Norwegian situation the view presented to the Minister was that, if the negotiations were starting now (June 1974), the comments of the International Court that the Norwegian Trough could not in any physical sense be said to be adjacent to Norway nor be its natural prolongation, would have encouraged the UK to take a much different stand. The note added that any move by the UK to re-open discussions on the boundary would undoubtedly meet with a very hostile reception from Norway and be rejected out of hand. It could lead to lasting bitterness between the countries. The Norwegians would resist with all means at their disposal any proposition which involved the boundary being relocated to the east of the present line. In any case, the treaty with Norway was binding on the UK.

This view was accepted by Mr Eric Varley, the Secretary of State for Energy. In a note he sent to the Secretary of State for Foreign and Commonwealth Affairs on boundary issues in January 1975, he regretfully acknowledged that treaties did not permit denunciation and that changes could only be made by negotiation. He accepted that the Norwegians, having now discovered Ekofisk and part of Frigg and Statfjord, would firmly decline to do so.

Nevertheless the CPRS pursued the issue further with the Department of Energy and Foreign and Commonwealth Office. The latter then produced a detailed exposition and defence of its negotiating position. Recounting the history of their position they pointed out that as long ago as 27th March 1958, at the Geneva Conference the UK delegate had specifically stated that in cases where – as off the west coast of Norway – there was a deep channel immediately off the coast, the provisions (i.e. the median line) would apply in the same way as to a continental shelf in the geological sense of the term.

The Foreign Office then argued that there was absolutely no reason to think that, had the UK Government taken the question of the UK/Norwegian delimitation to arbitration or judicial settlement in 1965, the International Court or an arbitral tribunal would have awarded an area of continental shelf extending up to the edge of the Norwegian Trough. In support of this view the Foreign Office argued that the International Law Commission commentary on the proposed definition of continental shelf already accepted in 1965 the concept that a feature such as the Norwegian trough would be ignored for delimitation purposes. The Foreign Office employed as additional evidence the UNESCO scientific report in 1957 which supported the view that the Norwegian Trough formed part of the North Sea Continental Shelf because of its sill. The conclusion reached by the Foreign Office was that in 1964/65 the weight of legal and scientific evidence was in favour of the thesis that the Norwegian Trough was simply a depression in the North Sea Continental Shelf and could not be regarded as interrupting Norway's claim to areas beyond the Trough.

The Foreign Office then argued that it was misleading to suggest, as the CPRS had done, that the International Court judgement in the North Sea Continental Shelf case in 1969 concerning Germany, Denmark and the Netherlands, said nothing that was not known in 1965. The judgement could be regarded as innovatory. Further, it had been strongly criticised by, among others, Professor Wolfgang Friedman, who regarded the Court's rejection of the equidistance principle as debatable, and the alternative criteria advanced for delimitation as both unconvincing and inconsistent. He suggested that the Court in not accepting the median line as the appropriate boundary may have been seeking to counterbalance the relative inequity resulting from the concave curvature of the coast of West Germany which, in his view rendered the Court's pronouncements suspect.

The Foreign Office pointed out further that the Court had specifically disclaimed any attempt to pronounce on the status of the Norwegian Trough and had been concerned to criticise the argument that only a line drawn on equidistance principles would satisfy the tests of proximity, adjacency, and the natural prolongation of the land territory, and illustrated the fluidity of all these notions by the case of the Norwegian Trough. The Foreign Office then argued that this cryptic and allusive reference to the Norwegian trough could not be interpreted as demonstrating that a court if confronted with the problem of the delimitation of the UK/Norway Continental Shelf in 1965 would have found that the natural prolongation of the United Kingdom into the sea extended up to the edge of the Norwegian trough.

Reflections on agreement with Norway

These then were the arguments and counter-arguments employed in the debate on the most important North Sea Continental Shelf boundary issue. The position of the Foreign Office consistently favoured use of the median line principle. When that was enunciated both in 1958 and in 1964–65 no serious objections were raised by other departments. The only audible opposition at the time was that of Lord Shackleton, but it received little or no support. For the Foreign Office in 1964–65 to have taken an approach different to their stance in 1958 would have been rather difficult. The Norwegians were well aware of the attitude which the British delegation had taken at the Geneva Convention on the issue.

Nevertheless, policies often change, and in the negotiation in 1964–65 there was certainly an opportunity to deploy arguments other than the median line. Lack of early agreement clearly did not hinder the licensing of large amounts of acreage. There would have been little or nothing to lose and the possibility of gain by advocating a dividing line to the east of the median line. If no agreement had been reached in 1965 and the question of arbitration or referral to the International Court had to be considered, assessing the likely outcome would have been very difficult. The median line would certainly have figured prominently in deliberations, but some attention would doubtless have been paid to the special circumstances raised by the Norwegian Trough.

The agreement in 1965 had an extremely strong legal basis as it was formalised in a treaty. This meant that the prospect of making retrospective adjustments was very slim. Given that discoveries had been made both on the median line and close to it inside Norway's sector the Norwegian government would have strongly resisted any attempt by the British government to have the boundary shifted eastwards.

This would no doubt have occurred if the agreement had been made through an Exchange of Notes with accompanying charts as the UK Government had suggested. The evidence is that the Norwegian Government could well have been persuaded to accept this arrangement. While the legal status of an Exchange of Notes is perhaps less strong than a treaty, and thus might have given the British Government an opportunity to reopen the issue, the chances of a favourable modification would still have been low.

Discussions with Denmark, the Netherlands and Belgium

The agreement with Norway was also important because it formed a precedent for the Government's negotiations with the other North Sea countries. Discussions with Denmark, The Netherlands and Belgium were under way through much of 1964. For these discussions ambassadors were presented with charts by the Foreign Office showing the British Government's calculation of the true median line. They were asked to transmit these to the Governments in question with the view expressed that they could serve as an equitable boundary.

Complications emerged. With respect to Denmark and The Netherlands these emanated from the uncertainties of the outcomes of the negotiations which these countries were having with West Germany. If the median line principle were employed for delimitation purposes the UK would not have had a boundary with West Germany at all. The latter country was, however, unwilling to accept that the use of the median line principle produced an equitable result. Its employment would have given West Germany a very small continental shelf emanating from its land curvatures in the North Sea in relation to those of Denmark and The Netherlands. Discussions continued among the 3 countries for a long time and eventually in 1967 the issue was referred to the International Court of Justice. The dispute did not affect the median line between the UK and the other 3 countries taken as a group, but it did affect the terminal points between the UK and each of them individually. The UK could not have sensible discussions with West Germany at all until the latter's boundaries with Denmark and The Netherlands had been determined.[6]

Agreement with the Netherlands

Discussions with the neighbouring North Sea countries proceeded with the UK Government's negotiating position continuing to be based on the median line principle. Those with the Netherlands led to an agreement being signed in October 1965. This agreement is noteworthy in that it makes no reference to any boundary with Germany. Thus to the north the termination points of the boundary line are defined as the point of intersection of the dividing line between the Continental

Shelves of the UK, the Netherlands, and Denmark. After the International Court gave its decision on the boundaries among the Netherlands, Denmark and West Germany the agreement had to be modified to accommodate the effect of the judgement to give West Germany a boundary with the UK. This was done by a Protocol in 1972 which made the northern limit with the Netherlands the tripoint where the boundary lines of the three countries met.

Both the UK and the Netherlands were keen to apply the equidistance principle. A particular point of detail was of some concern to the UK negotiators. The Dutch side had suggested that, in determining the median line the projected Europoort harbour works should be taken into account. This project had not then been completed and the UK side was not convinced that such future projects were relevant for this purpose. The Dutch Government subsequently agreed to accept the UK's position on this matter. The median line was thus based on the situation at the time of the signing of the Treaty in 1965, irrespective of subsequent changes in the Dutch baseline and outer limit of her territorial waters following the completion of the Europoort project. Small variations in the location of the boundary could, of course, be of major importance as was later confirmed by the pattern of gas discoveries.

A separate agreement with the Netherlands was also made in 1965 relating to the exploitation of discoveries straddling the median line. The principles of seeking agreement on the most effective way of developing such deposits and how the costs and revenues were established. It was also established that, if agreement on these matters could not be reached, and where such failure would prevent maximum ultimate recovery or lead to unnecessary competitive drilling, the matter would be referred to arbitration.

Agreement with Denmark

Discussions with the Danish Government commenced in the early part of 1964. The UK Government proposed a specific boundary line in April. The issue arose of the uncertainty of the dividing line between Denmark and West Germany and the consequential uncertainty of the location of the southern terminal point of the boundary between the UK and Denmark. On the issue of the development of discoveries made on the border area the Danish side suggested that the agreement between the two countries should contain detailed provisions about the procedures to be followed in that eventuality. The Ministry of Power had no objections to this in principle but made it clear that they did not favour joint exploitation. The UK side made some proposals on procedures which included formal consultations with the relevant licensees. The Danish side felt that it would be undesirable to give the concessionaires a formal legal right to be consulted. In practice, however, informal consultations would be made. The UK agreed to this request. The agreement was signed in March 1966. Following the International Court's ruling on the disputed Danish–West German boundary, a new agreement was concluded in 1972. This simply reduced the length of the boundary to eleven nautical miles.

Discussions with Belgium

With respect to Belgium the UK Government approached the Ministry of Foreign Affairs in June 1964, with a proposal that the dividing line be based on equidistance principles. It was understood that the northern and southern terminal points would depend on the outcome of negotiations between the Belgians and the Dutch and French authorities. In the event the Belgian Government gave priority to attempting to reach an agreement with the French Government. This postponed any agreement with the UK for a very long time.

Discussions with France

Discussions with the French authorities first took place in 1964. In May 1964, at an interdepartmental meeting held at the Foreign Office the British initial position was determined. The median line principle was again employed with simplifications made to eliminate irregularities. When the Hydrographer's Department produced a map it was apparent that the division would be based on a line between the Channel Islands and France such that the shelf to the north west of the Islands would fall to the UK. The group also noted that, if the French objected to such a claim, it was clear that a median line calculated as if the Channel Islands did not exist would not greatly increase the area which the French could claim.

In their deliberations the group anticipated that the French would argue that there were special geographical circumstances which supported a claim to a larger area than was justified strictly on median line principles. In that event the group agreed not to concede any principles relating to the Continental Shelf of small islands which might by extension to Rockall prejudice the UK's claims to the Continental Shelf in the Atlantic Ocean. The group also agreed that it would be appropriate to consult the Channel Island Authorities before proposals were put to the French.

The French were duly shown maps with the proposed dividing lines based on median line principles, and in 1966 detailed exchanges commenced between the parties. Given that there was no great interest among investors in the areas to be divided it was agreed to postpone formal negotiations. In 1969 circumstances changed when geological and geophysical surveys were published indicating prospects of hydrocarbons in the areas in question, particularly off the Isle of Wight and in the South West approaches. Similar information had been conveyed to the French Government regarding prospects in what they regarded as acreage falling under their control. This provided an impetus to the resumption of negotiations. In October 1970, the French gave their view that agreement on the boundary was necessary before any block designations could be made by either side. The UK Government agreed to this suggestion, a contributory reason being the need to avoid friction as application had recently been made to join the EEC. The negotiations which followed were extremely protracted and go beyond the scope of this history.

Internal and territorial waters

Attention had also to be given to other quite different boundary issues. The Regulations under the 1964 Act applied to activities in the seabed and subsoil under territorial waters. For onshore activities the Regulations under the 1935 Act applied. Uncertainty developed over the precise meaning of the term "territorial waters". One view within the Ministry of Power was that where there were bay closing lines they were simply a device which was employed to determine the seaward limits of the territorial waters, and that any tidal waters between "closing lines" and the low water mark of ordinary tide were part of UK territorial waters. On this view the 1935 Regulations ceased at the low water mark of ordinary tide. Other interpretations were possible particularly with respect to estuaries.

The issue was of academic importance until the summer of 1964 when the Ministry of Power received an application from Seaboard Oils requesting prospecting licences off the east, south and west coasts of the UK under the 1935 Regulations (rather than the 1964 ones). The areas in question were within "closing lines". The application was supported by legal opinion from Professor Sir Humphrey Waldock QC. In essence this stated that the terms "territorial sea" and "territorial waters" were to be understood as having the meaning given to them in the Conventions (which was their normal meaning). They should be understood as referring to the maritime belt alone, thus leaving internal waters outside the 1964 Regulations. If this were so it followed that internal waters remained subject to the 1935 Regulations. These were not the same as for the UKCS. It would be for the UK Government to determine the areas of internal waters.

The Ministry of Power took note of this view and felt that, even if the argument regarding the distinction between internal and territorial waters was accepted the crucial question of where the boundaries ("closing lines") should be drawn was unanswered. In 1960 the UK Government had ratified the Convention on the Territorial Sea and the Contiguous Zone which provided for alterations to the existing boundaries. At that time the maximum length allowed for "closing lines" was ten miles. Article 7 of the Convention permitted "closing lines" of up to 24 miles in length. In a further memorandum Professor Waldock gave his opinion that adopting the 24-mile "closing lines" for United Kingdom bays would affect the delimitation of the sea areas in several ways. Thus, it would push further to seaward the limit of the internal waters of bays whose entrances were more than ten miles wide. Further, it would bring within territorial (and conceivably in some cases within internal) waters certain adjacent areas of seabed previously regarded as forming part of the continental shelf. Professor Waldock further pointed out that, while the total area of land and seabed in which the 1935 and 1964 Acts had vested the petroleum rights in the Crown had not altered, the consequences of the revision to the delimitation altered the legal source of the Crown's rights in areas which passed from the Continental Shelf to territorial or internal waters. Any revision should not affect the status of existing licences, but only the legal basis of the Ministry's power to grant future licences.

The Foreign Office was very keen to preserve the distinction between internal and territorial waters which was important internationally, particularly in relation to navigation. Waters landward of a bay "closing line" were internal whether they were tidal or not. The Government was shortly to modify the length of the bay "closing line" from ten miles to twenty-four miles. This took effect from 30th September 1964, by way of an Order in Council. The Foreign Office emphasised the view that any changes to the Regulations should not involve any blurring of the distinction between internal and territorial waters.

Land areas and sea areas

The Ministry of Power consulted the office of the Hydrographer of the Navy on the issue which was its key concern, namely to define the line of demarcation between "land areas" and "sea areas" while acknowledging that internal waters were distinct from the territorial sea. The Ministry desired that the area of tidal waters defined as "land areas" should be kept to the minimum compatible with commonsense for rivers and estuaries. The Hydrographer confirmed that the 24-mile "closing line" would in practice enclose large areas which in everyday language would be described as "the sea", and that to regard all tidal waters within the baselines defined in the Schedule to the Order as being internal waters would mean the inclusion of stretches of the sea over 50 miles wide.

Following this the Ministry found difficulty in drafting any forms of words for inclusion in subordinate legislation which would meet its policy objectives. Thus a tight definition of internal waters could produce extreme examples of territorial waters such as the Thames up to Teddington Lock. The reluctant conclusion was that the only practical solution was to draw a map of demarcation around the *whole* of the coast, and the inward limits of the territorial sea should be defined by reference to this line. If this view were to prevail it would be necessary to overcome the anxiety of the Foreign Office regarding the blurring of the distinction between internal and external waters.

The Ministry of Power then proceeded to draft dividing lines between landward and seaward areas. The starting point was the low water mark, but modifications were made to satisfy the joint need for practicability and administrative convenience. The procedure was to draw the line at the most logical outermost points of estuaries and river mouths based on the perception of where the "sea" could reasonably be thought to begin. In some areas the use of this line meant that large areas of water would be enclosed with the land. Examples would be the Moray Firth and Humber mouth. For such areas alternative lines were drawn further inland. Other notable areas requiring changes to the line included the Wash and Morecambe Bay. Islands connected to the mainland by low tide elevations were defined as "land" while other islands not so connected were defined as "sea". An exception was the Isle of Wight. The Solent was proposed to be "sea". Harbours were generally defined as "land". It was clear that the area to the North West of Scotland had special difficulties because of the many islands. But as the geological prospects of petroleum in this area were perceived to be negligible there appeared to be no point in designating it at all, and the question of drawing lines did not arise. On further reflection it was decided to propose to adopt the base line between Cape Wrath and the Mull of Kintyre as was laid down by the Order in Council in September 1964. With respect to the Orkney and Shetland Islands following either the low water mark or base lines for territorial waters would have produced very odd shaped areas and it was proposed to follow the outer limits of territorial waters round the islands.

The Foreign Office reiterated its view on the importance of a clear distinction between internal waters, territorial sea, and high sea. They thought it important to ensure that licensees were made aware that the whole area within a licence might not be subject to the same legal régime with possible differences not only in licensing regulations, but in criminal and civil law. In response the Ministry of Power pointed out that licensees had already been awarded blocks which straddled the line between territorial waters and the designated Continental Shelf without giving rise to difficulty. The boundary lines proposed above were, with very minor modifications, incorporated in the Petroleum (Production) Regulations, 1966.

Revenue shares to Northern Ireland, Isle of Man and Channel Islands

A further boundary issue had to be addressed in this period. When the Continental Shelf Bill was under consideration in 1963-64 the Northern Ireland Government put forward the argument that they had a claim to the resources in the part of the Continental Shelf which was claimed by the United Kingdom by virtue of Northern Ireland's geographic location. The Home Office, which had prime responsibility for dealing with the Northern Ireland authorities, stated that there was inadequate time to pursue this argument, but also saw difficulties in admitting it on the grounds that the exploitation of the Continental Shelf had repercussions on several factors, including international negotiations, navigations, and submarine cables, subjects on which the Northern Ireland Government did not have competence. As a result the jurisdiction of the Government of Northern Ireland was not extended as requested, but the UK Government undertook to examine the possibility of ensuring that benefits accrued to Northern Ireland from the exploitation of the relevant part of the Continental Shelf. The Home Office also expressed the view that the arguments against conferring powers of extra-territorial jurisdiction applied to the Channel Islands and Isle of Man at least as strongly as to Northern Ireland, but also expressed the view that their position should be included in any review that was made of the Northern Ireland situation. The Islands were dependencies of the Crown, not part of the United Kingdom, but for whose international relations the UK Government was responsible. Thus the Continental Shelf Convention contained no indication of territorial extent and the United Kingdom's ratification was therefore deemed to extend to dependent territories. The Shelf claimed by the United Kingdom would thus include areas claimed by virtue of the Islands' geographic situation, though the administration of such areas would be in the hands of the UK Government and any revenue accruing from it would go to the Exchequer.

The Home Office then expressed the view that it was doubtful whether it would be useful to pursue the question of claims by Northern Ireland and the Islands on strict grounds of constitutional law, since the exploitation of the Shelf raised radically new principles which could well lead to a wearisome and inconclusive debate. The Home Office preferred that, on broad grounds of equity, since the UK Government was in a position to make claims for the people of the British Islands, by virtue of the geography of the British Islands as a whole, it was the Government's duty to see that any benefits that accrued were distributed to those on whose behalf the claims were made. Elaborating on the possibilities the Home Office felt that, to take an extreme case, if a valuable strike of oil were made just outside the territorial waters of the Isle of Man, it would be very difficult to defend to the Isle of Man Government a state of affairs under which they got no benefit whatsoever. The conclusion of the Home Office was that some payment should be made to the Governments of Northern Ireland, the Channel Islands, and the Isle of Man in respect of the exploitation of the Shelf. The two obvious alternatives were (1) that they should receive a considerable part of the revenues flowing from exploitation of that part of the Shelf to which they could lay claim under the Convention if they were sovereign states, or (2) that they should be given a much smaller proportion of the revenue flowing from all exploitation of the Shelf around the British Islands. The Home Office was inclined to favour the second alternative, partly on general grounds of fairness and partly because it was felt that this would be acceptable to the Northern Ireland Government. The first alternative would require that licences were distributed according to some principle which took account of median lines between the areas in question. This would be administratively difficult. The practical proposal made by the Home Office was that payment should be made to Northern Ireland and the Islands in respect of all exploitation of the UKCS, and that such payments should be determined on the basis of relative population. This would approximate to shares of 2.5% to Northern Ireland and 0.1% each to Jersey, Guernsey, and the Isle of Man.

The above Home Office views and proposals were shared by the Ministry of Power and sent to the Treasury for comment. The Treasury noted that the Northern Ireland Government first claimed a proportion of licence receipts when the Continental Shelf Bill was being debated. At that time the possibility of the Irish Sea being involved was thought to be extremely remote; and the claim was therefore brushed aside. It was agreed that the claim had to be taken more seriously now that some oil companies were seeking to explore in the Irish Sea. There were no inter-Governmental financial arrangements between the UK Exchequer and those of the Channel Islands. Thus a much stronger case was needed for any payments to be made. It was also not yet clear whether a part of the Shelf in the vicinity of these Islands would be allocated to the UK. Thus their case could be left on one side for the time being.

The Treasury accepted that the UK Government should be prepared to make some payment to Northern Ireland and the Isle of Man. There were, however, doubts about whether undertakings should be entered into regarding the basis of payments for the indefinite future. Given all the uncertainties it was reasonable to agree a basis for determining payments in the immediate future while leaving the longer-term arrangements to be settled at a later date. The view of the Home

Office and Ministry of Power that a population proportion basis would be tenable for all time was not felt to be credible. Thus if oil were struck just outside their territorial waters, the Isle of Man and/or Northern Ireland would not be content with so small a proportion of receipts and the two Ministers felt that whatever agreement was reached now, a larger share in the event of a large discovery in their vicinity would be difficult to deny.

A different consideration was the defensibility from a UK standpoint of making large payments if oil were found but only in the North Sea. In the case of Northern Ireland oil-related receipts would be an undeserved windfall, but, given the heavy subsidies currently received from the UK Government, this windfall would be welcome. With the Isle of Man, payments would be made to a Government which levied income tax at a rate well below that applicable in the United Kingdom. On the other hand if oil were found in the North Sea the UK Government might be able to use its "generosity" with respect to payments based on a population basis as justification for driving a harder bargain on some other financial arrangement. Similarly, if oil were found only in the Irish Sea, a fresh basis might have to be negotiated, but the UK Government would be in a stronger position at the beginning of such negotiations if there were a fixed agreement on a population proportion basis than if decisions on the basis had been deferred until the time came.

Agreed position on Northern Ireland case

An interdepartmental meeting was held among the relevant Ministries in March 1965, to discuss the whole issue of revenue sharing of the fees received by the Ministry of Power from the licences issued for oil and gas exploitation. It was recognised that, if exploration were successful, the associated royalty payments would become much more important. It was agreed that any revenue-sharing arrangement should include royalties. It was also agreed that Northern Ireland, as being a part of the United Kingdom and observing parity in taxation and services, as compared with Great Britain, should share in these revenues. Northern Ireland's share should be determined on a population basis relating to the whole of the UK rather than treating the receipts from some particular part of the UKCS as earmarked for Northern Ireland.

Channel Islands case different

The case of the Channel Islands was quite different because it was not part of the United Kingdom and had different (lower) taxes and services. The meeting recognised that negotiations with the French might result in the UK obtaining rights to a larger part of the Continental Shelf in the English Channel because of the Islands. In that event it was recognised that the Channel Islands would have a reasonable claim to a share in the proceeds. The best course would probably be to treat them for this purpose as if they were part of the UK and to allocate to them also a share of the total UK proceeds on a population basis. It was also agreed, however, that there would be no grounds for allocating them anything if the UK failed to secure enhanced rights in the Channel because of the presence of the Channel Islands.

Agreed position on Isle of Man case

The group regarded the Isle of Man as an in-between case. Thus the financial arrangements were close, but not identical, to those in Northern Ireland. It was recognised that the UK Government had larger rights in the Irish Sea because of the existence of the Isle of Man. The group thus agreed that for this purpose the Isle of Man should be treated as if it were part of the UK and should receive an allocation of the monies in question (licence fees and royalties) on a population basis.

The group also agreed that the settlements once concluded should be on the basis of "for better or for worse". That is to say, they should hold good whether in the event these territories got more or less money as a result than they would have done if particular areas of the Continental Shelf had been allocated to them. The group's thinking on this point was influenced by the notion that it was only on this basis that one could defend the situation which would arise if, for instance, Jersey were able to reduce its income tax still further because of its share in royalties from oil production in the North Sea.

Discussions with Government of Northern Ireland

The Home Office then proceeded to prepare a submission to the Secretary of State seeking approval to make proposals to the Governments of Northern Ireland, and the Isle of Man and the Channel Islands authorities on the lines discussed above. When this was given discussions took place with representatives of the Northern Ireland and Isle of Man Governments. The Northern Ireland Government raised the issue of discoveries which straddled the line between territorial waters (over which the Northern Ireland Government had jurisdiction) and the high seas. The issue arose of whether, in the event of a field development, a formal agreement was required between the two Governments on how the field should be exploited. The view of the Ministry of Power was that, while the issue could not be ignored, no formal agreement between the two Governments should be required to deal with this situation. Their suggestion was that in these circumstances the (UK) Minister should be able to direct the licensees as to the manner of exploitation of a field, part of which lay in an area outside his control, without the need for an international agreement.

Discussions with Government of Isle of Man

The Isle of Man representatives requested consultations regarding licences granted in the vicinity of the island. The Ministry of Power made no promises regarding genuine consultation, but indicated that some information could be shared with them. Consultation would certainly be possible with respect to applications for consents to drill. The Ministry would be willing to consult on the exploitation of fields straddling the boundary between the Continental Shelf and the Isle of Man territorial waters. The Home Office were reluctant to do anything which would admit that the Isle of Man had a valid claim to a part of the Continental Shelf.

The Isle of Man representatives asked whether the UK Government would consider licence applications made by companies registered in the Isle of Man. They had in mind a company, Isle of Man Petroleum, which had an exploration concession on the island and its territorial waters. The UK representatives discouraged this idea which was motivated by the possibility of receipts of profits taxes. The Ministry of Power representative did, however, note that there was a case for the Isle of Man to have a share of any tax (as well as royalties) accruing from the exploitation of the Continental Shelf, but did not pass on this thought to the Isle of Man delegation.

In subsequent discussions within the Ministry it was suggested that the UK Government could provide the Isle of Man Government with information regarding (a) blocks applied for in their vicinity, (b) details of licences awarded in respect of such blocks, and (c) applications for consent to drill wells in these blocks. Consultations would take place with respect to fields straddling their respective boundaries. Licence applications from companies registered in the Island would require an amendment to the Regulations for which there was not justification.

Agreements with Northern Ireland and Isle of Man

Offers on revenue-sharing on the lines of the main terms discussed above were then made to the two Governments. The Northern Ireland Government accepted the proposals without further debate. The Isle of Man Government requested that it have as much notice as possible before the Minister of Power published his decisions regarding the issue of licences. Requests were also made to consider revenue-sharing arrangements for minerals other than oil and gas. The UK Government agreed to make the latter issue a possible topic for future negotiations.

Implementation of agreements

Subsequently attention was concentrated on the need to obtain statutory authority to make the payments from 1967-68 onwards. The Exchequer and Audit Department had stipulated that this would be required. The Treasury informed the Ministry of Power in October 1966, that the appropriate method would be to secure an amendment to the Continental Shelf Act 1964, and it would be the Ministry's responsibility to make the preparations of the necessary clauses in a Miscellaneous Financial Provisions Bill.

The Ministry of Power felt that the issue could not be dealt with by making amendments to the Continental Shelf Act. This was because all monies received under the Act had to be paid to the Exchequer. Thus any share of the receipts which had to be paid to other Governments was solely a matter for the Treasury. The Ministry of Power could advise on some particular aspects. One problem would be the apportionment of receipts derived from licensed areas straddling territorial waters and the Continental Shelf.

This view was transmitted to the Treasury with the additional information that the Ministry had other very good reasons for not favouring amendments to the Continental Shelf Act 1964, because they did not want to open the door to other amendments on Continental Shelf matters. The reply from the Treasury argued that the Ministry of Power had the Departmental responsibility for the collection of receipts under both the Petroleum (Production) Act 1934, and the Continental Shelf Act 1964, and it must therefore follow that the Ministry had responsibility for any arrangements where payments were being made from these revenues. Thus an amendment to the Continental Shelf Act was the appropriate way of authorising the payments.

In reply the Ministry reiterated its view that amendments to the Continental Shelf Act were not the appropriate method of providing the legal basis for payments, and the Treasury response did not provide any prospect for an early Miscellaneous Financial Provisions Bill. The matter was debated further within the Ministry. Various views were expressed, including one which wondered whether the Ministry of Power should take any more action as the matter was essentially an agreement about payments between the Home Office and the two Governments.

The Home Office became concerned at the delay in effecting payments to the two Governments. They wrote to the Treasury in December 1967, seeking their help to establish that, come what may, the payments would continue to be made as an obligation incurred by the UK Government, until such time as suitable legislation had been enacted. The position with the Isle of Man in particular had become very sensitive. Thus in April 1968, the Home Office was presented with demands for constitutional changes amounting to a state of full autonomy with the option to negotiate for sovereign independence. The suggestion that the UK should default on payments because of lack of statutory authority was thus of great concern. The Home Office had just received an inquiry from the Isle of Man regarding payments.

In August 1968, the Treasury agreed to promote a Miscellaneous Financial Provisions Bill. The Ministry of Power agreed to provide background notes on the requirements of the legislation. Eventually no provision was made for the inclusion of the Channel Islands. The Ministry of Power view was based on several arguments. There was no agreement with France on where the dividing line between the two countries would be drawn and there was no current exploration interest in the region among the oil companies. There were several possible solutions to the issue, including one whereby the Channel Islands might even administer a Continental Shelf of their own. Until these matters were settled no provision to pay them a share of proceeds from the UKCS could be considered.

In December 1968, the Miscellaneous Financial Provisions Bill was passed. This provided for payments to the two Governments on the lines discussed above.

Care was taken to ensure that the relevant expenses of administration of all UK Government Departments would first be deducted in calculating any sums due. Where such expenses exceeded the licence proceeds (licence fees and royalties) the difference would be carried forward to the next year.

Line of jurisdiction between Scotland and England

A further boundary issue which had to be addressed related to the line of jurisdiction between Scotland and England. This was essentially for purposes of applicable civil and criminal law. In inter-departmental discussions on this issue when the Continental Shelf Bill was being prepared the Scottish Home Department gave its view that it might be necessary to take powers to apply the municipal laws of whatever was the appropriate part of the UK. There was particular concern that there should be proper arrangements for parts of the Shelf lying off Scotland. The Department added that, while the Foreign Office rightly pointed out that in international law the United Kingdom was a unity, and might feel that extending the Anglo/Scottish border into the middle of the North Sea was inappropriate, there was a presumption in favour of taking powers to apply some system of municipal law in its entirety, and so to give the Executive and Judiciary of the appropriate part of the UK all the powers they might conceivably need.

A debate ensued regarding the extent to which municipal laws should be selective or comprehensive in their application to the UKCS. At a meeting of representatives of seven interested Departments in April 1962, it was agreed that criminal and civil law should, with some exceptions, be extended to cover the whole of the UKCS. It was also felt that the UKCS would have to be divided into sections to be covered respectively by English, Scottish and other law. This could best be done by Order in Council so that a line of demarcation could be amended as the occasion arose. In the continuing debate about how criminal law would be applied the Scottish Home Department expressed its hope that it would be possible to avoid a presumption that English law applied except where specific provision to the contrary was made.

The opinion of the Lord Chancellor's Office was sought on this and related issues. The view expressed was that for practical purposes the choice lay between (a) permitting the courts of England, Scotland and Northern Ireland to exercise jurisdiction throughout the UKCS, or (b) dividing the Shelf up among the three jurisdictions. The second alternative was to be preferred because (1) there were some differences in procedures relating to criminal law in the three jurisdictions, and (2) overlapping civil jurisdictions would lead to conflicts and anomalies. Thus, with respect to fatal accidents, the rights of dependents differed under Scots and English Law. The conclusion was that the most satisfactory solution would be a geographical division of the UKCS with English Law applied to one defined part and Scots Law to another defined part.

The relevant parts of the Continental Shelf Bill were prepared in line with the above views. In the debates in the House of Commons Ministers had to defend their approach which eventually prevailed. It was indicated when the relevant clause was under discussion that single licences for overlapping jurisdictions would not be issued. Where an applicant sought a licence for an area in more than one jurisdiction two separate licences would be issued.

Udal Law off Orkney and Shetland Islands?

While the subject was being debated Mr J. Grimond, MP for Orkney and Shetland, raised a quite different jurisdictional issue, namely that, off the Orkney and Shetland Islands, Udal Law might apply. The Legal Branch of the Ministry of Power investigated this issue. Their understanding was that Udal Law could be described as the original common law obtaining in these Islands. So far as offshore was concerned the key point was that the foreshore and presumably the seabed under territorial waters, was vested in the owner of the land from which the fore-shore struck out. The respective legal rights of the onshore property owners and the Crown with respect to the foreshore and seabed under territorial waters were unclear. Whether Udal Law could extend beyond territorial waters was even more unclear. Legal Branch felt that the Lord Privy Seal was probably right in stating that if there was a conflict between Udal Law and the Convention on the Continental Shelf the latter would have to be made to prevail.

Consideration had next to be given to the location of the lines demarcating English and Scots Law. The Scottish Office revealed that for territorial waters an intensive search had failed to reveal a judicial decision. Legal Branch of the Ministry of Power was acutely aware that it was not within the Minister's powers to draw it arbitrarily. To do so would open the possibility of legal challenge. Legal Branch felt that the alternatives were either a projection of the land border or a line drawn at right angles from the base line of territorial waters at the point where the land border struck that line. The Branch felt that an East-West line from that point should be rejected because the countries did not in fact run North and South. The view of the Branch was that the idea of projecting the land border was illogical because it assumed that the border ought to be a straight line, and it was not. While there was an argument that a straight line frontier might be continued out to sea, there could not be any such argument for continuing a zig-zag line.

Assistance from Territorial Sea Convention

In the search for a solution Legal Branch felt that assistance could be obtained from the Territorial Sea Convention. Article 12(1) of that Convention was understood to mean that the dividing line in the case of adjacent States would be a perpendicular drawn from the coast at the land frontier. It, therefore, would be right to proceed by analogy and to draw blocks for licence purposes, using a line of demarcation between England and Scotland drawn on the basis of Article 12 of that Convention. After further discussion agreement was reached with the Scottish Office and Parliamentary Counsel was instructed to draft the necessary Order. In the North

Sea the Scottish/English jurisdiction boundary was Lat. 55° 50′ N. In the Irish Sea the issue was more complicated and the instruction was that the line should follow Lat. 54° 30′ N from 5° 00′ W (the outer limit of the then proposed designated area) to the points of intersection with the perpendicular bisector of the bay closing line across the Solway Firth and then along that bisector to the outer limit of territorial waters. The Order in Council became operative in 1968.

3   What role for the state?

Policy review by new Government

As soon as the First Licensing Round had been completed, stocktaking commenced even before the first offshore well was drilled. The change of Government gave an additional impetus to the review. At a meeting of the Ministerial Committee on Economic Development on 6th November 1964, when it was agreed that the licences issued by the previous Administration should not be disturbed, Mr Fred Lee, the Minister of Power, was invited to produce a paper setting out the considerations which had determined the system of licensing then in use, and to prepare proposals for allocating further licences. The Minister himself was keen to consider methods of substantially increasing the British share in new licences. It was noted that British participation in the First Round was only 30% of the total, though this rose to 42% in the area in which the greatest hopes were placed. Views were also expressed, that, because of the high risks involved, in current circumstances the nation could ill afford the necessary considerable risk capital. On the other hand the success in the Netherlands (onshore) and the eagerness of the international oil companies to invest indicated that the risks were justified. In developing policy it had also to be borne in mind that the UK had a very large stake in oil production overseas. Any actions taken with respect to terms in the North Sea could have repercussions on those imposed by foreign Governments. With respect to timing it was noted that exploration was now proceeding in other parts of the North Sea outside UK jurisdiction, and there was a need to ensure that we were not placed in a disadvantageous position with respect to our European neighbours.

The Ministry proceeded to undertake studies and consultations in response to the Committee's requests. Consideration was given as to how the British share could be increased in a future licence round. There were both private companies and nationalised industries which might have a greater involvement than in the First Round. With respect to state-owned organisations only the Gas Council had participated in that Round. The reasons for the Council's involvement were that (1) it should have a direct stake since success in the exploration for natural gas would have major consequences for the whole gas industry, (2) it might obtain gas at a lower cost if it were found by its own group and improve its bargaining position with other successful groups, (3) it would gain some know-how in regard to exploration and production, and (4) it would increase the British financial stake in the North Sea.

The Minister was under some political pressure to increase state involvement. In December 1964, he received a nine-man delegation from the TUC and was reminded that the 1964 Congress had carried a resolution calling for public ownership, and, where practicable, public control of any mineral resources that might be discovered in the North Sea Continental Shelf. The delegation felt that a Labour Government should have paid more attention to the part the national-ised industries might play in developing the North Sea resources.

The Minister argued that the 1964 Act had effectively nationalised natural resources found in the North Sea Shelf, and, in a sense, the oil companies were merely acting as agents of the Government. He defended his decision to confirm the licences issued by the previous Government, and emphasised the serious consequences of unilateral revocation of them by the new Government. He also argued that there was no public authority capable of carrying out the work. Thus neither the Gas Council nor the Coal Board had any direct experience of this kind of work. The Minister further expressed the view that it was a pity that the Gas Council had not joined forces with BP, although he believed it was not the Council's fault. In the event the Council's decision to team up with three American companies had in effect meant that they received some preferential treatment. In further discussion with the delegation it was pointed out that the licensees were committed to a minimum expenditure of £80 million. If oil or gas were discovered the expenditures would be much greater. Much of the expertise would be in foreign currency brought in by the foreign oil companies which would help our balance of payments. The building of drilling rigs would bring a brand new industry to this country. In the award of licences certain criteria had been laid down for evaluating the weight to be placed on a company's application. Full acknowledgement was given to UK nationality, and in the most generally favoured area British companies (including the Gas Council) were well represented. It was emphasised to the delegation that when companies were questioned about their work programmes favourable notice was taken of any intention they expressed to build drilling rigs or other equipment in the UK.

Attitude of Gas Council

The details of the Gas Council's involvement as a licensee went back several years. In September 1962, Sir Henry Jones informed the Permanent Secretary, Ministry of Power, that he was favourably disposed towards an approach by Standard Oil of Indiana because this company had expressed its willingness to tie itself unre-servedly with the Gas Council as regards the disposal of any supplies of gas from the North Sea, whereas the consortium of the three UK companies had not come forward with any such proposals. It was felt that Sir Henry Jones suspected that the UK companies might be harbouring ideas of marketing any supplies of North Sea gas themselves. The Permanent Secretary pointed out to Sir Henry that it was natural that Standard Oil of Indiana, which had no distribution organisation in the UK, would be keen to enter into a partnership with the Gas Council. He also stressed the undesirability of the Gas Council becoming identified with Standard Oil Indiana without at least giving their UK rivals an opportunity of entering into a similar association with the Council. He suggested that Sir Henry would do well to pocket his pride and seek a discussion with the leaders of the UK companies, even though they appeared to have gone ahead with their exploration project without consulting him.

The Gas Council continued its discussions with Standard Oil of Indiana and in January 1963, felt that proposals with respect to a seismic survey programme made by the company were satisfactory. Sir Henry reported to the Ministry of Power that, in return for bearing 10% of the cost of the programme, the Council would receive all the information generated. Following the seismographic work and its evaluation the Council would have the option of electing to join a licence application group for up to 50% of the total venture. The group, with Standard Oil Indiana as prospective operator, would then apply for production licences. All gas discovered would be delivered to UK markets through the Gas Council, until such time as the Council no longer had markets for the gas. A constraint on the Council's activities stated that it would not enter into any other producing relationships within a defined area of 20,000 square miles which would be competitive with the proposed partnership. Sir Henry sought the approval of the Ministry to proceed with discussions on the lines of Standard Oil Indiana's proposals.

Reaction of Ministry to Gas Council's views

The Council's proposal was received by the Ministry with caution. It was recognised that there were advantages in the Council becoming involved in exploration and production, particularly access to its own sources of gas and the know-how which it would acquire. The latter would enhance its bargaining power in negotiations with other producers. On the other hand the Ministry felt that the North Sea would be thoroughly explored by the oil companies, and the active involvement of the Council would ultimately require large amounts of risk capital. It was open to question whether the proposed direction was optimal. The Council had been involved in other expensive and risky enterprises, but they had been in areas where it was unlikely that anyone else would undertake the development in question. This was not the case in the present proposal.

The Ministry was also aware that the proposal was less attractive than it would have been if the prospective partners had been UK-based oil companies. The proposal would then have been a natural extension of the partnership which the Council had with BP in searching for gas onshore. It was also recognised, however, that the proposal was a very good bargain for the Council. The "entry fee" was so low that the Ministry wondered whether, despite what they had been told, Standard Oil Indiana had been influenced by the prospect that association with the Council would put them in a favoured position when licences were awarded. The conclusion of the Ministry's review was that the low cost and clear interest of the Council in the proposal should probably be the deciding factors. There was the prospect of some future embarrassment on licensing. It was recommended that before a final decision was made, the Council be informed that participation in seismic surveys would not be regarded, by itself, as an argument for the Council's participation in the further stages outlined in Sir Henry's letter. Standard Oil Indiana should also be under no illusion that they would gain preferential treatment over other applicants as a result of its association with the Council.

In the event the Council was permitted to proceed with its participation in the seismic surveys. By the middle of 1964 the Council had to declare the share in further exploration and development which it wanted to take up. A meeting took place in June of that year between the Chairman and the Deputy Chairman of the Council and the Permanent Secretary of the Ministry of Power to discuss the possibilities. It was explained that, as from July 1964, the Council would have to meet its full share of its final share in the joint venture. Thus, if it took 50% (the maximum) in the joint venture, it would have to pay the additional 40% above the 10% to which the Council was already committed. Following discussion there was agreement among all present that there were strong arguments in favour of the Council taking a 50% share in the joint venture. The Chairman would write to the Minister on the matter.

Following the meeting the Permanent Secretary consulted his colleagues on the issue. Several felt that the Council's participation in the consortium should not exceed 25%. Further, the Council should advise the Ministry beforehand of the absolute amount of their commitment since the sums involved could be very large. The considerations which led to this conclusion did not all point in the same direction. Thus it was felt that North Sea exploitation was likely to be a speculative and expensive affair where investment of state funds was unnecessary and doubtfully appropriate. Further, the entitlement of the gas industry to supplies of gas on reasonable terms was safeguarded under the 1964 Act and by the Minister's powers. Such powers extended to securing rapid exploitation of the fuel resources of the Continental Shelf. It was also recognised that it would be difficult to justify prevention of participation in promising North Sea areas by the Gas Council when it led the way and expended substantial sums on onshore gas exploitation and in the development of the UK gas market. The argument that further participation would enhance the know-how of the gas industry regarding exploration and production activities had considerable weight. If discoveries were made by the consortium of which the Council was a part its bargaining position vis-à-vis other groups would be improved because of its greater ability to arrive at settlements on gas contracts without bringing in the Minister to decide "reasonable terms" for supplies from such other groups. The Ministry would also find it very useful to have the Gas Council as a source of inside information. The Council's participation would also enhance the British financial share in the North Sea. On the other hand it was noted that the Council had no expertise to contribute and its interest in the joint venture would be purely financial.

Having considered all the above points the Ministry group felt that Gas Council participation was justified but not to the extent of as much as 50%. Involvement at that level would make the Council the dominant partner in a consortium where it would have the major financial responsibility but little of the operating responsibility. Further, a 50% stake could involve very large financial commitment. On balance, the group felt that the Council's involvement should not exceed 25%.

The Permanent Secretary subsequently informed Sir Henry Jones that, on the balance of the arguments discussed above, the Gas Council should participate in joint venture bidding for production licences to a maximum share of 25%. In the meantime Sir Henry informed the Minister that the Council had reached agreement with Standard Oil Indiana (now known as Amoco) and new partners Texas Eastern and Amerada on a consortium in which the Council had the option to participate up to a maximum of 50%. Sir Henry added that he foresaw the Council exercising this option to the full extent. In the event the Council elected for a share of 31% in the consortium which was successful in its licence application in the First Round.

Following the election and change of Government the position of the Gas Council was re-examined in the context of the objective of increasing the British stake and the share of the nationalised industries in a future licence round. Various ideas were examined. It was ascertained that BP had not been keen to have the Gas Council as a partner for two reasons. Firstly, it had already refused Gulf Oil as a partner, and it would be out of the question after that to take a non-oil organisation instead. Secondly, since the Gas Council would for practical purposes be the only gas buyer of North Sea gas it would be an unacceptable member of a consortium which was selling gas. Shell and Esso made the decision to apply for licences as a 50:50 partnership and were not available as partners to the Gas Council.

The Permanent Secretary met with Sir Henry Jones and the Deputy Chairman Sir Kenneth Hutchison in December 1964, and outlined the desired general approach to licensing of the new Government. He suggested that the Council might like to be involved in a new grouping for applications in the forthcoming Second Round. Such a new grouping would exclude Amoco and the other two US companies and could perhaps include the National Coal Board. The vehement response of the Gas Council was that it would be quite impossible for the Council to join any other group than the one with which it was then associated. The Deputy Chairman said that it would be a flagrant breach of business ethics to join another group. This was because plans for the exploration of any new areas in the North Sea adjacent to those for which licences had already been granted, would have to draw on information obtained from work done in the areas already licensed. The Gas Council could not pass on to others such information received from its present partners. The Council suggested that the National Coal Board might team up with BP, but that would not influence the attitude of the Council in its position as a gas buyer. The Council further suggested that it would be happy to increase its share in the group to which it belonged to 50% if the other members agreed.

While acknowledging that there was some force in this argument the Ministry of Power was not convinced that it was conclusive. A survey was conducted of experience in other countries. This revealed that in a few countries such as Algeria and Alaska one company could have joint venture arrangements with separate groups. It was not clear, however, whether these separate groupings were in close physical proximity with each other.

Preparing for the Second Round and enhancing the UK share

Meanwhile more wide-ranging work was progressing on preparations for the Second Round. Enhancing British participation was a main preoccupation, and a larger stake for the Gas Council was only one of several routes under consideration. There were three major British oil companies – Shell, BP, and Burmah, – and several smaller ones. It was recognised that there would be no particular administrative difficulty in giving these companies a greater share of any contested acreage for which they applied. The limiting factor was the companies' own abilities and willingness to invest capital and resources in the area. It was recognised that this constituted a real limitation and that it would still be necessary to award licences to foreign-owned companies if the maximum benefit to the UK was to be secured.

One rather radical idea had been considered whereby a preliminary allocation might be made administratively among the British companies before applications were formally invited, thus enabling the Minister to announce, at the time of issuing the invitations, what arrangements he had made for securing a bigger share for British companies. It was recognised that this procedure would not be possible under the Regulations as they stood. These required the Minister to award licences only after publishing a notice in the Official Gazette, and he could not announce a preliminary allocation before applications had been received. Prior informal consultation with British companies would be possible, but care would be required to ensure that suspicions did not arise that the Minister had prejudged his eventual decision by determining allocations before he had considered all the applications.

It was recognised that other British non-oil companies such as ICI and Courtaulds had taken stakes in the First Round. While they had no technical expertise they might have some genuine contribution to make besides their share of the capital and their British ownership by providing an assured market outlet for a proportion of any oil or gas which might be discovered. It was felt that further companies of this type might be found willing to participate, particularly if a hint were given that the Minister would look favourably on groups containing British partners. It was even thought that some of the larger Cooperative Societies might take a share. They could have benefits to offer a partner by providing potential outlets for petroleum products.

It was also recognised that a further source of British participation would be financial interests which might take up a share in North Sea exploration in a speculative investment. The Ministry felt that there was no objection to such companies supplying genuine risk capital. It was also felt, however, that it would seem wrong in principle to give licences to speculative interests whose object was merely to sell them again at a profit. It was also felt that it would be undesirable to give preference to foreign oil companies entering partnership arrangements with British financial interests on favourable terms merely in the hope of cashing in on their British name. Thus care was needed in arrangements designed to secure greater British participation, not to give any encouragement to purely speculative interests.

Giving state companies a larger stake

The Ministry recognised that there were many different possible ways by which state-owned enterprises could be given a greater stake in the North Sea. One method would be to entrust the whole task of exploration and production to public enterprise and reject all private sector applications. A second approach would be to form a large consortium of British public and private sector interests (such as BP, the Gas Council and National Coal Board) which would be awarded any territory for which it applied. A third approach would be to form individual partnerships between nationalised industries and oil companies. Such partnerships could be either an essential feature of all licences or only in specified areas.

Direct participation by a public enterprise was not essential to procure a public financial stake in the North Sea. This could be achieved more simply through the royalties and other provisions for payment direct to the Government. In fact direct participation by public enterprise could only give the *possibility* of greater profits but would also carry with it the real risk of loss. It was recognised that direct participation on terms which avoided risk might be possible, but would almost certainly have to be in partnership with one or more of the smaller foreign-owned oil companies.

The Ministry recognised that, if enhanced public sector participation was to be encouraged, careful consideration had to be given to the question of whether the risks should be fully or partially shared or whether a device had to be found which involved no risk. The large oil companies were able to diversify their exploration risks by operating in many parts of the world. They were able to write-off their abortive exploration losses against the proceeds of successful ventures. But exploration limited to one area was much riskier. If public sector bodies undertook all the exploration and production the Government would effectively have to provide all the capital and carry all the risk of failure, in return for which it would receive all the profits from successes (instead of somewhat over 50% under the current arrangements). It was noted that, based on the above arguments, it was rare for public sector enterprises to shoulder all the exploration risks, and in countries where it had been tried (such as Mexico), the results had not been outstandingly successful. In the Middle East national oil companies had been set up, but it was noticeable that the arrangements were generally that the state company negotiated an option to participate with a foreign oil company only after oil had been found.

Candidates for state participation

Candidates for participation included the Gas Council, National Coal Board (NCB), and Central Electricity Generating Board (CEGB). The Gas Council was the most obvious candidate as it was already a licensee. The NCB was a major supplier of energy and interests in oil exploration could be a useful diversification and possible new source of revenue. Legislation might be required to permit the NCB to apply for and hold a licence. It might be possible to negotiate an arrangement whereby the Board would have an option to come in as a partner with a licensee at a later stage, after it had obtained the necessary statutory powers. The CEGB was a potentially large consumer of natural gas (much larger than ICI). However, any switching of power stations to run on natural gas would raise major questions of fuel policy. Exhorting the CEGB to participate in a licence group would risk prejudging an important wider policy issue.

The alternative to using existing organisations was to set up a new state enterprise specifically to conduct oil and gas exploration. It was recognised however, that to establish such an enterprise involved complex and controversial legislation, and the need to recruit staff and build up an organisation from scratch would take a long time. There was a quite different concern, namely that if the British Government established a body of this kind, it would be regarded as a national oil company, and this could be extremely embarrassing for British oil companies in their international operations. This possibility was, therefore not considered further.

Conclusions of Ministry on options

In coming to conclusions on the various options the Ministry felt that the award of all licences to public enterprises was unlikely to be in the public interest. Neither the Gas Council nor the NCB were technically equipped to carry out the work, and in practice they would have to negotiate contracts with oil companies to ensure that the work was undertaken. This was unlikely to be a satisfactory procedure. A mixed consortium of oil companies and nationalised enterprises would get round this problem but there were still difficulties. The question of whether the nationalised companies should be full risk-bearers arose. If it were felt that public sector companies should not bear their full share of the risks it was very doubtful whether British oil companies would be willing to participate. The Ministry was aware that BP and Shell had declined to accept the Gas Council as a partner in a group to undertake seismic work, partly on the grounds that the Council was going to be the only effective gas buyer, which made it an unacceptable member of a group which was selling gas. Further, most of the relevant parties had already entered into other groupings which would be very difficult to unscramble. Attempts to force changes would encounter practical difficulties, particularly if they had to be carried through in the face of opposition from the Gas Council. In any case the Council might require the consent of its partners before it could join another grouping.

It was also understood that the interests of the British oil companies did not coincide and the negotiation of a contract acceptable to them all would be quite complicated and time-consuming. A further problem for the international British oil companies was that a joint venture with a nationalised company in the UK would make it hard for them to resist pressure in the Middle East to enter into partnerships with national oil companies there. From the Ministry's viewpoint the formation of a large consortium introduced another difficulty, namely to secure a satisfactory work programme, because the companies concerned would feel sure of getting the best territory available, come what may, and might not be inclined to accept such heavy working obligations as they would if they were competing against each other.

Given the problems of a very large consortium there was some merit in individual partnerships between nationalised industries and oil companies. These could take two forms. One was where partnerships were a pre-condition of obtaining a licence. The Ministry noted that some Middle East countries, particularly Iran in its recent offshore award, had stipulated that concessions would only be granted to companies which accepted the state oil company as a partner. Such agreements typically incorporated carried interest whereby the private sector oil company carried all the exploration risks. To a large extent the device was designed to increase the state's share of any profits. Success from this device depended on the acreage on offer being very attractive. The Ministry concluded that it seemed extremely doubtful whether many companies would be willing to accept similar terms in the unproved and difficult territory of the North Sea.

Individual partnerships were a quite different matter. An oil company entering into a joint venture with a nationalised industry would hope to secure preferential treatment in the award of licences. It was doubtful whether the British oil companies would be willing to enter into this type of agreement, but some of the American independent oil companies might well be prepared to do so, even on terms which would involve them taking all or most of the risk. The Gas Council was the most obvious vehicle for increasing the UK share. There were, of course, limits to the scale of effort which the American partners and the Gas Council were able and willing to undertake.

Mr Lee, the Minister of Power, himself played a central role at this stage, and conducted a series of meetings with key British investors. In March 1965 he suggested to Sir Henry Jones that the best arrangement for securing greater participation by British companies and the nationalised industries in the next round would be to establish a large consortium of British oil companies, the Gas Council and the NCB. Sir Henry responded that the Minister was asking something very difficult. He reiterated the problems involved in forming a partnership with BP. On the other hand he was very pleased with the joint venture with Amoco which was working well. He had a high regard for Amoco's technical competence. If the Council were to join forces with other partners in a different part of the North Sea its good relationship with Amoco would be put in jeopardy. With respect to its present joint venture Sir Henry felt that, for applications in a new licence round, there should be no difficulty in the Council increasing its share to 50%. On the existing licences renegotiation with the partners would be required. The Council would much prefer not to take this step. He also stressed that the Council lacked the necessary technical expertise to work a licence area by itself. Through its association with Amoco it was now party to first-class work on the geological interpretation of the structure of the North Sea Shelf. The work done to date had narrowed down the areas which were really promising, and thus the Council was well placed to know the best areas for which to apply in the next round. Sir Henry also thought that, if the Government felt that it could not allow the Council to take up further licences with its current partners, he did not want to take the responsibility for rejecting these partners and would prefer to say that it was acting under Government edict. He added one further point, namely that if only British-owned companies were allowed to exploit the North Sea, the repercussions on our overseas oil interests should be carefully considered.

Views of BP

The Ministry, with Mr Lee again in the chair, subsequently met with Sir Maurice Bridgeman of BP. The Minister introduced the issue of a desire to see a larger British share in the next round. He raised the idea of a large consortium of British oil companies, the Gas Council and the NCB. In his response Sir Maurice said that in the last round BP believed it had not done as well as might have been expected in the south-east of the area in which it was interested. There were several blocks presumably available for the next round in this area for which BP might apply. The issue of BP's participation with other companies presented difficulties. After careful consideration of possible partners (including Gulf Oil) BP had decided to apply for licences on its own. If BP went into partnership with another company it would want to do so with one whose interests matched its own. This did not apply to the Gas Council or ICI. In the later stages of its partnership with the Council in onshore areas the relationship had not been happy, and BP had felt that the Council expected BP to spend its shareholders' money searching for natural gas for the benefit of the gas industry. The interests of BP and the NCB were, however, in some respects identical, but, in view of BP's earlier attitude on partnerships, it would not be easy for the company to make a joint application with the NCB. If such a partnership were felt to be desirable it might be better if the NCB were to apply for a licence on its own account, and subsequently invite BP to participate. A problem with this approach was the lack of technical competence of the NCB in offshore petroleum exploration. The device would look like a transparent device to give preferential treatment to nationalised industries and British companies.

It was also suggested that the prospects of finding oil or gas in commercial quantities on the North Sea Shelf were about 30 to 1 against; and the cost of each well was of the order of £1m. Some licence holders would probably drill a series of unproductive wells and if this were to happen to a nationalised industry there might well be embarrassing questions in Parliament about the waste of public money.

Views of Shell

Shortly afterwards the Ministry held a meeting with Mr David Barran of Shell on the same subject. Mr Lee stated that he was keen to proceed with a Second Licence Round before the Dutch and the Norwegians invited applications for their part of the North Sea Shelf. A further consideration in proceeding quickly to the next round was the possibility that the early results of exploration might prove disappointing. He raised with Mr Barran the concept of a large British consortium of British oil companies, the Gas Council, and the NCB.

Mr Barran shared the Minister's view that there were advantages in proceeding quickly with a new round and he confirmed Shell's interest. With respect to partnerships Shell's position was unambiguous. It had a firm commitment for participation with Esso, either in the form of joint bidding for licences, or, in the event of either company's applying for a licence on its own account, of its offering participation to the other. This joint participation would apply also in any wider consortium on which the companies joined. Shell and Esso because of their joint partnership in the Netherlands had decided to apply for licences jointly, and without taking other partners. They both felt that there were severe disadvantages to having a large number of companies associated in a joint venture. This certainly applied to the Iraq Petroleum Company and the Iranian Consortium.

Mr Barran queried the desirability of having the nationalised industries play a larger role in the next round. He emphasised the extremely speculative nature of ventures of this kind. He noted that if gas were found the Gas Council would automatically be involved as a distributor in Britain. He was doubtful about the case for associating the NCB or the CEGB, the latter as a potential user, in the search for oil or gas. He emphasised the great risks involved. Shell was able to spread its risks and it was precisely because this was not practicable with a nationalised industry operating in the North Sea Shelf (and which might find itself involved in substantial losses without any chance of making offsetting gains) that made the venture unsuitable.

In discussions it was pointed out that Shell had entered into partnership with the National Iranian Oil Company. In response it was stated that the circumstances were different. The Iranian authorities had made it clear that Shell's involvement would not be accepted on any other basis. Further, the territory in the Iranian offshore was a good deal more prospective than the North Sea Shelf. There was also a basic difference between the economies of the two countries. Iran was almost wholly dependent on oil revenues, whereas Britain had a wide diversity of other industries and skills. It was, therefore, to some extent understandable that the Iranians should want their national oil company to participate closely in all the stages of exploiting their main natural asset.

Mr Barran felt it would be unfortunate if there were obvious discrimination against foreign companies in the next round. Shell was part Dutch and a truly international company. It was in a very vulnerable position when other countries decided to discriminate against foreign companies, and it would be unfortunate if Britain were to give other nations an excuse for increasing the degree of discrimination in favour of their own nationals.

Views of Burmah Oil

A meeting between the Ministry and Mr R. P. Smith of Burmah Oil Company was also held on the same issue. The Minister put forward the idea of a large consortium of British oil companies, the Gas Council, and the NCB. Mr Smith explained that Burmah was currently in partnership with ICI, Murphy Petroleum and Ocean Exploration, the latter two being American companies. He pointed out that there was an agreement among the partners that, if any one of them were allocated further licences for other areas of the UKCS, the others would be given the chance to participate on the same terms and conditions as under the present licences. As a consequence if the issue arose of Burmah joining other groups it would have to discuss the matter with its present partners. With this qualification Mr Smith saw no objection in principle to Burmah taking part in a wider consortium.

Ministry reviews its position

The Ministry reviewed its position in the light of the meetings with the companies. Officials concluded that it would not be practicable to specify preferences for British participation in a hard and fast way in the preliminary announcement of invitations to bid. It would be best to reserve the possibilities of doing more on these lines after the bids had been received and assessed. Participation in North Sea exploration in the early stages was a risky financial speculation, and full state participation would be a direct charge on the Exchequer. It was better for public enterprise to participate after some results had been achieved. In practice this could be after six years when 50% of the licensed areas would revert to the state.

Mr Lee acknowledged the force of these conclusions. A paper would have to be circulated to the Economic Development Committee on all the issues relevant to a new licence round. It should consider all the aspects relating to enhanced British participation, a subject on which he would have to address the Parliamentary Labour Party because of its political interest. Officials proceeded to prepare a detailed paper covering all the main issues. With respect to the question of enhancing the British share the arguments discussed above were summarised as were the findings of the meetings with the British oil companies. On balance it would be wrong to restrict allocations to British companies because this would reduce the competitive element. Foreign capital would benefit the balance of payments and secure more rapid development of the UKCS. It would be possible, however, to announce the results in two stages, the first covering the most heavily contested area (in which the British companies would be seen to have a large, though not exclusive share) and the second covering other areas (where there might be a greater proportion of foreign licensees).

The difficulties which the British oil companies and the Gas Council had in entering into new groupings were fully appreciated, and the disadvantages of forming a very large British consortium highlighted. The idea that the Government could employ its majority shareholding in BP and insist on its entering into a partnership with a nationalised industry had been considered but was not recommended. To do so would be a complete reversal of the policy followed consistently by Governments of all parties for over fifty years, of never interfering in the ordinary commercial management of the company. It could probably only be carried out by using the Government's voting power to replace the entire Board of Directors, and it would certainly cause incalculable damage to the company's position in foreign countries where it did most of its business.

The draft paper also found sympathy with the Gas Council's position vis-à-vis its existing partners. The NCB as a supplier of primary fuel was perhaps fitted to participate, but its legal position had first to be clarified and legislation might be required to ensure that it could be involved. Participation by the CEGB would enable it to use its share of production as power station fuel, but this would raise awkward questions in relation to the future utilisation of coal. This cast doubt on the wisdom of pursuing this possibility.

The paper highlighted the financing requirements as the major obstacle to large-scale involvement by the nationalised industries. One exploration well alone would cost £0.5 million – £1 million and the result was speculative. Exploration on a limited scale in a single area was particularly hazardous. Investment by a nationalised industry in a speculative venture of this type would be quite unprecedented. The sums involved would have to be large to secure any worthwhile participation, and might in the end have to be written off as a complete loss. If the oil companies bore all the risk, the UK Government would still take over half the profits of any successful discovery in the form of royalties and taxes. The paper added that if, despite the risks involved, further state participation was desired, the simplest route would be for the Gas Council to increase its share of the group of which it was currently a member. The notion that smaller American oil companies might be prepared to offer favourable participation terms to a nationalised industry (such as carried interest at the exploration stage) had somewhat dubious advantages, but any proposals made by the companies could certainly be considered.

The paper's conclusion was that the appropriate time for large-scale participation by nationalised enterprise would be in 1970 when 50% of the present licensed acreage had to be surrendered. By that time it would be able properly to assess the risks. This would enable the Government to allocate acreage to nationalised industry with a fairly full knowledge of what was involved and in the more confident expectation of a successful outcome.

Interestingly, the Treasury, when it received the draft paper from the Ministry of Power, was prepared to take a more liberal attitude towards increased participation by nationalised industries. In a Minute it was argued that, as the Government was going to take 60% of profits of the total risk capital involved, it was not unreasonable for the Government to be underwriting some proportion of it. It was also felt that some nationalised industries were already investing relatively large sums in equally risky projects in other fields (e.g. magneto-hydro-dynamic generation of electricity). In sum in this matter, initiative should be left with the undertakings concerned, nationalised and non-nationalised.

Checkerboarding of blocks?

While the issue of enhanced British participation was a dominant issue in the preparatory work for the Second Round several other subjects had to be addressed. One of these was the suggestion that a "checkerboarding" system be adopted in designing the areas to be offered to investors. Under this system the area to be offered would be divided into alternate "black" and "white" squares. Initially only the "black" ones would be offered. The "white" ones would be retained by the Government for later licensing on more favourable terms if exploration in the adjoining "black" squares was successful. A variant would be licence blocks initially in the conventional manner, but provide that areas must be relinquished on the "checkerboarding" principle (diagonally opposite quarters on each block).

The Ministry examined this scheme but concluded that it was not suitable for employment in North Sea conditions. The Ministry's understanding was that the system operated only in parts of onshore Canada, particularly Saskatchewan. One of the objectives there was to secure a wider geographical spread of production. Maximum production was emphatically not the object – on the contrary production was already subject to restrictions by pro-rationing. Conditions in the Continental Shelf were quite different. There was nothing to be gained by deliberate geographical dispersion of production, and the UK's interests lay in securing the maximum effort in exploration and exploitation.

The Ministry did not think it necessary to adopt a "checkerboarding" system in order that the Government retained rights for the future. Thus the existing provisions for surrender of acreage ensured that 50% of each licence reverted to the state after six years. It was also felt that use of the "checkerboarding" system would make the investment prospects less attractive to potential applicants. The Ministry was also concerned about perceived practical difficulties in implementing the scheme. If it were to be effective the blocks offered had to be fairly small, and this might lead to problems over the efficient exploitation of any oil or gas found.

This last point was probably the most important one. There was room for debate about the effect of a "checkerboarding" system on the size of the exploration effort and the value of licence blocks, but the possibility of discoveries overlapping block boundaries and the consequent need for unitisation agreements raised practical problems which were more difficult in offshore situations than onshore. The prospect of a substantial proportion of development plans having to incorporate unitisation agreements was generally unwelcome to both host Governments and investors.

Financial terms

The Ministry group also had to consider the financial terms for the new round. The idea of having an auction system for allocating blocks was reconsidered but fairly quickly rejected. In the present case there was particular concern that the result of adopting this scheme would be that the Minister would have little or no control over the result and would not be able to ensure that British companies or nationalised industries obtained a fair share of the more promising territory. Further, the potential of the North Sea was still unknown and the Government could not expect companies to be willing to pay a very high price for concessions. It was noted that a competitive element was still present with respect to the work programmes submitted. The possibility of putting some blocks to auction could be considered again in 1970 when 50% of the present licensed areas would be surrendered.

With respect to licence fees, royalties, and taxes the Ministry felt that those applicable to the First Round were broadly in line with those set by oil producing countries in the Middle East and elsewhere and were probably as favourable to the Government as any in other completely unproved areas elsewhere in the world. The effective Government take of around 60% was roughly the average in the Middle East, and had been regarded as stiff by the oil companies at the time of the First Round. The Ministry also felt that the bulk of the territory that could be offered, though reasonably interesting, was not by any means as attractive to the potential applicants as that taken in the First Round. It had also to be borne in mind that the oil companies would be well aware of the opportunities coming up in the Norwegian and Dutch sectors. It was felt that, at least in some respects, the Norwegian financial terms were slightly more favourable to licensees than the British ones. There was thus a concern that if the UK imposed stiffer terms than last time this would almost certainly discourage applicants, who would be disposed to hold off and bid on the other side of the Shelf. A further consideration was the need to avoid setting precedents which might be followed by Governments of oil producing countries abroad to the detriment of British companies and thus to the balance of payments. On the other hand there did not seem to be any reason to relax the terms and thus the recommendation was to leave them unchanged. It was noted that the change in company taxation announced in the budget of 1965 introducing corporation tax, would probably result in lower payments than the current system of profits and income tax, but there would be additional income tax received on profits distributed to British shareholders. The net effect should be somewhat higher total receipts. On the other hand tax payments from foreign-owned companies could be less because the tax on their dividends could be reduced under the double tax treaties.

The Treasury examined the Ministry's proposals on the financial terms and quickly agreed that they were as favourable to the Government as could be expected. The Foreign Office also agreed that the proposed terms were acceptable. They were very concerned that any attempt to stiffen the terms, apart from discouraging applications, might set a precedent to the Governments of other oil producing countries to the detriment of the interests of British companies.

As in the First Round the Ministry proposed to offer large areas for licensing. Agreement on the boundaries had now been reached with Norway, Denmark and the Netherlands, and it would now be possible to designate areas out to the median lines. It was also proposed to designate areas further off the north of Scotland up to the northern limit of the agreed boundary with Norway. Some interest had also been shown in the Irish Sea, and it was proposed to designate areas there, taking care to ensure that these were well short of the likely boundary with the Irish Republic, and excluding areas within the territorial waters of the Isle of Man. Finally, a narrow strip along part of the south coast of England could be offered. There had been some slight interest in this area. The total acreage proposed to be offered in the Second Round was around 66,000 square miles of which 54,000 square miles were in blocks offered in the First Round but not awarded. By way of comparison the total acreage put on offer in the First Round was 80,000 square miles.

Inter-departmental issues

At its meeting on 31st May 1965, the Economic Development Committee agreed to the proposals put forward by the Ministry of Power on the lines discussed above. This included the possibility that the NCB might join a group applying for licences. In view of the high political interest the First Secretary of State felt it appropriate to consult the Prime Minister about the proposals. Mr Wilson agreed, and the Ministry proceeded with the detailed preparatory work. One issue mentioned by the First Secretary in his Minute to the Prime Minister was the need to reconcile the safeguarding of essential defence interests with the licensing of large areas for petroleum exploration. The problem had been recognised in the later part of 1964. The Ministry of Power received from the Ministry of Aviation a map of the Danger Areas in the UK (including the UKCS). This caused concern as it included substantial areas off the Lincoln and Norfolk coasts which were heavily licensed in the First round. Helicopters could not fly through the areas in question during times of defence-related activity. When drilling took place large rigs with crews of up to 50 would be required as would regular helicopter services. The Ministry of Power informed the Ministry of Aviation that the Government had great hopes of economic advantages arising from exploration and exploitation of the Continental Shelf, and, having issued licences and received considerable sums by way of consideration, could not contemplate a situation where the activities of licensees were curtailed or even rendered impossible because of these Danger Areas. There followed a considerable dialogue between the Ministry of Defence and the Ministry of Power on the issue. The Ministry of Defence emphasised the importance of the Danger Areas in the North Sea to the Service Departments and the considerable expense which would be involved in moving their defence-related activities to other locations. But working arrangements acceptable to both interests could hopefully be developed. In the areas of immediate concern most activity of the Service Departments took place near to the shore, though this could still create problems relating to the safe passage of helicopters. A meeting subsequently took place between representatives of the Ministry of Aviation, Ministry of Defence and Bristow Helicopters (the relevant helicopter operator) at which agreements were made on liaison procedures and helicopter route determination.

When the Ministry of Power started preparations for the Second Round the Ministry of Defence, on the authority of the Secretary of State, asked that it be consulted before further licences were issued. A meeting was held in April 1965, among representatives of the Ministries of Power and Defence and the Board of Trade (whose concern was navigational issues). The Ministry of Defence outlined their interests which were (a) navigation (both surface and submarine), (b) bombing and mine-laying areas, and (c) exercise areas. If oil companies wanted to drill in areas coming in the (b) and (c) categories the Ministry of Defence would be in difficulty as certain bombing and exercise areas were linked to specific Air Stations. For this reason it would be impossible to move to other areas. It should also be noted that the Ministry of Agriculture, Fisheries and Food could well object to a movement of exercise areas because of interference with the fishing industry. The Ministry of Defence would require as much notice as possible to be given of oil-related activities. When there were no difficulties four weeks notice would be adequate. But there could be occasions when the Ministry of Defence would be obliged to ask for delays to drilling operations, request modifications to detailed sites and dates of drilling, or sometimes object outright.

The Ministry of Power felt that the system of notices to drill could be improved to be helpful to the defence interests. It felt that contractors could drill anywhere within a mile radius of a particular position or phase the order of drilling in different positions. The Ministry of Power wondered whether it would be possible to inform operators in advance of areas where exercises were planned, so that they knew in good time areas which they should avoid. The Ministry of Defence felt that, while they would look at this idea, there might be security objections to providing such information to outside parties. The Hydrographer's Department thought that in a large scale exercise on the high seas there should be no problems with drilling rigs, as ships taking part in such exercises had to take account of all other users of the sea and any other obstructions. Following discussion it was suggested that the Ministry of Defence might provide a map showing sensitive areas. The Ministry of Power would then advise licensees with concessions in these areas that they must consult the Ministry of Defence.

The possibility was raised of dangers that could arise if oil companies desired to drill in areas where bombs had been dumped or mine-laying exercises had taken place. The Hydrographer's Department noted that information about these areas had previously been made available to the Ministry of Agriculture, Fisheries and Food in order that fishermen could be informed of possible danger. This subject would be examined further. It was agreed that the Ministry of Defence would be consulted on all future proposals for new areas to be offered for licence.

The Ministry of Defence then produced a submission to the Economic Development Committee drawing attention to its interests in the forthcoming licence round. Having seen the proposed plans of the Ministry of Power, the Ministry of Defence found a number of areas where the presence of drilling rigs would be unacceptable, either because of the disruption they would cause to essential training and weapon trials, or because of the intensive use of the area by naval units. Several examples were given. These included the Moray Firth which was in constant use for training purposes by both aircraft and ships, four areas off the east coast used as air weapon practice areas by the RAF, and a range located to the north-west of the Isle of Man which was used by Bomber Command and the

USAF-Europe. The memorandum went on to state that the activities carried on in the areas in question could not be temporarily moved to another location because most of the areas were closely linked to a shore establishment or air station. If the use of the range in question were denied the land base would cease to be able to function for the purpose in question. The difficulties of finding satisfactory alternative areas were also very great. Over the years the Service Departments had relinquished large areas of land used as range and exercise areas. Thus the coastal and sea areas were now of great importance. The areas currently used had been arrived at only after prolonged discussions with several development departments and other bodies (such as the Society for the Preservation of Rural England). There would be very great difficulty in finding other areas at sea and even more resistance to the acquisition of bombing and firing areas on land. The Ministry of Defence, with the support of the Secretary of State, then recommended that licences should not be issued in areas where the Ministry of Defence certified that drilling would cause unacceptable interference with essential defence activities, and that licensees should be asked to consult the defence authorities about their operations.

The response of the Ministry of Power was that, in general, the recommendations were acceptable. It was felt, however, that in the event of failure to reach agreement among officials about areas which the Ministry of Defence would like to be excluded the matter should be referred to Ministers. It would not be satisfactory to give the Ministry a unilateral right of veto. The Treasury supported this view, arguing that the potential economic importance of oil and gas exploitation was such that the Ministry of Defence could not have the last word in deciding that a particular exploration could not go ahead. This could result in large areas where oil or gas might be found being sterilised. The final decision could be made by Ministers, and if the result went against the Ministry of Defence consideration could be given to reimburse the extra expense involved in rearranging defence facilities.

A considerable correspondence ensued concerning the details of the blocks where the Ministry of Defence wanted either prohibition or restrictions on drilling. In the final selection of blocks offered for licensing in the Second Round, (advertised in the London Gazette on 6th August 1965), all those which the Ministry of Defence felt were affected to a substantial degree by defence interests were excluded. Most of a further set where the defence interest was affected to a relatively small extent were included. For some the Ministry of Power proposed to inform applicants that drilling would be prohibited in certain specified Danger Areas. The applicant would be given the opportunity to accept the block subject to restrictions, accept a reduction in the area of the block, or withdraw.

The Second Round is launched

The Minister announced the Second Round in a Statement in the House of Commons on 21st July 1965 which reflected the recommendations of the Economic Development Committee. The Minister highlighted the considerations he would have in awarding licences. The most important objective was to procure the most thorough and rapid exploration and development of the UKCS. Towards this end particular attention would be given to the work programmes proposed and the capacity of the applicant to undertake the work. The record of work already performed by applicants would be taken into account. The facilities of applicants for disposing of oil and gas in the UK would be considered. With respect to foreign applicants the extent to which British companies received equitable treatment in the country concerned would be taken into account. The statement added that, other things being equal, weight would be given to the contribution which the applicant was currently or planned to make to the UK economy, including balance of payments, and the growth of industry and employment, with special reference to the regions. The Minister would also consider proposals made by applicants to facilitate the participation of public enterprises in the exploitation of any oil or gas.

Debate on revisions to Regulations with industry

In the meantime work had been progressing on the preparation of revisions to the Petroleum Regulations. Key drivers had been the need to incorporate provisions relating to discoveries straddling the median lines with other countries, and to clarify the position with respect to the landward and sea areas and the relationship of these to territorial waters. The Ministry felt that other Regulations could also be reviewed and in the process of doing this asked the oil industry for its views in January 1965. Forty-one companies responded by forming a committee which submitted its views and recommendations to the Ministry in March. Some related to very detailed issues. Of the main recommendations one requested that the period of notice required by a licensee to surrender all or part of a licence area be reduced from two years to six months for a part area, and twelve months for a whole licence area. It was argued that the effect of a long period of notice on a licensee who had decided to surrender acreage would be to sterilise it, while at the same time it constituted an unjustifiable burden on the licensee.

A second recommendation related to the fact that because drilling operations were very costly, delays were financially burdensome. The committee requested that the requirement to obtain drilling consent in writing, which could be a source of delay, should be removed. A further recommendation related to perceived difficulties relating to geological and geophysical surveys in the situation where many discontinuous blocks were held by different licensees. One operator, in evaluating the potential of his own block, might well wish to extend his surveys to blocks in adjoining areas. The operators in question would probably be in a similar position and would probably be willing to give permission for such work to be undertaken. It was recommended that Ministerial permission for such arrangements should be unnecessary.

Other recommendations included the removal of the requirement for Ministerial consent for the abandonment of wells. The committee felt that the removal of this requirement would not harm the interests of the Government, while its presence caused delays to a licensee. The committee also requested that the clause dealing with the licensee's landing obligation requiring him to provide details of the place of delivery, the price obtained, and the manner in which payment of that price was to be made, should be deleted. The committee argued that the Government already had wide powers to impose landing conditions, and was concerned that in other countries and contexts such requirements could be used against the interests of the industry. (By this was meant the fear that the clause in question might be used by OPEC countries as an excuse to regulate the export price and payments relating to their oil.) The more general recommendation of the committee was that it would be entirely inappropriate to apply a more severe régime to the remaining Shelf areas. There was no evidence that the prospects on the North Sea Shelf could be rated more highly now than a year earlier, while large tracts of the currently undesignated part of the Shelf might safely be regarded as possessing markedly inferior prospects or none at all.

The Ministry studied the report. On the question of the notice period required by a licensee to voluntarily relinquish acreage there was some sympathy with the industry's views, and it was decided to reduce the notice period from twelve months to six months within the initial six-year period, and to twelve months from two years in the second (forty-year) period. With respect to the current require-ment for the abandonment and plugging of wells the Ministry felt that it was necessary that the Minister should retain control in case problems relating to envi-ronmental or safety issues arose, but were prepared to make some technical changes. There was some sympathy with the request that joint geological surveys could be carried out without the Minister's permission.

The Ministry could not agree to the request of the industry committee that the clause outlining the detailed requirements relating to the landing requirement be deleted. The Ministry understood the companies' fears about the clause possibly being used by OPEC countries, but thought that the parallel was not valid. There were separate provisions dealing with valuation for royalty purposes. The purpose of the clause which the industry wanted deleted was solely to provide powers equivalent to those contained in the Exchange Control Act. These already applied to activities on the UK mainland, but as the UKCS was not part of the United Kingdom the Exchange Control Act did not apply there. The Government thus required the powers in question to ensure that offshore licensees were subject to the UK exchange control regulations.

Unitisation of fields straddling median lines

A particular issue which engaged the Ministry and the industry for some time was the regulatory arrangement to secure compliance by licensees with agreements which were made between states with respect to the exploitation of fields strad-dling the boundary between them. This issue had to be provided for because the agreements on boundaries with the other North Sea countries meant that licences could be awarded up to the boundary line. While the agreement with Norway, for example, provided that the contracting states, in consultation with the licensees, would seek to reach agreement on the manner in which a field straddling the boundary should be exploited and subsequent proceeds apportioned, the current Regulations did not contain provisions to ensure that such an agreement was implemented by the licensees. The view of the Ministry's legal department was that this would require a Regulation empowering the Minister to give directions to licensees to secure their compliance with any international agreement made.

A draft clause was shown to a number of oil companies. Several expressed disquiet. Gulf Oil expressed the view that the proposed reservation of an unrestricted and undefined power to impose restrictions on a licensee could result in the serious curtailment of the exercise by him of the rights initially granted under his licence. In support Gulf Oil pointed out that the UK-Norwegian boundary agreement provided for consultation with licensees. Further, the existing UK Regulations gave the licensee the right to submit his own development plan and also provided that, if he objected to a scheme prepared by the Minister, he could refer the matter to arbitration.

BP wrote in similar vein, arguing that it would be inequitable in the circumstances to deny at least the possibility of consultation with licensees. The company thus requested that the clause be modified to include prior consultation with the licensee before development plans and conditions were determined. Shell also conveyed their unease on this subject.

The Ministry considered these representations with some sympathy, given that provisions of the kind requested had been incorporated in the treaty with Norway. The legal adviser considered, however, that a distinction had to be drawn between provisions in a treaty and a clause in a licence which might be the subject of a dispute coming before the courts. He also argued that the circumstances envisaged in the proposed clause were such that consultation with the licensee would be a practical necessity. In the light of this the Ministry felt that the alternative procedure of giving written assurances to licensees that consultations would take place should be proposed. This procedure was broadly acceptable to the investors in question, and the proposed clause was essentially left unaltered.

It had been hoped that the revised Regulations would be brought into force in 1965 in time for the Second Round. In the event this did not prove possible. The settling of some detailed issues such as those relating to the definition of the boundary between landward and seaward areas, and the updating of the land regulations (unchanged since 1935) to make them broadly consistent with those applicable offshore consumed much of the Ministry's time. It was also concluded that the issue of new Regulations at around the same time as the Second Round was in progress might prejudice the speedy conclusion of the Round.

Accordingly it was not until June 1966 that the Minister was asked to approve the new draft Regulations based on the subjects discussed above. (The onshore proposals are not discussed here as the subject is outside the scope of this history.) Following approval the proposals were laid before Parliament and came into operation on 8th August 1966. The revised Regulations applied only to future licences and thus not to those issued in late 1965 under the Second Round.

Progress of Second Round

The Ministry was able to give a preliminary report on the applications for Second Round licences in late September 1965. Twenty-one companies or groups of companies had submitted applications for 127 individual blocks. Applications for 76 of these were uncontested. It was noteworthy that, compared to the First Round, there was now at least some revealed interest in territories east of the Orkney Islands, the Moray Firth, east of the Shetland Islands near the median line with Norway, and the Irish Sea. In these areas applications were mostly uncontested and the bulk of the interest was still in the Southern North Sea. The second clear feature was the very selective manner in which applications were made, particularly in the Southern Sector. Thus 11 applicants gave one block (49/4) as their first choice. It was clear from a preliminary look at the priorities attached by the companies for the blocks requested that it was going to be extremely difficult if not impossible to accommodate all the applicants, even those with a quite high ranking under the Minister's criteria. After discussions with the applicants, preliminary proposals for awards were prepared by Petroleum Division on the basis of the published criteria. Two companies, Gulf Oil and Allied Chemicals had included in their applications proposals to include the NCB in their joint ventures. Because of these proposals the two companies had been given more favourable treatment than they would otherwise have received. A decision on the NCB's participation was thus required, though this should not hold up the whole exercise.

Mr Lee held a meeting with officials to discuss the applications. He had been given the preliminary proposals plus further information indicating that on the basis of the proposals the UK content would be 31% overall, and in the most contested areas 41% – 42%. The figures were quite similar to those of the First Round. This was in a sense disappointing, given the policy intent of increasing the British share. Mr Lee was advised, however, that the policy of aiming at rapid exploration and development and the preponderance of American companies applying had made a high foreign content inevitable. He was thus advised to acquiesce with the outcome in this respect.

Officials asked for Ministerial guidance on the question of NCB participation. Lord Robens had written to the Minister in June 1965, putting the issue of decision firmly on the Government. Officials felt that it was preferable that decisions of this sort should be taken by the NCB rather than as a dictat from the Minister. It was anticipated that, given the favourable terms offered by Gulf Oil and Allied Chemicals, the amount of money involved over the next few years should not exceed £5 million and would reasonably be regarded as within the borrowing powers which had already been decided on for the National Coal Board. Allied Chemicals in particular had made an attractive offer whereby the NCB would have the option to acquire a 75% interest after a commercial discovery. This was on a carried interest basis and thus NCB would pay nothing if a commercial discovery were not made. Officials recommended that the Minister allow NCB participation.

Mr Lee felt that, before final allocations were settled, it was important to establish the role of the nationalised industries. He favoured NCB participation, though

Gas Council involvement should be given priority. Fortunately there was only limited overlap in the applications from the groups with which the Council and NCB were associated. The view was expressed that, before NCB participation was agreed, the positive willingness of the Board to do so should be ascertained.

Mr Lee was informed that, of the other British applicants, BP would be awarded their top-rated block. Shell would not come out so well because they could not be awarded their highest-related blocks without depriving either the Gas Council, BP or Gulf, all of whom were also in the top priority group and had better claims to the blocks desired by Shell. It was noted that the proposal by the Gas Council to take a 50% share in its group was intended to reflect the views of the Minister. It was estimated that if the Council took on this obligation it would have to find at least an extra £1 million per year to finance its share of the cost. This would have to be obtained by a levy on the Area Boards which in turn might need higher gas tariffs in order to pay for it. It was explained that this was the result of the Council's decision to charge Northern Sea exploration costs to revenue account. The Ministry was not convinced that this was the most appropriate procedure.

Negotiations with companies

Mr Lee generally accepted the proposals of officials who were authorised to enter into detailed discussions with applicants. The Ministry followed certain principles in this exercise. They wanted to ensure that highly prospective areas were not combined with less promising blocks. This was designed to safeguard the position in six years time when at least 50% of each licence had to be surrendered. Thus blocks in the Southern area, which was the most highly favoured part of the Shelf, could not be combined with other blocks further to the north. Because of legal differences blocks off Scottish waters could not be combined in the same licence with blocks off English waters.

In negotiating the basis for work programmes the main principle employed was to try to ensure that the minimum programme for each licence should be sufficiently intensive to cover the work needed to disprove the territory offered. Drilling commitments were generally being insisted on, although in some cases there was some conditionality. The Ministry was faced with cases where blocks now being considered were contiguous with blocks held in an existing licence. Another situation was where the seismic maps showed that potential hydrocarbon-bearing structures straddled blocks on which different groups of companies had been asked to submit work programmes. In both situations the Ministry accepted that the drilling of a well on the structure could demonstrate that there was no likelihood of reservoir conditions existing in any part of the structure. To deal with this problem the Ministry took the view that, on an *ad referendum* basis, the work programme for the block in question could be cross-referenced to an existing licence. The implication was that, if parts of the median line area appeared unpromising as a result of drilling, a well drilling obligation could be transferred to an existing licence.

The Ministry was able to report that the minimum work programmes negotiated amounted to 44 wells plus seismic at a total cost estimated at £30 million. If the NCB's participation was to the extent of 40% in the applications of Gulf Oil and Allied Chemicals the UK content could be in the 38.5% – 42% range. Amoseas (Caltex) had withdrawn their bid for acreage in the Irish Sea. This left the area open to Gulf Oil the other bidder, and it was proposed that this group be awarded a five-block licence in the area.

The awards are made

The final proposals of the officials were accepted by the Minister. They involved an overall British content of 37% if the NCB took up the options to the full extent. If it did not participate the British share would be 31%. The share of the nationalised industries would be 11% if the NCB took up its options. The Minister made a brief statement to the House of Commons on the awards on 24th November 1965. They involved 37 licences to 18 groups and comprised 127 blocks covering 10,000 square miles. The award of acreage covering 500 square miles in the Irish Sea was an innovation.

Involvement of NCB in UKCS

Meanwhile the Ministry was much engaged on issues resulting from the Second Round. In September 1965, the Economic Development Committee had agreed that powers to enable the NCB to participate in exploration should be included in wider legislation to extend the powers of all nationalised industries. Such wider legislation was omitted from the legislative programme for 1966–67, and this necessitated the preparation of separate legislation to honour the commitment which the Minister had given to Parliament in November 1965. In October 1966, the Minster submitted a draft Bill to the Economic Development Committee. It was pointed out that the Bill should be enacted rapidly to enable the NCB to take advantage of the most favourable options given by Allied Chemicals. Both Gulf Oil and Allied Chemicals had been pressing the NCB to clarify their intentions to enable them to finalise their exploration plans.

The Ministry's proposals involved granting the NCB the minimum powers necessary to operate on equal terms with their potential partners. This included the right to operate on their own. Powers to operate downstream or explore for oil and gas outside the UKCS were not proposed. The Bill on the above terms was enacted in December 1966.

Political profile of state participation in UKCS

Politically, the subject of state participation in the North Sea was taking an increasingly high profile. At the 1966 Labour Party Conference a resolution was unanimously approved calling on the National Executive to examine and report on the advisability of public ownership of all operations concerning the production of natural gas and oil in Britain or on the British side of the Continental Shelf. The Ministry had to respond to this. It was noted that the arguments put forward in favour of nationalisation included (a) the bringing of a new, growing sector under public ownership and control, (b) no "unnecessary profits" accruing to private business, in some cases to be remitted overseas, and (c) the increased ease of developing a fully coordinated energy policy.

The Ministry's reaction was that there were very strong arguments against such a course covering, *inter alia*, getting the job done, finance, compensation, the balance of payments and overseas considerations. The first issue was the most immediate. Nationalisation would be extremely controversial, both at home and overseas. If it were seriously mooted work in the North Sea would be greatly reduced. It was possible that the licensees would undertake only the minimum work consistent with their licence obligations. There would be delays in the attainment of production. In terms of implementation a Bill to nationalise North Sea operations could not be introduced before the 1967/68 Session at the earliest. Further, even if it were given top priority, Vesting Day for a new public corporation could not be before the middle of 1968 only two years before the first relinquishments were due.

On the issue of finance, while the initial success rate achieved was very good, on the basis of the experience of the other provinces it might not be maintained. Across the world success rates averaged one in nine or one in ten, and the chance of a major commercial discovery were very much less. The large oil companies could spread their risks geographically, but a national oil corporation was by definition restricted to one area, and was thus not so well placed. It might be very fortunate, but could lose considerable sums. It followed that petroleum exploration was not the kind of operation that Governments or public enterprises should lightly undertake. There were, of course, numerous examples of the nationalisation of oil operations around the world, but the benefits, to say the least, were questionable, and in some cases private enterprise had been recalled.

Petroleum exploration was a highly specialised activity. British oil companies had their share of the required skills, but they had to employ specialised contractors, normally American, to undertake the work. In due course British companies would develop these skills. But this required time, and it was inevitable that a British public corporation would have to rely heavily on foreign contractors and other specialists in its first few years. It could not be assumed that these would be forthcoming in the numbers and quality required when they were already committed to the private sector. It could also not be assumed that their organisation into a single new entity under state control would be easy or efficient. It was also felt that the diversity of technical expertise across many separate oil companies and contractors was important, and specialist sub-contractors working to a single employer could not be expected to provide an adequate substitute. The spread of skills then available was likely to be more effective than the efforts of a single unit created from scratch. A short-term problem related to the drilling rigs. It was feared that a decision to nationalise would result in the rigs currently being employed in the North Sea being transferred to other areas of the world.

A different consideration related to the effect on the overseas interests of British oil companies. These maintained oil supplies for the UK and earned substantial foreign exchange earnings from their overseas sales. There was a fear that nation-alising North Sea operations might encourage similar action by others affecting British oil property abroad, and of course it would be impossible for the UK to dissuade these others from such action.

Another financial consideration was the compensation involved. In practice this would require valuation of the assets. Expenditure in the North Sea up to late 1966 was around £100 million. Provision would also have to be made for loss of profits which, conservatively, could amount to another £100 million. Well over 50% of the compensation would have to be remitted abroad, given the ownership of the licensees. A new public corporation would have to find the capital to pursue operations in the North Sea. Such requirements could be several times the £100 million already spent.

The conclusions of the Ministry in late 1966 were that state involvement through the Gas Council and the NCB was welcome, but to go further and take the whole of the development into the public sector would be fraught with difficul-ties. To date the pace of work was very brisk compared to other parts of the world. If the UK wanted the job done quickly and thoroughly it should consider very carefully before throwing aside the skills and capital of private industry. Under the current arrangements the nation was obtaining the advantage that other people were risking their money and not the Government. It was virtually impossible to organise an effort by a public corporation comparable with that available through the combination of oil companies. The financial burden of compensation and financing the corporation would also be very considerable.

The Minister requested that the Ministry's views be sent to the Labour Party Research Department. The resolution at the Labour Party Conference had, of course, been widely reported in the press. The reaction of the Opposition spokesman, Mr Anthony Barber, was to state that to nationalise the North Sea operations would be a disaster for this country. The fact that these have been devel-oped so quickly has been due to private industry, and even to consider nationalising the industry at this stage would be against the national interest. However, there was a considerable body of opinion within the Labour Party in favour of nationalisa-tion. At a meeting with the Lord President in December 1966, the Minister deployed the various arguments against nationalisation and stressed the impor-tance for the Party of keeping clear of any commitment. The Minister agreed to produce a note for other Ministers and Labour Party MPs indicating the positive aspects of the present arrangements and the great risks involved in further explora-tion. The paper emphasised the substantial UK share under the current arrange-ments with a total stake in licences of 34% if the NCB exercised its options. Around 50% of profits would accrue to the Exchequer. The success rate to date had been good with six commercial gas discoveries, but the ratio of failure to successes was likely to increase. The international companies were accepting the high risks and costs. It would be very difficult to find UK substitutes for all the private capital and equipment which was being devoted to the North Sea.

The debate continued. The idea of effective nationalisation had already been mooted by the Parliamentary Secretary at the Ministry of Power from a rather different angle. If the oil companies were dissatisfied with the price at which they could sell gas to the Gas Council they should be invited to surrender their licences. The Government would then take over the activity via a national company. As an alternative BP might be required to take up any licences relinquished by others. The Ministry reviewed this suggestion. The balance of the arguments were against nationalisation on the grounds discussed above. It was most unlikely that BP would be willing to take up relinquished licences and it would be difficult to compel them to do so. The Government's shareholding power was limited to applying a veto to Board resolutions on grounds of high public policy. BP would not have enough money nor share the Parliamentary Secretary's judgement that the proposal would constitute a good investment. These views were passed to the Minister.

National Hydrocarbons Corporation?

Following the Labour Party conference of 1966 the National Executive Committee (NEC) established a North Sea Study Group under the chairmanship of Dr Tony Hart. Its membership included MPs, party members employed in the oil industry, and academics, including Dr Peter Odell. The Study Group started to develop ideas for the formation of a National Hydrocarbons Corporation (NHC). They presented their initial ideas to the Minister on 10th April 1967. The Group explained that they saw the role of the NHC as a means of building up a public stake without the expense of nationalisation and without the setback to current exploration and production which this would have entailed. Five functions of the NHC were identified. It would (1) take over concessions relinquished by licensees, (2) take over the licences held by the Gas Council and NCB, (3) exploit fields which were not sufficiently attractive to oil companies, (4) take over areas which had not been explored, and (5) examine the possibility of accepting responsibility for all offshore transportation. It was explained that exploitation of a field might be unattractive because of high transportation costs and these might be reduced if all offshore pipelines could be planned and coordinated by a single body. Under the fourth role the idea was to take over areas which licensees had made no effort to explore. The cost of this in compensation should be minimal. The Group explained that it would be better to have one public organisation rather than have the effort divided between the Gas Council and the NCB. A new body would be better able to concentrate on building up an efficient organisation covering the whole field of hydrocarbons than the Gas Council whose primary interest lay in marketing, and who had no direct concern with oil.

The Minister's reaction was that, while he naturally favoured an extension of public ownership, they had to take care that this was not simply a political gesture but would stand a good chance of bringing economic benefits. He felt that there was a main risk that a new organisation such as the proposed NHC would run into financial difficulties. It could not spread its risks so widely as the major oil companies. There would also be problems in obtaining sufficient skilled personnel. There was also a possibility that the effect of the NHC might be to reduce the efforts of the oil companies in the years before the Corporation became fully effective.

Report of North Sea Study Group of National Executive Committee

The Study Group's first report was produced in July 1967. The Ministry reviewed its main proposals which followed those already outlined to the Minister in April. The report suggested that the NHC would (a) have powers to explore for and produce oil and gas in the North Sea, (b) act as the monopoly buyer of all gas produced by the current licensees, probably on the basis of a price formula similar to that employed by the US Federal Power Commission rather than the "reasonable price" incorporated in the 1964 Act, and (c) be responsible for assessing the economic advantages of the various possible uses and the reselling or exporting of the gas. To pursue its exploration and production functions the NHC would have the various powers outlined by the Group when it met the Minister earlier in April. The Group did consider whether the Gas Council could perform the exploration and production functions, but came down against the idea because the Council was "town gas oriented" and had shown little interest in exploration hitherto. The Group felt that there were advantages, such as risk sharing, from the NHC operating internationally, something which would be difficult for the Gas Council. In the longer term the task of optimising the use of North Sea gas, particularly bearing in mind balance of payments considerations, should be given to the NHC rather than the Minister. With that in mind it was important that long-term agreements entered into did not conflict with this desired longer-term objective.

The Study Group also made other proposals, not directly related to the NHC, but still involving more state control. Thus closer supervision of the licensees was recommended, particularly with regard to the enforcement of conservation policies and unitisation schemes. Interestingly, the Group also recommended that legislation be enacted to give the Minister powers to regulate offshore pipelines and enforce common carrier provisions. This included the possibility of the state taking ownership of the offshore pipeline network. The Group felt that leaving responsibility for transporting the gas to the shore entirely to the producing companies was likely to lead to an economically irrational pattern of underwater pipelines. As an example the Group claimed that the most economic method of transporting gas from Phillips' find in Block 49/6 was via BP's pipeline (suitably enlarged) from their find in Block 48/6. The Group understood that BP had declined to offer Phillips transport facilities with the result that Phillips was faced with the prospect of building a much longer pipeline of their own which jeopardised the economic viability of the field. The Ministry agreed that the concept of an integrated network under the control of a single body could not be lightly dismissed. The advantages and disadvantages required further examination.

With respect to the financial viability of the exploration and production activities of the NHC, the Study Group argued that, while there could be no certainty that proven acreage would be returned to the Government in 1970, at least some of the acreage relinquished would be well worth exploring, and, along with the producing areas inherited from the Gas Council, these should produce the basis for a viable corporation. The report also envisaged that in the early years the NHC might contract out or farm out both production and exploration acreage.

The Ministry still felt that the financial risks facing the NHC were high. It was agreed that they would be reduced by farming out acreage, if by this was meant arranging for the private oil companies to drill exploration wells at their own expense in return for a share in any resulting production. The Ministry felt, however, that this was essentially an alternative to direct licensing by the Minister. On future occasions this could be done using the auction system and more stringent relinquishment terms. The only possible advantage that the Ministry saw in the procedure of private oil companies being enlisted through the agency of the NHC rather than the Government directly was that the NHC might be freer to discriminate and enter purely commercial deals without having any obligation to be "fair" as between different applicants.

The Ministry remained sceptical about the idea of the NHC developing into a national oil company with international exploration and production activities on the lines of ENI in Italy and ERAP in France where these companies looked after the respective interests of their parent countries. This represented a radical departure from existing wider UK oil policy which relied on the international oil companies to provide secure oil supplies from their widely-diversified, world-wide operations. Their role as a buffer between the main producing and consuming countries was beneficial. The foreign operations of the British oil companies also brought large benefits to the balance of payments. Neither France nor Italy had comparable private oil companies and so the comparison was perhaps not appropriate. Nevertheless, there might be advantages from a national oil company, but this question required much more study than that provided by the Study Group.

The Study Group proposed that the NHC would take over many of the functions currently undertaken by the Gas Council, including not only the purchase of gas from the North Sea but also its disposal. The Ministry felt that it was by no means obvious that a completely new organisation would function any better than the Gas Council, while there would undoubtedly be numerous demarcation and other problems.

The question arose of the advisability of publishing the report. On balance the Ministry felt that publication would be unlikely to cause serious difficulty or embarrassment for the Government. The references to the nationalisation of British overseas oil interests should be omitted, and perhaps also the reference to BP's offshore pipeline. It should be made clear that the proposals did not imply acceptance of them by the Labour Party or the Government. The Study Group had expressed concern that the adoption of their proposals was not prejudiced by long-term agreements entered into now with the existing consortia of companies. This point had been reiterated in a letter to Mr Richard Marsh, the Minister of Power, from Mr George Brown, the First Secretary of State in his capacity as Chairman of the Labour Party Home Policy Committee. The Ministry's view on this matter was that gas purchase contracts would contain provisions for price reviews after a period. With respect to licensing there were no current proposals for a new round.

The debate continued. The Study Group's proposals were examined by the NEC of the Labour Party which produced a Statement to the 1967 Labour Annual Party Conference. The Statement endorsed many of the Study Group's proposals, but wanted some of the unresolved issues raised examined in more detail. The Group was reconstituted to examine specific issues including (a) the relationship between the NHC and the Gas Council, (b) the mechanism for ensuring that the best use was made of the gas, and (c) the relationship between the NHC and the existing British oil companies.

Ministry studies options

At the Labour Party Conference the NEC Statement was approved. The Ministry took a keen interest in these developments. It was clear that the first priority of the NHC would be serious involvement in exploration and production in the UKCS with possible overseas operations coming later. The existing licence rights of the oil companies could be preserved, but the 50% of acreage due to be relinquished in 1970 could be taken over by the NHC. The Ministry examined this as one option among several. The other possibilities included (a) a continuation of the present system, (b) modification of the current system to incorporate bonus or royalty bidding and different surrender provisions, and (c) greater emphasis on public participation through the Gas Council, NCB or NHC.

The Ministry felt that, putting aside purely political considerations, the essential difference between a licensing system and direct operation through a public corporation lay in the degree of risk involved. It was arguable that with a licensing system the Government could not lose. It was not required to put up any capital, and it received royalty on any oil or gas produced, while the profits of successful operations were subject to tax. If an auction system were operated the Government would receive an approximation to the market value of the licences. If the NHC were employed instead it could not hope to do better than this except by taking risks and spending sums of money which could be large. The risks could be reduced if the NHC entered into farm-out arrangements with the oil companies whereby the latter would undertake exploration at their own cost in return for a share of production from discoveries. But the potential profits would be reduced accordingly.

It was acknowledged that if the NHC were in charge of arrangements for future exploration and development it would have greater flexibility than a Government Department. Thus if it wanted to minimise risks it could invite competitive bids for sub-licences, with the bids being made not for cash but as options for the NHC to participate in the exploitation of discoveries. In cases where the potential appeared to be particularly attractive it would go ahead on its own account. To successfully take advantage of this flexibility would involve the deployment of substantial skills. This would require first-class staff the recruitment of which could be difficult. This was especially the case because the NHC would start off with the areas which the oil companies considered to have the least attractive prospects. A further consequence would be that the NHC would be unlikely to show results as good as those of the more successful private companies, and its operations would be likely to

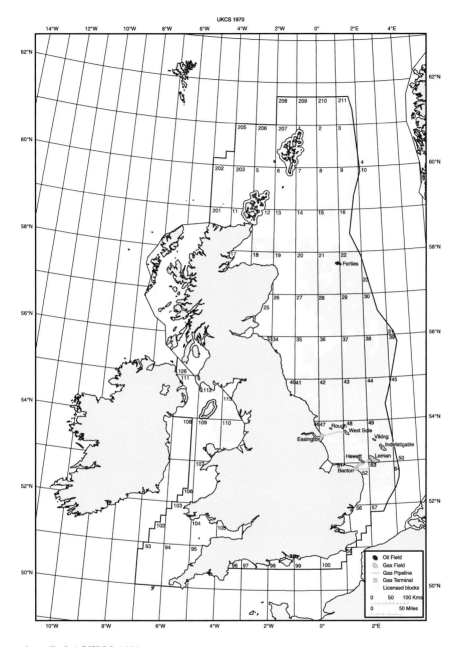

Appendix 3.1 UKCS 1970

attract a lot of Parliamentary criticisms, especially in the early years. If the worst happened the Government might even be accused of having promoted a second groundnuts scheme.

If Ministerial control over the issue of licences and policy more widely were desired, a less radical method of providing a direct public stake would be to set up the NHC not to take over all unallocated acreage but to operate under licence alongside private industry. The Minister would continue to issue all licences but could allocate blocks directly to the NHC or make a licence condition for private companies awarded licences that they had to take the NHC into partnership with them when commercial discoveries were made.

The Ministry felt that the longer term functions foreseen for the NHC, namely the implementation of a national fuel policy including control of the domestic oil industry, raised much more complex issues. While there might be political attractions it was far from evident that any real economic benefits would be achieved. International operations would cut across existing policies which recognised the benefits of overseas operations of British oil companies. There was no obvious need to create the NHC to give Britain a stake in this business, and funds devoted to this purpose would be better employed in supporting and strengthening the British oil companies against their foreign competitors. Regarding the other regulatory and policy functions proposed for the NHC these would more naturally fall to a Department under the direct control of a Minister. With respect to the proposed role of the NHC in marketing gas from the North Sea the Ministry reiterated its view that there was no reason to suppose that a completely new body would function more efficiently than the Council.

Conclusions of Ministry on NHC

The overall conclusion was that on economic grounds there was no strong case for the Study Group's proposals. Nevertheless, if the Minister wished to proceed for political reasons, the establishment of the NHC was a practicable proposition. There was no assurance that it would give better results than the present arrangements and the probability was fairly high that it would do worse. It could be made to function in such a way as to limit the risks to acceptable proportions. The legislation would be complex and controversial, but the Corporation could be established by the end of the six-year licensing period in late 1970 when relinquished acreage would become available.

The wider debate continues

The debate on enhanced state control continued both within the Ministry and more widely in Parliament and the media. The Minister had to answer questions in Parliament, but would not be drawn on his plans beyond saying that the proposal for the NHC was being studied. Within the Ministry a Working Party had been established to look at the Organisation and Structure of the Gas and Electricity Industries. In late November 1967, the Permanent Secretary asked the

Group to include the NHC concept in their deliberations. At its fourth meeting in December 1967, the Working Group was concerned that, if the role of the NHC extended to onshore gas transmission and direct sales of gas to customers, there would be a major overlap with the current functions of the Gas Council and Area Boards. The Working Group was clear that there should be no question of two gas supply industries.

The continuing debate on the possibility of fundamental changes in policy was creating some investment uncertainty within the industry. This affected many organisations directly or indirectly. The Director of the Institute of Geological Sciences wrote to the Minister indicating his concern that the proposals for an NHC were likely to result in the oil companies refusing to disclose to the Institute geophysical information which was indispensable to the synthesis of the geology of the North Sea which it had been asked to make. The Director was even more concerned with the prospect that exploration in the UKCS by the oil companies would fall as a result of the prospect of the NHC having a dominant position. The attractions of investing in other non-UK parts of the North Sea could well be greater.

Second Report of North Sea Study Group

The North Sea Study Group's Second Report added a considerable amount of information on the NHC's possible manpower requirements, its sales, and financial position to 1980. It argued that the NHC should take over from the Gas Council not only its current concessions and partnerships but also its storage, importation, onshore transmission, and initial processing of natural gas. It should recruit a considerable proportion of its staff from the Gas Council. With respect to marketing of gas the Study Group suggested that the NHC should sell gas to the Area Boards but for large industrial users (defined as those with a minimum demand of around 5 mmcf/d) the NHC should make direct sales to final customers.

Reactions of Ministry

The Ministry examined the report. With respect to the marketing proposals it was felt that there were very few large consumers located near the national transmission grid, and thus currently most bulk industrial users were likely to be supplied through the Area Boards' pipelines, and the Gas Council would only engage in direct supply in exceptional circumstances. Thus, in the scheme proposed by the Study Group, the NHC would be operating in direct competition with the Area Boards. However, the indicative prices in the Study Group report showed that the NHC would be selling to large industrial consumers at prices well below those it was charging the Area Boards. It could thus readily capture a large market. Substantial direct sales to industrial consumers by the NHC would deprive the Area Boards of their best method of improving their internal load factor. In turn this would mean that the Boards would have to buy gas from the NHC at a low load factor and thus a high unit price.

The Ministry was concerned that the Study Group's proposals would prevent the optimisation of the pipeline and storage system. A unified plan for the whole country was necessary for this. Currently the Gas Council and the Area Boards were linking together the grids in a single integrated information and control system. It was felt that a national high pressure system transmitting large amounts of gas from a variety of sources such as Easington, Bacton and Canvey Island was most efficiently and economically controlled from a centre with links to the Area Boards' distribution systems. With supply in the hands of the NHC and distribution remaining with the Area Boards no central control would be possible, Area Boards would have to work more independently, and full advantage could not be taken of the different sources of supply and strategically located storage units.

The Ministry was not convinced by the financial projections of the position of the NHC made by the Study Group, calling them factually inaccurate and over-optimistic. If the NHC were to maintain any reasonable exploration momentum the costs would be many times the Study Group's estimates. The Ministry thought that the report appeared to assume that any new discoveries by the NHC would be so situated that a single pipeline and a single shore terminal would suffice for several discoveries. On the contrary, the surrendered blocks available to the NHC would be widely scattered, and, even if discoveries were made at the rate envisaged, it was fantasy to presume that they would be so conveniently situated as to be served by one pipeline.

The Ministry queried both the cost and revenue projections of the Study Group. The Group had valued the Gas Council's main transmission system at £100 million whereas the Ministry reckoned it could be £250 million. For future expenditure on the system the Council had provided figures double those of the Study Group. The Ministry found the revenue forecasts equally dubious. Thus the figures on beach prices were expected to fall from 2.75d per therm in 1970–72 to 2.0d in 1975–80. The Ministry found these projections difficult to reconcile with known contracts such as the Algerian contract at 7.5d per them at Canvey Island which would run until 1979, and the Phillips contract at 2.87d per therm for 25 years. The Ministry did not deny that the NHC could be profitable, but the projections presented in the report were quite unrealistic and should not be used as evidence of its financial viability.

The Ministry's overall conclusions were that as a prospectus for a new public corporation the report was ill-conceived, inaccurate and unconvincing. They were particularly concerned about the fragmentation of the gas industry which they thought would be very damaging. The Ministry was prepared to accept that there might be a case for establishing an NHC to carry on exploration and production in the North Sea, but it was not made out in the report.

Meeting with Study Group

The Minister attended a meeting of the Labour Party Home Policy Committee on 10th June 1968. He suggested that the Study Group should meet with Ministry officials to discuss the financial projections and related matters. The result was a meeting on 19th June 1968. There was much discussion of the exploration prospects and effort, and the costs likely to be required. The Ministry felt that the Study Group's assumptions were optimistic but the Group still felt that their discovery rate was plausible. The Study Group clarified one major point. Their concept was that the NHC would act commercially in the North Sea and would not in any way be attempting the wholesale exploration of all the relinquished areas. With respect to the development of future discoveries the Study Group acknowledged that they had optimistically assumed that all of their three modelled discoveries could be linked into one pipeline. The discussion on the substantial differences in onshore gas investment requirements did not produce a consensus. There were differences in the prospective growth of the market with the Ministry's figures (based on Gas Council estimates) showing significantly faster growth. The Ministry felt that the meeting had been useful in adding considerable clarity to the thinking behind the Study Group's report.

The Minister, now Mr Roy Mason, was briefed to the effect that, while the meeting had clarified some matters, there was no change in the main views of officials. There was particular immediate concern on the idea that the Corporation take over the transmission and bulk sales of gas which was wholly inconsistent with the Government's current proposals for the reorganisation of the gas industry. Mr Mason felt obliged to write to Mr George Brown in his capacity as Chairman of the Labour Party Home Policy Committee indicating that he could not support the Group's proposal for truncating the gas industry. This would be a retrograde stage which would not only be damaging to the industry but would militate against the efficient exploitation of natural gas.

The Second Report of the Study Group as endorsed by the NEC, was published on 17th August 1968. The Ministry subsequently prepared a detailed paper on the report for discussion at the Natural Gas (Official) Committee. This outlined the proposals and the familiar comments of the Ministry, but did not make direct recommendations on the central issue which they felt was predominantly a political question. A financial analysis of the Study Group's projections was undertaken. The finding was that the internal rate of return for the NHC's activities up to 1980 was only 4.5% on central assumptions. Even on more optimistic assumptions the rate of return was only in the 6% – 8% range.

Views of Gas Council on Study Group Report

The report of the Study Group was also seen by the Gas Council. Sir Henry Jones wrote to Mr Mason about it. He indicated much disquiet. The fragmentation of the industry was in effect putting the clock back. The proposal eliminated any real prospect of coordinating national and area gas pipeline systems and of the investment programmes needed for the efficient use of North Sea gas. There was no reason to suppose that the new body could perform its functions as well as the existing gas industry. Sir Henry hoped that if the Government wanted the North Sea operation to be conducted as an efficient business enterprise it would not permit a wrecking proposal to proceed. The effects on the morale of the Council's staff and on its relationships with North Sea operators and potential customers would be very serious indeed if the Government appeared in any way to encourage such an amateurish and ill-thought-out plan.

The subject of the NHC was expected to figure prominently at the forthcoming Labour Party Conference, and it was felt that the Government's line had to be determined in advance. Accordingly, Mr Mason submitted a Minute to Mr Wilson, the Prime Minister, on the whole subject. This provided the background to the NHC proposal. Ministers had not yet collectively discussed the idea. Mr Mason stated that he had most serious misgivings about the detailed proposals of the Study Group report. He expressed particular concern about the inconsistency of the proposals with the Government's policy for the future structure of the gas industry. Thus to bring natural gas rapidly and efficiently into use firm central policy control was essential, and the main elements in the gas chain must all be subject to one centrally determined strategy and policy direction. Mr Mason was quite clear that the Study Group's proposals would take the Government in the opposite direction. He was concerned that divided responsibility for onshore matters would lead to wasteful duplication of the transmission and supply system and a fragmented marketing effort. The proposals would impede the rapid and efficient exploitation of natural gas. The Minister also felt that the Group's prospectus about the potential from released acreage was optimistic.

The Prime Minister's attention was drawn to other ways of obtaining a greater public stake in the North Sea without establishing a new public body. The licence terms could be modified in future rounds to procure a larger share of the revenues to the Exchequer, while leaving all the risks with the private sector. Alternatively, the Gas Council could be given a more prominent role. The Minister felt that there was no need to make immediate decisions, and to take a non-committal line at the forthcoming Conference. In the meantime further studies of the options could be undertaken.

Cabinet decision

At a Cabinet meeting on 24th September 1968 it was decided that the Government should be prepared to indicate at the Party Conference that they accepted the general objectives of the Report, but had not yet taken a view on the relative merits of the various possible implementation methods, including the NHC. It would be proposed that a joint Working Group drawn from members of the Government and the NEC would consider further the Study Group's proposals. It was agreed among senior officials at the Ministry and the Cabinet Office that on the Government side inter-departmental preparatory work should be undertaken by the Natural Gas (Official) Committee. The Prime Minister agreed with this, but added that the preparatory work should proceed as quickly as possible as there was some impatience at the National Executive Committee.

Further studies on options

Studies were undertaken for the Committee with the emphasis being on the different options viewed in the context of future licensing policy. Ministers had already decided on 17th September 1968 (MISC188 (68) 5th Meeting) that no further licences would be issued pending further consideration of policy. The Ministry of Power submitted a detailed paper to the Official Natural Gas Committee in December 1968. A decision in principle on whether to set up a NHC needed to be taken in the near future. The relevant considerations included the experience in the North Sea to date. Four substantial commercial gas discoveries had been made with recoverable reserves totalling around 24 trillion cubic feet (tcf). The total British stake was around 38% and the Gas Council's share 11%. Around 174 wells had been drilled with a total investment of £150 million. When production commenced the annual saving to the balance of payments would reach £50 million by 1970 and £100 million by 1975. A number of smaller gas discoveries had also been made. Little drilling had been undertaken in the Central and Northern waters of the UKCS with no discoveries in the UK sector. Phillips had made a discovery in the Norwegian sector but it had not yet been fully evaluated. The Ministry felt that, while further exploration would be justified in many parts of the UKCS, the prospects were speculative and the success ratio probably much lower than that achieved in the initial phase in the Southern Basin.

The Ministry felt that the gas fields already discovered could supply about 3.5 bcf/d after six or seven years and thus secure the greater part of the 4 bcf/d which was assumed to become available in the White Paper on *Fuel Policy* published in 1967. The Ministry was aware, however, that if the discouraging experience of the past 18 months, with no major finds, continued, by 1970 the UK could be faced with the prospect of having to curtail the expansion of the gas market after 1975. There would then be a need to embark on, or encourage others to undertake, a big exploration effort against a background of disappointment.

These were important considerations in deciding the level of public participation and the cost and risk which would fall on the Exchequer. It was now clear that the initial risk that the whole North Sea venture might turn out to be a failure had been eliminated but so also, perhaps, had the likelihood of making further big discoveries, at least in the Southern Basin. With respect to Central and Northern waters, on present evidence it seemed likely that only prolific fields with good quality crude and relatively high well deliverabilities would be economic to produce in competition with oil imported from the Middle East.

The options could be considered under three headings, namely (a) allocating licences exclusively to the public sector (existing bodies or a new one), (b) an auction system, and (c) a continuation of past policies, but perhaps with modified terms to secure greater public participation. The first involved the maximum chance of gain and loss for public funds. The second reduced the costs and risk to a minimum, ensured that the Exchequer gained the market value of the concessions at the time of their award, but provided no assurance of direct state participation. The third option offered great flexibility and the best prospect of securing an optimum balance between the objectives. It would permit a more discriminating approach tailored to the needs of the time.

If a public sector body were granted exclusive rights to the available acreage the issues of the scale of effort required and the expected costs and returns were paramount considerations. The Ministry had undertaken studies to indicate the possibilities. Based on somewhat optimistic assumptions about reserves and costs in the Southern Basin a rate of return of 18.5% might be earned. On less optimistic assumptions the result would be much less favourable. In Central and Northern waters the risks were greater and any appraisal of the economics of exploring and developing was largely guesswork. The Ministry concluded that even in the Southern Basin it was open to question whether a single body, public or private, could successfully undertake the whole future exploration of the areas that would be available to the Government.

There were other disadvantages of entrusting the territory available to one public body. There would be an initial loss to the balance of payments through the reduced inflow of foreign investment. In the longer run whether there was a gain or not depended on the degree of success and the profits which otherwise would have been remitted abroad. A further concern was the financial and staff resources required. The latter would take some time to build up. Another consideration was the negative effect that the exclusion of the oil companies would have on the overseas interests of the British oil companies.

For the above reasons the Ministry felt that it would not be in the UK's best interest to grant exclusive rights to a NHC or any other public body. The Study Group had also suggested that the NHC could enter into partnership agreements with the oil companies. The Ministry felt that, under this option the results might not differ essentially from those which could equally well have been secured without any new legislation.

The Ministry had given further consideration to the use of the auction system. The bids could be in the form of initial cash payments with fixed rentals and royalties or the latter could themselves be biddable items. Offers to give options to public sector bodies were a further possibility. There was no evidence that this system had led elsewhere to collusion among the companies. In any case the Minister would have the right to reject any bids. The advantages were early cash receipts. The Ministry also felt that there was some danger that, if heavy initial payments were made, less capital would be available for exploration. The main perceived disadvantage of the auction system, however, was that it removed the discretion which the Minister currently had in awarding concessions. The awards would go to the highest bidder which would have the politically unattractive consequence of smaller public participation in future licensed areas or even no public participation at all. It was agreed, however, that auctioning of selected blocks had advantages. It was one way of testing the market from time to time.

On balance the Ministry felt that the discretionary system because of its flexibility provided the most generally useful means of tailoring the licensing procedure to the needs and prospects of the times. The Minister could within limits give greater preference to favoured applicants, and could stiffen or relax the terms according to the perceived likely value of the concessions at the time. If this system were favoured the Ministry felt that in current circumstances the share given to British groups and to the public sector could be increased. Awards would be restricted to groups with a specified British or public sector holding, but this created practical problems in the form of the consequential need for a major reorganisation of the current, well established, operating groups. A preferred approach would be to follow the recent Dutch precedent whereby a licence condition was to require the participation of a state organisation when a commercial discovery was made. The state company would pay for its share of successful exploration and development costs but not for abortive exploration.

The discretionary system also permitted royalties and rental payments to be varied, for example across different areas or between oil and gas in accordance with perceptions of prospectivity at the time of licence awards. Surrender terms could also be varied to increase the state's share of acreage, but the procedures involved were cumbersome, and it was felt that state participation in discoveries was the better route.

Leaving political considerations aside the Ministry felt that increased public participation was best obtained via existing bodies. A new body would require a major Bill. It would be easier to build up the Gas Council. The grouping of the Council's onshore and offshore activities would eliminate the friction and administration problems that would arise if they were divided.

The Committee felt that the effects on the balance of payments and public sector borrowing of the three basic options identified by the Ministry should be quantified as far as possible. This was a difficult exercise involving many variables and great uncertainties. The Committee considered the information provided as part of revised reports at its meeting in February 1969, where it was agreed to recommend to Ministers that the idea of a state monopoly should be rejected. Further consideration should be given to limited state participation.

A report to Ministers from the Official Committee on the above lines was finalised. The Chairman's accompanying Summary Note emphasised the uncertainties surrounding future North Sea prospects, and stated that much of the territory which had not been allocated appeared relatively unattractive. Commercial discoveries would bring clear benefits to the national economy and balance of payments. Economic production by British interests would yield the greatest long-term benefits, but foreign investment brought short-term balance of payments advantages and longer term benefits if exploration was relatively unsuccessful. No single body could explore the very large area involved as quickly or as efficiently as the oil companies combined. The State's share could be increased at moderate cost by various means including the carried interest of a public sector body. The Committee thus advised against the idea of a state monopoly, and favoured further examination of the other options for enhancing the public sector stake.

Problem of discovery extending to open block 52/4

The Ministry and the Official Committee had other more specific licensing issues to consider in this period. One related to the Hewett field discovery which extended not only across three licensed blocks, namely 52/5 and 48/30 (Phillips) and 48/29 (Arpet), but also over an open block, namely 52/4. Given that the field was going to be developed a decision had to be made about how to deal with the open block. If nothing was done royalties would be payable on gas produced from Block 52/4, but the Ministry felt that it should be possible to obtain additional returns to the Exchequer. There were various options. One was that the Government itself might take over the block. Legal advice, however, was that the law was based on the Minister standing in a licensor/licensee relationship with organisations undertaking the exploration and it would be stretching legal concepts too far to envisage a situation, permissible by law, where the Minister issued a licence to himself. A further consideration was the likelihood that one or two appraisal wells would be required in the block in question in addition to a proportionate share of the field development costs.

The most obvious courses of action were to licence the block either by Ministerial discretion or by auction. If the former method were employed when there was only one block on offer and it were decided that the block should be awarded to a chosen instrument of the Government, the Minister might lay himself open to criticism for using the legislation in a manner not intended. The Ministry thus felt that the best method of dealing with the situation would be to offer the block for auction. It could be expected that Phillips and Arpet would bid. They would not welcome additional partners and could be expected to pitch their bid at a level which would ensure their success. Use of the auction mechanism would also provide useful information for the future. The Ministry suggested that two other neighbouring but unallocated blocks could also be auctioned at the same time. At its meeting on 17th December 1968, the Official Committee agreed to recommend to Ministers that Block 25/4 should be offered for auction, but the future of Blocks 48/27 and 52/10 should be considered at a later stage. This was the first case of a positive decision in favour of the auction method. The circumstances were, of course, somewhat unusual.

Large all-British group?

A different approach to the subject of the British stake was suggested at a Ministerial Meeting, on 18th March 1969. The proposal was that surrendered blocks could be administered by a British grouping which would be a joint enterprise comprising the Gas Council, the NCB, and BP. The group could exploit these assets itself or in effect hire them out to others. The suggestion of an all-British grouping had been examined for the Second Round but there was inadequate interest among the prospective partners. The Ministry was aware that there were now constraints on participation in new groupings by the Gas Council and the NCB. The Council had an agreement with its partners whereby it could not accept new licences in the North Sea without first offering its partners the opportunity to participate. The NCB arrangements were less restrictive, but its agreement with Conoco required either party to offer the other a 50% interest in any new acquisitions in specified areas of mutual interest. The then Minister had insisted that he should not be constrained by this clause in future licensing.

The Ministry saw some advantages in the suggested grouping. Thus it was not only all-British but would substantially increase the public sector stake. It had all the necessary expertise and it would represent a development of present arrangements. There were also disadvantages as none of the three prospective partners had shown any particular desire to join together with the others; the new grouping would therefore be something of a shotgun marriage. Relations between the Gas Council and BP had been edgy. If the group took over all relinquished acreage it would either be faced with a much bigger programme than it judged advisable and was prepared to finance, or it would require financial relief from the Treasury. If the new group did not want the entire relinquished acreage and hired some out to others it would be replicating a task already performed by the Ministry.

Mr Mason consulted informally the chairmen of BP and the Gas Council on the idea. The reaction was unenthusiastic. Sir Henry Jones found the NCB difficult to deal with, and he felt they would be pulled by conflicting interests. He also objected to a partnership with BP. He much preferred Amoco, his present partner. Sir Henry felt that the Council could play a bigger role and was interested in becoming an operator on the basis of a limited number of blocks and with the right to take on partners if necessary. The chairman of BP also opposed the idea of the British trio on the grounds of conflict of interest, possible adverse effects on its overseas position resulting from apparent preferential treatment in the UK, and from closeness to the UK Government.

Checkerboarding?

At the Ministerial meeting on 18th March 1969, the suggestion had also been made that future licensing might be undertaken on the checkerboarding or diagonal principle. The Ministry of Power undertook further study of this idea and prepared a note for the meeting of the Official Committee on Natural Gas in June 1969. The report noted that the main objective of the checkerboarding scheme was to ensure that the licensing authority procured a substantial share of any territory found to contain hydrocarbons. There were several variants but all had this basic objective. The diagonal method could be employed in either of two ways. The particular scheme suggested at the meeting divided the area to be allocated into rectangles each of which contained four blocks. When the initial exploration programme was completed the licensee would be allowed to select from the rectangle a diagonal of two blocks to keep for himself. The other two would be surrendered to the state. Under the second variant the area was still divided into blocks but alternate diagonal blocks would be left unallocated from the outset. They would become available for allocation subsequently when more was known about the potential of the area.

The scheme had been pioneered in Alberta and a variant adopted in Saskatchewan. A related procedure had been adopted in Victoria, Australia for offshore situations. There the objective was not to ensure a larger direct share to the state but to exact differential royalties depending on the prospectivity of the blocks.

The Ministry still considered that the disadvantages of the checkerboarding scheme were decisive. Making licensing arrangements more favourable to Government automatically made them less attractive to potential applicants. They argued that, to ensure that the state participated in any commercial discoveries, the blocks offered would have to be fairly small. This was certainly the case in Alberta and Saskatchewan where they were far smaller than in the UKCS under the current system. It followed that, unless the individual fields were themselves small, very small blocks in practice would almost certainly lead to problems over the efficient exploitation of discoveries. In the UKCS there were already difficulties from this. Discoveries had stretched across different blocks, and the consequential need for unitisation of development plans among different licensees was causing problems. The Ministry concluded that, although very small blocks might be acceptable for land operations in prospective territory, they were impracticable for unproven offshore areas when neither the geology nor the location – as for most of the UKCS – was specially promising.

The philosophy underlying the leasing schemes in Alberta and Saskatchewan was not to secure an increased direct state participation. In these provinces the exploitation was undertaken by the private sector, and the whole leasing arrangements were designed to obtain the best return to the state by selling rights to the highest bidder. Checkerboarding did not have any special attractions when the objective of policy was to secure a bigger public participation in licensing arrangements. It was not recommended. The Official Committee gave its approval to this view at its meeting on 10th June 1969.

Decisions are made

Mr Mason subsequently prepared a paper reflecting the views of the Official Committee for submission to the Ministerial MISC (188) Committee. It highlighted the notion of giving a greater role to the Gas Council and NCB. The Treasury briefed the Chief Secretary to note that an increased role for the Gas Council meant less financing by the oil companies and thus a lower capital inflow. The greater capital expenditure of the Gas Council and NCB would have to be kept under review. Mr Mason explained that, in his proposals, groups which included the Gas Council, NCB or BP would be favoured, while in the Irish Sea Gas Council (Exploration), a new subsidiary of the Gas Council, could become an operator of 10 blocks, and a further 15 should be licensed only to groups which included the Council or NCB. The idea of the Council becoming an operator was a distinct move to enlarge the public stake. Various other ideas were raised including the establishment of a new public corporation, and the financial involvement of the Central Electricity Generating Board and British Steel Corporation as major fuel users. The proposed new subsidiary of the Gas Council could be involved with oil exploitation as well as gas. The most important elements of Mr Mason's proposals were accepted, but he was asked to consider whether the proposed name of the Gas Council's subsidiary could be changed to incorporate the word "Hydrocarbons". He was also asked to consider whether an advisory body, perhaps to be called a National Hydrocarbons Council, could be established. At a further meeting of the Ministerial MISC (188) Committee Mr Mason said that the name change suggested earlier could readily be introduced. He further proposed that the Gas Council should be empowered to exploit and market oil. This was agreed.

Mr Mason made a Statement in the House of Commons on 23rd July 1969, indicating his plans for future licensing. Compared to the first two rounds there would be added preference for groups involving the Gas Council, the NCB and other British interests in the North Sea area. In the Irish Sea a stringent criterion would be participation by the Council or NCB in all groups, and the Minister would welcome applications from the Council to act as operator in a limited part of the Irish Sea. The Statement was greeted enthusiastically by Labour and Liberal MPs but with dismay by the Opposition spokesman, Sir John Eden, who stated that the proposals were wholly unacceptable to his side of the House. Sir John queried the use of taxpayers' money in a speculative area, and felt that the oil companies, who had been complimented by the Minister for their immense experience and resources, should be left to get on with the job, instead of being forced unwillingly into partnerships.

Views of Gas Council

The announcement concerning the enhanced role of the Gas Council reflected the fruits of much consultation between it and Ministry of Power officials. At a meeting in January 1969, the Council had intimated its desire to maintain an active interest in operations in the UKCS. The Council was convinced that its activities there to date had enabled it to conclude gas purchase contracts on favourable terms. They were happy with their present partners. If competitive bidding were adopted for the award of future licences it would not be practicable for the Council to be members of more than one bidding group. On the other hand there would be no difficulty in the Council entering into partnerships with a number of different groups in production operations (as in the Dutch legislation). It would also be possible for the Council to act as sole operator in an area allocated to it by the Government. Naturally the Council would prefer such blocks to be in an area of good prospectivity.

The Ministry queried whether the Council could be members of more than one bidding group, and after legal advice, the Council agreed that, outside the survey area already agreed with its current partners, it would be able to choose other partners. Much discussion ensued. The chairman of the Gas Council made it clear to the Minister that he was very happy with the notion of a specific Gas Council subsidiary to undertake exploration, but was most reluctant to have the words "National" or "Corporation" in the title. At a meeting shortly after the Minister's

Statement to the House, the Council explained to Ministry officials some of its concerns relating to its proposed enhanced role. In the North Sea area the Council would apply with its partners, the Amoco group. It expected that it would not be awarded all the blocks which it requested, but an awkward situation could arise where the licensees who were awarded blocks in preference to the Gas Council/Amoco group then offered the Gas Council an option to participate, perhaps on favourable terms.

In the Irish Sea the Council's arrangements with its existing partners were less formal, and, while it felt under some obligation to apply for some blocks with them, they would not be inhibited from bidding with other partners. There were potential problems with the NCB in the Irish Sea if both were approached by oil companies who offered participation in the same blocks and attempted to play off one against the other.

At a further meeting the Gas Council confirmed that, in the Irish Sea, it would apply for some blocks with the Amoco group, but had made it clear to its partners that it remained free to take up options with other groups. The Council remained concerned that there could be difficulties with the NCB's role, especially if oil companies played one off against the other. The Council understood that the NCB wished to have geographic spheres of interest in the Irish Sea, playing a leading role in the northern area where it had already undertaken seismic work. The Council was generally against the concept of spheres of interest, but did feel that it should be regarded as the public's main agency, and that the NCB's role should be to fill in the gaps they could not cover. The Ministry indicated that they were concerned to ensure that no reputable company should be barred from applying for licences just because it could not make arrangements for participation with the Council or the NCB. Thus the Council should not get drawn into making exclusive deals with companies which precluded them from taking up options with other groups. The Ministry also did not favour a deal between the Council and the NCB which defined respective spheres of influence as this would restrict opportunities for participation and limit flexibility. Applications from the Council with the Amoco group would be examined seriously but, if they were unsuccessful in any particular block, and that block was awarded to another group which in turn gave the Council the option to participate, there should be no recrimination.

The Council remained concerned regarding its prospective position in the Irish Sea. At a further meeting they requested that they would like the Ministry to agree arrangements with their current partners that they would (1) restrict partnership applications in the Irish Sea to their current group, (2) stipulate that the Council must be free to take on some territory on its own as operators, and (3) stipulate that the Council would be free to enter into option agreements outside their group for any territory. The Ministry was content with these proposals, but suggested that the Council should also be prepared to enter into partnership with other groups wishing to operate in the Irish Sea, provided that the blocks for which application was being made were not also being applied for by the Amoco group. The Council objected to this. The companies in their existing group would be unwilling to share the interpretation of the group's seismic data if the Council envisaged partnership with other companies, even for territory in which the Amoco group had no interest. The Amoco group would be most reluctant for the territory in which they were interested to become known. This could not be concealed if the Council were discussing with other companies potential partnerships and had to reveal that for some they were already committed. If the Council could not use their group's seismic interpretation they would in effect be applying blind with obvious disadvantages.

The Ministry felt that these objections were exaggerated. The Amoco group should realise that, because of their partnership with the Gas Council, they were exceptionally well placed for good treatment in applications, and should not risk their privileged position by being very rigid about the terms on which the Council could use seismic data.

Position of Hydrocarbons Great Britain

At yet another meeting the position of the new Gas Council subsidiary (now called Hydrocarbons Great Britain Limited) was discussed. The Chairman of the Gas Council asked whether it was true that the intention was that the operations of the company would be restricted to the UKCS. He had assumed that at least the whole European continental shelf would be open to the company, in particular the Dutch, Norwegian, and Irish parts. The Ministry confirmed that it was the intention to confine the company's activities to the UKCS. Sir Henry Jones found this most extraordinary and pointed out that the Gas Act, 1965 allowed the Council to supply gas to anyone in Great Britain or elsewhere. It seemed most odd to prevent the Council from exploring for and producing gas outside Great Britain when it had powers to market gas there. Both from a gas and oil production perspective it would be very unfortunate if the company could not operate outside the UKCS.

Partnership problems

At a further meeting between the parties the Council reported that, in the northerly part of the Irish Sea, Amoco were about to undertake a more detailed seismic survey and had proposed that before going ahead they should sign an agreement with the Council similar in intent and purpose to the existing one in the North Sea. The Council were not planning to agree to this and had counter-proposals. They proposed to say that, if the Council participated in the new survey, they would make an agreement only with respect to the blocks for which licences might be awarded to the Council/Amoco group. To try to accommodate the Government's objectives the Council planned to propose that in the defined area (Irish Sea north of Anglesey) the Council would apply for blocks as members of the Amoco group. Within this area it would not apply either on its own or as operator of another group for any blocks for which the Amoco group had applied. The Council would, however, be free to apply as operators in blocks in which their partners showed no interest. Further, the Council would be entitled to arrange options to participate in licences awarded to other groups. These could include blocks for which the Amoco group applied. The options could cover a range of possibilities such as the right to take up a specified interest shortly after a licence was awarded, or a right to take a share after a commercial discovery had been made.

The Ministry reiterated its argument that it would give added flexibility and perhaps be more attractive to some oil companies if the Council could freely make joint applications with other groups for blocks inside the defined area, but for which the Amoco group did not plan to apply. The Ministry felt that this was particularly important as a precedent for future licensing rounds. The Gas Council reiterated its views that there were difficulties in disclosing blocks in which the Amoco group was not interested. It was agreed that the Council could proceed on the basis it had suggested, but it would also endeavour to get their partners to agree that it should be free to apply as partners in other groups for blocks which the Amoco group did not want.

Later, the Gas Council sought clarification from the Ministry on the meaning of the term "option to participate". There were several issues including the timing of the exercise of the option, which could be shortly after licence award, after exploration drilling, or after commercial discovery. There was also the question of the appropriate proportion of the licence which the Council would acquire. If the timing of the option exercise was after commercial discovery a further question was whether the Council would pay its share of (past) exploration costs. In further discussions there was agreement between the Council and the Ministry that the maximum option which should be sought would be around 40%. It should be related to the drilling of wells rather than to time. The Ministry did not want a minimum to be specified as this would remove an important element of flexibility out of the Government's power when it came to award licences. The Council felt that in the absence of a specified minimum option the oil companies might play off the Council and the NCB against each other, leading each to reduce the terms in which they would accept options. The Council felt there was a danger that the companies would collude and settle among themselves options that would be offered. The Ministry did not think this was a likely prospect, and recommended that the Council should explain the broad range they had in mind in discussions with the oil companies, but leave the detailed figures for negotiation.

The Council was also concerned about the financing of operations in the Irish Sea. In blocks where they were in partnership with Amoco and where exploration was clearly justifiable they would expect to fund their operations from cash flows and borrowing on normal terms from the Government. In other blocks which the Council did not regard as adequately prospective they would not wish to risk their own funds. If they were to be explored the Council thought that this should be regarded as a Government risk, and the Council would want to work them as a Government Agency, keeping the accounts relating to them separate. The Council was concerned that it might be pressed by the Government to undertake exploration which they deemed non-commercial. The Ministry felt that they could not at the current stage set up a procedure whereby the Government would finance operations against the commercial judgement of the Council, but also agreed that it would be difficult to defend a situation whereby the Council had to commit its funds in options which they did not feel were economically justified. The Ministry was also concerned about another possibility, namely the circumstance where the Council rejected participation in blocks which subsequently contained large fields. The Ministry favoured a stance whereby, when the prospectivity looked attractive, the Council could agree to very early participation, but where there were doubts, it should aim to participate only after a commercial discovery had been made. There was no need to consider direct financing of exploration at this stage. If the Council were faced with a take-it-or-leave-it option situation that would be the time to consider financing arrangements.

Role of NCB

Meanwhile the Ministry had also been having discussions with the NCB in its possible role in the Third Round. The NCB had already exercised its options on Second Round blocks awarded to Gulf Oil and Allied Chemicals. These included Blocks 110/3, 110/4, 110/8, 110/9 and 110/13 in the Irish Sea with Gulf. The NCB met with the Ministry in August 1969, to discuss the vexed question of participation options. The NCB's understanding with Gulf was that, with respect to blocks for which they applied jointly, they would have no dealings with other companies, but they would be able to make other arrangements for blocks for which no joint application was to be made. The Board was concerned that, if they were to negotiate with other companies in the Irish Sea for blocks subject to joint application with Gulf, it would appear to Gulf that they were in effect backing both horses and there was likely to be strong suspicion of their intentions. The Board's proposal was to point out to Gulf that the NCB might be approached by other companies about any blocks, and if they were prepared to talk about some but not about others, this would reveal the blocks for which they intended to apply with Gulf. To avoid this situation the Board proposed to decline to negotiate on the blocks, but would be willing to receive offers of options from applicants.

The Ministry's objective was that the Board should be free to take up options from any company for any blocks. They expressed doubts about the Board's proposal, and would prefer them to take a more open line. If the Board's proposal was followed there was a danger that Gulf Oil might press them to undertake not to take up any options offered by other companies relating to blocks for which they were applying with that company. The Ministry thought that it would be preferable for the Board to explain openly to Gulf that a new situation had been created by the Minister's statement, and that, in order to comply with Government policy, they had to be free to take up options from anyone. While it was possible for a company to make an application to the Ministry incorporating an option for the NCB it would be ridiculous if in such circumstances the Board were precluded from taking up an option which they had done nothing to stimulate.

The NCB reflected on these points and at a subsequent meeting reported to the Ministry that there would now be no difficulty in taking up any options offered. The Board recognised that it had an advantageous position in the Irish Sea because of its existing involvement there with Gulf. The Ministry emphasised that, while it would be for the Board to decide whether to take up options offered, it should not refuse to consider any offered, though, of course, it need not accept them. The Ministry also emphasised that it was most important that companies prepared to discuss option schemes should not be able to say that they had not received a fair hearing.

Preparations for Third Round

Meanwhile the Ministry had been occupied with other issues relating to preparations for the Third Round. In April 1969 the view had been formed that roughly 100 blocks might be offered. This was substantially less than in previous rounds. About 75% would be in the North Sea and the rest in the Irish Sea. Different terms could apply in the different areas, and the Ministry was interested in the state participation scheme now applicable in the Netherlands and felt it could be introduced in the Irish Sea. Interestingly, the Ministry felt that in the Irish Sea prospects were wholly speculative; there was no reason to think that they were better than in the Northern North Sea Basin, but in the absence of any evidence many companies felt that they could not risk being left out in case something good came up, especially as oil or gas found in this area would cost less to bring onshore. There seemed, therefore, to be a better chance of getting applications for a limited number of blocks even on relatively onerous terms. The Ministry also felt that it was still very much in the dark about the attractiveness of further UK Continental Shelf licences to the oil companies. For this reason it was suggested to auction a limited number of blocks scattered in various parts of the North Sea to test the market.

Work of Institute of Geological Sciences

Other issues had to be settled before the new round could be formally launched. One was the level of licence fees. This subject became intermingled with a quite separate one, namely the role and work of the Institute of Geological Sciences (IGS) in the UKCS. This had been discussed at a Ministerial MISC 188 meeting and the Official Committee on Natural Resources had been asked to report on whether the work programme of the IGS in the UKCS was adequate in terms of size, and whether additional expenditure could be offset (at least in part) by a charge on the oil companies. The Natural Resources Committee supported an enhanced work programme for the IGS in the UKCS. The Parliamentary Secretary at the Department of Economic Affairs drafted a summary of the findings of the Committee lending support for an increase in seismic work and the creation of a network of shallow offshore borings, supplemented by a series of deep offshore boreholes. At least one such hole should be drilled in each sedimentary basin to confirm the strata and the hydrocarbon-bearing possibilities. The enhanced work would require an additional £1 million – £1.5 million per year. It was suggested that the extra cost should primarily be met from public funds, but the Ministry of Power should approach the oil companies to contribute to particular projects.

The Ministry of Power was interested not only in the specific financial issue, but also to ensure that any work undertaken by the IGS, especially drilling, should be coordinated with the licensing programme and commercial exploration. In particular, there was a need to ensure that public money should not be wasted on obtaining expensive information which would be forthcoming from work obligations imposed on commercial licensees. The Ministry was also clear that the oil companies would be most unwilling to commit funds to other exploratory work which they would regard as having less commercial value.

The issue of financing the work of the IGS continued. The Ministerial MISC group at its meeting on 21st July, requested the Minister of Power to consider whether the fees charged for licences could be increased to meet the enlarged programme relating to the UKCS.

Debate on licence fees

Mr Mason submitted a Minute to the Prime Minister on the idea. He explained the background to the existing fees, adding that they were broadly in line with those of the other countries with activities in the North Sea. They could not be changed for existing licences, and to find an extra £1 million – £1.5 million per year entailed a very steep increase in the terms for new licences. Even doubling the present licence fees for the initial six-year period would only bring in an extra £6 – £700,000 for 100 blocks. The Minister added that he was very much opposed to increasing the fees. He pointed out that the new licensing arrangements marked a considerable advance in the participation of the public sector in the North Sea. While they had been well received by Labour Party supporters they were bound to cause some concern to the oil companies. An essential part of the UK's strategy and the test of its success was to secure a good response from the industry: otherwise the momentum of exploration would fall off. The Minister's conclusion was that it would be most unwise to risk further discouragement of the industry, given that the balance was already shifting in favour of the public sector.

The Prime Minister was interested to know the Treasury's views. A meeting was held between Treasury and Ministry of Power officials. The Ministry explained that since the last round market conditions had tightened against the exploiting oil companies, not only because of the enhanced public sector involvement, but also from the gas price settlements. No changes in fees were thus proposed. The Treasury felt that, as a minimum, increases to reflect inflation should be made. There was also a danger that, if no increase were made, any future increases would become difficult to achieve on precedent grounds. The Ministry agreed to reflect further. The arguments against significant change were reiterated. It was particularly emphasised that the royalty should not be increased from the 12.5% rate which was now standard in OPEC countries. The Ministry did, however, agree that the initial and annual licence fees could be increased to offset the effects of inflation since 1964. The Treasury generally accepted these arguments, and proposed only a minor further upward adjustment to the annual increase to the annual payment.

Decision on work of IGS

The issue of licence fees was not finally settled until the question of the financing of the IGS work programme was resolved. At the Cabinet meeting on 29th July it was decided that, in the light of the recent statement by the Minister of Power on licensing arrangements, the Lord President of the Council in consultation with other Ministers, should reconsider the priority to be given to deepwater exploration by the IGS. An Interdepartmental Committee under the chairmanship of Sir Solly Zuckerman, Chief Scientific Adviser, met to discuss the issue. It felt that the situation had changed substantially with the recent new licensing announcement. Areas, including some in the Irish Sea, which had been earmarked for exploration by the IGS, had now been put on offer to the oil companies. The enhanced role of the public sector would ensure that more knowledge was received. Further, the oil companies were now supplying the information required by the Government, including seismic results and geological cores. If the oil companies took up the blocks to be offered in the Third Round the proposed IGS deepwater programme would not significantly add to the information becoming available to Government. The conclusion was that the deepwater programme should not receive financial support at the present time. The position should be reviewed after the results of the Third Round were known. If the oil companies did not respond positively to the offer of licences on the Irish Sea the case for IGS involvement in drilling there would become stronger. The views of the Lord President were endorsed by his colleagues.

Criteria for award of Third Round licences

Meanwhile work was progressing on finalising the criteria to be employed in awarding licences. Ministry officials had favoured the use of auctions for a few blocks. The Minister, after discussing the matter with the Prime Minister, decided that auctions would not be employed in the Third Round. He also decided that, of the nationalised industries, only the Gas Council and the NCB should be asked to participate, although the possibility of the CEGB and the BSC should be borne in mind for later rounds. A Press Notice on the criteria was released on 19th September, emphasising the importance of work programmes proposed, and the contribution of the applicant to the economic prosperity of the UK, including the balance of payments, growth of industry and employment, especially regional aspects. In line with the July Statement the importance of proposals involving the Gas Council and NCB was emphasised. Participation with these two organisations was clearly stated to be a stringent criterion for applications in the Irish Sea. The Press Office Guidance Notes indicated that the equivalent of around 140 full blocks would be offered. (There would be a number of part-blocks in practice.) The significant increase from the earlier thinking that around 100 blocks would be offered was due to receipt of indications of interest from the oil companies covering around 460 blocks, including some for which the Ministry had not anticipated interest. The Notes also confirmed that the Irish Sea was effectively unknown territory. The Gazette Notice on 23rd September provided fuller details. In total there were 157 full and part-blocks on offer of which 111 were in the North Sea, 42 in the Irish Sea (including 19 in the Cardigan Bay area), and 4 off the north of Scotland.

Minister's defence of policy stance

These announcements came shortly before the Labour Party Conference. The Minister was briefed on how he might deal with attacks on his North Sea policies, particularly the failure to introduce the NHC. The decision had been reached only after long and detailed consideration of all the issues, including consultations with other Departments at both official and Ministerial levels. There were three main reasons for the decision. Firstly, the costs of funding a reasonable exploration programme by a monopoly body was daunting. It could be around £80 million, with much greater sums required at the field development stage. The risks were also high with very little chance that future exploration would be as successful as that of the first 2–3 years. This was not the sort of situation in which it was proper to risk vast sums of public money.

The second reason for the rejection of the NHC was the continuing need to tap the technical resources of the international oil companies. A new state monopoly body would require time to recruit staff and become effectively operational on a significant scale. The pace of exploration and development would be considerably slowed, and this the country could not afford. Large reserves of gas had been discovered because of the expertise of the diverse oil industry. The third reason related to the balance of payments. An NHC would place a very heavy burden on the Exchequer during the first 5–10 years. The benefits would only accrue in the longer-term even if large discoveries were made. There were short-term benefits to the balance of payments through attracting foreign investment. There would also be substantial benefits from royalties, taxation, and reinvestment of profits. The policy recently adopted met the somewhat conflicting needs of the UK in the most practical way possible. There was provision for substantial increased public participation without placing an excessive burden on the Exchequer. The pace of exploration and development should continue at the maximum feasible rate while still procuring gas supplies at advantageous prices.

Conflict with defence interests

A quite different problem relating to the Third Round blocks emerged a little later. Following the Gazette Notice the Ministry of Technology (into which the Ministry of Power became absorbed) approached the Ministry of Defence (MOD) to ascertain any conditions with respect to timing and notice periods which would need to be imposed on licensees to accommodate essential defence requirements. For certain areas offered the MOD wanted to impose absolute prohibitions on drilling because of the unacceptable interruption to weapons testing and development. The areas related to much of Cardigan Bay and two other smaller areas in the Irish Sea. The Ministry of Technology's view was that, if it was accepted that the exploration of the areas in question for a potential source of energy was essential to the economy, some compromise had to be made. If defence considerations were judged to be paramount urgent action was needed with respect to the blocks in question. They could either be withdrawn from the published offer, or it could be decided to take no immediate action but to decline to issue licences for them.

The MOD and Ministry of Technology prepared a joint paper setting out their views. The Cardigan Bay area was used as a major guided weapon testing facility, with activities relating to research and development, acceptance and evaluation, and practice of guided weapons all taking place. The area was used intensively throughout the year. The conflict of use related to fourteen of the nineteen blocks on offer in the area. The two Ministries reviewed how the problem could be resolved. They thought that seismic operations could take place without undue difficulty, but considerable restrictions on other operations would be necessary for safety reasons. Even though the majority of missiles tested did not carry warheads they could still inflict considerable damage to any structure which they hit. Their recommendation was that it should be made clear to licensees that there would be considerable restrictions on drilling within specified areas. Licensees would also have to accept the risk of impact to their property within specified areas and any consequential damage to third parties.

The issue was brought to the attention of the Prime Minister in a letter from the Lord President of the Council. He was informed that 18 blocks in Cardigan Bay and six others in the Irish Sea coincided with experimental weapon ranges or crossed submarine lanes. The Lord President expressed the view that it was not necessary to take long-term decisions at present, but he proposed to publish an announcement in the Official Gazette warning that drilling restrictions would apply to certain blocks. The Prime Minister wondered how the conflict had not been anticipated and asked to be informed of the outcome. The announcement warning of drilling restrictions on 25 blocks was published in the Official Gazette on 22nd December 1969.

Assessing the applications

The closing date for Third Round applications was 15th January 1970. Thirty-four applications involving 63 companies were received for 117 of the 157 blocks on offer. The split was 115 for the North Sea and 42 for the Irish Sea. Most of the applications were highly selective in their choice of territory. The most sought after areas comprising two full and two part blocks on the median line with Norway close to the recent Cod discovery attracted 25 applications. Similarly, in Quadrant 16 in the Southern North Sea two full and part blocks attracted 21 applications.

The Ministry found the allocation problem more difficult in this Round than in the earlier ones because of the complex award criteria. The applications were provisionally graded on a points system based on these criteria. This produced a total UK content of about 50% (compared to 45% for all the applications) if the options offered to the Gas Council and NCB were taken up. This compared to 30% in the First Round and around 37% in the Second Round.

Because the Ministry was entitled to receive technical data from all the operating companies it was able to assess applications with the benefits of a reasonable knowledge of the seismic picture and the logs of all wells drilled. Applicants were interviewed to scrutinise the backing material behind the applications and to appraise their priorities attached to different blocks. With respect to the contested areas particular attention was paid both to the standing of the applications and to the priorities they attached to the blocks. This was to secure the maximum work effort. Ministerial approval was sought to engage in detailed discussions with applicants on their work programmes. This would entail hard bargaining. Applicants would be informed of the provisional awards that they could obtain subject to satisfactory work programmes on the particular blocks. In reporting progress to the Prime Minister in April 1970, the Paymaster General emphasised the prospective UK content of nearly 50% and the 25% share of the nationalised industries.

When acceptable work programmes had been proposed by each applicant, and when the terms of options offered to the Gas Council and NCB were found to be satisfactory by the Ministry, officials sought Ministerial approval for the proposed awards. In a Minute to the Prime Minister in late May 1970, the Paymaster General expressed satisfaction with the prospective outcome. The expected total cost of the minimum work programme was £35 million. The only area where negotiations had not been completed was in Cardigan Bay where the conflict of interest with defence had not yet been resolved. The Paymaster confirmed the likely UK and public sector contents and sought permission to announce awards. The Secretary of State for Defence wished to reserve his position on blocks in Cardigan Bay pending a resolution to the conflict problem.

Announcement of awards

The Ministry of Technology released the Press Notice on the awards on 8th June. Ninety-four bocks were licensed, of which 83 were in the North Sea and 11 in the Irish Sea, involving 24 companies or groups. The total area covered was 19,000 square kilometres compared to 26,000 in the Second Round and 80,000 in the First Round. The Press Release noted that applications for a number of other blocks were still under examination and further awards were expected. A noteworthy feature was the award of a sole licence to Hydrocarbons Great Britain Limited, the new subsidiary of the Gas Council, covering four blocks in the Irish Sea. The resulting total acreage under licence in 1970 is shown in Appendix 3.1. Key features are the dominant interest in the Southern Basin but also the growing interest in the Central North Sea and in nearly all areas close to the median line with Norway. The map also shows the early gas field developments which are the subject of Chapter 4.

Reflections on policy debates

The end results of the policy debates in the second half of the 1960s generally represented the triumph of pragmatism and caution over ideology and radicalism. The political mood of the time favoured increased state intervention and direct participation. The officials of the relevant Departments were generally well aware of the main issues involved. They were convinced that a state organisation was not the appropriate vehicle for accepting the full costs and risks of further exploration and development in a province which had not yet been substantially proven. They also saw clearly the various carried interest devices which could be employed to increase the state's share at lower risk.

Officials were able to deploy the above arguments to restrain the more radical instincts which Ministers may have entertained following the work of the North Sea Study Group. Perhaps because the proposals of the Group were so radical there was a disinclination to find favour with any of its recommendations. But the Group showed perception in specific areas. An example was the issue of the possible need for coordination of the developing offshore pipeline system and the related appropriate role of Government. This subject was to become a matter of continuing controversy, involving much debate on tariffing arrangements, and possible proliferation of pipelines. A fully efficient system for third party use of assets is perhaps not yet in place in 2010. The Study Group deserves credit for raising the issue in the 1960s though no worked-out solution to the problem was provided.

On the issue of the appropriate form of state participation the Government's decision that it would be easier to involve existing public bodies rather than establish a new one was based on pragmatism rather than on a theory of efficient business organisation. The Gas Council had a major influence on the policy outcome. In turn its thinking was influenced greatly by the advantages of knowledge acquired in North Sea operations in informing its negotiations with other gas producers. The Government's thinking was also influenced by this consideration. The possible advantages of vertical integration do not appear to have greatly influenced thinking within Government. Similarly, the possible advantages of an entirely new, focused, state organisation unencumbered with non-North Sea activities did not receive very serious examination because of the large amount of legislative time and other work involved in building up an organisation from scratch. No detailed consideration was given to any possible fresh benefits from a new organisation. The Government was also convinced of the benefits of a centrally coordinated onshore gas infrastructure system. The idea of competition in the supply of gas to consumers received virtually no consideration. The influence of the Gas Council on policy was pronounced and the Study Group's antipathy to it found little or no sympathy.

4 The early gas contracts

The first discovery

The first gas discovery in the UKCS occurred in Block 48/6 and was announced by the operator, BP, in September 1965. There were initially doubts about its commercial significance, but very soon afterwards the company reported that tests had indicated that the find was encouraging. Events thereafter moved with remarkable speed. On 10th December 1965, the BP Chairman, Sir Maurice Bridgeman, accompanied by Mr Steel and Mr Luard called at the Ministry of Power and reported that the results were so encouraging that the company had made a firm offer to the Gas Council to supply gas at the rate of 50 million cubic feet per day (mm cf/d) starting in early 1967 if a decision could be taken by January 1966. The company argued that an early decision was necessary because the pipeline needed to bring the gas ashore could only be laid in the summer months. A quick decision would also mean that they could obtain first use of a pipe-laying barge currently under construction in the Netherlands.

The company also reported that this initial supply of 50 mmcf/d would be obtained from the initial well plus four more soon to be drilled, but, if results came up to expectation, production could be increased to over 200 mmcf/d. Sir Maurice added that the minimum size of pipeline for transporting 50 mmcf/d was 8-inch diameter but, in the hope that output would greatly exceed this, BP would be prepared to lay a 16-inch line. There was considerable risk attached to this, however, and in recognition of this, BP proposed that the Gas Council should pay an extra 0.5d per therm over and above the basic price for the gas which it bought. This would represent the additional cost and interest payments on the larger line.

In response to questions Sir Maurice stated that the basic price of natural gas was very difficult to determine at this time when the size of the discovery was still unknown as were the prospects for other discoveries. He had therefore proposed to Sir Henry Jones that the price should be reviewed after a period which he would prefer to be seven years, but which could be as little as three years. Subject to this he had proposed an initial price of 6.5d per therm, to which the 0.5d surcharge would be added, for gas landed onshore. In his view this price would be less than the cost to the Gas Boards of imported gas from Algeria and the cost of obtaining town gas from LPG.

Sir Maurice added that the Gas Council had not made a significant response to this offer, but appeared to be contemplating a price based on production costs. It was not possible to estimate these with any accuracy, however, as both the size of the field and the drilling costs were still very uncertain. The price of 6.5d per therm could not be precisely related to costs. Sir Maurice was prepared to be flexible and, for example, BP would be willing to consider a sliding scale whereby the price might fall to, say, 6.25d per therm if production were 75 mmcf/d, and perhaps 6d at 100 mmcf/d. Hopefully the price would ultimately be substantially reduced, but in the meantime there were advantages in not fixing too low a price as this would discourage further exploration. He thought that the Government had little to lose as 80% of the profits would come to the Exchequer in royalty, tax, and the Government shareholding. He also thought that the Gas Council would gain much in public esteem if gas from the North Sea became available much earlier than had been thought possible.

Views of Ministry

The Ministry was grateful for being informed of BP's thinking. Negotiations on price were a matter for the Gas Council, but, even with an early review, the Council would have to acknowledge that what was agreed with BP would influence the pattern for the future. It was hoped that BP would be flexible in their thinking on all the relevant issues. Sir Maurice gave a positive response and indicated that he would be willing to let it be known in the industry that the initial price should not be regarded as setting a pattern for the future.

Officials immediately reported the news to Mr Lee. It was agreed that it was important to ensure that the earliest possible use was made of this new source of indigenous fuel. The price issue required very careful and thorough consideration. Any reasonable price had to include an allowance for the cost of unsuccessful ventures. The Minister would see Sir Maurice Bridgman and Sir Henry Jones as soon as possible. The meeting with Sir Maurice took place the very next day. He explained his company's position with respect to the recent discovery and their key proposals to supply gas to the Gas Council. The Minister confirmed that he was most anxious to see an early start to the project. He proposed to see Sir Henry Jones the following day and would ask him to approach the matter as helpfully as he could. The prospect of North Sea gas being used as early as the beginning of 1967 exceeded any hopes so far publicly expressed and, if possible, he would like to make a statement about it before Parliament broke for the Christmas recess. He was thus most interested to know more about the prospects.

Sir Maurice indicated that the total area of the structure was 25 square miles. An output of 50 mmcf/d could be obtained from some two square miles in the vicinity of the discovery well. If the gas extended to the limits of the structure the maximum production could be as high as 800 mmcf/d. BP believed that the price suggested to the Council was justifiable. It was on a par with Algerian methane. The cost of gas made from light petroleum distillate, calculated on the basis of a 30-year life for the gas-making plant as suggested by the Council, was not an appropriate comparison. Further a price below 5d per therm risked setting a precedent which would make it impossible to exploit profitably the marginal fields which would probably come later. Sir Maurice did not pretend that BP's asking price was low, but in a pioneering project the cheapest terms could not be expected.

Discussions between Ministry and Gas Council

The next day the Minister and officials met with Sir Henry Jones. Sir Henry was confident that the Council could absorb the gas which BP was offering. He was sceptical about the timescale for delivery which BP was suggesting, but the Council would be prepared. Even if there was some slippage in the date suggested by BP it should be possible to have the gas in use by the summer of 1967. Sir Henry felt, however, that there would be a difficulty in negotiating for the gas against such a deadline because BP's initial price indication seemed to him to be totally unrealistic and liable to put a premium on the use of North Sea gas. There were also technical questions of load factor and other contractual terms to be discussed.

The Permanent Secretary indicated that BP was keen to proceed with the project and would not be inflexible with respect to the price. Also, the price set for the initial supply need not be a precedent for later supplies. Sir Henry felt that once a price had become established there would be difficulty in avoiding its being treated as a precedent. Mr Lee's objective was to do what he could to facilitate the landing and use of the gas as soon as possible. He suggested that, while it was entirely proper for the Gas Council to be reluctant to bind itself to a long term contract at too high a price, especially before the means of establishing a proper cost for the gas were available, the fact that the initial gas price might be above that for which natural gas was obtainable in some other parts of the world, ought not to inhibit the drawing up of a short term contract. It would, of course, be strange if the ultimate price level of North Sea gas were not below that for which natural gas from thousands of miles away could be landed in this country.

Sir Henry emphasised that the main question was the basic price of the gas and on that we should be wary that in the national desire for haste nothing was done that would prejudice the long term prospects for utilising North Sea gas. He noticed that BP would not disclose their costs, and felt that the price range in which negotiations would take place had to be seen in relation to the prices at which Dutch and Nigerian gas had been offered to the Council.

The Permanent Secretary felt that negotiations for the initial supply had to be conducted with no firm knowledge of costs. Mr Lee thought it was important not to allow the speedy utilisation of North Sea gas to be inhibited by the question of its proper long-term price. If, in the event no further gas were discovered in the North Sea, the price paid for this initial strike of gas had no long term implications. If, however, it turned out to be only the first of a number of strikes, and large quantities of gas were found, the whole question of price would inevitably have to be reappraised. He had no intention of endorsing an artificially high price, but it might be justifiable to have a special price for this first supply.

Sir Henry's response was that both the Gas Council and BP were now faced with substantial investment decisions. He accepted the Minister's sense of urgency, and would consider how far it would be proper for him to advise the Council to accept the project in principle in the absence of a prior agreement on price. He added that it appeared that Dutch gas could be landed in the UK at little more than 4d per therm and BP's indicated initial price was therefore quite unrealistic.

Mr Lee felt that, leaving aside the question of price, it would be desirable to make an early announcement of the news that it was now considered physically possible to bring an initial supply of gas ashore by 1967/68. He thought it would be helpful if he could make a statement in Parliament in a week's time indicating that BP were satisfied that they had sufficient gas available in their Block 48/6 to justify piping it to land at a rate which, all being well, should be at least 50 mmcf/d by 1967/68. He subsequently conveyed the essence of this message to the Prime Minister and made his announcement to Parliament on 21st December 1965.

Agreement between BP and the Council, even for this limited gas supply, was not easily achieved. Differences between the parties were revealed in the press. It became apparent that BP was prepared to reduce its asking price to around 6d per therm for delivery of 50 mmcf/d, and would use their best endeavours to increase this to 100 mmcf/d. The Gas Council was willing to pay 4d per therm for 100 mmcf/d. The gap was quite substantial, and the Ministry felt it should intervene in an attempt to precipitate negotiations between the parties.

Ministry becomes involved in price discussions

The Permanent Secretary saw Mr E. Drake of BP and Sir Henry Jones in mid-January 1966. He indicated that it might be useful in arriving at a settlement if they were aware of the Minister's likely attitude if he were asked to determine a reasonable price in conformity with the 1964 Act. He informed both parties that it was in the national interest that North Sea gas should be made available as soon as this could sensibly be achieved. It was understood that the cost of producing it could not yet be accurately ascertained. This pointed towards a limited, temporary settlement of the price question presently at issue. Thus any price determined now should rule for only three years at most, and should be subject to renegotiation thereafter.

The value of the gas to the Gas Council was determined by the prices paid for comparable products. Thus the Council was importing Algerian methane at a price of 6.25d per therm delivered to Canvey Island. Discussions between the Council and Nigerian producers (Shell and BP) indicated that in the future gas might be available at 5.25d per therm. Other discussions with the Dutch indicated a price of about 4.5d per therm. In this latter case account had to be taken of the large nitrogen content. This could be removed but only at some expense. It thus appeared to the Permanent Secretary that a price of around 5d per therm was lower than any authenticated import price. He concluded that the Minister's likely view of a reasonable price was that it should be 4d per therm for up to 100 mmcf/d for a period not exceeding three years. The price for additional quantities would be subject to review, and in any case the whole price arrangement would be subject to renegotiation at the end of that period in the light of fuller information about costs and other supplies from the North Sea.

Mr Drake protested that a price of 5d was too low to cover all the risks and costs involved and to keep up the morale of prospectors. In response it was argued that, on present evidence, a price of 5d should be rewarding to BP. Mr Drake then suggested that the amount of gas that would qualify for the 5d price should be increased to 150 mmcf/d, and that price should extend to a period of five years. Sir Henry Jones felt that the proposed price was far too high. The Permanent Secretary reminded him that the Council had been promoting a scheme for the import of Nigerian gas at an even higher price. With respect to the costs of producing North Sea gas no reasonable view could yet be formed. From the Gas Council's viewpoint a price of 3d should still be quite profitable.

Sir Henry then argued that he felt he was being pushed into this enterprise in too great a haste, and perhaps it would be better if everything were to proceed more slowly. The Ministry pointed out that if Sir Henry felt that a slower pace were desirable he should so inform the Minister and give reasons. It was accepted that there were political and national advantages in securing rapid development, but this should not outweigh reasonable prudence. But delay had to be explained. Sir Henry was also concerned about the risk relating to the size of the (onshore) investment which the Council would have to make, given the uncertainty of the gas volumes that might come from the field. The Ministry was able to persuade both BP and the Gas Council to resume negotiations on the basis of the information on the Minister's likely attitude.

This was done, and, while some progress was made, differences still remained which prevented a contract from being signed. The Ministry intervened again. The Permanent Secretary requested both Sir Henry Jones and Sir Maurice Bridgeman to see him separately. Sir Henry said that there were three outstanding issues. The first was on the sulphur content of the gas which was greater than originally thought. This should be reflected in a lower price. The second issue concerned the maximum volumes, especially during the first year. The Council also wanted a clause whereby, if production turned out to be higher than anticipated, such extra gas would be offered to the Council at a reasonable price. BP wanted to preserve the right to use such extra gas for its own purposes. The Permanent Secretary attempted to persuade Sir Henry that these points were not really vital.

Sir Maurice Bridgeman was firmly of the view that, with respect to any extra gas, BP wanted to keep its options open, particularly as the whole matter related to gas which might not be there, and which the Council might not be able to take. Further the price for it was completely undefined. The Permanent Secretary persuaded Sir Maurice to reflect further on the issue. He also persuaded Sir Maurice not to state BP's full position in public, on the grounds that brawling in the press was not the most successful way to bring these difficult discussions to fruition.

Progress was made and the Minister felt he should inform the Prime Minister of the position. On 2nd February 1966, he sent a Minute indicating that the two parties were now ready to conclude a historic agreement. The Minister was satisfied that the Council had been given the opportunity to purchase at a reasonable price, and he had not had to invoke his statutory powers on this subject. The Gas Council was concerned about the supply and price of naphtha on which it had increasingly come to depend as a source of gas. The Minister had pointed out to the Council that it would be difficult to justify further imports of gas when it could be available from the North Sea.

The Minister emphasised that the negotiations between the Council and the company had been anything but smooth and he had felt obliged to intervene because in intervals of negotiations both were brawling in the press and lobbying wherever they could. He had to intervene later when they had reached deadlock, with the company asking around 6d per therm and the Council offering 4d plus a conditional contribution of 0.5d per therm for a limited period towards the installation of a pipeline (offshore) larger than BP considered justifiable. Eventually both parties had accepted 5d per therm on a temporary basis for a limited volume of gas. This price was significantly below the price in the existing Algerian contract which was 6.25d per therm, and was lower than the estimated price of imported Nigerian methane which was 5.18d per therm. The Minister also felt that the price was competitive with the estimated price of Dutch gas after account was taken of its high nitrogen content.

Other considerations of Ministry

The Minister went on to mention some of his other considerations. He wanted to ensure that the price would not be so low as to discourage exploration and production, or so high as to discourage its utilisation and the expansion of the market. He added that he would not care to give further impetus to it immediately by indicating a low price for supplies which would not be available for a year or two.

Finally, the Minister emphasised that at the present time there was no question of him fixing a price for North Sea gas generally. The costs of production were still unknown. He had instructed the Ministry to examine this issue. If larger quantities of gas were discovered we could expect a significant reduction in the price.

Shortly thereafter the Minister was able to make a statement to the House of Commons that BP and the Gas Council had reached an agreement. The key features were that BP was undertaking to deliver a minimum of 50 mmcf/d for 15 years and would use its best endeavours to increase production to 100 mmcf/d during the first three years of supply. These additional supplies would be offered to the Gas Council. A price of 5d per therm had been agreed, but this would apply only up to an average of 100 mmcf/d for a period of three years from 1st July 1967 or the date of commencement of the guaranteed supply, whichever was the earlier. For supplies above the stipulated quantity in the first three years, and for all volumes after the first three years, the price was negotiable. The Minister again emphasised that the price was below gas import prices and was for limited quantities. In the event of further large discoveries the price could be significantly below that prevailing in this very first contract.

In the briefing to the Minister for this historic occasion he was advised that a price of 5d per therm would produce gas competitive with that made from oil feedstocks. He was also advised that, as North Sea gas would replace oil feedstocks, it would reduce import requirements and benefit the balance of payments which was, of course, a major problem. To put this first contract in perspective, 100 mmcf/d constituted around 10% of the UK's gas requirements at the time.

Major exploration successes in 1966

The year 1966 turned out to be a very successful one for gas exploration. Three major discoveries were made in the Southern Basin, namely Leman Bank by Shell/Esso (Block 49/26) in April, Indefatigable by the Amoco/Gas Council Group (Block 49/18), Shell/Esso (Block 49/19) in June, and Hewett by the Phillips Group (Block 48/29) in October. At the time of the discoveries there was, of course, much uncertainty about the size of the reserves, and the operators were generally cautious in their pronouncements. The very first announcement about Leman made by Shell on March 28th 1966 referred only to encouraging indications of gas.

It was fairly clear to the Ministry of Power, however, that the initial discoveries had the potential to make a substantial contribution to the indigenous energy supplies of the UK. As early as the beginning of May 1966 the Ministry felt that the maximum potential production from West Sole and Leman Bank could be as much as 3,800 mmcf/d. Much work was initiated on the implications. Attention was given in particular to appropriate long-term contracts with the producers. In turn this necessitated fuller understanding of the market prospects for natural gas, the likely costs involved, and appropriate gas prices. While the Ministry of Power was clearly in the lead on these issues other Departments were involved. A Steering Group on Energy Policy was established as well as an Interdepartmental Working Group on Natural Gas. At its meeting on 1st July the Steering Group asked the Ministry of Power to prepare a preliminary paper on the principles that should be employed in the determination of prices for sale by the producers to the Gas Council.

Ministry studies gas pricing principles

In the preparation of this paper the Ministry used as planning assumptions availability from the North Sea of 200 mmcf/d by autumn 1967, 700 mmcf/d by autumn 1968, and 1,000 mmcf/d by autumn 1969. It was not possible to make a proper assessment of the long-term potential until much more exploration had been undertaken. While the Minister had no formal standing in the price to be paid by the Gas Council, it had already been impressed on the parties that the Government must take the closest interest in the price and other aspects of the exploitation of the natural gas reserves with a view to securing the greatest benefit to the economy and of encouraging continued vigorous exploration. Both the Gas Council and the oil companies had accepted the Minister's interest, and were willing to discuss pricing principles and the progress of negotiations with the Ministry.

Views of oil companies on pricing

The oil companies had already made their views known. Without exception they argued in favour of a market value approach to pricing related in the short-term to the cost of alternative feedstocks for gas-making (naphtha and imported liquefied natural gas), and in the longer term to that price for gas at the shore which permitted its sale to the mix of consumers after reasonable allowance for efficient transportation, distribution and marketing. The Ministry felt that, in its extreme form (which the companies might not seriously support), this approach would allow the gas industry no more than a cost of service return and, apart from this, the whole of the surplus derived from the difference between the price to the ultimate consumer and the actual cost of producing and supplying the gas would accrue to the producers. The Ministry noted the companies' arguments in favour of this approach, principally that other commodities, including petroleum products, were normally priced at market values, and that this should secure vigorous exploration, the optimal rate of developments of gas reserves and the appropriate balance in the energy market. The oil companies had also argued that the alternative approach of basing prices on costs would discourage exploration and would set a dangerous precedent which could have serious implications for British oil interests abroad. The companies had also pointed out that a pricing system based on costs would not be practicable because accurate costs would not be known for several years. The companies were also in principle opposed to any system of regulated prices as opposed to negotiated ones.

Views of BP

The Ministry received a note from BP in July 1966 setting out the company's detailed views. This emphasised that the uncertainties were so great that it was out of the question to devise an equitable formula which would be applicable to all future circumstances. The most important uncertainties related to the size of the reserves, the costs of producing them, the rate of gas absorption in the market, and the effects on overall energy policy. Against this background it was argued that the maximum price of gas should be determined by the relative cost of alternative sources of supply, while the minimum should be determined by the necessity for encouraging further exploration. It was felt that the difference between the maximum and the minimum would not be so large that a compromise reference price could not be reached by negotiation. Contracts could then be drawn up to include provisions for price adjustments every four or five years. The direction of the adjustment would be determined by supply and demand conditions. If supply were exceeding demand the adjustment would be downwards and vice versa. The size of the adjustment would be limited to a movement of 10% on each occasion.

Development of Ministry's thinking

The Ministry found some merit in the general approach suggested by BP. There was agreement that the large uncertainties precluded the design of a hard and fast long-term price formula. There were acknowledged disadvantages in a strict cost plus system, and provision in contracts for review of terms was sensible. The summary of the main uncertainties was also perfectly sound. Despite these, plans and decisions had to be made based on the best available information. This applied to all stakeholders. Companies had to decide whether to continue with exploration, the Gas Council had to determine its marketing plans, and the Government had to take a view on the rate of gas exploration and its role in energy policy.

The Ministry was clear that there were overwhelming objections against a strict cost plus formula whereby a producer's costs would be ascertained in detail and the price would cover these with an agreed percentage or fixed margin. The Ministry did not contemplate this, but did see merit in a form of fixed price contract where the agreed price would be related to estimated costs and would not be changed for a period of years, even if the producer succeeded in increasing productivity and secured a higher return than originally envisaged. It was felt that the determination of the minimum price as defined by BP must involve assumptions of the costs of finding and developing deposits and prospective returns despite the manifest uncertainties.

The Ministry was doubtful about whether it would be easy to reach an agreed reference price by normal negotiation, and felt that it was unlikely that a single price should be applicable to all producers irrespective of their individual costs. There was no disagreement about the bases of the maximum and minimum prices, but it was felt that agreed minimum prices would have to vary across fields as there would be substantial differences in costs on small, high cost fields compared to the recent Leman discovery. A price necessary to incentivise the development of small, marginal fields could provide very large profits to a low cost producer. With respect to price adjustments, the concept was attractive, but the circumstances for an adjustment required clarification. Would it be automatically determined by, for example, changes in the reserves/production ratio or entirely open to negotiation?

Discussions with BP

The Ministry invited BP to discuss all these issues. A meeting took place on 1st August 1966 between Ministry representatives, including Mr Marshall, the Deputy Secretary, and representatives of BP, including Sir Maurice Bridgeman. Sir Maurice found the cost plus approach unacceptable. BP had hesitated before investing in the North Sea. Had they known that a cost plus approach to pricing was to be adopted they would not have started exploration. He emphasised four points. Firstly, it would create a disastrous precedent in the oil industry. He was concerned that foreign Governments would take the same view and impose export taxes. Further, if the British oil industry were worse treated in the UK than other companies on their home ground, the British oil industry would not long survive. Secondly, Sir Maurice argued that a cost plus system would encourage the artificial inflation of costs. Thirdly, it would be very difficult to decide how widely costs should be averaged in calculations of this kind. Fourthly, marginal producers could be brought in by varying the level of royalty payment and by guaranteeing a high load factor.

The Ministry representatives emphasised that the Government's approach was not doctrinaire, and they were already convinced that the costs of production would vary widely according to field size and location. The Government intended to see that licensees were adequately rewarded, but at the same time they would not accept excessive profit margins. On royalties the Ministry was aware that there was an alternative view that the level was already too low. With respect to price levels the Ministry's current views were that the maximum was about 3.5d per therm and the minimum about 1.5d. The Ministry was interested in BP's views on these calculations. There was political pressure to obtain information on production costs and officials did not want to advise the Minister without giving the oil companies the opportunity to provide such information.

Sir Maurice indicated that he preferred not to give guidance of this kind. He did not subscribe to this pricing principle. It was highly desirable from the viewpoints of both the Government and BP that the price should be a negotiated settlement and not defended publicly by disclosing costs or profit margins.

Sir Maurice thought that the difference between cost and market value would not be so wide, and the negotiated price should fall between 2.75d and 3.5d. A marginal field, producing 50 mmcf/d and located 100 miles from shore could obtain a return on capital of 10% to 12% at a landed price of 4.5d. It was agreed that the first contract with the Gas Council at 5d per therm was a special case and too high for future contracts. It had been agreed in order to persuade BP to invest in a pipeline before the potential of the field was properly known. Sir Maurice agreed that varying royalties was a widely accepted practice, but if royalties increased, so would foreign royalties and the foreign exchange cost of BP oil to the UK. He was also concerned that estimates of cost would be arbitrary. He did not think that the Gas Council could offer different prices to producers for different quantities at the same point of time.

Sliding-scale price formula?

The Ministry representatives suggested that prices could be based on a sliding scale related to volumes. Sir Maurice thought that this would only be acceptable on long-term contracts without provision for review. He was concerned that geologists might deliberately underestimate the capacity of gas fields during negotiations. He also wondered whether, on a very small field, the price necessary to give the investor a reasonable return would be too high to be acceptable to the Gas Council.

Views of Gas Council on market situation

Meanwhile the Ministry had been having numerous discussions with the Gas Council. On 6th September 1966 senior Council Members and staff presented several papers on key aspects of the introduction of gas from the North Sea. The Deputy Chairman, Sir Kenneth Hutchison, opened his presentation by stating that they were faced with a problem of the sudden availability of very large quantities of natural gas and of producers who are naturally anxious to dispose of it all as quickly as possible. Gas demand in the UK was now growing at least at 10% per annum. Much of the expected increase would be in the domestic sector. A major implication of this was a low load factor and high seasonal demand. This demand had to be met, but the producers were exerting pressure on the Council to take gas at load factors which did not necessarily match the demand. He provided two scenarios of the future relating to different scales of possible discoveries. The first was where North Sea production was around 1,000 mmcf/d (around the current gas consumption level) and the second where it became 4,000 mmcf/d. Sir Kenneth felt that both scenarios would permit substantial reductions in price to consumers, but only after the period of extra necessary expenditure by the gas industry had ended. He thought that in the second scenario the price of gas could be halved. The expected large seasonal load meant that the Council would have to plan the supply system very carefully so as to match this variable demand with the optimisation of gas field outputs.

The Council had opened negotiations with the prospective producers. It had been agreed by all that it was premature to discuss price until supply conditions had been settled since these would be reflected in the price. Some prospective producers had expressed doubts about continuing exploration on the grounds that their potential market was likely to be saturated. The Council had been giving the companies assurances that this was not the case, and that it would either adopt some form of rationing system or be prepared to purchase reserves from the companies.

The Council had examined the assessments of likely reserves foreseen by the different producers, and in each case recalculated the proposed average daily rate of supply to one which they thought could be sustained for 30 years. It had become apparent to the Council that for the next two or three years the quantity of gas available would be in excess of its requirements, but after that, unless major additional reserves were found there would be a shortfall. To deal with these prospective trends in supply and demand the Council had come to the view that its appropriate policy would be to purchase a specified proportion of each producer's deliverability related to its reserves, the sum equalling the Council's total requirements for the year. The balance of what a producer wished to supply and the

Council's requirements would be carried forward to the next year. A new percentage would be worked out each year to determine the quantity from each producer. The Council reported that these ideas had been received with varying degrees of enthusiasm.

Gas Council's plan for National Transmission System (NTS)

The Council presented their plans for the development of the basic transmission system up to the beginning of 1970. This would involve about 1,250 miles of trunk main at an estimated cost of £110 million. This could absorb up to 2,000 mmcf/d. Further substantial investments in secondary transmission systems would be required by the Area Boards. There would be a heavy demand for steel pipes, and it was already clear that, although British suppliers would meet much of the requirements, some importation of pipe would be required, particularly of special steels which were not available in the UK.

Need for swing factor

To provide for the seasonality of demand it was hoped to incorporate a considerable swing factor in the contracts with the producers. But other means would also be necessary. Storage facilities were being developed, including storage for liquefied natural gas (LNG) at Canvey Island. The LNG received from Algeria could provide a very valuable source of peak load gas.

Need to convert all gas-using appliances

Natural gas from the North Sea was chemically different from the town gas which was then in use. There was a basic incompatibility between natural gas and all the using appliances. Natural gas had approximately twice the calorific value of town gas made from coal and required about twice as much air to burn it fully. The Gas Council, after prolonged study of the possibility of using intermediate gases, had concluded that this was less economic than the conversion of all appliances to use natural gas directly. The estimated cost of the conversion programme at September 1966 was around £400 million. The whole programme would take ten years. (The present author's appliances were not converted until 1977.) Substantial expenditures relating to the obsolescence of coal and oil-based plants as natural gas was substituted for town gas would also be required.

The Council had taken the view that, for planning and operational purposes, natural gas should be made available to all Area Boards through a common transmission system with all costs merged into a single account. The Council was intending that these pooled costs should provide the basis for bulk supply tariffs to the Area Boards. This would not mean that the price to the final consumer would be the same throughout the country. There was a need to vary the bulk supply tariffs to the Area Boards to reflect differing load factors. Also each Area Board would need to add its own (differing) costs of distribution to the wholesale tariff before the final price was determined.

Views of Ministry on pricing

Having heard the views of the main parties directly involved the Ministry's view was that the broad objective of the Government should be to ensure that the nation obtained the gas at the lowest price consistent with encouraging further vigorous exploration. In their extreme forms neither the market value nor the cost plus approach were compatible with this view. The case against relating price to market value was simply that it might result in paying more than was needed to secure the optimum development of the UK's natural gas resources. The Ministry recognised several problems with a cost plus system. Thus a scheme whereby each producer was paid on the basis of ascertained costs plus a stipulated profit margin would lead to abuse. It would certainly not encourage cost-reducing initiatives. Similarly, the Ministry felt that a regulated system whereby the price was closely related to average costs in an area (as was being attempted by the Federal Power Commission in the USA), was not practicable in the UK because of the lack of knowledge of the finding and development costs. Even if the costs relating to the present discoveries were known with some accuracy, these would not be enough to establish an average for the basin as a whole. The Ministry was also prepared to believe the strongly-expressed views of the oil companies that a strict cost-based system would severely discourage exploration and could set a damaging precedent to the UK's overseas oil interests.

It was also felt, however, that the above objections would not hold against an attempt to negotiate a price related more closely to cost than to market value. This was on the understanding that costs could not at present be accurately ascertained. Attempts to estimate them should recognise the need to allow producers a return sufficient to incentivise vigorous exploration.

An appropriate negotiated price should lie between "cost" and "market value". In the short-term the market value of North Sea gas was set by the cost of alternative sources of gas. These were reformed naphtha and imported LNG. Naphtha was available at around 4½d per therm and the cost of reforming it to town gas was about 1d. The current price for imported LNG was 6¼d per therm, though for large volumes it might be possible to obtain it at 5d. The Ministry thus felt that for practical purposes the upper limit could be set at 4.5d per therm.

The lower limit was more difficult to estimate. Preliminary work by the Ministry on a set of model fields suggested that on a large field producing 500 mmcf/d, and assuming an exploration success ratio of 1 in 20 and 100% load factor, a price of 1.25d per therm procured a post-tax rate of return of 15%. On the other hand for a field producing 100 mmcf/d with the other assumptions unchanged the price would have to be 4d per therm. For a small field producing 50 mmcf/d the price would have to be 5d per therm. It was stressed that there was as yet insufficient information to calculate the costs relating to any actual field let alone the average for the whole province. With these provisos the Ministry felt that it would be unrealistic to expect that initial contracts could be negotiated at prices of less than 2d per therm. The practical limits were thus likely to be between 4.5d and 2d.

Excise tax?

The Ministry was aware that, because of this wide range between "market value" and "cost", an excise tax could be imposed to narrow the gap and ensure that part of the surplus accrued directly to the Exchequer. There were several arguments in favour of this. Firstly, the tax would make gas more expensive and would avert the risk of supplies being diverted from the gas industry to petrochemical use, which would be less advantageous to the economy. A second advantage was that an announcement of the Government's intention to impose an excise tax would facilitate negotiations by reducing the area of disagreement, and removing the risk of the Gas Council being led into paying too high a price. The third advantage of the tax would be the welcome source of revenues. It would also avoid the risk of large profits being earned by the gas industry weakening its incentive to improve efficiency.

The Ministry felt that the risks of supplies being diverted to the petrochemical industry did not appear to be serious. The potential demand was quite small in relation to the likely supplies. Much of the potential demand was at ICI, Billingham, with other outlets on the west coast. They were remote from the current North Sea discoveries and could realistically only be supplied through the gas industry's distribution system. If another party wished to lay an onshore pipeline the Minister's permission was required. In any case ICI might not be in a hurry to buy gas from other companies while it had hopes of making discoveries of its own.

The immediate case for a tax was that it would facilitate price negotiations. While the Ministry felt that this argument had some merit the Gas Council had a very strong negotiation position as virtually a monopoly buyer, especially as it could count on the Government's backing. Thus although a tax might shorten negotiations it would not necessarily result in a better price than could be secured through the bargaining process. The Ministry also felt that a tax involved serious risks. The exploration and development costs were not yet known, nor was the price necessary to give adequate incentives to investors. A further problem was that a proper assessment had not yet been made of the extra expenditures of the gas industry on construction of (onshore) pipelines to distribute natural gas, conversion of equipment and appliances, and the writing off of obsolete plant. If all these were not taken into account there was a risk that the imposition of a tax could lead either to the sale of gas on uneconomic terms (from the perspective of the Gas Council and Area Boards) or the inhibition of further exploitation of the North Sea. The conclusion was that a tax would be a premature step which could prejudice the prospects for optimising the development of the offshore gas resources.

Price review provision?

Because of the great uncertainties surrounding reserves, costs, and market absorption the producers would expect the price to contain a substantial risk premium. It followed that it would be in the Government's interest to accept a reasonably generous settlement to encourage continued exploration and development. Over time the uncertainties would be reduced and it would be reasonable to hope that the price paid could be appreciably reduced. Thus provision for price reviews after four years or so would be appropriate. The producers would probably be happy with such a provision though the Gas Council was more doubtful. The manner in which the review would operate required careful definition at the outset, however, as there was a danger that it would result in a price increase rather than a decrease.

Matching supply and demand

Matching the potential supplies from the North Sea with demand was recognised to be a problem which was still being studied. The Gas Council had suggested a scheme whereby it would invite offers annually for deliveries to commence two years ahead. If the quantity offered exceeded the Council's needs each producer's offer would be scaled down by an equal percentage. The Ministry had not yet formed a view on this or alternative schemes. Nor had it come to a conclusion on the issue of price differentiation across fields. It was recognised that costs would vary widely across fields, and a single uniform price might give a low cost producer very high profits while a high cost field might have an unprofitable return in prospect. It was felt, however, that there were difficulties about discriminating prices as between different producers or fields; this would give the appearance of unfairness and would remove part of the incentive to explore. The above views were presented to the Official Committee on Natural Gas and to the Steering Group on Energy Policy.

Gas Council on prorationing

The discussions between the Ministry of Power and the Gas Council continued apace. In response to queries the Council amplified its views on gas sales prospects and its proposed market sharing scheme. It still felt that an over-supply situation would exist for the first two or three years. The Council's forward planning was based on a gas buying year which would start on 1st October 1968, the earliest date at which it could enter into firm commitments. (This particular yearly period was to remain the purchasing basis for many years ahead.) The Council proposed that all offers of gas should be based on the total proven reserves in each discovery. A uniform annual rate of delivery would be set at $\frac{1}{30}$th of the agreed total reserves. In each year the Council would examine any new offers of gas along with any gas held over from the previous year. The basis of these offers would be for delivery starting two years from the date of the contract. The Council felt that this would permit time for the necessary collecting and delivery facilities to be constructed.

In their calculations the Gas Council had adopted a load factor of 60% (equating to a swing factor of 1.67). Any increases in supply would take effect only from the commencement of a new gas year. To cater for peak demand in excess of the 60% load factor town gas and LNG would be employed. The detailed price of gas would be determined for each gas year. Any gas held over from an earlier year would be sold at the new price. Work was in hand for dealing with over-and under-estimation of reserves.

The Council elaborated its proposals for prorationing. The underlying principles of such a scheme would be to meet several objectives. These included (1) the optimal exploitation of each field (maximum economic recovery), (2) the preferential exploitation of lower cost fields, (3) the minimisation of development and transmission expenditures, (4) the attainment of equity among producers, and (5) the encouragement of further exploration.

One Ministry view was that the Council's proposed scheme to take an equal percentage of each producer's offer year by year up to its total requirements would be consistent with these objectives. The method had some advantages namely (1) flexibility, (2) the prospect of sale for every producer, (3) the encouragement of the exploitation of smaller fields, and (4) a reduced likelihood that producers would attempt to sell directly to industry. There were also acknowledged drawbacks, particularly the possibility that only a proportion of supplies would come from the lowest cost fields. It was also possible that producers would install facilities which in the event would operate at less than full capacity.

At least one Ministry view was that the pricing system should be the mechanism for stimulating exploration. With respect to flexibility there was a concern that the result of guaranteeing equal percentage takes and uniform load factors from fields regardless of their size, costs and location would constitute encumbrances rather than flexibility. The Council had noted that two other forms of prorationing based on different percentage takes and the purchase of lowest cost gas could avoid economic inefficiency, but had rejected them, presumably as failing to provide incentives to develop small fields and to encourage exploration. A Ministry view was that the Council should revise its proposed method to slant their gas taken towards low cost producers both quantitatively and chronologically, whilst using prices as judicious palliatives. Similarly, wasteful investment expenditure could be avoided by correlating the capacity with prorationing.

The Council had included a statement in its proposal that it would be under no obligation to include a producer who had opted out of its scheme and supplied direct to industry in any subsequent schemes. There was concern that in effect this meant that a producer could be locked into the Council scheme for fear of possible adverse treatment later. Producers with supplies available to and not taken by the gas industry, and/or with pipelines run at non-optimum load factors might find this implication intolerable. They would be justified in seeking to sell direct to industry if their supplies were under-utilised, and also in seeking an assurance that their future position would not be jeopardised vis-à-vis the Gas Council. It was a moot point whether direct supplies to industry should be discouraged on economic or fuel policy grounds.

One Ministry view was that the Council was "not expansive" on the methods of increasing the load factor and demand to alleviate prorationing. Effort should be directed at developing off peak and interruptible sales, and supplies to dual-fired power stations. The latter could provide excellent summer outlets for North Sea gas. Efforts should also be made to develop storage and peak-shaving techniques. It was noted that in the USA there were dedicated reserves contracts involving an annual redetermination of reserves resulting in adjustments to annual average deliveries over the agreed life of the fields. It was felt that the Gas Council's proposals ostensibly assumed that in the year of initial contract the total reserves in a discovery were known. Perhaps under the Council's approach reserves could be redetermined annually and any excess brought into the pool in subsequent years. It was also noteworthy that American contracts normally contained take-or-pay clauses which gave incentives both to producers and buyers. This was an alternative method of dealing with the problem of compensating producers for deferred sales as a result of prorationing and deserved further consideration.

The Ministry and Council representatives met to consider the prorationing and related issues on 12th September 1966. The Ministry stressed that the Government had to be able to avoid the criticism that natural gas was being absorbed too slowly into the economy and had therefore to be convinced that prorationing was necessary. The response from the Deputy Chairman was that the Gas Council could sell all the natural gas on offer just as quickly as could the licensees, but the Gas Council assumed that it was not the Government's intention to flood the general industrial market with gas. Further, supply would only match demand coincidentally in any given year. The Council were, however, assessing the potential industrial demand in case it was necessary to reduce pressure from the oil companies for consent to supply industry direct. The Ministry representatives confirmed that the Government would be reluctant to consent to direct supply.

The Council had been refining its prorationing scheme. Their current thoughts were that in the first year of a contract it could offer to take around 61% of the gas on offer from each producer which equated to 216 days take of the total amount. Of this about 50% would be taken in the winter. In the following year the Council would offer to buy a proportion of the gas carried over plus any additional finds on offer. This process would continue. In a few years time the Council hoped that the market would develop sufficiently so that it would take a very high proportion of the gas on offer.

The Council produced a revised paper on the reconciliation of supply and demand in October 1966. By this time specific offers of gas had been made from BP, Shell, Esso, Amoco/Gas Council, and Phillips relating to the first four major discoveries recently made. The Council was anxious to replace the industry's existing fuel sources with low cost natural gas and to develop new markets as quickly as possible, but it faced some constraints, principally the rate at which onshore pipelines and new, enlarged distribution systems could be constructed, and industrial and domestic appliances designed to burn town gas converted to the use of natural gas.

The current thinking of the Council was that there was likely to be an over-supply position from the start of major supplies in 1968 to 1970, but thereafter, unless large further discoveries were made, a serious shortage could develop in the early or mid-1970s. Though additional reserves could be expected it would be unwise, and could be extremely dangerous, to base firm plans on this assumption. This formed the background to the Council's proposed prorationing scheme.

The available demand would be shared among producers in proportion to the quantity they offered. In turn the offers would be based on the size of the established reserves less a specified amount for the producer's own use or non-fuel purposes. The offer would be provisionally set at a maximum of $\frac{1}{30}$th yearly of the total reserves. The limit had been set to ensure the security of future supplies over a period of years which had regard to the life of the transmission and distribution facilities involved, but could be changed later if the rate of discoveries of new gas reserves justified a faster depletion rate. The total amount offered in each year would be compared with the Council's requirements. Under the scheme each producer would then be invited to supply the appropriate proportion of his offered quantity such that the Council's needs were met. The system would commence such that quotas would be fixed each year for deliveries to start two years ahead. Any balance of gas not taken would be held over and would rate equally with any new offers based on newly discovered reserves in the next year.

To put the matter mildly the detailed implementation of the scheme would be quite complex. Thus each producer would have to provide the Council with information on its reserves sufficiently detailed to enable the latter to verify their adequacy. The Council would assess its yearly expected sales and, on the basis of the combined information, each producer would be sent a Requirement Notice specifying the required amounts. The Council would then assess the resulting quantities tendered, and, taking into account volumes preferred but not taken in the previous year, would then determine and allocate quantities to each producer. This procedure would be incorporated in the main contracts with each producer covering not only volumes but load factor, price, and delivery. The price of the gas would be settled with each producer and would, subject to any price revision arrangements, remain constant for any particular tranche of production for the whole period for which the supply was contracted, say 30 years.

The Council thought that it would be necessary to set a minimum size of reserves for entry into the proposed scheme. It might initially be set at 1 trillion cubic feet. For smaller reserves separate negotiations would be necessary. It might also be necessary to provide for revision of the initial estimates of reserves as better quality data became available.

From the Council's viewpoint the scheme established an orderly and fair method of purchasing natural gas during a period of over-supply. It would offer all producers the opportunity to participate with certain knowledge that all their reserves of gas would be taken up over a period of time. The alternative of separate contracts with producers would create difficulty in assessing the quantity to which the Council would be justified in positively committing itself in advance. The scheme thus reduced the Council's risks, but it felt that the risks of the producers were also accommodated because they would have a firm indication of the quantity to be supplied two years ahead, and would also know that the balance of gas held over would be spread over a limited number of years. Currently the Council felt that it would be able to take at least 50% of gas likely to be on offer in the foreseeable future. New discoveries would be fully taken into account as they arose, as would balances of untaken gas carried forward from previous years. There would therefore be a continuing incentive for new exploration. The Council anticipated that the annual capital investment of the gas industry would exceed that of all the producers combined. It followed that the Council had every incentive to develop markets for the gas as quickly as possible because the high throughputs would enable its very capital intensive system to be used more economically.

Debate on prorationing scheme within Ministry

The proposals of the Council provoked considerable debate in the Ministry of Power. A full review of the scheme was undertaken and a paper produced for the Working Party on Natural Gas. This involved much elucidation of the implications of the scheme. It was felt that, while supplies taken by the Council from a field could start at 50% of the attainable level, this would rise annually to 75%, 87.5% and 93.75%. The effect of having the gas year start on 1st October was to associate each winter with the following summer which would increase the load factor, given the annual growth in demand. It also had the advantage to the Council that adjustments to the rate of offtake to ensure that the quantity actually purchased matched the contract figure would be more easily made in the summer months. With respect to price the Council's system appeared to envisage a common price structure for all contracts made in any one year with negotiated differentials to take account of factors such as quality and pressure. The system appeared to envisage a two-part tariff related to volume with a high initial price for the first 100 mmcf/d and a lower one for higher amounts. The price would be fixed for all the quantities contracted in that year. That price would continue to apply to these quantities in subsequent years. Gas not taken up in the Council's original offer but carried forward would obtain the price applicable to the later year when it came into the quota.

The expected average load factor for gas from the North Sea was about 60% which was higher than for the Council's system as a whole. This was made possible by taking each winter with the following summer, and because LNG, LPG and naphtha would be used for peak shaving purposes. The producers would have to install capacity sufficient to supply the whole quantity offered at the 60% load factor, but it was understood that there would be a sliding scale whereby the price was higher at lower load factors and lower at higher load factors. The intention was to devise a scale to give both the Council and producers incentives to maximise the load factor. No price review clause was proposed.

The Council was taking a cautious view of future discoveries, and with the anticipated fast growth in consumption, availability would increasingly fall short of demand in the early 1970s. Following from this the Council was not planning to expand sales much beyond its traditional markets, though additional outlets could quickly be found by reducing prices to industrial consumers. The Ministry noted that the proposed thirty-year depletion period, which was designed to ensure long-term continuity of supplies, would increase costs compared to the twenty-year depletion period normally adopted in contracts in the USA. If more discoveries were made and anxieties regarding early declines in supplies were removed, the Council would offer to renegotiate the early contracts to provide for shorter depletion periods.

It was understood that the quota scheme had received a mixed reception from the oil companies who had already discovered gas. Companies which had expected to supply larger quantities without the scheme had reacted unfavourably.

In assessing whether the scheme was necessary at all the Ministry felt that there would inevitably be some imbalance between short-term availability and demand. This could continue depending on whether new discoveries were bunched or not, and some systematic means of reconciling supply and demand would be needed. This was a quite separate issue from keeping the *long-term* trend of supply and demand in step. This could be secured primarily by varying prices to consumers and possibly influencing the supply side through varying the rate of depletion.

The Ministry saw several disadvantages of the scheme. Thus it was complicated, it increased costs, and it could prejudice policies on other issues. It was admitted that there might be a need for a scheme to ensure the balancing of short-term supply and demand, but a simpler one had advantages. As an example it might be preferable to fix the price applicable to all gas supplied by a licensee from a field at the outset, rather than bring in separate quotas at the price applicable to new contracts signed in any year. A quota system would increase costs as compared to bringing fields on stream in a predetermined order such as lowest cost first, because the depletion of each field would be adjusted to the working of the Council's formula rather than in accordance with the most economic rate of drilling production wells. The result could be underemployment of capacity in the early years, and delay in building up the full potential of the lowest cost fields because of the need to bring on higher cost ones.

A different consideration was the effect on the Gas Council's negotiating position. This could be weakened because a licensee, knowing that he was assured of a quota, could adopt a more intransigent attitude in negotiations.

It was also necessary to consider the implications of the Council's quota system on other policy issues particularly price review, depletion period, improvement of load factor, and price differentiation. The Ministry felt that the scheme was consistent with a periodic price review, even though the Council itself had not been enthusiastic about this. It was noted that the mechanics of the scheme could readily be applied to depletion periods less than the thirty years proposed by the Council. Similarly, the operation of the system did not depend upon the 60% load factor suggested by the Council, and would be consistent with measures taken to increase it.

There was a concern that the quota system would necessitate restrictions to the possible methods of price discrimination. The Ministry's understanding was that the Council envisaged a common price structure for all contracts conducted in any single year involving a two-part tariff with a higher price for the smaller fields and a lower price for the low cost ones. The Ministry wondered whether the scheme could work with prices negotiated separately at different levels for each contract, because licensees participating in the scheme on equal terms would expect to be paid on a similar basis. There was a risk that if the quota system became a reality it would prove impossible to negotiate a two-part or sliding-scale tariff involving quantity differentiation. The Ministry felt the alternative of uniform pricing could make it uneconomic to develop higher-cost fields, unless that price was set at a high level.

The Ministry pointed out that the main alternative to a quota system for the reconciliation of supply and demand was ad hoc negotiation of contracts with different producers. In practice this meant that the Council would play off one producer against another by taking larger quantities from those who were prepared to offer lower prices, adjusting the build-up period and other terms of the contract by individual negotiation so as to keep the overall level of offtake in line with expected demand. The negotiations would certainly be complex and it was not clear whether this approach offered more benefits than the quota system.

A variation on the Council's scheme deserved further attention. This was still a quota system but was based on a variable (not equal) proportion of each field related to its size. In theory this would encourage lower cost production. It did, however, involve more complex administration, less apparent equity among producers, and might still give insufficient incentive to higher cost producers to continue. The whole issue deserved further debate and elaboration from the Council.

A different approach to the short-run reconciliation of supply and demand was the employment of short-term interruptible contracts with large industrial consumers. In such situations gas would have to be offered at low prices. There could be a problem of whether the offtake could be varied quickly enough to deal with the problem compared to the quota system. Because of this interruptible contracts might be regarded as complementary to the quota system rather than a substitute.

Further discussions with Gas Council

The whole subject was then discussed with the Council. At a meeting in October 1966 the Ministry representatives revealed their current thinking. They reiterated their position that on the basis of studies undertaken average costs for North Sea gas could not be calculated because of the inadequate experience to date. It would thus not be possible to fix contracts on a cost plus basis for individual fields. It was already clear that costs fell sharply as volumes increased. Studies undertaken indicated that costs might vary from 1.25d on a large field to 4.5d on a small one. The latter might be the highest price the Council would pay. The Ministry felt that it was important to discover to what extent oil companies' views on market values might be lowered when realistic negotiations began. Hopefully the assured market for their gas would have a positive effect on the incentives of the companies.

Sir Kenneth Hutchison acknowledged that strict cost plus pricing was unrealistic. Discussions with the companies to date had revealed their adherence to the principle that the gas should be bought at its commodity value. When serious negotiations started there would be a chance of arranging two-part tariffs. It was acknowledged that such tariffs were known in the industry already. Sir Kenneth indicated that the companies would be informed that if the gas market expanded as fast as they hoped the market value would be about 3d per therm delivered to the Area Boards. He felt that the companies would probably prefer this type of arrangement to the two-part tariff system, taking comfort from the idea that low cost production would earn higher profits.

The Ministry reiterated its concern that it was the Government's policy to make it worthwhile to exploit all the gas fields which could deliver gas at prices the Gas Council could afford. It followed that if the Council calculated that the cost of gas from a 100 mmcf/d field was around 4d per therm there were formidable objections to uniform pricing, without differentiation for size. Further progress on the whole pricing issue could not be made until the Council talked seriously with the companies on the subject. The time for this had now come. It probably did not matter if the price was thought of as cost-related or linked to the long-term market value of the gas, so long as the price settled in the right area. The Ministry would also like the Council to seriously test the two-part tariff scheme with the companies. If the companies would not accept this scheme (or a variant of it) as part of the quota system then the latter might have to be abandoned. The only acceptable alternative combination, of ad hoc contracts based on individual costs, would almost certainly be more distasteful to the companies. Sir Kenneth acknowledged that the Ministry's view was now clear. The Council thought that the average price under a two-part tariff should be low enough to permit gas to be delivered to the Area Boards at a price not exceeding 3d–3.5d per therm. This meant that the price delivered at the beach would be no more than 2.5d per therm, with lower values for interruptible supplies.

Gas Council's views on market absorption

On the subject of market absorption and growth Sir Kenneth indicated that the Council's intention was to build up their traditional markets quickly, but to generate large new industrial demands on the basis of the reserves so far proved would not be wise. They had studied the potential consumption by industry and envisaged that naphtha would first be displaced, then the middle distillates, and then black oil. They could not guarantee that this programme would not indirectly damage the coal market. Oil displaced in one place might well displace coal at another. The Council also noted that if the Government wished to give more definite guidance about the markets to be supplied, a different consumption pattern could be arranged. The gas could be piped to the power stations situated close to the terminals and interruptible loads could be accepted more generally. In the longer term, gas might drive turbines to supply power to cities.

Ministry's views on market absorption

The Ministry's view on market absorption was that currently they were not thinking of allowing gas to be supplied directly to industry by the producers, but if the Gas Council's capacity fell unacceptably short of available supplies this was not impossible. Thus the Council should plan to supply to industry and at the same time see that their traditional markets expanded fast enough. In determining the strategy on absorption the Council was advised to assume that the current duty on fuel oil would remain, and that the potential advantage to the balance of payments from displacing naphtha and other refined oil products was very important in the Government's thinking. The Council was invited to produce its own estimates of the potential savings to the balance of payments on different assumptions about the markets in which gas was used including direct supplies to the CEGB.

Gas Council's views on prorationing scheme

With respect to gas availability Sir Kenneth agreed that the thirty-year depletion period was longer than the optimum, and had been taken to enhance security. The proposed quota system could be modified to shorten the depletion period if substantial new reserves were found over the next few years. The Council was very conscious of another dimension to the availability question. If broad contractual agreement was not reached soon the oil companies would not be ready to deliver gas in 1968 because of the inevitable field investment lead-time to first production.

The Council's market sharing scheme was discussed at some length. The Ministry saw its administrative convenience and equity, but were concerned on a number of counts, including the possibility that the oil companies might reject it, the disincentive to the Gas Council to expand its markets quickly, and the possibility that the Council would be unable to cope if further large reserves were found in a short time period.

The Council argued that the presence of a guaranteed market for some of their gas should give the oil companies comfort. The Council was also planning to give an undertaking to expand its markets to match availability from the companies as quickly as possible. It was admitted that the discovery of enormous reserves would necessitate a fresh examination of the scheme. The Council thus proposed a clause whereby after ten years the operation of the scheme and the price provisions would be reviewed.

The Council provided the Ministry with details of their estimates of the recoverable reserves and prospective production rates from the four main discoveries already made. For the total the range of reserves was from 9.78 tcf to 24.18 tcf. The corresponding range of average daily production rates over the proposed thirty-year depletion period was from 950 mmcf/d to 2,210 mmcf/d.

Ministry advises on next steps

With respect to the next steps the Minister would have to be consulted before the Council proceeded further with negotiations on the central issues. Later, he would wish to consult his colleagues on all the principles involved in the first major contracts. Before that he would want to know the oil companies' reactions to the quota scheme and two-part pricing. He would also want to know the scope for interruptible supplies and direct supplies to industry, and more about the load factor issue from the perspectives of both producers and the Council.

Following consultation with the Minister, Mr Marshall, the Deputy Secretary, wrote to Sir Kenneth emphasising the importance which the Minister attached to being closely informed of the development of thinking on the main policy issues in the negotiations and about the progress of these negotiations. This was so that he was able effectively to discharge his responsibilities for fuel policy. He would need to consult his colleagues on some of the broad implications of North Sea gas pricing. The Minister had no objections to the Gas Council conducting preliminary negotiations on the central issue provided always that it took great care to avoid getting into a position of commitment or near-commitment on policy issues.

The letter proceeded to summarise the Ministry's key concerns as discussed above. Additional emphasis was put on the national benefits of an expansionist gas absorption policy. It was indicated that, given the broader perspective which the Government had compared to the Council, there might from a national viewpoint be overriding advantages in a period of depletion shorter than thirty years. Meanwhile the Minister prepared a paper for the Economic Development Committee which informed his Ministerial colleagues on the current state of play and outlined in some detail the strategy (based on the lines discussed above) which he proposed to adopt towards the contract negotiations with the oil companies. In that paper the Minister was able to include estimated production from a fifth discovery (by Arpet). The plateau aggregate production from all the significant discoveries to date was now estimated by the Ministry to be in the 1,080 mmcf/d–2,900 mmcf/d range.

Continuing high level contact between Ministry and Gas Council

Very frequent high level contact was maintained between the Ministry and the Gas Council, with the former being anxious to ensure that the latter followed its guidelines in negotiations. In a letter to Sir Kenneth in early November Mr Marshall reiterated the Minister's overriding interest in the outcome of price negotiations from the point of view of fuel policy and the effects of the settlement on the economy. It was made clear that the Ministry strongly supported a cost-related approach by the Gas Council to the price negotiations. Guidance was given on possible values. The cost studies undertaken had suggested that on a substantial field with production of 500 mmcf/d a price of around 2d per therm would yield an adequate return, which suggested to the Ministry that the Council's opening proposal would be below 2d per therm. It was again emphasised that it was vital that there should be the closest consultation at all stages. In a further letter to Sir Kenneth on the subject of the timing of a price review the Ministry indicated that, while the Council's view that it should come at the end of the seventh year had some merit, there might be strong arguments in favour of it taking place earlier, depending on the volumes of gas and the prices covered in the early contract. The Council was thus requested to avoid commitment on the issue at the present stage.

Political sensitivity of gas pricing

The subject of the gas contracts, particularly the pricing aspects, had become politically very sensitive. Mr Wilson, the Prime Minister, became concerned about newspaper leaks on the matter. He wanted to maintain Ministerial involvement in the major decisions, but requested that substantial matters requiring Ministerial consideration should be referred to the First Secretary of State, the Minister of Power, and the Chancellor of the Exchequer, rather than be submitted to the Committee on Economic Development. Where differences remained the Prime Minister himself would consider the issue. Mr Wilson also reiterated the Government's position that the Official Steering Group on Energy Policy should consider the instructions to the Gas Council on the price beyond which they must refer back to the Minister before final commitments were made.

Views of companies made public

At this time the oil industry was making its views on the gas contracts issues known publicly as well as privately. Mr David Barran, a Managing Director of the Shell Group, made a speech in New York in November 1966 and argued for the need (1) to take a more realistic view of the contribution which natural gas could make to the UK, and (2) to give a reasonable incentive to the companies to explore the North Sea thoroughly. He was cautious on the medium-term potential for gas production from the North Sea.

Limited progress with Shell and Esso

In mid-November 1966 the Council reported to the Ministry that detailed discussions with Shell and Esso, the licensees on Leman, the largest discovery, were under way but no progress had been made on the price issue. To date they had resulted in little more than arguments about the basis of pricing. The Council was now planning to propose a simple differentiated price structure with 3d for the first 100 mmcf/d followed by 1.5d for the rest, resulting in an average price of 2d for a field with 300 mmcf/d and 1.8d for one with 500 mmcf/d. The Ministry was content with this. The Council had been advised that another element in its purchasing policy, namely to negotiate each year the price for that proportion of the gas on offer which it was able to take, while leaving to subsequent years the negotiation of the price for the remainder of the gas carried forward and then taken up, was probably illegal as it infringed the Restrictive Practices Act. The Council would now probably have to determine at the beginning the price for each field. This made the case for an earlier price review stronger, and the Council was asked to keep the review date open pending the further development of the negotiations. On the above basis the Council was able to open detailed negotiations with Shell and Esso.

Gas Council's detailed proposals to oil companies

The Council then prepared a memorandum on its basic purchasing proposals which was sent to the companies. This made clear that there would be a single contract of the depletion type for each field. It would determine the price to be paid for all of the gas offered from the field (subject to periodic review). This would be in place of the earlier proposal for a series of contract documents which would have included prices for additional quantities taken up each year. There would be a depletion period of 25–30 years with the rate of take building up to an average of $\frac{1}{7300}$ x estimated reserves. The initial load factor proposed would be 60% for the Leman Bank field. Any difference in price between 60% load factor and the optimal load should reflect the additional cost of wells, equipment, and transmission on a cost of service basis. The document indicated that the price structure would be two-part. This was proposed in order to reflect the lower costs of large fields and the need to encourage the development of smaller ones. It would also enhance the cash flow to the producer in the early years when capital expenditure was being recovered. To deal with the problem of the take by the Gas Council exceeding or falling short of the contract figure a scale of values would be drawn up to compensate the producer for deferment of revenue in the case of a low take, and in the case of a high take to recognise the increased use of assets and the consequent shortening of the depletion period.

Further debate between Gas Council and Ministry on basis for pricing

The debate on the conceptual basis for the price between the companies and the Council continued. Sir Kenneth felt that had there been a free market in the licensed areas the commodity rate proposition would have been defensible, as the finder would have been rewarded according to his skill in preliminary surveys and the extent to which he had been prepared to commit his resources to outbidding his rivals in the purchase of concessions. This was not the procedure adopted, however, and licences were awarded on a basis that took into account many factors extraneous to the North Sea, and everyone paid the same licence fee for a block whether it was one like 48/6 for which most people applied, or some for which some did not think it worthwhile even to apply. It was thus reasonable to argue that the fortunate finders of large fields did not buy their licences in a free market, and should be content with a lower average price of gas, especially if this could be shown to give a high DCF rate of return on their investment. The step-rate mechanism in the multi-part tariff scheme was helpful to producers by increasing early cash flows. It should encourage them to continue drilling.

Complications on unitised fields

The multi-part tariff system raised complications when applied to unitised fields (such as Leman Bank and Indefatigable) in each of which separate licence groups had interests. The Gas Council proposed that each group would obtain the benefit of the higher price for the initial tranche of 100 mmcf/d. The Ministry investigated this issue further and prepared a paper on the subject. The focus of the Ministry's attention was on whether the Council's proposal was justified in terms of cost and what extra outlays were involved.

Their starting point was the proposition that the discovery and production of a shared field should cost little if anything more than one in single ownership. There might be some additional costs on appraisal wells to determine the limits of a field prior to unitisation, and there might be slightly higher overheads because of more than one operator. There was a problem with respect to the allowance for exploration which had been employed in estimating the long-run costs of finding a commercial field. This allowance was expressed as a dry hole ratio and in the Ministry's calculations had been set at a relatively high level. The allowance would be used once where a field was in the hands of one licence group, but where two groups were involved it would be given to each group separately. It was recognised, however, that appraisal wells could be dry. This had already happened in the Leman field, and it was acknowledged that there was a significant difference between appraisal wells drilled by the group which made a discovery and wells drilled by another group in a different block. In the first case the appraisal costs should be recovered from production income, but this might not apply to the second group if, as had just happened with the Phillips and Signal groups, the wells were dry. They could claim that the wells should be regarded as being for exploration and thus eligible for the allowance. This argument was not foolproof, and the chances of drilling a dry well located in close proximity to a discovery would be less than in a completely unlisted area.

The extra purchase costs incurred by the Council from the multi-tariff scheme in a unitised field compared to a single field also required consideration. The difference would become greater according to the steepness of the differentiated price scale. Using the cost estimates made by the Ministry the extra outlays falling on the Ministry would be very considerable. In detailed prepared examples the increased cost to the Council was in the 40%–132% range. Using a more moderately differentiated scale the extra cost was in the 9%–51% range.

The Ministry felt that the Council would initially seek to secure a fairly steeply differentiated scale to reflect the costs of exploiting different sizes of fields. The Ministry feared that the oil companies would resist this, and their resistance would be reinforced when they knew that the higher price for the initial tranche was not to be applied to their own gas, but to the whole field and thus shared with other groups. The Council would then be under pressure to concede that the differentiated price structure applied separately to production from each group. In that event the Council had to bear in mind not only the extra cost from the field in question, but the precedent which would be set for other fields.

Much discussion ensued within the Ministry on the design of a price structure which limited the extra cost to the Council from permitting separate block pricing. Various permutations were considered which produced the same revenues to the field investors from whole field and separate field pricing. This included the use of more than two tiers. General findings were that to produce this result the multi-tier system under separate block pricing compared to whole field pricing needed to be (a) far steeper in its initial stage, with a relatively low price for later tranches coming in quite quickly, and (b) lower along all the quantity.

Developing views of oil companies

Meanwhile, some of the oil companies, having engaged in negotiations with the Gas Council, contacted the Ministry to discuss their current views. Shell and Esso indicated that they had offered specified volumes from the Leman field rising to 500 mmcf/d in 1970 and 822 mmcf/d in 1975, but the Council were reluctant to enter into firm commitments above 500 mmcf/d because of the need to keep room for gas from other licensees. Shell/Esso were keen to agree minimum amounts. The quantities offered could not be wholly divorced from the price. Shell/Esso had not accepted the Council's rateable take scheme. The companies were disappointed with the prices offered by the Council (3d per therm for the first 100 mmcf/d and 1.5d for everything above this). The company representatives felt that the debate on whether the conceptual basis of the price should be cost related or market value was now sterile, and that it would probably be best to get down to hard bargaining about actual numbers.

Shortly afterwards the companies reported to the Ministry that they had broadly reached a settlement with the Council on volumes, subject to agreement on price. It might be possible to move nearer on price by changing the quantities involved. Esso had put forward counterproposals on price, namely 4.0375d per therm for 60% load factor, and 3.215d for a much higher load factor (which could be procured by interruptible summer supplies).

Other companies made their views known to the Ministry at this time. Texas Eastern (partners with Amoco and Amerada) indicated that they had found the Council's proposals unacceptable. The price offered might not encourage the development of their discovered field let alone encourage further exploration. In principle Texas Eastern was prepared to consider a price structure related to size of field though they had proposed a price related to achieved load factor. Texas

Eastern stated that they were officially negotiating with the Council separately from their partners, but the Ministry formed the view that they had found ways to coordinate their views. The company was very disturbed by press reports giving details of the Council's offer. They stressed the difficulties which this type of leak caused with their negotiations.

The same press report had been noted by others who interpreted the Council's reported offer quite differently. Dr Thomas Balogh at the Cabinet Office wrote to Mr Pitblado, the Permanent Secretary, Ministry of Power complaining that the price offer should have been discussed more widely within Government before being made. He also thought that the two-part tariff system was insufficiently flexible and that further tiers were more appropriate. In addition he felt that a figure of 1.5d per therm for volumes above 100 mmcf/d was distinctly on the high side and would create an impossible position at the later stages of the negotiations. It would be impossible to go much below 1.5d even if enormous gas fields were discovered.

Further studies in Ministry

The Ministry continued to undertake detailed studies of the effects of different pricing arrangements (uniform and multi-tier) in fields of various sizes and on assumptions of success rates varying from 1 in 10 to 1 in 30. At the beginning of 1967 Chief Scientist's Division was finding that for fields larger than 500 mmcf/d a price of 2d per therm gave an acceptable post-tax return to the investor with a dry hole ratio of 10 to 1. For fields with less than 100 mmcf/d a price of 4d per therm was necessary to produce an acceptable return with a dry hole ratio of 10 to 1.

Review with Gas Council

In early January 1967 a high level meeting was held with Sir Henry Jones to review the situation in the knowledge that negotiations with Shell/Esso and Amoco were imminent. Amoco had provided a memorandum to the Council with calculations showing that, for fields with production of 500 mmcf/d and 100 mmcf/d, and dry hole ratios of 10 to 1, with a price of 4d per therm the post-tax rates of return were 19.4% and 11.8% respectively. It was suggested that a much less optimistic dry hole ratio (such as 27 to 1) would be more realistic, resulting in much lower rates of return.

The Ministry and the Gas Council disputed many of Amoco's assumptions relating to subjects including royalty, investment grants, lead time to first production, compression costs, operating costs, overheads, load factor, production per well, and dry hole ratios. In view of the many uncertainties the Ministry felt that it would be quite unrealistic to attempt to relate the price solely to cost estimates, and that it would be necessary to adopt a somewhat generous approach. But care should be taken not to be generous twice over, once with individual items, and then by adding a margin in the total for the uncertainty involved.

With respect to negotiating tactics the Ministry felt that, at their next meeting with Shell/Esso when the price offer of 4.0375d per therm would be on the table, the Council should not improve its own offer, but should try to convince the companies that it was not prepared to discuss seriously figures in excess of around 3d per therm for a 500 mmcf/d field at 60% load factor. The Council might argue that it could not afford to pay more than this, which would indicate the reality of a market price from the Council's perspective.

Sir Henry Jones reported the results of the Council's last meeting with Shell/Esso. No progress had been made, but the companies had left a detailed paper to support their price offer. Sir Henry was baffled by the lack of progress. He had made it clear that a bid of 4d per therm did not provide a basis for negotiations but he had got no response. Accordingly, he had not been willing to improve on the Council's opening bid. He wondered whether Shell/Esso were waiting for Amoco to make the first move and to ease the way for them. An alternative possibility was that the two companies might not have resolved their own positions. Esso in particular was standing firm on market pricing. Yet another possibility was that the companies were banking on the Gas Council or the Minister giving way.

Mr Marshall discusses issue with Mr Barran of Shell

In the light of the stalemate the Deputy Secretary decided to see Mr David Barran, Managing Director of the Shell Group, to bring home to him the political delicacy of the position and the firmness of the Minister's stand on getting a price which would bring real benefit to the economy. Mr Barran was informed that the Minister would be very troubled that no progress had been made in negotiations, that there was intense political interest in the price for North Sea gas, and the Minister had to satisfy his colleagues, the House, and the public that satisfactory progress was being made. It was emphasised to Mr Barran that all the information available to the Ministry indicated that the companies' proposals did not offer a framework for negotiation. The Minister wanted to encourage continued exploration but he wanted the minimum price compatible with this. In particular, considerations of saving foreign exchange and providing low cost fuel supplies were of the utmost importance. The Ministry felt that the companies' price proposals were not compatible with these objectives. Mr Marshall felt that the concept of market price was meaningless in the context of the Continental Shelf legislation, and, while more meaningful in relation to the UK energy market, had still to be qualified by considerations of national interest, not to mention the need to expand the gas market if large quantities of gas were to be absorbed quickly.

Mr Barran understood the delicacy of the Minister's position, and hoped that the companies would not have to ask him to intervene. He hoped that the information which the companies had provided would help to narrow the gap between them. He pointed out that the negotiations presented difficulty because there were no points of reference for pricing such as existed in most oil transactions. He was also aware that if he were to make an important concession in order to get negotiations moving he had no means of telling whether the Gas Council would respond with some improvement on their terms or whether he would just have lost much of his bargaining position. He emphasised that the Council's offer totally failed to make the project worthwhile by comparison with other investment opportunities. With the greatest of caution he hinted at a price of 2.7 or 2.8d as possible if load factors and other material considerations could be got right. Mr Barran welcomed the idea of a differentiated price structure, but it would have to start higher than the Council's offer. The structure would have to be related to field size. Mr Barran undertook to bring about real negotiations in the very near future.

Meeting with Amoco negotiating team

A meeting was also held with senior members of the Amoco negotiating team at this time. The team was informed that the Ministry was deeply disturbed by reports of Amoco's price offer which made no kind of sense judged by criteria of national interest and which would yield ridiculously high returns. It was emphasised to the company that if it would recognise the necessity to have regard to the British national interests, particularly relief to the balance of payments and the provisions of low cost energy, they need not fear that the Minster would seek to grind them down to impossibly low rates of return, as this would frustrate his other objective of encouraging further exploration.

The senior Amoco representative (based in New York) emphasised that they would stay in the UK only if they obtained a return adequate in relation to opportunities elsewhere. They were expanding fast internationally and were not finding it easy to raise the necessary capital. A sensible agreement with the Council would help to promote a steady expansion in the UK. A new offer would be put to the Council in the near future. The differentiated pricing structure was welcome. They disliked the cost-related approach, and preferred a market-related approach reflecting the statutory and economic conditions of the UK market. It was agreed, however, that too much emphasis should not be placed on the method of approach as both parties had to consider costs and market conditions. Amoco also hoped that it would not be necessary for the Minister to intervene.

Ministry updates studies

The Ministry updated their studies on the possible costs and returns from the hypothetical fields under different price conditions. These were quite detailed. In general the Ministry was satisfied that its cost estimates were, if anything on the high side. Their findings in late January 1967 were that an average price of 2.5d per therm was generally enough on a 500 mmcf/d field to provide adequate incentives to investors. Prices above that were mentioned as being worthy of consideration in order to ensure agreement. The Minister of Power, Mr Marsh, sent a detailed Minute to the Prime Minister outlining the current position and his proposals. He summarised the background, highlighting the Gas Council's initial offer of 3d per therm for the first 100 mmcf/d and 1.5d for the remainder, giving an average of 1.8d for a 500 mmcf/d field with 60% load factor. Shell/Esso proposed 4d + per therm and Amoco 5d + per therm. After some negotiations Amoco were now proposing fractionally under 4d per therm, while Shell/Esso had made no further proposal. The Minister felt that the area of serious negotiation lay between 2d and 3d per therm. The difference in pricing philosophy had been a stumbling block. No progress could be made until the companies made a decisive move down to 3d or thereabout, though it was too early to say whether this figure would be a final settlement value or an important step towards one.

Minister's response to Gas Council's updated views

The Gas Council's latest views were that their original average price proposal of 1.8d was now no longer tenable as providing adequate incentives. The Chairman was now proposing an average price of 2.2d as a basis for realistic negotiations. He had been influenced after consideration of Amoco's calculations. To date he had been bound by the Minister's guidance to seek a solution in the 2d–2.5d range. Sir Henry had come to the conclusion that this range was no longer reasonable or realistic and that 2.5d was not the maximum but the minimum at which a price might be negotiated. Sir Henry was now suggesting that the range in which a settlement might be found was 2.5d to 3d rather than 2d to 2.5d. The Minister himself felt that earlier estimates had been on the low side. He therefore intended to tell Sir Henry that his aim should be to go all out for a settlement at around 2.5d. Offers in excess of this figure would be subject to further consultation with the Minister so that he could consider its effects on the Government's position in case he had to intervene.

Mr Marsh felt that this approach was preferable to personal intervention by himself. This possibility remained but the companies were anxious to avoid this and they knew his attitude to the negotiations. This included the need for his approval of any price before a deal was concluded.

Inter-departmental discussions

An inter-departmental meeting, involving Dr Balogh of the Cabinet Office and representatives of the Department for Economic Affairs (DEA) and Treasury, was then held to discuss the situation. The Ministry of Power representatives reported that the latest information was that the existing discoveries were capable of producing around 3,000 mmcf/d. A main point made was the need for a price structure with a relatively low level in relation to higher levels of output to ensure that unnecessarily high prices were not paid for very large fields. It was also necessary for the price paid for gas from smaller fields not to be so high that it could not readily be absorbed by the gas industry.

The news that the Ministry was planning to raise the price it was prepared to accept from the oil companies was received with alarm by Dr Balogh. In a letter to Mr Marshall he expressed the view that, given the Ministry's findings that an average price of around 2.2d per therm offered the prospect of a return of 25%

after tax, there was no need to offer more just because the companies had been a little tough. Given that the decision to change stance had effectively been made the way to retrieve the situation from the Government's viewpoint would be to impose a tax on gas production at, say, 1d per therm. This would prevent the economic rent from being left in the hands of the companies.

The Chancellor also submitted his views on the Minister of Power's plan to the Prime Minister. He was concerned that the guidelines to the Council should be clarified to ensure that the consultation about any offer in excess of 2.5d was not prejudiced in advance. He also thought that the price structure should incorporate a relatively low value for large volumes to avoid paying a relatively high price if very large volumes were found. It would be preferable to concede a fairly high initial price to get this result.

Shortly afterwards a meeting was held involving the First Secretary of State, the Chancellor of the Exchequer, and the Minister of Power to discuss the subject further. Mr Marsh outlined the current position with respect to the price negotiations. Mr Jenkins felt that the key question was the rate of return which the companies could expect. A figure in the region 20%–25% seemed reasonable compared to the net rate of return of around 10% which British oil companies were earning on their world-wide activities. In further discussions it was suggested that a price of 2d per therm would produce a handsome return on the capital employed, particularly in a stable country such as the UK, but a premium on this would be necessary to incentivise further exploration.

The Ministers were then joined by officials from the DEA, Treasury, Ministry of Power and Cabinet Office. Dr Balogh argued that at a price of 2.5d the oil companies' rate of return would be around 30%. This might be acceptable so long as the price was sharply reduced for volumes in excess of 500 mmcf/d from a field. The representative from the DEA suggested that the final settlement should be below 2.5d. The Ministry of Power representative argued that the Council would have to offer at least 2.25d to engage the companies in serious negotiation. A rate of return in the range 25%–30% for a 500 mmcf/d field was probably consistent with a price of 2.5d which would be reasonable. After further Ministerial discussions it was agreed that the Minister of Power should authorise the Gas Council to negotiate with the oil companies on the understanding that the final (average) price for a 500 mmcf/d field should not exceed 2.5d per therm, and that such a settlement should take into account the rate of return, the load factor, and reductions in price for volumes exceeding 500 mmcf/d from a field.

Personal intervention of Mr Marsh with oil companies

By early February 1967 Mr Marsh had decided that, in order to advance negotiations, he should personally intervene and see the oil company representatives. Negotiations between the Council and the Shell/Esso and Amoco groups had been proceeding (separately) since the summer of the previous year. A substantial measure of agreement had been reached on the terms other than price, such as depletion period, build up period, and load factor. Progress had been slow because the negotiators were breaking new ground, and both parties were anxious to agree terms which would set precedents for future fields. There had recently been some movement in the prices offered by the companies. Amoco's revised average price was now 3.83d per therm for a 500 mmcf/d field at 60% load factor. Shell/Esso were now proposing 3.775d per therm for a field with the same characteristics.

The Minister's objective was not to take over negotiations, but to induce the companies to move into a price range which he regarded as realistic, namely 2d–3d per therm for a 500 mmcf/d field. This was thought to be adequate to reward their enterprise and encourage them to further efforts. The Minister had also to consider that the full benefits to the nation would not be secured unless the price was kept as low as possible. The Government had to look at the effect on the balance of payments and the need to reduce energy costs to British industry. Politically there was much interest in the gas price, and it would be impossible for the Minister to agree to the Gas Council paying more than 2d-3d per therm unless it could be clearly demonstrated that this was necessary to give the companies a reasonable return on their investment.

The Minister met senior representatives of Amoco, Texas Eastern, and Amerada in February 1967 and outlined his concerns. On their side the industry representatives had explained that they had modified their price proposals in recognition of the requirement of the Council to make short-term industrial and interruptible sales to absorb the quantities on offer. The industry representatives had quizzed officials on the thinking behind the upper limit of 3d which the Council were prepared to offer. Ministry officials had given the familiar answers to the question, but also emphasised the marketing problems which the Council faced. It was argued that the prices which the companies were seeking would not enable the gas industry to market the gas and achieve the rates of absorption which were now physically possible. This was true even with the gas industry's present financial obligations. In discussions on the economics of the gas fields the Ministry informed the company representatives that on their calculations a price of 2.5d per therm produced a return to the investors in the 21%–31% range depending on specific assumptions made. The company representatives emphasised that their next fields were likely to be smaller, further from the shore, and thus more expensive to develop. They also pointed out that their estimates of capital expenditure were 30% above those of the Gas Council, and their operating costs were 40% higher. Thus their estimates of the expected rates of return were 6–8 percentage points below those of the Council.

Armed with this new information Mr Marsh emphasised the close interest he had been taking in the progress of the negotiations and his concern at the delay in reaching settlements. He was anxious to avoid having to intervene personally to fix a price. He reassured the company representatives that although there were some extremists in Parliament who publicly expressed the hope that the oil companies would be squeezed, the Government's position was that a fair settlement would take account of the risks involved and give a commercial return to the investors. The Amoco group stated that an expected rate of return in the upper part of the 15%–30% range which the Gas Council had indicated, was acceptable to them, but they were concerned that the Council's supporting figures greatly understated the likely costs. On their calculations nothing less than a 3d–4d range was realistic. The Minister responded by saying that he would have to publicly justify whatever figure was agreed. There were many journalists and others familiar with the calculations and he could not begin to defend to them a price in the 3d–4d range. Within Government the Ministry had been criticised for agreeing to an initial offer as high as 1.8d per therm. The Minister felt that the wide difference in price between the parties must be due either to a massive error in the calculations or very different assumptions. He had never met anyone outside the oil companies who did not think that 4d per therm would give a massive return on capital.

The company representatives felt that they could defend a 4d price. To date two factors had been given insufficient weight, namely (1) the lack of knowledge of the North Sea which made it difficult to forecast its future profitability, and (2) the extent to which the experience made the judgement of the oil companies more reliable than those of the Gas Council. The Minister reassured the representatives that the Government gave due weight to the experience of the companies, but would have to be convinced of the reasoning behind any figure. He also emphasised that experience in the North Sea to date had been much better than anticipated. It now looked as though the UK would have at least twice as much gas available in 1970 as it could use, and, to open up new markets, the Gas Council must get a low price conducive to a rapid build-up. The meeting ended with pledges speedily to pursue negotiations.

The Minister also had a meeting with Mr McFadzean of Shell who expressed the view that he himself had been concerned after his company's last meeting with the Gas Council when the latter had been arguing that gas could only be absorbed into the UK market at a price which was not economic for the companies. A cost-related approach could have an adverse effect on Shell's overseas operations because it might encourage other host Governments to adopt the same procedure. The Minister agreed that when a settlement was reached it would be necessary to avoid the suggestion that it was on a cost-related basis. Mr Marsh felt that rates of return in the 20%–30% range were surely attractive. Mr McFadzean's view was that at a price of 3.5d the rate of return might be 10%–17% though much uncertainty surrounded the calculations.

Mr McFadzean felt that one of the problems dealing with the Gas Council was the latter's relative ignorance of the going prices for competing oil fuels. Shell had much knowledge of this and were satisfied that 4d–4.5d per therm on a delivered basis would leave gas competitive. The Minister's response was that gas would have to be markedly cheaper in order to secure the conversions needed to make the necessary inroads into the UK market. Mr McFadzean was concerned that the Government was able to put much pressure on the companies because the latter had already spent considerable sums on the initial developments, but if they were squeezed too far they might not go beyond producing the existing fields. He felt that if there had been a competitive market the price could settle down in the 3d–3.5d range.

The Minister held a separate meeting with Mr Don Cox of Esso who argued that at a price of 2.25d it would hardly be profitable for Esso to develop their known reserves. He thought that a gas price related to the price of imported crude would be fairest and most politically acceptable. With a crude import price of 3.3d per therm North Sea gas might be priced at 3.4d.

Review by Energy Steering Group

Following the meetings with the licensees a Ministerial paper was prepared which was sent to the official Energy Steering Group. This reviewed the present position as noted above and reported on further work undertaken within the Ministry. To break the deadlock Shell had offered to discuss their cost estimates with Ministry officials, hoping to demonstrate that the price they had offered would not on an average field yield unreasonable profits to the producer. Esso had been unwilling as a matter of principle to put forward cost estimates but had agreed to comment on the Ministry's ones. Both companies would not agree to discuss this subject with the Council. Amoco, under pressure had agreed to do this. The discussions had been undertaken in a frank and forthcoming manner and were now completed. They had related to a hypothetical field with characteristics which might represent average conditions likely to be found. The Ministry's view was that the company estimates appeared to include ample margin for contingencies and to be based on a series of somewhat pessimistic assumptions, which, though individually plausible, would be unlikely all to be realised in the average case. The estimates of Shell and Esso were different in detail, but both indicated that a beach price of around 3.5d per therm for 500 mmcf/d at 60% load factor would produce a return in the 15%–20% range. Amoco's calculations suggested that a beach price of 4.3d per therm would give a 23% rate of return. Their data were quite different from those of Shell and Esso, and illustrated the very wide range of assumptions which could be made.

The Ministry had made its own full re-examination of the basis of its estimates of the costs of the hypothetical field of 500 mmcf/d. Their latest estimates indicated that a beach price varying from 1.7d–2.8d per therm would be consistent with rates of return in the 20%–25% range to investors. The range had now widened somewhat without significantly moving its centre point as the result of a number of mutually offsetting changes in the assumptions. It had to be borne in mind that the hypothetical field would probably not be typical of future discoveries. Seismic information and experience elsewhere suggested that they would be smaller and more difficult to produce. For this reason a price structure related to size of field was very appropriate.

Study of market value of gas by Shell and Esso

Shell and Esso had also produced a thorough and detailed study on the market value of the gas. They claimed that even with the larger quantities now expected and the consequent need to find outlets in the general energy market, a beach price of 3.5d per therm would enable the gas industry to absorb the gas without difficulty while earning an 8.75% DCF return on their operations which was higher than its present financial targets. The Gas Council disagreed with this statement. Their view was that with a price exceeding 2.5d there was a serious risk that the rate at which the gas could be absorbed consistent with its financial obligations would be slowed down. The studies of the companies and the Council had estimated gas demand from different categories of consumers over the next 15–20 years. Inevitably there was a large element of uncertainty surrounding the development of the market, and the Ministry was also aware that the assumptions necessary to make the estimates were influenced by their negotiating positions. The Ministry's view was that at prices of 2.5d or less the Council would be able to build up new markets quite rapidly. For prices in the 2.5d–3d range new market penetration became more difficult, but there was still adequate scope for the Council. At prices of 3d and above the gas industry might well have difficulty in expanding sales at sufficient speed in the early years and might be forced into uneconomic sales.

Position of Hewett field

One further new factor had emerged. The Phillips and Arpet groups which shared the Hewett field now had large amounts of gas to offer the Council. Their costs should be very low, and it was possible that they might be ready to offer an attractive price in order to assure themselves of an early share in the market. At the least it brought an additional element of competition into the negotiations.

Updated views of Mr Marsh

In the light of all the evidence the Minister had now formed several views namely, (1) under strong protest some, but not all, companies would be willing to exploit existing discoveries at a price of 2.25d, (2) none of the companies would consider this price adequate to explore the North Sea vigorously, and so their exploration effort would be reduced if a price of 2.25d were enforced, and (3) the companies were probably thinking that a price of around 3d was the minimum required to incentivise further exploration, but they might be induced to accept a figure towards the lower end of the 2.7d–3d range.

Based on all this fresh information the Minister had again discussed the position with Sir Henry Jones who believed that when negotiations resumed the Council should make a further all out effort to negotiate a price of around 2.5d. He feared, however, that this might be unattainable, and felt that a price of up to 2.75d would still bring advantages to the gas industry. The Minister concluded that the Council should be given the opportunity to take the negotiations further up to a limit of 2.6d. He also judged that the companies would be unlikely to willingly accept a price of 2.5d or 2.6d. If such a price were imposed it would have a severely negative affect on exploration. He thought that the companies could be brought to accept a figure up to 2.75d which would be preferable to an imposed solution. The Minister was satisfied that a settlement at this level would still bring great benefits to the economy. Accordingly, in the event that the Council could not reach agreement at around 2.5d, the Minister sought discretion to go up to 2.75d himself.

Reaction of Dr Balogh

The paper provoked a strong reaction from Dr Balogh at the Cabinet Office who sent a Minute to the Prime Minister arguing that on the evidence available there was no case for increasing the price to be offered to the companies; if anything there was a case for reducing it. Any concessions on the price beyond 2.5d should be considered only if a low price were obtained for gas above the 500 mmcf/d level, and if there was a break clause which would reduce the investor's return after a specified period. Dr Balogh also introduced a different argument, namely that the rates of return contemplated for investors were not only indefensibly high from a political viewpoint but would undermine the current prices and incomes policy. The Prime Minister himself felt that the Minister's paper did not provide an appreciation of the economic consequences of his proposals for the economy and energy policy.

Ministerial meeting

The result of the paper was a meeting between the First Secretary of State, The Chancellor, and the Minister of Power on 20th March 1967. Mr Marsh received very substantial briefing for this meeting. This contained some extra arguments and information in addition to those presented in his paper. It was argued that there was no reasonable expectation of finding further gas fields as big as Leman Bank or West Sole in the Southern part of the North Sea. Given the expected growth in gas demand in the 1970s and beyond, a sustained exploration effort would be required as the expected sizes of new fields would be considerably lower. If there were delays in bringing in natural gas from the North Sea there would be a loss of national benefits because industry would have to continue using higher cost feedstock and fuel. If the exploration effort did falter drilling rigs would be moved elsewhere and it would take some time to remount the effort. Under existing legislation there was no means of forcing the licensees to produce gas which they had discovered. Resort to nationalisation would involve very heavy capital expenditure and a severe delay in exploration.

Mr Marsh deployed the above arguments at the Ministerial meeting. The First Secretary of State and the Chief Secretary to the Treasury felt that the new evidence pointed towards a lower rather than a higher offer price. They were impressed with the substantial recent discoveries which meant that with the amount of gas now in prospect there was no need to accelerate the rate of exploration. After tax rates of return in the 20%–25% range were princely by normal standards, and the wide range of cost estimates meant that there would be prospects of returns even higher than this. It was difficult to envisage the companies pulling out with prospective returns of this order. The Chief Secretary now felt that with the new evidence it would be wrong to go beyond 2.25d. The First Secretary had some sympathy with this, but in view of the agreement reached in January he was prepared to adhere to 2.5d. He was quite clear that it would be wrong to go higher, and 2.5d should remain as the Minister's negotiating limit.

This was the decision of the meeting. Mr Marsh considered that the decision was wrong and the threatened dangers were very large. At this stage he would not take the issue to Cabinet, but might do so if events turned out as he feared. The Prime Minster agreed with the decision of the meeting, but requested that an early appreciation should be made of the economic consequences of North Sea gas for UK energy and investment policy, including the National Plan.

Ministry re-assesses situation

Following this decision the Ministry of Power took stock and re-assessed the whole situation. Negotiations would have to proceed on the basis of instructions to the Gas Council that 2.5d price was as far as the Government was willing to go. The Minister now wanted guidance on the consequences of (1) failure to reach agreement for some time, (2) an agreement with one or two producers but not others, and (3) a price which seriously curtailed exploration. Further work was also necessary on the foreign exchange costs and benefits at different gas prices. This would have to take into account different rates of gas absorption and the effects on both oil products and coal use, including the possibility that if gas displaced oil the latter might then displace coal.

The studies required priority within the Ministry. They would be necessary not only to enable the Minister and the Department to meet criticisms, but because the Minister might have to become directly embroiled in price negotiations, might need further discussions with the First Secretary and Chancellor, and might have to put a paper to the Cabinet.

Market value of gas

The Ministry's thinking on gas pricing had started from the view that it might be priced theoretically either according to its market value or to the cost of production. These would set the limits within which a negotiated price would settle. This had remained the Ministry's thinking. It had never made a thorough assessment of the market value of North Sea gas. The Gas Council had expounded two meanings of the concept namely (1) the value of alternative feedstocks for town gas manufacture, and (2) the price at which a given quantity of gas could be absorbed by the gas industry, assuming that the gas industry maintained its virtual monopoly of piped gas distribution. The Ministry had adopted the first of these as the appropriate description and had put this at 4d–4.5d per therm. This was on the assumption that natural gas would primarily displace naphtha.

The Ministry was aware of two other estimates of the market value. Thus A. D. Little had calculated for Amoco that the Gas Council could offer to pay 5d and still profitably dispose of natural gas. Another report by Merrett-Cyrax had estimated that at a price of 4.5d–4.75d natural gas could still compete with heavy fuel oil for the bulk heating market. Estimates had also been made by other potential users indicating that the steel industry put a market value at 4.5d and the petrochemical industry at 3.5d.

Perceived need for price structure

The Ministry had advised, and other Departments had accepted, that the broad aim of policy should be to obtain the gas at the lowest price consistent with encouraging further vigorous exploration. The market value of a 500 mmcf/d field was around 4.5d and the cost of producing it was around 1.25d, but the cost from a field of 100 mmcf/d would be around 4d. A price structure which took this into account was thus clearly necessary. This ruled out a single uniform price. There was virtue in one price structure across fields, and room for debate on how many tiers there might be, as well as how steeply the price fell as production moved into higher bands. There was merit in insisting that the price structure should apply to a whole field, rather than to individual groups in a unitised field. Under the latter arrangement the costs to the Council would escalate substantially. The Council had otherwise been given considerable discretion on the shape of the tariff structure for different production levels.

When the Ministry had recommended to the Council that its opening offers should be 3d for the first 100 mmcf/d and 1.5d for the rest the underlying basis had been 60% load factor, 20 year life, 30:1 dry hole ratio, 32 mile pipeline, and 20 mmcf/d average peak flow per well. This produced a post-tax return of 20%. The Working Party approved some modifications to these assumptions the most important of which was the employment of a 10:1 dry hole ratio.

At this stage in the negotiations there was a need to review again the detailed objectives. For example, should the objective still be to aim for a price structure based on average costs? Were the assumptions on costs appropriate? What would be the smallest size of field which should be developed? Should this be determined by market value? Was the Gas Council expecting to negotiate different prices with the various producers or would it feel committed to the same price for each? Much remained to be done to procure satisfactory agreements.

Reaction of oil companies to decisions of Ministers

Following the decisions of Ministers the Ministry lost no time in informing the producers of the up-to-date position. On 22nd March Mr McFadzean of Shell was told at a meeting with Mr Marshall that the Ministry had re-examined all their cost estimates in the light of their discussions with the licensees and had constructed a fresh set of assumptions. Their new calculations had been based on alternative rates of return for the investors of 20% and 25%. The Minister and his colleagues had been consulted on the resulting area of negotiation over price. The result was that the Minister felt that the possible range was still 2d–3d per therm, but that the eventual settlement should lie in the lower part of that range.

In reply Mr McFadzean said that he was quite unable to understand the Ministry's attitude. He felt that his company had tried honestly to explain their cost estimates and had put all their cards on the table. They had not seen the Ministry's new figures or had an opportunity to comment on them, and yet they were being faced with what amounted to a dictated price. He could only regard this as a breach of faith which would have repercussions of a far-reaching nature in other parts of the world. He had anticipated that the discussions would lead to the cost-related figures moving to approach the market price, but instead they had gone backwards. Mr McFadzean was not placated by the protestations of the Ministry that the bottom end of the cost range had been ignored and the objective was to encourage further exploration. Mr McFadzean felt that a figure of 2.5d could not be regarded as market-related. It bore no relation to prices in the industrial market on which Shell was well informed, and could only be regarded as a dictated price on an expropriation or salvage basis. He could see no point in resuming negotiations with the Gas Council on these terms. Mr McFadzean felt strongly on the issue and subsequently sent his own record of the meeting to the Ministry.

At a separate meeting on the same day Mr Cox of Esso was also informed of the conclusions of Government after their thorough review of the evidence. Mr Cox responded that the Minister's conclusions on the price range for negotiation had come as a complete shock and was deeply distressing. He would like to have a fuller understanding of the reasons behind the conclusions. He was reassured that the Ministry wished to encourage further exploration, but responded that the current suggestions were not helpful in this respect.

Shortly afterwards a further meeting took place between Mr Marsh and senior officials, with Mr Barran and Mr McFadzean of Shell. The Minister explained that the Government had been forced into the position of taking a view on the acceptable price and it would be necessary for Shell to consider whether it would be better for them to continue negotiating with the Gas Council, despite the fact that the Government had taken control of the negotiations.

Mr Barran explained that Shell had entered the North Sea on the basis that there would be a market for the gas. Their assessment was based on the need for a rapid expansion of the market and the price of 3.5d–4d which they had offered took this into account. It was considerably lower than the current price of naphtha which was 4.75d. Following the failure to reach agreement with the Gas Council the technical discussions on costs offered the prospect of breaking the impasse. These revealed significant differences between the parties. Shell had been anticipating further discussions to resolve the differences, and were dismayed to have heard the Government's findings that a price range of 2d–2.5d was still appropriate. This had left Shell in a difficult situation as their investment decisions had been made on considerably higher prices. He added that, if the Government were to insist on this level, which Shell considered unjustified both on a cost-related and a market-related basis, then the whole future of the project would have to be reconsidered. Mr Barran then added that, before doing this Shell intended to discuss actual prices with particular industrialists to see what they would in fact be prepared to pay, and, if as they expected, they were confirmed in their view that they could sell profitably direct to industry, they would apply for permission to do so under Section 9 of the 1964 Act.

Mr Marsh emphasised that the Government had done its own independent technical assessment of the costs, but the conclusion was that the 2d–2.5d price range was consistent with returns to investors in the 15%–30% range. In recent months the Gas Council had also become more convinced that it would have difficulty in profitably selling gas bought at a price above this range. In the light of all this the Minister could not see how the Government could go above a figure of 2.5d.

Both parties agreed that further discussions on differences in costs for model fields and on the appropriate assumptions regarding taxation were desirable. Mr McFadzean added, however, that, if the Government insisted on a price of 2.5d, then Shell would have to pull out of the North Sea. Mr Barran confirmed this, and also described it as a crushing blow to their aspirations. He added that it would not be possible for Shell to agree on such a low price with the Gas Council, and it would therefore have to be an adjudicated price. He then emphasised the dangers for British overseas oil investments, meaning that, if it came out that the Government regarded a rate of return of, say, 20% as being reasonable, then other Governments would be in a stronger position to argue for a much higher slice of the selling price. In turn this would lead to upward pressure on prices for consuming countries.

The outcome of the meeting was that further technical discussions between the parties would take place. Mr Barran reiterated his view that the Gas Council was putting too much stress on the need for cheap prices to secure a rapid build up of the market and did not appreciate the difficulties of basing 30-year contracts on such prices. A possible resolution to this problem was the price review clause which to date had only been discussed in a general way.

A further meeting was held with senior representatives of Esso on 10th April 1967. Coincidentally, a report had appeared that day in a newspaper stating that the Minister had decided that the price should be 2.5d per therm. Mr Marsh emphasised to Esso that neither he nor his Department were responsible for the story and that there had been no talk in any Government Department of nation-alising North Sea enterprises. The Minister added that the capital the Government would need for this would be colossal and unavailable at this time. The Esso representatives (Mr Campbell and Mr Cox) also denied that they were behind the newspaper report and emphasised that it was not in their interests to have spon-sored it. They considered that a price in the lower half of the 2d–3d range could not be justified as a commercial or market-related one. Such a price would inevi-tably appear to be imposed, and, as such, would lead them to a fundamental re-examination of their position.

The Minister emphasised that both his Department and the Gas Council had been working out prices which would provide investors with returns in the 15%–30% range. These were much higher than the average earned in industry generally. The Esso representatives expressed disappointment that their company's willingness to reveal their cost estimates had not led to an upward movement in the Ministry's views on an appropriate price. It was accepted that the large gap between the parties was substantially due to basic differences in judgement regarding costs. The Esso representatives stated, that, while they had discussed rates of return, they adhered to a market value approach, and considered that the world-wide commercial practice of relating the price of natural gas to other sources of gas should have been followed. The Gas Council were currently obtaining gas from naphtha at about 6d per therm and from imported LNG at 5.5d per therm. Esso now proposed to look at the industrial market in the UK and it was possible that they would seek the Minister's consent under the 1964 Act to supply industry.

The Minister indicated that the companies were quite free to examine the industrial market. He thought that it might be preferable from their viewpoint to keep the semblance of negotiations going, so that the final price, imposed or not, should be presentable as a negotiated price. In fact he felt that it would be advantageous if the companies continued discussions with the Gas Council and Government, and, when the price did become publicly known, both sides would know clearly the full reasons for any gap between them.

Detailed cost studies and meetings with companies

The result was a series of meetings at frequent intervals between the parties. The Ministry reviewed their assumptions on costs following meetings with Shell and Esso in particular, and also with the Gas Council which prepared its own estimates. The studies and related meetings on costs involved an extraordinary amount of detail. The concept in the studies was to concentrate on a hypothetical field producing at an average rate of 500 mmcf/d over a plateau period of 20 years at a load factor of 60%. The field would be located 50 miles offshore and the production horizon would be 8,000 feet. Estimates (which were vigorously debated among the parties) were made of the various cost elements including exploration and production wells, production platforms, pipelines, operating costs, and overhead costs. Further estimates were made about well productivity, numbers of dry wells, appraisal wells, and well replacements, taxation (including reliefs for the various cost items), and investment grants.

Summarising the position on areas of disagreement among the parties at 9th May the Ministry highlighted all main cost elements. For exploration the Ministry were assuming a dry hole ratio of 9:1 while Shell and Esso considered 10:1 to be appropriate. The Ministry put the average drilling cost at £720,000 while Shell and Esso considered £800,000 appropriate. There were also significant differences with respect to development well costs, and well productivity. On the subject of well productivity the Gas Council had more optimistic views than both the Ministry and the investors. With respect to platform and production facilities differences in cost partly related to different assumptions regarding the appropriate number, combination, and location of dehydration and compression facilities. There were also differences in several other items.

The Ministry's views on pricing were now based on returns to the investor at the wellhead of 20% and 25%, with 15% being allowed for the pipeline and shore terminal on the grounds that the latter involved less risk. This equated to total rates of return of 19% and 24%. Because the Ministry had agreed to some cost increases it was felt that the contingency element to be covered in the rate of return was now less, and so the 20% return case was the more relevant one.

Direct sales to industry and meaning of "reasonable price"?

Shell had informed the Minister that it planned to examine the price at which gas could be sold directly to industry. The Minister did not have to consent to this unless he was satisfied that the Council had been given the opportunity to buy the gas at a "reasonable price". Because the term was not entirely clear there was a possibility that there could be a legal challenge to the view that the Minister took. The Ministry felt that they needed to obtain a legal opinion on the matter. There was a possibility that Shell would find customers willing to pay (beach) prices in excess of the 2d–2.5d which the Ministry thought reasonable. The Ministry thought it unlikely that a court would find against Ministerial views in such cases (based on other historic cases), but as a precaution legal opinion was desirable.

The legal advice from the Law Officers was to the effect that the meaning of the term "reasonable price" in the current context was not necessarily the value of the gas to the Council. It could be strongly argued that the term referred to a price that represented no more than a proper return to the producers. Given the current policy it was likely that the Minister's position would be upheld. On another aspect the Law Officers found it difficult to imagine that the Minister would want to refuse permission to producers to supply gas to industrial users where the Council or Area Board had refused to take such gas at a lower price. If this became a real possibility he would like to consider the position in the light of the Minister's grounds for refusal.

Concern at slow progress and possible ministerial intervention

The Ministry was becoming increasingly concerned at the lack of conclusions to the negotiations. One possibility was that the oil companies might be employing delaying tactics to put pressure on the Government and Council to make concessions. The Ministry fully acknowledged that delays caused difficulty for the gas industry as well. If it were to absorb the volume of gas likely to be available in the 1970s it would not only have to increase sales to large premium industrial users, but would also have to find new outlets to non-premium markets at prices which were competitive with heavy fuel oil. The Council had been investigating these markets, but, until beach prices had been agreed, firm prices to potential customers could not be offered and neither could firm marketing arrangements. If agreements with producers continued to be delayed the gas industry's ability to develop new markets would at the least be delayed, and at the worst some permanent loss of market penetration could be experienced.

The Minister had come to the view that he might well have to intervene before the end of 1967. He had no statutory right to impose a price: he could not compel the producers to supply gas to the Council at a price which he felt was reasonable. A statement of what he thought was a reasonable maximum price could result in accusations that he had behaved improperly. These considerations made it difficult for the Minister to intervene formally.

But if formal action did become necessary the best procedure might be for the Council to make a final offer with the Minister perhaps informing Parliament that this had been done with his approval. The oil companies would not have to accept the offer, and might well respond by applying to sell the gas directly to UK industrial consumers or even to export it. The Minister would have to give the producers time and opportunity to prepare their case. The use of the final offer might thus not end the matter. Further difficulties could readily emerge because a price for the gas would only be meaningful in the context of other terms such as load factor, build-up, length of plateau, and provisions for price review. A price stated in isolation would lead to endless difficulties.

There was thus merit in avoiding formal intervention except as a very last resort, and to rely on more informal pressure to produce a settlement. The oil companies could be warned by the Minister that he expected them at least to settle heads of agreement by the end of 1967, otherwise he would have to intervene. Such an eventuality might even be worse for the companies than an agreement negotiated with the Council. The Minister might inform Parliament of his decision to set a deadline to the negotiations. This was essentially a political decision.

The situation was reviewed again within the Ministry a few days after the above thoughts on Ministerial intervention were composed. Substantial progress was reported in negotiations on all contract terms apart from price with Shell/Esso, Amoco, and the Arpet group. There was growing optimism that heads of agreement could be reached within a few weeks. The Gas Council thus did not want the Minister to intervene as this would upset the negotiations. It was agreed within the Ministry that the Council should proceed with the negotiations, but that they be informed that the most significant items should be discussed before irrevocable commitments were made.

In discussions on the possibility of formal Ministerial intervention the Ministry's legal adviser pointed out that the Minister had no legal powers to impose a price, though these could be given to him by further legislation. Mr Marshall indicated that the limits of the Minister's powers would be emphasised to him, and that it would be preferable that he pressed the companies privately to reach agreement by the end of 1967. Mrs Spencer of the Ministry argued that, while freely negotiated contracts were clearly desirable, if these broke down further legislation would have to be seriously considered. The Minister had clear responsibilities for the maintenance of gas supplies, and the gas industry's plans assumed that North Sea gas would be available. Another possible problem was that the Council might desire to agree terms which were not satisfactory to the Minister.

Ministry officials decided to advise the Minister to see the oil companies in the near future. The possible need for further legislation should be reviewed in mid-November.

Gas Council reports on progress

The Gas Council reported progress in the negotiations to the Ministry on 10th October. Shell/Esso were no longer talking about a price structure and had withdrawn their offer of valley gas. They were concentrating on an average price (which could subsequently be dressed up in any desired form). The companies had in mind a price fractionally under 3d per therm. Progress on other terms had been very considerable, but they had made it clear that if the Minister imposed a price these would no longer stand. The companies were also anxious to secure a strong tax clause on the grounds that if this were not included the Government could "nationalise" their interest by the back door by imposing a stiff tax which would make their operations uneconomic.

Mr Hetherington informed the Ministry that he had hinted to Shell/Esso that he would be willing to recommend an agreement at fractionally over 2.5d per therm, and had informally suggested a price of 2.75d for the first 300 mmcf/d, 2.5d for the remainder, and 2d for valley gas.

Amoco had also been talking in terms of an average price just below 3d. They were attaching great importance to a clause on devaluation. The company was firmly of the view that sterling would be devalued in the near future. The discussions with Arpet and Phillips had got bogged down in legalities. It was possible, but not certain, that they were deliberately aiming to keep behind the other groups.

Mr Hetherington's overall impression of the negotiations was that Shell and Esso might be prepared to settle at 2.7d per therm. The Gas Council were, of course, inhibited from reaching agreements at a price exceeding 2.5d without Ministerial approval. The companies were well aware of this. The continued lack of agreement was causing the gas industry increasing embarrassment. From the Council's viewpoint a quick agreement at an average price of 2.7d per therm for five years might be preferable to prolonged negotiations aimed at getting a somewhat lower price.

Further views of Amoco

Meanwhile the negotiations continued. In early October, Mr Morrow of Amoco visited Mr Marshall and informed him that his company had taken a very difficult decision to proceed with engineering developments in the North Sea to the value of £30 million. The positive decision meant that it was most important that the price negotiations should be concluded in the near future. On the price issue Mr Morrow indicated that Amoco would now seek a settlement at a price marginally below 3d. He thought that a price of 2.7d might be acceptable to the Council. Mr Marshall was pleased to hear Mr Morrow's news, and emphasised that the

Minister was not willing for the present uncertainty to drag on beyond the end of 1967, and would if necessary take action to bring about a settlement.

Discussions with Gas Council on negotiations

Mr Marshall met with the Chairman and senior executives of the Gas Council on 16th October to review the situation. The Council had recently engaged in further discussions with Shell/Esso. On matters other than price substantial agreement had been reached. Outstanding items also included force majeure, gas quality, and price review. The companies had stated that if the Minister intervened the terms which had been discussed would no longer stand. The Council felt that on price there could be no progress until the companies reinstated their offer of valley gas. The companies agreed that the price for this would be lower, but not to the extent that the Council wanted. There followed some informal and inconclusive discussion of an average price in the 2.7d–2.75d range, but it ended with neither side having altered their formal offer of 3.5d and 2.3d. Mr Hetherington's interpretation was that if the Council were to offer 2.7d with 2d for valley gas it could be accepted.

Mr Hetherington also reported on the latest talks with Amoco. The company would not contemplate a price below 2.2d for valley gas. A non-price clause on the obligations on the producer to maintain gas deliveries had caused difficulties. The company wanted the unqualified right, at six months notice, to reduce deliveries of gas if they were uneconomic, and this should not be an item which could be arbitrated. The Gas Council had obtained commitments by Shell/Esso to maintain supplies for fifteen years. Amoco did not feel that they should make a similar commitment because the Council already had rights under the joint operating agreement to continue production on taking over the partners' assets at cost.

Mr Hetherington reported that all the US companies were very concerned at the risk of sterling devaluation. While Shell/Esso were rather less concerned they attached much importance to a tight tax protection clause. They were very concerned that there should be no loophole for backdoor nationalisation by taxation. The recent endorsement by the Labour Part of a National Hydrocarbons Corporation had reinforced their suspicions.

With respect to future tactics Mr Hetherington felt that a price of 2.7d for the first 300 mmcf/d from Leman Bank, and 2.5d for everything in excess, with 2.0d for valley gas could constitute an offer with prospects of producing an agreement. Sir Henry Jones felt that a price of 2.7d left him a bit uneasy, but it might be preferable for the gas industry to settle for this rather than face prolonged uncertainty. The industry could probably live with this outcome.

Mr Marshall responded that the Minister would accept 2.5d but it was doubtful whether he would agree to 2.7d for all of the Leman Bank field. This might have to be extended to all fields. The Minister might, however, be willing to accept 2.7d for a tranche of production. Sir Henry Jones said the Council would continue negotiations in the hope of reaching agreement at 2.6d. It was agreed that a satisfactory price review clause should be developed.

Price review clause

The Ministry gave immediate attention to this issue. It was recognised that there were difficulties in producing provisions which were precise, particularly as the more easily measured factors such as inflation rates were likely to point to price increases. The elements would have to include cost factors, but there were difficulties in precise specification. It was also most likely that reference to a recoverable gas tax would have to be included. The oil companies were being very insistent on including a watertight clause which would enable them to pass on to the Council any tax imposed on them related to the quantity of gas. As noted above this was to allay their fears that the Government would impose further taxes on them. From the Council's viewpoint there was a danger that this could result in financial problems. They wanted a safeguard, and this could be provided for by ensuring that the imposition of such a tax would be incorporated in the price review.

The Ministry proposed that reviews could be undertaken after five years from contract signature and then after ten years. In conducting the reviews the parties should have regard to several factors, particularly (1) costs incurred or anticipated within the next five years in exploiting the gas, (2) changes in prices paid by consumers for fuels competing with gas (thus affecting the gas industry's ability to sell gas), (3) changes in the sterling/dollar exchange rate, (4) changes in the UK retail price index, and (5) changes in any recoverable gas tax. The Ministry felt that if no agreement had been reached within a specified time (say three months) the matter should be referred to arbitration. The Ministry was also of the view that extra or special reviews could be required by either party to the agreement in circumstances where there was a change of 20% or more in any of factors (2)–(4) noted above or in the recoverable gas tax when the latter had the effect of increasing the price paid by the gas buyer by more than 20%.

Legislation for price determination by Minister

At this time thought was also given to the legislation which would be required to enable the Minister to set gas prices. It was recognised that there was no existing statutory power which enabled the Minister to determine the price at which North Sea gas was to be sold to the Council nor to require the licensees to supply gas at that price. The only formal permissible action under existing legislation would be to arrange that the Council made a final offer, which could be publicised, in the hope that the companies would feel obliged to accept. There was a concern that the companies might procrastinate and pursue the possibility of selling direct to industry. They might even make formal application to do this. To forestall these possibilities further legislation was required.

The most obvious action would be to amend Section 9 of the Continental Shelf Act, 1964 by deleting the current provisions and instead provide that gas produced in the North Sea had to be supplied to the Gas Council, and that, in the event of a dispute regarding price, either party could refer the matter to the Minister for determination. These provisions would reduce the bargaining power of the oil companies and give the Minister a direct role in the price negotiations. The necessary legislation, while controversial, would be simple. The Ministry felt that it could actually be carried through without serious embarrassment to the Minister, and hence would represent a credible threat.

It was understood that this route had some disadvantages. Thus companies not involved in the dispute would suffer removal of their rights to use or supply gas for petrochemical purposes or to use it themselves. This could be regarded as high-handed retrospective changes in legislation that disadvantaged some companies which had already made investment commitments. Example companies would be ICI and Courtaulds which had entered the North Sea in the hope of finding gas to be used as a feedstock.

In the light of this less drastic legislative action might be considered. The main existing terms would be kept, but additions made to enable either party to refer the issues of contract dispute to the Minister for resolution. The Minister would be enabled to determine "reasonable price" as discussed in the 1964 Act. Having done this the Minister would then not consent to the use of the gas by the licensee unless he was satisfied that the Gas Council had been given the opportunity of buying at the determined price all the gas not required for the purposes for which his consent was currently sought. The advantage of this amendment was that the rights of parties not involved in the dispute were broadly preserved. It was acknowledged, however, that this amendment was complicated, and might have less of a deterrent effect on the oil companies.

There were wider considerations in introducing this amending legislation. All the perceived loopholes would not be closed, as there would be no power to require the oil companies to supply the Gas Council on the terms determined by the Minister. Thus it would still be legally open to them to shut in their wells and sit tight, in the hope that passage of time (and perhaps a General Election) would bring about a change in the Government's attitude. It was understood that this loophole could not be closed by directing the companies to supply gas to the Council. They might claim that the conditions were not practicable or were uneconomic. It would then be necessary to have further legislation which would confer on the Minister the power to require a licensee to deliver gas to the Council from named fields in named quantities and in other defined conditions. There would also have to be provision for arbitration if the licensee felt the conditions were inconsistent with good oil field practice. Further, there would have to be an option available to the licensee to relinquish his licence in return for compensation in circumstances where he claimed that compliance with the Minister's requirements rendered the activity uneconomic.

Such legislation would be both complex and controversial. It could be questioned whether it was worth embarking down this route. If the need clearly arose it might be simpler to proceed straight to the ultimate deterrent of nationalisation. This, of course, would be intensely controversial, and would drastically slow down the introduction of natural gas. Both this route and the complex alternative discussed above should not be contemplated except as a last resort.

Discussions with other Departments

Meanwhile the Ministry had been informing other Departments about progress. Mr Marshall informed representatives of the Treasury, Cabinet Office, and DEA at a meeting on 24th October 1967 that price discussions were at long last moving towards a conclusion. As evidence of this Shell had indicated that a price just below 3d could be negotiated. This could be regarded as a breakthrough into a negotiating range, and a price of 2.8d seemed a distinct possibility. Dr Balogh disputed this interpretation and referred to the conclusion of Ministers in March that negotiations should not go above 2.5d for 500 mmcf/d. An average price of 2.8d for more than 1,000 mmcf/d from Leman Bank was quite different. The whole basis of the negotiations had been changed by the Ministry. Mr Marshall denied that there had been a departure from the instructions of Ministers, and emphasised the great step forward that even informal talk of prices below 3d represented. One party could not dictate price to the other, and negotiations could proceed only in steps. The Ministry was working on calculations of the adjustments that would be necessary to make the present offers consistent with the costs previously presented to Ministers.

Dr Balogh was unconvinced regarding the stance of the Ministry, and informed the Prime Minister and the Secretary of State for Economic Affairs that an average price of 2.5d per therm for all gas (compared to 2.5d for only the first 500 mmcf/d per day) represented a major concession to the oil companies. He emphasised both the extra foreign exchange burden and the likelihood that a unitary price would discourage exploration in deeper waters. The Prime Minister responded by asking the Minister of Power to report to Ministerial colleagues on the current situation.

Ministry prepares detailed paper

The Ministry prepared a paper on the current position for discussion with other Departments and Ministers. After reviewing the historic situation it was felt that Shell/Esso would conclude a contract at 2.85d and might agree to 2.7d. Amoco might also settle for this figure. The Government might be able to force the price down towards 2.5d without resultant major adverse effects on exploration, but attempts to push the price below this would result in a reduction in the exploration effort. It should be noted that the effective royalty and tax take approximated to 50% and so the Government shared in any higher price received by the companies.

The Ministry's latest calculations indicated that at prices in the 2.5d–2.7d range the oil companies could obtain rates of return upwards of 20% on conservative assumptions. But such returns were by no means exceptional. High returns on successes had to pay for the inevitable failures. It was recognised that, from the viewpoint of foreign companies, political risks of investing in the North Sea (including possible devaluation) did exist, though they were much less than in developing countries. As far as future prospects were concerned it was expected that any discoveries would yield lower returns than Leman Bank. Thus prices in the range 2.5d–2.7d would cut out the smaller and more distant prospects.

A further consideration was that the companies would now be examining the situation overseas especially in the Netherlands. The export price at the Dutch border was between 3.4d and 3.8d per therm, depending on load factors and volumes, and it was to be expected that investors, particularly those with Dutch interests, would not want to see this price eroded via British contracts. Wellhead prices were around the equivalent of 2.7d. It was felt that, for new fields, the prospects of getting an export price of 3d per therm or more made this a very attractive alternative to exploration on the UK side of the North Sea. It was understood that most of the major companies active in the UKCS had applied for licences in the Dutch sector.

Sir Henry Jones had indicated that an average price of 2.7d was tolerable for all gas currently felt likely to be available by 1973, though he was much more comfortable with 2.5d. His advice would most probably be to accept a price not exceeding 2.7d. As far as the wider economy was concerned the Ministry was still confident that the balance of payments would gain from settlements in the above range.

Currently the Minister had no powers to impose a price, nor had he powers to oblige the producers to supply gas to the Council at a price which he thought reasonable. Neither side could directly enforce its will on the other. The results of a major reduction in development and exploration efforts would clearly be serious for the gas industry. The build-up by 1970 might then be to an annual rate of only around 800 mmcf/d which was half the amount otherwise expected to be available by 1971. The consequences would be that, not only would the current plans for expanding the industrial gas market have to be deferred, but substantial extra investment would have to be made in gas making plant using naphtha as a feedstock. The radical idea that the Government itself could take over the reserves and develop them through a state organisation would involve substantial delays.

The repercussions of this scenario for the balance of payments would probably be adverse at least for ten years, due principally to the reduction in inward capital flows and the outward flow of funds relating to compensation for nationalisation. In this context it was pertinent to note that the benefit to the UK economy from a price cut was only around 50% of the reduction, the difference representing the royalty and tax take. It was thus not in the national interest to push the companies beyond the point where they would not develop their fields. Even if they did do this but stopped further exploration the consequences would be serious, given the need for further discoveries to meet projected demand in the second half of the 1970s.

The Ministry also felt that the oil companies would not lightly provoke a showdown with Government. Some of them had already spent considerable amounts on field developments and exploration, and they would not want to risk losing expected future profits by pressing the issue to the point where the Government was driven to expropriate their interests. A long delay in reaching agreement was also not in their interests. They would also be sensitive to public opinion, and were aware that the UK was one of their largest markets for petroleum products. They also recognised that the Government had always supported them in their relations with other Governments.

With regard to the price structure the Ministry felt that, when an average price had been agreed, a structure could then be devised which provided adequate incentives to the companies to explore for and develop smaller, higher cost fields, without at the same time paying too much for the lower cost ones. A block pricing system varying with production per field, involving a relatively high price for the first tranche and lower values for subsequent tranches continued to have merit. In designing such a scheme the upper limit to the first block price would be set by the maximum amount which it would be worthwhile paying to get marginal extra quantities of gas. This could be around 2.7d, and it followed that the nearer was the average price to this value the less scope there was for a graduated price structure. While this pointed to the advantages of an average price well below 2.7d it was also recognised that, if the price paid for Leman Bank gas involved a graduated structure and the same system was applied to other fields, the result would be that the average price for such fields (which would include Hewett and Indefatigable) would be higher because their reserves were smaller.

It was thus prudent to bear in mind other possible price structures such as one where the price varied according to the distance from the shore. In practice this aspect could be handled by purchasing the gas at the wellhead. This scheme could facilitate the development of more distant fields. The disadvantage was that the Council would be more uncertain about the amount it should pay for future discoveries and might introduce an obligation to purchase some gas at prices at which it could not economically be sold. The conclusion was that this scheme should not be pressed on the companies.

With respect to the concept of price review it was noted that any disadvantage produced by paying a high price for gas now would be reduced if such a review could later procure a reduction. The Ministry also recognised, however, that the most readily measurable criteria which could be used in a review, such as indices of wholesale or retail prices, were more likely to point to a price increase than a reduction. The conclusion was that, while price revision clauses were sensible, they could not be relied on to obtain significant price reductions in the later years of contracts.

In sum the central issue facing the Government was to judge to what extent it would be possible to push the companies below 2.85d before they were driven to action which would cause more damage to the economy than the gain from the reduction in price. This risk existed at a price less than 2.7d.

Gas exploitation and the balance of payments

Meanwhile the Ministry had been conducting studies on the consequences for the balance of payments of a case with a price of 2.7d, with which was associated continued exploration and development by the companies, and one of 2.3d, which was associated with the development of fields on which significant investment had already taken place, plus the utilisation of a state company for further development and exploration. The studies were designed in particular to elucidate three main issues. The first was the foreign exchange cost of the gas taken. Emphasis was on the volumes of gas from foreign-owned companies. The second issue was the effect on North Sea investment. This highlighted the expenditure by the foreign companies as a credit to the balance of payments. Imports of goods and services were a debit. It was assumed that a state body would source more of its requirements from the UK. The third issue highlighted the reduced displacement of oil imports in the lower gas price and production case.

To obtain results involved many assumptions and calculations. The findings were that in 1970 the low price resulted in a moderate net extra cost to the balance of payments. In 1975, on the assumption that the state company's activities were quite successful, there was actually the prospect of a worthwhile net benefit to the balance of payments. Reduced profit remittances overseas constituted a significant gain. It was noted that the year 1975 somewhat fortuitously produced relatively favourable results for the low price case because of the phasing of investment and production, and in both earlier and later years the benefits were less. The results also took no account of compensation which would have to be paid for nationalisation. It was recognised that this would have a dramatic effect on the results. It was clear that the favourable 1975 result depended critically on this.

Effects of slower depletion rate

At this time a yet further study was undertaken in the Ministry on the consequences of a reduced rate of build up of gas production. The case emphasised was where the West Sole field would be exploited to the extent of the existing pipeline capacity, and output from Leman Bank would build up to the capacity of the pipeline which had already been laid. In this scenario no gas from other fields would occur until late 1971, when a further pipeline would have been laid and production wells drilled.

The slower build up would have major consequences for the gas industry, but the Ministry felt that there would still be adequate supplies available to justify conversion of the onshore gas network to use natural gas. The main reduction in demand compared to the fast build up scenario would be in the industrial market, and no supplies would be offered for electricity generation. There would be a greater problem in meeting peak demand, particularly as the reduction in industrial market sales would mean that the load factor would fall well below the 60% assumed for North Sea supplies. In the feedstock market many plants would be capable of using oil or natural gas, and to some extent oil could be used in the winter and gas in the summer. Supplementation from additional storage of imported LNG was also possible. The reduction in natural gas production would entail reduced investment in bulk transmission, though more would have to be spent on LNG storage and terminals.

Shell and Esso table formal offer for Leman

In the meantime Shell and Esso had formally tabled an offer for Leman Bank gas to the Gas Council. The main points were a price of 2.85d at 60% load factor with 2.15d for valley gas. Indexation would be provided for automatically every two years to reflect movements in official indices of the cost of basic manufacturing materials and the wholesale price of industrial products. There would be no full price reviews until 15 years from the date of the contract. Any major changes in economic circumstances which occurred before gas started to flow would entail renegotiation of the contract.

On 6th November Mr Marsh chaired a meeting of officials from his own Ministry and the Cabinet Office, DEA, and Treasury. He reported the Shell/Esso offer, and added that the Government's position of 2.5d for its model field of 500 mmcf/d entailed a price of 2.25d for the larger Leman field. His paper was discussed at some length. The DEA representative thought that the paper under-estimated the pressure which the Government could exert on the companies. In the longer term an arsenal of weapons including taxation and nationalisation was available. The prospective rates of return to investors were very attractive, and it was barely credible that the companies would pull out. A low price could slow down exploration, but, with the prospective production from existing discoveries being very substantial, this was not now a major concern. While the initial tranches of production would save foreign exchange higher levels of production would displace coal with less foreign exchange savings. When the market expanded further there would then be scope for additional displacement of oil. It was impor-tant to recognise that the Leman Bank price would set the pattern for all North Sea gas prices, including the price structure. Thus if a price of say 2.7d were agreed it would not be possible to have a steeply sloping structure. This might result in little incentive to explore for and develop small fields.

Dr Balogh from the Cabinet Office stated that the North Sea was an attractive investment environment offering returns of at least 20% after tax. These compared very favourably with those received by overseas British investment and with investment in gas supplies in Louisiana and Texas. The oil companies would not pull out before exploiting the existing discoveries, and, because of their large size, there was no reason to give a high price to encourage rapid exploration. In any case the Government could hire drilling companies to do such work. The Treasury representative agreed that the paper understated the Government's bargaining position, and, understandably, the Ministry had exaggerated the companies' case.

Mr Marsh felt that, after an agreement had been reached for Leman gas, the Government would be in a stronger buying position for further supplies not imme-diately required. They might even be able to negotiate the same price agreed for Leman for smaller fields. He doubted the effectiveness of any threat of nationalisa-tion. Some Ministry of Power officials felt that the promoted advantage of political stability in the UK would be weakened if threats of new taxation or nationalisation were made.

Mr Marshall felt that the Leman price would set the pattern for the other existing discoveries. A price as low as 2.25d would probably result in Shell/Esso developing their fields while Amoco might prefer to put its capital elsewhere. The Ministry appreciated that the companies were now concerned at the threat of devaluation and were looking at ways by which this risk could be covered in their contracts. The DEA representative reckoned that 10%–15% devaluation could reduce rates of return by around 3% which he did not regard as significant. The same representative expressed the view that a price between 2.25d and 2.5d for Leman with a sliding structure would be desirable. Dr Balogh also preferred a sliding price scale. The price should be based on the rate of return for comparable investments in advanced countries. He felt that the price should be driven down to retrieve what he perceived to be the undesirable situation brought about by the 1964 Act. Mr Marsh raised the possibility of tax being increased if settlements turned out to be too generous. The Treasury representative agreed that taxes could be varied but freedom in this area would partly depend on the terms of the gas contracts. Dr Balogh felt that a price review clause could protect the Government's position in this respect and thus a three-year initial settlement would be appropriate.

Mr Marsh meets with Shell and Esso

On the same day Mr Marsh met with senior representatives of Shell and Esso. They emphasised that their 2.85d price offer (with 2.15d for valley gas) was a rock bottom package. If all went well then the average would be around 2.65d. They were not saying that this was the appropriate price for other fields, nor that it was adequate to incentivise further exploration. They had, however, invested a lot of money, and, having no means of extricating themselves now, were anxious to come to a conclusion. All the non-price issues had been agreed with the Gas Council. Shell/Esso had suggested that the price review clause would not become operational for 15 years. This was to ensure that the investors received a secure return which would enable them to finance a commitment for that period. This was really forced on them by the insistence on the cost-related approach by the Ministry and the Council which had pressed them down to the low price that was now on offer. All the elements of the Shell/Esso proposals were interrelated, and if a change was sought in one part it would have consequences for the others.

Mr Marsh expressed his surprise at the length of the review period proposed. For Shell, Mr Barran stated that an early review could be just as difficult to settle as the initial price, resulting in much uncertainty for all. Comparative stability for a period of 15 years would go beyond the period of investment recovery which was important to investors. The Minister then indicated that on the basis of the calculations done in the Ministry the price for Leman gas should be substantially less than 2.85d. In reply Mr Barran said that Shell were building a fertiliser plant ideally suited for North Sea gas as a feedstock on a near 100% load factor, and had been offered gas by the Gas Council at a price which could be worked back to a price of around 2.9d at Bacton. He concluded that the Council must be thinking of something of that order.

Both parties agreed that a settlement was desired in the near future. Shell indicated that if agreement with the Council were not reached within a couple of weeks there was probably not much point in continuing to argue with them.

The Minister indicated that if no early conclusion were in sight he would think it best for him to be invited to secure a settlement. Mr Marshall indicated that the Minister would have to be able to say that any price agreed was a fair one from the exploitation of what was one of the nation's important assets. The price of 2.85d proposed by Shell/Esso produced a very high rate of return. Mr Barran indicated that initially the rate of return would be 20%–21%, but would fall over the period to around 15% because of inflation and despite the operation of the price indexation clause. Both the Shell and Esso representatives stated that 15% rate of return was essentially a break-even point for them, and Shell had recently rejected two projects offering such a return because of the risks involved.

Pressed on how they reconciled these numbers with overall company rates of return of 8.5% and 11.5%, Mr Barran responded that upstream profits were required to offset losses on refining and marketing. Mr Barran added that one of the reasons they were able to contemplate such low overall rates of return in the North Sea was because they were not themselves bearing the costs of distribution and marketing. A further issue stressed by the companies was the need to bear in mind the possibility that the price agreed might become unrealistic between now and the date of delivery in the event of unforeseen developments arising such as, for example, devaluation. The response of the Council had been that the same argument would apply to it, in the event of the fuel oil tax being removed! The Minister asked how significant was the risk of devaluation in the minds of the companies given the Government's clear determination to avoid devaluation. The response was that 70% of the companies' expenditure was on foreign goods, but neither Shell nor Esso believed that devaluation was likely!

Ministry discusses Shell/Esso offer with Gas Council

The 6th November was a busy day for the Minister and his officials. In the evening they met with the Chairman of the Gas Council and his senior colleagues. Sir Henry Jones was adamant that the Shell/Esso offer for Leman gas was unacceptable, especially on account of the indexation clause which would relieve the companies of most of the inflation risk. If the same price were applied to the Hewett field the result would be extraordinarily favourable to the companies, and, if applied to Indefatigable, it would be less favourable but generous. Sir Henry felt that a price of 2.85d would mean that the Council would have to turn away other producers because it would be unable to market more than the contract quantities from Leman. The pace of gas market development would be less than foreseen in the 1967 *Fuel Policy* White Paper. Sir Henry reiterated that the Council could live with a price of 2.7d, but even then there would be a very tough struggle on gas marketing. To procure large customers at 100% load factor required a maximum price of 4.5d per therm. The Council needed at least 2d to cover its own costs. This meant that they could not afford to pay more than a beach price of 2.5d at 60% load factor, with little more than 2d for valley gas.

Inter-Departmental discussions

Shortly afterwards an Inter-Departmental meeting of senior officials was held under the chairmanship of Sir Douglas Allen. The purpose was to prepare briefs for their respective Ministers on the price negotiations. Mr Marshall summarised the course of the negotiations to date as discussed above. With respect to price structure Dr Balogh favoured a graduated one for successive tranches of production with a low average value. The Ministry continued to have an open mind on this. A graduated structure would be possible with an average price around 2.5d per therm but would be difficult at 2.7d. The view of the DEA was that, other things being equal, the lower the price the greater the benefit to the balance of payments, but the constraint was the behaviour of the oil companies. Mr Marshall outlined the legal position under the 1964 Act as discussed above, and gave his considered opinion that a settlement with Shell/Esso could readily be achieved in the 2.7d–2.75d range, and, with difficulty, between 2.5d and 2.7d.

In discussion a general feeling emerged that, while a graduated structure was desirable to incentivise exploration, it should be centred on a low average value. This was needed if the Government was to ensure that the price and profits of the oil companies were publicly acceptable. Given the need for the Gas Council to earn a higher rate of return on its investment a price of around 2.4d should be the goal. It was appreciated that at this level the oil companies might abandon or delay exploration and even the development of less favourable discoveries. But the gain to the balance of payments to a great extent resulted from the replacement of imported naphtha by the first tranches of North Sea gas. Given this a fast rate of further exploitation was less necessary, and could even be embarrassing if coal was displaced. In these circumstances the effect of the temporary withdrawal of the companies would be less severe.

Mr Marsh determines his tactics

Mr Marsh was now determining his tactics for the next stage of the price discussions. He had come to the view that he should take a firm stand aimed at securing a price in line with the March instructions. Before proceeding he wanted full clarification of the Gas Council's views of the negotiating position. He asked the Chairman for his views on (a) the minimum price he thought he could negotiate, (b) the maximum price which the Council could pay, consistent with the build up of markets as envisaged in the White Paper and meeting its financial obligations, and (c) the price or prices at which the companies would not develop fields and seriously reduce their exploration. He also requested clarification on the ability of the Council to take over from Amoco the development of its share of the Leman and Indefatigable fields. He wanted to know the contractual situation, and the financial implications. Finally, he wanted to know the Council's view of how the next stage of the negotiations should be handled. He wondered whether they should be handed, perhaps in confidence, to the Ministry, or whether there was scope for further negotiation by the Council.

Gas Council clarifies its views

Sir Henry responded by letter in detail. He emphasised the gas market uncertainties and the difficulties of making accurate forecasts of gas penetration given the competitive environment. Costs were also uncertain. But the biggest uncertainty was the likely availability of North Sea gas. There were four large commercial discoveries of which Leman Bank was by far the largest with probable reserves of 13–14 tcf. The reserves of these fields were still subject to considerable uncertainty. There was also much uncertainty surrounding the development costs.

With respect to the price negotiations Shell/Esso had tabled an offer of 2.85d (with 2.15d for valley gas). Sir Henry had concluded after much consideration and meetings with the companies that, while they seemed convinced that this price would result in a level of profitability which was not particularly high by oil company standards, he fully expected the returns to be very satisfactory. He also felt that there was now not much margin for a price reduction before exploration would slow down. He also believed that the companies would produce gas from Leman and Indefatigable at a price considerably lower than that which would incentivise exploration. A settlement at 2.5d (with 1.9d for valley gas) would still result in the development of these fields. The Gas Council was unlikely to be able to secure in negotiations a price of 2.7d (with 2.0d for valley gas), unless the Minister made it clear to the companies that he had given a ceiling figure below 2.7d which had to apply. Attempts to push the price below 2.7d could lead to stalemate. There was some doubt about how the Minister could apply pressure under the 1964 Act. He had even heard informally that Shell/Esso, when they had finished the physical work, would produce gas and, in the absence of an agreement, invoice the Council at their price even if the Council paid at its price!

Sir Henry speculated that at a price of 2d companies would cease to produce from existing discoveries. But at a level below 2.5d relationships with the companies would substantially deteriorate, and could be followed by some non-cooperation. Sir Henry was quite clear that the escalation clause proposed by Shell/Esso was unacceptable. The annual price increase could be considerable. A 15-year period of reasonable stability would be attractive, but a review at, say, 5-year intervals would be more satisfactory.

In the event that a settlement with their Amoco partners was not achieved and the company pulled out the Council could hire rigs, but they would certainly miss the expertise of Amoco and time would be lost. The operating agreement allowed the Council to carry out sole risk exploration, but with respect to production the position was more complex. If Amoco pulled out it could be argued that the company could not claim that the gas discovered had any substantive value. On the other hand the Council might in effect purchase the gas in place in the absence of an agreement. Amoco could claim repayment of funds already spent.

Sir Henry made it very clear that scenarios involving voluntary withdrawals of investors were ones which should not be contemplated, especially from a large discovery. The wider consequences would be very serious. There would be allegations of bad faith on the part of the Government which could only be countered if an independent investigation could demonstrate that the companies would earn a satisfactory profit within the Government's own price proposals. There was another scenario which was that the companies did not pull out but just refused to spend funds on development. The legal situation was then unclear. If the Council proceeded to develop on its own the companies could apply to the courts to stop this on the grounds that the Council's operation would impair the potential future production from wells capable of production.

If the Council or another state body did take the place of the companies and undertook field developments on its own, with a loss of time of around one year, it was still doubtful whether operations could be conducted as skilfully as the best companies working in the North Sea. There would, of course, be longer term problems in attracting investors. With respect to the Shell/Esso negotiations Sir Henry felt that the Council should continue with non-price matters such as taxation, escalation, and review. On price he felt that the Council should offer 2.5d (1.9d for valley gas), but that this should be accompanied by a firm statement by the Minister to the companies.

Devaluation of sterling and its consequences

The day after the Minister of Power received this letter on Saturday 18th November, Mr Callaghan, the Chancellor of the Exchequer, announced (at 9.30pm) the devaluation of sterling by 14.3% from £1 = $2.80 to £1 = $2.40. This had obvious implications for the gas contracts as well as other aspects of economic policy. All interested parties immediately started examining the likely effects. Shell informed the Gas Council and the Ministry that their offer of two weeks ago should be regarded as in abeyance. Esso went further and said that theirs was withdrawn. A resubmission would be made after they had evaluated the effects. Mr Marsh had to reconsider his programme for consulting his colleagues. It was planned to await the fresh proposals from Shell/Esso before finalising a prepared position.

In the meantime the Minister and his officials met with the Chairman and Deputy Chairman of the Gas Council to discuss the new situation. It was agreed that further initiatives with Shell/Esso should await their revised proposals. The Gas Council representatives felt that the other oil companies were now sheltering behind Shell/Esso and taking great care not to undermine their position. There had been hopes that Amoco might have been prepared to undercut Shell/Esso, but this could no longer be expected given the recent price reduction made by the two companies.

Mr Marshall indicated the Ministry's preliminary views that on quite favourable assumptions to the Government, such as a significant shift in sourcing of equipment from US to UK sources, the minimum gas price increase to be expected was 0.1d. On unfavourable assumptions, such as maintaining dollar returns on earlier dollar expenditures, the increase could be as high as 0.3d for a US company. There were also complex secondary effects to consider such as the effect of devaluation on oil prices in the UK. Mr Marshall considered that the oil companies would expect the market to tolerate a higher gas price because the price of fuel oil, its main competitor, would go up in sterling terms. The Deputy Chairman of the Council thought that the companies might well try to obtain a price of the same order as the Dutch one. At the new exchange rate this was just over 3d per therm in the pipeline (compared to 2.7d before devaluation).

Sir Henry Jones reiterated his view that the Council would only be able to get a price below 2.7d if they were backed by a clear and firm Government view. The Minister appreciated this. The main issues on which he had lingering doubts was on the Council's apparent reluctance to commit themselves firmly to expand sales in accordance with the *Fuel Policy* White Paper[1] on the basis of 2.7d. The Minister felt that it would be a major catastrophe if the Council paid so much to the companies that they prejudiced their own sales effort and the financial performance of the industry. The reply from the Council was that even if the gas was obtained free of charge there would still be a few lean years ahead, a major uncertainty being the Council's lack of knowledge of the strategy of the oil companies, particularly with respect to fuel oil pricing.

Minister's meeting with Mr Peter Emery MP

The Minister raised another matter, namely an approach he had received from Mr Peter Emery, MP, in relation to the negotiations over the Hewett field with Phillips. A few weeks earlier the Phillips Group had submitted an offer to the Council based on a price of 3.15d. There had subsequently been a meeting on 13th November between the company and the Minister with his officials. The company representatives, emphasising the investment risks involved, had already experienced some dry wells in the UKCS. The Minister advised Phillips to find some way of reducing the price from its 3.15 offer. Lord Tangley for the Phillips Group reiterated the risks involved including devaluation. The Minister emphasised the Government's determination to maintain the existing parity.

Subsequently Mr Peter Emery had met the Minister informally. It had been emphasised to Mr Emery that the 3.15d offer was unrealistically high in relation to the Shell/Esso offer and that Phillips was in danger of being left out on a limb. Mr Emery had relayed this information to Phillips and subsequently returned to inform the Minister that Phillips would now like to discuss a revised offer. The Minister advised that such an offer should be submitted to the Council.

Detailed work on effect of devaluation

The Ministry's work on the effect of devaluation initially required the determination of the appropriate analytical framework. Several questions arose. One was whether costs already incurred should be included. The effect of devaluation clearly differed according to the assumptions about the timing of the costs. The companies would make their calculations in accordance with the phasing of their expenditures, but the Ministry was working with a hypothetical model field. If historic expenditure was included the effects on US-owned and UK-owned companies would differ. Thus, for UK companies which had incurred costs in sterling or in dollars at the pre-devaluation parity, but then received revenues in sterling, devaluation should make no difference. On the other hand US-owned companies would be worse off to the full extent of devaluation. Looking ahead both types of company would be affected equally.

Another question was the likely extent of import substitution in the purchase of equipment and materials following devaluation (which effectively increased the costs of imported equipment payable in dollars by 16.7%). The Ministry also wondered to what extent the additional sterling costs from devaluation should be offset by a reduction in the rate of return. This proposition was based on the notion that one of the investment risks had now been removed, with a further devaluation being very unlikely! The Ministry also wondered whether the case for a devaluation clause in the contracts was strengthened or lessened. It was recognised that market forces would increase the value of gas because oil prices in sterling would rise, but the Ministry also wondered whether this might not be realised in practice by policies such as those relating to national incomes and prices. The positive balance of payments effects of North Sea gas should be increased after devaluation. At any specified price the foreign exchange content of the gas would be lower because the profits of foreign-owned companies were reduced and tax receipts would be higher. If the naphtha and other oil prices rose the gain from displacing them with indigenous gas increased.

In further work on the subject the Ministry estimated that 70% of the expenditures on exploration and development were in dollars. Some switch to sterling sources could take place, but it would take time, and even then 50% sterling content was as much as could be expected. With 70% dollar expenditure, on the Ministry's model field (entirely discovered and developed post-devaluation), a price rise of 0.29d per therm would be required to give the same return as a price of 2.5d before devaluation. If 50% of the expenditure were in dollars the price increase would be 0.21d. If a price increase were also required to offset the proposed post-devaluation increase in corporation tax from 40% to 42.5% an increase of 0.05d. would be an average figure. The precise figure varied considerably according to the investor's tax position.

The companies offering gas to the Council had all incurred substantial expenditures prior to devaluation. Foreign companies had incurred costs in dollars or in sterling at the old parity, and would receive their revenues in sterling at the new parity. They (or their parents) would be worse off to the full extent of the devaluation. On the other hand UK companies had incurred costs in sterling or dollars at the old parity and would receive revenues in sterling. On this basis devaluation would not affect them. The final position depended on what proportion of the expenditures were incurred pre-and post-devaluation. The Ministry made estimates of this and, on the assumption that 70% of post-devaluation expenditures were still in dollars, came up with findings that full compensation would entail price increases of 0.38d (15%) for a foreign company, and 0.25d (10%) for a British company.

The Ministry noted that it would be possible to argue that pre-devaluation expenditures should be ignored in the calculation on the grounds that this was one of the business risks which overseas companies had to face. This would significantly reduce the required price increase. In dealing with the companies it would also have to be borne in mind that the latter employed higher cost figures which would produce a higher price increase for compensation purposes. The Ministry's conclusion was that devaluation could be held to justify price increases in the 0.2d–0.4d range. In negotiations the Council and Government should take their stand at the bottom of the range.

Post-devaluation discussions with companies

Meanwhile studies and consultations on the whole issue were continuing in the Ministry. Mr Marsh was under pressure from the Prime Minister to update him and his colleagues on the position, but argued that he had to await revised offers from the companies before producing a worthwhile report. To progress matters Mr Marshall met with Mr Barran of Shell to make suggestions regarding their revised offer. It was suggested to Mr Barran that the post-devaluation situation gave Shell an opportunity to narrow the gap on price between the parties. The Ministry had already undertaken some studies on the effects of devaluation. Mr Barran agreed with this approach, but was disturbed to hear that their last offer of 2.85d still left a substantial gap between the parties. For the two companies it had represented the farthest they could go to meet the Minister's requirements and permit vigorous exploration. He had thought that it could form the basis of an agreement, subject only to minor modifications.

Mr Marshall indicated that the Minister was still thinking that a price not in excess of 2.5d for Leman was reasonable. The recently published White Paper on *Fuel Policy* had stressed the importance of low cost energy. The Gas Council also had a major investment programme and the need to earn a reasonable return on it. Mr Barran appreciated this, but emphasised the risks and difficulties facing the producers. The pre-devaluation price of 2.85d represented the minimum return (barely 20%) for such a venture. He admitted that it did pay Shell to develop Leman at 2.5d, but they would do no more exploration in the UKCS. Shell had another angle on the situation. In the Netherlands it was the policy of both the Government and the companies to maintain the export price as high as possible. Any price agreed in the UK would influence the Dutch situation. This problem was now aggravated by the devaluation of the pound and the maintenance of the old parity for the guilder. The company was thus somewhat despondent about the situation.

Further discussions also took place with Amoco. In early December a meeting was held among representatives of the Ministry, Treasury, Bank of England and

Amoco to discuss (1) how much borrowing in the UK Amoco would be permitted to make in relation to North Sea gas developments, (2) the possibility of a clause in the contract covering cost increases, and (3) a possible clause to protect Amoco against devaluation. The company representative explained that it was under pressure from the US Government to restrict the outflow of dollars. Unless Amoco could borrow substantial sums in the UK its activity in the UKCS would be reduced. The company asked for exemption from the normal borrowing rules.

The Treasury representatives conceded that the amount which Amoco borrowed could have implications for the gas price, but, after consideration, it had been concluded that the normal 30%/70% formula should apply. It was explained that there would be some flexibility on the application of the formula, such that if Amoco borrowed less now (because interest rates were relatively high), it could borrow more later up to the 30% ceiling.

On other matters the Treasury had no objection in principle to indexation elements relating to movements in costs, and to a price review clause provided that the contract as a whole was acceptable. There was, however, no possibility of an exchange rate guarantee. This was not given to anyone.

A further meeting between Amoco and Mr Marshall was held a few days later. For Amoco Mr Morrow stated that the recent discussions had not been encouraging. They themselves had estimated that devaluation had raised their costs by around 0.5d. Their price bracket for negotiation was now 3.2d–3.5d on the basis that 90% of their expenditures was in dollars. There might be switching to around 80% post devaluation which would move their price range to 3.1d–3.4d.

Mr Marshall reiterated the Ministry's views expressed to Amoco over the past months. The effects of devaluation had now been examined, but none of the Ministry's estimates was consistent with an increase of 0.5d. There was room for differences of opinion on the matter. The Ministry could argue that the chances of a future devaluation were now less. Mr Marshall urged Amoco to put a new formal offer to the Council. He hoped that this would be as near as possible to the range which had been advised at previous meetings with an allowance for the recent devaluation.

Mr Marshall's meeting with Mr Peter Emery

Shortly afterwards Mr Marshall had a meeting with Mr Peter Emery. From the tenor of the discussion the impression was gained that Phillips had concluded that they had to offer a price below 3d. Mr Marshall also thought that Phillips was keen to procure an early settlement, at least in part to ensure a quick production build-up and rapid depletion. Mr Emery had sought a view on (1) the price which might produce immediate agreement, and (2) a range within which they might make an offer which could open conclusive negotiations over a short time frame.

Mr Marshall responded that a post-devaluation price of 2.7d, covering all costs, could be the basis for a quick agreement, on the assumption that the other clauses could also be resolved. Any price offer under 2.9d would also be regarded as a move into a sensible area of negotiation. But there would then be further stiff argument and bargaining as this figure was still too high from the Government's viewpoint.

The response of Mr Emery was that 2.7d was out of the question. Their own estimate of the effect of devaluation was 0.3d. After further discussion Mr Emery summarised the position to be that (1) a price offer of 2.99d, while it would evoke serious interest, would not bring a settlement, (2) an offer of 2.89d would produce serious negotiations, and (3) an offer of 2.7d would be close to a price acceptable to the Government and Gas Council and could lead to an early agreement. On the following day Mr Emery contacted Mr Marshall expressing some optimism about the prospects.

Ministry reflects further on tranche pricing

Meanwhile the Ministry was giving further thought to the issue of price structure, particularly the need to give higher prices to small fields than to large ones. The negotiations had all been aimed at settling an average price. The Ministry considered the possibility of designing a structure based on the average price agreed for the first contract (assumed to be Leman Bank). While there would be no explicit promise to pay for other fields on the basis of this structure it would certainly be the implied position. One consequence would be that, on the assumption that future fields would be smaller than Leman, the Council would be committed to paying a higher average price in the future. This might even apply to Hewett and Indefatigable which were smaller than Leman.

Because of this perceived problem the Ministry considered other possibilities. One would be to announce, after the initial contract for Leman had been agreed, that future purchases would be based on a price structure which gave the same average price for a field smaller than Leman and a lower price for larger ones. The latter could be justified on the grounds that large further quantities could only be absorbed in the market at a lower price. It was recognised that this could reduce incentives, but would still offer better incentives than a flat price.

Bulk Gas market and tranche pricing

The Ministry was quite concerned about the upper limit to which it would be sensible to pay for first tranches of gas. The concern centred on the ability of the gas industry to sell extra quantities and the price obtainable. This required the estimation of marginal costs and marginal revenues to the Council. It was important to note that, when the Council reduced its prices to increase its sales, it would have to offer the lower prices to existing customers as well. In looking at marginal revenues the Ministry felt that the appropriate market was the bulk one. Thus, in the Ministry's view, the prices obtainable in the bulk market determined the ceiling on the price which could be paid by the Council for new supplies.

It was also recognised that putting a (relatively lower) ceiling price for new first tranche gas could lead to less discoveries being made. The premium market would also continue over the long period of a contract, and it might be worthwhile for the

Council to buy extra gas over the next few years, even though it had to be sold in bulk markets at a small loss, in order to profit from the future growth of the premium market. Extra gas should also enable the load factor of the whole system to be increased. After estimating the likely growth of the two markets the Ministry concluded that there was a case for offering only a small premium for first tranche gas above the corresponding value sold to bulk consumers.

Tranche pricing and balance of payments

There were other wider national considerations unrelated to the position of the Gas Council which could point to the offer of a higher first tranche price. Thus royalty and profits tax were payable on gas production, and the balance of payments would benefit so long as the foreign exchange cost of the gas was less than that of oil products. The Ministry had undertaken considerable work on this subject and had concluded that the "danger price" (that is the price at which the foreign exchange cost of the gas equalled that of oil products) was 4d per therm in 1975 for gas in the 3,000–4,000 mmcf/d range. There were further considerations. When gas replaced oil the tax revenues from the fuel oil tax would decrease. This had been included in the balance of payments calculations, but there would be an effect on tax receipts which was difficult to estimate.

The appropriate post-devaluation price of first tranche gas had to recognise that fuel oil prices would go up by the equivalent of around 0.25d–0.5d per therm and gas prices to consumers could be modified accordingly. First tranche prices at the beach were estimated at 3d–3.5d on the basis of the Council's financial objectives. Higher prices would only be justified on wider considerations.

Tranche pricing and parity across fields

The Ministry devoted much attention to the practical details of a price structure. On the assumption that the Leman contract would be settled first there was a reluctance to pay more for Hewett and Indefatigable. Parity across the fields could be achieved if a flat price were agreed, but would be difficult with a differentiated structure. On the question of the slope of the price structure it was important to ensure that it did not give licensees an incentive to restrict production by lengthening the depletion period. In this respect the sliding scale price structure was akin to a production tax as far as the producers were concerned. An efficient system should produce higher returns for higher output even when the average price was less. This meant that the steps between successive tranche prices should be progressively less steep. There were complex trade-offs providing incentives to producers to explore for and develop small fields, production efficiency, and the costs of gas to the Council.

Attractions of flat average price

In the light of all the issues discussed above the Ministry wondered whether on balance there was a net advantage to be gained by a differentiated price structure.

A flat average price for the initial contracts entailed less commitment for the future by the Council. A price agreed for an initial contract would form the starting point for future negotiations, but the Council would be free to vary the terms whether to ensure absorption of gas into the market or to encourage exploration. There was a particular concern about the effects of a graduated price structure in committing the Council to take future supplies at higher prices when there was still much uncertainty about what volumes the Council could profitably sell. Unless an agreed flat price seriously discouraged exploration there were advantages with it, even at the cost of some extra quantities.

There were attractions in offering flat prices for the initial contracts and then to await results before deciding whether and how further exploration should best be incentivised. The Ministry's own calculations indicated that, with a flat price of 2.75d, there were still adequate incentives for exploration. It was recognised that from 1968 some of the exploration effort would be transferred to the Dutch sector, and rigs might be taken away from the UK sector. But they could readily return at a future date, given the short distances involved. There could also be difficulties in absorbing large quantities of gas into the UK market, particularly if the need to give preference to coal for electricity generation continued.

The conclusion was that the balance of advantage lay in agreeing a flat price for gas now on offer and to defer the question of additional incentives for a year or two. It was recognised that this was a departure from earlier views, principally because the estimate of the price required to acquire gas now had risen, while the assessment of the ceiling price obtainable in the market had gone down. The reduction in the gap between the average price and the first tranche price was now narrower, and thus the potential incentive which a graduated price structure could give had diminished.

Revised post-devaluation offers from companies

Meanwhile contacts between the parties continued. On 13th December Mr Barran of Shell wrote to Sir Henry Jones with an offer revised in the light of the devaluation. The letter indicated that their costs would increase, and as a result their price offer had to be increased by 12%, giving a base price of 3.2d, and, for quantities in excess of their annual contract quantities, 2.41d. The letter emphasised that Shell had tried to disturb the other terms as little as possible in order that the large area of the terms already agreed need not be reopened. It was reiterated that the package offered should be seen as a whole, and thus if one element were changed adjustments would have to be made elsewhere in the contract. Esso wrote in similar terms.

On hearing the details, Mr Marshall informed the Minister, indicating his disappointment. He interpreted the offer as providing a warning that a very stiff battle still lay ahead. To put the issue in perspective the pre-devaluation price of 2.5d on the hypothetical field equated to around 2.8d post-devaluation.

Mr Marshall also expressed some optimism regarding a future meeting between representatives of Phillips and Sir Henry Jones, (scheduled for New Year's Day!)

The offer was to supply at a base price of 2.95d (with excess gas at 2.35d). Officials incorporated this information in a paper being prepared for the Minister to circulate to his colleagues, some of whom were anxious to obtain an update. The paper quoted the new Phillips offer, and added that there was a prospect of a deal at around 2.85d which would certainly be a breakthrough as this price was equivalent to a pre-devaluation one of around 2.55d.

With respect to physical prospects the position in early 1968 was that enough reserves had been discovered to produce 3,000 mmcf/d by 1975, and thus further exploration was required to meet the figure of 4,000 mmcf/d envisaged in the *Fuel Policy* White Paper. The success ratio had declined in recent months. The paper recounted the status of the offers made by other groups–Shell/Esso, Amoco, and Arpet. Any new offers made by the Council would have to reflect the extra costs from devaluation, estimated at 0.2d–0.4d per therm. Given the predominance of foreign-owned companies it would be reasonable to allow at least 0.3d. On this basis the gap between Phillips and the Government's earlier position was quite close. To put the issue in perspective for the Phillips offer a difference of 0.25d amounted to around £1 million per year, about 50% of which would return to the Government in royalty and tax.

The Gas Council's post-devaluation position was that it would find a price in the 2.7d–3d range acceptable if the other terms were also acceptable. The Minister's overall assessment was that a price between 2.8d and 2.9d could be attained with Phillips. Further, he did not believe that better terms could be obtained. If such prices were agreed with the other companies rates of return upwards of 20% were likely to be earned on Leman Bank and higher figures on Hewett. While high in relation to the profitability of manufacturing industry, such returns were not exceptional in the oil industry, given the need to cover unsuccessful exploration. Prices in the 2.8d–2.9d range were also unfavourable in comparison to those now available in the Dutch sector where, with favourable geological prospects, beach prices of well over 3d could be expected. Thus exploration in the UKCS should continue on a reduced scale with some movement of rigs to the Dutch sector being inevitable.

Urgent need for settlements

It was now becoming increasingly urgent that settlements were reached so that the gas industry could make firm offers to potential customers and finalise investment plans. There was also a need to obtain early commitments from US companies because of the dangers from US Government restrictions on foreign investment. There was a danger that attempts to force the price down would produce a long period of deadlock, and possibly a withdrawal of oil company cooperation in other areas, such as placing orders for tankers and equipment in the UK. There was also no guarantee that attempts to depress the price would be successful. If agreement was reached with Phillips it was likely, but not inevitable, that their partners, the Arpet group, would settle on the same terms. It was less clear whether Shell/Esso would settle on the same terms, but the Council's negotiating position would be greatly enhanced.

Summarising the overall position the Minister's view was that there was an opportunity to reach a quick settlement with Phillips on terms which would bring substantial benefits to the economy and the gas industry. The Minister thus invited his colleagues to authorise the Council to negotiate an agreement with Phillips at a price not exceeding 2.9d, and to continue negotiations with the other groups within the same limits.

Ministerial views on offer from Phillips

At this point Mr Marsh was sufficiently encouraged by the news from Phillips that he sent a Minute to the Prime Minister indicating that the negotiations could be brought to a head within a few days. He requested directions on how to obtain clearance for proposals which he was putting to the Energy Steering Group. In a Minute to the Prime Minister the Cabinet Secretary summarised the historic situation and the current arguments in the Minister's new paper. There were now two possibilities facing Ministers. The first was to sweat it out for a further time period in the hope of obtaining a better offer from Phillips. The second was to make an agreement with Phillips now on the basis of the Minister's proposals, and to negotiate with the other companies on the same basis.

At the Ministerial meeting Mr Marsh recounted the negotiations over the past eighteen months. He argued that an agreement at a price of 2.9d was still advantageous to the balance of payments with the benefits rising to £60 million per year by 1972. In discussion there was agreement that the Gas Council be given authority to negotiate with Phillips (and the Arpet group) up to 2.9d for the Hewett field. But the group of Ministers could not agree at this stage that the same price limit should form the basis for negotiations with other groups. The Leman Bank was larger and the same price could result in excessive returns to the licensees. Further, too much emphasis should not be placed on exploration incentives, given that 75% of the market requirements for 1975 were already discovered. The Minister of Power was requested to report back to the Ministerial group on the outcome of negotiations with Phillips and of any discussion with Shell/Esso, the latter being without commitment.

Abandon tranche pricing?

Mr Marsh suggested that the concept of tranche pricing should now be abandoned. There was a danger that use of the concept would lead to excessive returns on small fields and could push up the general acquisition cost of supplies. It would be better to avoid use of the scheme in the early contracts, but could be introduced in later ones if the need to stimulate exploration was felt to be necessary. With respect to the negotiations with Phillips, the company had proposed an indexation provision related to costs, and for a wider review of the terms after a period of years. The meeting felt that a review clause would not necessarily work in the interests of the Government, as costs would probably rise with the expected decline in the success ratio and in the profitability of fields. It was also recognised that the

Council's negotiating position might be stronger for a few years if and when large gas supplies were developed. The meeting felt that an escalation clause could be conceded if it were combined with a general review clause which would consider the basic contract price as well as cost changes. The Minister of Power was thus asked to ensure that the proposal for a review clause was not abandoned without prior consultation with the group of Ministers.

Dr Balogh continues to favour tranche pricing

The results of the meeting attracted the interest of Dr Balogh who sent a Minute to the Prime Minister protesting strongly that the case for flat-rate pricing was unconvincing, and that tranche pricing was essential to meet the twin objectives of ensuring that (a) profits from large fields such as Leman Bank and Hewett were not excessive, and (b) incentives for exploitation of small fields were maintained. If the prospect of a large number of small discoveries threatening to increase the average gas acquisition costs did emerge there would be ample opportunity to reduce first tranche prices in new contracts. The Secretary of State for Economic Affairs supported Dr Balogh's view, and suggested to the Prime Minister that the Inter-Departmental Steering Group on Energy Policy assess the relative effects of flat-rate and tranche pricing for contracts other than Hewett.

Ministry studies price indexation clauses

Following receipt of the feedback from the Ministerial meeting officials in the Ministry of Power examined in detail the price adjustment clauses proposed by Phillips and the Council for the Hewett field. Phillips had proposed a clause applying a weighted average of three indices to 90% of the base price from the base year of 1967. The indices were comprised of (a) a price index of the output of the engineering industry (30% weight), (b) the average earnings of all employed (30% weight), and (c) the retail price index (40% weight). The justification for this indexation was to preserve the real value of their return.

The Ministry noted that the choice of 1967 as the base year would lead to some escalation in the price over the next two or three years as the effects of devaluation permeated the economy. The Ministry felt that devaluation had already been accounted for through the raised base price, and thus acceptance of 1967 as the base year would involve double counting in favour of Phillips. The Ministry also felt that the base year should be that when supplies actually commenced. This could be October 1969. The idea of annual adjustments was felt to be too frequent. A period of stability covering the build-up period was considered desirable. It was also felt that inflation risks should not be fully safeguarded: they should be shared by investors. In determining their ideas on a reasonable rate of return the Ministry had allowed for annual inflation at 3%.

It was also felt that the indices suggested by Phillips were not well adapted for the purpose which the company had in mind. To preserve the value of revenues the retail price index was appropriate but not the earnings index. The company may have had in mind the concept that the engineering index was a proxy for capital costs, the earnings index for labour costs, and the retail price index for the return. If this were the case the weighting seemed incorrect. Further, the earnings index was not a good proxy for costs, because it took no account of any higher productivity which was achieved and which was associated with higher earnings. Thus it would be preferable to use an index of earnings divided by an index of production.

The Ministry did concede that there should be a provision to cover changes in costs through the duration of the contract. The Gas Council had proposed indices relating to items of costs but applying them to only 10% of the price. Because annual operating costs might be only 5% of annual gross revenues, and little capital expenditure was expected after the initial investment, an index of costs applying to 10%–20% of the price could be a reasonable negotiating stance. The Ministry felt that the cost escalation index should apply only to the basic contract price and not to that for valley gas. Purchase of valley gas was an option to the Gas Council. If it were exercised the return to the oil company was increased.

Phillips had proposed that a price review of the annual adjustment should take place if the Council were placed in an uneconomic position. The Ministry felt that it would be very difficult to prove hardship and the operation of the clause was too limited. There was also no provision for a general review of the basic price after some years, and no safeguard against a fall in the price of competing fuels or a reduction in fuel oil duty.

In the light of all the above the Ministry felt that in further negotiations routine escalation should be limited to costs applied to a modest proportion of the basic price. Escalation should in any case only commence after the build-up had been achieved, and should take place at two or three year intervals. A further restriction to escalation in the form of an effective "top-stop" related to the price of competing fuels should also be incorporated into the scheme. A general price review after some years should also be part of the contract. A composite index was acceptable, but for cost escalation the index of weekly wage rates was felt to be preferable to the index of earnings, and should be applied to a maximum of 20% of the price.

The Ministry was keen to promote the concept of a top-stop to the escalation index reflecting the prices of competing fuels. There was, however, no satisfactory existing one. There were indices of wholesale prices for basic materials but the coverage was not comprehensive enough. An index of oil and coal prices, relating to prices paid by the CEGB, could be devised. If an index of oil prices alone were deemed appropriate this could be obtained from existing published information. There would be problems in negotiating a contract provision to use whichever index was devised for use as a top-stop. For example, a difficult issue would arise if the price as escalated by the index reached the ceiling and the index subsequently fell. Should the price then be reduced or not?

While a general price review clause was desirable there was a difficulty in determining the criteria on which it should operate. A vague formula relating to changes in economic circumstances would be difficult to negotiate, and would not be helpful to an arbitrator. The Ministry had general sympathy with the idea of an index which would measure "abnormal inflation" and be used to compensate investors for situations where inflation exceeded the rate which could reasonably be expected. Such an index would again only be applied to a proportion of the price. There would be no overlap between this and the provision for cost escalation. Thus if the cost escalation index applied to 20% of the price, the maximum proportion to which the abnormal inflation index could apply would be 80%. The index could be based on the general retail or wholesale price index. Escalation would only come into play when the index had increased more than an already pre-determined rate for "normal" inflation.

Preparing for resumption of negotiations

Meanwhile steps were being taken to resume negotiations with Shell/Esso and Amoco. When Sir Henry Jones heard of the decision of Ministers that they were unwilling to consider a price for Leman Bank in excess of 2.75d, he informed Mr Marshall that in negotiations he would have to offer 2.5d or 2.6d and did not feel this a reasonable proposition to make to the companies given the past history of negotiations and his assessment of the position. He would, therefore, be obliged to ask the Minister to take over the negotiations. Mr Marshall was also extremely gloomy about the wisdom of resuming negotiations at 2.5d or 2.6d, believing that it would cause intense ill-feeling, and make the companies more determined to obtain the maximum possible price, and perhaps withhold wider cooperation with the Government. He then proposed a price structure in the form of a tranche with negotiating limits of 2.85d for the first 600 mmcf/d, 2.75d for the next 600 mmcf/d, and 2.6d for all further gas. Corresponding opening offers for the tranches would be 2.8d, 2.7d, and 2.5d. The advantages of this strategy were that the average for Leman would be less than what was being aimed at for Hewett. Sir Henry Jones would also be willing to negotiate on this basis.

Ministerial approval was given for this and Mr Marshall wrote accordingly to Sir Henry Jones, adding that the Minister also saw advantages in postponing the resumption of negotiations with Shell/Esso in the hope that an agreement with Phillips could first be reached at a price in the 2.8d–2.9d range. The Minister also felt that the offers to Shell/Esso should be made firmly on a take it or leave it basis, as he wanted the negotiations to be brought to a head as soon as possible, and, if the offer was rejected, he would be willing to see them and put to them the Government's strong views on what was a reasonable price. In amplification of his views on strategy the Minister suggested that, as long as there was a possibility of an agreement with Phillips on acceptable terms, it would be unwise to become involved in protracted negotiations with Shell/Esso, possibly leading to unnecessary concessions in the event that agreement with Phillips were reached.

Meetings continued among the parties. The Gas Council made its revised offer to senior executives of Shell/Esso on 9th February. On all items except the base price there was no strong reaction, but extreme disappointment was expressed on this subject, and the response was that the offer was quite unacceptable. At such prices the development of Leman Bank could only be regarded as a salvage operation.

Further meetings with Phillips

Meetings with Phillips also resumed. On 15th February 1968 the company indicated to the Council that its proposed price of 2.9d was "near the bone", but might be prepared to reduce it slightly. There were several other issues which were of major importance to the company, and their representatives proposed that (a) the Council should accept the principle that the sellers' equity should have some protection against inflation, (b) the base year should be the average of 1968 and 1969, (c) the indexation component proposed by the Council (wholesale price of basic materials and fuel), should instead be either the wholesale price of all manufactured products or the index of capital goods published by the National Institute for Economic and Social Research, (d) adjustments above the basic price could be subject to a top-stop, but this should not operate below the basic price, and (e) escalation should apply to 40% of both the basic and valley gas prices.

At the same meeting Sir Henry Jones counter-proposed a package which (a) while not accepting publicly the concept of safeguarding the sellers' equity returns would give some comfort, (b) accepted 1968/69 as the base year, and (c) would consider further the sellers' proposals on (1) the specific indices for indexation and (2) top-stop variation. Sir Henry would also try to persuade the Government that escalation should apply to a maximum of 25% of the price. If valley gas were to be subject to escalation its base price would have to be reduced from 2.1d to 1.9d.

The parties resumed discussions the following day. The company dropped its request for a statement that the Council should accept the principle of compensation for the equity of the sellers. It also proposed that the top-stop to the price should not be automatic, but subject to review by a panel of experts who would consider a list of factors in making a judgement on the matter. The effect of the counterproposals was to water down the Council's proposals.

Immediately after these meetings Mr Marshall had a series of meetings with a representative of Phillips, and was able to state on 23rd February that he had agreed key terms with them which would form the basis of a final settlement. The key terms had been agreed with the Minister and Sir Henry Jones. The base price was 2.87d, that for valley gas 2.025d, and indexation would apply to 25% of the price (both basic and valley). The representative of Phillips had informed the Minister and Mr Marshall that he would guarantee acceptance of these terms as well as a compromise set of provisions dealing with indexation, arbitration, and other matters.

Key provisions were that the rate of build-up would lead to a full depletion rate by the sixth year. This was slower than Phillips had desired, but it allowed the Council to take account of other deals which it might make with other companies. The escalation clause was based on two indices–a cost index and a top-stop one. The former applied to 25% of the basic price, and would be reviewed in 1972 and every third year thereafter at the request of either party. This index was composite and would protect the investors against escalation of specified wholesale prices, wage rates, and the prices of capital goods. The initial price could thus increase or decrease according to movements in costs. In order to prevent the gas price from increasing so high that it became uncompetitive with other fuels, the second index based on movements in the prices of kerosene, oil purchased by the CEGB, and the average price of electricity, became operative. Thus the gas price might increase following upward movement in the cost index, but could not go over the limit indicated by the top-stop index.

Further articles provided that the price and escalation clauses were open to review if either party felt that, through a substantial change in economic circumstances, they were suffering hardship. The review would initially be conducted between the two parties, but, if agreement were not reached, provision was made for arbitration by three experts, one appointed by each side and the third by the Minister of Power.

Agreement with Phillips a major breakthrough

The agreement with Phillips was a major breakthrough, not only for its own sake, but because of its implications for negotiations with the other oil companies. It was decided in the Ministry that an early announcement was desirable. To this end the Council and the Phillips Group were going all out to get the full contract completed. Pending this great secrecy was required. Mr Marshall had informed the Permanent Secretary at the DEA (the Chairman of the Inter-Departmental Steering Group on Energy Policy) of the position, and he had advised that the Prime Minister should be involved but nothing should be put on paper.

Preparations were then made for a statement by the Minister in the House of Commons. The contract was signed on 2nd March 1968 and the statement was made on 6th March. It highlighted the price for the Phillips Group's share of Hewett with brief details of some of the other clauses. The expected plateau output was 600 mmcf/d. Opposition spokesmen expressed general satisfaction. Some Labour MPs had concerns about the possible adverse effects of natural gas exploitation on the market for coal.

Continuing negotiations with Shell and Esso

While negotiations were being concluded with Phillips discussions had been continuing with Shell/Esso. At a meeting with Dr Hoare of Esso on 21st February it was revealed that the company was rejecting the Council's latest offer which, it was argued, was in any case not in the best interests of the whole country. The company was in the process of reducing its investment plans. There was now a doubt about the second platform for Leman, and the exploration effort could well be transferred to the Netherlands. Dr Hoare argued that his company's price offer of 3.2d represented a major effort to produce a settlement. It incorporated only a very reasonable allowance for devaluation and the company was absorbing the increase in corporation tax. The price also had to be seen in relation to other opportunities. Dr Hoare indicated that one serious alternative was to export the gas to Italy. He also felt that the Council was unnecessarily apprehensive about its ability to market gas in the UK. A marginal improvement by the Council to its offer would be a waste of time. In the absence of an agreement with the Council based on direct negotiation there was no alternative but to bring the matter to the Minister, though this was an outcome which Esso had wished to avoid.

Inter-Departmental meeting on Phillips agreement

News of the agreement with Phillips had widespread repercussions. Dr Balogh complained to the Prime Minister that the DEA, Treasury, and he were not satisfied with the information at their disposal and thus found it difficult to judge whether the basic interests of the country were being safeguarded on this important subject. This was followed by a meeting of the Inter-Departmental Steering Group on Energy Policy at which the main elements of the agreement with Phillips were outlined. In discussion the view was expressed that it would have been preferable if the contract had a break clause which allowed full renegotiation after a specified number of years. This was desirable because a situation could arise over the long life of the contract where productivity offshore increased, but there was no relevant provision to take account of this in the indices. The underlying assumption was that prices would rise. Further, there was no provision for the Council to reopen the contract if the companies made very high profits. The Council could only call for a review if it was suffering hardship. If the companies made very large profits the only course open to the Government to procure a review would be to alter the tax position of the companies. The conclusions of the meeting were that, when contracts with the other oil companies were nearing completion, the Minister of Power should report to his Ministerial colleagues so that they could consider whether the indexation and break clauses applicable to the Phillips contract were suitable for other agreements.

Dr Balogh, a member of the Steering Group, pursued the matter further with the Prime Minister. He reiterated the concern about productivity increases not being accommodated in the escalation clause. He was unhappy with the review clause which did not permit the whole contract to be reviewed if the price moved very favourably to the oil companies. He thought that Phillips could obtain a return of 60% on its investment! He also queried whether the profits would be subject to full UK taxation. If the Council and the Ministry had been thinking that the agreement with Phillips had advantages in breaking the solidarity among the companies, it should be clear that this argument could not be used to give similar terms to Shell/Esso for the much bigger Leman field. He suggested that the Prime Minister himself chair the Ministerial meeting to which the Minister of Power should report on the position with respect to the Leman contract.

New Minister assesses position

In the Ministry the new Minister, Mr Ray Gunter, was briefed on the up-to-date position with the gas contracts. This included a short review of the alternative approaches to pricing. It was pointed out that a strict cost-plus approach was inappropriate. It was unrealistic for a situation where there was a risk of complete failure. The cost-related approach incorporated the idea of unsuccessful exploration. It was pointed out that the initial success rate was high, but that no new major finds had been made for over a year. The market value approach had not commended itself to the Gas Council or the Government, principally because there was a risk that the result could be an unnecessarily high price, but also because of the differences of view on what constituted the market value. Various studies had been undertaken, but these had not established such a value with any certainty. The contracts being negotiated provided that the Council had to take or pay for the volumes indicated. It was thus important that the price paid was such that permitted all the gas bought to be profitably marketed. This involved the penetration of new markets at a rate matching the purchases.

Following the agreement with Phillips negotiations were continuing with Arpet, which had a licence that also included a share of the Hewett field. This group was still debating provisions relating to security of supply, but the Ministry felt confident that they would have to settle on terms very similar to Phillips. The arrangements for unified development of the field were well advanced.

The new Minister was informed that the last offer made to Shell/Esso in February had been rejected with some asperity by the two companies, but discussions had been re-opened. The Ministry had some sympathy with the companies' views on the effects of devaluation on their costs, and had also calculated that the costs (per therm) of developing the Leman field would be higher than for Hewett, despite its larger reserves. To produce the same rate of return as currently foreseen for Hewett would entail a price of 3.1d for Leman. The proposed counter-argument was that the Phillips price was indicative of the going rate for North Sea gas. This pointed towards a settlement for Leman at a similar price. It would be very difficult to find reasons to settle at a significantly lower level. Attempts to force the price lower would cause extreme bitterness and could cause reduced exploration.

The Minister was also informed that Amoco had made an unacceptable offer of a base price of 3.25d for their share of the field. This did not constitute a basis for negotiation, but discussions were proceeding on other issues. Such other issues included price indexation and price review clauses. The Government was concerned that provision should be made in the contracts for review, after a period of years, to ensure that very large profits were not made. The indexation provisions commonly employed, such as those in the Phillips contract, were likely to result in price increases. To modify this possibility the top-stop condition had been agreed. The intention was to include such a provision in other contracts. This would not permit a review on the grounds that the investor was thought to be making very large profits. To attempt to incorporate such a provision now would be unacceptable and could be regarded as a breach of faith. The whole basis of the contracts would be altered. It was relevant to note that there was no statutory authority to obtain information on costs.

Prime Minister requests further paper on pricing

The Minister then sent a Minute to the Prime Minister offering to circulate a paper to the Ministerial Committee on the subject of the contracts. The Prime Minister responded that he wanted the paper to cover the subjects of price reviews and tranche pricing, and to be submitted first to the Steering Group on Energy Policy. The Ministry paper outlined the main features of the Phillips agreement and commented that the Gas Council had achieved a considerable success in the negotiations, particularly with the indexation and review clauses. The Arpet group had been offered the same terms, and, although they had not yet been accepted, it was fully anticipated that this would happen.

The paper argued that the success of the negotiations with Phillips would greatly enhance the chances of other contracts being settled at the same price. On the other hand lower prices would be very difficult to achieve. While Leman was larger its unit costs would also be higher. Indefatigable would be even costlier. Cost-related pricing had been adopted by the Council and Government, and this would make it harder to obtain a price as low as 2.87d. With respect to tranche pricing this had been employed by the Council in its latest offer to Shell/Esso but had been rejected. The companies were interested only with an average price for all the gas offered, but the Ministry felt that the companies might agree to a differentiated structure so long as the average was acceptable. There was, however, a concern that at prices above 3d per therm, marginal sales by the Area Boards might not be profitable. In this context it should be noted that future discoveries would probably be smaller. With an upper value of 3d and an average of around 2.9d there was only limited scope for differentiation.

Review clause

With respect to the review clause issue the one negotiated with Phillips was triggered when either party claimed that it was suffering hardship, but it did not provide for a review of the price on the basis of large profits being made. The paper argued that such a review clause was neither practical nor desirable. Companies were not obliged to reveal their costs. The effect of an attempt to introduce this type of clause would be to spur the companies to insist on a price for the early years of the contract sufficiently high to achieve an acceptable profit calculated on the basis of relatively low post-review prices. The Gas Council would also be faced with much uncertainty about the post-review price of gas which they had to market. The conclusion on this particular issue was that at this stage in the exploration and development of the North Sea it would be both damaging and wrong to attempt to force on the companies what they would regard as quite unjustifiable and unreasonable price controls. This was not ruled out at a later stage if, for example, further very large discoveries were made.

The Minister's paper concluded by seeking the approval of his colleagues to inform Sir Henry Jones that he had the Government's support to negotiate with Shell/Esso and Amoco within a price limit of 2.9d. Attempts would be made to improve on the Phillips terms, such as with escalation and review clauses.

Danger price of gas

Among back-up briefing materials for the Minister were updated calculations of the so-called danger price of gas. This indicated the price at which no further balance of payments net benefits would accrue from extra gas production. For 1970 with production in the 790 mmcf/d–1,300 mmcf/d range it was estimated at 4d. For 1975 for production in the 2,000 mmcf/d–3,000 mmcf/d range it was 6d, and 4d for the 3,000 mmcf/d–4,000 mmcf/d range. With respect to absolute benefits to the balance of payments in 1970 with production of 1,300 mmcf/d they were estimated at £47 million. In 1975 with production at 3,000 mmcf/d they could be around £80 million. These were based on prices of 2.87d and 2.75d on a tranched basis.

Considered views of Official Group

Following the meeting of the Steering Group on 29th April, the Chairman (Mr Neild of the DEA) produced an agreed note to reflect the views of the Official Group. The only substantial issue that arose from the Phillips settlement was the review clause. This protected the company from some of its risks, but not the Council against the very large profits which the investor might make. The Minister of Power had proposed that the contracts with Shell/Esso should incorporate a fixed price for a very long time, but without tranche pricing or review clauses. The absence of these required very careful consideration. The expected level of profits to the companies was a most important factor in deciding what was an appropriate price. The expected profits should reflect the risks involved. The Ministry had estimated the returns on the Hewett field to be in the 25%–30% range, though the companies might have lower values. At the same price the Ministry estimated the return on the Leman field to be 20%–25%, although it was believed that Shell/Esso had estimates in the 15%–20% range.

The Group agreed that, given national policy as set out in the White Paper on *Fuel Policy*, and the related needs of the Gas Council, a price below 2.9d was desirable. The key question was whether and how safeguards against excessive profits and consequential reductions in benefits to the balance of payments might be procured. Tranche pricing was one possibility. The first tranche would have to be at more than 3d per therm, which, if many small fields were found, would result in the Council buying considerable amounts of expensive gas which it would have difficulty in marketing at a profit. Some members favoured tranche pricing, however, to encourage exploration for smaller fields. If many were discovered the Council could gradually reduce its offer price in successive negotiations.

Review clauses were another method to meet the Government's objectives. They were likely to produce in effect a short-term contract within a long-term one. There would be a strong demand by the companies for higher prices in the pre-review period, and much uncertainty about the consequences of the review. The Group found it difficult to reach a definite view on this subject.

The agreed conclusions of the Group were that the critical issues were (a) whether the average price of Shell/Esso should be similar to that for the Phillips contract, (b) whether tranche pricing should be included, and (c) whether a review clause on stiffer terms than the Phillips one should be included. If negotiations were to reach an impasse new legislation could be introduced which would permit the costs of the companies to be examined, thus allowing prices to be fixed. All this would be very controversial, and would hold back exploration. In all the circumstances a stiffer review clause was probably the best option, though the Ministry of Power considered the scope for negotiating such a clause very limited.

Ministerial meeting on gas contracts

Mr Pitblado, the Permanent Secretary, briefed the Minister in advance of the Ministerial meeting that colleagues in other Departments were giving undue importance to tranche pricing. He also informed the Minister that a review clause which could be used to claw back profits above a certain level was entirely unnegotiable.

Other Ministers were also given briefings for the Ministerial meeting. Dr Balogh sent a Minute directly to the Prime Minister. Using colourful language he disputed the claims by the Ministry of Power that large fields were unlikely to be found in the future, and, therefore, the case against tranche pricing based on high prices being paid for a large number of small fields was also disputed. Dr Balogh also argued that the settlement with Phillips was generous, and, if repeated, could result in a deplorable situation where on the basis of supposedly cost-plus pricing, the oil companies could earn pre-tax profits of 60%–70% while the Gas Council found difficulty either in absorbing the gas or in meeting its financial target of 10.2%. To ensure that the contracts were nationally beneficial Dr Balogh felt that it was essential to have a review clause to come in after five or seven years, and that the principle of quantity discount should be maintained. In the case of Leman Bank the average price should not exceed 2.5d, and for the tranche of production over 1,500 mmcf/d it should be 2.0d.

The Secretary of State for Economic Affairs was also briefed to argue in favour of a review clause in future contracts and a system of tranche pricing. The review clause should be triggered after five years. The oil companies wanted to protect their oil markets and to get the maximum return on their risk investments. The Gas Council wanted to get the maximum amount of gas as soon as possible. But the national interest was best served by getting the lowest price to maximise balance of payments and resource benefits.

At the Ministerial meeting the Minister of Power outlined the up-to-date position with the negotiations and presented his proposals and the reasoning behind them. There was general support for the upper negotiating limit of 2.9d. It was also considered that a price review was necessary. Without this the oil companies might earn excessively high profits which would mostly be remitted overseas. There was also a concern that the Gas Council might not be able to meet its financial target and would have to ask either for price increases to consumers[2] or Exchequer support. While the contracts were legally determined in negotiations between the Gas Council and the oil companies there was also a concern that the Government could be exposed to criticism if a contract were condoned which led to excessive profits. The cases of Ferranti and Bristol Siddeley were still fresh in Ministers' minds.[3] If a full-scale review clause was not possible the alternatives of tranche pricing or a top-stop should be considered. These should allow a reduction in the price of Leman gas if there were to be a fall in the price of other fuels (including further discoveries of North Sea gas). If the companies were uncooperative the Government should be prepared to force a cost-related price review clause by new legislation. There were some risks attached to this course of action. Exploration might falter and balance of payments benefits might be lost when they were most needed.

After discussion the meeting concluded by inviting the Minister of Power to authorise the Gas Council to pursue negotiations with Shell/Esso and Amoco within a price limit of 2.9d, subject to a price review clause, which should preferably provide for the price structure to be reviewed in the light of subsequent experience, including information on costs and profits. If this could not be achieved consideration should be given to introducing tranche pricing or a top-stop index. The Minister of Power should report back to the Ministerial Group on progress. In the meantime the Steering Group should advise the Minister further on the contents of a review clause.

Further report of Steering Group

The Steering Group pursued the matter and produced another report for the Ministerial Committee. The Group considered that review clauses were essential. They could be considered under two main heads. The first would provide for radical review and redetermination of the price after an initial period. In effect a long-term agreement of 20 to 25 years would be converted into two or more short-term ones. Under the second heading review clauses could establish principles including a formula for adjusting the price during the course of a contract.

The Group felt that the first view was unsatisfactory, principally because the oil companies would react to the uncertainty of the outcome of a redetermination by bidding up the price for the first period. The open-ended nature of the price for the second period was also a concern. There was a worry that there might be deadlock between the parties when redetermination was being renegotiated. The second appraisal was thus preferable. A pre-determined formula could be based on specified cost-and/or market-related factors. A cost-related review related to actual costs would have the advantage that it should prevent excessive profits from being earned from the exploitation of a national asset. Such a clause could take many forms but there were some key features. The oil companies had to disclose their costs, and there had to be a pre-determined formula which would prescribe an agreed level or range of profits or rate of return. There were many plausible cost indices and ranges of acceptable profitability. If the objective was to prevent unduly high profits from being made either a maximum permissible rate of return would need to be established or the price could be progressively reduced as profits increased.

The Group also noted that a cost-plus contract would disadvantage the Government by transferring the risks to the buyer. In any case the oil companies were unwilling to have costs directly incorporated in each contract. The Gas Council had also expressed the view that to introduce a new element into the negotiations after 18 months would be regarded as a breach of faith. Difficulties for the Council in marketing the gas profitably could emerge. If a cost-related clause were introduced it might be necessary to pass legislation to alter the rights and duties of the parties. This would be required to compel the companies to disclose their costs and to give the Government powers to regulate prices. (The agreement on the Hewett field was not based on actual costs, but was justified as it broke the deadlock on the price issue.) The only way to ensure that the oil companies did not make excessive profits was to secure a review clause based on actual costs, and the question was whether Ministers were willing to legislate to obtain the necessary extra powers.

The Group then considered that, if on balance Ministers felt that the imposition of a cost-related clause was undesirable, it was all the more necessary that the Gas Council press for review clauses which safeguarded the national interest. The price review in the Phillips contract had three main elements, all of which were useful, but they also had limitations. Based on three published indices, the indexation provision, while it protected the companies against some of their cost risks, did not acknowledge that the Government had a similar risk that the companies' profits might be excessive. The top-stop index, while it would keep the gas price down if the price of other fuels fell, was defective because the index was subject to a floor of the original price of 2.87d.

The Group felt that the price review provisions would be improved by the inclusion of an element related to the size of future supplies (reserves) of gas. This would reflect not only the competitive situation but could also indirectly put some control over profits. Thus if large reserves became available unit costs should be reduced and there would be strong downward pressure on prices across the whole energy market. If the gas price was automatically adjusted downwards a restraint would be put on profits. The Group outlined a method whereby the idea could be implemented. A reserves index would be constructed. Three possible ways by which it could be applied were identified. It could be included in the top-stop as it would reflect the competitive situation. If a lot of gas were discovered a substantial fall in the top-stop could occur. This should include the possibility of a reduction below the initial level. Another possibility was to include the reserves index in the escalation index. Thus a proportion of the price could be subject to de-escalation by the reserves index. A further possibility was to use the index as a multiplier of the final price after it had been adjusted under the other review provisions. This could be the most attractive method as the effect of reserves would not be diluted to the extent that would occur when it was incorporated as part of a composite index.

The definition of the reserves index and the method of applying it would be a matter for negotiation. The key objective would be to adjust the escalated price by an amount which would vary in inverse proportion to the change in net reserves available to the Council between the signature of the contract and the review. In the event of the discovery of large new reserves, necessitating price reductions for their effective marketing, the price under existing contracts would also be reduced. If new reserves were discovered at the same rate as they were being depleted the multiplier would have no effect. If discoveries were smaller than the depletion rate the price would be increased. As an illustration of how the index might work the Group calculated the effect of varying the price by 20 per cent of the percentage change in net reserves. If the initial price for Leman gas was 2.9d, and if two further fields the size of Leman and Hewett were discovered, the operation of the index would result in a price reduction of 0.35d per therm. If no further reserves were discovered the price would increase by 0.08d. The Group noted that one possible effect of the scheme could be to reduce exploration incentives. Faced with this index the companies might also demand other concessions in their contracts, including a higher initial price. It was felt that the companies would find it hard to oppose the principle behind the reserves index. The Government could argue that it was justified to include the index given that the companies were being protected against cost inflation.

The Group judged that, once cost was abandoned as the basis of price, there was a much greater risk that excessively high prices would be paid to the oil companies leading to very high profits, than the risk that investors' rates of return would be inadequate. The overall conclusions of the Group were thus that there was a clear choice between contracts which contained cost-plus, cost-related review clauses (which might require new legislation), or price-variation provisions which were related to the future position of the energy market (including future gas reserves).

Views of Gas Council

The Minister in a note to the Ministerial Committee agreed that these were the key choices. He had requested the views of the Chairman of the Gas Council. The latter was strongly opposed to the introduction of any proposals aimed at relating prices to costs and profits in a review clause. He was convinced that the companies would react by negotiating on a new basis aimed at enhancing early returns. Further, he felt that a pricing system based on an element of cost-plus would lead to inflation of these costs. If higher prices had to be paid in the early years the Council would have difficulty in building up sales quickly. It would also have difficulty in concluding long-term sales contracts with consumers if a review were to take place after, say, 5 years. The Chairman also felt that exploration could be adversely affected.

ication gas contracts   219*

Minister favours stiffer price adjustment and review terms

The Minister was convinced by these arguments and concluded that a cost-plus basis for pricing was inappropriate and would involve serious technical problems. He thus supported the alternative approach of seeking stiffer price adjustment and review terms based on the future position of the energy market. He defended the price variation terms in the Phillips contract, and supported the view that these should be strengthened in other contracts. He also felt, however, that the Council should not be tied to a closely defined remit which gave it no freedom of manoeuvre and no scope for exercising its own judgement. Thus, while the proposals for stiffening the price variations had merit, he felt strongly that these should be put to the Council in general terms, to be secured if possible, but not as firm conditions of settlement.

Ministerial Committee favours price-variation provisions

The Ministerial Committee considered the memoranda of the Chairman of the Steering Group and the Minister on 31st May. The Minister summarised his views and recommended that the Government should accept the Steering Group's proposals for price-variation provisions. In discussion it was agreed that, although a cost-related review clause would have been desirable, it was now impossible to negotiate it. The Council should thus be asked to negotiate price-variation provisions on the lines set out by the Steering Group. The Chairman of the Council should, however, report to the Minister either his success or failure to negotiate successfully on the suggested lines. Ministers would then decide whether the proposed contract was acceptable. On the wider issue the view was expressed that there was a fundamental problem of differences of objectives among the oil companies, Gas Council and the Government. The prime concern of the Government was to secure maximum import savings which was not a prime concern of the other parties. Perhaps the Government should have been undertaking the primary negotiating role backed up by professional advice.

Reserves index practical?

Ministry officials examined the practical issues involved in designing a reserves index. The only firm figures available for reserves were those proposed to be dedicated under contracts being negotiated. To obtain regular updates for these from the operators might require an amendment to the Regulations. This was, however, a minor problem. There could well be endless arguments over the interpretation of data on which a determination could be made, and on the classification of what was commercially exploitable. The only firm figures would thus be dedicated volumes. Gas sold to parties other that the Council had to be included. Gas on offer was too imprecise as a basis for the index.

The concept of a reserves index introduced an entirely new element into the negotiations, and there was a danger that doing this at a time when the other price review terms were nearing finality could mean going over all the same ground again. While there was a case for making the reserves index part of the escalation provision, there were presentational advantages in proposing it as an element in the top-stop as it was another competitive energy market factor. The weighting of the reserves index would obviously have an important effect on the outcome, but much would depend on the lead[1] given to the top-stop. If the other components of the top-stop remained as in the Phillips contract and a 20% weighting was given to the reserves index, the discovery of a 15 tcf field by 1972 would broadly eliminate the 10% lead to the top-stop. The idea of a bottom-stop would be of only academic importance if a lead of 10% were conceded and the weighting of the reserves index were around 20%. But if the lead could be reduced to around 5% the bottom-stop would become more important. It had to be recognised, however, that the oil companies would try to keep the floor to the initial price. The implication of this was that the reserves index could not procure the big price reductions which Ministers might expect from it. It was recognised that the introduction of a reserves index into the negotiations would highlight the existing debate with the companies over the proportion of the price subject to escalation and de-escalation. If it were really believed that further large reserves would be discovered, from the Government's viewpoint there were advantages in applying the escalation and reserves indices to a higher percentage of the price. But the risks were high. The two indices need not be applied to the same percentage, but it would be difficult to argue that a higher proportion should be subject to de-escalation than to escalation.

The views of the Ministerial Committee were conveyed to the Chairman of the Gas Council. Accompanying this was a note from the Ministry indicating how a reserves index could be formulated and the consequential contractual and administrative problems. The Ministry was now clear that a reserves index could only be negotiable if (a) it was symmetric (capable of operating more or less equally in favour of either party), and (b) higher prices for the initial period were conceded. To obtain symmetric operation in a clear cut manner the adjustment would have to be based on the next increase in reserves between the contract date and the adjustment date. The oil companies would then receive a higher or lower price for their contracted gas depending on the relationship between discoveries and quantities already delivered.

There were serious difficulties in defining total reserves of commercially exploitable gas which was conceptually the appropriate definition. The only precise definition was in terms of reserves under contract to the Council. A further problem emanated from the likelihood that discoveries would be made in a discontinuous, lumpy manner. Thus the price adjustments would move irregularly. A three-year adjustment was suggested.

Having acknowledged these problems the Ministry's note then indicated how the reserves index could be grafted on to the price escalation formula. This could be either in the form of a multiplier applied to the price as revised by the escalation formula or it could be incorporated additively into the escalation formula. Either approach was acceptable.

Views of Gas Council on reserves index

Sir Henry Jones was dismayed to receive the above news from the Ministry. In preparing his response he noted that the negotiations with Shell/Esso had been proceeding since the autumn of 1966. Since then both the Council and the companies had expended large capital sums in anticipation of gas supplies starting in October. (It was now mid-June, 1968.) It should also be recognised that the agreement with Phillips was a shock to the other oil groups in the North Sea, and had been hailed in the gas industries in Europe as a triumph for the Council and UK Government. It was quite likely that Shell/Esso were aware of the main terms of the Phillips contract.

Against this background it was unfortunate that the Council was being asked to introduce two new elements (the reserves index and the alteration to the top-stop formula to include a price reduction below the base price). It was felt by the Council that the latter objective could be achieved by linking the gas price to the fuel oil price, as was the case in Dutch and French contracts.

The proposal to take into account in price determination future discoveries and cumulative consumption was also without precedent, and would provide an incentive to the companies to conceal or play down the size of discoveries. In sum the Chairman felt that both of the new proposals were misconceived. They would certainly delay the conclusion of the negotiations, and could well entail higher prices in the near term. The needs of the Council and the nation for a rapid build-up of gas sales did not seem to be served by proposals which appeared to stem from a dislike of oil company profits rather than from any national or commercial motive. The Council was also concerned with the risk to its reputation in the negotiation and implementation of contracts. The Council would have to work with the companies for many years. With the new proposals the reputational risks were such that the Chairman did not wish the Council to introduce them into the negotiations.

The Minister met with Sir Henry Jones to discuss the matter. Sir Henry explained how both new proposals would cause difficulty for his negotiations on the lines discussed above. At this late stage he would have to inform the companies that he was acting on Government instructions. He thought that they knew the terms of the Phillips agreement, and the Council would have difficulty in obtaining similar terms from the other companies. Currently Amoco were insisting that 60% of the price should be subject to escalation while Shell/Esso wanted 100%. The introduction of the two new proposals could certainly incentivise the companies to seek to recoup the costs of the extra risks in other parts of the contract, and the net effect would be higher prices.

In response the Minister expressed understanding of Sir Henry's difficulties. Some of his Ministerial colleagues took a very strong line on the subject of oil company profits, and he wondered whether Sir Henry could put the two new proposals informally to the companies on the understanding that, if they appeared likely to be unnegotiable, he should report back to the Minister. Sir Henry felt that it would not be appropriate to put the proposals to their own partner (Amoco), because they would react strongly and insist on a higher price. He would, however, speak informally with Mr Barran of Shell to obtain some assessment of the likely reaction. The Minister indicated his appreciation of such an approach.

Negotiations with companies continue

Meanwhile negotiations were continuing with the various licence groups. A notable event had taken place at the end of May. Mr David Barran of Shell had written to the Chairman of the Gas Council stating that, in order to achieve an accommodation, Shell was now prepared to offer a base price of 2.87d for gas from both Leman and Indefatigable. Further, the company was now willing to acknowledge the prices of other fuels in the indexation provisions. A similar letter and identical offer was received from Esso.

The reply from Sir Henry was less than grateful. This was because other elements of the contract had been varied from earlier versions to the disadvantage of the Council. He listed a number of such factors which included an increase in the load factor for Indefatigable, a change to the pricing of make-up gas (gas not taken by the Council in one contract period but taken later), and the variation to the price adjustment clause. In Sir Henry's view this clause as redrafted gave substantial escalation (favouring Shell), with only a theoretical protection of the Council's position in the market in which it would be selling. Sir Henry was thus disappointed, but indicated that the negotiating teams should meet again.

Discussions had also been taking place with Amoco. The company had expressed the view to the Ministry that a price of 3.25d for Indefatigable and an average of 2.97d for this field and Leman were reasonable. Both these fields were more expensive to exploit that Hewett. Mr Marshall indicated that the 2.87d price should be regarded as a ceiling, not a floor. For Amoco Mr Morrow indicated that such a price would not encourage exploration. He also felt that the proposal from the Council that the escalation index should only apply to 20% of the price did not adequately protect his company against cost inflation. He felt that 50%–60% of the price should escalate. Mr Marshall's response was that, while it was reasonable to provide some protection against cost inflation, there was no justification for preserving the real value of income. Allowance for this was included in the rate of return expected by the investor.

Mr Mason assesses position

At this critical time a new Minister of Power (Mr Roy Mason) was appointed. He had rapidly to be briefed on the up-to-date position. In early July 1968 the Ministry produced a briefing paper which indicated that agreement with Amoco was close, with the main difference being the proportion of the price that should be subject to the price review indices. Discussions with Shell/Esso had been in abeyance since the end of May. The Council and the Government had found their escalation proposals unacceptable. The idea of a reserves index had not yet formally been presented to them. Amoco were keen to restart discussions, and the Ministry felt that the final round was approaching.

Negotiations with Shell/Esso resume

The negotiations with Shell/Esso resumed and revised price review proposals were received by the Council. These contained three key elements namely (a) escalation based on one index (manufactured products) and weighted by 30%, (b) a trigger clause based on the basic materials and fuels index, and (c) a top-stop similar to that in the Phillips agreement with a 30% weighting. The Council discussed these with the Ministry on 15th July. It was agreed that the proposals represented the limit which could be conceded and should be accepted by the Council only as a last resort. The provision would produce an escalation rate similar to the clause in the Phillips contract. It was also agreed that the trigger could only operate as a time mechanism for setting off a price review earlier than otherwise, but not as a formula for adjusting the price as had been suggested by the companies. If the trigger came into effect (that is, if the index moved up 7 points in six months), the basic price would be increased in proportion to the rise over that period, and the new price would become the basic one subject to past and future escalation. This was regarded as double counting, because the manufactured products index would sooner or later reflect movements in the basic materials index. It was also recognised that, if the trigger did no more than justify a price review, a mechanism was necessary to bring the basic materials index to bear on the price.

Mr Denis Rooke's suggestions

Shortly thereafter Mr Marshall reported at a meeting of the Departmental Working Party on Natural Gas that Mr Denis Rooke of the Gas Council had suggested to him that there were reasonable prospects of being able to negotiate an agreement with Shell/Esso incorporating (a) a fixed price for 15–25 years, (b) tranche pricing (perhaps 2.87d, 2.85d, 2.80d), and (c) an abnormal inflation hedge at perhaps 70% of the basic materials index. A variant would have lower initial prices for the second and subsequent tranches, but would incorporate an abnormal inflation hedge during the fixed price period and a top-stop with, say, a 10% lead.

It was agreed that these packages were to be encouraged in negotiations with the companies, but it was also necessary for the Council to report to the Minister if and when they decided that the reserves index could not be negotiated. There then followed a discussion on what indices might best be employed for an abnormal inflation adjustment. The Treasury had advised that there could be no overt statement of a devaluation provision. As an indirect measure the basic materials and fuels index was appropriate, and the risks of marked movements in it for reasons other than devaluation could be tolerated. The movement of the indicator employed to trigger the abnormal inflation adjustment should be specified in percentage terms, not index points. The group also felt that any abnormal inflation provision should be symmetrical. It must allow for a price decrease as well as an increase. It was noted that the composition of the chosen escalation index had substantial consequences. Thus the inclusion of the basic materials and fuels index would restrain the normal inflation movement, but would result in a more immediate response to a devaluation.

Further proposals from Shell/Esso

It had become apparent that Shell/Esso were unenthusiastic about the inclusion of a reserves index. The group discussed the respective merits of having the reserves index as a direct price regulator or as part of the top-stop, but agreed that there was no point in pursuing the matter at this stage until the Council had examined the fixed price route further.

Following the meeting of the Working Party Ministry officials met again with the Gas Council and were informed that Shell/Esso had now turned against the idea of a fixed price contract with an abnormal inflation adjustment mechanism. They had now put forward a package with several price adjustment components namely, (a) automatic escalation of 30% of the price determined by a composite index based on the output of the engineering industry and men's wage rates, (b) a hardship review clause to apply to changes in the fuel oil tax and the surcharge on oil prices (following the Suez crisis), as well as to more general changes in economic circumstances, (c) a top-stop as in the Phillips contract, but with the surcharge and fuel oil tax excluded from the index base, and (d) a bottom-stop framed to prevent the top-stop (in the event that it fell) from reducing the price further below the initial level than it would otherwise have exceeded the initial price by the operation of the escalation provision.

The group felt that there were serious disadvantages in excluding the oil surcharge and fuel oil tax from the top-stop base. The removal of the fuel oil tax alone would have affected the top-stop in the Phillips contract by 10.5%–12%. There was disagreement on whether a four or six months trigger was in the best interests of the Council. Sensible scenarios could be produced to support each period.

On the same afternoon Shell/Esso tabled fresh proposals for the Leman field. They were on the lines indicated earlier by Mr Denis Rooke. The key elements were (a) a fixed price of 2.87d at 60% load factor for 15 years (with 2.025d for valley gas), and (b) this price to be varied upwards or downwards in the event of a sharp movement in the index of basic materials prices. If this were brought about by devaluation (the main worry) the indexation provisions would increase the price by around 40% of the amount of the devaluation, (c) after 15 years, and in the event of no price revision for abnormal inflation, there would be a tranche price system with 2.87d for the first 600 mmcf/d, 2.8d for the second 600 mmcf/d, and 2.75d for the rest, all subject to escalation for cost inflation alone, and (d) a top-stop with a 5% lead, but with a variation capable of reducing the price below the starting point.

The scheme had attractions to the Council. The possibility of a fixed price for 15 years greatly reduced their marketing risks, though they were exposed to the risk of the oil tax being reduced. While the terms would not directly meet the desire of Ministers for the inclusion of reserves in the formula, the long fixed price period offered some compensations, and Mr Marshall felt that there was now a good chance that the Phillips' terms could be bettered.

Mr Mason immediately met with Sir Henry Jones to discuss the Shell/Esso tentative offer. The Minister asked about the relative advantages of the fixed price arrangement compared to the incorporation of a reserves index. Sir Henry was very clear that a reserves index could not be included without conceding a price increase, and that it would be better to accept the broad lines of the offer, but attempt to improve on the price in negotiations. One possibility was to introduce the tranche pricing arrangement earlier than in the Shell/Esso proposals.

Mr Mason favourably disposed to latest Shell/Esso offer

Mr Mason then submitted a Minute to the Prime Minister on the position and requested a meeting with the relevant group of Ministers. After briefly outlining the history of the negotiations with Shell/Esso, and noting the expressed desire of Ministers to have oil reserves included in the price indexation formula, he reported that the Council had been unable to persuade the companies to accept such an index on acceptable terms. The companies had argued that the concept increased uncertainty, and was not superior to other direct and fairer methods of obtaining lower prices relating to further discoveries.

The Council's insistence on obtaining terms more favourable than in the Phillips contract had, however, elicited a fresh, tentative offer. He outlined the terms for Leman as noted above and suggested that this package was attractive to the Council and Government. The price stability was clearly attractive and was subject to risk only in abnormal circumstances. The tranche pricing for the later part of the contract offered the prospect of negotiating lower prices on further discoveries. The proposed terms for the Indefatigable field were the same as for Leman except that the price was 0.03d higher to reflect the higher expected costs. The whole package represented a good bargain.

Mr Mason reported that Sir Henry Jones felt that the companies had stretched themselves to the limit to produce the terms now on offer. Sir Henry felt that he should now be given authority to negotiate a settlement not less good than these on offer. He might be able to improve on them to a small degree. The Minister accepted Sir Henry's assessment and sought his colleagues' agreement that the Council should seek to negotiate a settlement on the lines indicated.

Official group has reservations

The North Sea Gas Official Committee examined Mr Mason's Minute and prepared a note which was submitted to the Ministerial Committee. The group agreed that the proposed terms were better than the Phillips contract. Some concern was expressed about the consequences of the (indirect) provision for devaluation being repeated in other contracts. The group felt that the tranche pricing provisions were not very advantageous. The contract was also open-ended on quantity, and the group raised the idea that the terms might be limited to, say, 2,000 mmcf/d in case much larger reserves were discovered.

In the light of the importance of the decision for the whole national economy, especially the balance of payments, the group felt that Ministers might like rather more time to reach a decision. However, given the need to obtain early agreement Ministers could either (a) meet again shortly to make a final decision or (b) authorise the Council to proceed with negotiations on the broad basis of the proposals but not to conclude an agreement without reference to Ministers.

The Prime Minister received other Minutes on the subject. One member of the Official Committee expressed concern that the apparent advantages of the fixed price had three offsetting factors namely (a) the devaluation hedge, (b) the absence of a top-stop for the first fifteen years, and (c) the receipt by the companies of much larger volumes at lower unit cost than in the Phillips case. The idea was also raised that the opposition of the companies to the inclusion of reserves in the price formula could be due to their belief that much bigger reserves would be found than the Ministry believed. The figures on reserves were based on company estimates which would certainly be conservative. In sum, the offer, while an improvement on the Phillips one, was still not good enough. A decision of this magnitude should not be taken in haste, and there were advantages in postponing a final decision. This would allow time to improve on the terms, especially those which would come into effect after 15 years. This could be achieved by having steeper tranche pricing.

Sir Burke Trend's reservations

Sir Burke Trend, the Cabinet Secretary, also briefed the Prime Minister on the issue. As well as preferring caution in taking an immediate final decision he raised the issue of the wider aspects of the guarantee against devaluation. This had further implications, including the Treasury's current negotiations on sterling balances. The Government would not want anything in the nature of a precedent for guaranteeing private balances against devaluation. It was also pertinent that Shell were currently negotiating with the Government about diversification of their large sterling balances.

Ministers discuss latest Shell/Esso proposals

At the Ministerial meeting on 2nd August the Minister of Power outlined the history of the negotiations with Shell/Esso and their latest proposals. He expressed the view that the current proposals were more favourable than could be obtained under a contract with a reserves index on any reasonable assumption regarding the volume of reserves likely to be discovered. The Gas Council should thus be authorised to proceed to negotiate terms on the basis proposed in his Minute.

In discussion it was suggested that, while the substance of the review clause for abnormal price movements was acceptable, it should not be included in the contract as it would be clearly seen as a hedge against devaluation. It was proposed that it should be agreed with the companies on a confidential basis, such as by a secret exchange of letters. Any such document should be couched in guarded terms and agreed with the Treasury.

There was also a feeling that there were risks attached in being committed to a fixed price for fifteen years for whatever volumes of gas were produced. There was a case for confining the fixed price to a limited volume. It was recognised, however, that there were objections to this, because the Gas Council was anxious to obtain all the gas under the proposed contract. If it did not do this the companies would be able to sell quantities in excess of the limit. Such sales would be damaging to the Council in terms of possible lost customers and revenues. On balance it would be better that the Council took all the gas on offer.

The Ministerial group felt that a more promising approach would be to shorten the period during which the fixed price would apply to less than the fifteen years proposed. This would bring forward the timing of the introduction of tranche pricing. The Council could also attempt to procure more favourable tranche pricing provisions. It was agreed that the Chairman of the Gas Council should be authorised to negotiate on the lines indicated above. The Minister of Power should report back to the Ministerial Committee the outcome of the further negotiations by the Council before final commitment to a settlement. The Minister of Power should also have an assessment prepared of the benefits to the balance of payments of a settlement on the contract terms most likely to be achieved. An assessment of the implications for such a deal on gas prices to domestic consumers was also requested.

What length of fixed price period?

Immediately following the meeting Mr Mason wrote to the Prime Minister informing him that the idea of shortening the period over which the price was to be held fixed from fifteen years to ten had already been examined and found to be less favourable to the Council. The Prime Minister received another Minute on the same day acknowledging that this might happen because the creeping increase resulting from the earlier introduction of the indexation formula to cover cost inflation would more than offset the benefits from tranche pricing. But a different conclusion was drawn. The result indicted the inadequacies of the proposals for tranche pricing! The lesson was to negotiate hard for more radical tranche pricing which would swing the advantage of an earlier date for the end of fixed pricing to the Government's advantage. In addition there should be a limit on the quantity to be taken under the contracts. There was a case for a complete break in the contract terms after ten years when much more information would be available on reserves, unit costs and profits. The odds were that the whole market situation would have changed by then, and it would be regretted that commitments had been made to a price as high as 2.87d (plus) for a number of years thereafter. The

Prime Minister's decision was that the best course of action was to try for more radical tranche pricing provisions which might swing the advantage of an early date of the end of a fixed price to the Government's benefit.

Reaction of Gas Council and Ministry

The Ministry conveyed the conclusions of the Ministerial meeting to the Council. The Council was much concerned about the idea of incorporating the provision for abnormal inflation in a secret letter. They feared that such a letter would not in practice be any more secret than the contract itself. It would become publicly known as soon as the deal was announced that there would be provision for abnormal inflation. The detailed provisions would soon get round to the large number of companies involved. There was no possibility of concealing this. A secret letter would highlight the fact that there was something to hide and arouse suspicions. A second concern was that a secret letter would damage the Council's credit with the oil companies and prejudice their future negotiating ability.

The Ministry generally agreed with the Council. Officials also recognised that the companies could insist on the right to refer to the provision in general terms, since otherwise they might appear to have failed in their duty to shareholders. The Gas Council could not deny the existence of the provision. They might even need to refer to it in discussions with their own customers on contract terms. The Ministry also thought, however, that it would be in the interests of all parties to prevent the detailed terms from becoming known. Thus the companies would not wish the restricted aspects of the price adjustment terms from becoming known, since this might constrain future negotiations. Another aspect was the possibility that the detailed terms might have to be disclosed in Court proceedings. In such an event a secret letter would be treated like the rest of the contract. A review provision for abnormal price agreements had now been agreed with the Treasury. It did not mention devaluation, and, in the view of the Ministry, would not arouse special interest in a contract in which the price was fixed for fifteen years. But, despite this, Treasury officials still firmly believed that the clause should only appear in a secret letter. It was argued that, even if the terms eventually became known, this procedure offered the best change of delaying disclosure. Both the Ministry and the Council took the opposite view, and felt that a secret letter would be more likely to draw immediate attention to the provision it was designed to conceal.

After further inconclusive discussions among the Ministry, Gas Council and Treasury, Mr Mason wrote to Mr Roy Jenkins, the Chancellor, on the issue. He summarised the arguments against a secret letter. The Chancellor replied that he now accepted that there was force in the arguments and agreed that the abnormal inflation provision could be included in the contract itself. He emphasised another point. It was important that the (disguised) devaluation hedge clause should not be included in any of the sales contracts which the Council was about to negotiate with its own large customers. He felt that this would be quite inappropriate.

Negotiations continue

The negotiations continued. The Council concentrated its efforts on trying to improve the tranche pricing arrangements. These were successful. Mr Mason was then able to report to his Ministerial colleagues that, for the initial fifteen year period instead of a flat price for all of the Leman gas the companies had agreed to prices of 2.87d for the first 600 mmcf/d, 2.85d for the next 600 mmcf/d, and 2.83d for the remainder. The average price for this period would now be just over 2.85d. But similar arrangements could not be negotiated for the Indefatigable field. The Minister reported that Sir Henry Jones was satisfied that this was the maximum concession which could be negotiated. Mr Mason regarded the outcome as highly satisfactory.

Implications of Shell/Esso proposals for balance of payments and consumer prices

Mr Mason also reported the findings of the study by his officials on the implications of the Shell/Esso settlement for the balance of payments and for domestic gas prices. Officials had presumed that the settlement with Shell/Esso would strongly influence subsequent deals and assumed that all the gas now in prospect (apart from the Hewett field and the short-term BP agreement) would be bought on similar terms with an average price in the 2.8d–2.9d range. The study concentrated on the likely position in 1970/71 and 1975. Availability was presumed to be 2,000 mmcf/d and 4,000 mmcf/d respectively in these years. The consequential savings to the balance of payments would be around £50 million and £75 million in the two years. The results were not very sensitive to small variations in the price. For example, a variation of 0.1d per therm would make a difference of less than £1 million in 1970/71, and less than £2 million in 1975.

With respect to the effects on gas prices the Ministry estimated that, after allowing for transmission costs, natural gas would produce a saving of around 4d per therm over gas manufactured in a modern oil plant, and about 8d per therm over the current average cost of the present mix of plant which included coal carbonisation plant. The very large expenditures on transmission, distribution and the conversion of consumers' appliances would limit the scope for early price reductions, even though they would be spread over a long period. To maximise the benefits from North Sea gas the gas industry needed to make large gains in the industrial market. This entailed price reductions in that market. In the near term price reductions in the domestic market could be around 0.5d–1d per therm, though by 1975/76 they might be reduced by 4d per therm.

Ministers again discuss proposed Shell/Esso contracts

Mr Mason invited his colleagues to agree that he should authorise the Gas Council to conclude an agreement on the lines suggested earlier, as adjusted by the new proposals on tranche pricing for the Leman field. The Prime Minister also received other briefing ahead of the Ministerial meeting. The claim that the tranche pricing in the initial fifteen year period was more advantageous than a shortening of this period to ten years was disputed. There was also no change in the very limited tranche pricing in the later period. It was noted that there was no tranche pricing in the initial fifteen years for Indefatigable. The argument that the outcome of the recent negotiation was highly satisfactory was thus open to dispute. The view was expressed that the average price was still far too high. There was a concern that the Gas Council would not be able to meet its sales targets. There had been press reports to this effect. There was a risk that the UK's industrial competitiveness could be undermined. By comparison US prices were stated to be around 1.25d per therm.

In the current circumstances where the negotiations were far advanced the best that could be done was to introduce some limitation on the volumes of gas supplied so that the Council's hands were not tied for 25 years if large extra reserves were found. There should also be tranche pricing in the Indefatigable field during its first 15 years as for the Leman field. For the future, 2.87d should not be regarded as a precedent for negotiations of new contracts. It was also necessary to ensure that the Government had direct access to information about exploration and reserves. This had handicapped negotiations to date. These suggestions were little more than palliatives, but they could do something to reduce the untoward effects of the present proposals.

At the Ministerial meeting the Minister of Power outlined progress since the previous meeting as noted above. In discussion it was generally agreed that, taking into account the prolonged and difficult negotiations to date, no better settlement for Leman could be procured, and so the Council should be authorised to settle with the companies on the terms discussed above. Mr Mason reported that the Chairman of Shell would not wish to take part in any press conference because in his view the contract was not satisfactory to Shell.

In further discussion it was felt essential that, following signature of the main contracts, the rate of substitution of gas for oil envisaged in the White Paper on *Fuel Policy* should be attained. There was a concern that the oil companies had no incentive to work to this end. If they perceived that their oil revenues were suffering through competition from gas they might hold back gas supplies or reduce oil prices to particular customers. It might become necessary to adjust the fuel oil duty to ensure that gas remained competitive. On the other hand, the companies had to earn a reasonable return on their North Sea investments. Thus it was unlikely that they would want to hold back gas supplies. The Ministerial Committee felt that it would be highly unfortunate if, having contracted supplies for 25 years from existing fields, there were other substantial discoveries from which gas could be obtained more cheaply.

Conclusions of Ministers

In summing up the discussion it was agreed that, while the Council could proceed to finalise the terms for Leman with Shell/Esso, no authority should be given for a settlement for Indefatigable until the Minister had provided an explanation of why there could be no tranche pricing on this field for the first 15 years.

Reaction of Gas Council and Ministry

The results of the meeting were conveyed to the Gas Council. The Chairman and Deputy Chairman were wholly opposed to making a further effort to secure a tranche price system for the first 15 years of Indefatigable. They had attempted to do so, but the companies had been absolutely intransigent in their refusal to make the concession. It was acknowledged that the Indefatigable field was smaller than Leman and would have higher unit costs. The structure was complex and faulted, and many more wells would have to be drilled before the recoverable reserves were known with any confidence. The best estimate was that it would yield around 600 mmcf/d, which meant that tranche pricing would make no difference.

In the circumstances Mr Marshall recommended that the Minister make a submission to his colleagues urging acceptance of the present proposals. A memorandum was prepared accordingly. It was argued that the difference of 0.03d in the initial price compared to Leman was amply justified by the cost differential. The Council had tried hard to obtain tranche pricing for the first fifteen years but had been unsuccessful. The strong and emphatic advice of the Chairman of the Council was not to reopen the issue. If this were done concessions relating to other parts of the contract would be sought and might have to be conceded. The result might be a worse deal than that currently on the table. The Minister strongly urged his colleagues to authorise the Council to finalise both contracts. Such agreement was confirmed on 20th September 1968. The First Secretary of State had been absent from London at the time of these deliberations, and subsequently wrote to the Minister of Power indicating that she was still opposed to the acceptance of the terms.

Taxation issues

The news was no doubt received with much relief by the Gas Council. But many other issues, mostly technical, remained to be settled before contracts could be signed. One issue of much importance to the companies related to taxation. They had been very keen to have a clause in the contracts which stated that any taxes based on gas production would in effect be paid by the Gas Council. In the contracts they were generally defined as repayable gas taxes. They referred to taxes based on gross income, but not those based on profits or price. Local authority taxes were also excluded from the definition of repayable taxes. The precise definitions and coverage of repayable and non-repayable taxes involved a considerable amount of negotiation and some involvement of the Inland Revenue in advising the Gas Council.

Negotiations with Amoco succeed

Negotiations with Amoco which had substantial but separate licence interests in Leman and Indefatigable had been continuing. The Council had impressed on their representatives that they could not obtain terms more favourable than those applicable to Shell/Esso. The company had been holding out for terms similar to those for the Hewett field. The representatives were having difficulty in persuading their parent board in the USA to agree to the same terms as for Shell/Esso. There had also been problems resulting from the difficulties Amoco was having in agreeing their respective shares of the two fields with Shell/Esso. Eventually, however, agreement with Amoco was reached in December.

Mr Mason announces agreements

On 17th December 1968, the Minister of Power announced in the House of Commons that agreements had been signed between the Gas Council and Shell/ Esso for their shares of the Leman and Indefatigable fields. Remarkably, details of the price terms were given in his statement. Agreement had also been reached with Amoco and its partners for similar terms for their share of the two fields. In back-up notes it was argued that the complexities of the issues and the sizes of the fields had been responsible for the long period of negotiation. It was also pointed out that this had not delayed the physical development of Leman. In fact under an interim arrangement gas had actually been flowing since August and production was now 300 mmcf/d. The price agreed was believed to have struck the right balance between providing a fair reward to the producers, including an incentive for further exploration, while enabling the Council to achieve its gas marketing objectives. The price was generally lower than in Europe but higher than in the USA. A big expansion of gas into new markets was in prospect. Priority would be given to increasing sales in industrial markets, principally at the expense of oil products.

Reflections on gas contracts

The conclusion of these agreements was a major landmark in the history of North Sea gas. The volumes from the three fields constituted a very large proportion of all the gas produced in the UKCS for many years ahead. Further, the agreed terms set the pattern for the contracts on later fields. This was the expectation among all the main parties. In turn this affected the attitude of the oil companies towards new licensing rounds. This was to become particularly important when oil discoveries were made in the Central North Sea. A further legacy of the contracts was the mutual suspicion between the Gas Council and the oil companies. This was to last a very long time, perhaps because of the prolonged involvement of key personalities at this time from within both the Gas Council and the oil companies.

The more fundamental questions relate to the wisdom of the underlying policies. The case for the cost-related pricing rested on the view that this would maximise the benefits to the UK balance of payments. At the time this was a major recurring problem, and it is understandable why attention centred on it. North Sea gas would substitute for imported oil. This meant both naphtha employed to manufacture town gas and oil products used in industrial markets where gas could compete. At lower gas prices there would be more scope for such import substitution. At lower purchase prices the Gas Council could extend its profitable sales from premium to base energy markets.

There was a general concern, expressed in the White Paper on *Fuel Policy*, to promote reductions in energy prices in the UK generally. This would help to foster the competitiveness of British industry which used energy on a substantial scale as an input. Heavy, energy-intensive industries such as steel making and shipbuilding played a major role in the economy at this time. The issue of the competitiveness of UK manufacturing industry in world markets was a major concern.

Concentration on the balance of payments also drew attention to the major role of the foreign oil companies and the effect of their profit remittances. Estimates were often made of the magnitudes involved. The conclusions from such calculations were that, other things being equal, smaller remittances were better than larger ones. Lower gas prices would result in lower overseas remittances because profits would be less.

Relatively low beachhead prices were also seen to be very beneficial to the Gas Council and the Government because they made the very large financing costs of the development of the National Transmission System and appliance conversion programme more manageable at gas prices to customers which were competitive. The financial targets of the Council and Area Boards could be achieved at lower prices to consumers.

Putting all the above arguments together produced the conclusion that the national benefits of North Sea gas were maximised the lower the price. Such views were indeed expressed from time to time. Estimates of the benefits to the balance of payments increasing with lower beach prices were frequently produced.

But a different conceptual framework might have been considered and was indeed used later for North Sea oil exploitation. The alternative approach would have based the gas price on its market value as was suggested by the oil companies. Market prices for this purpose is defined in terms of a competitive market price. The general case for this approach is that the market price represents the true value of the gas to the economy. If the gas were exported it would certainly have been at a price reflecting its full market value, and it is arguable that the same principle should have been used for sales to the home market. Such pricing is consistent with the opportunity cost principle.

The result of such market-related pricing could well have been that the oil companies earned economic rents from the gas production. These may be defined as returns in excess of the supply price of the necessary investment. The appropriate mechanism for ensuring that the state collected a share of these rents would be to impose a special, profit-related tax targeted on the rents with elements included to encourage further exploration and development. This whole approach would have meant that the economic rents were not diverted away from the whole nation to gas consumers. It is now generally accepted that economic rents from the exploitation of a natural resource should accrue to the whole nation rather than one element such as consumers of the product. Introduction of a resource rent tax would also have ensured that post-tax returns and overseas profit remittances were not excessive. The idea of special, profit-related taxation was occasionally mentioned in discussions but not given serious consideration.

Market-related pricing in a framework where the Gas Council remained the monopsony buyer would not have been straightforward. There would have been much debate about the appropriate values. North Sea gas would substitute for different oil products such as gas oil and fuel oil whose values also differed. The initial volumes would be used to substitute for the highest priced products and subsequent volumes for the lower priced ones. Translating this into long-term gas contracts involving very large quantities of gas would not have been easy, but, just as cost-related ones were concluded, they could have been achieved and did happen elsewhere. In the Netherlands the model was that Gasunie purchased gas from new fields at prices which were related to the final selling prices of the competing oil products. The producers were subject to a special profit-related tax somewhat confusingly termed the State Profit Share. This scheme was in operation in 1967 when the State Profit Share was introduced. The details would certainly have been known in the UK.

The contract prices eventually arrived at were the outcome of prolonged bargaining. They were widely referred to as cost-related prices, but, if fuel oil was taken to be the alternative fuel the initial prices were in practice not very different from market-related ones. Only if emphasis is put on the higher-valued alternative fuels was there a substantial difference. It was the indexation provisions which ensured that in later years gas prices from the early contracts diverged markedly from any reasonable estimates of market values.

A still more radical alternative would have removed the monopsony buying rights, and at least some of the monopoly selling rights, of the Gas Council. Thus the producers would have been able to sell directly to consumers. The case for the Council's monopsony/monopoly rights had been put in terms of the advantages of a centrally coordinated system of transmission, distribution, and supply. Having full control would enable the huge investments in pipeline systems, conversion of appliances, and allied activities to be undertaken in a well-coordinated and efficient manner.

The possible advantages of competition in the supply of gas to (industrial) consumers were not seriously considered, though competition with petroleum products was a recurring theme. There was some discussion of the possible disadvantages of competing pipeline systems, and passing acknowledgement that the Gas Council's pipeline network could be used to transport gas on behalf of others for a fee. In the absence of the Council's monopsony/monopoly rights a piecemeal transmission/distribution system would have developed to the main markets. The oil companies would have been primarily interested in the larger industrial markets. But it is certainly not clear that the comprehensive network built up by the Gas Council and its successor body could have been completed so expeditiously in the absence of its privileged rights.

While an enormous amount of attention was given to the price terms of the contracts other important elements also had long-lasting consequences. Thus there were field depletion contracts with strong take-or-pay obligations placed on the Gas Council. These provisions effectively removed the market volume risk from the producers and put it clearly in the Council's hands. Long-term contracts with such a clause were, and are, very valuable to the gas producers, and can facilitate the financing of field developments.

The contracts were a product of their times. The widespread media comment generally did not query the conceptual framework employed but concentrated on the prices and the expected profits of the oil companies. The Conservative Party in Parliament did not seriously query the conceptual framework either. A free-market alternative approach was, however, very clearly articulated as early as 1967 by George Polanyi.[5] Interestingly, he had worked for several years for the North Western Gas Board. This paper presented the case for a radical free-market alternative. He appreciated that economic rents might be earned by the producers, and suggested that an excess profits tax should be put in place to collect these to the state. In the editorial comment the editor felt it necessary to warn against this element!

5 The coming of oil, the Fourth Round controversy and its consequences

Early oil discoveries

The first oil discovery in the UK Continental Shelf (UKCS) to satisfy the Ministry's definition of "significant"[1] was made as early as November 1966 in Block 48/22 by the licence group led by Burmah Oil. At the time it was not regarded as significant and for many years was not included in the table of significant discoveries published by the Department of Energy. It remains the only significant oil/condensate discovery in the Southern North Sea and has not yet been developed. The first commercial oil discovery was made in December 1969 by Amoco in the Central North Sea in block 22/18. For a long time this was referred to as the Montrose field, but, after separate field status was given to the structure in which the discovery was made, it became known as Arbroath. In the Norwegian sector the giant Ekofisk field was discovered in late 1969. This added much interest to UK as well as Norwegian waters.

Wider significance of discovery of Forties field

While these finds encouraged exploration interest in the Central North Sea it was the discovery of the Forties field by BP in October 1970 in Block 21/10 that transformed the perceived outlook. It was quickly realised that the field was likely to be very prolific. This encouraged the view that there might be substantial deposits in other parts of Central and Northern waters. It was perhaps surprising that BP had made the discovery. As late as April 1970 the chairman, Sir Eric Drake, had stated publicly that there would be no major oil discovery in the British sector. The acreage in which Forties was discovered had been awarded to BP in the Second Round in 1966. It is clear that the company had only reluctantly expanded its exploration northwards from the Southern Basin, and even came close to withdrawing its application for blocks in the area when it was pressed by the Ministry to increase its drilling commitments. Further, drilling in Block 21/10 did not take place for over four years after the award was made.[2] By the autumn of 1971 the company was announcing that the Forties field was a giant one with the potential to produce at least 400,000 b/d.

Discovery of Brent field

The summer of 1971 also saw the discovery of the Brent field in Block 211/29, which turned out to be the largest hydrocarbon field in the UKCS to date. This dramatic event was not publicised whatsoever at the time, and an announcement was not made by Shell until over a year later. The lack of publicity was not unconnected with the launch of the Fourth Round in June 1971. The announcement of a large discovery would have encouraged very great extra interest in the surrounding acreage among all prospective investors.[3]

Preparations for Fourth Round

These dramatic events coincided with the preparations for the Fourth Licensing Round which also turned out to have very far-reaching consequences. Preparatory work had in effect commenced as early as 1968 because of the need to clarify the detailed arrangements for the relinquishment of acreage from the First Round in 1970. Such relinquished acreage would then become available for relicensing in the Fourth Round.

Several issues had arisen, with some investors asking whether they could be relieved of drilling obligations in Central and Northern waters, which they considered unpromising, on condition that they drilled an equivalent number of wells in the Southern Basin which they regarded as more prospective. They could, of course, relieve themselves of drilling obligations by surrendering their licence, but the Ministry was clear that they could not escape from their obligations while still retaining 50% of each licence area after the six-year period.

In 1968 the Ministry conducted a study on the prospects for relinquishment of both First and Second Round acreage in 1970 and 1971. The conclusions were that Southern Basin acreage was likely to be the most attractive, and, in very broad terms, around 60% might be retained while only 40% of the acreage in Central and Northern waters might be retained. In a subsequent update in early 1969 the conclusion was that part of the Southern Basin remained the most prospective, while in Central and Northern waters interest was considerably less and only about 20%–25% of the acreage might be retained.

Details of permitted relinquished areas

With respect to the details of what specific areas could be relinquished Legal Branch of the Ministry agreed that variations to the licence conditions covering the minimum area could be permitted through agreement between the parties. It was also felt that, consistent with the Regulations, the boundary lines of a surrendered area must run either due North and South *or* due East and West. Thus it would not be possible for the surrendered area to have a stepped form or any other geometrical shape apart from a rectangle or square extending either lengthways or transversely across the whole block. Legal Branch also felt, though with less conviction, that the area surrendered should be in one piece and not two or more parts, citing in support of this view the Interpretation Act 1889 which had a provision stating that, unless the context otherwise required, the singular should include the plural!

Within the Ministry there were other views, namely that the adoption of this interpretation of the Regulations was very restrictive and would make it difficult for the licensees to select the areas they wished to retain. It was also quite likely that they would object to this interpretation of the Regulations. It was recalled that the intention of the Regulation was to prevent undue fragmentation at the time of surrender. Such an objective was consistent with surrendered areas having stepped forms. In several other countries, including Nigeria, Norway and the Netherlands, there was very little restriction on the shape of the surrendered area. It was arguable that the size and shape of relinquished areas should be governed by the need to ensure that they were suitable for relicensing. Further, a licensee should not be obliged to surrender proven and retain non-productive acreage. Consistent with this it was arguable that any retained or surrendered area should be at least 80 sq.km. in area and compact in shape. The minimum width of any part of a surrendered or retained area should be at least two minutes of latitude or three minutes of longitude. Wherever possible boundaries should be in lines of whole minutes of latitude and longitude.

The debate continued within the Ministry and consultations were held with the North Sea Operators' Committee at which the Ministry put the view that surrendered areas should not have a stepped form. The representatives of the Committee argued that this would cause difficulties for some licensees and they could not accept the Ministry's interpretation and proposals. It was agreed that lawyers from both sides would consult on the legal aspects.

The lawyers acting for the Operators subsequently produced an opinion which argued that stepping of surrendered acreage was permissible. The Ministry's Legal Branch then felt that some doubt had crept in, and that it could no longer be said without qualification that stepping was inconsistent with the Regulation. In the circumstances it was felt that a compromise solution was in order whereby some measure of stepping would be allowed but the details should be subject to an agreement between the parties. This would protect all parties against any subsequent challenge, and would give the Ministry the opportunity to ensure that surrendered and retained areas were manageable with regard to size and shape. The Ministry's specific proposals were on the lines outlined above.

At a meeting with the Operators' Executive Committee in February 1970 the main proposals of the Ministry noted above were agreed. With respect to details it was agreed that where stepping was to be permitted the minimum size of each step would be two minutes in each direction. Further, the minimum width of any part of an area surrendered would be two minutes in either direction. These proposals were accepted by the full Committee.

The Ministry felt that, to implement surrender provisions which involved stepping, to avoid subsequent legal challenge it would be necessary for the terms of the relevant Regulation to be varied by a formal deed. A draft Deed of Variation was sent to operators. Members of the Operating Committee were unhappy with this procedure. They felt that it was inappropriate that some licensees had to have their surrenders covered by a deed while others had no such requirement. The Ministry felt that the operators were making very heavy weather of the issue and the Under Secretary pressed them to accept something which was really designed to help them.

Need to revise Regulations

By the Spring of 1970 the Ministry was convinced that, before the Fourth Round was launched, the Petroleum Regulations should be revised. It was decided that there should be full consultation with the Operators' Committee. The review was wide-ranging. It was felt desirable to have separate, clear-cut provisions for the auction of licences. Auctions might have been possible under the existing arrangements, but detailed provisions were thought to be desirable. It was felt that the operators would not object to an auction system as all companies operating in the USA were familiar with it.

Another change contemplated by the Ministry was to abolish the current invitation procedure for offshore licences. This would make it possible to allocate acreage to a single licensee and to do so without the publicity attendant on the current invitation procedure. The granting of discretionary powers to the Minister to make awards without calling for applications was felt to add flexibility to the procedures. It was recognised that the simple abolition of the invitation procedure would in effect put on offer the whole of the unlicensed designated area. While the suggested change would have been controversial with the oil companies under a Labour Government because it might have been regarded as a back door measure to enhance the state's share, it was felt that there would be no direct opposition under a Conservative Government.

Changes to the royalty obligations in licences were also contemplated. The current rules provided that costs of treatment and conveyancing the petroleum from the licensed area were deductible from the sales value in determining the royalty base. The provisions left the licensee with freedom to determine the conveyancing costs. There was also a lack of clarity regarding the treatment costs. Discussions between the parties to date were long and drawn-out. There was no incentive for the producer to reach a speedy agreement, and in the absence of agreement the only recourse available to the Minister was to go to arbitration. The Ministry wanted to reverse this, with the Minister having powers to impose an initial settlement and the licensee having resort to arbitration.

The Ministry also proposed that a sliding-scale royalty levied on the landed value be introduced. The rate(s) would be lowered to take account of the transport and treatment costs. The deductibility of these costs was to compensate to some extent for the higher costs of producers in fields located far from the shore, but the same effect could be achieved by a sliding-scale rate where the rate decreased according to the distance of the field from the landing point. An illustrative schedule of rates produced in the Ministry had a top rate of 12% where the field was located within the three mile limit, falling to 5% when the field was located more than 100 miles from shore.

Other changes to the Regulations were also proposed. When licensees agreed to unitise a common field without being directed to do so by the Minister there was no obligation on them to discuss the development plan or to supply a copy of the agreement. The Ministry proposed that the licensees be obliged to keep them fully informed. Subsequently the Ministry felt that licensees should be required to submit development plans for all fields, and proposed that the Minister should have the power to impose conditions on production policy. In the event of disagreement the matter would be referred to arbitration.

It was also recognised that the Regulations regarding records and returns required of licensees were inadequate. The Ministry now proposed that they be obliged to supply copies of their interpretation and geophysical and geological maps of licensed areas. They should also be required to provide information on development plans, including estimates of reserves. Under the then current rules all information had to be kept confidential for an indefinite period unless the licensee gave his consent for disclosure. The Ministry felt that this hindered the dissemination of geological knowledge and was detrimental to exploration and production. It was thus proposed that all information relating to a licensed area during the first six-year period should be made public six months after the expiry of this period. Further, information on the retained part of the licensed area should be made public two years after it was obtained.

The Ministry also contemplated reductions in the initial period of the licence from six years to perhaps four years, with another possibility of adding a condition to provide that specified work had to be undertaken within, say, three years. The experience since 1964 suggested to the Ministry that weather conditions had not been such a seriously inhibiting factor as the industry had argued.

Discussions with Operators' Committee

Several meetings were then held between the Department (by then DTI) and the Operators' Committee with the first being in October 1970. Some issues, including the minimum size of relinquished and retained areas, were readily agreed. Formally, each block would be divided into 120 sections, one minute by one minute in size. The minimum area retained or surrendered would be thirty sections. The operators were reluctant to supply estimates of reserves. The Department gave assurances that the information would only be used in aggregate form such that any one company's figures could not be identified. The companies did not want a specific clause requiring the provision of reserves estimates as this could provide a precedent for Governments of other countries who might be less scrupulous in using the information. It was agreed that a solution would be sought via an enabling clause and an exchange of letters requesting the data.

The issues of disclosure of information and the proposed royalty changes provoked much debate between the parties. The Department's considered view was that information should be made public after a certain time because (a) it would prevent duplication of information, (b) a specified limit on the period of confidentiality would encourage the exchange of information during that period, (c) the information could attract other companies and new entrants into areas which had been discarded by a licensee, and (d) much fuller information on the potential hydrocarbon resources of the UKCS could be publicly disclosed by the Minister. To obtain the appropriate balance between the genuine commercial interests of the existing licensees and the nation, at the end of 1970 the Department felt that (a) information gained under an exploration licence should be freely available three years after the expiry of the licence, (b) information gained in areas surrendered at the end of the initial six-year period should be freely available three years after the surrender date, and (c) information gained in retained areas should be freely available six years after being acquired.

The representatives of the Operators' Committee expressed particular resistance to the application of the proposals to licensed areas already awarded. The Department felt that there was also an inclination to preserve something akin to a closed shop against newcomers. By the end of 1970 the majority of the operators had agreed to periods of confidentiality of six years after (a) the expiry date of exploration licences, (b) surrender date of acreage in production licences, and (c) acquisition in the case of information obtained in retained areas after the initial six-year period. The Department felt that this was a genuine offer, and indicated that a reduction in the six-year period to five years would probably be acceptable.

With respect to royalties the Department now proposed that, because it might be sold at the wellhead rather than at a terminal, the method for calculating transport and treatment costs would be prescribed at the time of licence applications. Further, licensees would be required to make provisional royalty payments at the end of each royalty period. The operators felt that provisional payments were unnecessary if the detailed method of calculating eligible costs was specified. The Department made two further proposals on royalties: firstly that the Minister could elect to take royalty in kind, and secondly that the offsetting of licence fees against royalty should be done on a block basis rather than whole licence basis. By mid-January 1971 the operators had agreed to the information disclosure proposals and the manner in which royalty should be calculated. They remained opposed to the proposals to take royalty in kind and the limitation on the offset of licence fees against royalty.

Further deliberations within the Department and with the Operators' Committee ensued. Eventually by May 1971 it was decided that no provision should be made for taking royalty in kind nor to change the rules regarding the offset of licence rental fees against royalty. With respect to provision for auctions Legal Branch advised that a major modification to the Regulations would be required to permit an auction procedure in the strict sense of the term. Accordingly a scheme of competitive tendering was suggested. It was also advised that it would be extremely dubious to engage in any negotiations with applicants in the period between receipt of tenders and the awards. It would be best to use the sealed bid concept, leaving the tenders unseen until the specified date when they would all be looked at together. After some discussion it was decided that work obligations would not be required with competitive tendering and that the tendered amounts would be offered over and above the standard rent. The amended Regulations were signed by the Secretary of State on 18th May 1971 and came into operation a few days later.

Debate on licence fees with Treasury

Meanwhile, in preparing for the Fourth Round, the DTI had to consult with the Treasury over the financial terms. The DTI proposed that the fees for the first six years be raised from £30 to £35 per sq. km., but that the rental payments of subsequent years be unchanged from the Third Round when they were set at £50 per sq. km. rising in annual steps of £30 to £350 per sq. km. No increase was felt appropriate to maintain the balance between incentives to investors on the one hand and the flow back of territory for re-licensing. In making a judgement on this the Department had been influenced by the fact that 75% of the First Round territory had been relinquished in 1970 compared to the obligatory 50%. It was also proposed to leave the royalty unchanged at 12.5%, as any increase would discourage applications, have an adverse effect on exploration, and create an undesirable precedent in the international context.

The Treasury felt that both the initial annual payments and the annual rentals should be increased further than the DTI proposed, though by moderate amounts. Their thinking was influenced by the Forties and Ekofisk discoveries. The Treasury also raised several other matters with financial implications. They wanted to know the attitude to be taken to state participation which had implications for public expenditure. The attitude towards the attainment of a high British content also required elaboration. The change in Administration in 1970 warranted clear elucidation of any changes in policy. The DTI had referred briefly to bids by tender but it was unclear whether this method would be widely employed.

DTI's views on roles of Gas Council and NCB

The Minister for Industry clarified the position on the role of the Gas Council. It should participate with its partners as gas production was closely associated with its main activity of gas supply. The Minister felt that the NCB case was not so obvious. Participation might be criticised by Conservative Party supporters and could involve increased public expenditure. On balance, however, the Minister felt that the NCB should be allowed to participate. If it were to withdraw their partners would have ground for complaint and could not easily make new partnership arrangements at this late stage. While a review of the NCB's activities was under way Parliament had been assured that no hasty decisions would be made. Exclusion from the Fourth Round would constitute such a decision. It would also be difficult to discriminate between the NCB and Gas Council in this matter.

Views of Treasury

The Chief Secretary felt that a meeting with the DTI on the full range of issues raised was required. Treasury officials asked whether it would be possible to award all licences by tender or to place an initial batch by tender, with a view to establishing a market price, rather than an administered one, for licences. The DTI persuaded the Treasury that there were serious technical objections to this procedure. The current discretionary policy had fostered rapid exploration and development with consequent economic benefits, and the Treasury was persuaded that there was no strong reason to change it. The Treasury remained somewhat uneasy, however, as the policy could be regarded as inconsistent with the stated Government aim of encouraging competition. It depended on administrative judgements about the suitability of applicants rather than what was judged to be a commercial price for a licence.

Debate on NCB participation

The case for NCB participation was discussed. The Chief Secretary asked what would happen to the NCB's interests if it were allowed to participate but was subsequently required to withdraw. The DTI advised that the NCB's joint venture agreements gave their partners the right to buy the NCB's interests on terms no less favourable than an outsider if the partnership were dissolved. It could thus not be assumed that any successor body to the NCB which wished to take over its interests would have prior rights over the partners. Thus a requirement on the NCB to dispose of its interests might lead to an increase in the non-UK stake in the UKCS.

The Minister for Industry gave his view that to allow the NCB to participate only on condition that its partners could be persuaded to waive their first refusal rights was tantamount to refusing to allow participation at all, as the partners would not agree to waive their rights. It would also be prejudging the current review of the Board's activities. A further issue was the pre-emption rights in respect of the Board's existing interests. The Minister felt that his power to give consent to licence assignments could be used to ensure that the Board's interests stayed in UK ownership. Thus on balance he favoured NCB participation in the Fourth Round.

The Minister subsequently met with the Chief Secretary and explained that the NCB's operations in the UKCS were to be converted into a limited company with an NCB holding. In due course a public limited company would be established. The arrangements would be made in consultation with their partners, Gulf and Conoco. The plans would be made clear to them and so there would be no danger of subsequent accusations of bad faith. The Treasury was content with these proposals.

The discussions on the licence fees ended with a decision to raise the initial payment for the first six years to £45 per sq. km. The rental payments for the remainder of the licence period remained unchanged based on the arguments put forward by the DTI.

Decision to have large Fourth Round

The Department had decided in late 1970 that the Fourth Round should be a major one. They were encouraged in this view by (a) the recent discoveries in the Central North Sea, (b) the limited nature of the Third Round which had left a number of companies with a modest amount of acreage to explore, (c) the need to maintain the momentum of exploration activity, and (d) the rising interest in the UKCS because of the activities of OPEC Governments in relation to their concessionaires. It was decided that some 450 bocks should be put on offer. The geographic coverage was to be wide. The main interest of investors was now in the Central and Northern waters of the North Sea, but there was also scope for re-offering surrendered acreage in the Southern basin. In addition there was interest in the Western Approaches, the English Channel, the Irish Sea and West of Shetland. To permit exploration in new areas a further Continental Shelf Designation Order was made in April 1971 covering areas in the English Channel, off the West of Scotland, and off Shetland. The provisional list of blocks was revised from time to time during consultations with other interested Departments. Blocks in the English Channel were excluded because of lack of agreement with the French Government on the position of the boundary and because of conflicts regarding the use of the territory for defence and navigational purposes. In fact discussions with the Ministry of Defence in particular, plus the time required to complete the amendments to the Regulations delayed the launch of the Round by several months.

Discussions on blocks with other interested Departments

In February 1971 a provisional list of blocks was sent to six other Departments. There ensued fairly prolonged negotiations with the Ministry of Defence/Ministry of Aviation Supply. They strongly objected to the whole idea of drilling in many of the proposed blocks. At this very time the DTI was already having discussions with the Ministry of Defence on licensing areas in Cardigan Bay under Third Round awards. This created problems because of the missile testing range at Aberporth and the submarine lane which crossed the area. The MOD agreed to drilling in the submarine lane subject to restrictions on the amount of drilling and the provision of underwater sonar beacons. The missile testing range presented more serious problems. Few of the trials could be relocated. After much discussion restricted drilling within the testing area was agreed, with the Department reluctantly agreeing to accept liability against the risk of damage to a drilling installation.

Similar prolonged discussions took place relating to many of the blocks proposed for the Fourth Round. The MOD had strong objections to many of them. Eventually a compromise was reached whereby the DTI withdrew some blocks, and substituted others, while the MOD accepted the case for exploration in some defence areas subject to restrictions on the timing and number of rigs operating in certain areas. In some blocks the rigs were again required to be fitted with underwater sonar beacons.

The discussions with Marine Division (of the DTI) centred on the issue of potential conflict in established shipping lanes. There was a concern over the idea of Government encouragement of drilling in areas where there had been accidents, some of which had involved tankers with resulting problems of oil pollution. These anxieties plus those of the MOD led to the exclusion of blocks in the English Channel from the Fourth Round.

Only fifteen blocks for tender bids

It was decided to put out to tender only 15 blocks. The whole idea was regarded as an experiment to discover the reaction of the companies and thus to determine which method was most appropriate for UK conditions. The blocks chosen for tender were those which reflected intense interest by the oil companies as a result of discoveries made in the surrounding areas. The prospectivity of the blocks was thus regarded as high. Nevertheless, the Department had little idea of what weight of applications would be received. The majority of existing licensees were against the whole notion of tender bids. Interestingly, US Government Departments also expressed concern though the system was established practice in that country. The particular conditions governing tender applications included a 20% deposit with each tender, with successful applicants being required to pay the balance of each tender within 14 days of an award. The Secretary of State reserved the right to reject any bid (including the winning one) where (a) in cases of tenders by foreign-owned companies there was no equitable reciprocal treatment for British companies in the foreign country, and (b) he was not satisfied that the applicant had the necessary technical competence to undertake a work programme. No work programmes were required to be submitted. The Department felt that (financial) bids would not be made unless the applicant had the serious intention of undertaking a work programme. Applicants making tender bids were also not to be assessed on other criteria used in making discretionary awards such as their performance to date and contribution to the UK economy.

Assessment criteria for discretionary awards

The assessment criteria for applicants for discretionary awards were essentially the same as those used in the previous Round with one exception. There was no provision for preferential treatment for participation by the nationalised industries. Officially, policy was to treat applications by nationalised industries equally with others. Similarly there was no overt preference for British companies, though it was anticipated that they would gain some advantage under the discretionary system with respect to the criterion of contribution to the UK economy.

The Round is launched

The Round was launched on 22nd June 1971 when a total of 436 blocks, including the 15 under the tender bid system, were put on offer. No serious thought was given to sequential rather than simultaneous licensing under the two methods. In the period between the announcement and receipt of applications the Department had meetings with many prospective licensees, seeking information and providing evidence of their competence. Applications for the competitive tender blocks had to be submitted by 20th August. Elaborate precautions were taken to demonstrate the impartiality of the DTI in the process of handling them. Thirty-one groups involving 73 companies submitted a total of 78 bids for the 15 blocks. On the same day the bids were opened by the Treasury Solicitor and the results immediately made public in front of a large number of representatives of applicants and the media. The total value of the bids amounted to £135 million. The aggregate value of the highest bids made for each block was £37.2 million. Bids were highly concentrated in favour of acreage in the Central and Northern North Sea, with 17 bids for Block 9/13, 10 for Block 15/26, and 18 for Block 211/21. The last attracted the winning bid of £21 million from Shell/Esso. Full details were published, with the winning bids being confirmed a few days later after the Department had satisfied itself that the high bidders had met all the other conditions for acceptability.

Assessing applications for discretionary acreage

There were 92 applications covering 271 blocks for the discretionary acreage which covered 421 blocks. There was much overlapping with the number of applicants for the 25 most sought-after blocks ranging from 15 to 28. Given these large numbers much work was involved for the Department in assessing them. The rating of applicants in relation to the announced criteria involved judgements. Out of a maximum possible aggregate of 100 marks the maximum points for technical and financial competence were each set at 25. For a British applicant 10 marks was possible with a due proportion being given for a consortium with a British interest. The downstream interests of applicants in the UK were considered, with a maximum of 10 marks for large refining interests and a similar maximum for large petroleum product distribution interests. Applicants who were already licensees could have their earlier initiative rewarded to the extent of 5 marks where work programmes had been executed in a normal manner. Added marks were awarded for above-normal performance. Up to 10 marks could also be awarded where other relevant contributions to the UK economy were perceived.

The procedure then adopted was to rank the applicant companies according to a schedule ranging from "highly outstanding" to just "qualified". Next, the blocks requested were divided into five geographic areas. For each geographic area they were then ranked in order of attractiveness as indicated by the number of applications for each, the priority assigned to the block by each applicant, and the ranking of each applicant. This meant that greater weight was placed on a high priority assigned to a block by a highly-rated company compared to a more lowly-related one.

The procedure was then to allocate blocks as far as possible by matching the blocks to the applicants. This meant that a top-tier company could have been awarded any of the blocks. A second-tier company would be awarded a block in the highest sought-after category only if the top-tier companies had assigned it lower priority. Efforts were made to provide what the Department described as the best overall satisfaction. To procure this a so-called "satisfaction ratio", was calculated for each company. This took into account the blocks they had (provisionally) been awarded, and the priorities assigned to them compared to all the blocks for which they had applied. This procedure sometimes resulted in some reallocation of awards.

Interviews and work programmes

Interviews with applicants commenced in August 1971 and continued to February 1972. It was decided to deal with the various areas sequentially with the Southern Basin having first priority. Invitations to submit work programmes were issued in mid-October 1971. Offers were made in early December and on 22nd December 1971 details of the awards on the Southern Basin were published. The Minister was able to report that forty-three per cent of the territory involved had been awarded to indigenous British companies. The NCB and its partner Conoco received seven blocks, the largest number of awards to any group.

Discussions of work programmes relating to applications for the other areas on offer in the Central and Northern North Sea, West of Shetland and Western Approaches continued apace from late December 1971 to late February 1972. Offers were made in early March and public announcements made on 15th March 1972. Taking the Round as a whole 282 blocks were awarded involving 75 companies or groups of companies (213 individual companies). A total of £2.8 million was received in initial payments and the work programmes provided for at least 224 exploration wells to be drilled within six years. This number exceeded the total obligatory wells in the first three rounds. The expected expenditures were over £200 million. The UK participation in the total acreage awarded was 43%. The Gas Council and its partners received 13 blocks in Central and Northern waters. The NCB and its partners received 8 blocks in the same regions. As many as 60 blocks were awarded in the frontier West of Shetland area.

Reflections of DTI on Fourth Round arrangements

The Fourth Round was of momentous importance. The number of awards with the associated work programmes alone guaranteed that it would have a major impact. A high proportion of the nation's petroleum was to be discovered from the acreage awarded. The licensing and tax terms were to be subjected to detailed dissection leading to major changes. Following the completion of the Round Mr Angus Beckett, the Under Secretary responsible for the arrangements, provided his detailed reflections on the experience. Despite the success of the tender bid experiment he remained of the view that it should not be employed as the sole method of awarding licences, except in the event of an extremely limited round comprising highly prospective acreage. The oil companies had limited exploration budgets, and money spent on tender bids reduced the amount available for drilling. On its own the system could not facilitate rapid and thorough exploration. It would be quite wrong to extrapolate the results of an experiment covering 15 blocks to the whole UKCS. If all the acreage on offer in the Fourth Round had been subject to premium bidding the weight of applications would have been concentrated on the better blocks and other acreage would probably have been ignored altogether. This would have applied particularly to the Orkney/Shetland Basins where there had been no drilling to date. It was recognised that a sizeable sum would have accrued to the Treasury, but this would have been at the expense of a drilling programme secured under the discretionary system which comprised over 220 wells. Mr Beckett felt that the national economy was likely to benefit more from a rapid and substantial exploration programme than a substantial one-off payment. It was also noteworthy that in the premium bid awards the UK content was just over 21% while in the discretionary awards it was 43%. Within the latter UK companies were given favourable treatment in relation to their priorities and in the awards of the most highly-rated blocks. The discretionary system was also superior to any other in ensuring the maximum concentration of risk capital and technical expertise to the exploration activity.

Several variants on the straight tender bid method were possible, including bidding on royalty rates, expenditure of funds, and even rates of carried interest to nationalised industries. Mr Beckett considered that all these had serious disadvantages. He was concerned that increasing the royalty rate could be construed by overseas Governments as a direct invitation to follow suit. A combination of premium and rate of royalty bidding was possible, but could result in combinations which made it difficult to determine the winning bid. Bidding amounts of expenditure or physical activity on exploration could well result in bids being made which were out of proportion to the requirements for thorough exploration. There had been some evidence of this in the Fourth Round. The best approach was to seek realistic work programmes as one of several criteria as had been done in the Fourth Round. Mr Beckett saw no merit in basing awards on options or carried interest to nationalised industry. These were simply political gestures. If it were felt necessary to improve on the straightforward premium system employed in the Fourth Round he felt that it would be possible to make an award to the highest bidder contingent not only on technical and financial competence but on subsequent agreement to a reasonable work programme. In sum there was merit in a dual system with the weighting between premium bidding and discretion depending on the type of acreage on offer. Premium bidding should be reserved for highly prospective acreage.

A lesson from the Fourth Round was that the initial licence fees could be raised substantially. Mr Beckett felt that they could be set at five times the current level without seriously jeopardising applications. A further refinement could be to differentiate the payments according to perceived prospectivity with a low figure in untried areas and a higher one in areas where petroleum discoveries had been made.

On other licensing matters Mr Beckett felt that the present arrangements were generally satisfactory. On the size of block the Chairman of Shell had suggested that they were too small, and had argued that there was a significant chance that discoveries would straddle blocks leading to difficulties in developing a field. In deeper and more distant waters the minimum economic size of field was significantly larger and the chances of a discovery extending into two or more blocks would be greater. Mr Beckett felt that these fears were exaggerated. While one company's discovery extending into another licensee's blocks was a nuisance, the national interest was safeguarded through the right to impose compulsory unitisation. The existing size of blocks also permitted a larger number of operators with the associated greater financial resources and skill than would have occurred with bigger blocks. Nevertheless there might be a need to consider larger blocks in frontier areas. Mr Beckett felt that any attempt to introduce a checkerboarding system with respect to relinquishment terms should be resisted. He felt it had produced poor results in Alberta and would have a depressing effect on activity in the very different offshore situation.

Report from Public Accounts Committee

These were the considered views of the senior official at the DTI most closely concerned with the subject. By this time the Public Accounts Committee was showing a keen interest in the subject. Its report, following a penetrating, long-lasting inquiry into licensing and taxation arrangements, was widely quoted and became very influential in the development of later policies.[1] On the licensing terms the Committee made several points. It felt that it would have been preferable for the licensing of blocks by the two methods (tender bid and discretionary) to have been undertaken on a sequential rather than a concurrent basis. The lessons of the tender bids would have added substantial further information to inform the design of the discretionary terms, or even whether to offer more blocks under the tender bid method. The DTI felt that the need to proceed quickly with a large round was the more important consideration, as sequential licensing would have entailed some delay. DTI witnesses admitted that the results of the tender bids had exceeded their expectations in terms of the sums offered. Some blocks put on offer which had not been regarded as highly prospective had produced substantial bids. This in effect meant that the results had indeed produced valuable new information. On balance the Committee's argument had considerable merit.

The Committee also felt that, as a condition for participating in the tender bid procedures, prospective applicants could, with advantage, have been asked to produce acceptable work programmes. In evidence, Sir Robert Marshall, the Permanent Secretary agreed that this would have been possible. Although the Committee expressed some enthusiasm for the concept it could have produced substantial problems. Investors could well react by reducing the size of their bids when the work programme was given some prominence in the award criteria. There would be less clarity about the respective weights to be attached to the two elements. In other countries where tender bids were practised they were unencumbered with work programme commitments which were left to the judgement of the bidder. Familiarity with respect to the investment environment is generally a positive factor among petroleum companies, and adaptation to novel conditions undertaken gingerly. It must be doubtful whether the hybrid-type terms would have produced extra benefits to the UK in terms of combined cash bids and work commitments.

The Committee expressed surprise that, when the results of the tender bid competition became known on 20th August 1971 consideration was not given to withdrawing the invitations relating to the discretionary blocks or at least reconsidering the matter. It was acknowledged that there would have been no legal impediment to reconsidering or even withdrawing these invitations, but in evidence the Department argued strongly against this course of action. Their first argument was that the results did not invalidate the decision to have a large round based on ministerial discretion. This is open to question, and it could certainly be argued that, given the interest, further significant cash bids as well as substantial work programmes would have been forthcoming if more North Sea blocks had been put out to tender.

A second argument deployed by the Department was that the suspension of the discretionary element would have constituted a serious breach of faith which in turn would have had a negative effect on activity. This argument has some weight. The degree of trust between oil investors and their host Governments is certainly important in determining the formers' behaviour. At the very time in question the international companies were experiencing problems with host Governments demanding changes to agreements, particularly in the Middle East. The Tripoli/Tehran agreements in 1971 were of great concern to the companies. A more predictable regulatory régime would clearly have held attractions. A decision to suspend the discretionary element of the Round would certainly have attracted much comment and would have been remembered for some time ahead. On the other hand the perceived prospectivity of the acreage might have outweighed any negative effect of postponement on investor confidence. On balance the Department's decision to continue with the Round on the original timetable was justifiable.

The Committee also argued that the Department could have tightened the terms generally in the light of the perceived increased prospectivity in the North Sea and the tougher terms being introduced in other countries. The oil price had also been increasing. The Committee noted that in 1972 the Norwegian Government had (a) modified its royalty terms to a sliding scale system with rates ranging from 8% to 16% depending on production, (b) decreased the total licence duration from 46 to 36 years, and (c) introduced state participation with the new state company Statoil in the range 20%–50%.

The Committee expressed concern that on the completion of the Fourth Round the most promising areas in the North Sea had been allocated on terms very favourable to the investors. It might have been preferable to have held a smaller round which could well have been adequate to maintain a rising level of activity. It felt that the dominant feature of the four rounds, apart from the limited tender, was the small changes in licence fees with the increases reflecting only general inflation. The first licences had been issued before any discoveries had been made.

In all rounds they covered total periods of 46 years, and the committee wondered why they had not incorporated break clauses which would have permitted reassessment or renegotiation of the terms during this long period when circumstances could change markedly. The Department's view was that the terms were in line with international practice and that the relinquishment obligation after six years permitted different terms to be applied to surrendered acreage which was subsequently relicenced.

While this is certainly the case it sidesteps the issue of the position with respect to the 50% of acreage which the investor retains after the six-year period. The licensee was permitted to retain what he regarded as the most promising acreage without incurring specific work obligations. It would have been possible for work commitments to have been attached to retained acreage. These could have been negotiated at the time of the surrender of the initial 50% of the territory. The failure to require further work obligations as a condition of the retention of acreage along with the non-indexation of licence fees for inflation sowed the seeds of the fallow acreage problem which was to become increasingly troublesome from the mid-1980s onwards. In 2005 the great bulk of the fallow acreage (as defined by the DTI) still emanated from territory awarded in the first four rounds.

The Committee also examined the question of the opportunities for British industry provided by North Sea oil and gas. By this time the report of the International Management and Engineering Group (IMEG) on the subject had been published. In January 1973 the Government had announced that it would implement its main recommendation and establish a special office to facilitate the enhanced involvement of British industry. The Committee expressed surprise that, to date, the Department had regarded the response of British industry as primarily a matter for industry itself, though administrative pressure had been put on licensees to use British suppliers wherever possible. The Committee noted the differences in the UK share of the market as estimated by the Department in evidence and by IMEG with the former indicating a figure in excess of 50% for the period 1964–1971, while the latter suggested a range of 25%–30%. The difficulties of defining and measuring the UK share were to become a continuing subject of debate, and the Committee welcomed the establishment of a system by the Department whereby operators were to provide regular, quarterly information on orders placed at home and abroad.

The Committee also raised the subject of depletion policy. It noted that, to date, policy had been to encourage exploitation as quickly as possible to alleviate the balance of payments problem and to enhance security of energy supply. It appreciated the reasons for this emphasis, but felt that the issue of the optimal depletion rate should be kept under constant review and welcomed the assurance of the DTI that this would be done.

Full policy review in DTI

The report was generally very perceptive and justifiably influential in policy developments over the next few years. A full-scale policy review had in fact started by the completion of the Fourth Round. This anticipated some of the findings and recommendations of the Committee. The issue of the respective merits of awarding licences via auctions or the discretionary method produced a lively debate. The results of the experiment in the Fourth Round had forced some rethinking on the subject, but the majority preference within the DTI remained with the discretionary system. It was acknowledged that the auction system produced early revenues, but if the attainment of rapid and thorough exploration was deemed to be more important, the discretionary system was superior.

Wider advantages of discretionary system

More generally the discretionary system had advantages whenever there were policy objectives extending beyond the raising of revenues to the state. Thus its retention would permit the Government to favour UK applicants. It would also permit more effective promotion of opportunities for British contractors and supply companies. An auction system was likely to entail low or even zero bids for some blocks with perceived poor prospectivity. It would probably result in the exclusion of small companies, though this might be avoided by the formation of consortia, something which would not be easy to arrange. It was now acknowledged, as the Public Accounts Committee had argued, that it would be possible to incorporate some work programme obligations within an auction system, though this would be more difficult compared to the discretionary system. There was now less concern that the tender bid system would reduce the exploration effort on the grounds that the ranking of future investment should not be influenced by past expenditure. It was acknowledged, however, that smaller companies could allocate their resources in this way with some negative consequences for the exploration effort.

On balance the view in the DTI at this time (Autumn 1972) remained that the emphasis should continue to be discretionary licensing. But the idea of offering some blocks for tender found favour. The proportion so offered could be in the 25%–50% range. The Department felt that, although most of the blocks offered for auction should have high prospectivity, a substantial number of attractive ones should still be awarded through the discretionary mechanism. It was now felt that there should be sequential rather than simultaneous use of the two mechanisms in any round. Simultaneous licensing could reduce the size of the bids, and so a specified percentage of the blocks should be held back and subsequently auctioned. It was felt that such bidders should be informed that they would have to drill one well per block.

With respect to financial aspects the review devoted much attention to the issue of additional taxation on petroleum production activities (see Chapter 7). At one point it was considered that, if auctions were employed, there might be no need for special additional taxation. As with the great majority of host Governments around the world the final conclusion was to prefer to collect realised economic rents through taxation rather than rely on bonus bids which by definition can only collect anticipated rents. There could well be major differences between the two.

Royalties

With respect to royalties the Department felt that a large increase was not appropriate as special taxation was the more flexible device to deal with large profits earned by producers. The Department was also influenced by the danger that a major increase might trigger corresponding increases in OPEC countries to the detriment of British oil interests in these countries. Consideration was also given to the issue of whether royalty should be levied on the wellhead as at present or the landed value of the oil. Deduction of the transport and treatment costs was complicated, but disallowing them could discourage marginal production in fields where transport costs were high. Further, to do so with existing licences would be a breach of contract, and the DTI then felt that to base royalties on new licences on landed values while retaining the wellhead value for existing ones would be complicated and anomalous.

In similar vein it was felt that other possible and complex changes to the royalty system which did not have much effect on revenues should be avoided. This judgement applied to (1) a sliding scale system related to production, (2) royalty bidding, which it was felt had the general disadvantages of the auction scheme without bringing substantial immediate revenues, and (3) royalty in kind. It was felt that the last scheme had no advantages because the UK did not have a national oil company.

Licence fees

With respect to initial licence fees it was felt that, while they were not burdensome, to increase them to substantial figures would result in no applications for mediocre blocks. For retained acreage (after six years) it was felt that the annual increases should be much steeper to ensure that licensees did not retain fallow blocks. A doubling of the annual increases would be appropriate. It was also felt that the current arrangements whereby the rental payments were fully credited against royalties due by a licensee on *any* blocks covered by that licence encouraged the retention of fallow acreage. It was thus felt that rental payments should only be credited against royalties on the same block.

Assessment criteria

The assessment criterion of contribution to the British economy had involved (1) preference for British companies, and (2) pressure to purchase British goods and services. The first had received most emphasis, but was inconsistent with the Treaty of Rome, though it was felt that in practice it could continue. There were very great advantages to the UK balance of payments. It was estimated (in 1972) that the foreign exchange cost of North Sea oil produced by a foreign company in 1980 would be nearly £8 per ton compared to £1 per ton by a UK company.

With respect to the purchases of equipment, materials, and services it was estimated that by the end of 1971 operators had spent around £470 million of which some £250 million was paid to UK residents. It was understood that for some supplies foreign companies would be able to quote better terms on price, quality, or delivery, and it was important not to slow down the pace of development. But it was felt that even still larger foreign exchange and employment benefits could be obtained from purchases of goods produced in the UK where the terms were equally or nearly as good. In spite of possible EEC objections it was thus felt that this criterion should remain.

Full and fair opportunity for British industry

The DTI also considered whether further provisions were necessary to encourage purchases of British supplies. Any formal requirement to buy British equipment would be inconsistent both with the Treaty of Rome and GATT. Further, it was felt that any formal requirement to buy British whenever the terms were equal to or better than those from abroad would be difficult to administer and could lead to disputes. There was thus a preference for administrative action which gave flexibility and avoided international consequences. The statement that the Government wanted full and fair opportunity for British suppliers to compete for orders could be backed by a requirement that licensees provide information on their major purchases. This was consistent with the Government's international obligations.

Participation by nationalised industries

Participation by the nationalised industries had the advantage that all profits came either directly or indirectly to the Exchequer. A similar effect was produced from participation by BP due to the 48% Government shareholding. But nationalised industry participation also involved the provision of substantial risk capital. Current Government policy was to restrict nationalised industries to their main activities, and discourage them from doing what the private sector could do equally well. Their further involvement in the North Sea would result in the Government having to make judgements in a risky area in which they had no expertise. If the emerging ideas within Government on tax changes were implemented the case for further public sector participation was weakened. Obtaining a share of the profits through the taxation mechanism meant that the state procured the advantages at less risk and cost. The position with respect to BP and other British oil companies was different, and the discretionary system could with advantage be used discreetly to give preference to them.

Reserve powers in event of reluctance to produce

Other changes to licensing terms were also contemplated. It was possible that a company would be unwilling to produce petroleum of uncertain commercial value. There had already been some evidence of this. There might also be situations where operators turned out to be incompetent or very slow to exploit opportunities. Accordingly, it was felt desirable to introduce a reserve power whereby the Minister could terminate a licence if, after a specified number of years, the licensee was failing to produce. Such powers could apply to existing as well as new licences. It was felt that this proposed power, while strictly in breach of contract, would be easier to defend on existing licences than increasing the rental payments.

Surrender provisions

With respect to surrender provisions it was felt that they should be tightened to ensure that companies did not retain fallow acreage and to increase the Government's freedom of action for the future. For future licences 50% should be surrendered after six years (the current arrangement), but 50% of the remainder should also be relinquished after another few years. These provisions would apply on a whole licence not block basis to ensure that fields did not have to be split up.

EEC issues

UK accession to the EEC was imminent. This had several consequences for North Sea policies. Thus there would be a need to reconsider the requirement of British nationality on licensees. It was felt that this could be given up as it had no practical effect. A second current requirement was that central management and control should be in the UK. It was felt important that this obligation be retained, principally to ensure that taxation could be effectively levied on the companies. The third current requirement was to land oil and gas in the UK. It was felt essential that this obligation be kept to enhance security of supply.

The implications of joining the EEC had been considered by the Government for some years. Back in 1969 the view had been formed that the Continental Shelf was not part of the Community. Legal advice had emphasised this, highlighting its absence in the relevant Treaties. It was acknowledged that there was a contrary view. Thus the Commission took the view that the provisions of the Treaty of Rome should generally apply to the Continental Shelf. The issue was important because if the Continental Shelf were within the Community the Gas Council's monopsony could be open to challenge.

EEC and oil exports

Another issue relating to the EEC resulted from the revelation by BP in a presentation to Ministers in late 1971 that the Forties field could be expected to produce around 400,000 b/d at plateau, of which 50% would be used in the expanded Grangemouth refinery, and the remainder exported. (The projection of the proportion likely to be exported was later modified to somewhat less than 50%.) This aroused much debate. Lord Rothschild emphasised to the Prime Minister that if 200,000 b/d were exported a similar volume of imports would be required from less stable parts of the world. This was making life unnecessarily hazardous for the UK. The Prime Minister agreed and ordered an inquiry into the matter. It was quickly agreed that there were several inter-related issues namely (a) self-sufficiency balanced against treaty agreements, (b) the optimal depletion of oil within the context of wider energy policy, (c) the need for cooperation within the EEC, and (d) qualitative differentials between the crude oil from the North Sea and those most suitable for refining to meet the UK's demand for products. The Prime Minister was informed that the prohibitions of quantitative restrictions on exports would apply to North Sea oil, and there was no credible case for seeking exclusion of this item from the scope of the Treaty. The other international obligation arose under the OECD oil-sharing agreement originating from measures taken during the first Suez crisis whereby oil supplies available to Western European countries, including indigenous production, were pooled and shared equitably. This obligation remained for defined crisis situations.

Meanwhile a quick study had been undertaken by the Central Policy Review Staff (CPRS) on the subject of oil exports. The framework for the analysis was to consider the various ways of disposing of 50% of production from the Forties field. The calculations were quite detailed involving assumptions about the origin of oil displaced by Forties production, whether the displaced oil was transported by British tankers, and whether BP's total (world) sales were increased by the Forties output. Key findings were that there was a modest advantage to the balance of payments from exporting Forties oil because the low sulphur content produced a price premium over imported oil. Further, for every *extra* ton that was produced from Forties the UK balance of payments could benefit by around £9 (1972 prices). The UK economy could also gain an additional £1 for every extra ton refined in the UK. There was thus a case for increasing the refining capacity in the UK. Given the large magnitudes involved the Government should consider enhancing its influence on the behaviour of oil companies in relation to production, refining, pricing and marketing decisions. A national oil policy which maximised the benefits to the UK should be considered even if it conflicted with the sectoral interests of oil companies.

The CPRS further developed their examination of the issue in more dramatic terms by considering whether it should be mandatory for companies producing oil from the UKCS to market such oil in the UK to enhance security of supply and to keep down industrial costs. With respect to security of supply it was recognised that it would be unwise to oblige the companies to sell their oil in the UK while there were net gains to be made from the OECD sharing obligations. When more oil became available from the UKCS than from the OECD sharing arrangements there was a case for reneging on these obligations. Price rises induced by OPEC could be followed by tax increases on production from the UKCS. If the preservation of UK industrial competitiveness was a priority price controls could be introduced, but these would involve technical problems. On balance, in current circumstances mandatory controls on the marketing and pricing should not be introduced, but at some time in the future there could be advantages.

BP's plans for oil from Forties field

BP had by this time provided a fuller description of their proposed disposal of Forties oil. The company wanted to take advantage of the world-wide premium available for low sulphur crude by exporting a substantial proportion to Western Europe where the requirements for low sulphur fuel oil were substantially greater than in the UK. If BP were obliged to refine all the Forties oil in the UK but exports of products were permitted then the company would plan to export the extra low sulphur fuel oil and import higher sulphur oil. This would involve extra costs in the form of tanker movements of £6 million per year. BP felt, however, that higher product exports at the expense of Continental refineries could be ruled out because most Governments wanted maximum local refining. If BP had retained Forties crude oil *and* the low sulphur products for the UK market the company would then either have to buy its equivalent at higher cost or build desulphurisation plant(s) to meet the requirements for low sulphur fuel oil in Europe. Such measures would be expensive for the company. Thus the DTI concluded that the apparent national advantage from retaining North Sea oil in the UK would be offset by loss of BP profits and by the extra costs involved in getting other companies to refine the additional oil for them.

Government relations with BP

While the DTI appreciated these arguments the notion that there could be a divergence between the national interest and those of the oil companies was gaining increasing attention. In a review of policy produced in March 1972 the issue of whether BP should be brought under closer Government control was aired, despite the fact that it already had a 48.4% holding. The idea that Government might involve itself more deeply in the formulation of company strategy was raised, but so were the resulting disadvantages namely that the Government would become involved in commercial decisions and in BP's relations with foreign Governments. In any case the licence terms already gave the Government much influence over their activities in the UKCS.

Ministerial Committee examines North Sea policies

The review within Government on all aspects of North Sea policies was thus clearly in full swing well before the report of the Public Accounts Committee was published. This event and the widespread publicity surrounding it gave a further impetus to the review and ensured that it received high level attention. Through much of 1973 the subject was discussed by a Cabinet Committee chaired by Mr Heath, the Prime Minister. Considerable attention was given to how the Government take from North Sea revenues could be enhanced in the light of the increase in world oil prices and the expectation that oil exploitation would be highly profitable. Tax and non-tax measures were examined and the two became intertwined in the debate. Ministers were conscious of the change in public opinion in relation to the exploitation of oil resources, and Mr Heath was convinced that it was no longer realistic to allow this resource to fall into foreign hands or to permit foreign interests to make excessive profits from it.

Three main options had been identified by officials to increase the state's share. Two involved taxes namely a severance (or production) tax and a special profit-related tax provisionally called an Excess Revenue Tax. The third option involved direct state participation in the fields on a carried interest basis. There was some disposition to favour the participation route because of the associated control which it gave. Ministers were concerned, however, that it might be represented as a form of expropriation without adequate compensation and could even expose the Government to international claims. It would involve a breach of existing agreements, and there could be repercussions on the foreign operations of UK oil companies. Substantial participation would also introduce the prospect of direct Government involvement in management, and the method could be criticised by Government supporters as a form of nationalisation. On the other hand there could be Parliamentary approval for the interventionist nature of state participation. It was argued that while participation would involve Government expenditure in the early stages it would not involve a drain on national resources, and would be acceptable because it would produce a much earlier yield than taxation.[5]

Ministers favour state participation

The Ministerial meeting in late June 1973 ended with general support for the state participation route. But before final decisions were made Ministers recommended that an urgent study involving outside consultants as well as several Departments be undertaken. The opinion of the Law Officers should be sought on the legal implications of the options. The European implications should also be examined. Finally, confidential discussions should be held with BP and British Gas on the subject.

Report from officials

Detailed studies were undertaken on these subjects and reports made to the Ministerial group. Officials reported that there were no existing EEC obligations which would debar the Government from introducing any of the three devices though they all raised particular EEC issues. Thus state participation was not a tax and would avoid any proposals for tax harmonisation. State participation was already well-established in the Netherlands. Severance tax would have to be clearly seen to be an internal UK tax and not an import duty. An Excess Revenue Tax would need to be clearly separate from the normal tax on corporate profits for which harmonisation was possible. State participation might arouse attention because of the enhanced role which the Government would have in matters such as orders for equipment, depletion policy, and refining policy.

Views of FCO

On the question of overseas reaction to the implementation of any of the three measures the Foreign and Commonwealth Office (FCO) reported that there was likely to be a negative reaction from the US Government which was particularly concerned that policies by Western Governments should do nothing to enhance the increasing demands of the OPEC Governments. The FCO also felt that the introduction of state participation or a severance tax would probably permit host Governments of licensees to instigate successful legal proceedings against the UK in the International Court of Justice. Foreign companies might also be able to bring successful actions against the UK Government before the Human Rights Commission and Court at Strasbourg. There might also be further international consequences such as the encouragement to OPEC Governments to break their contractual agreements with the oil companies. In any event considerable protest should be expected, but direct legal or other retaliatory action by foreign Governments was thought unlikely.

Views of Mr Eli Lauterpacht

Officials consulted a variety of other parties on the issue. On the legal aspect Mr Eli Lauterpacht felt that there would be no problem with the Excess Revenue Tax which represented nothing more than the sovereign right of the Government to levy taxes. State participation with carried interest was likely to be defensible as it was essentially a tax by a different route. He felt, however, that severance tax was an objectionable last alternative because it was very close to a royalty increase which was in breach of the licence. The FCO legal advisers agreed with Mr Lauterpacht on Excess Revenue Tax and severance tax but felt that state participation carried legal dangers.

Views of British Gas

British Gas recommended adoption of state participation with carried interest, mainly because it would leave the producer's rate of return on commercial fields unchanged, and because it would give increased control over an important national resource.

Views of Mr Walter Levy

Mr Walter Levy, the consultant to the DTI, emphasised the disadvantages of severance tax, particularly its insensitivity to costs, and its substantial effect on profitability because payments were triggered early in field life. It also had the appearance of a royalty increase. Excess Revenue Tax was much less open to international challenge, but might provoke an increase in taxation by the OPEC countries. There would be a need to build in a mechanism to reduce the risk of deterring the development of marginal fields. State participation with carried interest was the mechanism preferred by Mr Levy. He emphasised the non-reduction in the rate of return on commercial fields and the increased power to influence or control petroleum operations. It was also a familiar device in other producing countries and was the only practical way of obtaining a very high share of profits to the state. It would, however, embarrass the UK in its attempts to urge OPEC countries not to break existing agreements in a unilateral manner. Mr Levy also noted that it would involve large payments by the Government before any return was received. To reduce the disadvantages he suggested that the companies should be induced to accept participation on a voluntary basis by informing them that they would otherwise have to pay Excess Revenue Tax.

Recommendations of officials

Having heard all these views officials gave their recommendations to the Ministerial group. They recounted all the advantages and disadvantages of the three devices as discussed above and concluded that severance tax should be rejected. They left open the other two options and the mixed one (state participation with carried interest and Excess Revenue Tax). The Inter-Departmental group of officials also prepared a further paper for Ministers on non-fiscal licensing changes with respect to current licences. They covered a wide range of topics. On royalties they proposed that powers be taken to impose an interim settlement of value on which royalty would be paid. Great delays had been experienced in reaching final agreement on royalty values with consequential delays in receipts. They also proposed that power be taken to receive royalty in kind as well as cash. This was now common internationally. The group also suggested that powers be taken to require licensees to begin and sustain exploration with due diligence and to produce at a reasonable rate, with the implicit power otherwise to revoke the licence. There was concern that currently there was nothing to prevent total inactivity by the licensee in the forty-year period following the initial six-year one. The group also recommended that Government consent should be required for substantial changes in the ownership of a licensee. There was a concern that such changes could affect the nationality, resources, and competence of a licensee, but there was no control over these transactions because formally the identity of the licensee remained unchanged.

The group also thought that Government consent should be required for any agreement made by a licensee under which another party shared in the profits of the licence. It was felt that the Government should be able to control profit-making by someone other than the licensee. A particular aspect was tax avoidance. Assignments by a licensee could be very valuable, and it was felt that the Government, which had granted the licence for a low initial fee, should share in the gains from an assignment.

Officials also recommended some tightening of the terms in several other areas. Thus Government consent for change of operator should be required to ensure continued competence in operations. There should also be power to require licensees to provide specified information about their development and production plans including the relevant costs. The absence of this requirement had become the subject of much criticism. It was also proposed that powers be taken to require licensees to provide parent company guarantees that their obligations would be met. Currently the licensee could be a subsidiary company with no significant resources of its own. The potential obligations could be large. Further powers to publish technical data, such as well data, much earlier than was currently provided for would be helpful in better informing the exploration potential in neighbouring blocks. Powers to regulate offshore pipeline developments were also desirable to deal with (a) the possibility of their uneconomic proliferation, (b) the sharing of pipelines, and, if necessary, to fix tariffs, and (c) the fixing of standards of construction and maintenance.

Officials felt that the oil companies would find it hard to argue that these proposed new powers were unreasonable. They were generally applicable in Norway. It would not be contrary to international law to take these powers and to use them so long as there was no discrimination against foreigners and no expropriation without full and prompt compensation. The ultimate sanction would be licence revocation, but it was not envisaged that this would be employed.

The issue of whether the depletion rate should be controlled by Government was a major issue worthy of further consideration. There were many issues involved, including not only the relationships with the oil companies but the international legal and political consequences.

The official group did not feel that a break clause in the licences, such as had been recommended by the Public Accounts Committee and Walter Levy, should be introduced. It would constitute a clear breach of contract and was unnecessary if the other fiscal and non-fiscal recommendations were implemented.

For its meeting in late October 1973 the Ministerial group also had the benefit of the advice of the Law Officers on the international legal aspects of the introduction of (a) state participation with carried interest, (b) severance tax, and (c) Excess Revenue Tax, so far as these impacted on current licensees. In essence the advice was that the imposition of participation with carried interest would be contrary to the rule requiring prompt and full compensation, but, if it were combined with an Excess Revenue Tax, a valuation of the licence interest which took account of the reduced rate of return resulting from the tax, was probably defensible. The advice of the Law Officers was that the imposition of a severance tax would be contrary to international law, while an Excess Revenue Tax either on its own or as part of a mixed system including participation would not conflict with international law.

Ministers' further reflections

The Ministerial group considered all these submissions. There was now less enthusiasm for the state participation option on existing licences and more for an Excess Revenue Tax which could provide an equivalent amount of revenue over the life of a field (though state participation might provide more in the early years). The group felt that the oil companies would prefer the Excess Revenue Tax, a sentiment which would probably be shared by the Government's supporters who might be concerned about a policy involving enhanced interference with the industry's operations. The Chancellor was invited to produce a detailed scheme of Excess Revenue Tax. It was further felt that, rather than seek increased involvement in the management of companies, the essential Government objectives should be to control the rate of production and the destination of the oil. But, to seek powers which enabled the Government to accelerate or decelerate production against the wishes of the companies with existing licences, could raise difficult legal issues which required further examination. Similarly, control on the destination of oil required further consideration, particularly in relation to EEC obligations.

State Participation/Excess Revenue Tax permutations

Much further work resulted from this meeting. Several papers were prepared for the subsequent Ministerial meeting in December 1973. Mr Peter Walker, the Secretary of State for Trade and Industry, submitted a memorandum on controls over production and trade backed up by detailed papers. With respect to export controls, powers to control exports to non-EEC destinations already existed under the Import, Export and Customs Powers (Defence) Act, 1939. This would apply to North Sea oil, and it was recommended that exports to such destinations should require a Government licence. With respect to the OECD sharing mechanism the Government could use its veto to avoid the obligation. This would cause a row, but the requisite power was available if necessary. With respect to exports to the EEC, it might be possible to employ the 1939 Act, irrespective of obligations under the Treaty of Rome. But inconsistency with the Treaty was a very serious threat and could lead to legal action in the European Court. Mr Walker proposed that no overt action should be taken to prevent North Sea oil exports which would inevitably produce conflicts with both the EEC and OECD. But informal pressure could be used to ensure that as much North Sea crude as possible was refined in the UK. This would help both the balance of payments and security of supply. If the companies were pressed now to refine and use the oil in the UK it would help to create a pattern of distribution and expectation which would enhance the likelihood of being able to retain North Sea oil when it was most needed. The issue of the potential loss of the premium value of North Sea oil on the world market was understood, but security of supply considerations would be the more pressing consideration.

The only means of substantial direct control short of nationalisation was through state participation. With 50% participation the UK could then have direct control over half of the oil without explicit breach of the Treaty and would be better able to influence the disposal of the remainder. While Ministers had earlier expressed scepticism about state participation with the carried interest mechanism, it was now agreed by all the relevant Departments that not only should this be taken on future licences, but should also be taken on current licences renegotiated at the licensee's option. In both cases the imposition of the Excess Revenue Tax would then be waived. A further advantage of this would be the greater influence over the rate of production. This could be provided for by direct control, but with state participation no legislation or action in breach of licence terms would be needed.

Because future licences would not result in production before 1980, and because only a minority of current licensees would voluntarily accept state participation, there was the question of whether powers should be taken to impose it as part of a hybrid participation – Excess Revenue Tax mixture, whereby all licensees would be subject to the tax, but the Government (not the licensee) would have the option to impose participation, and remit Excess Revenue Tax payments as partial compensation. The CPRS favoured this tougher approach because it would give more state participation and thus more control over exports. It was the only effective method of controlling exports to the EEC. The 1939 Act could only be employed in times of non-emergency if Ministers were prepared to breach EEC obligations. The CPRS also felt that informal pressure on the oil companies without credible sanctions would not work, and the availability of North Sea oil in times of shortage was too critical to the national interest to rely on informal pressures. The CPRS further argued that the complexity of the participation – Excess Revenue Tax combination was not a reason to reject it.

Other Departments preferred not to go beyond the licensee option to have state participation. They felt that exports to the EEC could be controlled under existing powers, despite the weak legal position. Further, the compulsory participation – Excess Revenue Tax mixture would still produce incomplete control over exports, because only 50% would be under the Government's control. The scheme would not only be very complex but expensive to the Government. The legal advice of the Law Officers was that, where participation was adopted, a capital payment might have to be made in compensation in addition to remission of the tax. The mechanism was also not free of legal risks as it could be challenged in international tribunals. Other Departments felt that informal pressures from the Government as licensing authority could be exerted more strongly than they had been to date. The DTI preferred a high state participation but without excessive complications. The optional approach was preferable, and to expedite agreements the Excess Revenue Tax should be set sufficiently high to induce the companies to choose participation with carried interest. It was also suggested that when consent to assignments was requested the parties should be pressed to accept participation.

State participation options in practice

If state participation were to proceed the question arose of who would administer the scheme on behalf of the Government. In his memorandum to his Ministerial colleagues Mr Walker felt that this depended on the prime purpose of the participation. If it was revenue-raising only the commercial decisions could all be left to the companies, and participation would essentially mean only checking development plans and subsequently auditing financial accounts. The DTI could readily do this with a modest increase in staff. If, however, the intent was to be an active, full partner to the extent of 50% or so in a field, with involvement in all the major decisions, a much larger number of staff would be required. The role could still be undertaken by the DTI but a separate body was also a possibility. There was a fairly strong case for full partnership based on the size of the financial stake, the benefits from influencing operations, and a clear response to public pressure to take an active part in the management of an important natural resource.

Use of BP to administer the rights was not recommended. It would mean changing the character of the company which was run on wholly commercial lines. The duties of the BP board to their shareholders could not be reconciled with duties as custodians of the Government's interest. Use of the DTI directly could ensure that the national interest (as seen by the Government) was clearly pursued. External organisations would develop interests of their own. There were disadvantages such as the difficulty of taking commercial decisions unhampered by political considerations. Using British Gas as the vehicle would give comparative freedom from political pressures. It would, however, look close to conventional nationalisation, and would radically change the character of British Gas because oil would soon dominate gas.

Mr Walker prefers new state company

A new organisation would have the advantage of comparative freedom from political pressure. The new organisation could be developed into a full state oil company. It would develop its own interests, but if the Secretary of State had powers of direction over it this problem would diminish. On balance Mr Walker preferred a specially-created company with powers of direction conferred on himself.

Study on depletion policy

Officials also produced a more detailed paper on control of depletion rates. Powers to accelerate and slow down exploration and production would be useful. As well as the concern about the lack of work obligations for the forty remaining years of licences after the first relinquishment period it was desirable to be able to take powers to procure increased production in an emergency. The taking of such powers was legally defensible though their execution could amount to expropriation, at least in part. The existence of the power might be enough to secure the desired response from the licensees. Powers could also be taken to achieve slower depletion by prescribing reduced production rates on fields shortly coming on stream, but new legislation would be required, and licensees would seek compensation. Similarly to warn licensees of fields not yet developed or even discovered could hardly be less controversial. There were also associated postponements in the balance of payments benefits and royalty and tax receipts. There were consequences for the contracting sector. Slower depletion would give more time for British industry to gear up to supply the new, growing market. But it would also reduce the overall size of that market. The advantages and disadvantages seemed finely balanced. Using a time-discount rate of 10% and current expectations of oil price growth there were national resource benefits from slower depletion.

Importance of security of supply

While all the above considerations were relevant the DTI felt that security of supply was of overwhelming importance, and thus the key objective should be to manage the depletion rate such that the greatest possible contribution was made to supply security. In practice this meant that, so long as imported oil remained insecure, indigenous production should not exceed demand. Discoveries made to date would be insufficient to produce self-sufficiency, but if further discoveries were made, there could come a time when curtailment of production was appropriate. While powers to do this could be taken now it would be preferable to wait until their use was required. There was a risk that the announcement of the powers would have a negative effect on investment.

The DTI noted that state participation would make it easier to introduce production cuts as the Government could reduce its share of the oil. But this would result in less Government revenue, and there would be practical difficulties in the determination of the offsetting increase in the Government's share at later dates.

Further deliberations of Ministers emphasise security of supply

The Ministerial meeting in December 1973 discussed all these memoranda and papers. Doubts were expressed about the advantages of state participation compared to Excess Revenue Tax as a device to raise revenues. The former should be viewed primarily as a means of controlling the disposal of the oil. Doubts were expressed about the willingness of the companies to accept participation, and the rate of Excess Revenue Tax required to produce the necessary inducement might have to be penal. There would also be demands for compensation. Other devices for controlling depletion such as licensing of production could also be used discreetly to influence the disposal of oil. Ministers were also greatly concerned about the rising price of oil on the world market and wondered whether UK consumers could be protected from its effects.

The conclusions of the meeting were that the most important issues were to ensure security of oil supply to the UK at reasonable prices. State participation was not obviously the most appropriate method. Before making a final decision Mr Walker was invited to examine the merits of enhancing security of oil supply from the North Sea by the licensing of production and refinery operations. He was also asked to examine the possibility of disassociating the price of North Sea oil from the inflated levels of the world market.

Revisions to Regulations

Meanwhile the DTI was continuing its work on revisions to the licensing regulations which had not received the full attention of Ministers. Consultations were held with BP and Shell on their views on the DTI proposals and consultants (Petroleum Studies) were also asked to provide a report on the subject. By late

February 1974 the new Department of Energy had formulated its revised views on the main issues. Thus the power to impose an interim valuation for royalty pending arbitration remained, but the earlier idea of basing royalty on landed rather than wellhead value, which had been strongly opposed by BP and Shell, was dropped. The proposal to have discretion to take royalty oil in kind was kept, even though Shell and BP had argued that this should only apply to exported oil. The proposal was now refined to provide that the Government would reimburse conveying and treatment costs in that event. A new proposal was to take discretionary powers to remit royalty (free of tax) in circumstances where production was not otherwise economic. Royalty payments could also subsequently be restored when remission was no longer justified.

Lack of industry enthusiasm for enhanced Government regulatory powers

With respect to the proposed powers over approval of field development plans, commencement and maintenance of production, and variations to production profiles, both BP and Shell indicated their opposition. They disliked the whole concept of Government intervention in economic decision-making, and felt that existing powers over the drilling of wells were sufficient. Intervention to vary production rates should be used only in an emergency. By February 1973 the DTI was convinced that it needed all the powers noted above. With respect to the encouragement of continued exploration after the end of the initial six-year surrender period, several alternative proposals had been made to Shell and BP for comment, namely that the Department could (a) have power to require licensees to undertake an agreed work programme on retained acreage, (b) that the offset of rental payments against royalty be terminated, (c) that the annual increments to rental payments be made much bigger, or (d) that licences be terminated if after, say, ten years no petroleum were produced. BP was unhappy with all the proposals, and suggested instead a further surrender of 25% of the original area after a second six-year period. Shell preferred alternative (a) on a rolling three-year basis. Following the consultations and further deliberation the Department in February 1973 felt that all their earlier ideas were defective, and proposed that they be empowered to call for exploration programmes on a discretionary basis where they felt the level of activity was inadequate. The Department would also be empowered to reject a proposed programme where it was deemed unsatisfactory, and to revoke the licence if no satisfactory programme was forthcoming.

The proposed powers to control changes in the ownership of a licence had not been objected to by Shell and BP, but they objected strongly to the idea that, in the event of an assignment, the Government should receive part of any premia. The Department decided to drop this idea. The companies did not object to the proposal that DTI consent be required when a change of operator was mooted. The Department remained keen to have the power to call for information on costs and profits despite the lack of enthusiasm of Shell and BP. Similarly, the Department was keen to be able to release technical data at any time after a period of five years from its acquisition. The companies wanted a longer period of confidentiality for exploration licences. The Department had become more concerned about gas flaring, and suggested to the companies that the Government have power to forbid flaring, and, where it was permitted, to charge royalty on flared gas. The companies objected strongly, and the Department now proposed that licences should have to obtain consent for any flaring. The proposals to have controls over offshore pipelines were not strongly objected to by the companies, and it was now proposed to include powers to ensure that the Government could prevent unnecessary proliferation of pipelines and provide for third party access on terms which could be fixed by the Secretary of State.

Reflections on position at end of Heath Government

By the end of the Heath Government proposals were thus well advanced to tighten up the detailed licence terms to accommodate not only the criticism of the Public Accounts Committee but to deal with other perceived defects as well. Some of the points made by the Public Accounts Committee had been understood long before publication of the report. The philosophy was one where detailed intervention relating to the behaviour of the companies was readily defensible. There was little change in the development of thinking in the Department on the detailed issues under the Conservative Government compared to the previous Labour one. Officials in the Department were guided by the evolving practical experience which had highlighted perceived defects in the existing Regulations.

On the bigger issues of control over the disposal of oil and its depletion rate, Department officials generally found favour with the state participation approach because it offered the prospect of achieving the desired goals without being in obvious conflict with the Treaty of Rome. Officials also found favour with state participation as a means to increase the Government's share of the revenues. The Secretary of State favoured the use of a new state-owned body to look after the state's participatory interests. Given that this was a Conservative Government it was not surprising that this view was not readily endorsed by other Ministers.

The debate on the respective merits of extra taxation and state participation was surprising. Much weight was given to the early revenues which participation would bring compared to the Excess Revenue Tax which would permit all field exploration and developments costs to be recovered before tax payments became due. But state participation on a carried interest basis as conceived at the time would have entailed large and early expenditures on field investments before profits were generated. This received surprisingly little emphasis in the debate. In general, participation even with carried interest at the exploration stage involves the state in more front-end risk-sharing than taxation based on field profits or production. Security of oil supply was becoming increasingly dominant in Government thinking following the four-fold increase in world price increases, and the perceived multiple benefits of state control were becoming more apparent irrespective of political philosophy.

6   Further gas developments and the Frigg contracts

Unique features of each field

It had been expected that the long-term gas contracts for the Hewett, Leman, and Indefatigable fields would greatly facilitate agreements on other fields. This did not prove to be the case. While the operators of other fields were aware of the main features of the agreements in negotiations they tended to emphasise the special features of their own fields which necessitated variations from existing contracts. The result was that negotiations were prolonged. The fields in question included West Sole, Viking, Deborah, Dotty, Hewett North, Rough, and Ekofisk, each of which were deemed by the operators to have their own unique characteristics deserving special consideration in contracts. Within Government, while thinking on some terms relating to gas contracts remained unchanged, variations relating to others were emerging. On pricing the cost-related approach was still stoutly defended. On utilisation the Ministry, in evidence to the Select Committee on Nationalised Industries in 1968, reiterated principles enunciated earlier in the 1967 White Paper, namely that initially there should be concentration on the premium market, and subsequently on the bulk market when prices should be lower. A controversy arose over this matter in early 1969 when the British Steel Corporation signed a large contract to purchase (imported) fuel oil. Arguments were produced that natural gas should have been used instead. Mr Mason explained to the Prime Minister that the quantities of gas required were not yet available, and that bulk fuel supply to industry did not represent the best use of North Sea gas at this stage.

Longer depletion periods for future contracts?

By the summer of 1969 the view was emerging that there might be advantages in providing that in future contracts depletion should be spread over a longer period. There might also be advantages in delaying field developments for a few years. It was decided to undertake a pilot study which would examine the additional costs and benefits to the Gas Council and the national economy of such changes. Consultations with the Gas Council might be delicate because, following the Leman and Indefatigable agreements, the Ministry had decided that it did not need to get so closely involved in the details of contracts. Mr Mason had so informed the relevant Cabinet Committee, and it was agreed that only substantial variations from the guidelines established for the three contracted fields should be reported to Ministers.

Slow progress

The Department thus did not have detailed meetings with licensees but kept in touch with the Council on progress. By September 1969 the Council reported that for the Viking field it had proposed to Conoco depletion over a thirty-year period with only 50% take-or-pay liability, with an expected price of around 2.87d per therm. It was expected that Conoco would argue that a substantially higher price was required because of the very long depletion period and the need for a long pipeline. Progress in negotiations had been good on other fields except West Sole where they were quite slow. On the question of incentives the Council recognised that it was essential to maintain the exploration momentum, but was unconvinced that higher prices stimulated exploration! The Department explained to the Council their studies on future gas absorption policy with emphasis on the costs and benefits of slower depletion.

By the end of 1969 the Council reported little further progress. On West Sole the Council wanted a contract with key features similar to those of Leman, but BP had a different framework in mind. The company also appeared to be content with the ad hoc agreements which had backed up the three-year contract already signed. On the Rough field Gulf and Amerada were seeking prices well above those contemplated by the Council. For the Viking field the Council again wanted a Leman-type contract, but with a slower build up and a tighter ceiling on the plateau level. With respect to the Dotty and Deborah fields the Council had now accepted that they would produce simultaneously with the Hewett field under "piggy-back" contracts. The Department was concerned that the Council were taking a hard line on the question of incentives for further exploration.

Ekofisk gas

The Department took a closer interest in the possible contract to purchase gas from the Norwegian Ekofisk field because of its wider implications, particularly those relating to the balance of payments. An inter-departmental group had begun examining this issue in early 1969. The group had considered two possibilities, the first being where the gas displaced coal in the bulk heat market. In this case the whole of the purchase price of the gas would represent a foreign exchange cost. The second case was where the gas displaced oil. In the later case it could be assumed that North Sea gas displaced an equivalent volume of average imported oil. But North Sea oil could become available in substantial volumes and perhaps at a lower cost. This would complicate the cost-benefit calculation. One case would be where Ekofisk supplied 600 mmcf/d which, with expected domestic production of 3,400 mmcf/d, would ensure that the 1967 White Paper projections of 4,000 mmcf/d were met. Alternative prices of 2.75d and 3.5d per therm could be employed. Reflecting the great concern with the balance of payments, the Ministry considered that it would be advantageous for the Gas Council to buy the gas at the wellhead. This would greatly reduce the foreign exchange cost, unless the Council had to employ foreign pipe and related equipment. A question had also arisen over whether investment grants could be paid to a Norwegian company building a pipeline from Ekofisk to the UK. If this work were undertaken by the Council no doubts would arise. A quite different angle on gas trade had been raised by Ian Mikardo MP, who had written to the Paymaster General arguing that the absorption of 4,000 mmcf/d by the mid-1970s (as foreseen in the 1967 White Paper), could only be achieved by using gas in power stations which in turn would involve an excessive cost to the coal industry. Selling more gas into the industrial market would not be possible because of keen competition from oil products. He therefore suggested that a state body should be established to consider export possibilities. The Department agreed that when the White Paper was prepared it was assumed that 25% of the 4,000 mmcf/d could be into power stations. But the estimates at late 1969 were that only 6%–7% might be available for power generation. The Gas Council felt that it could sell 4,000 mmcf/d without relying on power generation.

Detailed studies on depletion periods

By late 1969 the results of the modelling of variations to field depletion rates were becoming available in the Department. Using a hypothetical field with recoverable reserves of 2.5 tcf and financial simulation modelling, it was found that the optimal depletion period (from the seller's viewpoint) was fifteen years or even less. The Gas Council generally agreed with this finding, and both parties considered the implications for the Council's purchasing policies. Shorter depletion periods would have implications for the rate of absorption of gas and would bring forward the time at which further replacement gas would be required. On these grounds it was perhaps unlikely to be in the national interest to adopt shorter depletion times. The Council felt that another implication would be that, with the prospect of increased returns to the producers, the price of valley gas should be negotiated downwards below the prevailing 2.025d per therm level. On the other hand the Department also found in its modelling that extending the field depletion rate from twenty to thirty years would involve an increase in price to the producer of 0.5d per therm. Similarly, a postponement of field development by five years would entail a price increase of 1d per therm.

The Department developed scenarios of long-term future availability and demand. In early 1970 these pointed to a sharp fall-off in availability from around 1985, even after inclusion of future discoveries. Thus rapid absorption in the early years implied large LNG imports in later years. The notion of gas exports raised by Mr Mikardo had also to be seen in this light. The Department was undertaking modelling using linear programming on the relative costs of alternative depletion rates. To date the main finding had been that the optimal depletion pattern (including intervention to delay new field developments) was very sensitive to assumptions about the total quantity of reserves likely to be discovered. There was much uncertainty about future discoveries, and so there were advantages in obtaining flexibility in depletion terms in new contracts. More attention could usefully be given to the sequencing of new field developments in optimising the overall depletion rate.

In the ongoing negotiations on several new fields the Gas Council had been trying to obtain more flexibility (in its favour) compared to the early contracts. For the Viking field Conoco and the NCB had initially been offered only 50% take-or-pay terms. This had been received with much hostility, and at February 1970 the Council had proposed a 75% limit to this liability but was prepared to go to 90%. This was still quite unacceptable to the producers who felt that there should be no breach of the 100% take-or-pay provisions of the early contracts. There was also disagreement on the plateau rate, with the Council wanting a lower level than the investors. The NCB had requested protection against sterling devaluation, to which the Council had replied that it could not provide a compensation clause to a British company, though it would be prepared to do so for an American one. However, the Council would be prepared to move away from a clause triggered by devaluation to provision of additional payments in the event of devaluation.

With respect to the West Sole field the discussions with BP over a long-term contract were unfruitful and acrimonious. The Council had tried to reduce the price from the 5d in the initial three-year contract to 2.87d over the whole life of the contract. Agreement was not going to be easy, but BP had now been referring to a 3d price.

Department queries price and monopsony assumptions

In March 1970 the sacred cows of (a) the Gas Council's monopoly and (b) the ceiling on prices for new contracts of 2.87d were queried inside the Department. The price ceiling had been justified on the grounds that the Council could be in a position to meet the costs of developing the NTS, conversion of appliances, and accelerated depreciation of gas manufacturing plant. Other arguments such as the need to minimise the cost to the balance of payments and to keep the overall cost of energy down had been added, but they were not convincing in the context of a price margin of around 0.3d per therm. Looking ahead it would be inviting inefficiency to insist that the Council should continue to pay no more than 2.87d for future gas. For gas beyond the 4,000 mmcf/d level the Council should be prepared to pay a price which would ensure them a margin for further expanding their market with no further reference to their historic position. This was the only way to maintain vigorous exploration and ensure the development of small fields. There was little prospect of a "surplus" of gas emerging, especially with the continuation of the fuel oil duty. There were, however, signs of a protectionist attitude by the Council, manifested in a recent complaint about competition from LPG. With respect to the current set of negotiations the Rough field was an example of a marginal field where a price of 3d or even more would be justified to indicate that the 2.87d figure was not immutable and to provide exploration incentives. It would also make an insignificant difference to the Council's financial position in view of the modest volumes of gas involved.

With respect to the Council's monopoly position there was a case for allowing some competition in the industrial market. An example would be in relation to LNG. If, for example, Shell were to import it and use it at their Carrington petro-chemical complex they should be allowed to supply industrial demands in the nearby area if they had first of all offered it to the local Area Board at a reasonable price. There were advantages in permitting competition at the margin to the nationalised industry.

These ideas were received with some scepticism. Based on the evidence of Third Round applications there was still an appetite for exploration. A relaxation of pricing policy could encourage licensees on small fields to hold out for much higher prices, rather than a marginal increase. The suggested advantages of competition in the industrial market were queried on the curious grounds that it would lead to a situation such as prevailed in the steel industry where there were private and publicly-owned companies to the satisfaction of neither. Other reservations highlighted the notion that paying high prices for marginal North Sea supplies to meet an expanding premium market overlooked the prospect that the true marginal market was the bulk one where low prices were required to be competitive with oil. Competition with LNG was queried on the grounds that the supply of gas through pipelines was a natural monopoly, as had been recognised for over a hundred years.[1]

Debate on contract terms continues

While these longer-term issues were being debated attention had to be given to the current contract negotiations. The Paymaster General met with the Chairman and Deputy Chairman of the Council in March 1970 to discuss pricing policy. The Minister was informed of the current state of the negotiations as discussed above. The Paymaster subsequently informed the Prime Minister that he approved of the Council's tough but realistic stance of keeping prices within the framework established by Ministers for the earlier contracts, while seeking greater flexibility in supply conditions. The Prime Minister's response was that the Council should not commit to any new contracts without the Paymaster's approval. The Treasury should also be kept informed on negotiations and have the opportunity to comment prior to Government approval of a contract. At a subsequent meeting the Treasury expressed approval of the Council's stance on pricing and on procuring greater flexibility in supplies. The idea that a higher price could be set alongside greater flexibility was approvingly discussed. The Treasury was unhappy about an overt devaluation clause, and preferred a provision for price review in the event of special circumstances such as currency and cost changes.

The Treasury raised a quite different and perceptive point about long-term pricing. If the Council paid a fixed price for gas over a very long time, while costs, including those of competing fuels, were rising, a market distortion could ensue which could result in natural gas, a desirable fuel with limited supplies, being (artificially) used for non-premium purposes, entailing a misallocation of resources. There was thus a case for a price review after some years. In the early contracts the idea of a price review had, of course, been considered, but with a view to procuring a price decrease in the event of abundant supplies becoming available. The Ministry agreed that the environment had changed radically since the early contracts were signed. Inflation had been higher than anticipated, and expectations of the size of further reserves were now not so bullish. In the meantime, however, it was decided that the Council should continue its negotiations on the agreed lines.

At the end of April the Council received an offer from Conoco/NCB for the Viking field. The proposed price was 3.7d for the basic contract quantity and 2.5d for valley gas. A higher daily contract quantity than the Council had planned was suggested, but the 90% take-or-pay recently offered by the Council was accepted. It was clear to the Council and the Ministry that this offer would have to be rejected.

Progress was now being made with BP on the West Sole contract. The company had agreed to a field depletion contract (rather than a volume one as had earlier been the case). By early July agreement was in sight with a twenty-year contract, a basic price of 2.9d per therm and 2.025d for valley gas. There would be a price review after twelve years.

For the Viking field, by the end of September 1970 all main items except price had been settled. The Council was prepared to give a price trigger clause (for devaluation) to Conoco but not the NCB. The Council wondered whether the new Conservative Government took the same view on a devaluation clause as its predecessor. The answer was that there could be a clause covering a change in the parity of sterling, but it must cover with equal emphasis a change in either direction, and the clause should relate only to goods where the contract price was expressed in foreign exchange.

Ekofisk and Viking gas and competition from West Germany

By the end of September some progress had been made on the North Hewett fields, on Rough, and on Ekofisk where talks had started. The Department's view was that the chances of obtaining Ekofisk gas were quite problematic. Much depended on the price the Germans were prepared to pay, but also on whether UK investment grants were likely to be available. The issue of the German offer price came back with a vengeance later in the year when the news came through that Ruhrgas had made a firm offer at the equivalent of 4.5d per therm for the Viking field. As noted above the concept of gas exports had been raised earlier by Mr Mikardo as a device to protect the coal industry, but had also been raised more recently by Professor Odell. He had argued that to sell 4,000 mmcf/d of North Sea gas would involve the sale of up to 1,000 mmcf/d to power stations at a low price of around 2.5d, and that such gas could be sold abroad more profitably. The

Ministry disputed this and calculated that the great majority of the 4,000 mmcf/d could be sold by the mid-1970s to sectors other than power generation at much higher prices. The Ministry also disputed Professor Odell's estimate that UK gas could be delivered to consumers at around 3.5d per therm. Their estimate was a price at the German beach of 4.3d – 4.5d which they felt would be too high to compete with Dutch gas. Ruhrgas presumably felt they could make a profit.

In any event in December 1970 Lord Robens of the NCB requested an urgent meeting with the Minister for Industry. He said, that, as the Viking licensees had been unable to reach agreement with the Gas Council on a price for the gas after having negotiated for seventeen months, he would like the Minister's approval to be allowed to export the gas to the Continent where a better return was anticipated. The Minister requested that he present his case in writing. This was promptly done. Lord Robens highlighted three critical issues – the contract price, the price review clause, and the build up of the gas flow – where agreement had not been reached. It had been agreed by both parties that the contract should be related to the Indefatigable one, but the respective interpretations of the relationship with that contract differed markedly.

The NCB and Conoco maintained that there were five reasons why the Gas Council's offer was unreasonable. Firstly, the build-up to plateau was slower than in the Indefatigable case. Secondly, Viking was more valuable to the Council at Mablethorpe (where it was planned to land the gas) than at Bacton, as the former was nearer major centres of consumption. But the cost to the licensees was higher through the provision of a much longer pipeline. Thirdly, the Indefatigable price was no longer appropriate as fuel prices had risen significantly since 1968. In that year the beach gas price was 120% of the fuel oil price while now it was only 55%. Fourthly, it was expected that fuel prices would continue to rise as would general inflation. In a 25-year contract account should be taken of this by fixing the gas price in relation to current fuel prices and adjusting through time for inflation. Fifthly, it was apparent to the NCB and Conoco that the Council was attempting to use its monopoly powers to hold down gas prices in order to put gas in a favourable competitive position with other fuels. Lord Robens added that it was reasonable to seek to compete, but not to use monopoly powers in an arbitrary and discriminatory fashion.

In the light of the above the NCB and its associates would have to review their attitude to exploration in the UKCS. Lord Robens noted that this activity was now at a low level, almost certainly due to the lower returns expected compared to elsewhere. This had been forced on the companies by the use of the Council's monopoly powers. It was doubtful if these were in the public interest. In the light of the above circumstances Lord Robens requested that the Viking licensees be allowed to conclude an export contract for the gas.

Views of Gas Council on Viking gas

In giving its views on the matters to the Department the Council emphasised that it had already offered more generous terms for Viking gas than in other contracts.

They felt that that agreement would almost certainly have been possible with Conoco and that it was Lord Robens who had withheld agreement. The Council felt that it faced a particular difficulty in that the NCB negotiators had no negotiating discretion and could merely take note and report back. This had dictated the slow pace of negotiations. While oil prices had risen they could fall back in the future. Further the Government might abolish the fuel oil duty and rescind approval to use gas for power generation.

Because of the dispute on the Viking contract negotiations relating to other fields were at a standstill, as other licensees believed that precedents might be set by Viking which had implications for their own contracts. The Council also felt that rapid development of North Sea gas meant low prices not high ones! The Council was still keen to purchase Ekofisk gas and hoped to do so at less that 3.5d per therm.

The Department's views in early 1971 were that the latest Gas Council offer for Viking gas was not overgenerous bearing in mind the longer pipeline and the sharp rise in costs since 1968. The Council's offer price was only 0.028d above the Indefatigable price, and there was scope to be rather more generous. By February the Council's revised offer was 3.1512d compared to 3.48d requested by the licensees.

Government refuses export permission for Viking gas

The Government had no hesitation in refusing export permission for Viking gas, but in February 1971 the Minister for Industry expressed concern about the logic of this while encouraging the further use of gas in CEGB power stations. He requested an analysis of the comparative merits of exporting gas or using it in the UK for power stations. A quick report was produced for him. This emphasised the current world shortage of energy, and the UK's major reliance on imported oil from politically unstable countries. No country in the world exported gas unless it was clearly surplus to its long-term energy needs. All the known UK reserves were needed to meet the level of 4,000 mmcf/d in 1975 as indicated in the 1967 White Paper, and further reserves could be absorbed later. It was estimated that, at February 1971, coal delivered to the CEGB cost 7d per therm, and fuel oil 5d. The delivered price of natural gas would not exceed 4.5d. The DTI understood that the Viking licensees were hoping for a delivered price to Germany of 4.3d – 4.5d. This was higher than the price paid by Germany to the Netherlands.

In current circumstances the UK would be exporting gas at around 4.3d per therm, but paying 5d if the CEGB was prepared to increase its exposure to imported oil or 7d for replacement coal. The CEGB's position did not represent the national position, however. The true social cost to the nation of UK coal could be around 6d rather than 7d per therm. But the export price of gas would have to be reduced by imports of equipment and overseas remittances by licensees. Imports of the necessary pipe to transport the gas to Germany could cost between 1d – 2d per therm depending on the export route chosen. The effective net export price to the nation would probably not exceed 3d per therm. In sum the UK would be paying around 6d. to gain foreign exchange worth around 3d per therm.

The Department also argued that, if the CEGB continued to burn UK coal in stations which otherwise would have been converted to burn gas without resulting in any further increase in fuel oil being burned, there would be no foreign exchange costs, but gains of around 3d per therm. But if the export of gas resulted in the CEGB burning more imported oil directly or indirectly the foreign exchange cost would be around 4d per them, leaving a net foreign exchange loss of 1d per therm. The Department's conclusion was that in current and foreseeable circumstances gas exports would only be in the national interest if very much higher export prices were available.

Agreements reached with North Hewett and Viking fields

Meanwhile there had been substantial progress with the North Hewett contracts, and by March 1971 agreement had been reached in principle with all the licensees involving a main price of 2.87d with 2.025d for valley gas, and escalation as for the main Hewett contract. The Council was able to obtain greater flexibility in the gas take provisions. Progress was slower with the Viking contract but later in the year agreement was reached with a base gas price of 3.6d per therm and valley gas at 2.025d. The higher price was justified because of the higher offshore transportation costs. The Viking contract was also important because the estimated reserves (4 tcf at the time) would make a substantial contribution to the total supplies from the mid-1970s. The contribution of the North Hewett fields was estimated to be considerably less with reserves of around 1 tcf.

Desire to acquire gas from Ekofisk

The Government and the Gas Council maintained a keen interest in acquiring gas from the Ekofisk area. In February 1971 the DTI heard from Phillips (Norway), the operator of the Ekofisk complex, that the company had in mind a price of around 4d per therm. The company was planning to talk to a variety of possible purchasers including several on the continent, namely in Denmark, Sweden, Germany, and Netherlands (for re-export), and also the CEGB, South of Scotland Electricity Board (SSEB), and Gas Council in the UK. The company felt that the Conservative Government would remove any impediments to such deals including new legislation if necessary.

This news precipitated a meeting among the SSEB, Gas Council, Scottish Development Department (SDD), and DTI. The SSEB confirmed their interest, adding that neither coal nor oil offered them a particularly stable base on which to plan future electricity production. Further, the Gas Council did not appear to have sufficient quantities available for sale to them in the next few years. In discussion the view emerged that direct purchase of Ekofisk gas by the SSEB was not a practical proposition, not only because of the current legal situation, but also because a power station wholly dependent for its fuel on a 200 mile pipeline was felt to be risky. The likely very high continuous load factor (because gas from Ekofisk was associated with oil) would impose difficult obligations on the SSEB which they might not be able to honour, unless the Council was prepared to buy gas from the SSEB at times when it did not require it. There were also advantages in the Gas Council being the sole purchasing negotiator! There was also discussion on the likely landfall for the gas, with both Teesside and the Forth being regarded as candidates. The Scottish representatives were interested to ensure that, as far as gas supplies were concerned, the SSEB should be treated on a par with the CEGB.

Progress in the negotiations was slow. The Norwegians had decided that in the first instance the gas should be reinjected into the field to enhance oil recovery and so there was no pressure to make an early agreement. By the autumn of 1971 Phillips had prepared revised offer terms, key features of which were large volumes of 1,000 mmcf/d (compared to 450/650 mmcf/d earlier), and a price of 5d per therm (compared to 4d earlier). It was proposed that the price be expressed in US cents with an annual review to reflect UK cost inflation in relation to 30% of the price and heavy fuel prices in Europe as to 50% of the price.

Given the benefits of reducing dependence on oil from unstable areas there were advantages from an energy policy viewpoint in obtaining this gas if the terms were acceptable. The Ekofisk supplies would become available at a time when production from fields in the UKCS would be levelling off. This would enable the gas industry to meet growth in the premium market without diverting supplies from bulk industrial users who would then have to turn to oil. Ekofisk gas would initially have to be absorbed in the bulk industrial market. In the power generation market the Gas Council had expressed confidence that they could absorb the gas without further conversions to gas beyond the three stations for which consent was currently being sought. At plateau production the foreign exchange cost would be £62 million per year at 1.7 pence (4d) and £77 million at 2.1 pence (5d). The DTI had also calculated that the savings from displacing around 10 million tonnes of fuel oil would be the equivalent of around 1.9 pence to 2.1 pence per therm in 1977 when plateau production from Ekofisk would be attained. Thus the balance of payments savings in 1977 would be around £73 million. The higher the price paid for Ekofisk the less the benefit, and it was estimated that if the price exceeded 2.0 pence (4.8d). the net benefits would disappear.

Because of the long length of the contract the escalation clauses were of particular importance. Contracts to date had provided for escalation to apply to only a part of the price. In the most recent Viking contract it had applied to 38% of the price. As noted above Phillips had proposed escalation to 80% of the price with an annual review. Given the high current rate of inflation in the UK there was a need to obtain improvement to the escalation terms. Because the Phillips proposal was based on continental fuel oil prices there was no protection for the Council in the UK market if the Government were to remove or reduce the tax on fuel oil.

The price terms would also have consequences for the Council's ability to market the gas profitably. The Council estimated that at a price of 1.8 pence per therm they could sell the gas at a minimum price of 1.9 pence, a level which was lower than prices currently being received. A further aspect of the proposed deal was the expectation that the base price agreed would be regarded as setting a new minimum for future contracts in the UKCS.

A relevant factor included the price that continental buyers were prepared to pay. If the price quoted by Lord Robens of 1.9 pence for sales to Ruhrgas was realistic then, from Phillips viewpoint, because of the lower costs of transporting the gas to Teesside, the comparable UK price could be nearer 1.7 pence than 2.1 pence. Another factor to consider was the possibility that no further large discoveries would be made in the UKCS, and the alternative for the Council would be to import Liquefied Natural Gas (LNG) or manufacture Synthetic Natural Gas (SNG) from oil feedstocks. At late 1971 regasified LNG would cost the Council around 2.4 pence per therm.

Debate on Gas Council's monopoly rights

While these deliberations and the Ekofisk negotiations were continuing two related policy issues had to be settled. In making preparations for the forthcoming Gas Bill a decision had to be made on whether changes should be made to the Gas Council's effective monopsony buying rights of gas from the UKCS. The issue was considered by the Ministerial Committee on Economic Policy in November 1971. The Minister of State for Industry reported the views of oil companies that the result had been unduly low gas prices with negative effects on the exploration effort. The CEGB had pressed strongly for the right to buy direct from the producers. The forthcoming Gas Bill gave the opportunity to end the Council's monopsony rights, but the current energy policy review had led to serious doubts about the wisdom of so doing. The Minister argued that the only likely direct purchaser would be the CEGB which would use natural gas to displace coal on price grounds. With the need to close unprofitable mines following the fall in demand for coal, it would be unwise to do anything which would allow the CEGB to become free to buy as much gas direct from producers as they wished, given the consequential implications for power station conversions.

A different aspect was the implications of EEC membership, where conservation of natural gas and purchase by state bodies was not inconsistent with the Treaty of Rome. However, the question of whether the Treaty applied to the Continental Shelf was unclear. In these circumstances it was not sensible to free the supply of gas before entering the EEC, without knowing the applicable rules, and before any changes or concessions had been made by other EEC countries. The Minister thus proposed that no change should be made to the statutory position, but that in the debate on the Gas Bill it would be made clear that the Secretary of State was fully prepared to use his existing powers to allow direct supply to industry in suitable cases. The Ministerial group endorsed the Minister's proposals, stressing the need to emphasise that the Secretary of State was indeed ready to use his discretionary powers.

The issue came up shortly thereafter at a meeting between DTI Ministers and their officials when the draft passage of the Second Reading speech on the Gas Bill was being considered. The Minister for Industry expressed misgivings about the policy line indicated above on the grounds that both the oil companies and the Government's supporters had wanted a more radical change. After discussion it was agreed that the term "reasonable price" (in negotiations between licensees and the Gas Council) should be interpreted to include incentives to explore for and develop new discoveries. Officials emphasised that Ministers should not suggest that large quantities would be permitted to be sold directly to consumers by the producers because of anxiety regarding the supplies required to sustain the Gas Council's needs.

No competition from CEGB in bidding for Ekofisk gas

At the same meeting the issue of dissuading the CEGB from bidding for Ekofisk gas was discussed. The Minister for Industry expressed misgivings about this as it ran counter to the Government's policies on competition and non-intervention, and was also inconsistent with the proposed announcement in the Gas Bill. He added that, as others were free to bring gas to the UK for their own use, the CEGB should be allowed to do the same. The Secretary of State felt that the national interest dictated that, since the Gas Council and the CEGB were the only prospective large scale buyers of Ekofisk gas, the UK would pay more for the gas if they bid against each other for it. The Government should reserve its position, pending the completion of the review of energy policy, on whether the CEGB should be allowed to use gas on a substantial scale. The prudent policy was thus to advise the CEGB to come to an arrangement with the Gas Council. The Parliamentary Under Secretary of State was concerned about prospective criticism from the Government's supporters and the Select Committee at this departure from its policy of disengagement and the method of implementing it. In discussion the arguments were produced that there would be a big risk to the CEGB in committing itself to buy Ekofisk gas without any assurance that it would be allowed to use it. There were attractions for the CEGB in having an optional agreement for gas supply from the Council. This line was eventually agreed and the Permanent Secretary was asked to meet the chairmen of the Council and the CEGB to persuade them of the wisdom of coming to an agreement over Ekofisk gas.

Thus ended the mild attempt to introduce modest competition into the gas industry. Nowhere were the wider potential benefits of competition adequately ventilated, the impression being left that energy prices were more likely to be raised rather than lowered. Policy was dictated primarily by the perceived need to maintain the dominant role of the Gas Council and minimise the possible disruption to the coal industry.

Rough field assignment

Meanwhile the Department had to attend to a policy issue involving two state companies, namely the assignment of licences under which the Rough field had been discovered. The discovery had been made by Gulf Oil in Block 47/8, but it extended into Block 47/03 which was operated by Amoco with the Gas Council as a partner. Reserves were estimated at 0.35 tcf. Gulf had incurred a considerable amount of expenditure and was anxious that work be progressed in Block 47/03. But this was not happening, and Gulf was now prepared to farm out its (100%) interests. The Conoco/NCB group was interested in buying the Gulf interest. Gulf was asking for a cash payment plus an overriding royalty of 3/32nd of the value of the relevant gas production. The proposed assignments on the terms indicated had some attractions. The UK share would increase and the NCB would be operating jointly with private enterprise in accordance with Government policy. The proposal could, however, lead to criticisms. The use of an overriding royalty might attract the criticism that the Government royalty was too low. Secondly, there might be unease over the sale of the Rough gas production which involved two nationalised industries playing a major role in price determination.

There were other considerations. The Gas Council intimated that it had an interest in becoming a licensee as well as a purchaser of Rough gas. The Council was also concerned that if the NCB became a licensee the result might be a higher price for the gas. The Department considered the matter further. It was agreed that the proposition constituted a sensible investment for Conoco and the NCB with a satisfactory expected return, but problems could ensue with the NCB having a middle-man role. There was more merit in the Gas Council having the licensee role. It would not involve a significant increase in the Council's investment. Officials obtained the approval of the Minister for Industry that the Department should facilitate the assignment of the Gulf interest to the Council, and if this failed, the NCB should be allowed to pursue its offer.

The Department then suggested to Gulf that they approach the Council with an offer, emphasising the advantages of avoiding the introduction of a third party who would be acting the role of a middle-man. Unsurprisingly Conoco/NCB were unhappy at this development, and, at a meeting with Department officials, outlined their case for concluding the deal. They explained their plans to extend their interests in the Southern basin and how their overall unit costs could be reduced by involvement in Rough. There was a concern that the Gas Council was being accorded a special position. The response was that the Council had a statutory role as monopoly purchaser of gas, but apart from that was treated on a par with all other operators.

This saga was to continue for quite a few years before British Gas eventually obtained control of the Rough gas field in 1980. The manoeuvres in the first half of the 1970s indicated how political considerations were influencing the debate. Thus factors such as the prices which the prospective farming-in parties were prepared to pay, or their respective abilities efficiently to develop and operate the field, were given little consideration.

The Frigg field

While the Ekofisk negotiations continued interest developed in another major gas discovery and potential contract. The large Frigg field had been discovered in the Norwegian sector in 1971 and its extension into the UKCS was proven in May

1972. The fact that it straddled the boundary with the consequential need for unitisation ensured that the UK Government took a keen interest in the project. By April 1972 the operator on the UK side, Total, was informing the Department that reserves could be 10 tcf and production in the range 1,150 – 2,300 mmcf/d. The company was considering three disposal options, namely (1) pipeline to the UK, (2) liquefaction (perhaps on the Shetlands) and subsequent export to USA, and (3) pipeline to the continent. The Gas Council was very interested in acquiring Frigg gas, and in July 1972 informed the Department that it was prepared to take both the Norwegian and UK shares. By this time total reserves had been estimated at 9.5 tcf with 4 tcf being in the UKCS.

Enthusiasm of Gas Council for UK and Norwegian Frigg gas

A meeting was held between Department officials and senior executives of the Gas Council to discuss attitudes to the Frigg opportunity. The Council was in no doubt that the UK share of Frigg should come to the UK. The Council also indicated that it would be more than willing to take all that Frigg and Ekofisk could produce. If necessary it would use this gas, and pay to leave some of the reserves in the Southern basin in the ground in short-term contracts. Given the opportunity to sell gas for power generation the total quantity from Frigg and Ekofisk could be absorbed.

The Department recognised that the Council might have to negotiate two prices for Frigg gas, with that for the UK element being based on the Department's guidelines of a "reasonable price", whereas the Norwegian part would be based on an estimated world value. By this time (late July 1972) the Council felt that it was unlikely that Ekofisk gas could be obtained. Their understanding was that their offer price was well below the continental one. The Council was prepared to raise its offer price, but there were other problems. The escalation clause put forward by Phillips was based on the average cost of energy in the UK and related to 100% of the price. The Council also needed more flexibility in the disposal of the gas, including interruptible contracts with the CEGB. Without such flexibility the Council would have to sell the gas at much lower prices and thus could offer less for its purchase. The Council felt handicapped because of lack of knowledge of Government energy policy.

Leisurely approach of Norwegian authorities

Officials then obtained the approval of the Minister for Industry to inform the Council that it should continue negotiations for Frigg gas, including the Norwegian element if it wished. Progress was slower than the Council, the UK Government, and the French licensees desired. The leisurely approach of the Norwegian authorities reflected the lack of a home market for the gas and the notion that the value of the gas in the ground was probably a sound investment in current market circumstances. The Government and the French licensees were so concerned on this issue that they examined the possibility of developing the UK part of the field in the absence of an agreement with Norway. The Council was keen to procure an early agreement, even before the conclusion of the Ekofisk negotiations, progress on which had not been satisfactory.

Complications between Gas Council and CEGB on Ekofisk gas

The Council had become concerned about the uncertainties it faced in relation to the marketing of Ekofisk gas and thus in its negotiations with Phillips. An agreement had been reached with the CEGB whereby the Council would make available to it 50% of the gas from Ekofisk on a fully interruptible basis but without a take-or-pay obligation on the part of the Board. The Board had every intention of keeping to this agreement, but the Council was concerned about the uncertainties caused by the need for the CEGB to obtain Ministerial consent to convert power stations from coal to gas. If such consent were not forthcoming the Council would have to absorb all the Ekofisk gas elsewhere. As Ekofisk gas was associated with oil a very high load factor was inevitably involved. By comparison with the Frigg contract, although a relatively high load factor would be required for other reasons, the Council had greater flexibility and would not see CEGB involvement as essential. This was a difficult political issue for the Department, and eventually the Council was persuaded that an unambiguous statement from the CEGB that gas would be taken at the expense of oil would be satisfactory.

Unilateral development of UK Frigg?

Meanwhile the Council was anxious to progress negotiations on Frigg against a background of concern that the Norwegian authorities were adopting a leisurely approach. Total, the operator on the UK side, was keen to progress to the development of the field, and in November 1972, wrote to Elf, the operator on the Norwegian side, indicating that, while a unitised development was clearly optimal, if an agreement on this was not reached by spring, 1973, they would plan to develop the UK part unilaterally. This raised the question of the consistency of a unilateral development with the Treaty with Norway signed in 1965. The DTI solicitors felt that as (inconclusive) talks had already been held with the Norwegians the relevant Article of the Treaty had been satisfied and unilateral development of the UK side could proceed. The FCO legal advice was more cautious, confirming that unilateral action was possible, but only if serious negotiations with the Norwegians, involving officials of a high rank, had occurred with no ensuing agreement. The DTI concluded that this stage had not yet been reached.

DTI discussions with Norwegian Government

Accordingly, in early December 1972 the DTI wrote to the relevant Norwegian Ministry indicating a desire to reach an early agreement on unitisation, and stated that, if the operators on the two sides could not reach agreement among themselves quite soon, direct talks between the two Ministries should take place in the near future. At the meeting which took place on 14th December the DTI reiterated the wish of the Gas Council to purchase all Frigg gas. The response was that the Norwegians were studying all possible markets with a view to obtaining the highest possible price. This included the USA (LNG) as well as European markets. Nevertheless the Norwegian authorities hoped that speedy progress could be made. It was agreed that a definitive decision on the reserves would not be possible for some time, but that field development could proceed on the basis of provisional figures.

Ekofisk gas to go to Germany and lessons for UK

By this time the news had been received that the Gas Council had been unsuccessful in its bid to buy Ekofisk gas which was to be purchased by a European consortium with the gas being delivered at Emden. The DTI's information was that the price was at an equivalent in excess of 2.3 pence per therm with escalation in relation to European oil prices. The DTI was also informed that the Norwegians wanted the gas to be delivered to Germany because the licensees were anxious to bring the Ekofisk oil to the UK. The Minister for Industry was anxious to ensure that the lessons were learned for the Frigg negotiations. Thus the respective effects of the proposed UK and European escalation provisions should be examined. There was also a concern that Norwegian Frigg gas could be sent to Ekofisk and then to the continent employing a common pipeline which might produce a cost advantage for that route. The Department calculated the comparative effects of this possibility with those of landing it in the North East of Scotland. The conclusion was that there were likely to be extra costs of taking the gas to Germany of around £150 million at early 1973 prices. Thus extra booster stations would be required if the Ekofisk line were to be employed. A single large diameter line with booster station could take all the Frigg gas to the UK. It was also pointed out that booster stations involved significant operating and maintenance costs with a greater risk of breakdowns and interruptions to supply. This prospect could even lead to a decision to have a second line with less requirements for booster stations.

Currency aspects of Frigg contracts

The currency aspects of the Frigg contract negotiations involved BGC, DTI, and Treasury as well as the investors and the Norwegian authorities. The early 1970s had seen much turbulence in the currency markets with two major realignments, including the devaluation of the dollar, and the floating of the pound. Investors were naturally anxious to protect themselves, and this involved the choice of currency and the indexation provisions for the sales contracts. It was felt that neither the UK nor the Norwegian groups would be prepared to accept a starting price without some protection. The issue with respect to indexation had arisen with the ill-fated Ekofisk contract. In that case the Treasury had agreed that the purchase price could be expressed in US dollars, but this depended on (a) the seller not being a resident of the Sterling Area, and (b) the Gas Council not alone assuming any exchange risk (that is no one-sided protection). In the case of Frigg the Treasury view was that, for the Norwegian part, payment could be in sterling, Norwegian kroner, or French francs because they were the currencies of the licensees, but other currencies such as the mark were regarded as irrelevant and not favoured. For the British part of the field the currency should be sterling with no direct provision for devaluation, but, given the current unstable situation, the Treasury would be prepared to consider some proposal for currency protection. BGC understood that the currency for the UK part should be in sterling, but in the present case it had to be recognised that the parents of the UK licensees were French, and the same companies were the parents of the main investors in the Norwegian part. They would thus expect the price for both parts to be denominated in francs.

Protection to investors against increased taxes

The Frigg investors became increasingly concerned about the possibility of increased taxes being imposed on their operations and sought protection in their proposed contracts with BGC. Total requested that they should be safeguarded against rates of taxation which would cause them to make a loss. The company proposed that there should be a "bottom price" which was intended to represent their costs plus conventional tax and royalty to which any increased Government take would be added. The increased take would all be borne by the seller until the "bottom price" plus the increased take exceeded the contract price of the gas. Above that level BGC would bear the additional take. The protection would relate only to taxes on production and not to those based on profits. British Gas was given guarded approval to agree to some form of tax reimbursement clause, though this term was generally frowned upon. By June 1973 agreement was close for the British part of the field at a base price of 2.27p per therm with 75% escalation linked to oil, gas, and electricity price indices. The tax reimbursement clause stipulated that, if the agreed "bottom price" (1.5p per therm) as increased by 0.04p per year, plus the net increase in Government take, exceeded the base price adjusted by the price review, then the contract price would be mid-way between these two prices. Thus BGC would accept 50% of the increase or in effect reimburse the sellers for half of the increase in Government take as defined.

The Government accepted this provision on the grounds that it was felt necessary by British Gas in order to reach an agreement. In fact there were tax reimbursement clauses for Southern Basin contracts which applied to 100% of any extra tax or royalty on gas production. The DTI also felt that tax reimbursement was unlikely to occur, estimating that the Government could impose a tax of over 30% of the beach price before British Gas became liable to make any reimbursement. The field investors had also sought assurances that the British Government would not seek to participate in the ownership of the pipeline from the field to the

UK. The response was that there was no present intention of the Government to do this, but future Governments could not be restricted.

Negotiations for Frigg (Norway)

Separate negotiations proceeded for the Norwegian share of the field which by mid-1973 was estimated to contain around 60% of the total reserves. In this case BGC was not a monopsony buyer and competition from the continent was experienced. By July 1973 the financial terms proposed by the sellers included a base price of 2.55 pence (1971) with 100% escalation against three indices of oil and other fuel prices. A mix of currencies was involved with sterling given a 40% weighting (compared to 60% in the contract for the UK part). The proposed tax reimbursement clause was tougher, involving a bottom price of 2.4p plus 0.048p per year and the increase in Government take. If this price exceeded the escalated base price BGC would bear the whole difference. This meant that it would effectively bear the cost of all the increase in Government take.

BGC fears terms may be uncommercial

In these circumstances DTI officials felt it necessary to warn Mr Boardman, the Minister for Industry, that BGC was being asked to accept terms which were commercially doubtful, on the assumption that there would be no constraints on gas prices to consumers apart from competition with other fuels. If the British Government were to constrain gas prices over the longer term the contract could be regarded as very dubious indeed. This was the view of BGC, who were unsure not only of their bargaining position but also of the Government's view, as there was now an apparent conflict between the desire to see the gas secured to the UK and the constraint on prices to consumers. The Corporation thus wished to consult the Minister on their stance. The Minister's response was to request a fuller assessment by officials, and to ensure that BGC consulted him if they were contemplating turning down the whole contract.

The Corporation indicated that they saw no prospect of improving on the escalation terms or the currency formula, but hoped to achieve some reduction in the base price. The view of both BGC and DTI officials was that the Norwegian Frigg proposals viewed solely as a commercial proposition was only just tolerable. The DTI conclusion was based on assumptions relating to future oil prices which turned out to be very low, namely 86.4% increase in real terms between 1973 and 1980, but which were regarded as plausible by many observers at the time.

BGC's views on implications of loss of Frigg contract

BGC understood that if Norwegian Frigg gas were not secure there were other potential supplies from the UKCS, but were convinced that they would not make up anything like the Frigg volumes. Further, if new supplies were to come from UK sources further measures would be needed to control the producers to ensure that the price did not rise to Norwegian Frigg levels. There were further serious implications of the sale of this gas to Germany. A pipeline from Frigg to Ekofisk and then to the continent would constitute an invaluable main line to which supplies from future Norwegian discoveries could readily be linked. This could lead to Britain being cut off from future Norwegian supplies.

Government to acknowledge security of supply benefits

BGC felt that there were two further reasons why they could not treat the negotiations on a purely commercial basis. The weakness of sterling made them unhappy about having a currency clause on top of a price escalation clause. The two taken together could result in a (sterling) price increase over the years in excess of the increase in the sterling price of oil. BGC felt that the Government should bear the additional cost of the operation of the currency clause. BGC also argued that for some time it had not been allowed to fix the prices to customers at a commercial level and feared that this situation might persist.[2] Accepting large volumes of high-priced Norwegian gas would thus expose them to a greater risk of making substantial losses in future years, and it might even be preferable not to take this gas and revert to a less significant role in the UK energy market. The Corporation felt that it should have a Government direction to buy the Norwegian gas or be assured that it would have Government support for rejecting the offer of the sellers. After discussion with officials BGC agreed instead to accept explicit Government encouragement to take account of the national interest in security of supply by being ready to go to the limit of what was commercial and possibly a little beyond that.

Mr Boardman met with the Chairman of BGC and discussed these issues. He then reported to the Prime Minister that the sellers of Norwegian Frigg were trying to obtain severe terms for the gas, such that the offer was only marginally worth accepting. For security of supply reasons he felt it important that the gas should be acquired. The volumes from the Norwegian part of Frigg were very large, contributing a significant element of the total energy requirements of the UK by 1980. He informed the Prime Minister of the concerns of BGC and their desire for Government assurances that, if the gas were bought, they would be free to charge customers prices reflecting these costs, and further that the Government should guarantee BGC against losses emanating from the operation of the currency clause. The Minister had felt unable to give such assurances, but had advised BGC that, in making their calculations, they should assume that they would be able to make commercially realistic charges to customers, and that there would be no adverse effects resulting from the operation of the currency clause. In short BGC had been advised that they should not lose the gas on either of the two grounds, and should go to the limit of what they could justify, taking into account the security of supply benefits. There was one further item of concern relating to the tax reimbursement clause which would apply not only to extra UK taxes levied on the gas but to those of the Norwegian Government. This was unacceptable on an open-ended basis, and BGC had earlier been urged to avoid such clauses unless the whole contract was put in jeopardy. In the present situation

BGC had been urged to seek improvements on this item and report back before negotiations were concluded or broke down.

The Treasury's view on the requests of BGC was also sought. The Chief Secretary indicated that the Corporation should certainly not assume that the current restraints on their pricing would continue indefinitely, and that they would be free to set commercially realistic prices. While the current constraints continued compensating financial arrangements were part of Government policy. There were, however, major policy objections to the provision of exchange cover to deal with the currency clause. The Government could not be put in the position of giving compensation for exchange rate losses. The issue had arisen in many other circumstances where hardship was pleaded and the Government had to take a consistent firm stand on the matter. The Chief Secretary felt that any specific compensation to BGC should be related not to the exchange rate issue but to the national interest which necessitated the signing of the contract on grounds of security of supply. The Minister for Industry should propose and defend a measure of this type.

The escalation formula

On 19th July the Chairman of BGC informed the Minister for Industry that agreement with the Frigg licenses was imminent. He emphasised that BGC would be in deep trouble if the pound depreciated to a significant extent, and was still hoping that the Treasury would give some assistance in this matter. Officials were conducting urgent work on the effects of the proposed terms. The sums involved were very large as the current estimates of the recoverable reserves for the field were 7.2 tcf of which 60% – 65% could be in the Norwegian sector. The expected plateau contract quantity was 1,450 mmcf/d. The general approach to the evaluation of the terms was to consider that the purchase of Norwegian Frigg was in the national interest if it cost less in resource terms than the alternatives of fuel oil, SNG and LNG. Over the contract period the price paid depended on the base price and the escalation and currency clauses. Because of its profound effects and later importance it is useful to set out the complex escalation formula as follows:

$$P = P_0\left(0.40\left[\frac{R_1 + T + S}{R_0 + T + S}\right] + 0.30\frac{E}{E_0} + 0.30\frac{F}{F_0}\right)$$

P = gas price
R = index of low sulphur fuel oil (Rotterdam) published in Platt's oilgram and converted at average exchange rate during month preceding price review from dollars to sterling (R_0 = £7.13 per tonne)
T = cost of transport (£1.22 per tonne)
S = fuel oil tax (£2.3 per tonne)
E = General Index of Retail Prices – fuel and light, as published in CSO Monthly Digest of Statistics. (E_0 = 160.9)
F = DTI Digest of Energy Statistics, fuels used by industry – fuel oil. (F_0 = £13.975 per tonne.)

DTI officials calculated that, given the base values for R, T, and S an x% increase in general oil prices would be reflected by 0.272x% increase in P. With respect to the RPI the weightings for the various fuels would result in an x% increase in oil prices being reflected in an increase in P of 0.46x%. The UK fuel oil index included cost of delivery and the fuel oil tax. The effect on P via this term was estimated at 0.24x%. The combined effect of all the terms in response to a general increase in oil prices of x% was thus 0.556x% (56% escalation with oil prices). Thus the greater the oil price increase the bigger the potential benefit from the contract. The currency clause involved the gas price being denominated to the extent of 40% in sterling and 60% to 5 (strong) European currencies and the US dollar. Parity changes would also be reflected in the operation of the escalation formula. The DTI estimated that sterling depreciation of 10% could lead to a 12% increase in the contract price.

Implications of contract terms in UK

In the early years of the contract BGC would be supplying its premium markets from sources already contracted from the UKCS. Thus the Frigg gas would be sold in the non-premium market where it would make a loss. Later, the gas would displace SNG/LNG in supplying premium markets which produced net benefits from the contract. The size of the discounted return to the project in terms of net present value (NPV) at 10%, on the DTI central view of oil prices (increasing by 95% in real terms between 1973 and 1980), but assuming no change in the parity of sterling, would be £50 million at a base price of 2.55p, and £80 million at a base price of 2.45p. If sterling depreciated against the basket of currencies in the contract at 2% per year the total payments for the gas would be increased by £225 million. However, without Norwegian Frigg gas the same depreciation of sterling would involve additional substantial sterling costs on BGC in producing SNG or buying LNG to supply its premium markets, estimated at around £90 million in discounted terms. There would also be additional sterling costs to the nation from the burning of oil by customers who would have used Frigg gas of around £73 million in discounted terms. From the above, the additional cost to BGC of buying Norwegian Frigg would be £135 million (£225 million minus £90 million) which would produce a negative NPV for the project. But, because of the higher price of fuel oil resulting from the depreciation of sterling, BGC would be able to increase its prices to non-premium users, producing additional revenues of around £70 million. Thus the full additional cost from sterling depreciation would be around £65 million and, seen in this light, the contract as a whole would show a positive NPV if the base price were below 2.5p per therm.

The DTI evaluation thus confirmed that the project was very marginal even when the indirect consequences were considered. There was acknowledgement that the net benefits would increase if oil prices increased above their central estimate (which they did for the period to the early 1980s). There was no discussion of the possible effects of removal or reduction of the fuel oil duty which later became a major issue (See Chapter 11). There was also little discussion of the notion that the UK might not need this gas at all for the foreseeable future because more could be discovered and developed from the UKCS. As noted above, alternatives examined were that BGC would manufacture SNG or import LNG and more fuel oil would be used. The volumes from Norwegian Frigg formed a very large part of total UK gas supplies in the 1980s, accounting for around 25% in the first half of the decade.

BGC pursues concerns over currency risk

It was clear that emphasis on security of supply dominated the thinking both of BGC and the Government. Very late in negotiations the Corporation was able to procure a base price of 2.47p (compared to the earlier proposal of 2.55p), and to limit the reimbursement of further taxes imposed by Norway or the UK to a maximum of 50% rather than 100%. A special right of termination by BGC was also agreed in the event that Government taxation became too onerous. The Corporation pursued its concern over currency risks, asking the Government for protection. The DTI, in consulting the Treasury on the matter, indicated the long length and onerous escalation terms of the contract, and gave their findings that, if in the next fifteen years sterling did no more against other currencies than it had done over the preceding twenty years, the BGC could break even. But if sterling performed as it had done since 1968 the price of the gas would be above that of the relevant oil products through the life of the contract. On this basis, and having told BGC to make the assumption that there would be no worsening in the parity of sterling, there was a case for at least some compensation for adverse currency movements.

Further debate within Government on currency risk compensation to BGC

The DTI felt that the Government could reasonably offer one of two schemes. The first would undertake to compensate BGC only to the extent that the currency clause together with the price escalation clause took the cost price of the gas under the contract above the corresponding oil cost. Further, the Government should be paid a bonus if the clause led to a contract cost more than a specified percentage below UK fuel oil prices. The alternative scheme would offer compensation as in the first one (without provision for a bonus payment) in return for a fixed annual premium payable by BGC. A problem was the need to inform Parliament. This could cause problems if the arrangement became known to other suppliers of North Sea gas (who could exploit it to squeeze BGC in negotiations), or to the EEC, who might regard it as a subsidy and make representations about North Sea policies more widely. Fresh powers or those requiring Parliamentary approval should be avoided.

This was the DTI view sent to the Treasury, but it did not reflect a unanimous position within the Department. Another view was that, if the BGC had paid a premium to enhance security of supply, then it should be gas consumers not taxpayers who should pay for any insurance premium and bear the consequential risk of overinsurance. Energy policy did not lay down market shares for the different fuels but left the market to determine the balance. Removing one of the gas industry's risks from the consumer to the taxpayer lessened the incentive to consumers to switch to other fuels if the current policy put too high a price on gas. BGC should only be relieved of the responsibility of accepting the risks if the Government had decided to overrule the Corporation's judgement. This was hardly the case in the present situation.

Discussions between the DTI and Treasury on the matter continued for some time. Eventually in November 1973 agreement was reached. Mr Boardman was informed of this, and updated on the latest calculations on the effects of the contract. The contract was still only marginally commercial. At late 1973 gas from the Southern North Sea was costing 1.03p per therm while UK Frigg would be costing 2.76p and Norwegian Frigg 3.14p. This was more than the cost of fuel oil including duty.

With respect to the request from BGC for currency protection there was no existing legislation covering the specific assurance which the Corporation requested or which could be given without publicity (which was unwanted by both parties). Accordingly, a statement had been proposed to send to BGC which refrained from making direct commitments on compensation. It confirmed the right of the Corporation to make commercially realistic charges to their customers over the life of the contract. This would be interpreted to include reactions to adverse currency movements or the operation of the escalation clause.

Contracts agreed but late complication from France

The contract for UK Frigg was signed on 13th December 1973. While the Norwegian Frigg terms had been agreed they required ratification by the Storting. It had to be satisfied that all feasible options had been thoroughly examined, including in particular the landing of the gas in Norway. During this time a somewhat surprising twist occurred to the Frigg saga. Earlier in August 1973, the French Minister for Industry wrote to his UK counterpart indicating that France (through Gaz de France) was interested in acquiring Frigg gas. The company had not competed with BGC for the gas, but was interested in buying some of it from the Corporation, which in turn had indicated that the matter should be referred to the Government.

DTI officials discovered that Gaz de France apparently had in mind 50% of the supplies from the field. If this were the case the idea appeared to be unsatisfactory as it would take a large part of what had been welcomed as a major contribution to the long-term energy security of the UK. On the other hand a short-term contract for a few years could relieve BGC of a problem in the early years when it would be selling the gas to non-premium users, perhaps at a loss. This sort of scheme was, however, unlikely to be what the French had in mind. A further consideration was that once a cross-Channel pipeline were built it could readily be used to export other gas from the UKCS which could have an adverse effect on security of supply. Mr Boardman was advised that there were three possible responses. The first was to politely reject the idea on the grounds that all the gas was required to meet demand growth in the UK. The second was to temporise and endeavour to ensure that negotiations between BGC and Gaz de France did not succeed. The third option was to open the way for valley gas to be supplied to Gaz de France.

The views of the FCO were that the request was rather odd, but that it was primarily a matter for BGC and Gaz de France. A possible consequence of a refusal to supply might result in a complaint by the French to the European Commission. But good legal arguments on the landing requirement were available. The FCO's conclusion was that the Government should not oppose a deal in principle but that it was primarily a commercial matter for BGC. The Chairman of BGC informed the Minister that the Corporation could market all of the gas in the UK, and had no desire to negotiate a sale to France.

Mr Boardman thus considered sending a polite but negative reply to the French request, but Mr Heath felt that such a response should not be given so soon after his meeting with the French President at which the subject had been discussed. He asked for further proposals on the subject, and Mr Boardman reiterated the arguments noted above, but included the idea of an energy exchange. The French were, however, unlikely to be in a position to offer to the UK an assured energy supply in return for what the UK could provide. The matter dragged on for some time and eventually in February, 1974 the British Ambassador to France was asked to explain verbally the British Government's position to the Elysée. This emphasised the expectation that all the Frigg gas would be required for UK consumption. On other matters relating to oil, gas, and energy more widely the UK was very happy to cooperate with France.

Enormous repercussions of Frigg contracts

The Frigg contracts had enormous repercussions. The very large volumes contributed markedly to security of supply for many years. Those from Norwegian Frigg alone were to account for around 25% of the UK's gas needs in the first half of the 1980s. Within the then established conceptual framework the price for Norwegian Frigg was quite high, due principally to the operation of the escalation clause. Thus in 1978/79 while the average price paid by BGC for *all* of its gas was 4.47p per therm, for Norwegian Frigg it was 12p per therm. Of course, the resource cost to the nation of imported gas is the price paid. For indigenous gas the resource cost is less than the price paid, since royalties and tax paid to the UK Government constitute an internal transfer payment. The escalation formula was also to emerge as a major but quite unanticipated issue in the early 1980s when there was great pressure on the Government to reduce the fuel oil duty to alleviate the problems of the manufacturing sector which was suffering from the high value of the pound as well as high oil prices. The Government's embarrassment in being unable to provide adequate relief stemmed from the very large compensatory payments which would become due to the Norwegian Frigg sellers under the escalation formula outlined above where the fuel oil duty played a prominent role. This problem was certainly not foreseen by the DTI or the Treasury in 1973.

The large volumes contracted from Frigg by BGC had repercussions on North Sea activity relating to gas exploration and development. Given secure supplies the Corporation was under little pressure to provide price incentives to producers in the Southern North Sea or indeed to conclude further agreements. The Viking agreement was concluded in 1972 with a base price of 1.5p and limited escalation provisions, but after that exploration and interest in the Southern basin fell dramatically to near zero in the second half of the 1970s. There were little or no incentives for producers whose attention was in any case diverted to the exciting oil opportunities in Central and Northern waters. When substantial price incentives were introduced from 1980 onwards the response in terms of exploration and subsequently production was dramatic. With the benefit of hindsight it is arguable that from the nation's viewpoint the Frigg contract, in particular the Norwegian element, was sub-optimal. Adequate supplies could have been forthcoming from the British sector if incentives in the form of market-related prices had been offered. In 1973, when security of supply was a major issue as a consequence of the international oil crisis and industrial problems in the coal industry, the emphasis within Government on security of supply was such that an insurance premium was felt to be justified. In the widest sense this premium turned out to be quite expensive. On the other hand the continued presence of the two substantial pipelines from the Frigg field to St Fergus after the field depleted, has turned out to be very beneficial to the UK given the later need to import large quantities of gas from other Norwegian fields. The Vesterled pipeline in particular may be regarded as a valuable legacy of the decision to purchase Norwegian Frigg gas.

The Gas Act, 1972

The Conservative Administration also saw the passing of the Gas Act, 1972. Work on this had started under the Labour Administration and a Bill was introduced in Parliament but was lost at the General Election. There were three main ideas behind the Bill, namely (1) to make the Gas Council clearly responsible for the central direction of the industry, (2) to give the Council specific powers through subsidiaries to search for, exploit, refine, and sell oil, and (3) to promote safety in the use of gas. In the summer of 1969 the view in the Ministry was that the oil powers of the Council should be restricted to operations in the UKCS, although it was recognised that the Gas Act 1965, perhaps inadvertently, did give it the right to acquire gas from Great Britain or anywhere else. The Ministry was also anxious to ensure that any subsidiaries did not have wider powers than the Council itself. It was recognised that there could be no strong objection to the involvement of the Council in the Dutch or Norwegian parts of the North Sea, but, as it was difficult to draft a provision in politically acceptable terms differentiating among foreign territories, and given the perceived need to restrict the range of the Council's operations, a blanket ban on overseas petroleum activities was felt appropriate. In the draft Bill the word "petroleum" was deliberately employed to *include* natural gas and thus not to highlight the diminution in the Council's powers!

Debate on BGC's overseas operations

Many discussions followed on the issue. There were external pressures on the Government. Dr Colin Phipps, a leading member of the Labour Party's North Sea Study Group, published an article in the *New Statesman* in August 1969 welcoming the announcement by the Minister of Power of the formation of a subsidiary of the Gas Council to engage in exploration for both oil and gas. He then expressed the view that there were national advantages in letting the company operate internationally, on the grounds that the industry was inherently international in character, and noted that ENI and Elf were becoming much more influential after expanding their international operations. This view did not find favour within the Ministry. Concerns were expressed that there might be negative effects on the willingness of foreign companies to invest in the UKCS. It might also be seen as an indication of a lack of confidence by the Government in BP's ability to further the UK's oil interests overseas. But fundamentally the Ministry was not at all convinced that the Council and its subsidiaries would be in a position to explore overseas for many years. However, an odd position was reached when the draft clauses of the Bill indicated that subsidiaries of the Council would be unable to pursue petroleum activities outside Britain and the UKCS while the powers of the Council itself to get natural gas still referred to the UK and elsewhere. Such powers were really to enable the Council to acquire imports of gas such as LNG from Algeria, and it was perhaps inconsistent that the Council could also engage in gas exploitation beyond the UKCS. It was felt that this possibility was very remote as all the Council's exploration and production activities operated via subsidiaries. Under the proposed legislation for activities outside the UKCS this would not be possible and the Council would have to undertake the activity itself or use contractors. These were unwelcome complications.

Gas Council unhappy at restrictions on overseas operations

The Gas Council was quite unhappy with all the proposals relating to overseas activities, and Sir Henry Jones forcibly informed the Permanent Secretary, indicating that, while he understood that a Minister could put pressure on the Council to limit its activities to a specified zone, to put such restrictions into primary legislation would be exceedingly unwise. The Ministry remained determined to limit the overseas activities of the Council, particularly with respect to oil, while the Council highlighted situations where it was desirable that its activities be allowed to extend further, such as when discoveries extended beyond the boundary line of the UKCS with that of Norway.

Views of BP and Shell widen the debate

The Bill fell as a result of the General Election in 1970. The Conservative Government examined the issues afresh and asked BP and Shell for their views. BP expressed the hope that the earlier proposal to turn the Gas Council into an oil company would be dropped. BP also requested that gas producers be permitted to sell gas for fuel purposes direct to customers. The company also thought that the Council should be obliged to act as a common carrier for third party gas for a commercial fee. BP also requested that gas producers should have the right to export gas as well as the Council under the earlier proposals. It was also thought inappropriate that the Council should be able to use taxpayers' funds to engage in the risky business of overseas exploration. Shell presented detailed proposals which would enable gas producers to purchase stakes in the gas transmission system (NTS), and be enabled to compete in the bulk gas market. The Council and Area Boards would compete with the oil companies. DTI officials felt that Shell's proposals probably reflected concern that the low price of valley gas and the large volumes which the Council could take, was enabling the Area Boards to compete strongly with petroleum products in the bulk industrial market. Officials felt that the Council's behaviour in this respect was commercially and ethically justifiable.

Competition in bulk gas market not favoured by Department

The proposals to introduce producing companies into the NTS and allow them to compete in the bulk gas market were examined but rejected. The Minister emphasised that this would involve a major reversal of the policy laid down by the Conservative Government in the Continental Shelf Act, 1964. It would also cause a damaging dislocation to the development of North Sea gas which had already involved major contracts with producers and a very large public investment. Finally, it was felt that the transmission and sale of gas in bulk markets did not offer the most promising areas for obtaining the benefits of greater competition. The pipeline company would have to be subject to close regulation as had happened in the USA.

The Minister proposed that the Gas Council should be entrusted with the duty of securing the efficient and coordinated development of the whole industry, with overall financial responsibility for the industry, and powers to coordinate its investment programmes, and marketing policies. The Area Boards would be given freedom to price natural gas competitively with other fuels. With respect to exploration and production it was proposed to give powers relating to gas only, with such powers being restricted to Great Britain and the UKCS.

Gas Council argues for overseas gas activities

The Chairman of the Gas Council wrote to the Minister of State arguing that there were advantages in having no geographical restrictions in the Council's powers to search for and produce gas. Natural gas from the UKCS was a wasting asset, and overseas operations of the Council, perhaps in partnership with oil companies, could help to ensure continuity of supply. The Minister would in any case have the power to approve investment programmes and prohibition by statute of activities outside the UKCS was quite unnecessarily restrictive.

Sir Henry Jones reiterated his arguments at a meeting with the Minister. The latter emphasised his view that the ability of the Council to be able to continue buying gas from the UKCS on a monopsony basis should enable competitive supplies to be acquired. The Minister also asked the Council to consider putting all its exploration and production activities into a single subsidiary in which in due course there could be private investors. At a further meeting in October 1970 Sir Henry further reiterated arguments in favour of the Council being allowed to produce and procure gas from beyond the UKCS, citing the possibilities of fields straddling the boundaries between the UKCS and neighbouring North Sea countries, but also indicating more distant possible sources such as Trinidad and Nigeria. The Minister indicated that, for activities beyond the UKCS, his consent would be required, and any Gas Council exploration and production should be conducted through "Companies Act" companies with private sector participation, preferably publicly quoted ones. Officials had consistently been opposed to a Ministerial consent provision on the grounds that Ministers should not bear the risks of making such a decision because they would not have all the necessary technical and economic information on which to make a sound decision. Eventually the Minister decided that he would support the continuation of the Council's ability to obtain gas from operations outwith the UKCS, but that this should be subject to Ministerial consent. Where this was given it would only be where the operations were being carried out by a separate "Companies Act" company with private sector participation. It was decided that this condition would not be incorporated in the Bill itself, but would be a condition of Ministerial consent.

Gas Bill enacted

The Gas Bill was not introduced until January 1972 and received Royal Assent in August. It dealt with many other matters not directly related to the UKCS. The more centralised structure of the industry was a main feature reflected in the name of the new statutory body, the British Gas Corporation (BGC). In effect its activities were restricted to Great Britain and the UKCS. No major changes directly affecting North Sea matters were introduced. Consent was no longer required for the supply of gas by a producer to parties other than BGC for non-fuel purposes. If, in the course of looking for gas in the UKCS, BGC found oil it could produce and sell it but not engage in refining.

The Conservative Government came to an end in February 1974 with only modest changes to the policy stance of the previous Labour Administration. Officials were clearly unenthusiastic about making more radical changes to the structure of the gas industry and the role of BGC, and Ministers did not strongly press the advantages of more competition. The Gas Council/BGC continued to have a substantial influence on policy making. This was also the case with the Frigg contract where the prime importance of security of supply over other relevant considerations was very apparent. The international oil crisis and the problems in the coal industry ensured that this issue was uppermost in the minds of Ministers and officials alike. The idea that the large imports from Norway could substantially retard the development of gas from the UKCS was given little or no consideration.

7 Designing the tax package

Early interest of Government in taxation of oil companies

Close interest within Government in the particular taxation issues relating to the petroleum industry started in the later part of the 1960s. This did not directly concern North Sea oil and gas but the issues raised had a major influence on the structure of the tax package eventually introduced. The Inland Revenue had become concerned that the oil industry in the UK was paying little or no (UK) corporation tax despite its large-scale activities here. A detailed investigation of the causes was conducted, and eventually a substantial report was prepared and submitted to the Chancellor in February 1970. The reasons for the lack of tax payments in the UK were the effects of the tax and posted price systems in operation in the main oil producing countries overseas and the resulting transactions between the affiliates of the major oil companies. In these countries the profits for taxation purposes were determined by the employment of a posted price which by early 1970 was estimated to be about 25% above the free-market price. The posted price was used for transferring the crude oil to the UK affiliates, and the result was little or no profit and frequently losses incurred by the downstream companies involved in refining, distribution and petrochemicals. The research by the Inland Revenue indicated that the loss of UK corporation tax from the operation of this mechanism was around £65 million per year.

Prospective effects of current arrangements

There was also evidence from the Inland Revenue's research that the companies were not fully exploiting the opportunities provided by their tax position because they were not utilising all their losses generated by the transfer pricing arrangements. Under group relief provisions the losses of one company could be set against the profits of another member of the same group. The Inland Revenue estimated that the tax losses could double or even treble if no action was taken. There was a concern that the ability of oil companies to invest in projects without paying effective tax would give them an advantage over other non-oil companies. Further, the then current policy of encouraging inward investment partly rested on the premise that the national economy would gain from enhanced corporation tax payments. As matters stood this would not apply to inward investments by foreign oil companies.

The Inland Revenue had found evidence that, while intra-group transfers were being made at the posted prices, sales to third parties were made at lower prices reflecting the market value of the oil. Intra-group transfers did not have to be made on the basis of posted prices, but it paid the companies to do this. Larger profits would be made in the producing countries, but no further UK tax was payable either because of downstream losses or because the liability would be covered by double taxation relief. Interestingly the (substantial) document did not mention the potential effect on tax revenues from the North Sea. These could be reduced or wiped out by the losses incurred by affiliate companies. North Sea gas production had commenced in 1967 and some corporation tax from the UKCS was actually paid in the tax year 1970–71.

Artificial posted price root of problem

The Inland Revenue felt that the problem was urgent and should be tackled at its root which was the artificial price at which oil was transferred. It was proposed to strengthen by legislation the Revenue's powers to substitute for tax purposes arm's length prices for artificial ones in trading between associated companies. It was recognised that such an initiative had to be seen in the context of wider Government policy towards oil and gas. Because of the large accrued losses it would be several years before at least some of the major companies would be paying tax. The Inland Revenue felt that 75% of the tax would be passed on to consumers in higher prices for petroleum products with the companies bearing the remainder. Other effects on the balance of payments were examined namely, (1) the current account effects of existing operations, (2) the capital and current account effects of changes in future refinery construction, and (3) the current and capital effects of changes in the terms on which oil companies expanded (other) UK activities. Following detailed studies the Revenue concluded that under the first heading there could be a current account gain of around £10 million per year, mainly through reduced remittances by the companies. Under the second heading it was estimated that, with the reduced incentives to expand refineries in the UK (rather than elsewhere in Europe), there would be a capital account loss of around £5 million per year with a growing current account loss of around £8.5 million from four or five years ahead. Under the third heading there would be a capital account loss from reduced outflow of dividends and interest. The Revenue estimated that there would be a net gain in due course, rising to £40 million in the late 1970s. It is again noteworthy that the effects on North Sea investment were not specifically examined in this exercise.

Prolonged discussions with companies

The overall findings were supportive of the proposed tax change, but officials felt that, before final decisions were taken, there should be consultations with the oil companies to see if a voluntary agreement could be reached, which would mean that legislation would be unnecessary. The proposals were viewed with some dismay in the Ministry of Technology. There was concern on several counts. The context of the review was felt to be too narrow, the result of the proposals would be a net addition to the total tax take on the oil companies, rather than a reduction in the take from the overseas producing countries, the net benefit to the balance of payments was quite small, there was a reduction in the incentive to invest in UK refining and petrochemicals, and the proposal would hit British oil companies harder because they had a higher share of their activities in the UK compared to foreign ones. If there was a need for more revenues from the oil sector indirect taxation on petroleum products could be raised! There was, however, no discussion of the implications for North Sea activities in the deliberations of the Ministry at this time (March 1970).

The Chancellor decided that discussions should take place between officials and the companies on the issue and ruled out early legislation. The Conservative Government endorsed the idea of detailed discussions which were prolonged and became bedevilled by the proposed change in corporation tax from the classical system to the imputation system (which occurred in 1973). This would disadvantage companies which received the greater part of their income from abroad (such as the UK oil companies) compared to those whose income was primarily domestic. By 1972 little progress had been made, but the idea that North Sea oil production could well be very profitable had become widely appreciated, and this was included in the deliberations within Government. There was a great concern over another matter, namely that the oil companies would use their accumulated tax losses to advantage by taking over non-oil businesses, competing unfairly with non-oil companies. The Inland Revenue thus made a proposal in February 1972 which in effect would draw a ring fence round all the companies' oil activities on a "no profit, no loss basis" (thus preventing further artificial losses), while their non-oil operations, including petrochemicals, would be put on a "normal" footing for tax purposes. It was hoped that all this could be achieved without new legislation.

Recognition of possible high profitability of North Sea oil

There was now growing recognition of the potential high profitability of North Sea oil and the need to ensure that the UK received a reasonable take from the activity. The DTI argued that the take could be increased without adverse consequences. The respective values of a ring fence around North Sea activities or a special tax on the producers were debated. In May 1972 the Inland Revenue stated that the question of the take from the North Sea introduced an entirely new factor, and that the DTI proposals for corporation tax would require two ring fences, namely (1) between oil and non-oil activities, and (2) between North Sea and other activities. The Revenue felt that there was no defensible tax reason to draw a ring fence round North Sea activities. The only fiscal reason for taking any action was because the present tax losses were artificial. If they were real (which they could be at some future date) there would be no reason to refuse loss reliefs. This would be clearly discriminatory against the oil industry, and corporation tax was supposed to be non-discriminatory. The appropriate course of action was to attack the problem at its root, namely the artificial transfer prices. The aim should be to tax the oil companies on their genuine profits and losses, not to sterilise genuine losses as well as artificial ones. Genuine losses should be relievable against any other profits, whether from the North Sea or non-oil activities. This procedure would, of course, only "normalise" the situation with respect to the oil companies, and would not by itself markedly increase the take from the North Sea.

The debate on the issue of appropriate take gathered pace in the second half of 1972. The Treasury became more deeply involved in examination of the appropriate level of take, and the possible ways of achieving this. Its position at July 1972 was that the combination of existing royalty plus corporation tax (with the artificial losses stopped) was inadequate. At this time the Treasury felt that the mode by which the national benefits of gas exploitation accrued (through the monopsony buying of BGC) was not in question. The Treasury also supported the Inland Revenue's opposition to the suggestion that a ring fence for corporation tax should be put round North Sea activities. To increase the overall level of take the royalty could be increased or a specific commodity tax could be introduced. A variable royalty or production tax was a possibility.

Inter-departmental Working Party

At the end of August 1972 a Working Party of officials from the Treasury, Inland Revenue, CPRS and DTI was established to review North Sea Licensing Policy. In practice much attention was paid to taxation issues. It produced a report in November of that year. There was a strong case for increasing the level of take from the UKCS based on estimates of projected profitability. To do this efficiently a new tax was required. Auctions of future licences could not achieve the objective because it was estimated by the DTI that 80% of the most promising acreage had already been licensed. The idea of state participation with carried interest had also been examined, but there was a major disadvantage in the costs to the Exchequer of paying for the state's share of development costs. These could amount to £100 million per year. In addition there was the difficulty of avoiding involvement in management decisions.

Excess Revenue Tax?

A commodity (or production) tax would be administratively simple and could produce early revenues. It would, however, be virtually indistinguishable from an increase in royalties and thus open to the criticism of a breach of licence terms. Another possibility was a new tax provisionally termed an Excess Revenue Tax by the Inland Revenue. The concept was that for each field a running account would be kept to which all expenditures (capital as well as operating) would be debited, and all receipts would be credited. When cumulative receipts exceeded cumulative revenues by a specified margin the investor would become liable to a special tax on the amounts by which subsequent annual receipts exceeded expenses. In effect no tax would be paid until the investor had recovered his outlay plus a reasonable return.

With respect to the detailed features of the tax expenditures on the cost of the acquisition of rights and in constructing and operating terminals and pipelines would be eligible, but preliminary costs such as the formation of a new company to exploit the rights would not be deductible. Where expenditures were attributable partly to the North Sea but partly elsewhere rules to define the allowable element would be designed. Two items which might otherwise be deductible, namely loan interest and corporation tax, should be disallowed. The Inland Revenue felt that the inclusion of interest would be an invitation to finance exploration companies by loan capital and to manipulate the rates payable, especially between associated companies. The inclusion of corporation tax would involve the difficult task of negotiating the tax appropriate to North Sea profits, and in principle it would be preferable to keep the ordinary corporation tax on total profits entirely separate from a special one on a limited geographic activity. Thus the corporation tax would not be deductible in arriving at the base for the Excess Revenue Tax nor would the latter be deducted in calculating the tax base for the former. The exclusion of loan interest would be taken into account in fixing the size of the exempt margin, and the exclusion of corporation tax in determining the tax rate. The tax could be levied on a field basis or on the entire operations of the investor in the North Sea. Clearly the oil companies would prefer the latter, but the result would be the postponement of tax payments for a long time. Levying the tax on a field base would lead to the objection that abortive exploration was not deductible, but it would be possible to permit such deductions on a cross-field basis.

With respect to the size of the margin the relevant considerations were the investment to production lead time and the non-deductibility of interest. If the investor had to pay interest for around four years the margin might be 40%. But it was arguable that the investment risk element should also be considered, in particular the dry holes likely to be drilled. Using a success ratio of 1 in 20 the abortive expenditures might be 6% of the total investment costs of a very large field and 12% of a smaller one. Taking weighting into account a margin of 50% might be appropriate.

With respect to the rate, only illustrative figures could be given at this stage, but a rate in excess of 30% might be regarded by the industry as penal when combined with royalty at 12.5% and corporation tax at 50%. A rate of 25% should thus be considered. With this package producers could expect returns of around 36% on large fields and 25% on small ones, with the Government take being in the 63% – 65% range over the lifetime of the fields. The idea of a sliding scale related progressively to profits should also be considered. This could more readily ensure that marginal production would not be discouraged and high rates levied on very profitable fields.

Senior officials examine options

The report of the Working Party was considered at a meeting among senior officials of the Treasury, DTI, Inland Revenue, and CPRS. The meeting felt that, although the Working Party had concluded that state participation should be ruled out, its disadvantages were not insuperable and it was a sufficiently serious candidate to submit to Ministers. On the commodity tax the view was that a sliding scale would be necessary to avoid deterring marginal production and there would be much difficulty in determining the appropriate level. There was a worry that it could be represented as a breach of the licensing terms.

The senior Inland Revenue representatives outlined the thinking behind the Excess Revenue Tax as outlined above, and argued that the Revenue did not think that corporation tax should be allowed as a deduction in determining the tax base. The special tax and corporation tax should be entirely separate. This was disputed by others who felt that the limitation on the deductions for the Excess Revenue Tax would make it less acceptable. It was agreed that further consideration should be given to this issue. There was a concern that revenues from the proposed tax might not be received until 1980. The general view of the meeting was that the Excess Revenue Tax produced the fewest problems, but that participation with carried interest should not be ruled out. The agreement of Ministers that the principle of increasing Government take was acceptable should now be sought.

Prolonged debate

The debate thus continued. By late 1972 the Inland Revenue felt that legislation, rather than negotiation with the companies, was necessary to deal with the problem of artificial prices employed for intra-group transactions. The Treasury had misgivings on this matter, doubting the ability of the Revenue to determine arm's length prices which would not be disputed by the companies resulting in continued court cases. There was no transparent world price for oil and information on third party sales was difficult to obtain. A further consideration was the possibility that other European countries might follow any legislative lead given by the UK to the detriment of the overseas earnings of BP and Shell which were a substantial positive element in the UK's balance of payments. Given the above the Treasury felt that the Inland Revenue should try again to reach a negotiated settlement with the companies. The proposal of the Revenue to have a special tax on North Sea oil also weakened the objection to having a ring fence round the North Sea for corporation tax purposes. Finally, the Treasury very perceptively observed (in late 1972) that, with growing state participation in the Middle East, market prices would have to be negotiated and these could become increasingly common in the next few years. Thus artificial transfer prices might gradually disappear.

The debate continued with the Departments involved having difficulty in arriving at a settled position. In February 1973, Mr John Davies, the Secretary of

State for Trade and Industry, sent a Minute to Mr Heath stating his preference for state participation, emphasising the revenues which the Exchequer would obtain. The Prime Minister met with Ministerial colleagues to discuss this proposal. There was some opposition to it on the grounds that the UK should not do precisely what it was telling OPEC Governments not to do. The state participation approach was not approved, and the Prime Minister asked his colleagues to further examine the tax options. Accordingly, a memorandum was prepared discussing the respective merits of a production tax and Excess Revenue Tax. This reiterated the pros and cons of the two taxes as discussed above, but did not come down clearly in favour of any one scheme. At a Ministerial meeting in March the decision in principle was finally made to increase the take from the North Sea, but the options had to be further considered. The DTI prepared another paper which reiterated the pros and cons of the three identified options, and noted the support of the Public Accounts Committee for the production tax.

The international legal and political consequences of increasing take from the North Sea had to be considered. The FCO had warned that state participation and the production tax on existing licences would be regarded as a form of expropriation, and would encourage OPEC Governments to break their agreements with the oil companies. On the other hand foreign Governments would understand that, following the large oil price hikes, any host Government would be entitled to procure a share of the increased revenues. With respect to the behaviour of OPEC Governments the UK's ability to influence their decisions was in any case quite marginal.

The conclusion was that on future licences carried interest was the best option. As well as providing large and early revenues it gave non-fiscal advantages relating to depletion and security of supply. On current licences, if the legal obstacles were deemed to be strong, the use of state participation could be restricted to voluntary agreements. For the remainder of current licences there was a majority view in favour of a production tax (now referred to as a severance tax because of its widespread use in the USA), on the grounds of its delivery of early revenues and administrative simplicity. Some Departments preferred the Excess Revenue Tax. This included not only the Inland Revenue but the FCO because of the legal risks involved in the other two instruments.

The debate among Departments continued, involving interminable exchanges and redrafting of the paper. A revised version was discussed at an interdepartmental meeting of senior officials in June 1973. The representation had by this time been extended to include not only the Treasury, DTI, FCO, Inland Revenue, and CPRS but the Scottish Office and Customs and Excise. The last Department had been brought in because it was thought that the administration of a production or severance tax should fall on it. There was broad agreement that carried interest was the preferred approach. An odd argument in favour of this approach was produced by the DTI namely that it had the advantage of injecting funds into the companies at an early stage! The FCO emphasised its concerns about carried interest and severance tax being possibly in contravention of international law and being akin to expropriation. This view was not universally shared by the meeting which was belatedly recognising that severance taxes were common in the USA. The Inland Revenue objected to the proposal for two different régimes for existing and new licences. Apart from the administrative complications, to apply tax only where state participation was not adopted implied tax exemption for companies in which the Government had a shareholding.[1] Customs and Excise felt that severance tax could raise difficulties with the EEC because if it was charged on oil landed in the UK it would resemble a customs duty, the imposition of which would be contrary to the Treaty of Rome. The Commission was submitting to the Council of Ministers a draft directive which would require oil in Community countries to be subject only to excise duties and value-added tax. At the end of the meeting the DTI was invited to revise the paper yet again and to avoid recommending a hybrid solution.

Following the meeting an FCO representative wrote to the Inland Revenue suggesting that a criticism of the Excess Revenue Tax, namely the delay in tax receipts from a field until such time as all investment costs plus a margin had been recovered, could be met by an obligation to make instalments from the time of initial production with these payments being treated as credits when normal liability was reached. This imaginative suggestion would have ameliorated later problems relating to the timing of tax receipts.[2]

A revised paper was submitted to the Ministerial group in June 1973. This went through the issues as discussed above, and concluded that most Departments considered that carried interest for all licensees was the best option. If Ministers objected to this on political grounds the Treasury and CPRS favoured the severance tax. In the event that international legal difficulties were felt to be a major consideration the severance tax would also have to be ruled out. In that event the choice would be between the Excess Revenue Tax and a mixed system whereby the Government would impose state participation with carried interest on future and renegotiated licences, and Excess Revenue Tax only to increase the take from current licences. The DTI preferred this mixed system to levying Excess Revenue Tax on all licences.

The debate continued and the DTI lawyer gave his opinion that products from the UKCS were already treated as domestic products. Further, he argued that EEC harmonisation of excise duties did not apply to crude oil. Many calculations were undertaken on the respective tax/Government takes and the timing of the receipts under the three approaches. The Chancellor remained opposed to state participation despite strong briefing in favour of it by Treasury officials. The Minister for Industry (Mr Tom Boardman) was also unconvinced, stating that he opposed it on almost every ground particularly for existing licences. The Minister was concerned about Government interference in management. When the Permanent Secretary explained that the Department's interests would be represented either by Departmental members on the Boards of the joint companies or through a public holding company of some kind, Mr Boardman's response was that these ideas were repugnant, and he foresaw, for example, that a field's development would be delayed on public expenditure grounds. He felt that state participation with carried interest would undermine the commercial nature of operations. He did not believe that the BP situation of non-involvement in management could exist in a new company which lacked the long BP tradition.

Mr Boardman also disputed the claim that carried interest would not reduce the investor's return so that incentives would not be diminished. Investors would bear the full costs of abortive exploration losses which would reduce the profits of the integrated operation. He also thought it odd that the proposals were being made because the investor's return on capital was felt to be excessive but the carried interest mechanism left it unchanged! The Minister's point had some substance. The official paper had emphasised how the carried interest scheme would leave the rate of return on a commercial field unchanged (and produce revenues to Government), but did not discuss the negative effect which it would have on the expected monetary value or full cycle rate of return facing a company contemplating an exploration investment.

Mr Boardman also disputed the assertion that state participation with carried interest was the best way of ensuring that marginal fields did not become uneconomic as a result of measures to increase Government take. This could be done in other ways such as in the detailed terms of the special tax. He also disputed the assertion that a major disadvantage of the Excess Revenue Tax was the delay in producing tax receipts. He pointed out that this could be avoided by spreading the relief for the capital expenditure over a longer period rather than on 100% first year basis as proposed. His point was certainly valid, but the effect of extending the period of capital recovery in reducing the discounted rate of return also needed consideration. This problem could have been surmounted by adjusting the size of the margin or better still by expressing it as a percentage of the declining balance of the investment.

The Inland Revenue did not favour Mr Boardman's proposal because it would in essence be an additional corporation tax on a particular industry with special rules for depreciation which would conflict with the important principle that taxes on profits must be generally and uniformly applied throughout the jurisdiction. Further, it would be difficult to defend an additional tax on the profits of North Sea operations which incorporated especially unfavourable allowances for depreciation. The Revenue also thought that the acceleration of revenues produced would be quite modest, perhaps by one year, if the allowances were on 25% straight line basis. These objections do not appear decisive and certainly did not inhibit the introduction of differential capital allowances in the North Sea compared to other sectors of the economy in later years.

Options for accelerating tax receipts

The Inland Revenue was, however, stirred into thinking about alternative methods of accelerating tax receipts and several were considered. One idea would be to introduce payments on account starting with first production. There was a concern that this might be considered a severance tax in substance. It would also encounter opposition from the industry as being unrelated to profitability. It would also set a highly undesirable precedent in terms of fiscal policy. Removing the margin would accelerate payments, but its retention was an integral part of the Inland Revenue's proposal. Finally, a system of quarterly accounts could be introduced which would accelerate payments by over a year compared to the scheme currently designed. This would leave the structure of the tax unchanged and was the Revenue's preferred option.

Officials in the Treasury were persuaded by the Inland Revenue's arguments against moving the Excess Revenue Tax closer to a profits tax, but DTI officials did their own calculations on the whole subject and concluded (a) that the Inland Revenue's own proposal produced a worthwhile acceleration, and (b) Mr Boardman's proposal produced a very substantial acceleration. The DTI thus promoted Mr Boardman's idea, but the Inland Revenue remained opposed to it on the grounds discussed above. The DTI felt that these objections were exaggerated, with the main one (discriminatory treatment of one industry) applying also to Excess Revenue Tax. Mr Boardman was keen to promote his scheme, but the Permanent Secretary advised that it would be difficult to overcome Treasury and Inland Revenue opposition.

Views of outside parties sought

Because of the difficulties in coming to firm conclusions Ministers decided to obtain opinions from other parties. Thus the views of BP, BGC, Cooper Brothers and Walter Levy were sought, and on legal aspects those of Eli Lauterpacht and the Law Officers. The views of several Ambassadors on the likely reactions of overseas Governments and investors were also sought. Mr Lauterpacht's opinions were that in international law (a) Excess Revenue Tax was clearly a simple exercise of a Government's right to tax, (b) state participation with carried interest was only marginally less defensible than Excess Revenue Tax if it procured the same revenues as the tax but by another means, (c) the mixed carried interest/Excess Revenue Tax system had the advantage of emphasising the equivalence of participation and tax, and (d) the severance tax was objectionable. The response from the embassy in Washington was that retrospective carried interest would be the worst option for political reasons, and severance tax was the best one because it was well known in the USA.

Mr Walter Levy's views emphasised the disadvantages of the severance tax because of its insensitivity to costs and large effect on profitability given its early impact. He also felt that Excess Revenue Tax was not fully sensitive to costs and risked deterring marginal production. It might provoke reaction in OPEC countries against the very large profits being earned there. He also criticised it for the non-tax reason that it would not assist the Government to obtain greater control over the industry which on grounds of substance and presentation he felt should be the aim. For these reasons he favoured state participation with carried interest. It was the only practical way to procure a high share of profits to the Government and it had been adopted by many other oil-producing countries. But introducing it on existing licences created formidable problems as it gave a precedent to other overseas countries, including Libya, where the Government was being exhorted by the British Government not to break agreements unilaterally. He thus thought that the companies should be induced to accept participation voluntarily by telling them that otherwise they would have to pay Excess Revenue Tax. Further suggestions were that the Government should pay interest on its contributions to past costs, and pay 50% of the costs.

Further debate within Government

Following this the DTI felt that severance tax should now be rejected, and that, if Excess Revenue Tax was to be adopted, powers to remit royalties were needed to avoid discouraging marginal fields. If priority was attached to raising large revenues plus achieving control over the exploitation of the oil state participation was the most effective method. To deal with the problems from imposing this on existing licences the options for Ministers were (1) to accept the risk and legislate, (2) to avoid the risk and hope to persuade licensees to renegotiate voluntarily, and (3) to renegotiate on the understanding that the Government would impose Excess Revenue Tax on companies who were unwilling to renegotiate.

Understandably the mixed participation/Excess Revenue Tax proposal did not receive automatic support, and the Permanent Secretary at the Treasury requested that the substance of the scheme be examined further. It had to be acknowledged that it was contrary to taxation principles to make liability to tax contingent on a commercial transaction with the Government (such as renegotiation of a licence). The Excess Revenue Tax would have to be assessed in all cases but would be allowed as a credit against liability under a participation agreement. There was a potential problem in comparing the two schemes in situations where they produced equal yields to the Government (in present value terms). The applicable Excess Revenue Tax might then not be high enough to persuade companies to opt for state participation. The loss of control would be a reason to prefer the tax option. Thus the required rate of tax necessary to encourage participation would have to be higher. But this would raise a problem of disincentives to investment by new licensees. The DTI's response to this was to suggest that Excess Revenue Tax should be imposed on all present licences and state participation on all future ones. The Inland Revenue felt that this contravened a firm tax principle that trading activities carried on under public ownership, either alone or in partnership with private sector companies, should be taxable in the same way as other trading activities. This principle did not disappear because the activities were confined to a single sector. A quite separate objection to the latest DTI proposal was that participation in all future licences would include those of dubious commercial value.

Ministers debate options

The Ministerial group met to consider the options in late October 1973. In preparation for this meeting officials prepared papers. One new element in the debate was the Law Officers' Opinion on the three methods. Legal advice on state participation with carried interest on existing licences was that prompt and adequate compensation would be required, but, if it were combined with Excess Revenue Tax, a valuation which took account of the reduced return would be defensible. On severance tax the advice of the Law Officers was that its imposition in existing licences would be contrary to international law. Excess Revenue Tax either on its own or as part of a mixed system would be consistent with international law. Given these judgements officials felt that state participation in all licences was no longer a practical proposition. Despite its manifest complications the DTI, CPRS, and Treasury (but perhaps not the Chancellor himself) still felt that the mixed system offered the best solution in terms of early revenues and control over the activity. The latter was assuming ever greater importance in thinking because of enhanced concern over security of supplies. Two mixed systems were now suggested to Ministers. Under both of them all licences would be subject to Excess Revenue Tax, but payments would be waived as partial compensation when participation was taken. Under the first option participation would be chosen at the Government's option while under the second the licensee would have the option. The CPRS favoured the first option, while other Departments favoured the second, principally because the advice of the Law Officers was that the scheme whereby participation was at the Government's option would only be consistent with international law under quite restrictive circumstances. These were that (1) extra compensation in addition to remission of Excess Revenue Tax would probably be required, and (2) such remitted tax would have to be of the same value as the state participation taken. The latter would be difficult to achieve and the rate of tax would probably have to vary among licensees. There would also be difficulties in making further discretionary changes to the rate of tax.

At the meeting Ministers did not make final decisions and requested further work on the subject. There was continued difficulty in obtaining interdepartmental agreement. The CPRS felt that compulsory state participation was necessary (principally for reasons of control rather than revenue-raising), and in a further draft paper for Ministers the DTI suggested that, while they preferred the voluntary approach, the rate of Excess Profit Tax should be fixed at a level sufficiently high to induce the licensees to choose state participation. While the Secretary of State gave his approval to this Mr Boardman remained unconvinced about the merits of the mixed schemes, commenting that they constituted a socialist-bureaucratic dream with which he did not want to be associated. It is very doubtful whether the Minister was fully informed of the complexities that the DTI had in mind. Thus it was felt that maximum flexibility in the degree of participation was desirable, and this could be obtained by designing a sliding scale of the extent of participation with a corresponding sliding scale of the extent to which the full Excess Revenue Tax would be payable: the lower the degree of participation the greater the extent of the full tax payable. An illustrative case of five steps was designed. The Inland Revenue did not see overriding objections to the sliding scale scheme. By the time of the fall of the Conservative Government no final decisions had been made, but some officials were contemplating that the Excess

Revenue Tax might be levied in addition to state participation, so that a licensee who had agreed participation would still pay the tax on his (reduced) share.

Labour Government favours enhanced state control

The Labour Government had been elected on a manifesto which included the pledge to obtain majority public participation in North Sea exploration and production. Officials thus felt able to consider participation shares in excess of the 50% maximum contemplated under the previous Government. Thus it was estimated that with participation at 60% the total Government take (including royalties and corporation tax) would be around 83%. There would be further clear advantages of enhanced control (see Chapter 8). The CPRS in a fresh note re-emphasised the point that a special tax had the serious disadvantage of not providing enhanced control to the Government. Thus participation on existing licences, but on a negotiated basis, was the recommended route. Failing that it favoured a hybrid scheme with participation and the special tax with remission of the latter on existing licences as compensation. Some officials were prepared to contemplate more radical measures. A senior CPRS official enquired why expropriation could not be employed as he believed (generally mistakenly) that this had happened in the Middle East. The Treasury agreed that there was a case for such a course, but international legal complications had prevented this.

Pursuing more conventional methods, Mr Varley, the Secretary of State for Energy, quickly prepared a paper for his Ministerial colleagues, proposing state participation on future licences, and a special tax on current licences which would be set at a level sufficiently high to persuade licensees to opt for state participation. The Paymaster General, Mr Edmund Dell, was unhappy with this approach. He was concerned that, despite an incentive to accept participation, the companies might prefer to pay the tax. Thus he felt that a special tax *plus* participation of at least 51% would be necessary, and the Government should have the flexibility to vary the tax. The Paymaster also felt it was necessary to stop the loss of corporation tax revenues from the use of accumulated losses. The Inland Revenue emphasised the adverse reaction by the companies to the introduction of a ring fence around North Sea activities. The Revenue reiterated to the Paymaster their opposition to a severance or barrelage tax and in favour of one based on the excess of receipts over expenditures including a margin on investment. It was acknowledged that the capital allowances could be spread over a number of years. If it were imposed on a field basis the timing of receipts could be accelerated. The Revenue had mixed feelings about the idea of the special tax being employed as a device to accept participation, noting the potential conflict between the objective of maximising the yield and letting it be seen that participation was a good bargain for the Government.

Mr Varley submitted another Memorandum to his colleagues in the middle of May on North Sea policies generally. This recommended a special tax, but, where participation (at 51% or more) was negotiated, it would be remitted to the appropriate extent. Further work was needed on the appropriate rate of tax and its relationship with participation. This was immediately followed by a note to the Ministerial Committee from the CPRS arguing strongly for the participation route because of its non-revenue advantages. In the meantime the Inland Revenue had been developing its own thinking on taxation. The concept of the Excess Revenue Tax with a margin as designed earlier was still favoured, but now included the possibility of spreading the capital expenditure allowances over a longer period. Given the dramatic increases in oil prices currently taking place another variant was to include a base profit figure. The excess of profits above this base would be subjected to tax at a high rate. A further possibility was a graduated tax related to a unit such as a barrel. The tax would then be progressively related to profits per barrel.

Complications of interaction of participation and special tax

The Revenue also showed how the interaction of participation and the special tax could lead to very great complications, given the possibility of different participation at different percentages. A further issue, abortive exploration, required attention. To allow such costs to be deductible against any current profits for the special tax could be done but was not recommended. It might be impossible to tell whether the expenditure was abortive until much later, and in such circumstances if it turned out to be successful there would be a need to withdraw the relief retrospectively. The Inland Revenue also thought that BGC and the NCB should be liable to the special tax, but not the proposed national oil company because of its proposed special position as the Government's vehicle for holding the state participation interest.

Valuation issue

A number of more technical but still important issues in relation to the tax system had to be resolved. One was the valuation of the oil in situations where it was transferred between affiliate companies and where sales by companies to non-affiliates might not be at unfettered arm's length prices. The problem was how to determine the appropriate arm's length price. The Department of Energy favoured an administered price which could be related to the value of an equivalent oil produced outside the UKCS with adjustments for any discounts and transport to the UK. There might have to be provision for appeals which could be the Department, the existing Tax Commissioners or a special commission. There was a danger that an appeals system could lead to a loss of tax revenues. The Department's first preference was for one common tax and royalty reference price, determined by the Inland Revenue and based on estimated market value, and without scope for appeal. The Inland Revenue expressed concern that one reference price might not be appropriate for the whole industry. Rights of appeal were conventional and could hardly be removed when large amounts of revenues were at stake.

Artificial losses and group relief

The debate on valuation became intertwined with the issue of relief for artificial losses and group relief arrangements. The current rules were that the artificially high posted price at which a UK resident company bought oil from an overseas associated production company could not be displaced in the UK tax computation under the relevant transfer pricing legislation (Section 485 of the Income and Corporation Taxes Act, 1970). Thus there would be difficulty in establishing that the posted price was not an arm's length price. Further, the provision did not apply where both companies were resident in the UK. The result was that the purchasing company made artificial losses and the production company made artificially high profits on which no UK tax was payable because of double taxation relief for the overseas taxes.

The results of the studies under the Conservative Government had resulted in a proposal by the Chancellor in 1973 to provide for an administered price to be used for these purposes. Legislation had been deferred to allow for consultation with the industry. Mr Barber had also proposed to introduce legislation to deal with the issue of accumulated past losses whereby losses up to the end of 1972 would not be available to set against profits from the North Sea or any other new activity. Legislation was also deferred on this issue to permit industry consultations.

Mr Edmund Dell, the Paymaster General, reviewed all these issues and by June 1974 he concluded that (1) on current losses Section 485 of the 1970 Act should be amended, (2) there should be a ring fence around the North Sea to restrict group relief, and (3) accumulated losses should be sterilised, but some might be utilised in year 1973/74. At a meeting among Treasury and Inland Revenue colleagues the Chief Secretary expressed broad agreement, but felt that not all the accumulated losses were artificial. In discussion the idea of a future date for the cancellation of past losses should be considered. The Financial Secretary expressed concern at the proposal for a ring fence on the grounds that it would cause short-term distortions. The Paymaster emphasised the acceleration of receipts. The modification to the transfer pricing rules probably would not procure adequate taxable profits. He also thought a worse form of economic distortion would be the use of North Sea profits to fertilise other activities which on their own would not be economic. Inland Revenue officials felt that the argument of economic distortions could be used against all group relief and should not be emphasised publicly, but the Paymaster felt that the scale of North Sea profits was enough to make them a special case.

North Sea ring fence to be established

Mr Dell subsequently informed Mr Varley that the decision had now been made to establish a ring fence around the North Sea to insulate profits from losses and capital allowances arising elsewhere. The existing defects on the rules on transfer pricing would be removed and this should ensure that artificial tax losses would be eliminated from January 1973. Losses accumulated up to the end of 1972 arose from the artificiality of the posted price system and would be cancelled, not just restricted as the Conservative Government had proposed. Given the potentially retrospective element of complete cancellation some losses should be allowable against 1973 profits and part of 1974 profits. The cancellation of accumulated losses would not apply to foreign-owned groups because the clear defects of the transfer pricing system did not apply in these cases. No action was proposed in relation to the unilateral double taxation relief in respect of profits taxes imposed by Middle East Governments.

White paper on North Sea policies is published

To respond to much political pressure the Government was anxious to make a public statement of its policy stance towards North Sea oil and gas even before final decisions had been made on the detailed aspects of the tax package. A White Paper entitled *United Kingdom Offshore Oil and Gas Policy* (Cmnd. 5696) was published on 11th July 1974. It emphasised the large prospective profits, estimated at £4,000 million before tax at current oil prices by 1980, with the expected Government take being little more than 50%, and half of the post-tax profits being remitted overseas. The Government take had to be increased as had public control over such an important national asset. The increased take would be achieved by the introduction of an additional tax on the profits and by closing loopholes in the current tax system as described above. Thus accumulated past losses would be cancelled on the grounds that they did not represent a real commercial loss. Limited concessions would be given to meet the criticism of retrospection, and in addition each company would be allowed to carry forward a minimum amount of losses of £50 million to be set against profits (except those from the UKCS). With respect to the UKCS a ring fence would immediately be established disallowing group relief relating to the offsetting of losses and capital allowances arising from outside the North Sea. In addition where a group company carried on North Sea and non-North Sea activities losses from the latter could not be offset against profits in the former. The White Paper also announced that in future licences a condition of award would be majority state participation on a carried interest basis, while in existing licences the companies were invited to negotiate participation.

Effects of oil discoveries on Scotland

A quite different issue was also raised in the White Paper, namely the Government's response to the effects of the oil discoveries on Scotland. Expectations had been much aroused, both economic and political, with the growth of support for the Scottish National Party. This had produced concern and even alarm within Government and the other political parties. The Scottish Office had given their detailed views on the subject to other Departments in late May, arguing that there was now a need to devise a means whereby oil revenues could be brought to bear on the long-standing economic problems of the country in a visible manner. Mr Ross, the Secretary of State for Scotland, felt that the appropriate mechanism was to set up a development agency which would be financed at least in part, from North Sea oil revenues. Scottish Office officials produced a draft paper on the possibilities. They felt that the forthcoming statement and White Paper dealing with taxation should be accompanied by a statement of interest about how and the extent to which North Sea revenues should be used for the benefit of Scotland. The paper considered principally a Regional Development Fund akin to the proposed European Regional Development Fund, but found more favour with the concept of a Scottish Development Agency which would have its own powers of initiation, assessment and execution. This was accepted within Government and the White Paper included a short statement indicating that such an Agency would be established. The Treasury was implacably opposed to the idea of hypothecation of any oil revenues, and the statement emphasised that the Agency would be financed by the UK Exchequer. No reference was made to the debate on devolution following the Kilbrandon report nor to the sharing of licence fees and royalties with the Isle of Man and Northern Ireland Governments.

Discussions with industry on proposed new tax

Meanwhile further work continued on the details of the proposed new tax. Consultations were held with oil companies. Shell gave its views in writing, conceded that extra taxation was justified, and highlighted its opposition to a production/barrelage tax on the grounds that it was unrelated to profits and was effectively another royalty dressed up in another form. Fluctuations in oil prices would also mean that the appropriate rate of barrelage tax would have to be changed. On new concessions sliding scale royalties could be introduced, but much care would be required to ensure that marginal fields were not rendered uneconomic. Similarly, the company argued that, while state participation was internationally quite common, if compensation for past costs were given, this device would not apply to the investor's share of the profits and thus the problem would remain unsolved. Shell thus favoured a supplementary petroleum tax. This should only come into effect after a certain profit norm had been achieved. It could be a sliding scale one, but should always leave a margin sufficient to make new investment worthwhile. Its structure should take into account all operations in the UKCS, including exploration and the large differences in field sizes and costs.

BP also accepted that a new tax régime for the UKCS was justified to secure a proper return to the Government, but emphasised that it should not damage international confidence in the UK, including not only the oil industry directly but also the international banks who would have to provide enormous funds to finance developments. It would also be important to ensure that there was no retaliation by overseas Governments (such as Alaska) against British interests. (For this reason BP was also strongly opposed to state participation in existing licences.) Any new tax should also not discourage the development of marginal fields.

The company did not favour barrelage or severance taxes because they were not related to profits. Even sliding scale ones were unsatisfactory as they were in effect clumsy income taxes. BP was also opposed to a scheme which imposed a penal rate of tax on the excess over a specified rate of return as this would penalise the efficient more than the inefficient. The preferred option was a higher rate of corporation tax applied to North Sea profits. This would have several advantages, namely it would (a) allow for any level of take required, (b) not damage international confidence, (c) not (if designed properly) erode the credit rating of the North Sea and thus encourage the banks to lend, (d) not hinder the development of marginal fields (perhaps by taxing small ones at a lower rate), and (e) would be relatively simple to administer.

Gulf Oil also indicated to the Chancellor that extra taxation on large profits (above returns in the 25% – 30% range) were justified. The company favoured the introduction of an Oil Profit Levy or Windfall Profit Tax geared to overall profitability from all licences. It could be graduated according to the average after-tax return on all North Sea investments. As an incentive it should be reduced by expenditures ploughed back into further exploration and development. State participation was not favoured because (a) it was unnecessary given the powers already available to the Government, and (b) it would be very costly in terms of public expenditures.

Relationship between PRT and corporation tax

The Government considered these arguments and continued with detailed work on several issues which, though of a technical nature, had major implications for the operation of the tax system and the revenues which might be obtained. One such issue which caused considerable debate was how the new tax (now termed Petroleum Revenue Tax (PRT)) should interact with corporation tax. Professor Nicholas Kaldor, now a Special Adviser at the Treasury, argued rather strongly that the proposed PRT should be a prior charge (deductible) for corporation tax and levied at a rather high rate in order to procure substantial "early" revenues. Treasury and Inland Revenue officials had looked at several options namely (a) PRT deductible for corporation tax, (b) corporation tax deductible for PRT, and (c) a high PRT rate and exemption from corporation tax. The Inland Revenue had concerns about option (a) on the grounds that, as companies would be in very different corporation tax positions the value of deductibility would vary greatly across licensees. The same argument would, of course, apply to option (b). Because different licences would inevitably be in different tax positions it would be extremely difficult to equalise effective liability. There was also concern that a high rate would have other efficiency-related disadvantages. It would encourage further exploration and development by companies paying the high rate (because of the associated high rate of relief), but would give a disincentive to new entrants because they would have no North Sea income against which to offset their costs. A further concern was that a very high rate would make it difficult to resist the claims that PRT should be levied not on a field basis, which was desirable on timing arguments, but on a whole North Sea basis.

The decision to impose a ring fence around the North Sea for corporation tax purposes greatly increased the effective rate of that tax, and thus reduced the case for having a high rate of PRT and making it a prior charge. (It was of course recognised that investors in multi-field situations would still have different effective corporation tax positions.) The perceived need to resist Scottish nationalist pressures to hypothecate some of the revenues also pointed to the collection of as much revenue as possible from normal corporation tax. In further discussions between the Permanent Secretary at the Treasury and senior Inland Revenue officials on whether to recommend (a) a high-rate PRT deductible for corporation tax or (b) a lower rate-PRT not deductible, it was felt that the advantages of the deductible route were that (1) it would generate a high yield, (2) there would be a less complicated interaction between PRT and corporation tax so that when the rules for the latter were changed there would be no need to adjust PRT, and (3) it would be easier to change the net North Sea take by adjusting a non-deductible PRT. It was recognised that a main disadvantage of this option was to highlight the larger share of the total take coming from PRT which gave ammunition to those who wished to hypothecate North Sea revenues. When everything was considered officials did not have a strong view to recommend to the Paymaster General.

Detailed paper on PRT produced by Inland Revenue

By July 1974 the Inland Revenue had prepared a paper dealing with all the main aspects of the new tax. The change in title to PRT was recommended as the term Excess Revenue Tax might leave the misleading impression that it was intended to tax an element of excess profits above a certain level. This latter idea had been raised with disfavour by BP. Another issue was whether PRT should apply to gas production. The Inland Revenue felt that it should so apply. It was recognised that BGC had been using its monopsony buying power to keep down wholesale gas prices and thus producers probably would not make excessive profits. But because gas and oil were competing fuels a "reasonable" price for gas would be influenced by oil prices. It was also noteworthy that the most resent BGC contracts provided for the gas price to reflect a large measure of increase in the oil price. This trend would probably continue. It might also become difficult to justify holding gas prices below a market level when the same producers were allowed to sell oil at world prices. There was also the prospect of more gas being sold to parties other than BGC (including direct exports). Even if gas production was on average less profitable than oil there was still an expectation that it would be sufficient to justify extra taxation. There would also be a cushioning effect from the tax-free margin. Alleviation of the tax on gas would be particularly difficult in fields with associated gas, where the need for cost allocations would pose serious difficulties. It was agreed, however, that special arrangements would be necessary in gas fields where substantial production had already occurred prior to the introduction of PRT. It was proposed that receipts before the introduction of the tax should be exempt, with a corresponding reduction in the proportion of capital expenditure allowed against chargeable receipts. The apportionment could be determined in relation to the proportions of reserves before and after the introduction of the tax. The Department of Energy was unconvinced that PRT should apply to gas production, and the matter remained unresolved.

Disposal receipts

Other dimensions of the scope of the tax also had to be considered. These included receipts other than from producing oil and gas. One was capital receipts from the disposal of an interest in a field in excess of the capital expenditure necessary to achieve production. The issue was complex. If capital sums from asset disposals were not taxed an easy route to tax avoidance would be available, though the tax would accelerate rather than increase the yield if the purchaser was able to claim the price paid as an allowable deduction. The Revenue recognised that there were arguments against making capital receipts taxable. In these circumstances the tax would no longer apply just to field profits but would become one on the total financial operations of the participants. This increased the complexity of the tax, but on balance it would be odd if a licensee could effectively dispose of his assets on which he had obtained tax relief without paying tax on the sums involved, and thus the Revenue favoured their inclusion in the tax base.

Field basis of PRT

With respect to the unit of charge the Revenue view was that it could either be the field or the whole of an investor's North Sea activities. The field basis would clearly produce an earlier yield since investment relating to a second or later field could not be offset against the income from the first one. A field basis would also be easier for keeping control over allowable costs as the expenditures on a field had to be acceptable to all field partners, while a company-based tax would allow each company to make independent claims. The Department of Energy advised that identification of separate fields was quite possible. If the complication of the interaction between taxation and state participation had not existed the Revenue would have preferred that tax for each field should be charged on the profits of the field as a whole and not separately on each licensee. As well as enhancing control of field expenditure this would have permitted the tax to be collected in one sum. However, the proposals for state participation, whereby in existing licences each partner would be able to concede participation or not, plus the proposal that the tax charge would depend on whether there was state participation, meant that each licensee had to be charged separately.

Abortive exploration

With respect to exploration expenditures those which led to commercial production would clearly be deductible, but on this basis abortive expenditures would not be allowable. This would produce disincentives and so it was proposed to permit these costs to be deductible when they were clearly shown to be unsuccessful. Interestingly, the Revenue felt that, if exploration relief were so allowed, there was a strong argument in favour of charging onshore production to PRT, otherwise the right to allow onshore exploration costs against North Sea profits would introduce a major incentive to onshore exploration.

Exempt slice of profits?

The Revenue had given some consideration to the possibility that the new tax could be levied only on exceptional profits above an exempt slice. The tax rate on the exceptional element could then be higher than if it were charged on all profits. The more progressive scheme would be open to the criticism made by Sir Eric Drake of BP that it would be penalising the more efficient. The Revenue was not entirely convinced by this argument, but, given that the tax might have to be related to state participation, felt on balance that it might be best not to pursue the notion of the tax being related to the rate of return.

Loan interest

On the question of interest on loans the Revenue was aware that debt finance was being widely employed to finance field developments. PRT was planned to be a field-based tax, and so if interest were allowable it would be necessary to allocate it among different fields, and also between North Sea and non-North Sea activities. This was felt to pose intractable problems. Further, if interest were deductible for PRT there would be no question of charging PRT on the lender. Equality of treatment between equity and loan capital would be achieved by disallowing interest relief to the borrower. The problem of allocation among fields would then disappear. The burden of the disallowance would fall on the licensees, and this led to the concept of a margin or uplift on the capital investment as an alternative. It was recognised that it was a somewhat rough and ready alternative as it would be available irrespective of whether debt or equity capital were employed.

Treatment of hire payments

A problem was also raised in relation to hire payments for capital equipment. To produce equitable treatment between licensees who borrowed money to finance capital investment and those who hired the facilities from financiers it would be necessary to identify and disallow the interest element in hire payments, while the capital element should qualify for uplift and deductibility. This was not a practical procedure, however, and it was proposed that both interest paid and hire payments made for major permanent assets should be disallowed. It was recognised that these proposals would be controversial with the industry.

Six-month charge period

The Revenue recommended that the period of charge should be six months on a calendar year basis. This was consistent with the royalty periods, and, while quarterly periods were possible, it was felt that the industry would object to the shorter period. The original idea had been to levy it on a cumulative basis (that is, the excess of cumulative receipts over cumulative expenditures), but it was felt on further reflection that, as this would not affect the eventual amount payable, there was no need to recommend this. Payments would become due three months after the end of each period. By mid-1974 the Revenue was adopting an open-minded attitude about whether the capital expenditure should be deducted on 100% first year basis or spread over a number of years.

Tariff receipts

The Revenue at this time felt that where a licensee hired out surplus facilities such as pipelines to other licensees there was a strong practical argument for charging the receipts to PRT. If they were not charged there would be a need to apportion the owner's expenditure between his own use and the use by others. This would be complicated and so the Revenue recommended that tariff income should be charged. It was recognised that this introduced a possible inconsistency with the notion that the tax was related to production income.

Tax position of BNOC

The proposed British National Oil Corporation (BNOC) should clearly be charged to corporation tax, but the Revenue felt that PRT was more difficult. The notion that PRT was to some degree an alternative to participation, the key role which BNOC would have in that activity as the Government's agent, plus the special financing arrangements in mind for the company, suggested that BNOC should not be charged to PRT. On the other hand BGC and the NCB should be chargeable to the tax.

Inter-departmental debate

The proposals were debated with the Department of Energy (DEN), CPRS and Treasury. The DEN were not convinced that gas from the Southern North Sea should be subject to PRT because of the low price paid to producers. The Inland Revenue emphasised the practical problems in mixed fields if oil were taxed and gas exempt, the expected high profitability of gas from the Northern gas fields, and the increasing indexation of gas to oil in contracts.

The effects of the creditability of PRT in the parent countries of the oil companies were discussed. The Inland Revenue had calculated that in the USA any substantial further taxes paid in the UK would result in the credits being above the ceiling in accordance with the current rules (excess foreign tax credits). This meant that the burden would fall on the companies rather than the US Treasury. The CPRS felt that this was an important issue as the companies would be more willing to accept participation if they, rather than the US Government, bore the full burden of the new tax.

The debate on the individual features of PRT continued. The issue of whether it should be a prior charge for corporation tax or entirely independent received a surprising amount of attention. Mr Dell asked for a further review of the issue by the Inland Revenue and Treasury. They produced a further report for him which reviewed the arguments already discussed above, concluding that the main argument for the prior charge was the accelerated tax receipts and the greater security to the overall yield (with more leakage likely where corporation tax was based on all the UKCS). The main arguments against the prior charge were that there would be questioning of a high rate tax with unusual features, and the danger of exposing more revenues to claims for hypothecation to Scotland. The balance of the arguments was mildly in favour of complete tax separation. The Treasury subsequently preferred a neutral conclusion while the Inland Revenue continued to prefer separation.

The DEN was understandably concerned about the various effects which the new tax might have on activity levels in the UKCS. One such effect was on the financing arrangements for the development of fields. Large loans were required involving, for example, £180 million and £468 million for Forties, and $240 million for Piper. It was important that the ability of the companies to borrow should not be impaired. Immediate depreciation, allowing the companies to reach payback before the tax became payable, was important from the banks' viewpoint and was thus favoured.

At the end of July 1974 officials in the Inland Revenue summarised the state of debate for the Paymaster General. On the question of whether PRT should be based on a field or corporate basis the need for the link with participation which was on a field basis remained a deciding factor. The DEN had attempted to quantify the tax rate which would be required to be imposed on a corporate basis to procure the same revenues received on a present value basis with a rate of 30% applied on a field basis. This exercise required several sweeping assumptions but the surprising finding was 31%. The difference in yield in the first year or two was felt by the Revenue to be quite substantial. The Paymaster was advised to retain the field as the basis of the charge.

The DEN had also calculated the costs of allowing abortive exploration as a deduction against PRT at the earliest possible time. To maintain the revenues from PRT would require an increase in the rate from 30% to 33%. The Inland Revenue recommended examination of delayed relief for abortive exploration. On the question of whether field investment should be deductible on 100% first year basis or spread over a number of years, officials acknowledged that spreading would increase the yield in the early years but other arguments pointed to allowing 100% relief at the outset. These were (a) consistency with the immediate relief under corporation tax for most items, (b) the large amount of loan finance being employed, and the associated need for relatively quick repayments, and (c) the fact that the overall tax rates on North Sea oil would be exceptionally high.

With respect to the appropriate uplift on capital expenditure a 50% rate was now recommended. Studies had been undertaken to ascertain how closely this corresponded to deduction for interest paid. The then current high interest rates had been employed in the exercise and the conclusion was reached that 50% uplift would represent over 90% of the interest payments on a hypothetical large field situation.

Tax remission or tax offsets to incentivise state participation

The thorny subject of the tax inducement required to entice investors to accept state participation occupied the attention of officials at this time. There were two techniques, namely tax remission and tax offset payments, but each had advantages and disadvantages. Tax remission could deal with the levying of PRT and its abatement all in one operation and thus was presentationally attractive. There would be no awkwardness relating to the taking with one hand and giving back with the other. The Inland Revenue, however, felt that remission constituted the use of tax legislation for non-tax objectives which was contrary to established practice. Further, sliding scale remission (which was necessary to accommodate different levels of participation) would breach the principle of non-discrimination in taxation and cast doubts on the genuineness of the tax. It would also be less flexible than offset payments where, for example, it was felt necessary to give relief in excess of the PRT liability.

Tax offset payments did not cause any problems of tax principle and they were very flexible, but they involved two operations where one would suffice, and introduced presentational difficulties of making payments to the oil companies and much Parliamentary scrutiny, particularly if annual Votes for the sums involved were required. Both schemes involved substantial complexities, particularly where varying rates of participation were involved and where the rate of PRT were set at a relatively high level. In such cases companies accepting participation might still have to pay some PRT. The PRT rate had not yet been decided, and one of the factors causing this was the unresolved controversy over whether PRT should be entirely separated from corporation tax or made deductible for the latter. In that case the rate of PRT would be considerably higher.

In a meeting among Ministers and senior officials of the Treasury, Inland Revenue and DEN Mr Dell argued in favour of tax offset payments, emphasising the advantages of the new tax being entirely separate from participation, the easier accommodation of a sliding scale system relating to varying degrees of participation, and the complete freedom to vary the rate of PRT. The offset payments scheme provided greater flexibility to the actions of Government. The Minister of State for Energy, Lord Balogh, was concerned about the presentational difficulties of the offset payments scheme, particularly the payments made to oil companies which could be interpreted as a quasi-nationalisation measure.

Oil Account

On the mechanics of implementing a tax offset scheme the Treasury proposed that an Oil Account be established to meet the expenses and receive the revenues of the proposed BNOC and from which the net proceeds of state participation would be paid to the Exchequer. This arrangement would remove the requirements for offset payments to be made out of Parliamentary votes. Whether or not BNOC paid PRT as well as corporation tax would be a relevant consideration because, if both were payable and offset payments were made, it was very doubtful whether BNOC would have a positive net cash flow. It was agreed that a positive cash flow was desirable and thus BNOC should be exempt from PRT. At a subsequent meeting in mid-August Ministers agreed that the offset payments mechanism was technically preferable, but tax remission was preferable on presentational and political grounds. No agreement was reached.

Ministers expressed disquiet about fixing offset payments or tax remissions on the basis of once and for all calculations related to the life of the fields. Officials had produced calculations indicating that the association of 51% participation with a PRT rate of 27% was fairly insensitive to variations in oil prices and costs, but Ministers wondered whether, given the likely volatility of oil prices, offset payments might better be calculated yearly on the basis of actual outcomes. Ministers also showed concern that the rate of return on (development) investment for companies which accepted participation could be very high. With respect to the proposed Oil Account a choice had to be made whether it should relate to BNOC or the Government. Again no agreement was reached but it was acknowledged that the issue was primarily for DEN.

PRT a prior charge

Further studies were thus requested, but Mr Dell did report an Inland Revenue decision to the Secretary of State for Energy in August 1974, namely to make PRT a prior charge for corporation tax rather than an entirely independent tax. By this time the thinking in the Revenue was that the rate could be over 70% rather than around 35% if the tax was entirely separate. The decision was based on the benefits of tax revenue acceleration. The immediate response of Lord Balogh, the Minister of State for Energy, was to express doubts on the grounds that the wider public might deduce that, with corporation tax at 50%, the Government was levying an overall rate of 120% on profits.

Enormous complexity of tax remission/offset schemes

The debate on the above subjects continued with many revisions and refinements being made to papers. The issue of the tax offset/remission scheme remained a particularly vexed one, with highly complex arrangements having to be devised to produce the appropriate equity and incentive effects (to encourage acceptance of the state participation option) in an environment where the degree of participation was not fixed and provision had to be made for the rate of PRT to be changed. Given these factors, the majority view among officials was that the size of the offset payments would have to be determined annually in the light of the outcome for the year rather than pre-determined in a formula extending over the whole life of a field.

Further complications with the scheme were unveiled. Thus it was arguable that the offset payments made to the oil companies should really be taxable for corporation tax purposes. This would distort the intended equity and incentive effects. To leave the companies in the same post-tax position would require the payments to be grossed up at the corporation tax rate. In turn this would cause presentational problems with apparently large sums being paid to the licensees. If the payments were directly exempt from corporation tax issues of discrimination with other sectors could arise. Corporation tax was designed to apply to the whole corporate sector on an essentially non-discriminatory basis. It was also recognised that, while arrangements could be made to make the offset payments in the UK free of corporation tax, the tax authorities in the parent countries of the foreign oil companies could well take a different view and subject the payments to tax in their jurisdictions. The debate was prolonged. It was decided that decisions were not required in the near term as it would not be necessary to include details of the scheme in the Bill planned for the autumn of 1974.

Paymaster makes decisions and authorises consultation with industry

Mr Dell had decided by the middle of August 1974 that, for PRT, capital allowances would be on 100% first-year basis and that relief should be given for abortive exploration (without uplift). In authorising consultation with the industry on PRT he did not favour revealing at this stage its relationship to participation nor did he want to reveal any indication of the tax rate beyond hinting that it would be substantial. The consultations should be about the structure of the tax. The Inland Revenue prepared a consultation note accordingly. It thus did not refer to participation, the prospective rate and whether it would be a prior charge for corporation tax. It was proposed to apply PRT to third-party tariff income.

UKOITC expresses concerns

At early meetings with BP and subsequently the Oil Industry Taxation Committee (UKOITC) on the ring fence proposals for corporation tax, strong opposition was expressed to the cancellation of losses which was regarded as retrospective legislation. There was a view that the industry was being attacked twice over in relation to North Sea profits through the introduction of the ring fence and the cancellation of losses. It was felt that it was unreasonable to refer to the "artificiality" of the losses as they had been computed under the law at the relevant time. The industry clearly distinguished between losses relating to the pricing arrangements and capital allowances. The latter related to expenditures actually incurred and the related allowances were in no way artificial.

In October 1974 the Inland Revenue had meetings with UKOITC about the document on the structure of PRT. UKOITC raised several concerns on what they deemed to be matters of principle. One was a general apprehension about the differentiation between PRT and corporation tax. The Revenue felt that this essentially reflected a dislike of novelty and the fact that PRT would be paid earlier than corporation tax. A second concern related to whether PRT would be a creditable tax in other jurisdictions particularly the USA. The view of the Inland Revenue at this time was that it was likely to qualify and would certainly be proposed as such by the Government in any future negotiations.

UKOITC was particularly concerned about the field basis for PRT. It was regarded as unreasonable that tax on an established field was payable without obtaining concurrent relief for investment in another field. The Revenue view was that this could not be conceded in advance of the negotiations on participation (which were quite separate). The companies felt that there should be a statutory upper limit to total Government take, partly to assist their long-term planning and to reassure their bankers. The Revenue felt that this could not be met currently, but could be examined when the results of the participation negotiations became clear.

UKOITC argued that PRT would put the development of marginal fields at risk. This included large as well as small fields. Suggestions for a graduated tax were made. The Revenue was sceptical and asked the industry to provide a further analysis of the effects of the tax on marginal fields even though the rate was not yet known. The companies also argued that it would be unreasonable to apply PRT to gas which was already contracted to BGC, as the negotiated price was designed to ensure that large profits were not made by producers. The Inland Revenue agreed to consider this subject further. The consultative documents had proposed that no allowance would be made for expenditures which were dependent on the proceeds from the field. This would mean that no deduction could be made for overriding royalties payable to a financier or a licensee who had farmed into a block. UKOITC argued that this would impact adversely on most existing financing arrangements. The Inland Revenue was concerned about the potential loss of revenue, and did not feel that the case for deductions had been established.

UKOITC agreed that the proposed uplift of 50% was not unreasonable to the larger companies which had relatively cheap finance, but was oppressive for small companies which were very reliant on bank finance. They proposed that companies should be able to choose between the 50% uplift and actual interest paid to third parties (but not to other members of the same group). The Revenue was concerned about the additional complexity of this arrangement and the possibility of excessive interest being paid to financiers and thus were unwilling to meet the request.

Individual oil companies, including all the majors, made their own representations. These largely reiterated the views of UKOITC. There was some surprise in the Inland Revenue that the US-based companies complained about the proposed cancellation of accumulated losses for corporation tax purposes as they were not affected to nearly the same extent as UK-based companies. UKOITC subsequently submitted a document summarising their main views. These reiterated the points made above and added some others. One was the need for a mechanism which would automatically reduce or eliminate PRT as a consequence of falling oil prices, rising costs or disappointing production. This would also help to encourage the development of marginal fields. The Committee also expressed the view that PRT should be entirely independent of corporation tax.

Views of DEN

Senior officials at DEN felt that the encouragement of marginal fields was best done through the remission of royalties (free of any further PRT or corporation tax). They felt that this was preferable to a variable rate PRT. They also did not favour putting PRT on a whole North Sea basis. This would delay receipts and, as participation had to be on a field basis, would cause great practical complications.

Views of banking sector

Other representations on PRT were received, especially from the banking sector. A detailed note from Morgan Guaranty emphasised the adverse effects of the combination of a high overall tax rate with the field-by-field basis for PRT on the investor's debt service capacity. Lenders would be inclined to require amortisation of field development loans out of close to 100% of the available cash flow from the field. This would be more rapid than the wishes of the licensees, and could provide a substantial disincentive to make the investment. It was also argued that on some (but not all) assumptions the non-deductibility of loan interest was not compensated by the proposed uplift. The company also argued that the charging of PRT on third-party tariffs would make the financing of pipelines more difficult.

Lazards reiterated the concerns about the field-by-field basis for PRT and emphasised the view that lenders instinctively distrusted a system where interest payments were not tax deductible. Morgan Grenfell emphasised the extra risk to lenders in providing development finance on limited or non-recourse terms based on prospective field production. Such finance was increasingly in demand in the UKCS, and the disallowance of both interest and over-riding royalty payments for PRT would materially impair the ability of investors to finance their field developments. The Association of British Independent Oil Companies (BRINDEX) also emphasised the importance of debt finance to the smaller oil companies and the range of circumstances where 50% uplift would not compensate for the non-deductibility of interest for PRT. They also felt that over-riding royalties to lenders were true financing costs and should be deductible.

Mr Dell meets the companies

In the light of these representations Mr Dell reviewed the position with senior Treasury and Inland Revenue officials in early November. It was noted that there was universal concern among respondents to the field-by-field basis and further work on the cost of this to the companies was felt necessary. The Paymaster also decided that soon, when the Oil Taxation Bill was published, he would meet with representatives of the companies to discuss the provisions and provide them with illustrative calculations of the effects of the tax on a set of fields based on rates of 50%, 55%, 60% and 65%. The companies would be given the opportunity to comment and submit their own calculations. The Paymaster would also make it clear that, while he understood the need for tax stability, the companies should also understand that the rate might have to be changed in the event of major oil price movements.

The Bill was published on 19th November and the Paymaster met with senior representatives of around thirty oil companies that afternoon. The discussion centred on how the profitability and acceptability of investments should be measured, including choice of appropriate discount rates and whether absolute profits or profits per barrel were appropriate. The Paymaster emphasised that he was wanting to have a full dialogue with officials and himself when appropriate.

Further studies within Government

Meanwhile work was continuing on a range of elements of the package. The Inland Revenue produced estimates of the amounts of tax revenues which would be postponed if PRT was levied on a company rather than field basis. With a tax rate of 55% these amounted to £20 million, £75 million, and £60 million over the first three years. Work also progressed on the question of the appropriate rate. This had to be determined in the context of the total Government take, the expected returns to investors, and the need to encourage the companies to opt for state participation. By mid-October there was agreement within Government that PRT should be a prior charge which reduced the range of possible rates. Officials from DEN, Inland Revenue and the Treasury made calculations based on the indicative PRT rates noted above. The DEN employed oil prices of $10, and $7.50 in this work. A further dimension to the calculations which now had to be taken into account was the cost escalation relating to field developments. This was reaching alarming proportions, and a case where the costs were double their original values was now considered plausible. For PRT rates in the 50%-65% range the corresponding total Government takes as a share of profits were in the 78%–85% range. The effect on investment depended on the criteria employed by the companies, and DEN's view at this time was that with a 20% real rate of return as the economic cut-off, a PRT rate of above 50% would be risky. The Treasury felt that minimum rates of return in the 15%–18% range were appropriate and that the PRT rate could be in the 55%–60% range. The corresponding total Government takes of 78%–85% could be compared with 78% under the state participation route.

Nicholas Kaldor's suggestions

After the Oil Taxation Bill was published the question of the appropriate rate then became intermingled with the question of the protection of marginal fields. As noted above the DEN favoured royalty remission (free of tax) as the most efficient way to tackle the problem, but there was some interest in a system with a variable rate PRT. Lord Nicholas Kaldor, Special Adviser in the Treasury, proposed an alternative mechanism whereby the rate would continue to be flat, but, where the profit per barrel fell below a specified level, there would be a tax repayment to bring the net position into line with this minimum. A further possibility suggested by Kaldor was to establish that the tax should not exceed the amount which would leave profits equal to a specified percentage of the total capital expenditure relating to the field in question. The issue was discussed further among senior officials at the Policy Coordinating Committee in early December. There was no support for the idea of underwriting a minimum rate of return to encourage marginal fields (which had been suggested by a director of Shell), but the idea of a graduated tax related to the return on investment with the rate increasing to its full rate after field pay-back was felt to be more interesting.

Further taxation plus state participation prohibitive?

Further strong representation was received by the Chancellor from the Chairman of BP in mid-December. The view was expressed that, because of the Government's combined approach on taxation and participation, several companies were contemplating pulling out of the North Sea. The Chancellor met with the Paymaster and a senior official to discuss this alarming prospect. The uncertainties over the details of participation and the PRT rate were felt to be troublesome for investors, but these would shortly be clarified, and the companies would surely not abandon their North Sea stakes before the terms were fully known. The general view was that the alarm was not justified, but that confidence required some restoration.

Further representations from industry

Meanwhile UKOITC had assembled voluminous comments on the provisions in the Oil Taxation Bill. These dealt both with the large issues discussed above and many more technical ones where substantial monetary values were still involved. Among the latter were requests (1) that speedy relief be given for abortive exploration, (2) that an overall field loss be allowed against the profits of another, (3) to allow the full price paid by a purchaser of a stake in a block to be deductible, and (4) to allow initial storage and separation costs to be allowable. The view of the Revenue on the last issue was that there was a case for allowing separation costs but that storage was better regarded as part of the refining function and should not be deductible. UKOITC also argued that all decommissioning costs should be allowable instead of only those related to safety and anti-pollution requirements. The Inland Revenue's view was that they had followed the existing corporation tax rules which disallowed expenditure incurred in closing down a trade. Many other technical questions were raised, and the Inland Revenue agreed to consider further some issues both large and small.

This decision had also been encouraged by the bombardment of representations received in the closing weeks of 1974 from individual oil companies and other institutions particularly banks. Many of the points made repeated those made by UKOITC with the emphasis varying across companies. The Paymaster General felt that two of the larger issues frequently raised, namely possible relief for marginal fields, and the application of PRT to gas fields where contracts with BGC were already signed, deserved further attention. Amoco was particularly vociferous in protesting about the application of PRT to its gas contracts, and followed up its written and personal protests with a press advertising campaign. The Oil Taxation Bill had provided for limited relief for the Southern Basin fields by allowing all past capital expenditures as deductions but exempting receipts up to Budget Day. The companies argued strongly that this provision gave relief for only a quite limited time and that significant amounts of PRT would subsequently become payable.

Debate on PRT and Existing Gas contracts

The DEN also continued to feel that a more generous view should be taken of the treatment of the contracted gas fields. BGC pointed out that wholesale gas prices had increased somewhat, and that the producers should benefit to some extent. The Inland Revenue considered the matter further and indicated various options to the Paymaster. One straight-forward possibility was to completely exempt from PRT all Southern Basin gas fields where contracts had been signed with BGC. But it would not be easy to find a statutory formula for exempting Brent gas, for which Shell was pressing, but where the contract had not yet been signed. There would be an even greater difficulty in exempting Brent gas without also exempting Frigg where the contract was signed. The latter field had predominantly foreign licensees, and lack of consistency with the Government's publicly-stated policy of safeguarding the balance of payments could be alleged. Exempting all contracts from a specified future date with the implication that all future contracts be at a price which incorporated PRT liability might lead to much higher prices. Another possibility, namely making exemption depend on the gas price terms in the contract would be very difficult to translate into an acceptable statutory principle. Any formula would constitute a controversial form of tax exemption. The year ended with the matter unresolved.

Mr Dell requests studies on reliefs for marginal fields

Following receipt of the many representations Mr Dell requested further studies on reliefs for marginal fields. This generated much work and several possible methods, some of which reflected suggestions made in the industry representations. Remission of royalty (free of any subsequent PRT and corporation tax) was favoured by the Paymaster, with the decision being left to the discretion of the Secretary of State for Energy. This meant that there was no need to define a marginal field in the tax rules. The Inland Revenue was somewhat concerned that the deduction of remitted royalty for tax purposes would represent a major departure from tax principles, and could set a dangerous precedent for corporation tax.

The problem would be alleviated if royalty were actually paid and subsequently refunded. Another way to avoid the unfortunate precedent would be to remit royalties free of PRT but not of corporation tax. On balance the Revenue was against the notion of royalty remission free of either tax because of its conflict with sound tax principles.

With respect to mitigating the PRT burden the Revenue distinguished between measures which applied to all fields and those which applied only to identified marginal fields. Generally there was an objection of tax principle to discretionary determination and also a problem of objectively defining a marginal field. There was thus a *prima facie* case for giving particular attention to schemes which avoided the need to do so. Thus increasing both the uplift and the PRT rate was one possibility. This could reduce the liability on a marginal field while maintaining it on a highly profitable one. A drawback was the postponement of tax receipts from all fields. Other non-selective devices considered were (a) an extra allowance of a percentage of the revenues, and (b) a lower rate of PRT related to the first slice of revenues.

The employment of selective schemes required the identification of marginal fields. The Inland Revenue felt that this caused problems because the use of a plausible measure such as internal rate of return (IRR) required forecasts of future values which could well turn out to be quite wrong. This would necessitate provision of periodic reviews and retrospective revisions which would produce great complexity in the implementation of the scheme. A discretionary rather than statutory definition of marginal field could be employed, but the relevant authority (Treasury) would either have to disclose the definition to the industry or appear to act arbitrarily. Neither was attractive, and there were doubts about whether Parliament should be involved in taxation arrangements where substantial discretion was left to a Minister or Department.

The debate on marginal field reliefs continued inconclusively to the end of the year. Nicholas Kaldor added several suggestions including (a) a PRT exempt slice of income per barrel, (b) a guaranteed minimum profit per barrel, and (c) a guaranteed minimum profit per field expressed as a percentage of capital expenditure. None of these ideas found much favour with the Inland Revenue. Senior Treasury and Inland Revenue officials had a further meeting with the main investors. The result was a Minute to Mr Dell from the Deputy Secretary at the Treasury indicating that there was now a crisis of confidence with the industry, and the Government might now be resorting to overkill with respect to the combined tax and state participation proposals. There was now a need for sustained consultation and for substantial changes to the Oil Taxation Bill, as otherwise further exploration and development could be deterred. He himself favoured an increase in the uplift, exemption from PRT of Southern Basin gas contracts where the price was below equivalent energy prices, and for marginal fields either a further PRT-free tranche or a scheme with multiple PRT rates.

At the end of the year Mr Dell met with Treasury and Inland Revenue officials to consider further proposals for marginal fields. He expressed disapproval of a general increase in uplift and of the use of all schemes which entailed the use of measures of profitability of general applicability which would be difficult to justify and implement. He was also very lukewarm about multiple rate schemes which he felt could only be workable if the majority of fields paid at the standard rate. He favoured a scheme which had no explicit method of measuring profitability, and help for marginal fields could be given by a volume allowance or an equivalent cash allowance and by a simplification of one of Nicholas Kaldor's suggestions, namely an overriding limit on the PRT charge. The volume allowance would help small fields but would not help large ones such as Ninian whose expected rate of return was quite low. Thus another relief was necessary and he favoured a form which provided for a minimum profit per barrel ignoring capital allowances and before corporation tax. Discretionary relief of royalties could also be incorporated in the package.

Views of banking community

The year 1975 opened as the previous one had ended with hectic activity among all concerned with the Oil Taxation Bill. A new voice of concern was raised early in the year by the Governor of the Bank of England who reported to the Prime Minister that he had heard the disquieting news that some oil companies, particularly American ones, were thinking of leaving the North Sea. The DEN had been in direct touch with four of the main banks involved in financing North Sea developments and, in brief, they had indicated that there was no fundamental problem. There was, however, some deterioration in the climate of lending attributable mainly to (a) cost escalation in the UKCS, (b) uncertainty about the future of the British economy and (c) more selectivity in lending by all banks. The uncertainties of Government policy had also contributed to the changed climate. The work on the PRT Bill continued apace with renewed emphasis on the possible alleviation of the prospective burden on marginal fields. Inland Revenue officials examined the Paymaster's suggested scheme for a guaranteed minimum profit and (correctly) emphasised that this could not sensibly function without taking account of capital expenditure which was a main determinant of profitability. They also emphasised the distorting effect of the 100% marginal rate which would apply to a range of profitability just above the guaranteed level before the normal PRT rate triggered in.

Examination of proposed amendments to Bill

The suggestions of nineteen oil companies and other organisations which had proposed amendments to the Bill on the subject of marginal fields were closely scrutinised by officials. Eight organisations proposed a company rather than field basis, six suggested a production allowance, twelve suggested a form of variable or graduated tax (though not all on the same basis), and five supported an excess profits tax (often ill-defined). The suggestions were not mutually exclusive, with some companies requesting several reliefs. Mr Dell with senior officials held a meeting with representatives of the United Kingdom Offshore Operators'

Association (UKOOA) to discuss a report which the latter had prepared arguing that 25% was the highest tolerable rate of PRT. The Paymaster suggested that the rate could surely be higher when account was taken of (further) reliefs for marginal fields. In discussion the industry representatives suggested that only Forties, Brent, and Piper were not marginal fields at the current levels of costs. They indicated that at a price of $12 a field of 40 million tons was economic with no PRT but uneconomic with PRT at 25%. Viability was measured against criteria of 25% IRR and 0.4 profit/investment ratio. The Government representatives continued to argue that marginal field reliefs would eliminate PRT payments on such fields. The industry representatives feared that most future fields would be marginal. They highlighted the dramatic increase in construction costs and the delays in achieving first production.

UKOOA had proposed that individual companies be given options regarding which type of relief they could claim for marginal fields. It was explained that this reflected the differential impact of the various measures across fields. The Government representatives emphasised the practical difficulties of a system under which investors could choose from a menu of optional reliefs. On gas UKOOA argued that *all* fields should be exempt from PRT because all gas would be subject to price control given BGC's monopsony powers. UKOOA concluded by stating that the industry was basically opposed to PRT, but if the Government was determined to levy it then the various amendments proposed would be helpful.

A few days after this meeting on 16th January 1975, Mr Dell made a statement at the opening of the debate at the Committee Stage of the PRT Bill. He emphasised the Government's willingness to consider reliefs for marginal fields and proposed discretionary relief in the form of royalty remission free of PRT and possibly corporation tax as well. A number of non-discretionary reliefs had been proposed by the industry including (a) a lower PRT rate for marginal fields, (b) a graduated PRT perhaps related to profit per barrel, (c) an increased uplift, (d) exemption from PRT of a slice of revenues, and (e) a guaranteed minimum return. Consideration was also being given to further reliefs for gas. A considerable number of Government amendments were tabled on technical aspects in response to industry requests. The Paymaster said that he had now agreed in principle to other amendments which had not yet been tabled because consultations were still in progress. These included acceptance of the principle that initial treatment and storage costs should be deductible as should unrelieved losses over the life of a field at the time of its eventual abandonment.

Decision on PRT and old gas contracts

With respect to gas Conoco had submitted that on its Viking field the expected IRR was 25% without PRT and 21.5% with 50% PRT rate. Total had indicated that on Frigg its expected IRR was 13.8% without PRT and 11.3% with 40% PRT rate. Shell had been lobbying for the exemption of Brent gas. Heads of agreement had been reached with BGC, and the company was likely to sign the full agreement if PRT was not applied, but to renegotiate the terms if PRT was imposed. Because the gas was associated with oil, exemption created practical tax administration problems. At a meeting on 23rd January between the Paymaster General, Minister of State for Energy and senior officials the gas issue was discussed and agreement reached that there should be a PRT exemption for all gas contracts concluded with BGC by 30th June 1975. This would give time for the Brent contract to be finalised. The decision was made irrespective of the outcome of whatever proposals were agreed for reliefs on the grounds that these would not be sufficient to remove the fields from PRT. The need for apportionment of expenditure between oil and gas on the Brent field was troublesome but not impossible.

Further work on reliefs for marginal fields

Much inter-departmental work followed involving many computer-based calculations of the impact of the various reliefs for marginal fields referred to by the Paymaster. Sometimes there was concern that a relief (such as increased uplift) gave considerable benefit to fields which were clearly non-marginal. The associated difficulty of the definition of an acceptable rate of return to the investors also exercised officials. The oft-mentioned statement by the companies and banks that 25% in money-of-the day (MOD) terms was reasonable was not accepted without question by the Treasury which was mindful of the evidence it had received from industry (principally manufacturing) that a return of 10% in real terms was acceptable on low risk projects. It was acknowledged that the UKCS, particularly given the current frontier status of central and northern waters contained significant risks. Taking these and the current rampant inflation into account led to the tentative conclusion that real rates of return in the 12%-15% range were adequate. By today's standards the discussions with the companies and within Government were highly subjective.

In January 1975 when amendments to the PRT Bill were being actively considered the DEN submitted a report on prospects for the UKCS to the Official Committee on Energy. While a rapid growth of oil production was still foreseen the tenor of the report was to emphasise the cost escalation relating to construction costs and the delays to completion times. Uncertainty over PRT was now felt to be one factor (but not a major one) contributing to the uncertainties over finance which was now making it more difficult for the smaller companies to raise funds for field developments. Unusually in such documents an appendix was attached giving details of six recent press reports, all of them rather gloomy, about field development prospects. Mr Varley felt that the reports were exaggerating the true position.

Suggestions for PRT modifications continue

The Treasury continued to be bombarded with suggestions for PRT modifications. Conoco and Gulf proposed a scheme whereby the basic rate of PRT would be modified in accordance with a ratio where the numerator was taxable income as proposed in the PRT Bill and the denominator was cumulative investment costs (including exploration). The effective PRT rate would go down as the ratio went down. This would provide protection for marginal fields. Illustrative ranges for the ratio and PRT rates were attached. Senior officials at the Inland Revenue were unenthusiastic about pursuing the concept. One objection was the practical one that it was now too late in the progress of the Bill to undertake the detailed modelling necessary to evaluate the effects of the scheme. Another objection queried the whole idea of exempting some profits up to a defined return on investment. Practice had been to charge all profits to tax. This objection is difficult to defend when the object of the tax is to collect the economic rent from the exploitation of a natural resource. In fact the Conoco/Gulf Scheme with modifications, particularly redefining the numerator to be cumulative income (with no account of uplift), now forms the basis for the progressive sharing of profit oil between host Governments and oil companies in many countries under Production Sharing Contracts. The scheme and another very broadly similar one proposed by Patrick Jenkin the energy spokesman for the Opposition were not pursued further.

Decisions reached on further allowances

Following further experiments with the types of reliefs already identified, a meeting between the Paymaster General, Minister of State for Energy and senior officials was held on 31st January at which it was decided that uplift should be increased by an extra 25% and an oil allowance of one million tons per year with a cumulative total of ten million tons should also be introduced. In addition it was felt that there should be a safety net by which there would be a guarantee that the investor's rate of return would not as a consequence of PRT be brought below a specified figure. How this should be calculated was left for further discussion, but it could relate to (a) return on investment, (b) a minimum ratio as in the Conoco/Gulf proposal, or (c) a minimum profit per barrel. The Inland Revenue pointed out that the specified return would have to be on a pre-corporation tax basis as the latter was not levied on a field basis. They did not favour option (c) because it required the allocation of capital expenditure to each year of a field's life which would be difficult and complex. The Revenue also did not favour use of the income/investment ratio because there would be pressure to use it for calculating taxable capacity generally for PRT, which, as noted above, they did not favour. The favoured scheme was one where, if the profit in any year was less than, say, 30% of the field investment to date the PRT charge would be restricted to permit (if possible) the investor a 30% return (pre-corporation tax). It was recognised that this scheme would result in a profit zone immediately above a 30% return being wholly taken in PRT. This would be difficult to defend and a marginal relief provision would be desirable.

Further consultations with industry

By 10th February Treasury and Inland Revenue Ministers and senior officials had agreed on a package with 25% extra uplift, oil allowance, and a safety net the details of which should ensure that there was no tax rate of 100% immediately above it, and a PRT rate of either 45% or 50%. But further confidential consultations would be held with individual investors on the prospective effects on their own fields to gauge the likely reaction to final proposals. These consultations would not reveal the safety net idea. Work continued on the detailed design of the allowances. It was agreed that spreading of capital allowances through time to enable the utilisation of a greater proportion of the volume allowance in any year should not be permitted. It was agreed, however, that the limit of ten million tons should be available without any time restriction. By the middle of February the Revenue concluded that the safety net would specify that PRT was not payable when profit (excluding capital expenditure) was less than 30% of accumulated field investment on an annual basis. To ensure that 100% marginal rate did not apply, an overriding limit to PRT payable was specified as 80% of the excess of that profit above 30% of the accumulated field investment.

The oil companies quickly responded to the Inland Revenue proposals. They generally queried the worked examples provided to them on the grounds that the price employed by the Inland Revenue ($12.5 in real, 1974 terms) was too high and the costs of the fields too low. Generally they argued for larger allowances and a PRT rate below 50%. The largest companies continued to favour a flat rate of PRT while the medium-sized ones favoured a variable rate. The Deputy Chairman of BGC raised a particular point which was to prove troublesome. He argued that the application of PRT to new gas contracts produced anomalies from the application of the volume allowance. The Bill had specified that 40,000 cubic feet equated to 1 ton of oil for this purpose. He stated that on a thermal equivalence basis the gas figure should exceed 49,000 cubic feet. Further, because gas was sold at prices far below the thermal equivalence of oil the allowance for gas should be larger.

Ministers decide PRT scheme

Mr Dell presented his proposals to his Ministerial colleagues on 21st February. His memorandum summarised the feedback from the oil companies and his conclusion that the PRT package with 75% uplift, oil allowance of 10 million tons, safeguard as described above, and a rate of 45% constituted his recommended package. Using a price of £40 per ton total Government take on a large profitable field such as Forties would be around 77% and around 70% on a somewhat less profitable one. Discretionary royalty remission free of tax was included. Marginal fields received a substantial protection from the allowances. In discussion some of the Paymaster's colleagues showed concern that there might be criticism from their supporters with a rate as low as 45%. The CPRS had just reiterated its view that 50% was a more appropriate rate. Overall the view of the meeting was that the rate should be 45%. It was most important that field developments should not be held up. Accordingly the Paymaster was invited to make a statement on the subject. This occurred on 25th February. A Press Release showed how the system would operate with examples of hypothetical fields showing total Government take of around 71%. A case where the take was 73% is shown in Appendix 7.1.

Reaction of companies

The reaction of the oil companies and the press to the statement was generally favourable in the sense that the package was expected to encourage developments. Some backbenchers felt that the favourable reaction meant that the terms were too lenient. Work still continued on the detailed terms as the Bill still had some way to run. Many analysts were modelling the effects of the announced package. Petroleum Studies, consultants to the DEN, pointed out that, on a hypothetical and reasonably profitable field, the safety net provisions could ensure, that over a substantial part of its life, either reduced or zero PRT would be payable. The Press Release had not indicated this possibility. Walter Levy also noted this point and indicated further that, while the Treasury would benefit from oil price increases it would share significantly in the consequence of oil price falls. The company also compared the proposed terms with those announced by Norway and found that the UK terms were rather more favourable to investors. The conclusion was that investment should be encouraged. The Inland Revenue had difficulty in reconciling its own calculations of the impact of the safeguard provision with those of Petroleum Studies, but agreed that under plausible assumptions the hypothetical field could benefit from the safeguard, particularly in its later years. The Paymaster reported this, and added that it would be for the Government of the day to decide whether it should permit such a field to benefit from the safeguard after it had already yielded substantial returns on the investment.

Gas volume allowance

The subject of the treatment of gas for PRT involved further debate both within Government and with the industry. With respect to the oil allowance the DEN disputed BGC's claim that the conversion factor should be nearly 50,000 cubic feet = 1 ton of oil compared to 40,000 cubic feet in the Bill, but agreed that 45,000 might have been better, but it was not felt worthwhile to amend the Bill. The industry had also made representation to the effect that, because gas prices for the Central and Northern North Sea were in the range 33%-50% of those for oil on a thermal equivalent basis, the volume allowance for gas should be increased by a factor of two or three to give comparable relief. A further relevant point was that unit costs were higher for gas. The DEN had some sympathy with this argument and felt that there was a case for a separate volume allowance for gas. The Inland Revenue remained sceptical, but agreed that in a mixed oil and gas field the allowance could be used first against oil to the maximum extent possible. In a field such as Brent where oil was to be subject to PRT but gas was exempt, complex rules regarding apportionment of costs between the two would be necessary.

Valuation

Pricing and valuation issues provoked substantial controversy as the Bill progressed. The Treasury and Inland Revenue had decided at an early stage in the life of the Labour Government that an administered price for North Sea oil was impracticable given the volatile nature of the world market and the preferred approach was to extend existing legislation in Section 485 of the Income and Corporation Taxes Act, 1970 by which an arm's length price could be substituted where a sale took place at an artificial price between associates, one of which was non-resident for tax purposes. The Section did not apply to sales between associates which were both resident in the UK for tax purposes. The Inland Revenue proposed to reinforce and extend the Section to provide a remedy against artificial transfer pricing by substituting an arm's length price in such transactions. There would also be a need to modify the concept of arm's length price because of a perceived concern that there were many third party transactions which were not a fair guide to the price at which large volumes would change hands. In the design of the detailed provisions of the Bill the Inland Revenue generally followed the rules on price determination contained in the Petroleum Regulations for royalty purposes. Thus for PRT the profits would be based on open market values. Following the Regulations these would be fairly closely related to spot prices. It was appreciated that these would be more volatile than those relating to long-term contracts but over time this would be a matter of swings and roundabouts as far as Government take was concerned. For non-arm's length sales the intention would be to apply values which could be expected to obtain in transactions between third parties. In determining such values account would be taken of the circumstances of third party sales. For example, the case of a transaction involving a small, weak seller to a non-associated company should not be conclusive evidence of the value to be adopted for a national sale by a major producer to its refining affiliate. Attention would be paid to the bargaining powers of the parties involved. In determining whether a particular transaction was arm's length or not tests would be applied concerning particularly (a) whether the contract price was the sole consideration for the sale, (b) whether the terms of the sale were affected by any other special relationship between the parties, and (c) whether the seller had any interest in the subsequent disposal of the oil.

During the passage of the Bill there was much debate on the details of the valuation provisions. Originally the Bill provided for half-yearly valuations, but, in response to Opposition arguments that these would lag too far behind current values, monthly valuations were proposed. Some companies objected to this on the ground that it would tie the tax value to the spot market, but the Inland Revenue argued that the yardstick was not a spot sale (which might be a single cargo), but an arm's length sale involving the same quantity as that delivered to the affiliate during the month in question. The Paymaster emphasised to Esso that isolated and minor third party sales would not be the determining factor in valuation, and appropriate account would be taken of all types of actual third-party sales. At Report Stage an Opposition amendment that contracts between connected parties should be treated as at arm's length was rejected.

Amendments during passage of Bill

Nevertheless, a considerable number of Opposition amendments were accepted during the progress of the Bill. These included provisions to permit for PRT (a) some hire payments to qualify for uplift, (b) overall loss relief for an abandoned field, and (c) treatment and storage costs as deductions. Some relaxation of the rules on interest allowable for corporation tax was also made on the Opposition's initiative. The amount of consultation with the industry was reckoned to be unprecedented. The debate in Parliament was very long but was not curtailed. Substantial Government Amendments were made as a consequence of the consultations. The eventual very complex package reflected the serious attention given to the proposals of the industry. The volume allowance, increase in the uplift to 75%, and the safeguard, all emerged from the protracted discussions with the industry. In his own account of the origins of PRT published long after the Oil Taxation Act, 1975 was passed[3] Mr Edmund Dell emphasises the lack of detailed knowledge within Government of the likely investment costs of the oil fields and how attention had to be given to the (rapidly increasing) cost estimates of the oil companies.

Reflections on PRT package

In retrospect it is clear that, after the uncertainties of the long consultation process were over, the enacted 1975 package did not hinder the pace of exploration and development. With the benefit of hindsight it is easy to state that the total Government take could have been greater, but it should be remembered that the estimates of profitability were made on the basis of oil prices of around $12 and nobody was predicting the very much higher levels achieved only a few years later, with the North Sea price averaging over $36 in 1980. It was also clear that macroeconomic considerations made the attainment of early production with the associated balance of payments benefits the first priority. At this time the balance of trade was in very serious deficit due in no small part to the escalation in oil prices.

The concept of a special tax tailored to collect a share of the economic rents from petroleum exploitation is widely acknowledged around the world to be justifiable. Such a tax should be targeted on the economic rents and so a profit-related scheme is more efficient than a barrelage or severance tax which was rightly rejected. The scope for debate is with the detailed structural features. Modern thinking favours schemes which are directly targeted on the economic rents measured by the size of the expected returns. That proposed by Conoco/Gulf was such a scheme with the rate of tax increasing with the income/investment ratio. Another scheme based on returns above a specified achieved threshold rate of return was published in a famous article around the time when the package was enacted.[4] The Inland Revenue was unenthusiastic about such schemes, preferring more orthodox ones with a conventional tax base and single rate. The introduction of the safeguard concept was a recognition of the need for a device to ensure that the tax would not bite on very low investment returns. Unfortunately the chosen device also produced benefits to fields of high profitability in the later years of their lives.

The concept of basing the new tax on project cash flows was certainly unorthodox at the time but fully consistent with conceptual thinking on the subject of resource rent taxation. The decision to make the individual field the basis of the tax was controversial and quite tough by world standards. To levy it on a company-wide basis would certainly have delayed receipts and the device adopted by the Norwegians which restricted the commencement of the utilisation of capital allowances until the field to which the expenditures related came on stream would have substantially moderated the deferment of revenues without attracting so much controversy. Another alternative which is now widely employed around the world makes the contract area activities the basis of the tax. This accelerates revenues but still gives incentives to explore for and develop satellite deposits without provoking the many subsequent debates over the definition of a field.

The concept of the investment uplift instead of loan interest, while controversial at the time, is defensible as a proxy, at least in part, for the necessary return on investment. It can be compared with the threshold rate of return under the resource rent tax. It also substantially contributes to making the tax progressively related to profits, and assists marginal fields relatively more than highly profitable ones. The concept was also employed in the corresponding legislation in the other North Sea countries, though the deductibility of loan interest as well in these countries is less easy to justify.

The volume allowance was justified by the need to protect small fields in particular which were presumed to be generally less profitable. The net present values (NPVs) would be small and the allowance would shelter a higher proportion of these returns compared to those on larger fields. The allowance is quite crude, however. Its value varies directly with the oil price. When downside protection is most required its value becomes less. The issue came up when the problem of its value in gas fields was debated but, given the volatility of oil prices, it surfaced more widely later. The assumption that small fields were inherently less profitable could also be questioned. This issue was to surface when the application of PRT to the Southern gas basin was re-examined.

In the evolution of the PRT system there was a tendency to look at the various allowances separately. This was understandable as in the consultation process the industry highlighted individual issues and proposed solutions. Less attention was thus paid to the interaction of all the various allowances. This had unintended consequences such as the possible incentives to "gold plating" of investments and reliefs to projects of high profitability. The decision to exempt "old" gas contracts from PRT was made before the safeguard allowance was determined. Given the final form of the combined allowances it is possible that the total reliefs for the "old" gas fields would have left tolerable returns to investors.

The eventual decision to separate the taxation system from state participation was fully justified. The notion of employing taxation differentials to exhort investors to accept state participation was a very odd one. The activity of collecting a perceived adequate share of the expected economic rents is separate from issues of control and regulation. A well-recognised principle in policy design is that the number of policy instruments should match the number of policy objectives. The intermingling of the two through PRT would have produced dramatic complexity and uncertain consequences for Government revenues.

To administer PRT and corporation tax as it applied to the UKCS the Inland Revenue established the Oil Taxation Office (OTO), in 1975. This was an imaginative and forward-looking decision. Given the emerging importance and specialised nature of the sector a corresponding specialist group of officials was highly appropriate. The large sums at stake justified the existence of the group whose responsibilities included the assessment of the PRT liabilities of the relevant companies and the corporation tax liabilities of oil companies within and outside the ring fence. Over the years it worked closely with the Inland Revenue Policy Division which dealt with the interpretation and implementation of the legislation and advised on the need for any changes. This arrangement has advantages both from Government and taxpayers' viewpoints.

Resolving doubts over taxation of foreign companies

In the 1970s attention had to be given to the issue of effective taxation of foreign companies operating in the UKCS. There were doubts surrounding the effectiveness of reliance on the licence condition of central management and context in the UK (as discussed in Chapter 1). To eradicate these doubts, in Section 38 of the Finance Act 1973, the Government introduced specific legislation extending the territorial charge to tax following the principles established in the Law of the Sea Convention on the Continental Shelf (referred to in Chapter 1). This deemed designated areas of the Continental Shelf to be part of the UK for the purpose of all direct taxes and treated all profits and gains from exploration and exploitation activities on the Shelf as profits and gains from activities in the UK proper. It also ensured that non-resident employees engaged on the Shelf could be taxed in the UK by treating earnings from duties performed on the Shelf as earnings from the UK proper. This legislation enabled non-resident contractors and employees to be taxed. Prior to 1973 the only way by which non-resident contractors' profits could be taxed was to try to attribute the profits to some base on the UK mainland. And prior to that date the UK could not tax non-resident employees working on the Shelf.

However, even with the Finance Act 1973 in place, there were still situations where the UK could not tax overseas companies. The problem was the UK's tax treaties. Firstly, some of them did not include the UKCS as part of the UK and the business profits articles (applying to companies) and the independent services articles (applying to partnerships and self employed individuals) provided that the UK could only tax profits attributable to a permanent establishment or fixed base in the UK proper. There were similar problems with taxing employees of non-resident employers. It became important to ensure that those tax treaties that did not extend to the Shelf were amended to do so. In practice this was not a big issue for profits from the disposal of oil and gas because of the safeguard of the licence condition referred to above and the fact that in practice it was difficult to exploit the UK's reserves (particularly with a landing requirement as a condition of the licence) without having a base on the UK mainland.

But there was a further major problem so far as overseas contractors were concerned. The OECD-based terms of UK treaties that required a "permanent establishment" or "fixed base" raised considerable doubts over whether offshore facilities could be regarded as such. Some suggested that even a production platform could not be regarded as a fixed base, but clearly there were even more doubts in relation to mobile vessels. The result was that it was likely that a significant amount of ancillary profits derived from the UKCS could not be taxed in the UK unless the network of tax treaties was amended speedily to incorporate provisions similar to those included in Section 38 of Finance Act 1973 (thus overriding the normal OECD-based tax treaty articles). So in the late 1970s and throughout the 1980s the Inland Revenue had the difficult task of attempting to amend/renegotiate treaties, especially those with other North Sea countries from which offshore contractors could operate directly, but also with other countries with companies engaged in offshore activities – particularly those with lower tax rates than the UK. This was not always easy as many countries without offshore oil demanded important concessions in return.

The 1973 legislation also included provisions which enabled the Revenue to collect tax unpaid by non-resident contractors and employees from the UK licensees in whose area they were engaged. There were provisions which exempted the licensee from this obligation if the Revenue was satisfied that the contractor in question would definitely meet its tax liabilities. These provisions were disliked by the oil industry because they were at that time the only provisions in UK tax law that make one person liable for the tax debts of another.

Taxation and transmedian fields

Another issue which caused some controversy was that of taxing transmedian line fields. The UK and Norway Governments realised that normal OECD-based principles that enabled tax to be charged if there was a permanent establishment in the country would create enormous problems in relation to transmedian line fields, particularly where the platform(s) were situated wholly on the Shelf of one country. So special rules were agreed with Norway that provided for tax to follow the unitisation principle. This meant that the UK could only tax its own licensees in respect of profits derived from its own oil or gas, and Norway could only charge its own licensees on profits from Norwegian hydrocarbons, irrespective of on whose Shelf the installations were situated. However, while Norway swiftly accepted this principle, it was very difficult to persuade other countries, particularly the Netherlands, to follow suit.

Two important personal tax issues

The Tax Treaty with Norway provided that employees should pay tax solely to the country on whose Shelf they worked. It is understood that this rule generally worked well. However, it did create problems for workers in the Frigg field where installations were situated on both sides of the median line, three of which were linked with bridges. A practical solution had to be found to divide tax between the two countries based on the principles established in the Tax Treaty. The agreement between the two countries led to some enforced adjustment of working routines in the field to give employees the opportunity to work on the UK side and pay the (lower) UK taxes! Because of the amount of gas being supplied to the UK from Frigg it was very important to both countries that the division of tax between the two countries should not be a cause for discontent to the workforce.

The second personal tax issue concerned North Sea divers most of whom claimed they were self employed. The Revenue concluded that they were not and insisted that PAYE be charged. Self-employed status meant that the divers could claim substantially more expenses and pay a lot less tax as a result. The outcome of the Revenue decision was uproar among divers who threatened to leave the UKCS in droves, and from those that preferred to remain there was the persistent threat of industrial action which would have severely delayed work on a number of offshore developments. After prolonged debate it was decided in the late 1970s to introduce a special tax provision that treated all divers as self-employed regardless of whether they were actually employed. The result of this special tax treatment reveals the concern at that time to remove impediments to the development of the North Sea.

Appendix 7.1

Effects of Tax Structure on a Hypothetical North Sea Field: Total over Life of Field

		£ million (rounded)	% of Net Revenue
	REVENUE		
1.	Production (million tons)	80	
2.	Price per ton (£)	35	
3.	**Gross Revenue (1×2)**	**2800**	
	EXPENSES		
4.	Operating Costs	400	
5.	Capital Expenditure	400	
6.	Interest Payments (say)	200	
7.	**Total Expenses (4+5+6)**	**1000**	
8.	Net Revenue (before Royalty and Tax) (3–7)	1800	100
9.	**Royalty**	**310**	**17**
	PRT LIABILITY		
10.	Allowances for PRT (4+ (175% of 5) + 9)	1410	
11.	Oil Allowance (10 million tons maximum)	350	
12.	**Total PRT Allowances (10+11)**	**1760**	
13.	Taxable Base for PRT (3–12)	1040	
14.	**PRT at 45%**	**470**	
	CORPORATION TAX LIABILITY		
15.	**Allowances for Corporation Tax (4+5+6+9+14)**	**1780**	
16.	Taxable Base for Corporation Tax (3–15)	1020	
17.	**Corporation Tax at 52%**	**530**	**30**
18.	**Total Government Take (9+14+17)**	**1310**	**73**
19.	**Company Take (8–18)**	**490**	**27**

Note: The Table does not illustrate the effect of the "safeguard" or the remissions of royalty. No remission of royalty would be necessary in this example. It is possible, depending on costs, prices and the profile of production, that the safeguard might affect the PRT liability in a field of this size when production began to decline towards the end of the life of the field.

8 Providing for BNOC and enhanced state control

Mid-1970s period of high drama in exploration and development

This period of major and controversial legislation was also one of memorable exploration successes and field developments. The remarkable volumes of reserves discovered and the large average size of discovery are shown in Appendices 8.1 and 8.2. The number of significant discoveries was also notable (Appendix 8.3), while the exploration success rate (Appendix 8.4) was high by international standards. Expenditures on field developments grew dramatically at this time, and in real terms attained their highest ever levels (Appendix 8.5). Oil production commenced in 1975 but was confidently predicted soon to overtake gas production (Appendix 8.6). These years saw the development of some of the historically most important fields in the history of the province (Appendix 8.7). In many respects this was the most exciting time in the whole history of North Sea oil and gas.

Multiple facets of enhanced state involvement

As already indicated, following the change of Government in 1974, the policy debates on how to increase the state's control proceeded apace in parallel with those on the taxation side. The issues involved were wide-ranging including not only participation in fields by the state, but depletion policy, the enhancement of opportunities for UK contractors, refining and disposal policy, and the case for a state oil buying agency on the lines of that performed by BGC for gas. Following early decisions by Ministers that all these subjects deserved detailed consideration the DEN was requested to prepare proposals. It was also asked to consider how the negotiations over participation with the other companies should be conducted.

What state body?

The DEN paper for the Ministerial group was produced in early May 1974. With respect to the structure of participation it was argued that the state body which administered participation would have three main functions namely (a) securing

Government revenue, (b) exercising control over depletion rates and the disposal/ destination of oil, and (c) direct participation in production, including possibly exploration in future licences held on its own account. While the state body would be an agent for central Government it should act in a commercial fashion. It would have to be responsive to Government on policy questions and would have much less autonomy than a conventional nationalised industry. To fulfil its upstream functions it would need a staff of 1,000 or more, and further specialised personnel would be required if it entered the downstream business.

With respect to the choice of state agency DEN considered afresh the case for employing (a) BGC, (b) BP, (c) DEN, and (d) a new Corporation. Employing BGC had some advantages, namely comparative freedom from Parliamentary pressures, the existence of a nucleus of relevant staff (albeit small), and the avoidance of two public sector bodies in the petroleum area. On the other hand there were disadvantages of employing BGC. The character of the company would be radically altered as oil interests would soon dominate the gas ones. Further, BGC was already heavily involved with downstream gas and should not be distracted from these responsibilities. There would also be a conflict between BGC as the buyer of gas and the oil companies as gas producers. The idea of making BGC the agent for buying gas alone with another agent buying oil introduced practical difficulties. These would be most obvious with mixed fields. The conclusion was that there were overriding arguments against the employment of BGC as the state entity.

With respect to BP the perceived advantages were that there would be fewer problems with staff recruitment and that the company's position inside the UK and perhaps internationally would be strengthened through its enhanced access to oil supplies. There were numerous perceived disadvantages, however. Effective Government control would be unlikely and the company clearly wanted to maintain its commercial freedom. Given the 52% private shareholding the company could not act in a non-commercial way as the Government's agent, such as for cutting back production. There would be a potential cause of conflict in the valuation of oil sold to BP's downstream subsidiaries. There would most likely be charges of discrimination, as the net effect would be to transfer oil mostly from foreign-owned companies to the only wholly British major company. This could imperil the commercial status of the company in other parts of the world which in due course would result in a loss of earnings remitted to the UK. The conclusion was thus that there was a clear case against the employment of BP as the agent for participation.

There were also strong arguments against the use of the DEN as the state entity. The principal one was that the Department was not suitable for undertaking commercial activities, because of lack of familiarity and the difficulties of taking decisions unhampered by political and Parliamentary pressures. Looking ahead a distinctly odd situation could arise where the Department could award licences to itself. In general the Secretary of State could not be his own licensee. There were further complications such as potential penalties in respect of pollution and safety which it would be inappropriate for the Secretary of State to share.

What role for BNOC?

Given all the above a new body was the most appropriate solution. Government control could be asserted uninhibited by attitudes and constitutional arrangements inherited from the past. The new British National Oil Corporation (BNOC) could be made subject to specific and general direction by the Secretary of State. With respect to the form of participation there were two main possibilities. The first one would involve the creation of new companies in which BNOC had a shareholding determined by the degree of participation. These companies would become the licensees and would take all decisions relating to licence activities. The second approach would involve commercial agreements with the oil companies. BNOC would become a joint licensee and relations among all the licensees would be determined by an Operating Agreement. Each partner would own its appropriate share of the oil produced.

The DEN felt that the first approach, while it had the attraction of giving BNOC a direct voice in the disposal of all oil produced, had several disadvantages. The oil companies would be very unwilling to renegotiate for participation on the basis of the new company structure because the disposal of the oil would be determined by the company in which BNOC would probably have a majority holding. There could also be problems with Companies Act requirements giving safeguards to minority shareholders when the Government wanted the company to act in a non-commercial fashion. In practice the company structure would not give substantially greater control than a commercial agreement giving right to, say, 51% of the oil plus royalty oil. Thus the commercial agreement was the favoured approach. The appropriate details of the Operating Agreements required further study.

Relationship between Government and BNOC

The financial relationship between the Government and BNOC required clarification in primary legislation along with a statement of its functions and constitution. Provision needed to be made to control BNOC's capital expenditure and for the receipt of profits. A mechanism would be necessary to ensure that BNOC conducted its work economically and did not divert its (prospectively ample) funds to activities not desired by the Government.

State Buying Agency?

The DEN paper also considered the case for and against the establishment of a State Buying Agency which would buy all the oil produced from the UKCS at a price which could be the market value, a cost-related value, or an intermediate value. There were several arguments in favour of the Agency. It would provide control over the disposal of all oil produced, while participation at 51% plus royalty oil gave just over 57% of the total. If the oil were bought at values below world prices the benefits could be passed on in the form of lower industrial costs.

The Agency would have an option on whether to sell the oil back to the companies or refine and distribute it itself. The Agency, unlike BNOC, would not require a public contribution to costs.

But there were felt to be serious disadvantages to the scheme. The notion of passing on the economic rent from North Sea oil in lower prices to consumers rather than in taxes and dividend payments to the state was unlikely to be in the public interest. The energy market would be distorted with oil demand increased at the expense of coal and nuclear power which current energy policy wanted to promote. The resource value of North Sea oil was measured at its world market value, and its sale in the UK at a price below this level represented a misallocation of reserves. The extra tax revenues which the Government would receive were expected to be substantial (in 1980 more than the current total revenue from corporation tax), and could be deployed in the wider national interest. There would be great practical difficulties in importing OPEC oil at world values while maintaining lower prices for North Sea oil. These arguments were very cogent and convincing. The contrast with the current position with respect to gas was not discussed!

The DEN paper also recognised several other practical problems with the Buying Agency concept. Compelling current licensees to sell the oil at below the world price would probably be contrary to international law unless compensation was given based on the difference between the stipulated selling price and the world value. This would frustrate the object of the exercise. The policy would have a disincentive effect on oil company behaviour. Thus there could be no assurance of what prospective profits would be on future discoveries since the buying price would be fixed separately for each field. Further, there would be no assured access to crude which was very important to integrated companies. Borrowing to finance field developments would become more difficult, particularly through the increasingly common production payment method. A State Buying Agency would not actively engage in the management of fields. This would require participation as well. It was also felt that the Buying Agency concept would be more likely than participation to run foul of the Treaty of Rome. Article 37 specifically forbad the establishment of new state monopolies restricting trade among member states. This was more vulnerable than participation, and was important because a policy objective was to control exports without explicit breach of the Treaty. The danger of a challenge under Article 37 would be reduced if only a proportion of the oil was sold to a state body. The overall conclusion of DEN was thus that a State Buying Agency was not the best method of achieving the Government's objectives relating to (a) increase in state take, (b) participation in exploration and development, and (c) control over the disposal of the oil.

Changes to licensing Regulations

The DEN paper also produced proposals for substantial changes to the licensing Regulations. These were to apply to existing as well as future licences. The legal advice from the FCO was that the exercise of the proposed new powers could amount to expropriation of proprietary rights (at least in part) without compensation, would be contrary to international law, and would justify claims against the UK Government. The mere taking of the powers would not be unlawful, however, and DEN felt that, where use of the powers was likely to involve international difficulties, they would not be applied. The extra powers would constitute a deterrent which need not be used, but which would ensure that licensees were more ready to adhere to the Government's wishes without formal direction.

Proposed powers far-reaching

The extra powers were numerous and far-reaching. A major one related to depletion policy. It was proposed that the Secretary of State be empowered to order the start of production, and/or an increase in the rate of production to a level specified by him in exercising judgement on what was in the national interest. It was also proposed that development plans for all new fields should be submitted to the Secretary of State for approval. He would be able to suggest amendments and even reject plans if they were not in accordance with good oilfield practice. He would also be empowered to call for exploration programmes on a discretionary basis where he felt there was insufficient activity, be able to reject a proposed programme which he felt was unsatisfactory, and revoke a licence if no satisfactory programme were implemented. The Secretary of State would also have powers to require a licensee to give him any information relating to his operations in licensed areas. Such powers would cover financial, technical and geological information. The Secretary of State would also have the power to appoint an auditor to inspect a licensee's records where the response to a request for information was deemed unsatisfactory. In addition, the Secretary of State would have power to authorise early release of all information supplied by a licensee concerning his operations. This was to promote interest by new players. A further proposal was that licensees would have to obtain permission before any gas was flared. This would be granted only if it were necessary for technical or economic reasons. Yet further proposals were that the Secretary of State be empowered to take royalty in kind and to remit royalty at his discretion to encourage production which would not otherwise be economic. Others were that the Secretary of State would have authority to revoke a licence in the event of a substantial change in its ownership or control. There was a concern that such changes could affect the nationality and/or competence of the licensee. It was noted that there would be EEC implications of this power if it were exercised to the detriment of EEC nationals. Finally, it was proposed that the Secretary of State have powers to approve any arrangements whereby the profits from a licence were to be shared between a licensee and another party (such as a bank). This was to preserve the Government's take from the North Sea.

Proposed powers on pipelines

In addition to all the above the DEN paper also made separate proposals with respect to pipelines. Back in 1963–1964 when preparations were being made for the Continental Shelf Bill the issue of control over pipelines had been discussed within the Ministry of Power. At that time the Pipelines Act, 1962 gave the Government substantial powers over onshore pipelines, including control over their development, and safety regulations surrounding their construction and use. The Ministry had considered applying the totality of the Act to the UKCS, but this would have included a large number of provisions which could not conceivably apply to offshore situations. To select only certain provisions would have been quite complicated, and in the end adequate powers had not been included in the Continental Shelf Act. Several new controls were now proposed. Thus the Secretary of State would have powers to authorise the construction of all offshore pipelines. These would have to be constructed such that third parties could use them. Third party use on existing pipelines would also be required at charges which could be fixed by the Secretary of State. This would help to facilitate the development of small fields and curtail the proliferation of pipelines. The Secretary of State would also be empowered to instigate measures to control pollution and protect the health and safety of workers. He would also have powers to call for all relevant information, including that relating to arrangements whereby profits from using a pipeline were shared with persons other than the owner.

The DEN paper considered at length the question of whether BNOC should participate in pipelines as another means of increasing control. While the case was not as clear-cut as for participation in fields there were sound reasons in favour of so doing. Thus pipelines were generally an integral part of the exploitation of a field and the oil companies would be more readily persuaded to accept participation in fields if the related pipeline costs were also included. BNOC should acquire a capability in all aspects of the business and participation in pipelines would be consistent with this objective. BNOC involvement would give the Government more information and assurance regarding the control of pipeline developments. BNOC should have the power to participate in all pipelines, but priority would be given to pipelines associated with fields where participation was sought.

The paper even considered whether powers should be taken to bring some or all future pipelines under complete public ownership. Such a step would be politically attractive, it would give the Government complete control, and could put pressure on licensees. It would avoid the need for complex controls, and would give BNOC the opportunity to build a pipeline where it was in the national interest. It was recognised that there were arguments against such a measure. There would be a substantial increase in public expenditure probably without a commensurate increase in Government returns, and there could be friction with the oil companies regarding the operation of the pipelines. The arguments appeared to be fairly evenly balanced, but the DEN concluded that there was not a case for full national ownership of all pipelines. But to ensure full flexibility there was a case for providing that BNOC could take full ownership in a future line where it was in the national interest so to do.

Finally, the paper raised the question of whether BNOC should participate in downstream activities. An answer to this required the completion of major studies on the use of North Sea oil, but BNOC should be given the powers to participate, though these powers should be kept in reserve to minimise investment uncertainty.

Mr Varley's proposals

In a covering Memorandum to his Ministerial colleagues Mr Varley, Secretary of State for Energy, referred to the unsettled state of the world oil market, the importance of security of supply, the importance of being able to control North Sea oil exports, and the heavy economic penalty from having to share North Sea oil with others in emergency situations. These had all been emphasised in a paper produced by the CPRS. Mr Varley pointed out that explicit control of exports to EEC countries would certainly contravene the Treaty of Rome in a non-emergency and might even be contrary to it in an emergency. To avoid a confrontation the best course of action was to set up a system which would permit control over supplies without explicitly breaching the Treaty. The best means was to take Government ownership of the oil which would reduce to a minimum dependence on directives, formal and informal, to the oil companies, which in any case might not be obeyed. Thus BNOC oil could be sold to companies which would refine and distribute it in the UK. While this would constitute only just over 57% of the oil there would be considerable leverage over the disposal of the remainder because the oil companies would not wish to imperil their chances of buying back some BNOC oil by disposing of their own oil contrary to the Government's wishes.

Covert control over the companies could also be strengthened by the necessity of the licensees to obtain consents under their licences, and their desire to obtain new licences in the next Round. While this policy did not ensure that there would be no challenge, there was a reasonable chance that it would procure a major share of North Sea oil without confrontation with the EEC. Mr Varley noted further that there was a case for moving towards a managed market as in France where refineries, imports, and petrol sales required state authorisation. This would increase the Government's leverage over the companies and help ensure that North Sea oil was kept for internal use. Such measures were designed to ensure that the UK had the ability to retain North Sea oil when required, but separate studies were being conducted on the question of whether in more normal world market conditions it was desirable to do so or not. Mr Varley was confident that state participation was consistent with the Treaty of Rome and that there should be no retaliation by foreign Governments (such as the USA) because the measures would not discriminate against foreign companies. Regarding tactics for the renegotiation of contracts Mr Varley was keen that they commence straight away to convey evidence of the Government's determination to secure participation. He also felt it important to ensure that the companies were not allowed to present a united front, and to concentrate on those most vulnerable to pressure such as those very dependent on an assured supply of North Sea crude.

White Paper indicates main policy headings

There was broad Ministerial agreement to the main proposals of the Secretary of State and further work proceeded with emphasis on the complex taxation/participation relationship and what should be published in the forthcoming White Paper. Because of the perceived need to make an early statement and the substantial time required to finalise details, the White Paper (*United Kingdom Offshore Oil and Gas Policy*, Cmnd 5696, 11th July 1974) provided only the main policy headings apart from those relating to taxation where fuller details were given (see Chapter 7). The intention to take majority participation in future licences, to procure such participation by voluntary agreement in existing commercial fields, to establish BNOC, and to extend powers to control physical production and pipelines were highlighted. The White Paper also made specific reference to Scotland and Wales. To placate Scottish opinion it was agreed that it be reaffirmed that Scotland and other regions in need of development should obtain benefits from the exploitation of North Sea oil. It was decided that the headquarters of the Offshore Supplies Office and the main office of BNOC should be in Scotland. While Ministers were anxious to ensure that Scotland should be seen to benefit from North Sea oil they were even more anxious to avoid any direct linkage between oil revenues and the financing of the proposed Scottish Development Agency (a new organisation proposed by Mr Ross, the Secretary of State for Scotland). Any direct linkage would raise the question of hypothecation of revenues. The White Paper thus took care to refer to the funding of development activities from central Government funds. The Chancellor of the Exchequer was even more cautious, highlighting the dangers of making individual spending commitments before the overall macroeconomic situation and national priorities had been clarified.

Functions and constitution of BNOC

Meanwhile detailed work continued on issues raised in the DEN's large paper. One was the functions and constitution of BNOC. By the summer of 1974 the DEN saw the Corporation's key functions on the lines of those described above in relation to participation, but also highlighted its trading functions, including importation of oil, exploration and production abroad, and its ability to raise funds from overseas. Securing Government control was regarded as paramount given the vast prospective sums involved. Thus DEN recommended that the Secretary of State have specific as well as general powers of direction which could be applied to any aspect of BNOC's activities. Such powers would be more extensive than those generally applied to nationalised industries. With respect to capital structure it was felt that an orthodox arrangement, with capital being remunerated by interest and dividend payments was not appropriate for the special circumstances of the North Sea, because BNOC would effectively be an agent for the Government in raising funds and collecting (non-tax) revenues. It was felt that Government must have complete control over the likely enormous cash flows. This could best be achieved by an arrangement whereby BNOC would automatically pay the Government all its participation receipts. A National Oil Account would be established and initially amounts equivalent to BNOC's needs would be paid into it from the Consolidated Fund. Participation revenues would then be paid in and the balance returned to the Exchequer. The absence of a conventional capital structure would not impair BNOC's ability to borrow from abroad. This would be important for balance of payments reasons. The main advantages of the scheme were felt to be (a) administrative simplicity, (b) a clear reflection of one of BNOC's prime functions, namely to collect money for the state, and (c) the elimination of arguments over claims by BNOC to retain some of the revenues!

Continuing on the theme of financial control the DEN gave consideration to two specific issues, namely (a) how to ensure that BNOC minimised its costs given the likely large disparity between revenues and costs and the partly non-commercial character of its operations, and (b) how to reconcile the exercise of control by Government and the legitimate interests of BNOC's prospective private sector partners, including the Operating Agreements. It was felt that, for future discoveries, the Secretary of State should decide expeditiously whether to exercise his participation option. This would be based on the field development plan. For ongoing expenditures and revisions to development plans it was acknowledged that there would have to be give and take with BNOC's partners. One reassurance which could be important to the private sector would be to provide that budgets require a majority stake of 60%-70% to be carried. Normally there would not be a divergence of interest, but where this did arise, such as when the Government wanted the licensees to act non-commercially, the 51% BNOC vote plus its position as a licensee would give the Corporation a very strong position.

Detailed work on depletion policy

Concurrently with these studies work was also proceeding on the subject of depletion policy with the DEN again in the lead role. The context of the perceived need for a depletion policy was that, as a barrel of oil could only be used once, a depletion strategy was necessary to ensure that it was used at the time which produced maximum benefit. A major feature of the problem was the great uncertainties surrounding the size of oil reserves both in the UKCS and the world as a whole, and about prospective oil prices. These made it unwise if not impossible to come to a firm view on the subject and indicated the merits of having flexible arrangements. At late 1974 the DEN estimated ultimate recoverable oil reserves in the 3 billion – 5 billion tons range with the higher and lower volumes having a broadly equal probability.[1]

Oil price forecasting difficult

Following the four-fold increase in 1973, oil price forecasting was extremely uncertain with past experience giving little guide. It was felt that up to the mid-1980s consumer response to high prices could be limited as was the scope for substitution for OPEC oil, and OPEC could be able to maintain high prices ($7 per barrel or more at 1974 prices). In the long-term the UK would again be dependent on imported oil. So long as the oil consuming world was substantially dependent on OPEC oil imported oil could be regarded as insecure. Domestic production clearly gave protection against this, and adequate security could be achieved if home production was in the range of 75% – 80% of consumption.

Macroeconomic considerations relating to depletion rates

Macroeconomic considerations, particularly the balance of payments, were also important, and these pointed to a higher degree of self-sufficiency than the security arguments. The current economic strategy was based on achieving a broad balance in the current account by 1978–1979, by which time the accumulated debt could be £15 – £20 billion. The strategy involved attainment of oil self-sufficiency by 1979. This would require the maximum possible production currently foreseeable. If the medium-term strategy were successful then it might be possible to deplete the oil reserves more slowly at around self-sufficiency levels. But if balance of payments problems persisted an oil export surplus of around 20 million tons per year, which would be available with reserves of only 3 billion tons, would make a substantial difference to the balance of payments. If total reserves turned out to be near the upper estimate of 5 billion tons production could rise to a plateau of 90–120 million tons above consumption by 1990 and the choice of depletion rate would become much more significant. A fast oil depletion rate would permit a higher growth in consumption in the 1980s but in the 1990s there would need to be a curtailment to the growth of consumption which could cause problems. Alternatively the proceeds of depleting oil in the 1980s could be productively invested either at home or abroad to provide for future needs. But there would be practical problems of chan-nelling such large reserves into profitable investments particularly at home, and there might be advantages in leaving substantial amounts of oil in the ground, particularly if prices were to rise beyond the early 1980s. Rapid depletion for purposes of personal or public consumption would be difficult to justify if, from around 2000, adequate growth with a large oil import bill were to be sustained.

The DEN produced several possible scenarios of UK oil production and demand. On the basis of high reserves of 5 billion tons unrestrained production could rise continuously to as much as 250 million tons in 1990. One (high) demand scenario indicated 160 million tons in 1990 indicating a surplus of 90 million tons. If reserves were only 3 billion tons unrestrained production could increase to 140 million tons in 1980 and maintain a plateau at around that rate until 1990 with self sufficiency disappearing just after 1988.[2]

Case for slowing depletion rate

Against this background there was a case for intervening to modify prospective depletion rates. Any combination of delaying the issue of new licences, delaying new field developments, and reducing production on existing fields was possible. Combinations of controls which could achieve the twin objectives of maximum production to 1980 and maximum flexibility thereafter were produced by DEN on the basis of the high and low reserves indicated above. Common assumptions were that production cuts of 20% would be imposed on all finds made before the end of 1975, delays of two years in the development of later discoveries in present licences followed by production cuts, and development delays of three years imposed on finds from future licences. The effect under the case with high reserves was to curtail production by as much as 80 million tons in the late 1980s, while in the case of the low reserves the reduction was much smaller at around 20 million tons in the early 1980s. Varying the extent of production cuts and development delays could produce the flexibility which was desired given the uncertainties.

The DEN also examined the effects of these controls on the profitability of fields. Using large, medium, and small model fields for illustrative purposes it was found that on the basis of oil prices of $7.50 per barrel in real 1974 terms, while rates of return and net present values at 10% were reduced by the various measures, they remained attractive to investors.

Mr Varley's proposed statement

On the basis of these arguments and studies Mr Varley proposed to make a statement to Parliament. This noted the case for an interventionist policy in short summary form and emphasised a number of safeguards for investors. With respect to new field developments no delays would be imposed on finds made before the end of 1975, and if they were imposed on later discoveries there would be full consultation with the industry so that premature investment was avoided. With respect to production there would be no cuts imposed on fields from discoveries already made or from new finds made before the end of 1975, until 1982 at the very earliest. Further, no cuts in production would be made from any later discovery made under an existing licence until 150% of the capital investment in the field had been recovered. In deciding on the allocation and extent of the use of the powers full regard would be given to the technical and economic characteristics of the fields in question. Consultations would take place with the industry in the period of notice before any production cut would be implemented. These proposals were approved by Ministers.

Industry opposes depletion controls

Meanwhile the oil companies had been expressing their strong opposition to the whole concept of depletion controls ever since the subject was raised in the July White Paper. By November when it had become clear that the Government was determined to press ahead with an interventionist policy, the industry decided that it should concentrate on obtaining what it perceived as damage-limiting measures. In a submission UKOOA argued that, with respect to production controls, as a preliminary to any system of control the Secretary of State and the licensees concerned should agree for each discovered field for which development expenditure had commenced, a production profile which would serve as a base during the life of the field.[3] A profile would similarly be agreed for future fields when their development was approved. The profiles would be based on good oilfield practice, and by mutual agreement this would be reviewed in the light of the performance of the field. UKOOA then argued that at any given time the minimum rate of production for the UKCS would be defined as the sum of the output profiles as agreed above, and the Secretary of State should have this sum firmly in mind before the development of new fields was agreed. If the Government then determined that production should be reduced below the total of the agreed profiles UKOOA argued that the Government take (in royalty and tax) should be adjusted so that the licensees were not penalised by the cutbacks. The industry should also be fully consulted in advance of any Government decision. UKOOA also argued that after such consultation an affirmative Statutory Instrument should be laid before Parliament, and this should provide that a period of notice would be required before any statutory control came into effect. The suggested minimum period of notice was six months and one year if the production cuts exceeded 10%. It was also argued that field development controls could result in undue delays between discoveries and development/production. Accordingly, licensees so constrained should receive compensation. Finally, UKOOA noted that the envisaged controls could also give the Government power to compel licensees to start up development and production operations. Such powers were felt to be unnecessary as licensees would quickly develop all commercial fields given proper incentives.

Mr Varley's depletion policy statement and assurances

These arguments went unheeded and Mr Varley made his Statement to Parliament on 6th December 1974 based on the terms approved earlier by his Ministerial colleagues. The only additions were that production cuts would generally be limited to 20% at most, and that in coming to decisions the Government would take into account the needs of the offshore supplies market in Scotland and elsewhere and the benefits of stability in that market. The Varley Assurances as they became known certainly did give the Government much flexibility from 1982 onwards. Whether they adequately reduced the areas of uncertainty remained an issue. With respect to field development delays the length of the period was left unclear. It was also unclear whether delays would apply selectively or not, and, if selectively, how choices would be made. Similarly, if production cuts were to be made it was unclear whether they would apply to all fields or not, and again, if selectively, how the unfortunate ones would be chosen. But the whole subject of depletion policy was to be considered further in the forthcoming Petroleum and Submarine Pipelines Bill, and the famous Varley Assurances were essentially regarded as a necessary first statement to clarify the general intentions and reduce the uncertainties, albeit to a modest degree, with the facilitation of field development financing agreements being a prime motive.

Disposal and refinery policy

On the very same day that he made his Parliamentary statement on depletion policy Mr Varley also made a statement on North Sea disposal and refinery policy. Work on this subject had been proceeding for several months, and had gained extra momentum when it became clear that BP planned to export a substantial proportion of oil from the Forties field. In November 1974 a report with policy proposals was produced by the DEN. It was estimated that, if left to themselves, the companies generally would export much North Sea oil while substituting it for similar quality crudes currently being imported. If the British Government pursued further sulphur restrictions, the free-market degree of substitution would amount to about 30% – 40% of the crude oil refined in the UK. It was also estimated that about 20% of the UK's crude oil intake could not be reasonably met by North Sea oil which lacked the characteristics needed to make products such as bitumen and lubricating oil.

Conflicting considerations in determining policy

The DEN recognised that most distortions of the market pattern of disposal would involve economic costs to the companies, possibly to the nation as a whole, and be incompatible with EEC obligations. It was also recognised, however, that the retention of extra amounts of North Sea oil would add slightly to security of supply. It was felt that it was commonly expected that North Sea oil would be used mainly in the UK. Policy decisions had to balance these conflicting considerations.

The Department identified three main commercial factors in determining the pattern of disposal of North Sea oil. The first was its sulphur content which was very low and gave it a price premium over most Middle East crudes, worth about $3.5 per ton in Europe and as much as $6 per ton in the USA. The North Sea oil premium emanated from its ability to produce low sulphur fuel and gas oils without expensive desulphurisation. The second commercial factor was freight costs. These were substantially more expensive for products than crude. The differential was currently $1.10 – $1.70 to Rotterdam and $2.80 – $4.20 to the US East Coast. The expected continuation of the surplus of crude oil tankers could increase this differential. The third factor was refinery capacity. Consumption growth had slowed down due to the recent dramatic increase in oil prices, and on current plans excess refining capacity of around 30 million tons was foreseen in the first half of the 1980s. But further refinery upgrading would be required to meet the likely increased demand for light distillates, while demand for fuel oil and heavy distillates would fall.

With the aid of a study prepared for the Department by the consultancy company Petroleum Economics the effects of these three factors were calculated for the current situation, and the costs of many other patterns of disposal were compared with the pattern likely to be adopted by the companies on strictly commercial grounds in the early 1980s. The latter was calculated to involve

120 million tons being refined in the UK of which 24% would be from North Sea oil.[4] One main finding of the study was that a policy which involved a higher utilisation of existing refinery capacity would result in higher freight costs which could be offset by the refinery margin gained on the additional production. But because Europe was expected to have a surplus of refining capacity the net effect was likely to be a loss of around £60 million in foreign exchange. Similarly, a policy requiring the construction of additional refining capacity in the UK would involve not only additional product exports with the associated freight costs but also the capital costs of the extra and arguably unnecessary capacity, estimated at £3 per ton. Refining a higher proportion of North Sea crude would involve extra freight costs without any offsetting gains in refining margins. The overall cost could be £85 million in foreign exchange. It was also estimated that a policy of self-sufficiency in light distillates would involve some loss in the low sulphur premium from North Sea oil but would eliminate high cost imports of naphtha and petrol.

Security of supply issues and EEC

There were complex security of supply issues relating to disposal and refining policy. The UK was likely to be a participant in an international emergency oil sharing scheme. With respect to the EEC, Article 34 of the Treaty of Rome prohibited quantitative restrictions on exports among Member States. Article 36 over-ruled Article 34 if restrictions were imposed on grounds of public policy or national security. There was doubt about whether a restriction on the disposal of North Sea oil would be permitted under Article 36, but it would be illegal under Article 34. The DEN considered that covert action in peacetime to retain North Sea oil in the UK would be less likely to be challenged than such action in an emergency. But the Commission would be aware of the commercial considerations affecting the disposal of North Sea oil, was probably already suspicious of UK intentions, and would probably challenge any unlikely commercial pattern of its disposal.

Role of BNOC in security of supply

The emergence of BNOC would be helpful with respect to oil security. It would not be subject to Article 34 but to Article 37 which forbad discrimination by nationalised industries among nationals of Member States. If BNOC were to supply its 57% of North Sea oil (royalty plus 51% participation) to the UK market in normal times, it would be difficult for the Commission to claim discrimination, as it would be natural for a new company to concentrate on its home market. But in normal times even if the UK were supplied 100% from the North Sea it would be publicly and economically advantageous to share some of it with EEC partners. Even if a large proportion were normally exported to the EEC in an emergency somewhat more of the UK's share of the total could probably be retained without provoking adverse comment. There were advantages in covertly increasing the proportion normally disposed of in the UK market. From a security viewpoint there were advantages in exports being in the cargo market or short-term contracts rather than long-term ones. It was also noteworthy that exports to non-EEC destinations could be banned in an emergency without infringing the Treaty of Rome.

The DEN emphasised the security gains from ensuring that in normal times the UK market was supplied from UK refineries. Elimination of reliance on imports of any product would put the UK in a better position to choose which products should bear the demand restraint in an emergency. If there were no international sharing scheme product self-sufficiency was even more important. While refinery policy had little effect generally on industrial development it was particularly important to ensure that feedstocks to the petrochemical sector were not interrupted as the result would be an immediate reduction in that industry's output.

Conclusions of DEN on disposal/refining policy

Summing up, the DEN estimated that to increase refining of North Sea oil to around 60% of the UK's needs would cost around £45 million per year, which should be acceptable on political and security grounds. If all the products were retained the cost would rise to over £100 million per year with no significant gain to security. Because of all the uncertainties policies needed to be flexible. Thus the recommendation was that there should be refining of North Sea oil equivalent to 50%–60% of UK demand with product exports allowed in normal times. Refinery projects should be supported in general terms and there should be an aim to procure self-sufficiency in products by the early 1980s. Companies should be pressed to achieve the substantial increase in catcracking capacity required to achieve this.

Mr Varley's statement

Mr Varley prepared a draft Statement based on the DEN studies, received approval from his Ministerial colleagues, and made the Statement to the House of Commons on 6th December 1974. It referred to the reasonable expectation that up to two-thirds of North Sea oil should be refined in the UK depending on the level of production. He stated that he was looking for an increase in upgrading capacity to minimise imports of products. The implications for national oil policy of new refinery developments were so important that powers were needed to include this aspect in their evaluation. Measures to this effect would be included in the forthcoming Petroleum Bill.

Proposed functions of BNOC

Work on the Petroleum Bill had been proceeding for several months and in the summer of 1974 Mr Varley prepared a paper for his Ministerial colleagues on BNOC's proposed functions. With respect to current licences BNOC's main role should be to act as the Government's agent for participation in renegotiated licences. This involved the collection of revenues as well as control. By 1980 with 51% participation in all fields the excess of revenues over costs could be £1,800 million. BNOC would also be a licensee in the fields in which it participated, and would have the same responsibilities and powers as the other licensees. But the Corporation would not behave purely like a commercial licensee because a main objective was to enable the Government to influence the licensees' decisions in the national interest which could sometimes be against their commercial interests. It was recognised that such influence would often have to be covert because it might be contrary to international obligations, particularly under the Treaty of Rome. Thus BNOC could be used to control the rate of depletion. This would be through its influence on the management of the fields and distinct from the power which the Secretary of State would have. BNOC could also influence co-licensees to buy British goods and to ensure that all gas was offered to BGC.

Adequate Government control

It was recognised that some of these actions would be against BNOC's commercial interests, and so, in determining the structure of BNOC, it was important to ensure that there was adequate Government control. In considering the method of control international obligations had to be borne in mind. Decisions on the terms and acceptability of renegotiation had to remain a matter for the Government, though detailed negotiation of the terms might be a matter for BNOC. But this should take place in accordance with principles laid down by Ministers which would cover the important elements of Operating Agreements including (a) voting procedures, (b) capital budgets, (c) appointment of operator, and (d) sale of gas. With respect to future licences BNOC would have the option to participate in future discoveries. The percentage share would be left open. In due course BNOC would also be able to acquire licences entirely on its own account.

Control over disposal

In due course when it acquired experience BNOC would have a more pro-active role including participation in pipelines, terminals, and storage, handling royalties in kind, and eventually engaging in refining and distribution, as well as selling back its oil to co-licensees or other oil companies. The Government was keenly interested in the disposal arrangements, as one of the main purposes of participation was to ensure that North Sea oil was kept in the UK. The Government thus had to have full powers to enable it to ensure that BNOC's oil was sold only to companies which would keep it in the UK if required. Thus the power of direction on the sale of oil was required. BNOC should also be able to operate overseas with the consent of the Secretary of State. This would include the acquisition of licences abroad and the importation of oil.

Constitutionally BNOC would be in a different position from other nationalised industries and would be a statutory body under the control of the Secretary of State for Energy. It would thus not be a Crown corporation and the staff would not be civil servants. The additional powers which the Secretary of State would have compared to other nationalised industries would include specific as well as general powers of direction applicable to any aspect of BNOC's activities. Occasional specific directions could be kept secret and it might be necessary to ensure that directions were not published.

Members of BNOC Board

The members of the BNOC Board would be appointed by the Secretary of State. As one of the main objectives was to ensure that BNOC was responsive to the national interest there should be official representation on the Board. It was recognised that this raised questions of (a) the effect on the relationship of other Board members to the Secretary of State, (b) the Secretary of State's accountability to Parliament, and (c) the degree of independence which BNOC enjoyed. These issues required further consideration. BNOC would require a large and expert staff, and it was felt that within a few years at least 1,000 employees would be required. There would be problems in finding staff of the desired calibre.

Ministerial decisions on BNOC

Mr Varley presented his proposals to his Ministerial colleagues at a meeting in early July 1974. In discussion some concern was expressed that the industry might be caused unnecessary alarm if all the functions proposed for BNOC were paraded at the outset, and some Ministers felt that if negotiations with the oil companies on participation were still in progress when the Bill was introduced to Parliament, there might be merit in delaying the introduction of clauses likely to cause particular concern to a later stage in the Bill's progress. The view was also expressed that the calculations of the expected revenues were based on market prices, and there was a case for reserving the right to sell North Sea oil at below world market values. Some concern was also expressed about the proposal that the Government must have full power to enable it to ensure that BNOC oil was sold only to companies which would keep it in the UK if this were deemed necessary. It would hardly be able to exercise such powers discreetly, and there was a strong probability of a protest from EEC partners that the Treaty of Rome was being breached. But it was also argued by some Ministers that the Treaty did not compel the UK to offer oil abroad if on commercial grounds a more attractive home market existed. One of the reasons for establishing BNOC was to ensure that the domestic market should become the natural outlet for North Sea oil. At the end of the meeting Mr Varley was given approval to prepare the necessary legislation based on his submission, but he should take into account the points raised above by his colleagues, particularly those of the Foreign and Commonwealth Secretary on the issue that BNOC oil would only be sold to companies which should keep it in the UK. This subject deserved further study.

Need for National Oil Account?

Work continued on these and related matters particularly within the DEN and Treasury. Although the concept of the National Oil Account had support there was not unanimous approval. One Treasury view was that although it was a lesser evil than the idea of an Oil Fund it was (a) unnecessary, (b) an attempt to make respectable tax arrangements which the Inland Revenue believed would be unacceptable if normal accounting procedures were employed, and (c) a standing invitation to the Scots to claim that the income belonged to Scotland. The main reason for having the Account was apparently to provide a mechanism for handling PRT offset payments, but it was not obvious what advantage this mechanism had compared to the alternatives of (a) payments directly by BNOC, and (b) payments directly from DEN Votes. The Oil Account was unnecessary under either method.

As work developed on the subject the case for some form of Oil Account gained support, but views differed on whether it should be a Government or BNOC one. By August 1974 there was agreement that the Corporation would be initially funded from the National Loans Fund into an Oil Account, and BNOC would pay all revenues less operating costs, other expenses, and corporation tax into the Account. BNOC capital expenditures would be met from the Account and by borrowing on its own account. Offset payments would also come from the Account. The remaining balance would be paid into the Consolidated Fund.

A Government account had four advantages namely (a) it avoided Estimates procedures, (b) it met Treasury and Parliamentary financial proprieties, (c) it gave the Government absolute control over BNOC's finances because BNOC would have to request any retention of funds, and (d) it gave Parliament a proper opportunity to question the Accounting Officer on the administration of the Account. The disadvantages were (a) that direct payment of large sums to the oil companies from a Government Account would be readily identifiable, and could inflame some elements of Parliamentary and public opinion, and (b) the ability of the Comptroller and Auditor General and the Public Accounts Committee to scrutinise the Account could lead to unwelcome interventions, particularly with respect to offset payments.

The advantages of a BNOC Account were (a) it would not be subject to Estimates procedures, (b) the DEN would not be directly accountable for offset payments made by BNOC on its own account, and (c) large sums paid to the oil companies in offset payments from a BNOC Account would be somewhat concealed and thus less provocative to public opinion. The disadvantages were (a) surplus revenues would lie with BNOC, and there was some risk of friction between the parties with the Government having to claim revenues from a BNOC Account, (b) BNOC and its accounts would still be subject to Parliamentary scrutiny, and Government involvement in offset payments would become known, and (c) tax and participation were Government responsibilities and it would be inconsistent if equalisation payments were made from a non-Government account.

On balance DEN officials favoured a Government Account. This would be transparent and was in accordance with the reality of Government responsibility and control. Interestingly, the Permanent Under Secretary (the Accounting Officer) had reservations. In the Treasury the preference was for a BNOC Account with the reduced DEN accountability being emphasised as an advantage. The Paymaster General and Lord Balogh, Minister of State at DEN, favoured a Government Account, and in the event this view prevailed.

Location of BNOC head office

The July White Paper precipitated attention to a quite different issue regarding BNOC, namely the location of its head office. The White Paper identified Scotland but left the precise location for later decision. Immediately after the publication of the White Paper the DEN received many submissions in favour of particular locations from local Chambers of Commerce and Councils. The Leith Chamber of Commerce cited Leith's strategic location in relation to North Sea developments and its proximity to Edinburgh. The Edinburgh Chamber emphasised the proximity of the Scottish Office and the financial institutions. The Scottish Council for Development and Industry writing from Aberdeen emphasised the advantages of BNOC's location alongside the operations of the oil companies which were now concentrating in Aberdeen. Lothian Region Liberal Council argued that the local facilities in Edinburgh were the best available in Scotland for commercial activity.

DEN officials approached the issue by listing the relevant considerations in determining the optimal location. These were felt to be (a) the attractiveness of a location to professional staff recruited from elsewhere, (b) the ease of recruitment locally of both professional and support staff, and (c) travel facilities to (1) oil company main headquarters, (2) oil company operations centres, and (3) Government headquarter offices in London and Scotland. The Civil Service Department which was currently involved in an exercise on the dispersal of Government offices from London had been asked for their views on Glasgow, Edinburgh, Aberdeen and Dundee. The Under Secretary involved had little to say about Aberdeen and Dundee, but gave his opinion that Glasgow was generally regarded by his staff as a black spot, and was bottom of the league of a number of possible dispersal sites being considered.

Views of DEN on BNOC office location

After further deliberation DEN officials summed up their views at late July 1974. Any location in Scotland was felt to be inferior to London as the offices of the companies in Aberdeen were executive ones only, while decisions on policy and expenditures were made in London. BNOC's involvement in oil operations in Aberdeen was regarded as unimportant, and comparisons could thus be based on other factors. It was even suggested that future oil activities might not be based in Aberdeen! An important consideration was the ease of communications with

London. Glasgow was best placed in this respect as it had more direct flights to London than any other Scottish city. Aberdeen was furthest from London and there were few flights between the two, though it was acknowledged that these could be improved. Recruitment of local personnel, mostly for support purposes, would be easier in Glasgow. There was already intense pressure on clerical and secretarial services in Aberdeen and to a less extent in Edinburgh. There was a need to attract high calibre oil men into the location chosen for the new company. It was felt that on this score Edinburgh was clearly the most attractive. Glasgow had a bad image though it was noted that it would be possible to commute from Edinburgh! Aberdeen, and even more so Dundee, would not offer a sufficiently sophisticated social life to attract top people! This last point had been made to DEN by the Chairman of UKOOA. The DEN took all this seriously, arguing that the importance of location image should not be underestimated. With respect to office space it was noted that Glasgow had most to offer, with Dundee likely to have space readily available, but Aberdeen, and to a less extent Edinburgh had less available.

With respect to proximity to other organisations it was noted that the Scottish Office was in Edinburgh and there was an Industrial Development Office in Glasgow where the Offshore Supplies Office (OSO) was already located. It was acknowledged, however, that BNOC would not have any formal links with either. It was also acknowledged that Edinburgh and Glasgow were far from Aberdeen, the centre of operations.

The conclusion of DEN officials was that on the basis of present transport patterns BNOC should be cited in Glasgow. But if air services from Edinburgh could be improved then Edinburgh should be chosen. There was no systematic discussion of industrial logic or the concept of critical mass or oil cluster in the formation of these judgements.

Views of Scottish Office on location of BNOC office

By the end of July 1974, Scottish Office officials expressed their view to DEN that the serious contenders were Aberdeen and Glasgow. Aberdeen was the centre of action for North Sea oil, but labour and housing were more readily available in Glasgow, which also had the advantage of the presence of the OSO and a Department of Industry Office. The Secretary of State for Scotland, Mr Willie Ross, sent his views to Mr Varley in early August 1974. In his view the principal candidates were Glasgow and Edinburgh and his preference was for Glasgow. He dismissed the acknowledged obvious claims of Aberdeen on the grounds that it was very overcrowded with pressure on housing and office buildings, and because decisions which were the concern of BNOC were taken elsewhere. Locating BNOC in Dundee would merely serve to spread the centres of decision-making on oil and would not be attractive to senior management. Edinburgh had no strong links with oil operations or need of the type of employment offered. Glasgow was the industrial and commercial capital of Scotland and boasted superior communications with London. The presence of BNOC and the OSO in Glasgow could counteract the attractions of Edinburgh to the oil companies. Accommodation was easier to provide in Glasgow.

Views of industry and continuing debate

DEN officials considered this and informally consulted BP and Shell at a senior level. Both were quite convinced that BNOC should be located in Aberdeen. Each was moving the control of their operations to Aberdeen and expected the industry generally to follow. Edinburgh was their second choice because it was an attractive city. Glasgow was a bad third mainly because it would be hard to attract staff there. The senior executive of Burmah consulted preferred Edinburgh because of the high pressure on local resources in Aberdeen, though DEN officials noted that Burmah was itself contemplating the relocation of its Northern operations to Aberdeen. On balance DEN officials supported Edinburgh over Aberdeen because of the resource pressure in the latter, with Glasgow being the least attractive. The Minister of State, Lord Balogh, also preferred Edinburgh on the grounds of easier staff recruitment. The Parliamentary Secretary, Dr Gavin Strang, supported Edinburgh on the grounds that the case for Glasgow was weakened by the decision of the Ministry of Defence to announce the relocation of 6,000 jobs from London to Glasgow! On the other hand another decision, namely to accord Edinburgh development area status, made Mr Ross firmly against Edinburgh being the location for BNOC!

The debate between DEN and the Scottish Office continued. In mid-August Mr Varley informed the Scottish Secretary that he would not press the claims of Aberdeen, despite the evidence that the oil companies were moving their offices there, on the grounds, stressed by Mr Ross, that local resources were overstretched. These judgements were made without detailed examination of this subject, and in particular without considering whether the industrial logic and synergy were more important considerations. A thoughtful editorial in the *Press and Journal* put the matter in perspective by pointing out that most oil companies had chosen Aberdeen as their Scottish location for carefully thought out cogent reasons of operational effectiveness, and were not blind to the obvious but essentially short-term soluble problems of housing and labour shortage.[5] Mr Varley continued to prefer Edinburgh to Glasgow on the grounds of recruitment advantages and so informed Mr Ross. The response of Mr Ross was to remind Mr Varley that the original decision to locate BNOC's headquarters in Scotland was the scope it would afford to draw the decision-making capability of the offshore industry and its suppliers to Scotland. He argued further that the greater the concentration of oil-related activities in one place the more likely it was to attract the industry. This conforms with industrial logic and synergy and the cluster concept, but Mr Ross argued that Glasgow was still the preferred location compared to Edinburgh on the grounds of readier availability of accommodation and communications with the south. On this occasion he did not even mention Aberdeen, despite its clear consistency with the criteria for the original decision to locate BNOC's head office in Scotland and the absence of such consistency with the other contenders.

The saga continued for some time. Officials and Ministers agreed that there was merit in leaving the decision until after the General Election. The issue was arousing increasing interest among Scottish politicians and local authorities. DEN officials also argued that there was merit in allowing BNOC itself to have an input into the decision. The lobbying continued. In November the Lord Provost of Glasgow met Mr Varley and argued that, because of problems of congestion, infrastructure, and communications, Aberdeen and Dundee were unsuitable, and the choice lay between Glasgow and Edinburgh. The former already had the largest proportion of civil servants for this type of employment. The city had more capacity to fill the job opportunities which would arise and had superior rail, road and air communications.

Mr John Smith, Parliamentary Under Secretary of State at the DEN, also gave his views. He did not even seriously consider Aberdeen and supported Glasgow over Edinburgh on what he termed regional and industrial considerations. The only case for Edinburgh was that it might be more attractive to senior management. But they could easily live in Edinburgh and work in Glasgow. This was now a common practice. Managers could also live in other areas outside Glasgow within easy travelling distance of the city centre. Local recruitment would be easier in Glasgow as would the availability of office space. Glasgow was closer to the industrial scene and he wanted to see oil developments more tilted towards the west to balance the picture.

Decision in favour of Glasgow

The issue dragged on to February 1975 when Mr Varley decided that he could agree to Glasgow as the location but asked Mr Ross to give him assurances of the ready availability of good quality office accommodation of an adequate size. The reply from Mr Ross was unhesitatingly positive: the Glasgow area, in addition to making the most commercial sense, offered the greatest assurance of good quality accommodation. This view was not endorsed by the Secretary of State for the Environment, Mr Crosland, whose Department incorporated the Property Services Agency (PSA). Reflecting the views of the PSA Mr Crosland informed Mr Varley that it would not be easy to find suitable accommodation in Glasgow.

The DEN had indicated to PSA Scotland that the initial requirements would be for around 200 staff (40,000 square feet), rising to around 160,000 square feet for the staff required by the early 1980s. PSA Scotland informed DEN that there was no accommodation in Glasgow of the magnitude of 160,000 sq. ft., and only one building, the Savoy Tower, which could house 200 staff. If this were not suitable then the staff would have to be dispersed across a number of smaller buildings. The advice was that in other Scottish cities there was no accommodation of adequate size in one building for 200 staff. The DEN felt that the two options were (a) to utilise the Savoy Tower in the first instance and then have a new office built for the longer term, or (b) to disperse the staff in a number of buildings. The latter would permit other cities to be considered. The preferred option was the first one.

This had the enthusiastic support of Mr Ross who urged an early announcement of Glasgow as the location to end the continuing pressures for the location to be elsewhere. Mr Varley duly made the announcement of Glasgow as the location to the House of Commons on 30th April 1975 during the debate on the Second Reading of the Petroleum and Submarine Pipelines Bill.

Predictably the announcement received a mixed reception. *The Oilman* surveyed political opinion in Scotland.[6] The Liberal Party's oil spokesman, Mr Malcolm Bruce, stated that the location decision was about as logical as citing the Fisheries Office in Birmingham! He felt that political expediency had outweighed the need to establish a significant Government presence in the region of the country in which the oil activities were concentrated. The Scottish Tory party spokesman, Mr Iain Sproat, similarly argued that as private industry had already chosen Aberdeen the Government should have done likewise. BNOC's employees would be isolated from the centres of activity. The Labour Party's Scottish Research Officer, Mr Alex Neil argued in favour of Glasgow on the grounds that (a) the Offshore Supplies Office of the DEN had already been established there, and (b) there would be a boost to employment in Glasgow which was one of the depressed regions of Britain. There were also longer term benefits from attracting more oil-related activity to Clydeside and of giving contracts to local industry. The North East of Scotland Development Agency, in further representation to the Scottish Office, reiterated the advantages of BNOC being located in Aberdeen close to the centre of oil operations and the people involved in the activity. The example of the location of Statoil, the Norwegian national oil company, in Stavanger the oil operations centre, and a very much smaller city than Aberdeen was cited with approval. The eventual total employment of around 1,000 people would be built up gradually over a number of years and the necessary accommodation could be developed accordingly. The City of Aberdeen Council similarly expressed its regrets at the Government's decision and requested that it be reconsidered in favour of Aberdeen.

The original decision prevailed and BNOC's head office was eventually established in Glasgow, but via a tortuous route. PSA Scotland was asked to negotiate terms for the Savoy Tower, but agreement could not be reached on the details of the terms. BNOC itself was unenthusiastic about the Savoy Tower. It examined several other buildings and eventually expressed a clear preference for Trident House, a new office block located near Glasgow airport. Scottish Ministers strongly opposed this site because it was outside the Glasgow city boundaries and could be regarded as a breach of the commitment made by Mr Varley in his speech in the House of Commons during the Second Reading of the Petroleum and Submarine Pipelines Bill. Trident House was in the Paisley local authority area. A further political irritation to the Scottish Secretary was its location in the constituency of an MP who had broken away from the Labour Party over the hotly debated subject of devolution. Mr Ross urged BNOC to consider other sites. This led to the suggestion of space in a large building in St. Vincent Street being built for the Scottish Amicable company. This had the support of Mr Ross, even though the rent was higher than for Trident House, and the Corporation relocated to 150 St. Vincent Street in January 1977 from the temporary buildings it had been occupying since its establishment.

The whole episode clearly highlighted the narrow political dimension to decision-making. In depth cost-benefit studies of the merits of different locations were not undertaken, nor did Ministers request that they be made. The result was a decision largely based on judgements. The industrial logic hardly favoured Glasgow and pointed to Aberdeen where a large oil cluster was already developing. When BNOC's activities started to develop it found it necessary to open an office in Aberdeen which constituted the Corporation's third office. Over the years many more oil companies located in Aberdeen and new ones were born there. The presence of BNOC in Glasgow did not become a catalyst for the emergence of other oil companies there: the industrial logic was absent. For the same reason it was not surprising that, following the take-over by BP of Britoil the private sector successor company for BNOC's upstream assets, the office in Glasgow was closed and operations concentrated in Aberdeen.

Preparations for Petroleum Bill

The key decision on the location of the head office of BNOC was only one element in the preparatory work for the Petroleum and Submarine Pipelines Bill. Much of this work centred on the role/functions of BNOC and its precise relationships with central Government. The July 1974 White Paper had not discussed these in any detail, but by that time the wide-ranging role of the Corporation had been agreed within Government as described above. But much work was required on the details covering a range of issues. One which produced a surprising amount of discussion was the proposal by the DEN to have civil servants as members of the BNOC Board to facilitate the closest possible relationship between the Corporation and the Government. The Civil Service Department was unconvinced that this was necessary and could cause problems. Thus the officials in question would only be present as representatives of their Minister who would be answerable to Parliament for their actions. If the Minister were to argue that the officials were Board members in their personal capacities and not as his representatives there would be a contradiction with the declared aim of the arrangement. Further, in the performance of their duties, officials could not claim to represent a view of the public interest which differed from the Minister's view. Under normal board procedures civil service members could be outvoted by their colleagues which could raise problems for the Minister, if, as could be expected, the votes of officials reflected the views of the Minister. The Civil Service Department felt that the precedent of directors appointed by the Government to serve on the boards of particular companies (such as BP) was not relevant, because in such cases the Government directors were essentially individuals chosen to represent the Government's interests in a situation where there were responsibilities to all shareholders. In the circumstances of BNOC the Civil Service Department favoured the notion of civil servants having observer or assessor status.

The consequence of the submission of these views was an inter-departmental meeting. The outcome was an agreement that there should be two members (from the DEN and Treasury) who would be expressly appointed as agents of Ministers, and whose main function would be to improve communications and the flow of information by giving early indications of Government thinking and relaying BNOC plans to Government. The representatives would not have voting rights nor receive any fees for the duties undertaken.

Multiple objectives of BNOC consistent?

In the autumn of 1974 officials were wrestling over the implications of the earlier endorsement by Cabinet of the multiple objectives of BNOC. Principally these included (a) acting as the Government's agent in collecting revenues other than tax (i.e. participation), (b) acting as a licensee in fields with the same commercial responsibilities as the private sector companies, and (c) acting in a non-commercial manner to execute Government policies relating to depletion rates and procurement of supplies (from UK sources). Some officials in DEN felt that one body was being asked to pursue inconsistent aims. These became particularly noticeable when the questions of the appropriate financial objectives of BNOC and Government financial controls were being considered. Following discussions it was agreed that, in situations where BNOC was acting as the Government's agent, the Secretary of State should have complete and unambiguous control over the Corporation's actions and finances. But where BNOC was acting as a commercial company more conventional controls and consents such as applied to other nationalised industries would be sufficient. The question of which functions should be regarded as "commercial" or "agency" in nature was less easy to resolve. It was clear that any downstream activities should be conducted on a commercial basis, and where BNOC was disposing of its own and participation oil it was acting as the Government's agent, and should be subject to general and specific Government direction. But as a partner in a field and being involved in investment and other field development decisions the position was less clear. The Minister of State, Lord Balogh, felt that BNOC should behave commercially in this situation. A consequence of this decision was that state participation and BNOC could not be employed as an instrument of depletion policy which would have to be operated directly by the Government.

Financial provisions in Bill

Work continued on the details of many of the other concepts already agreed by Ministers relating to the role of BNOC which required inclusion in the forthcoming Bill. By the end of 1974 officials had agreed interdepartmentally some main financial provisions. Thus the Secretary of State for Energy would have the responsibility for the National Oil Account (NOA). BNOC would be required to transfer gross revenues which it obtained from its activities to it, and the Secretary of State would have powers to issue funds from the NOA to BNOC for specific purposes set by legislation, particularly initial capital, capital and operating expenditures, loan servicing and repayments, and offset payments (in return for the acceptance of state participation). The legislation would also provide for monies to be issued from the Consolidated Fund and/or the National Loans Fund as necessary to keep the NOA solvent subject to an overall limit. The Secretary of State would also be responsible for transferring surpluses to the Consolidated Fund. All these arrangements were to ensure that the Government had very close control of BNOC's activities.

Financial duties of BNOC

Officials also agreed that BNOC would not have the conventional financial duty of a nationalised industry, but would be required to conduct its business in accordance with plans approved by the Secretary of State. Such plans would cover both capital and current operations. BNOC would be given powers to borrow both in sterling and foreign currencies, but again only with the approval of the Secretary of State and the Treasury. The Treasury would be able to guarantee borrowings made by BNOC. All these provisions would also apply to wholly-owned subsidiaries of BNOC. With respect to partly-owned subsidiaries officials felt that BNOC should become involved with them only with the approval of the Secretary of State who would also have the power to direct BNOC to divest itself of such holdings. BNOC would pay royalties and corporation tax in the normal way, but would not be subject to PRT on the grounds that its revenues were to be paid into the NOA.

Transfer of NCB's oil interests to BNOC

The new Bill had to provide for the transfer of the NCB's North Sea oil and gas interests. This decision had been made earlier and incorporated in the July White Paper against the strong objections of Sir Derek Ezra the chairman of the Board, who had argued that the Board should be allowed to retain at least part of its interests, with BNOC taking 51% for example. The subject was left for later clarification, but by late 1974 DEN officials had concluded that there should be a clean break, and in November 1974 Mr Varley wrote to Sir Derek informing him that all the Board's interests would be transferred to BNOC.

Two issues arose of particular importance to the NCB. It wanted to expand into petrochemicals including the use of oil from its North Sea licences as feedstock. The DEN did not wish to encourage such plans, but, to obtain the Board's acquiescence to the transfer, the Secretary of State's letter emphasised that the transfer itself would not jeopardise this objective. The second issue concerned compensation which the Board would be seeking. DEN officials felt that when BNOC took over the NCB's North Sea subsidiary it would repay the loans which had been used to finance the Board's North Sea activities. But compensation for profits foregone could not be provided for, because this would send an embarrassing precedent for the participation negotiations with the oil companies. Further, there did not appear to be a conceptually sound reason for compensation when the transfer of assets was entirely within the public sector.

Provision of information by/to BNOC

The issue of provision of information aroused much debate. It came up in planning for the Bill because the DEN was anxious to ensure that it had (a) right of access to all information which BNOC acquired, and (b) the right to request any information from the oil companies in matters relating to their licence operations. The oil companies were very concerned that information provided by them would be held in strict confidence and should not be disclosed to BNOC or to suppliers of goods and services. When it later became known that civil servants would be on the BNOC Board the companies were anxious to ensure that in that capacity they did not pass confidential information provided to DEN to BNOC as a potential competitor. At the outset officials also recognised that restrictions should also be placed on BNOC from releasing information of their own, and information about their partners, to the outside world, and particularly to other oil companies. There were different views within DEN about the coverage of the information which should be provided to BNOC. One was that BNOC should be able to receive from DEN (a) any *aggregated* information compiled from detailed information initially obtained from individual licensees, and (b) *any* information about an individual licensee's activities where this was relevant to BNOC's operations as a Government agent (rather than a licensee). An example of the latter would be where BNOC was asked by the Government to drill in a specified location on its own account and information on adjacent acreage was available to DEN. A further proposal was that BNOC should have information on specific licensees to enable it to perform its role as an agent of Government. All this was justified on the grounds that knowledge of operations on the UKCS should be put at the disposal of the Corporation to enable it to operate more effectively in the national interest.

The case against these privileges had several strands, but they all related to the souring of relations with the oil companies and the danger of prejudicing the chances of successful participation negotiations. UKOOA had already argued strongly that BNOC should not have access to any information supplied in confidence by licensees to the DEN. Further, in the participation negotiations which were already underway, the Government had stressed the argument that BNOC, when in partnership with the oil companies, would act commercially and that this should be reflected in Operating Agreements. To permit disclosure of information to BNOC beyond which it was entitled as a party to an Operating Agreement would undermine the commercial credibility of the Corporation. Some officials felt that the provision of information about specific companies would be very strongly opposed by the licensees. They would be unlikely to appreciate the distinction between BNOC as an agent and as a principal, and would regard it primarily as a competitor. It was also debatable whether the planned agency functions required the proposed sweeping powers of disclosure. Eventually it was decided that, for purposes of introducing the Bill, powers to release specific licensee information to BNOC when it was acting as a Government agent should be sought only for future licences and put accordingly in the Regulations. But if the arguments were well received an amendment to the Bill could be sought to apply the proposal to existing licences.

Relationship between BNOC and BGC

The Bill dealt with the relationship between BNOC's activities and those of BGC, a subject on which the latter developed strong views. The issue related to the potential overlap of their activities in a situation where both had a right to operate in the UKCS. DEN officials felt that, while the two Corporations could make some arrangements between themselves, both bodies were accountable to the Secretary of State for Energy, and thus a statutory oversight of the arrangements made between them was appropriate. But the circumstances were impossible to foresee, and the proposal was to require the two bodies to jointly examine any activities specified by the Government to determine the respective roles which were in the national interest. The Secretary of State would be given powers of direction in the determination of the national interest.

The Deputy Chairman of BGC, Mr Denis Rooke, was concerned about these proposals, principally on the grounds that they could give the Secretary of State powers of direction which could be more far-reaching than those currently applicable under the Gas Act 1972. In principle the proposed powers could extend to the transfer or divestment of any assets or even the removal of BGC's privileges with respect to gas purchase. Following discussions of the issue some assurances were given to BGC whereby relevant sections of the Continental Shelf Act 1964 and the Gas Act 1972 applied to BNOC, in order to preserve BGC's gas purchasing monopsony. Further, a clause was eventually inserted in the Bill, which ensured that the Secretary of State's powers of direction did not override restrictions incorporated in the Gas Act 1972. In particular this meant that BGC could not be directed to dispose of assets to BNOC if this conflicted with BGC's obligations under the Gas Act. Mr Rooke's suspicions were eventually very well-founded. Part of the problem in the design of this part of the legislation in 1974–75 was the absence of guidance on the matters to be subject to joint examination, along with the determination of the national interest being the exclusive right of the Secretary of State. But officials were firmly of the view that this was the appropriate approach.

Keeping some directions confidential

Another particular issue which caused debate was the desire within DEN to ensure that directions given to BNOC could if necessary be given in secret and withheld from publication either in its Annual Report or elsewhere. The main reason for some directions to be kept secret related to the disposal and destination of North Sea oil. State participation through BNOC gave valuable extra control on this matter, but there was a danger that directions might give the appearance of conflicting with international obligations such as those under the Treaty of Rome. There were also other areas of BNOC's operations which justified powers to suppress directions, namely the Corporation's proposed management of the (onshore) defence pipelines and storage system, and its possible involvement in arrangements for the defence of offshore installations. There might also be other circumstances involving sensitive commercial information which would justify directions being made secretly. Ministers accepted these arguments, though they were warned by Mr Liverman, the Deputy Secretary, that vigorous criticism could be expected during the Parliamentary debate about the non-publication of directions.

Appointment of BNOC Chairman and Board members

Concurrent with preparatory work on the Bill officials were also busy on non-legislative issues dealing with BNOC. These dealt with several practical matters including the appointment of the Chairman, Chief Executive, and Board members. By early 1975 Mr Varley had decided that the Chairman should be a political figure with business experience. The Chief Executive would be the driving force within the company and DEN employed a firm of consultants to search among senior oil executives for an appropriate person. All Board members would have to be of the highest quality if BNOC was to compete with the major companies and fulfil its objectives. Accordingly, it would be necessary to pay competitive salaries and the Secretary of State was planning to put his case to the Top Salaries Review Body.

BNOC Organising Committee

The Prime Minister personally intervened in late February 1975 to give an impetus to the forward planning for the commencement of BNOC's operations. His interest had been aroused by a letter from Sir Kenneth Berrill, Head of the CPRS, stating that one of the uncertainties which was threatening to delay the financing and development of North Sea oil was the interval before BNOC was established and subsequently becoming operational. The Prime Minister suggested that this problem could be mitigated by setting up an Organising Committee in advance of the passing of the legislation. Officials in DEN then proceeded to determine how the Committee would function, how its members should be chosen, where it would be located, how its costs would be met, and what precisely would be its tasks. The initial thoughts of DEN officials were that it should concentrate on a variety of subjects including BNOC's corporate plan, initial budget, staff structure and recruitment, marketing strategy, and draft North Sea oil participation and disposal contracts. All these matters were agreed with remarkable rapidity and the decision was made that the Committee become operational soon after Second Reading of the Bill (set for April 1975). The intention was to appoint the Chairman and Chief Executive of BNOC as soon as possible after Second Reading with both becoming members of the Organising Committee. By the beginning of March a list of potential members had been drawn up including industrialists, bankers, trade unionists, and oil men.

Depletion control Regulations

As discussed earlier Ministers had approved in principle substantial changes to licence Regulations in the summer of 1974. These were to be implemented in the Petroleum Bill along with the establishment of BNOC. DEN officials decided that the proposals should be discussed with UKOOA and licensees. A major topic of debate was depletion controls. Before the Ministerial statement on the subject on 6th December UKOOA had expressed strong objection to production controls. The view was also expressed that if the Government was determined to introduce constraints this could be achieved with minimum damage by a scheme which controlled the time when new field developments commenced. If licensees encountered delays in the timing of new field developments as a result of Government policy they should be compensated. Further, if the Government wanted to reduce production from a field below the levels approved at the time of the initial field development the adjustment should be made through a variation in the Government take (such as royalty), so that licensees were not penalised. The Varley Assurances announced in December thus did not fully meet the industry's concerns.

Officials felt that stronger powers were needed to deal with both emergency and longer-term problems. Accordingly, they drafted sweeping powers in the Bill to enable the Secretary of State to control depletion in several ways. Firstly, he would be empowered to order an increase in the rate of production notwithstanding any previously agreed rates. No limitations or safeguards were proposed. The purpose was to deal with exceptional or emergency circumstances. Officials had been pressed to make the Varley Assurances statutory, but felt that such a safeguard would deny Government the necessary flexibility in an emergency. They were, however, well aware that an order substantially to increase production could require large extra investment which could justify a concession during the passage of the Bill.

The second power proposed was to order a compulsory start-up of production. This would be exercised over a licensee who had found oil but for no good reason had not developed it, or who genuinely felt that the discovery was not commercial. It was recognised that this power could be very controversial, but that it would be unwise to have no powers over an "unwilling" licensee.

The third power proposed was to order a deferral of field development. This would be much less controversial and was (reluctantly) accepted by the companies. The central idea was that the Government, having formed an overall depletion strategy, should be able to decide when a particular field should come on stream to procure the required profile. By deferring both the investment and the income the damage to the economics of the field would be minimised, unless during the period of delay the investment costs increased and/or the price of oil fell.

The planning system proposed in the Regulations was comprehensive. The licensee would be required to prepare and submit a development/production plan to the Secretary of State who could approve or amend and even impose plans. The Secretary of State would consider a development plan from the viewpoints both of good oilfield practice and depletion policy. He would then inform the licensee that he (a) approved the plan on both counts, or (b) accepted the plan subject to the development being postponed for a specified period, or (c) rejected the plan on grounds of good oilfield practice (subject to arbitration), or (d) rejected the plan on the grounds that the proposed production rates did not accord with depletion policy. If a plan were rejected on depletion policy grounds the Secretary of State would have to tell the licensees what production rate was in the public interest. In turn the licensee would have to submit a plan allowing for different production rates within the bounds of good oilfield practice. Once a plan had been agreed or served on the licensee he would be obliged to carry it out.

Officials warned Ministers that there would be strong industry and Opposition criticism of the proposed powers on a number of grounds. Thus the Secretary of State was to be given apparently unlimited powers over depletion. The industry preferred the deferral of developments to production cuts and would also prefer the powers to rest on good oilfield practice which would be arbitrable. Officials were unenthusiastic about arbitration because only the Government could define the national interest. Reliance on deferment alone would also lose an essential element of flexibility in a supply crisis.

The argument of the industry that production cuts imposed a severe penalty and should be compensated caused problems because it could be very costly, though difficult to calculate. UKOOA also objected to the proposed powers to alter the rate of production after a programme had been agreed. While understandable, DEN officials still felt that the power was necessary as an element of flexibility to meet unforeseen circumstances.

On the fundamental issue of what should be a detailed long-term depletion strategy the view of officials was that it was not possible to lay one down in 1975 before oil production had commenced because of the many uncertainties surrounding (a) the timing and size of future discoveries, (b) domestic oil demand, (c) likely supplies from foreign sources, (d) prospective oil prices, (e) the prospects for the UK balance of payments and tax revenue requirements, and (f) the effect on the contracting sector of rapid or slow rates of development. It was clear, however, that there was a national need for a rapid build-up of production to 1980 or so. The Varley Assurances were designed to facilitate such developments.

Interim determination of royalties

While the discussion on depletion controls was probably the most important subject of debate with the industry in the period prior to the publication of the Bill other subjects were also debated. Some were not regarded as particularly controversial. With respect to royalties the Government was proposing several changes. There had been long drawn-out discussions between the DEN and licensees on how the allowances for conveying and treatment costs should be calculated. There was a loss of revenue to the DEN and it was decided that powers to make an interim determination should be taken. These were instigated in time for the Fourth Round but it was also proposed to apply them to pre-1971 licences. While this was retrospective UKOOA had no basic objections, and the only debate was over the interest rate which should be paid on any excess or shortage in the interim payment until the final figure was agreed.

Remission of royalties discretionary

Powers to remit royalties when they caused production to become uneconomic were also being discussed with the industry. The DEN was keen to make such powers discretionary while the industry had initially requested that they be non-discretionary to enhance investment certainty. Officials made attempts to define a marginal field or project in a manner which could be reflected in printed Regulations, but found this very difficult, and decided to retain the discretionary power which removed the need for fully specifying the definition of a marginal or sub-marginal project. In late 1974 UKOOA welcomed the proposal, adding that any royalty reduction should be for an agreed minimum period subject to revision if a large price increase substantially improved the economics of the project.

Royalty in kind

To enhance security of supply DEN was now proposing to be able to take royalty in kind from old as well as new licensees. UKOOA was concerned about the retroactive element and proposed that this be dealt with separately between the Secretary of State and each licensee. With respect to new licences UKOOA felt that licensees should be given twelve months warning before royalty was taken in kind rather than cash. UKOOA also argued that, in recognition of the problems taking royalty in kind raised, the Government should take into account several factors. Thus, as far as possible there should be non-discrimination among licensees. If this was really necessary, because of limited demand, for example, the Government should endeavour to mitigate the effects of such discrimination. This could be done by rotating the obligation over time from one field/licence to another. The Government should also consider the effects of any obligations to pay royalty in kind on a licensee's total access to oil from his licence, bearing in mind possible state participation as well.

Powers to impose work programme

UKOOA was opposed to the proposal to give the Secretary of State powers to impose an exploration programme on existing licences, arguing that this violated very important and fundamental rights granted for the full licence period. For new licences it was appreciated that the provision would only apply to the second term of the licence, but limitations on the Secretary of State's powers of licence revocation under this article were desirable. Thus licensees should not be required to relinquish proven production areas. The Secretary of State should also be obliged to take into account the licensee's submissions regarding the geological prospects for the block concerned plus the economic aspects of any prospective production.

Approval of development plans

With respect to the proposed powers to approve all field development plans UKOOA had no objection in principle, but argued that the Regulation should clearly state that the sole criterion for rejection of a development plan would be that it did not conform to good oilfield practice. The Secretary of State should also be obliged to set out clearly his reasons for rejecting a proposed development plan.

Approval for assignments

The Government had become concerned about the transfer of licence interests which sometimes occurred through company reorganisations or mergers and takeovers. This raised concerns about the suitability of the new owners. It was thus proposed to take strong powers to ensure that any changes in licence ownership could only take place with Government approval. Many licensees expressed concern over the proposed powers, and UKOOA suggested that the Regulation be framed to avoid deterring transactions beneficial to activity, and provide that the DEN would issue guidelines so that licensees would know in advance whether a farm-out, sale, or granting of an overriding interest would be likely to receive approval. UKOOA wanted a large number of exemptions from the guidelines including mergers, corporate reorganisations, security interest schemes (such as pledges of shares), and, in general, situations which did not breach criteria established by the Secretary of State. A further proposal was made that if one licensee was deemed to be in default of the licence ownership provisions this should not cause revocation of the licence for any co-licensees.

Controls on construction and use of pipelines

The Bill contained proposals to give the Secretary of State powers to control the construction and use of pipelines. These powers were quite wide-ranging, including not only the authorisation of schemes but the facilitation of their use by third parties. The Secretary of State would have powers to consider whether changes in routes and capacities were desirable, and, in the event of these being suggested by parties other than the initial proposer, to require a contribution to any extra costs from that third party. The Secretary of State would also be able to require third-party use of pipelines and to regulate the charges for such use. The proposals in the Bill also enabled the Secretary of State to make Regulations concerning safety and related issues on work taking place on pipelines. In the consultation period prior to the publication of the Bill UKOOA had not formed a collective view.

Discussions with UKOOA on proposed Regulations

Several meetings on the proposed Regulations were held between DEN officials and UKOOA in the period leading up to the publication of the Bill. DEN officials had sympathy with some of UKOOA's suggestions. For example, rejection of a field development plan should only occur when it was inconsistent with good oilfield practice. The exercise of this power and that to revoke licences should be arbitrable. On the subject of changes in licence ownership there was a readiness to consider the issue of non-statutory guidelines on transactions likely to receive approval, but officials could not agree that revocation of a licence should affect a defaulter but not his co-licensees, as this would be inconsistent with the joint and several liability principle. On restrictions on gas flaring, officials were willing to accept that, before exercising controls, the Government should have regard to both technical and economic considerations.

Offset payments

Other main items contained in the Bill provided for offset payments to be made by BNOC to or on behalf of licensees who accepted state participation. The full rules for this had not been worked out by the publication date. The Bill also stipulated the proposed borrowing limits of BNOC, with an initial level of £600 million and a further £300 million subject to Order in Council.

Comments on Bill

The large, complex, and controversial Bill was published on 8th April 1975. Comments quickly followed, even prior to the Second Reading. BP expressed concern to DEN officials on two main points relating to BNOC. The first was the applicable financial régime for the Corporation and how this affected its competitive position. There was a specific concern that exemption from PRT would give the Corporation an unfair advantage, and it was unclear how the operation of the National Oil Account would affect its position. On consideration DEN officials felt that the financial régime for BNOC required further examination. It was felt that the three key activities of (a) co-licensee, (b) sole licensee, and (c) downstream player could have distinct financial régimes, but these needed elaboration with possible incorporation in Amendments to the Bill. The second concern expressed by BP related to the confidentiality of information obtained by BNOC. Anxiety was expressed about the extent of knowledge which BNOC would acquire through partnership in all or most of the commercial fields. BP was also concerned that, in BNOC's advisory role, it would receive information from the Government which had been obtained by the latter in its regulatory role. Mr Liverman promised to consider safeguards, but noted that the matter was not straight-forward. Thus the companies themselves could benefit from BNOC's widespread partnerships, and if the nation was to obtain the benefit of comprehensive knowledge BNOC had to have access to much information.

Second Reading debate

The Second Reading debate took place on 30th April. Mr Varley emphasised the need for enhanced control over North Sea oil, and indicated how the Bill would achieve this by establishing a framework for state participation and the establishment of BNOC. He emphasised how state participation had become common around the world where there were substantial oil reserves. BNOC would behave commercially when in partnership with the oil companies, but not always when it was a sole licensee and acting as the state's agent. Mr Varley then briefly summarised the proposed changes to the Regulations and the enhanced powers to be taken on the lines discussed above. The Opposition spokesman was Mr Patrick Jenkin who emphasised the lack of clarity in the Government's intentions with respect to participation which left considerable uncertainty among investors and would lead to a reduction in exploration. Mr. Jenkin argued that the Government had not made out a case for participation while the objectives specified for BNOC were vague and confused. It would be so much under the control of the Secretary of State that it would have great difficulty in acting commercially. He had some sympathy with the objectives of controlling depletion, but was not convinced that the powers needed to be applied retrospectively. If that were done then the licensees should be compensated. Mr Jenkin then argued in favour of an independent, impartial regulatory authority, citing with approval the example of the Alberta Energy Resources Conservation Board. He agreed that Government had the duty to determine the aggregate depletion rate, but how this was translated into detailed provisions required special expertise, and the parties involved should be able to present their arguments before an expert tribunal which would make decisions.

Other Opposition speakers queried the need for a national oil company and the likely vast cost of acquiring 51% participation. Mr Gordon Wilson, the Leader of the SNP, favoured the establishment of BNOC and participation, but emphasised the need for Scotland to obtain "a proper share of her own oil resources". Winding up for the Government Mr John Smith emphasised the advantages of participation as essentially being the gaining of a profitable share of the North Sea oil resources and a say in its disposal.

Prolonged Committee Stage

The detailed examination of the Bill in the Commons (Committee Stage) started on 13th May and lasted for nearly three months, occupying no less than twenty-five sittings. In the middle of these proceedings Mr Tony Benn succeeded Mr Varley as Secretary of State for Energy. Many Amendments were proposed both by Government and Opposition. Much of the debate on policy issues centred on the role of BNOC and participation. Mr Jenkin queried the Government's claim that participation would give greater control over the disposal of North Sea oil as it had to be landed in the UK under existing Regulations. He queried the need for additional powers, noting that emergency powers over exports and imports had existed since 1939 and had been employed in October 1973. He did not feel that the additional powers were necessary. Mr Benn emphasised that the proposed greater controls reduced the nation's dependence on the actions of the oil companies. In the Parliamentary exchanges there was little or no overt reference to the increased ability of the Government provided by 51% participation to influence the disposal of the oil with reduced risk of challenge by the EEC in particular. This was a sensitive subject, and it is probable that the speakers did not want to highlight the full nature of the issue which was in possible conflict with the Articles in the Treaty of Rome dealing with trading restrictions.

BNOC exemption from PRT

The Opposition made repeated and strong attacks on the exemption of BNOC from PRT, arguing that this privilege would produce unfair competition and lead the Corporation to make investments in projects which would be uneconomic for full tax-paying investors. Several oil companies also emphasised their opposition to this concession. The exemption was also queried by the EEC Commission (Competition Directorate). All this led the Permanent Secretary at the DEN to reappraise the issue. The Treasury felt that, so long as BNOC had to sell oil at the world market price, exemption from PRT was merely a book-keeping point as the Government had already argued. Only if BNOC became involved in refining and marketing would a tax-induced incentive to undercut rivals in selling products arise. The case for making BNOC liable to PRT had several strands. The assurance given by Mr Varley that the Corporation would act commercially in investment decisions left open the possibility that the tax concession could produce a different assessment from the other companies. It could also be argued that the exemption would unnecessarily poison BNOC's relationships with the industry. The argument that the concession simplified administration was a thin one, and it was arguable that confidence could be significantly enhanced at negligible cost by making BNOC liable to PRT. The claim that it was administratively pointless to subject BNOC to PRT but to ask it to assess investments as if it were liable would in practice involve a notional tax calculation.

There were, however, other consequences of making BNOC pay PRT. It would reduce the Corporation's net cash flow, thereby increasing its call on advances from the National Oil Account and thus producing a deterioration in the net cash flow for the whole Account. It effectively meant that the Exchequer would for some time put money into the Account to enable BNOC to pay its tax bills. It would also raise BNOC's cumulative borrowing, and accelerate the time when its borrowing limit had to be raised. There were, however, no resource implications for the economy.

DEN officials felt that if no concession on PRT liability were made it would be necessary to give further assurances about BNOC's commercial behaviour. They were not fully convinced that the Treasury and Inland Revenue proposals that Ministerial assurances that BNOC would always sell crude and products at full market value were adequate. The conclusion of DEN officials was thus that the PRT exemption should be given up, which would cost virtually nothing, but produce a big increase in goodwill, and enhance the prospects of successful participation negotiations.

Complexities of offset payments and taxation

In debate among the DEN, Treasury, and Inland Revenue other complexities were raised. DEN officials wondered whether the offset payments, made by BNOC to licensees to persuade them to accept participation, could be made deductible for PRT. The Inland Revenue pointed out that the existing rules did not provide for this, and they were in any case unconvinced that this would affect BNOC's overall position. Further, they had resisted demands from the oil companies to permit deductions of payments made to acquire interests in a field. If BNOC were given a deduction for offset payments there could be renewed demands by the companies for what they would regard as equivalent payments. The Inland Revenue also felt that permitting a deduction of offset payments for corporation tax would mean giving BNOC more favoured treatment than other companies in the private sector, and it offended against the principle that nationalised industries should be treated in the same way as private ones.

PRT and National Oil Account

At a meeting in late June 1975 between the Paymaster General and the Minister of State at the DEN the former emphasised that if BNOC paid PRT the National Oil Account would be in deficit to a greater extent and for a longer period than would otherwise be the case which would have presentational disadvantages. The whole issue deserved further study and a final decision on the issue was postponed to the Report Stage of the Bill. In the meantime in the Standing Committee Government spokesmen reiterated the arguments for exemption outlined above but promised to listen to representations from the industry. For the Opposition Mr Patrick Jenkin made another proposal, namely that in the National Oil Account BNOC's non-paid PRT be shown separately. Mr John Smith proposed to consider this. The Inland Revenue was very concerned at this suggestion on the grounds that the calculation would be irksome and imprecise and no definitive figure could be produced. The Treasury broadly agreed with this and the suggestion was made to DEN that an order of magnitude estimate of notional PRT on a non-auditable basis could be provided. This was agreed.

The debate on the Bill moved to the House of Lords and the issue of PRT exemption reappeared. Lord Balogh was willing to make further concessions on the subject, but the Treasury and Inland Revenue were keen that the existing agreed stance be maintained. In the debate Lord Campbell of Croy pointed out an anomaly that would follow from the exemption. This concerned the volume allowance for PRT. An exempt BNOC would not utilise this allowance which would eventually become available to the co-licensees in the field. This was an unintended consequence which the Inland Revenue agreed would have to be remedied. Eventually, in late October 1975 at Report Stage, Lord Balogh moved a Government Amendment stating that BNOC would be required to publish what its PRT and corporation tax liabilities would have been were it not for the PRT exemption.

Representations from oil companies

The Government also had to deal with direct representations from many of the oil companies on the Bill. These dealt with a range of issues but with some common elements. Thus all complained about the PRT exemption, arguing that it conferred an unfair competitive advantage both upstream and downstream. In downstream activities competition was already severe, with excess refining capacity and there was no case for privileged treatment to a new rival. ICI argued that the tax exemption of BNOC would enable the latter to enter and compete in the petro-chemicals market on favoured terms. Esso submitted a detailed memorandum on the Bill. On BNOC, as well as arguing for the removal of its PRT exemption, Esso argued that a procedure be established whereby any activities in which BNOC was not intended to operate commercially would be identified and accounted for separately. Separate accounts should be kept for each activity and published to show a true picture of the profit and loss for each. The Corporation should have a more orthodox capital structure with funds being obtained from the Consolidated Fund in competition with the rest of the public sector or from the outside capital market.

With respect to the proposed changes to the Regulations, Esso argued that, if they were applied to existing licences, prompt and adequate compensation should be paid for the resulting reduction in the value of licence interests. Esso felt that the proposed power to ensure that companies explored acreage was too sweeping, as it involved an open-ended commitment on the licensee to carry out exploration over unspecified periods against the severe sanction of revocation of the entire licence. The provision could be used to force the licensee to surrender acreage which he felt was uneconomic to work at that time, or alternatively he might work acreage which he felt was uneconomic simply to preserve the validity of the licence. The sanction of licence revocation was particularly unfair because it applied to the whole licence and not just to the area on which exploration was sought. This could mean the loss of promising blocks for failure to explore a less promising one. Further, the absence of compensation on revocation would mean that the DEN or BNOC would obtain the benefit of all expenditure made in the licence area. Esso suggested that the power of revocation exclude those parts of the licence which included producing fields, discoveries under appraisal, and discoveries with a reasonable likelihood of being developed. In the event of revocation compensation should be paid.

With respect to the proposed Regulation on Development and Production, Esso had no objection to the concept of Government approval to ensure good oilfield practice, but the provision now included powers to delay developments and to compel licensees to develop acreage. Esso argued that it would be grossly unfair if a licensee were forced to make uneconomic investments to preserve his licence rights and safeguard his prior investment. The power to delay field developments, while undesirable, was a preferred alternative to production controls. In general Esso felt that a licensee should not be required to carry out a development against his commercial judgement. Any imposed development delays should be for a specified and non-extendable period. Compensation should be provided for adverse financial consequences of forced delays. If production controls really had to be imposed the legislation should clearly state the extent of the reduction in production rates and provide for the establishment of an independent body to administer the scheme in a non-discriminatory manner. With respect to the proposed powers to authorise and control pipelines Esso argued that the Bill needed to specify the grounds on which authorisation could be refused. The provision dealing with the use of pipelines by third parties could lead to the owners incurring increased costs with no effective assurance of being recompensed. Esso felt that if a change in pipeline route or increase in capacity were required the third party should be required to make a contribution in respect of the increased costs. If the Secretary of State required a change in route or capacity then the cost contribution should be made from public funds.

Response of Government to representations

Other companies made similar comments, though generally not in such a detailed and systematic manner. The Government certainly considered them and felt able to agree with some but not others. Pressure for compensation was generally resisted. It was argued that the proposals in the Bill were not retrospective in their effects, but imposed new obligations which would only affect licensees at some time in the future. These might operate to the disadvantage of those affected, but were no different in principle from other obligations relating to safety, health, or pollution. The national interest was behind the compensation principle and it was the Government's function to interpret this.

Limitation notices to be introduced

With respect to depletion the Government did make significant amendments in response to industry representations. The original proposal gave the Secretary of State unlimited power to cut back or increase production from any field not protected by the Varley Assurances. To alleviate these anxieties, at least in part, a Government Amendment required the Secretary of State to issue a Limitation Notice when approving a field development plan. The Notice would specify the maximum cutback in production which could be required and after what period. A further Amendment restricted the power of the Secretary of State to order a licensee to increase production only in national emergency situations and to cost no more than the drilling of a new well. With respect to requirements to undertake additional exploration it was made clear that this would be that which a conscientious licensee with adequate resources would undertake. Further, partial revocation would be permitted at the option of the Secretary of State. But the option of full revocation would remain, and this would apply to breaches of depletion controls. Matters of good oilfield practice would be arbitrable but not those affecting the national interest. The Secretary of State would also retain the power to require development of a field at times of his choosing.

Opposition proposes Oil Conservation Authority

At the Report stage the Opposition proposed the establishment of a UK Oil Conservation Authority. Its functions would be to appraise the UK's reserves of oil and gas, prospective demand, and to implement conservation, pollution and safety policies subject to directives by the Secretary of State. Interestingly, BP had proposed this concept in its evidence to the House of Commons Select Committee on Nationalised Industries. The concept was based both on the Alberta Energy Conservation Board and the Texas Railroad Commission. Mr Jenkin argued that the staffing problem which was widely recognised to exist given the rapid expansion of activity in the UKCS could be more readily solved in this manner rather than by establishing BNOC. Mr Benn did not accept the Opposition's proposal, and argued that the regulation of oil and gas activities was so important that it had to be undertaken directly by the Government rather than delegated to another body.

Lord Kearton to be Chairman of BNOC

The debates involved several other proposals on less important matters. But at Third Reading on 29th July 1975 Mr Benn made a most important announcement, namely the appointment of Lord Kearton as Chairman of BNOC. The debates in the Lords and Commons continued into the Autumn. A Government Amendment enabled BNOC to borrow in any currency with Treasury permission. The Lords passed an Opposition Amendment requiring compensation when retrospective alterations were made to licence terms, but the Commons subsequently reversed it. The Opposition tried in vain to limit the flows of royalties into the National Oil Account only to the end of 1978. In the Lords the Opposition also introduced an Amendment to prevent the Secretary of State from using his powers of consent or the terms of a licence to obtain state participation. It was argued that, if participation in existing licences was truly voluntary as the Government was maintaining, then it should not use its powers in this way. Lord Balogh replied that the Government would fully employ the arguments and bargaining power at its disposal. The Amendment was subsequently withdrawn. The argument that the Government might make improper use of its discretionary powers by acting in the way indicated, and could even be subject to legal challenge for misuse of these powers to achieve purposes other than those for which they were granted, could have been deployed more directly, and officials were relieved that this did not occur.

Reflections on Bill

The Bill was finally enacted on 12th November 1975. The marathon had involved use of the guillotine. No less than 71 substantive Amendments had been tabled of which 32 were by the Government unaided, and 21 in response to proposals from UKOOA. All this reflected the size and extensive coverage of the Bill and its controversial nature. Behind the Bill, but *not* a main feature of it, was the concept of state participation, which was certainly controversial, particularly with respect to its application to existing licences, and this added greatly to the emotion of the debates and exchanges with the companies. The concept of the establishment of a national oil company was hardly radical at this time. There were plenty of precedents around the world. Similarly, attention to security of oil supply was being given by all consuming country Governments following the crisis of 1973–74, and it would have been very odd if the UK had not taken some interventionist steps to enhance supply security. Further, the notion that host Governments should be able to influence depletion rates was by this time hardly a radical one.

The roots of the controversy surrounding the Bill stemmed from a combination of the multiple functions of BNOC, involving, according to the critics, conflicting duties, and the wide and fairly open-ended discretionary powers granted to the Secretary of State for Energy. The notion that BNOC could simultaneously function as a commercial oil company competing with other licensees and provide advice to Government as its agent was felt by critics to have inherent conflicts. Thus the issue of supply of data to BNOC aroused much suspicion. On all these issues it is surprising that little attention was paid to the alternative model developed in Norway. This was already operational by the time of the debate in the UK. Thus in July 1972 the decision was made to establish the state oil company Statoil and the Norwegian Petroleum Directorate (NPD) both of which commenced operations in 1973. Statoil essentially had a business role, including holding the state's participation shares in licences. The NPD was concerned with the administration of policy including matters such as inspection and surveying. It reported to, and provided advice to, the Ministry of Industry which was responsible for the determination of overall official policy. Broadly there was a separation of (a) the business and (b) the administration/regulatory functions. It is arguable that this division of responsibilities reduced the level of controversy surrounding the introduction of a highly interventionist policy. Further, the arrangements have stood the test of time quite well.

In some ways, however, the 1975 Act has also stood the test of time in the sense that it implemented policies effectively in areas which were in some ways ventures into the unknown. There have, of course, been criticisms and changes to the Act, but these have generally reflected changes in policy rather than problems with the operation of the legislation.

Appendix 8.1

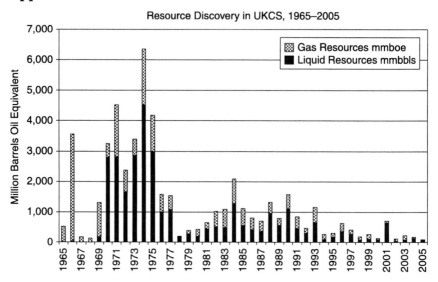

Source: IHS

Appendix 8.2

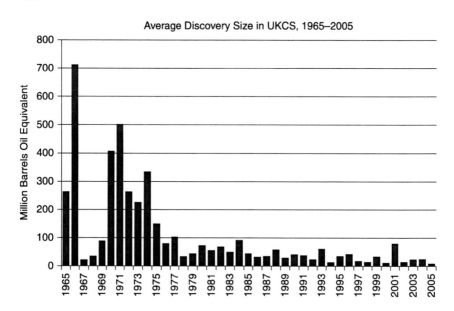

Source: IHS

Appendix 8.3

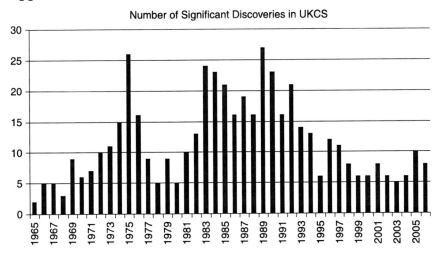

Appendix 8.4

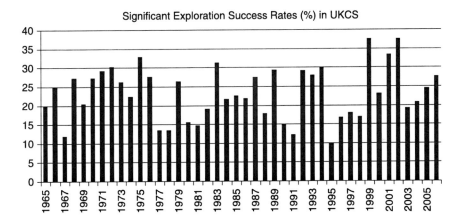

Appendix 8.5

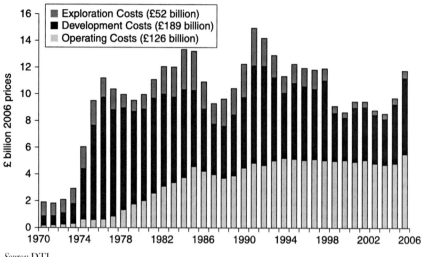

Source: DTI

Appendix 8.6

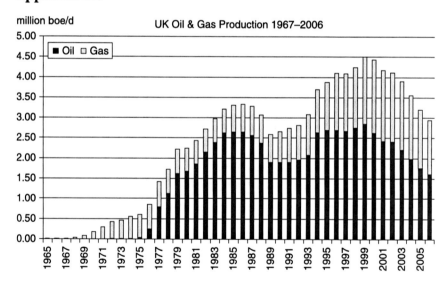

Appendix 8.7

Characteristics of Historically Important UKCS Fields

Field Name	Start-up	Operator (i)	Location (ii)	Type	Facilities	Const Site	Comments
West Sole	1967	BP	SNS	Gas	3 small steel platforms plus 2 satellite platforms. An additional platform removed in 1978. Two 70km long export pipelines to Easington.	Holland	First commercial gas find. First producing field. First platform to be removed from UKCS. (Field still producing)
Leman	1968	Shell and Amoco	SNS	Gas	14 small steel platforms operated by Shell, 19 small steel platforms operated by Amoco. Three export pipelines to Bacton. Twenty infield pipelines.	Holland	Largest UKCS gas field. BK compression platform removed in 1996. (Field still producing)
Indefatigable	1971	Shell and Perenco [Amoco]	SNS	Gas	6 small steel platforms operated by Shell, 9 small steel platforms operated by Perenco. 35km export pipeline to Leman. Ten infield pipelines.	Holland	Production from Shell part of field ceased in 2005. Decommissioning Programme currently under consideration. (Perenco still producing.)
Argyll	1975	Hamilton Bros	CNS	Oil	Floating Production System (converted drilling rig), CALM loading buoy, 2 subsea manifolds, 5 infield pipelines. Facilities were removed in 1992/93.	N/A	First producing UKCS oilfield, first floating production system. Ceased production in 1992 and decommissioned. Field redeveloped in 2003 as the Ardmore field (see Ardmore entry).

(Continued overleaf)

Field Name	Start-up	Operator (i)	Location (ii)	Type	Facilities	Const Site	Comments
Rough	1975	Centrica [British Gas]	SNS	Gas	5 small platforms. Two 30km pipelines to Easington plus 1 infield line.	Holland/ Ardersier/ Methil.	1986: first development in the world to use partly depleted reservoir for summer gas storage to provide additional peak supplies in winter.
Forties	1975	Apache [BP]	CNS	Oil	4 large and 2 small steel platforms. Two 170km export lines (1 out of use) to Cruden Bay. Seven infield pipelines.	Teeside/ Nigg.	First major UKCS oilfield to be developed. (Field still producing.)
Beryl	1976	ExxonMobil [Mobil]	NNS	Oil	1 concrete platform, 1 large steel platform, 1 riser platform, 2 SPM loading columns, 1 flare tower. One 325km gas pipeline (SAGE) to St. Fergus.	Norway/ Methil.	First concrete platform to be installed on the UKCS. (Field still producing.)
Brent	1976	Shell	NNS	Oil	3 concrete platforms, 1 large steel platform, Spar storage and loading buoy (removed 1995, anchor blocks removed 2006) and flare column (removed 2006). 30km oil export pipeline to Cormorant, 448km gas line (FLAGS) to St Fergus, 12 infield lines.	Norway/ Methil/ Ardyne Point.	Largest UKCS field to be developed in terms of total oil and gas reserves. Major controversy over proposed sea disposal of Brent Spar in 1995 which led to new international (OSPAR) regime for disposal of disused offshore installations in 1998. (Field still producing but initial stakeholder dialogue meeting held Jan 07 to consider future options.)

	Year	Operator	Region	Type	Facilities	Onshore	Notes
Piper	1976	Talisman[Elf][Occidental]	CNS	Oil	1 large steel platform, 169km oil export pipeline to Flotta, 53km gas line to MCP01.	Ardersier.	Piper Alpha disaster 1988. First UKCS decommissioning programme. (Field still producing.)
Frigg	1977	Elf and Total[Total]	NNS	Gas	3 concrete platforms (2 UK, 1 Norway), 2 small steel platforms (1 UK, 1 Norway), steel flare column (UK -removed 1996), damaged steel jacket (Norway), two 362km gas export lines (1 UK, 1 Norway) to St Fergus plus midway concrete compression platform. 14 infield pipelines.	Norway/France/Ardyne Point.	First joint UK/Norwegian field to be developed, first Norwegian gas to be delivered to St Fergus. Production ceased in 2004, joint decommissioning programme approved in 2003. First UK concrete installations subject to OSPAR derogation. First UKCS project to be archived under the 'Capturing the Energy' initiative.
Thistle	1978	Lundin[DNO][BP]	NNS	Oil	1 large steel platform, 1 SALM loading buoy (removed 1978), 12km oil export pipeline to Dunlin, 8km gas line to Northern Leg Gas Pipeline system, 2 infield pipelines.	Teeside.	Second deepest development in North Sea. Fourth largest steel jacket. Facilities return to BP for decommissioning. Field still producing.
Ninian	1978	CNR[Kerr McGee][Oryx][Chevron]	NNS	Oil	1 concrete platform, 2 large steel platforms, 161km oil pipeline to Sullom Voe, 16km gas line to FLAGS, 4 infield pipelines.	Methil/Kishorn/Nigg.	Ninian Central, heaviest concrete gravity structure on the UKCS. (Field still producing.)
Beatrice	1981	Talisman[BP]	MF	Oil	4 small steel platforms, 67km oil export pipeline to Nigg, 4 infield pipelines. Two wind turbines providing power.	Spain/Methil/Stornoway	First development in the Moray Firth (12 miles from shore). Proposed eventual reuse of facilities in offshore windfarm development.

(Continued overleaf)

Field Name	Start-up	Operator (i)	Location (ii)	Type	Facilities	Const Site	Comments
NW Hutton	1983	BP[Amoco]	NNS	Oil	1 large steel platform, 13km oil export pipeline to Cormorant, 11km gas line to WELGAS.	Ardersier.	Ceased production in 2003, decommissioning programme approved 2006. First 'footings' of large steel installation subject to OSPAR derogation.
Magnus	1983	BP	NNS	Oil	1 large steel platform. One 92km oil export pipeline to Ninian Central, one 79km gas line to Brent.	Nigg.	The largest, deepest and most northerly steel platform on the UKCS. (Field still producing.)
Maureen	1983	Phillips	NNS	Oil	1 steel gravity base platform, 1 articulated loading column (ALC). One 2.3km pipeline. Facilities removed in 2001.	Kishorn.	Only steel gravity based platform on UKCS. First ALC in the world to incorporate concrete shaft and gravity base. Ceased production in 1999 and decommissioned. Only gravity based installation to be re-floated.
Hutton	1984	Maersk[KerrMcGee][Oryx][Conoco]	NNS	Oil	1 steel tension leg platform (TLP), 6km oil export pipeline to NW Hutton, 7km gas import line. Facilities removed in 2002.	Nigg/Ardersier.	First ever tension leg platform. Ceased production in 2001, decommissioned in 2002.
Morecambe	1985	Centrica[BG]	IS	Gas	1 large steel platform, 6 small steel platforms. One 38km gas pipeline to Barrow-in-Furness, 8 infield pipelines.	Methil/Ardersier/Kishorn.	First development in the Irish Sea. Field developed principally to provide peak demand winter gas supplies. (Field still producing.)

Field	Year	Operator	Region	Type	Description	Refinery	Notes
Arbroath	1990	Talisman[Energy NS] [Paladin][Amoco]	CNS	Oil	Small steel wellhead platform tied-back to Montrose platform. Four 8km pipelines	Nigg.	First oil found in UK waters in 1969. (Field still producing.)
Miller	1992	BP	NNS	Oil	1 large steel platform, 8km oil export pipeline to Brae, 242km gas line to St Fergus/Peterhead Power Station.	Nigg.	First platform to incorporate post-Piper Alpha safety requirements. First proposed decarbonised fuels project with CO_2 recovery and ultimate offshore storage.
Markham	1992	CH4[Lasmo]	SNS	Gas	1 small steel platform, gas line to K13 platform in Dutch sector and there to Den Helder.	Holland.	Only UK/Netherlands development. (Field still producing.)
Foinaven	1997	BP	WOS	Oil	Floating Production System (FPSO) with offshore loading.	Spain.	First major development West of Shetlands. (Field still producing)
Ardmore	2003	Tuscan	CNS	Oil	Converted jack-up drilling rig, oil export via 2 Single Anchor Line (SAL) mooring sytems to shuttle tankers. Facilities removed in 2005 and 2006.	N/A	First redeveloped field (previously Argyll). Production terminated in 2005 when operator ceased trading. Decommissioning Programmes approved.
Clair	2005	BP	WOS	Oil	1 Small steel platform, 102km oil pipeline to Sullom Voe, 10km gas line to WOSPS.	N/A	First oil discovery West of Shetlands in 1977.

(i) Current operator. Previous operators shown in square brackets.
(ii) SNS: Southern North Sea
CNS: Central North Sea
NNS: Northern North Sea
MF: Moray Firth
WOS: West of Shetland

Source: DTI

9   The new policy in action: state participation

State participation: NSRC is established

In parallel with the preparations for the Petroleum and Submarine Pipelines Bill policy debates and related discussions with the industry continued apace, particularly on the subject of state participation. This did not feature prominently in the Bill, but both the Government and the oil companies were fully aware that this subject was probably the most important element of all the emerging policies. In the late summer of 1974 it was decided to establish a North Sea Oil Renegotiation Committee (NSRC) to progress matters. The Committee was a mixed Ministerial/Official one, chaired by the Secretary of State for Energy, and included senior representatives from the DEN, CPRS, Treasury, Inland Revenue, FCO, and the Law Officers' Department. Before the Committee met it had been decided that the Chancellor of the Duchy of Lancaster, Mr Harold Lever, would lead the negotiations supported by the Paymaster General, Mr Edmund Dell, and the Minister of State for Energy, Lord Balogh.

What state participation share?

The NSRC held its first meeting on 28th October 1974 to discuss the Government's negotiating position. This had to be based on the July White Paper which had made only fairly general statements. The DEN identified several key aspects of their negotiating stance which required clarification. The first was the percentage participation which should be sought. The White Paper had simply stated that it would be a majority, and no figure had ever been quoted though the industry was assuming that it would be 51%. DEN officials felt that, whether more than this should be sought, depended on considerations of control rather than state take, since, with the proposed offset payments system, further participation would not increase the state take because of the corresponding increase in the size of these payments. The question of control was regarded as a central one, and it was felt that the companies' main objection was that it would permit the Government to interfere with commercial decisions. Thus there would be very strong resistance to participation in excess of 51%. DEN officials advised that it was unlikely that more than 51% could be obtained.

Further, even if a higher figure were achieved, there might not be much extra control because this was determined by the rules of the licence Operating Agreements and, for major decisions, the companies would press for the qualifying majority vote to exceed the Government's participation share. In any case if BNOC had a 51% share it could veto all proposals by its partners until its own views were accepted, though this would doubtless involve great acrimony. Officials noted, however, that the Government's opening bid could exceed 51%, and might be 60% which could be reduced to a bare majority as a negotiating concession. It was to be noted that in the consortia which included BGC and the NCB the shares of these companies counted towards state majority participation. Thus the private sector partners would have to give up a smaller percentage of their holdings which should be regarded as a valuable concession. It was possible to argue that a similar concession might be considered for BP given the Government's 48% shareholding, but officials did not recommend this, given the difficulties of controlling BP and the implied discrimination between BP and the other companies.

At the meeting of the Committee on 30th October 1974 it was agreed that an opening negotiating position of 60% state share followed by a retreat to 51% would represent a damaging position. It was therefore agreed that a firm and clear intention to secure 51% should be stated from the outset.

Which companies to approach?

The second main issue considered was the companies that should be approached. DEN officials noted that the three largest companies in the North Sea, namely BP, Shell and Esso, all felt that they had a special relationship with the UK Government (though for different reasons). It was thus felt that the first approach should be made to them, starting with BP because it was wholly British and partly state-owned, and because to start elsewhere might look odd. It was recognised, however, that these three large companies did not offer the best prospects for success. Thus BP depended less on any favours from the Government than foreign companies. Shell had taken a very strong public stance against participation. Esso seemed a better prospect, and, as the biggest foreign company, was of strategic importance, but it was a partner with Shell in all their commercial fields and could be expected to follow the same line as Shell was doing.

DEN officials felt that one of the best prospects would be the NCB-Gulf-Conoco group because the NCB share was substantial (33%) which would count towards majority participation. Further, Conoco had already indicated that it had no objection in principle to participation, and Gulf was recognised as one of the least doctrinaire of the major companies. The group also had holdings in at least three fields for which participation would be sought, namely Thistle, Dunlin, and Hutton. Occidental was also felt to be a good prospect, both because it was very dependent on the North Sea, and because it had conceded participation on severe terms in Libya. There were, however, doubts about the reaction of their partners in the relevant fields (Piper and Claymore). It was expected that an approach would be made by other licensees, and in general it was likely that the smaller companies might find it attractive to concede participation because of the difficulties they would have in financing their field development costs. In this context it was noted that these were currently escalating at an alarming rate.

At the NSRC meeting it was agreed that it was essential to negotiate with the companies individually not collectively, so that the effort could be concentrated on the most promising candidates. Mr Varley felt that Gulf, Conoco and Occidental should be included in the first round of companies. It was agreed, however, that the process should be started by the Secretary of State writing to all licensees on the subject.

What Government contribution to costs?

The third main issue was Government contribution to costs. The starting point was again the July White Paper which stated that the Government would meet its share of costs including past costs. Officials emphasised the importance of maintaining the stance that, apart from offset payments, no payment should be made for profits foregone. It was anticipated that the negotiations would be much concerned with the issue of *when* the Government paid its share of the costs and how they would be measured. It was envisaged that the Government would make its contribution to field development costs as they were incurred. It was also noted, however, that in Norway some agreements were providing that the state would pay its share of costs out of its share of the field's production income. This was much less favourable to the companies as they would have to wait for a considerable time before they obtained payment. But the carrying of the state's share of development costs was a plausible opening negotiating position from which a concession could later be made.

Several other questions on costs also arose. One was whether interest should be paid on past costs. A second was whether costs of (successful) exploration should be included, and, if the answer to this was positive, a third was whether abortive exploration costs should also be included. Officials felt that the Government's opening position should be not to allow any of these concessions. Conceding abortive exploration and interest would be quite expensive. DEN officials estimated that if participation at 51% on all commercial fields was activated from January 1976 the gross cost for development costs alone would be around £700 million, but if abortive exploration and interest were included it would become £1,150 million. It was recognised, however, that if all exploration costs were to be allowed for PRT it would be difficult to avoid making the same concession for participation. Allowing interest on past costs should be resisted as far as possible, though it might have to be conceded as a last resort. The conclusion of the discussion on this subject at the NSRC meeting on 30th October was that the Government should put the onus of suggesting the details of how the costs of participation should be met on the companies.

Clarification of offset payments

The fourth key subject which required clarification concerned offset payments. By this time it had been agreed that all licensees except BNOC would be subject to PRT which meant that those who accepted participation would be in a worse financial position than those who did not agree to it. It had also been agreed in principle that offset payments would be made to licensees acceding to participation to ensure that the present value of their profits would be the same as for companies rejecting participation. The payments would be made by BNOC directly to the Inland Revenue towards the discharge of the companies' tax liability. Officials felt that until negotiations commenced it would not be possible to decide on the precise method of calculation of the payments. Decisions had to be made at the outset whether to declare that the Government accepted the principle that the companies should be no worse off with participation. There would be no reason for a company to accept participation without offset payments, and if this was not clarified the negotiations would soon founder. Officials thus felt that the principle of offset payments should be mentioned at the outset, but without specification of the details. It was noted that financial equivalence might not constitute a sufficient inducement to accept participation because some had strong objections on other grounds. Consideration should thus be given to the notion that it might eventually be necessary to provide offset payments sufficiently large to put the participating companies in a better financial position than those which refused. But such an offer should be regarded as a last resort. In discussion at the NSRC meeting in was concluded that it was premature to take decisions on the method and extent of offset payments. Mr Lever expressed his view that either the companies would accommodate the Government because they believed it was in their interest so to do, or the level of financial incentive required to overcome their reluctance would be so great that it would prejudice the whole Government policy in this area.

BNOC and operating agreements

The last major issue identified related to Operating Agreements among co-licensees. These determined how major decisions were made. Officials suggested that the general principle should be that where BNOC participated the existing Operating Agreement should continue unchanged as far as possible. Thus BNOC would expect to acquire the rights of a 51% shareholder. It was felt that if a brand new agreement were negotiated there was a danger that the private sector companies would attempt to cut down BNOC's powers below those which its share should confer. Officials also felt that even if BNOC obtained the same rights as the other co-licensees it would be necessary to renegotiate the voting arrangements in the Operating Committee. These would be disturbed by the entrance of a new 51% shareholder. Officials understood that generally where there was more than one major licensee the Operating Agreements were such that, unless a decision had to be unanimous, major decisions could not be taken by one licensee on his own. It was expected that this would remain the case with BNOC involvement, and that this would be a sticking point in the negotiations. But the Government's opening position could be to state that the assumption was that a majority share-holder could put its resolutions through the Operating Committee. The size of the voting requirement was of course closely connected to the size of the shareholding, and it might be tactically desirable to treat the two together, but leaving the possibility of making a concession on one without also making a concession on the other. Officials felt, however, that if an agreement were to be reached on 51% participation, a requirement that important resolutions needed a higher percentage than BNOC's to be carried, would probably have to be conceded. At the NSRC meeting the principle was agreed that where BNOC participated it would do so on a basis which allowed present Operating Agreements to continue.

Security of supply in negotiations

Enhancing security of oil supply to the UK market was a major consideration for the Government at this time against the background of the 1973–1974 oil price shock and Arab boycott. But it was also appreciated that the integrated oil companies would wish to obtain possession of as much as possible of the North Sea oil they produced. There were obvious advantages in terms of security and quality, but additionally the companies would generally not wish participation oil to fall into the hands of competitors or, in the medium-term, to BNOC which could become a downstream competitor. It was thus appreciated that an offer to sell back participation oil to the companies was a key negotiating card. Bearing in mind that royalty oil would be taken in kind tactics which could be employed included making the buy-back of royalty oil conditional on participation, or selling royalty from non-participating licensees to those conceding participation. It was also noted that non-integrated companies might be perfectly happy to sell their oil to BNOC, and this could be offered to companies acceding to participation. In the early years the Government's room for manoeuvre might largely be confined to switching oil between the existing companies.

Participation could help North Sea disposal and refining policy which was just being finalised (see Chapter 8). Royalty oil in kind plus 51% participation meant that 57% of North Sea oil would be publicly owned, but to exploit this control required either a threat to withhold participation oil (which might stall the negotiations), or attach conditions on disposal which would make the negotiations more difficult and might be inconsistent with EEC rules. The achievement of participation would bring a greatly enhanced understanding of the destination of North Sea oil. Regarding tactics, officials felt that the Government should not give the impression that, if the companies conceded participation, they would be subject to greater restraints on disposal than if they did not agree to it. Thus the Government's objectives concerning destination should be clearly stated to all licensees at the earliest opportunity. This would permit the discussions with the companies on destination to be seen as separate from the participation negotiations, though they would proceed in parallel.

Buy-back contracts

The DEN felt that the key terms of buy-back contracts relating to duration and price should be discussed with the companies at an early stage. Regarding duration, a fixed term agreement, unless it were for a substantial number of years, would provide limited security, since the whole agreement would become open to negotiation. Thus an evergreen contract of no fixed total length, but subject to annual review with respect to quantity and satisfactory break clauses, would be preferable. This could involve agreeing a minimum period during which the break clause could not be invoked, while giving each party the right to terminate subject to a notice period. Abrupt termination would cause problems for either party. But too lasting a commitment would lessen the Government's influence on the destination of the oil. With respect to price long-term fixed price contracts would be unacceptable even with adjustment clauses. Clearly the Government had to take account of the values employed for royalty and tax. Any discounts to encourage participation would have to be clearly defined to avoid any reaction on the tax take.

In the light of the above Mr Varley felt that the Government's opening position should be to inform the companies that disposal policy with a substantial requirement to refine North Sea oil in the UK would apply to all licensees irrespective of participation, and that the Government would be willing to discuss proposals from the companies for the buy-back of participation oil, bearing in mind the keen interest in disposal and security of supply.

Opening meetings with companies

The NSRC approved Mr Varley's proposed negotiating stance and this was followed by no less than nine opening meetings with the companies (sometimes in groups) between 29th November and Christmas 1974. The early ones with Shell, BP, and Esso (separately) had all the three designated Ministers present. Some of the others were chaired by the Permanent Secretary or the Deputy Secretary at the DEN. At the very first meeting with Shell on 28th November Mr Lever emphasised that the participation sought was to be voluntary and fair, and the company would be no worse and no better off as a consequence. Participation should not be confused with nationalisation. The relevant 51% of future field expenditures would be met by the Government, but past expenditures would probably be covered by future income flows though suggestions from the company for a capital repayment would be considered.

Shell fears loss of control

The Shell representatives, led by Mr Baxendell, emphasised that a main concern was the prospective loss of control over their North Sea operations. There were grave doubts concerning the expertise and managerial proficiency of BNOC and they were worried about impediments to their speed of operation. BNOC would also be a partner with many other companies and would thus have to examine many plans and budgets. Its lack of expertise meant that it would have to spend a considerable time trying to understand complex problems involving enormous sums of money. There was a prospect of undesirable delay to projects. This might be a particular issue with the more difficult projects as BNOC could be expected to concentrate its attention on the best prospects. Mr Baxendell then questioned the purpose of the 51% state participation if the companies were to be no worse off as a consequence. Mr Lever emphasised the need for the Government to secure an automatic legal right to 51% of the oil.

BP's concerns

The meeting with BP representatives, led by their chairman Sir Eric Drake, took place on the same day. Mr Lever stated the Government's objectives in general terms on the same lines as those outlined to Shell. Sir Eric Drake emphasised the Government's existing shareholding in BP (now at 48%) and how, if 51% participation were negotiated, there would be a 75% Government stake in BP's North Sea activities. He felt that the current situation was quite delicate as he had recently been approached by a number of American oil companies whose confidence in the Government's intentions to the North Sea was less than that of BP. He had assured them that the British Government had never reneged on its obligations and hoped that his confidence was justified. He did not object in principle to the amendment of existing licences but was concerned about the details. He was also much concerned about BP's position in Alaska where the company had secured very large reserves. He was aware that contingency legislation had been prepared so that any discrimination against US companies operating abroad could be countered by action against offending countries' companies in the USA. It would thus be very undesirable for BP to be the leader in concluding a participation agreement as this might be interpreted as following from the Government's use of its large shareholding. Mr Lever emphasised that the Government would not discriminate against US companies. Sir Eric Drake then suggested that 51% participation would result in a substantial management responsibility as well, which could be a handicap to decision-making, given that decisions involving large sums sometimes had to be taken urgently. Sir Eric also pointed out that his main responsibilities were to all shareholders and he could not give away rights. There were also many detailed issues requiring clarification. For example, was participation to be based on licences, blocks, or fields?

In discussing the means by which BNOC's participation would be financed Mr Lever stated that the Government wanted to avoid any traditional form of capital payments and were thinking in terms of adjusting the future flow of income in an appropriate way. The Government would certainly meet its share of future expenditures, but with respect to past costs the Government hoped to agree an income flow which would meet the requirements of the companies by providing an adequate *quid pro quo* for participation and would consider proposals by which future income streams would be reduced in consideration of an earlier capital payment.

Esso's concerns

On the very next day a meeting was held with Esso who were represented by senior executives including Dr Pearce, Chairman of Esso UK, and Mr Dean, President of Esso Europe. Mr Lever outlined the Government's objectives on the same lines as indicated to BP and Shell. The Esso representatives indicated that, if given a free choice, they would prefer not to cede participation, but promised to cogitate on Mr Lever's suggestions. The company was concerned about the proliferation of new Government measures which would hit their operations including the forthcoming PRT, depletion controls, and new licence Regulations as well as participation.

Mr Lever's optimism

Following these meetings the NSRC met to review the position. Mr Lever felt that it would be possible to do a deal on the basis he had outlined, and safeguards could be included to deal with the companies' worries about interference in normal operations. He now felt that it was important to consider the rate of PRT in the context of participation, even though it was being emphasised that they were separate exercises. There could be merit in starting with a low PRT rate and increasing it later when circumstances permitted if this would facilitate participation. It was agreed that it was important to maintain the momentum of initial discussions. These continued apace and included a number of smaller companies who had their own distinct perspective on the issue. An example was the Argyll field partners who were interested to know that having BNOC as a partner could be helpful when fund-raising for future developments was involved. For example, a Government guarantee to banks for BNOC's 51% share would be possible. On another aspect, as none of the Argyll partners had its own refinery, the idea that BNOC could buy the oil was of considerable interest.

DEN's reflections on industry views

The DEN reflected on the comments received from the industry. It was then agreed that the Government's basic objective was to participate in commercial oil fields, but not in unproven acreage. Thus sharing in licences as they stood would not be appropriate. To participate effectively in the manner intended would involve carving out new licences covering only commercial fields. The private sector companies would remain on their own in the remainder of the old licences. It was also noted that the licence did not say what share was held by each co-licensee: this was clarified in the Operating Agreement. It would thus be necessary for the Agreement to provide that BNOC had 51% of the relevant undertaking. With respect to the composition of the 51% in a field it would be preferable to start by seeking 51% from each partner, but, if that proved difficult, unequal individual shares adding to 51% of the total would be acceptable. There were further complications when a field extended into more than one licence area. The preference was to acquire 51% in each consortium in the field rather than unequal shares adding to 51% as the latter could produce complications, given the continuing uncertainty about the proportions of the field being located in each block. On the timing of participation it was agreed that generally this should be immediately when a field was declared commercial.

Officials reflected further on the claims by oil companies that BNOC's involvement would delay field developments. It was felt that there were some positive advantages to the industry from BNOC participation. Thus BNOC would have more access to investment funds than many of the private companies. It could become a useful intermediary between the companies and the Government which could facilitate the resolution of disagreements. It was recognised that the introduction of a new partner owned by the state and having a 51% share could create difficulties. It was felt that assurances could be given to allay their worries. Thus it could be made very clear that BNOC would behave commercially in its role as a field partner. It would adhere to development plans already agreed. Participation in Operating Agreements was recognised to be particularly sensitive, and an assurance could be given that the intention was to enter into existing agreements with only the minimum changes needed to reflect the entry of a 51% partner. While changes would be needed to the voting arrangements adherence would be given to existing arrangements regarding items such as the timescale for major decisions, delegation rights of operator, and sole risk developments. It would also be made clear that existing operators would remain unchanged.

Possible buy-back arrangements

In the early part of 1975 in the light of early feedback from the oil companies, further consideration was given by officials to the stance that should be taken on some elements of the participation package. One concerned the details of buy-back contracts. There was ready agreement that the buy-back price should reflect the full market value of the oil. With respect to the appropriate volumes and length of contract it was hard to define a suitable negotiating position when it was unclear how much oil BNOC would require for trading. One possibility would be that BNOC could sell back virtually all of its oil for a moderate period (say three years), but then a lower proportion for a much longer period. It was also noteworthy that some licensees which were not orthodox oil companies or which had no downstream interests would not be very interested in buy-back contracts at all. The integrated companies would be very anxious to purchase participation oil, however, and it was felt that a flexible approach should be taken on this whole subject.

Relationship of buy-back contracts to refining policy

Buy-back arrangements had to be seen in the context of disposal policy, which suggested a target of the refining of up to two-thirds of North Sea oil in the UK. But contractual arrangements to ensure that a satisfactory proportion of buy-back oil was refined in the UK could well conflict with Article 34 of the Treaty of Rome. One alternative was to sell much of the participation oil back to the companies and get them to agree outside the contract to refine it in the UK. At May 1975 the view in the DEN was that the objective should be to aim for buy-back contracts with various durations and of varying volumes to minimise the cost of providing BNOC with adequate flexibility. The initial negotiating position should be to offer back 100% of participation oil for 2–5 years, followed by 75% for 3–5 years with a 2–3 years taper-off thereafter. The companies should also be prepared to clearly state that they would take account of the Government's disposal policy.

Great cost of oil disruption

Further studies by DEN officials resulted in a detailed paper being prepared for the NSRC. The context was felt to be the great cost to the British economy which would result from a disruption to oil supplies. The Treaty of Rome permitted export restrictions in a national emergency but, under the international sharing arrangements, in an emergency the UK would be forced to forego perhaps a substantial proportion of its normal supplies from abroad. Thus the best safeguard of supplies in an emergency would be to have a high proportion of the UK's needs met from the North Sea. Taking all royalty oil in kind would make substantial volumes available to BNOC, but it would be preferable to satisfy BNOC's needs through participation and keep royalty oil as a reserve. It was not expected that UK oil consumption would increase in the next decade,[1] and it would be difficult for BNOC to break into a stagnant downstream market. With a static market BNOC would not expect to have a downstream market exceeding ten million tonnes in 1985 with five million tonnes a more realistic target. If BNOC exported a third of its oil as crude (which might be politically contentious) its ability to handle oil would be increased by up to five million tonnes giving an upper possibility of fifteen million tonnes per year. DEN officials also calculated that by 1982 over 20 million tonnes per year could accrue to BNOC without participation oil if all royalty oil and the NCB's share were taken.

In determining policy for the buy-back of participation oil it was recognised that there were disadvantages in seeking to obtain more oil for BNOC than it could effectively handle. It was important not to reduce the confidence of the oil companies to such an extent that they were unwilling to commit themselves to continued large investment in the UKCS. Given the differing requirements of the companies negotiators might best seek a variety of buy-back contracts, with the variations related to their downstream requirements, and with all having reducing percentages through time. The oil should not be sold back to the companies at a discount, and any financial adjustments should be made through offset payments. It was inadvisable, and possibly in breach of the Treaty of Rome, to include firm commitments on disposal in buy-back contracts, but written undertakings from the companies that they would adhere to the Government's disposal policy should be sought. At the NSRC meeting in late July 1975 it was decided that officials should try to devise a form of declaration which the oil companies might be persuaded to sign during the participation negotiations, committing them to consult the Government about safeguarding security of supply in an emergency. This would require careful wording to avoid objections by the industry or internationally under EEC and International Energy Agency (IEA) obligations.

Meaning of "no better no worse off"?

Meanwhile several other issues relating to participation were being given urgent attention by officials and Ministers. There was a lack of clarity on the precise meaning of the term "no worse off" which had been employed by Mr Lever, and Government negotiators should be in a position to put forward firm proposals on the financial terms. Different situations could be distinguished. In a case where the Government made no direct contribution to costs and the oil company financed all development costs from its own funds its post-tax cash flow before and after participation would be calculated and an offset payment equal to the difference would be made. In the case where contributions to past costs were contemplated and paid from income from field production, the size of the offset payment could remain unchanged, except that part or all would be termed a contribution to past costs.

It was recognised that the companies might ask the Government to pay interest relating to what would become the Government's share of past expenditure and that there could be differing views on how the revenues from the early years of field life might be shared. But it was also noted that, where BNOC shared in the costs before commencement of production, the oil company would be relieved of some costs and risks. It was then arguable that BNOC's contribution should attract interest. The interest rate should be no lower than that payable by a company on its borrowings. Treasury officials suggested that such an interest rate would be very difficult to determine and proposed that an uplift which the Government would recover and retain should be used instead. It was further argued by DEN officials that, because of the risks involved, such as from technical failure, falling oil prices, or escalating costs, BNOC's cost contribution should attract a premium interest rate. In the typical situation where the oil company was borrowing to finance the development of a field the Government could have other options, including taking over its share of a loan and becoming involved in the negotiation of loan terms with the lending banks. At its meeting in mid-May 1975 the NSRC generally endorsed the approach proposed, including the interest risk premium concept, and authorised a worked illustrative example to be shown by Government negotiators to the oil companies.

Possible costs of participation

DEN officials also prepared estimates of the likely costs of participation. In the long run the net cost would be zero, but there would be heavy net outgoings in the early years. For sixteen fields officials estimated that, using the approach noted above, the cumulative net costs to the Government would be £810 million by 1977 (at 1974 prices), falling to £240 million by 1980.

Participation in pipelines and terminals?

An issue which had been raised in early discussions with the companies was whether participation should extend to pipelines and terminals. It had already been agreed that BNOC would be legally able to construct pipelines or participate in others by agreement. DEN officials examined the policy case for and against such participation, paying particular attention to the Forties pipeline to Cruden Bay, the Piper line to Flotta, and the Brent and Ninian lines to Sullom Voe. The case against participation was felt principally to relate to the costs involved. The costs for the four pipelines were very high. The costs of the terminals at Sullom Voe and Flotta would also be very high. The introduction of state participation at Sullom Voe might also complicate the tense relationship between the companies and the Shetland Islands Council. After much difficult negotiation a complex agreement regarding the terms for use of the terminal had been reached. Participation by BNOC might reopen the problems.

The case *for* participation contained several strands. It would provide very useful experience to BNOC and help it to become an integrated oil company. The information which it acquired would also be useful to the Government. But the main argument was that the companies themselves would probably argue strongly for it, and its absence could seriously hamper the negotiations. The companies could be expected to argue that the fields and associated pipelines were viewed as integrated investments and the costs of both should be shared by participants. They could also argue that there was clear merit in using the same boundaries for participation as had been stipulated for PRT. The compatibility of offset payments consistent with the PRT ring fence was simple and logical. The recommendation of DEN officials was to indicate that the Government's objective was to secure 51% interest in pipelines and terminals relating to the commercial oilfields. There was no present intention to participate in gas fields or gas pipelines, but this would be further considered in the future. The Treasury was not persuaded by these arguments, and argued that state participation in pipelines and terminals was expensive and unnecessary. Ample control was provided for third-party access at negotiated or imposed tariffs. Participation was not necessary as the provision of help with development finance could be given under a clause of the Petroleum Bill. In sum participation in the four oil pipelines was irrelevant to the Government's present objectives.

The issue was discussed at the NSRC in late July 1975 when Mr Lever, Mr Dell, and the CPRS broadly supported the views of Treasury officials and felt that the DEN proposals went too far. Further information on (a) the likely costs and (b) the consequences of participation and non-participation was required. In the meantime negotiators should take the line that the Government would prefer not to participate in pipelines and terminals where heavy expenditures were involved, but, if pressed a willingness to discuss such participation would be conceded, but only on an *ad referendum* basis.

Discussions with companies on "no better no worse off"

While these deliberations on policy and negotiating strategy continued discussions with the companies had been gathering pace. Thus on 23rd May 1975 DEN officials met with Conoco and Gulf representatives and presented to them the illustrative example of the "no better no worse off" Government proposals. The two companies responded then, and subsequently, with several proposals of their own, with the general objective of being less complicated than the Government's model. DEN officials found some ideas of interest but others unacceptable. There were three main suggestions, termed the Twin Assignment Proposal, the Call Proposal, and the Deferred Purchase Proposal. In examining the details it should be noted that the NCB already had a one-third share in the fields (namely part of Thistle, part of Dunlin and part of the UK share of Statfjord). Thus only 27% participation was necessary to ensure a Government majority share.

Twin assignment proposal

In essence under the Twin Assignment Proposal the companies would assign 27% of their interests in the relevant licences to the Government which would then reassign the oil rights relating to that 27% interest back to the companies. BNOC would thus have legal title to 27% of the companies' licence interests, but the latter would have the right to own and receive 27% of all oil produced under these licences. The companies would be in an unchanged financial position so long as (a) the twin assignments did not constitute a taxable transaction (either in the UK or USA), and (b) the Government would not unreasonably withhold consent to any assignment to a third party under the new Regulations. The proposal from Gulf and Conoco also envisaged that after x years (to be negotiated) BNOC would have the option to purchase 27% of the oil produced by the companies, thereby raising BNOC's full share to 51%.

Call proposal

The Call Proposal would eliminate the double assignment procedure. In essence the companies holding the interests in the licences would grant to BNOC a call (option to purchase) on 27% of the oil they produced. This right would be exercisable after x years (to be negotiated) and not from the beginning of the agreement. It would again be necessary for the tax authorities in the UK and USA to recognise that this did not constitute a taxable transaction, and for the Government to acknowledge that its participation obligations had been met, and that it would not unreasonably withhold consent for any assignment to a third party.

The companies claimed that, because of their special position as BNOC partners, the two proposals should satisfy the Government's objectives, because the NCB holding gave BNOC adequate knowledge of, and an effective voice in, the licence interests, no public expenditures were involved, and BNOC would obtain full title to 51% of the oil in due course. DEN officials agreed that the proposals were considerably simpler than their scheme, involved no additional claim on public funds, and, because of the special circumstances with the NCB, would not create a precedent for other schemes. On balance the Call Proposal seemed preferable on grounds of simplicity, though the Twin Assignment Proposal had presentational advantages.

Deferred purchase proposal

The Deferred Purchase Proposal involved an option for BNOC, to be exercised after, say, five years, to raise its share in the blocks from 33% to 51% at a negotiated arm's length price based on the asset value of the blocks. BNOC would thus end up with a 51% equity interest. In the interim there would be an agreement whereby the companies would assign to BNOC a bare legal title to 27% of their licence interest. This was also a simple scheme, but had the disadvantage of a claim on public funds. There would also be difficulties over the valuation. On balance the Call Proposal was the most attractive to DEN officials.

Mr Lever favours twin assignment proposal

At its meeting in late July 1975 Mr Lever expressed support for the Call Proposal, felt that the Twin Assignment Proposal was also acceptable, but did not favour the Deferred Purchase scheme. Following discussion it was agreed that, given the presentational advantages of the Twin Assignment Proposal, negotiation should give first preference to it, secondly to the Call Proposal, but the Deferred Purchase scheme should not be encouraged.

Progress at July 1975

By 10th July 1975 discussions had taken place with twenty-two companies which had earlier been categorised as offering reasonable prospects for procuring an agreement, and with several others where the prospects were felt to be somewhat less promising. As well as Conoco/Gulf and BP negotiations were in progress with Burmah, which had well-known financial problems, (and were under pressure from their bankers to cooperate), the LSMO group, Tricentrol, and RTZ. Officials were also optimistic that negotiations would soon start with Thomson, and possibly with their partners Occidental, Allied Chemicals and Getty. Other companies had formally adopted a neutral position but had sought the illustrative details of the Government's position. No formal approach had been made to Shell and Exxon, but no company had refused outright to consider participation. Because of the importance of field development financing arrangements DEN officials felt that banking groups preparing financing proposals should also receive a presentation on participation. Officials also recommended that Shell and Exxon be invited to meetings at which they would be given the same presentation as other companies had received on the financial proposals.

Bankers to be informed of proposals

At the NSRC meeting in mid-July Mr Lever felt that it was particularly important that bankers should be made aware of the flexibility of the participation arrangements. He emphasised the large borrowing requirements which were implied by the participation costs and the consequential advantages of negotiating forms of participation which involved the lowest increase in borrowing. With this in mind he was not convinced that Shell and Exxon needed to be approached at this stage. The Committee decided that relevant bankers should be informed of the Government's proposals while Shell and Exxon should be approached informally to discover whether they would welcome a presentation.

What details to make public?

In anticipation of agreements being reached consideration had to be given to the question of what details should be made public. There was already a panoply of obligations on the Government to keep Parliament and the public at large informed. Disclosure would bring credit for the discharge of the political commitment to secure participation. But full disclosure could negatively affect the negotiators' position in successive deals. The companies would also have some disclosure obligations but these would vary. A strong company might require to disclose very little of its agreement whereas a weak one which was dependent on Government financial assistance might have to disclose extensive details. Ministers would obviously wish to inform Parliament as soon as commitments had been made in principle, and a standard announcement would confirm the 51% interest and the proportion of oil sold as buy-back. Where offset payments and/or financial guarantees were involved, more extensive disclosures would be involved. Because the circumstances of each case would vary the disclosures would also vary, but the general aim should be to make the announcements as full as possible consistent with commercial confidentialities and the conduct of later negotiations. The NSRC agreed to these proposals, with Lord Balogh suggesting that publicity should be given to the progress which the Government had made on North Sea oil policies and the generous concessions which had been made to the companies (such as with buy-back arrangements).

Safeguarding supplies in emergency and EEC/IEA obligations

Officials had to give further consideration to declarations which might be included in buy-back contracts committing the companies to consult with the Government about safeguarding supplies in the event of an emergency. An inter-departmental paper was agreed on this subject which raised the basic questions of the retention of North Sea oil in an emergency and its likely effectiveness. The international obligations were clear. Under Article 34 of the Treaty of Rome quantitative restrictions on exports to partner countries were prohibited, and, while Article 36 permitted such restrictions in an emergency, there was legal advice that this would not justify action which affected EEC partners. These considerations underlaid the announced refining and disposal policy. Membership of the IEA contained both constraints and safeguards. In an emergency oil would be allocated by the IEA, and it was anticipated that the UK could expect to obtain up to 90% of its normal domestic requirements, at least up to the point when 50% of the IEA's emergency reserves had been consumed. Thus overt action to restrict exports in an emergency would put the UK in breach of both EEC and IEA rules. Implementation of currently-stated refining and disposal policy might enable more oil to be kept in an emergency without arousing hostility, but action specifically designed to evade these international obligations would certainly be criticised and could result in infraction proceedings. It was noted that the difficulties would not arise immediately if the undertakings with the companies were kept confidential, but it was doubtful if this was feasible. A consequence of confidential agreements would also make it impossible to demonstrate publicly how North Sea policies had increased the UK's security of supply.

It was also noted that in an emergency the Oil Industry Emergency Committee would take control over the disposal of oil and an undertaking by the companies simply to consult would have little practical value. Further, knowledge that such undertakings were being sought would arouse suspicions that there was an intention to default on international obligations. The oil companies would be conscious of their own obligations under EEC and IEA rules, and would in any case dislike constraints on their supply flexibility.

These problems suggested a possible alternative to officials. This was to include in a buy-back contract a condition that in any emergency it could be broken at, say, six months notice. This might be drafted such that it did not breach the Treaty of Rome, and the economy could probably survive for six months on stocks plus some demand constraint. But it was recognised that such a condition in a contract would arouse suspicions and the oil companies might well look for some compensation as their own security of supply was threatened. It was also noted that BNOC would be subject to EEC and IEA rules, and flouting of these could not be undertaken irrespective of who had title to North Sea oil. The conclusion of officials was thus that conditions attached to buy-back contracts aimed at safeguarding UK supplies in an emergency would be open to international criticism and could be costly to obtain. Further, they would not add significantly to supply. But the whole development of North Sea oil would substantially increase security of supply. If there were spare producing capacity it should be possible to retain the related extra production in the UK. In all the circumstances it was not recommended that additional measures should be sought through the medium of buy-back contracts. At its meeting in October, 1975 the NSRC agreed that negotiators need not seek these additional safeguards on security of supply, that a public statement should be made on the Government's powers to control North Sea oil in an emergency, and that Lord Kearton, the Chairman Designate of BNOC, should be invited to suggest guidelines for negotiators on buy-back arrangements.

Single assignment proposal

Concurrent with these deliberations negotiations with the oil companies continued. Gulf and Conoco had tabled a revised proposal and a list of associated points. Officials sought further negotiating authority in the light of these. The Twin Assignment Proposal now became a Single Assignment Proposal which involved a technical change but no new issue of principle. In the original proposal the economic interest in the licences held by the US parent companies under agreements made with their UK subsidiaries would have been transferred to BNOC and then reassigned to the companies. The Single Assignment method preserved the transfer of title from the UK subsidiaries, but made this conditional on the parent US companies retaining their economic interest.

Negotiations with Burmah Oil

Negotiations were also continuing with the Burmah Oil Company at this time. The company had increased its interests in the North Sea as a consequence of its purchase of Signal Oil. Thus it became the operator of the Ninian field (with 20% interest) and Thistle (with 19% interest). Complications then arose emanating from the company's financial difficulties. Following several acquisitions and contractual commitments involving the volatile tanker market the company had became financially over-extended, and by late 1974 was in danger of defaulting on large dollar loans. The full details of this and the rescue operation undertaken by the Bank of England with Government support are outside the scope of this history. In essence, in spite of the high risks involved, and to maintain confidence in North Sea investment it was decided to support the company. The measures included transfer of the company's 21% holding in BP to the Bank of England.[2] Burmah confirmed its firm intention to proceed expeditiously with the development of Ninian and Thistle and to accept the principle of participation. Following the rescue announcement events moved at a fast pace. Mr Alastair Down, formerly a director of BP, was appointed Chairman and Managing Director of Burmah. The partners in the large Ninian field subsequently expressed concern at Burmah's operatorship of the field. From discussions among them the suggestion was made to DEN that Chevron which had an 18% share should be appointed as operator. DEN was initially unenthusiastic, because the replacement of Burmah as operator might further reduce confidence in the company. The views of the partners had to be recognised, however, and DEN approached BP (who had a 12% stake) that it take over the role to preserve British operatorship. But BP did not feel able to do this because their resources were already stretched with Forties and other North Sea interests, though they did agree to take over the main responsibility for the Ninian pipeline. DEN subsequently agreed that Chevron should become the operator. Burmah remained operator for Thistle.[3]

In March 1975 the Government asked Burmah to confirm that it would continue to meet its remaining share of future development costs (after taking account of BNOC's prospective participation share), but the company was unable to give a categorical undertaking. Nevertheless the Government decided to press on with the negotiations on the grounds that an early agreement would be advantageous and could reduce the likelihood of delays to the field development if Burmah had difficulty in raising its share.

The negotiations were prolonged and complex. From April 1975 the Government's negotiating stance reflected its bargaining power and the NSRC approved the view that the term "no worse off" should be interpreted in the manner most favourable to the Government. Any participation terms offered to the company were also to be based on the understanding that Burmah would raise its 49% of investment funds unaided.

There were several sticking points in the negotiations. Burmah proposed that it should be able to buy back substantial volumes of any participation oil, namely 100% for the first ten years, 50% for the following five years, and 25% for the remaining years, with an option to extend the 100% element if it could demonstrate that it could utilise all the oil in its downstream operations. Originally the company wanted royalty oil to be included in the buy-back arrangement, but later conceded that it be excluded. In October 1975 Ministers were asked to approve the negotiating stance whereby BNOC would be given the rights to receive 25% of the oil (including royalty oil) over the life of each field, on the understanding that this could be reduced if Burmah could demonstrate that it thereby received a material financial benefit which would reduce the cost of the support operation. But the minimum which BNOC received could not be less than the royalty oil. It was felt that to request less than 25% of the oil would set an embarrassing precedent, but DEN officials were also aware that BNOC did not have a demonstrable need for as much as 25% of the oil from all the fields. At its meeting on 15th October the NSRC was quite concerned at reports of Burmah's continued financial difficulties, and Ministers decided that participation and possible further financial support would have to be jointly considered. The Committee also agreed to Burmah's request that a rate of interest should be substituted for uplift in the calculation of offset payments which had been proposed by officials. It was noted, however, that 75% uplift would have given Burmah a rate of return in excess of 20% which was felt to be very high. It was agreed that the interest rate should be related to the cost of finance to the borrower and 3% over LIBOR was suggested to be an appropriate rate.

At a further meeting between officials and Burmah at the end of October 1975 the company was informed that the Government would now agree to the request that participation would cover pipelines and terminals. A thorny issue was the extent of participation in the context of the possible disposal by Burmah of some of its assets to third parties. The company was very keen to ensure that, in the words of Mr Alistair Down its Chief Executive, the share which Burmah would retain after participation would be a "clean 49%", meaning that it could dispose of part of this without the buyer being involved in further BNOC participation. The Government side was concerned about the likely extent of such disposals before coming to a view on the issue, but the company was not yet in a position to provide a firm estimate.

The subject of the detailed calculation of offset payments became extremely complex. Burmah proposed a post-PRT and pre-corporation tax scheme with offset payments for capital recovery (including interest) starting from first production with the computation essentially being on a cash-flow basis with a capital contribution. Thus BNOC would retain sufficient of the revenues to reimburse it for its capital expenditure and interest charges, and the remainder would be paid to Burmah as reimbursement of 51% of past costs and offset payments, all of which would leave the company no better and no worse off. Officials debated the acceptability of this formula. There were complex problems principally involving taxation. A main issue was how the notional PRT that would have been borne by Burmah on the 51% interest transferred to BNOC would be calculated. This would be required for calculating offset payments and the rate of reimbursement of past costs. Burmah had also asked for a notional corporation tax payment to be made to provide for BNOC to compensate it for any disadvantages attributable to the offset arrangements. The Inland Revenue was in no doubt that such calculations involved serious difficulties. These were both conceptual and practical. There were too many variables to design workable rules for all the plausible situations that could arise, though some rules could be laid down to reduce the areas of uncertainty. Thus valuation of gross revenues used for calculating Burmah's PRT should be grossed up for calculation of the offset itself and the notional PRT. This should also apply to field and other expenses.

In the midst of these deliberations it became clear that Burmah's financial difficulties were continuing and that further Government support would be required. Mr Benn, the Secretary of State for Energy, made a Statement to the House of Commons on 3rd December 1975 indicating that the Government would renew its guarantee for the company's dollar borrowing for another nine months in order to give it further time to sell its US assets at a satisfactory price. He also announced that the Government had offered to purchase the whole or part of Burmah's North Sea assets at a fair, arm's length price. Attention was diverted to this issue and away from participation, and at the end of the year work on the complexities of offset payments had been suspended.

Mr Lever reports progress to colleagues

In late 1975 Mr Lever reported to his Ministerial colleagues on the overall progress of the negotiations. Seven companies, including BP and Burmah had publicly agreed in principle to 51% participation, and negotiations with Gulf and Conoco were felt to be at an advanced stage. It was hoped that Heads of Agreement with one or two companies could be reached in the near future. It was acknowledged that some of the other companies, including Shell and Exxon, had reacted coolly to the Government's proposals. Mr Lever felt it was clear that, given the size of the PSBR, participation should be sought with the minimum call on public expenditure. He hoped that in some agreements at least it would be possible that BNOC would not be required to provide 51% of ongoing development costs, let alone historic costs. In some cases, such as Burmah, it was inevitable that finance for ongoing development costs would have to be provided. He warned his colleagues of the importance which the companies attached to command over the North Sea oil which they produced, and this had to be borne in mind in the negotiations, given that participation was designed to be reached by voluntary means.

Lord Kearton intervenes

All these pain-staking deliberations and negotiations were interrupted in the later weeks of 1975 by the forceful intervention of Lord Kearton. Although still Chairman-designate of BNOC he had been appointed a member of the NSRC. He had become increasingly frustrated at the slow pace of the negotiations and in particular at the likely negative effect of the buy-back arrangements on the position of BNOC. In a note to the NSRC he indicated that, if BNOC were to be a credible company, it had to build up its activities quite rapidly. He felt that the prospective slow rate at which BNOC would acquire effective control over significant oil supplies – perhaps only 10% of production in ten years time – would make it difficult for the company to recruit staff of high calibre. He felt it essential that BNOC should get involved in downstream activities within a fairly short time period to establish its credibility and to prevent it being in an impossibly weak position as a seller of crude oil. He acknowledged that this was not the time to build new downstream capacity, as there was a growing surplus, but other routes could be explored, including acquisitions (not favoured), partnerships, and agreements with other companies to process and sell BNOC oil on an agency basis. A target of 30 million tonnes of downstream capacity for BNOC by 1980 was felt to be reasonable.

Lord Kearton then argued that to achieve such targets attention should be concentrated on the large oil companies, which in practice meant BP, Shell, and Exxon, plus to lesser extent Occidental and its partners. The particular package which he had in mind included (a) a minority BNOC stake (perhaps 20%) in the fields, possibly on a full partnership basis, (b) a Government assurance that BNOC would not seek further participation for the life of the current Parliament, and (c) a provision that BNOC would pay PRT. Lord Kearton felt that the attractions of this package for the companies were (a) the removal of uncertainty about further participation demands, (b) the avoidance of having BNOC as a downstream competitor, and (c) a positive long-term supply arrangement with BNOC which in the 1980s would have command of more North Sea oil than any other single producer.

Mr Lever's reaction to Lord Kearton's proposals

Mr Lever set out his reaction to Lord Kearton's proposals. He queried the notions that BNOC's credibility depended on having control of large quantities of oil and being substantially involved in downstream activities. Providing expert assistance to the Government was also valuable. The Corporation's credibility did not depend on substantial near term downstream involvement. BNOC could avoid being a weak seller of North Sea crude by simply taking those quantities which it could readily market. Even royalty oil could be taken in kind or cash at the Government's discretion. Mr Lever felt that the participation negotiations had little chance of success if the radical approach proposed by Lord Kearton were adopted. He misunderstood both the strength of the Government's negotiating position and the attitude of the major oil companies. Participation was voluntary and the companies did not need to surrender control over the oil. They would not be impressed by an offer that BNOC would help them sell the oil from the outset as they, and not BNOC, had the downstream facilities. It was also unlikely that they would agree to be refining and marketing agents for BNOC, it being more obviously in their interests to buy back participation oil and sell it themselves. The Government's best negotiating card was the assurance from a voluntary participation agreement that the subject had been completed. Mr Lever added that even this might not convince some companies which might feel that they could do better to exploit their existing licences alone and deal with future problems as they arose. They might well feel that BNOC could not become a serious competitor for a considerable number of years. Finally, Mr Lever felt that there should be no concern from the Government side about precedents being set on any agreement. Different contracts were defensible because there were clear differences in the position of individual companies. For these reasons Mr Lever was against changing strategy towards participation.

At its meeting on 10th November the NSRC discussed these memoranda. No agreement was reached on Lord Kearton's specific proposal, and it was decided that he should prepare a fuller paper on the strategy which he thought BNOC should adopt. In the meantime to avoid confusion his own informal talks with the oil companies should cease. On a particular aspect of participation there was support for the notion that buy-back contracts should generally be restricted to a three-year period.

Lord Kearton's radical proposals on BNOC strategy

Lord Kearton quickly produced a detailed paper on BNOC strategy. After reviewing the existing situation on the lines of his earlier memorandum, and recognising the financial constraints on the Government, he concluded that there should be four elements of strategy. The first was to secure options to purchase considerable quantities of oil in order to give BNOC leverage to promote national and commercial objectives in its relations with the existing companies. The second and near term element should be to build up maximum understanding of upstream and downstream operations in the UK. The third element should be to obtain options to become minority partners in downstream activities. The fourth element was to pursue partnership arrangements with existing companies, particularly BP, because of the Government's existing major shareholding which already provided an opportunity to influence the company's strategy. Several arrangements between BNOC and BP were possible, and Lord Kearton raised the idea that the whole of BP's UK operations could be transferred to the Corporation. He recognised that there were formidable reasons against this proposal, but insisted that the potential existed for fruitful cooperation between BNOC and BP as well as with the other major companies. Less radical arrangements were also possible. Examples were a joint BNOC/BP company in which BNOC had a 51% share, and another would involve BNOC initially only taking control of BP's North Sea interests. To discover what relationships were plausible it was important to exchange views with BP.

Officials have serious reservations on Lord Kearton's proposals

The subject of Lord Kearton's proposals was deemed to be so important that a special Ministerial Group was set up to consider them. The Prime Minister, who chaired the Group, requested officials to examine Lord Kearton's idea that BP's UK operations should be used as the nucleus for BNOC, and an inter-departmental group from DEN, Treasury, Inland Revenue, FCO, Department of Industry and Bank of England prepared a paper on the subject. The scale of the operation was a concern. The value of BP's UK assets was estimated to be well over £1,000 million, and, though the Government had a large shareholding, the value of the private stake would be far above the total bill for nationalising shipbuilding and aircraft (estimated at £170 million). It was assumed that the cooperation of BP would be required, and so any deal had to be acceptable to the company's Board and private shareholders. Contrary to Lord Kearton's belief officials felts that the negotiations would be very protracted.

The case for the proposal was that it would establish early on a credible powerful and expert enterprise provided that the majority of the staff could be retained. Such a company could readily be awarded sole licences which would lead to extra state revenues and control over the disposition of North Sea oil. With downstream assets BNOC would no longer be a weak seller.

The effect on BP would be dramatic given the great importance of its UK North Sea and downstream assets to its worldwide operations. The proposal would be repugnant to the company which would claim heavy compensation for the disruption. The loss of its entire UK base would weaken its credit rating and its ability to borrow internationally. With respect to the financing of the scheme Lord Kearton had suggested that this could be facilitated by the cancellation of the BP shares currently held by the Government and the Bank of England to the extent necessary. Officials could see no advantage in this for BP's management and private shareholders. The reduction in BP's capital would require difficult negotiations with the current lenders to the company, and it would result in an increase in its debt: equity ratio with an impairment to its capital raising ability. Other methods of payment involved major tax problems. It appeared inevitable to officials that any settlement with BP would involve very large public expenditure.

Officials identified other possible negative effects. The apprehensions of other companies operating in the North Sea regarding participation would be intensified. Their fear of unfair competition from BNOC could turn to outright opposition if BNOC's development proceeded in the way proposed. The change in the rules applicable to the participation talks could create a crisis of confidence. The entire participation subject would require to be reviewed if BP's UK assets were acquired wholly or in part. A particular effect would be the dashing of hopes to develop the UK as a petrochemical growth centre.

The conclusions of officials were that it was essential that BNOC's capability should be built up without the disadvantage to the economy and to BP in terms of disruption and confidence as well as in financial terms which Lord Kearton's proposal would bring. It was thus recommended that other possibilities for expediting participation and building up BNOC should be explored, and BP should be urged to provide cooperation to BNOC in staffing and in marketing by other means.

Ministers consider BNOC/BP relationship

The inter-departmental paper was submitted to the Ministerial Group chaired by the Prime Minister and considered at its meeting on 23rd October 1975. The Secretary of State, Mr Benn, made it clear that he did not agree with the views of officials and felt that Lord Kearton's views should be considered further. He planned to prepare a paper of his own indicating how the difficulties identified by officials could be overcome. In discussion strong concern was expressed that Lord Kearton, by talking about his ideas in the City and elsewhere, was causing confusion and anxiety by proposals including the threat of nationalisation. There was a danger of great damage being caused to BP, and, if it were deprived of its UK assets, it might even relocate outside the UK with a loss to national tax revenues and the balance of payments.

In further discussions Ministers also considered whether a merger between BNOC and BGC would produce a fast build-up of expertise. It was noted that BGC had built up a strong expertise in North Sea gas activities, but it had to be acknowledged that it was neither big nor expert enough in oil operations to fulfil the required role.

The conclusions of the Ministerial Group were that officials had examined only Lord Kearton's most radical proposal. There were other possibilities, and it was decided that a mixed committee of Ministers and officials should examine them and report to the Ministerial Group. The Secretary of State for Energy would submit his provisional paper on Lord Kearton's proposals. In the meantime Lord Kearton should be informed that his proposals for the present had not been accepted, and that he should desist from canvassing them further as this could do more harm than good.

Soon after Lord Kearton met with the Prime Minister and impressed on Mr Wilson his concern that BNOC had very little credibility because the participation terms currently being negotiated seemed likely to give it very little oil to market. Further, no progress had been made in finding high quality, oil-experienced staff. The Prime Minister recognised these difficulties, but the procedure to be followed should be on the lines of the conclusions of the Ministerial Group.

Mr Benn's memorandum

Mr Benn prepared a Memorandum for the Ministerial Group giving his views. He expressed support for Lord Kearton's interpretation of the current and prospective position regarding the build-up of BNOC. He examined several other possible routes by which the Corporation could develop. These included the takeover of BP's UK assets, a joint venture with BP, a management contract with BP, cooperation agreements with other major companies, and takeover of Burmah. The conclusion was that a bolder approach was required and that the options noted above should be urgently examined.

Further Ministerial discussions

At the meeting of the Ministerial Group on 10th December 1975 Mr Benn reiterated his position, emphasising the need for BNOC to obtain options to retain a high proportion of participation oil and to form some form of partnership with BP. The advent of a new chairman of BP presented an opportunity for a fresh approach to the company. Mr Lever noted the departure from existing policy in some of Mr Benn's proposals. He was not against BNOC having access to downstream facilities which could help to maintain prices, but this should not involve the creation of new capacity which already exhibited an excess. In wider discussion it was agreed that the acquisition of Burmah's North Sea interests should be pursued. It was noted that, if sales of sufficient ex-Burmah shares in BP held by the Bank of England were made to finance the Burmah deal, the Government would be left with around 60% of the shares in BP. But there were doubts about whether this majority shareholding could be used to force BP to cooperate with BNOC, as this would be tantamount to oppression of minority shareholders. The meeting agreed that officials should further study the options about how the build-up of BNOC could be accelerated.

While this study was being undertaken it was acknowledged that negotiations with BP were at a standstill pending further Ministerial guidance. But at the end of 1975 officials felt that a package deal based on effective 51% option on Forties oil, collaboration on downstream activities, and secondment of good quality technical staff to BNOC offered promise.

BNOC's human resource needs

The human resource aspects of BNOC's activities had also been engaging both officials and Ministers at this time. Possible candidates for Board appointments were even examined by the Prime Minister. Difficulties were experienced in finding suitable candidates with direct oil industry experience. BP, for example, had refused to allow one of their Board members (Mr Pennell) to serve on the BNOC Board. There was a lack of success in the search for a chief executive, though there was some suspicion that Lord Kearton wanted to be his own chief executive. Just before Xmas 1975, Mr Benn announced ten Board appointments with Lord Kearton as full-time Chairman, and Lord Balogh, who had just retired from his Ministerial post, as Deputy Chairman. The striking feature of the composition of the Board was not its so-called geriatric nature as was rather misleadingly stated in the media, but the absence of members with oil industry experience. The membership strongly reflected the political environment within which the Corporation was being established including Ian Clark, the Chief Executive of Shetland Islands Council, who had been heavily involved in the negotiations with the oil companies over the Sullom Voe terminal, Denis Rooke the chairman-designate of BGC, Sir Robert Fairbairn, Chairman of the Clydesdale Bank, and Gavin Laird, a senior official of the Amalgamated Union of Engineering Workers. The two official members were John Liverman, Deputy Secretary at DEN, and Lawrence Airey, Deputy Secretary at the Treasury. Further appointments were promised and in the meantime Lord Kearton would be Chief Executive.

DEN considers options for build-up of BNOC

Very early in 1976 DEN officials prepared a paper on the options for the build-up of BNOC. The negotiations for the purchase of Burmah's interests in the Ninian and Thistle fields had made progress and a successful outcome was foreseen though the complication of the company's financial difficulties remained. But the reserves in question were comparatively small, and the success of participation policy required satisfactory agreements with BP, Shell and Esso who together held about half the reserves in the fourteen commercial fields. BP should be tackled first because it was the only wholly British major company, was mainly Government-owned, and had agreed in principle to participation. It was also felt that Shell and Esso would wait to see what deal was concluded with BP before committing themselves.

It was recognised that under their new chairman, Mr David Steel, BP remained implacably opposed to the takeover of their UK interests. This meant that any of the takeover proposals would involve protracted negotiations and would not advance BNOC's short-term development. It was thus felt best to make a three-fold attack on the BP position involving (1) the resumption of negotiations with the prime aim of obtaining for BNOC a vote on the Forties Operating Committee, plus options to take a share of the oil rising to 51% over a reasonable time period, (2) the negotiation of the secondment of a substantial batch of expert staff, and (3) the examination of the scope for downstream cooperation between BNOC and BP. All three elements should be pursued simultaneously, and it should be made clear to BP that they were all regarded as important from a Government perspective, and the ex-Burmah shares would not be disposed of until the objectives had been attained. It was felt that the Government's holding should be no lower than 51%.

Lord Kearton's response

Lord Kearton, now formally working as BNOC's chairman and chief executive, was shown the paper detailing the above proposals. He wrote to the Permanent

Secretary at the DEN reporting that over the past five months he had had over 300 meetings with oil company and related representatives, all of whom had been primarily interested in whether the provisions of the new 1975 Act would be activated in a meaningful sense. The oil companies did not like the idea of a state company, but Lord Kearton felt that they would become more cooperative if they were convinced that the Government intended BNOC to be taken seriously. There had been a retreat in Government purpose and intentions in recent months, and the oil companies felt that their firmness in opposition and lobbying had brought this about. He felt that the touchstone for BNOC was its relationship with BP, and that if the Corporation did not have a real share in BP's UK affairs it would be broken-backed from the start. Everyone in the industry he had talked to held this view. Lord Kearton's current proposal was to establish a joint company in which BNOC would have a 51% share, but would be content for BP to undertake day-to-day management. Career prospects for BP staff would be unaffected, but the Government's shareholding would involve membership of Boards and Committees, and permit the Government to have a voice in BP's affairs which it had not had in the sixty years of being a major shareholder.

Mr Benn supports Lord Kearton

To progress matters Mr Benn sought a meeting with the Prime Minister to enlist his support for the twin ideas that BP should be told publicly that no disposal of the Government's shares would be contemplated until a satisfactory participation deal had been concluded, and that negotiations with the company on the lines outlined above should now proceed. The Treasury had rather different views on these matters. They were anxious to sell the ex-Burmah shares as soon as possible, and wanted to restrict negotiations with BP to downstream participation arrangements which involved no cost in public expenditure. As far as the North Sea was concerned Forties had now come on stream, BP had satisfactory financing arrangements, and no Government contributions to costs were required.

Meeting with BP at Chequers

At his meeting with the Prime Minister Mr Benn suggested that Mr Wilson might meet with Mr Steel and Lord Kearton to impress upon them the importance of breaking the deadlock and concluding an agreement between BNOC and BP. Mr Benn also indicated that if BP made a participation agreement other major companies would follow suit. A dinner meeting at Chequers on 25th January 1976 was immediately arranged to exchange views but not to negotiate. It was attended by Mr Wilson, Mr Benn, Lord Kearton, and from BP Mr David Steel and Mr Monty Pennell. Mr Steel stressed the desire of BP to maintain its independence as a commercial company. In this context the prospect of an excessively close relationship with the Government was a matter of concern. The company wanted to use the cash flows from the North Sea to finance operations elsewhere. It also wanted to protect its overseas position, and in particular to ensure that any relationship with BNOC did not adversely affect its position in Alaska. The need for the Government to regulate North Sea activities was recognised, however, as was BNOC's role as the instrument for implementing some of these policies. Participation on a no gain no loss basis was accepted in principle, and BP still awaited a response from their proposal on how that might be implemented. The company remained unclear on what were the Government's objectives in this area, but suggestions of an all-embracing partnership were disturbing.

Lord Kearton indicated that BNOC wanted partnership with all oil companies operating in the North Sea. BNOC required knowledge and expertise to become an effective organisation and participation arrangements would facilitate this. The BP representatives indicated that they would be willing to help in providing expertise, but would prefer to do so on an arm's-length consultancy basis. The Government representatives felt that BNOC required a wide range of information and expertise which could not be provided on an arm's length basis. BP remained concerned about a close partnership which could jeopardise their independence and thus their competitive position overseas. Lord Kearton felt that a partnership arrangement in the North Sea need not include any BNOC involvement in BP's overseas activities. The notion that BNOC could acquire technical staff by secondment was mooted, as was the idea that BNOC's key staff ought to participate under a partnership agreement in the BP North Sea Operating Committees. The BP representatives reiterated their views that the Government should divest itself of the ex-Burmah shares because the very large Government/Bank of England shareholding could jeopardise the company's position in Alaska in particular. The Government's view was that the disposal of the ex-Burmah shares was a quite separate issue from participation in the North Sea. Summing up, Mr Wilson felt that there were some options which might be mutually attractive to both BNOC and BP, and these should be explored further by Lord Kearton, Mr Steel and Mr Pennell. On being informed of the outcome of the meeting the Chancellor of the Exchequer expressed relief that the ideas being considered further were less radical than some earlier ones, and indicated that the sale of the ex-Burmah shares would help to reduce the PSBR.

BP supplies detailed proposals

Soon afterwards Mr Benn sought BP's detailed views on the options discussed at the Chequers dinner. These were duly submitted by Mr Steel on 10th February. In his covering letter he made it clear that the proposals were made on the understanding that at the time of the announcement of an agreement it would also be stated that the ex-Burmah shares would be sold, and the British Government was not interfering in the commercial affairs of the company.

The document dealt with five proposals discussed at the Chequers meeting. The first considered the possible acquisition by BNOC of 51% of BP's North Sea assets via provision of loan finance. BP were now working on a proposal which restricted the Government's loan to an amount equal to future capital expenditure. For Forties this was estimated at £98 million. This would be left with BP for some years in order to acquire the 51% interest in the field. Compensation for past expenditure would be met through deferment of the loan repayment. BP required North Sea oil for its own markets over the next number of years, and proposed that the percentage of field production available to BNOC be on a sliding scale from 12.5% in the first nine years rising to a maximum of 57.125% (including royalty) from the sixteenth year onwards.

The second subject was the notion that all BP's UK assets be transferred to a new company owned 51% by BNOC and 49% by BP with payment by the cancellation of a negotiated number of the Government's BP shares. BP felt that this proposal failed to meet the commerciality test. Several reasons were given for this view including (a) the impairment of the BP Group's technical base for its worldwide operations if a substantial number of staff were transferred to the joint company, (b) the great difficulty of valuing BP's worldwide assets for the purpose of agreeing the number of shares to be cancelled, (c) the impairment of the company's ability to raise future finance following a reduction in its equity without a reduction in its debt, and (d) the international effect (particularly in the USA) of the perceived loss of BP's commercial independence in the UK.

The third subject was the purchase option of 51% of BP's North Sea production by BNOC, together with voting rights on Operating Committees. On the latter point BP felt that only non-voting seats could be given to BNOC in the absence of financial participation. While BP had some difficulty in understanding the logic of a purchase option the company was prepared to offer to BNOC from 1980 onwards an option at one year's notice to purchase at market price an amount of oil equal to the difference between North Sea oil processed in BP's UK refineries, and the lesser of either two-thirds of the total UK demand for BP's oil or 38.5% of BP's North Sea production, which, together with BNOC's royalty option, was close to 51%. This would protect the Government's crude oil disposal policy. The result could be that 51% of BP's North Sea production from 1980 onwards could be refined in the UK.

The fourth subject was the notion of a joint BP-BNOC offshore services company. BP indicated its willingness to provide offshore services to BNOC provided that BP's capacity to meet its own needs was not thereby impaired. A small joint company could be established to procure the technical services as either participant required. If BP could not meet the requirements the joint company would approach suitable third parties.

The fifth subject was the processing arrangements and possible participation by BNOC in BP's refineries. BP was prepared to offer capacity in its refineries for the processing of oil bought under the options or crude from BNOC emanating from other sources. A commercial fee would be charged for this. BP was also willing to consider a future partnership with BNOC which could grow out of the acquisition of a minority equity stake in BP's refineries via finance provided for new plant.

Ministers consider BP's proposals

The Ministerial Group on Lord Kearton's proposals for BNOC considered BP's suggestions at its meeting on 23rd February. With respect to the first idea, namely the acquisition by BNOC of 51% of BP's North Sea interests via loan finance, concern was expressed that the Government was being asked to loan £98 million for which they would eventually receive back £255 million but no return for the first nine years. It was arguable that, as BP could raise all the capital they needed, the Government should not make such a capital contribution. It was not clear whether the seats on the Operating Committees had voting rights. The pattern established for Forties would be important in subsequent negotiations relating to other fields. On the option issue the Group understood that a right to purchase was of little value unless facilities were available for its refining. But if BNOC wanted to support the price obtainable by small producers to ensure the maximum PRT yield, it might have to intervene in the market and make large purchases. Refining arrangements as discussed by BP were important in enabling BNOC to dispose of its oil.

The meeting concluded that most of the possibilities raised by BP should be explored further but with the objective of obtaining terms more satisfactory to the Government. There was less enthusiasm for the joint company concept as outlined by BP. It was agreed that all involved in negotiations should be guided by the outcome of the Group's deliberations.

The Group also discussed the question of the disposal of the ex-Burmah shares. There was general agreement that they should be sold as soon as practicable with the Government to hold 51%. Studies should be undertaken of the various methods by which the shares should be marketed. It was generally agreed that disposal to the Shah of Iran or the West German Government should not be contemplated.

Government response to BP

Following the meeting the BP suggestions were considered further in the DEN. This resulted in a model being prepared for negotiation with BP. The key features were that BP would assign to BNOC 51% of its licence interests in commercial fields in the UKCS but would retain its beneficial interests. BP would be responsible for all the costs. Mr Benn wrote to Mr Steel giving the Government's response to the company's proposals. It was felt that capital contributions with BP, either on Forties or in Ninian, were unnecessary, given BP's ability to finance the investments itself. With respect to voting rights the objective of the Government was to achieve full access to information and an effective voice for BNOC on the Operating Committees. Mr Benn invited BP to propose how this could be achieved. With respect to the volumes of oil to be made available to BNOC Mr Benn wanted an option starting after 2–3 years, building up to 57% no later than five years after first production. With respect to the notion that BNOC's entitlement to North Sea oil should depend on the amount that BP refined in the UK Mr Benn was concerned that in practice this could mean that BNOC's entitlement would only be around 12.5%, given BP's UK refining needs. He thus found this proposal unacceptable. The proposals from BP on cooperation with respect to technical services and training were gratefully received and should be pursued with Lord

Kearton. The issue of downstream cooperation should be pursued further among a group from BP, BNOC, DEN, and Treasury.

DEN model for upstream participation

The model for upstream participation proposed to BP reflected the outcome of further deliberations within Government on the objectives of participation and how they might best be achieved. The Select Committee on Nationalised Industries had published a report[1] indicating that the aims were obscure. In February 1976 the Government published its reply stating that the Government's aims were essentially four-fold, namely (1) to assist the development of a national exploration capability through BNOC, (2) to secure better technical and economic knowledge of operations in the UKCS, (3) to secure title for the nation in the licences under which oil was produced, and control over a share of the oil, and (4) to enable BNOC to have some say in decisions about the exploitation of North Sea oil in partnership with private sector companies. It was added that the achievement of these aims would enable the Government to formulate licensing, depletion, and other policies on a better informed basis.

Admission that complexities of offset payments scheme are prohibitive

Further consideration had been given to the types of participation models which should be pursued. It was eventually recognised that the computational and tax problems arising from the offset payments method of achieving the no gain no loss position were so complex that every effort should be made to find alternative routes, although negotiators should not withdraw proposals already tabled. Fortunately, the oil companies had already arrived at similar conclusions on this matter. The new approach also included the notion that a capital contribution from BNOC was no longer a prerequisite to an agreement given the desire of the companies to avoid tax complications and the Government's desire to reduce public expenditure.

Key minimum objectives

Following interdepartmental discussions it was agreed that key minimum objectives should be to obtain (1) 51% of title to the licence, (2) a seat and voting rights for BNOC on the Operating Committees, and (3) an option to buy up to 51% of the oil. In ranking specific schemes the criteria which should be employed were (1) the ability to demonstrate that the scheme had substance, (2) administrative simplicity, especially on tax, and (3) requirement of little or no legislation.

The preferred scheme was felt to be one where (1) the company assigned to BNOC 51% of its interest in the field, (2) the company was responsible for all the exploration, development and production, and in return had a beneficial interest in all the assets and petroleum produced, (3) the company gave BNOC the option to purchase up to 51% of the oil produced at market price, and (4) BNOC would be a licence holder, would participate fully in the relevant Operating Committees, and be a party to all relevant agreements.

The second choice was based on BP's proposals with the main elements being (1) assignment of 51% interest in the field or licence, and title to 51% of the oil to BNOC, (2) payment by BNOC of its share of operating costs and royalty with the oil company paying the full exploration and development costs, (3) transfer by BNOC to the original licence the oil at cost to it (operating cost plus royalty), (4) payment of all taxes by the company and claims to all the allowances, (5) the option of BNOC to purchase up to 51% of the oil, and (6) capital contribution by BNOC via a loan separate from the participation agreement.

The second choice had the advantage that BNOC obtained title to the oil as well as the licence and had a (small) financial interest in the field. But there were disadvantages which were perceived to be serious, namely (1) that the sale of the oil at cost was presentationally awkward, and (2) the tax problems relating to the definition of operating costs and the effect of transfer of title to the oil.

A third choice was a simple call option whereby BNOC had the right to purchase up to 51% of the oil at market price. From a tax viewpoint this was attractive because there was no change in the tax position of the companies. But it was very transparent and should be considered only where the BNOC relationship with the licensees was reinforced by other factors.

Rethink on negotiation procedures

Meanwhile a rethink on the procedures on how the negotiations should be conducted was also taking place. Mr Lever felt that they were not as effective as they could be and he wrote to Mr Benn in late October 1975 suggesting that (1) the negotiating officials should come to the three negotiating Ministers to resolve points of difficulty, (2) reports and references regarding negotiations to the NSRC should come from himself, and (3) Ministerial letters to companies on the subject should also come from himself. Mr Benn could not agree to these suggestions, arguing that responsibility for the participation talks was properly with the NSRC which he chaired. The matter remained unresolved until Mr Callaghan became Prime Minister. Shortly after that event Mr Benn wrote to him suggesting that he, as Secretary of State for Energy, should be responsible for the participation negotiations. Mr Callaghan agreed that this should formally be the case, but added that Mr Lever and the Treasury (through Mr Joel Barnett) should also be involved in a team effort on the subject. The Prime Minister made an announcement on the new arrangements on 4th May 1976.

Breakthrough with Conoco/Gulf

Meanwhile a breakthrough had been achieved in late February 1976 in the form of an agreement with Conoco and Gulf. The overall agreement had five documents. The first was the Assignment Agreement whereby the companies assigned to BNOC 26.5% of their interests in the licences relating to the Thistle, Dunlin and Statfjord UK fields. (This figure took into account the NCB's existing interest which was transferred to BNOC, resulting in a total BNOC share of 51%.) The companies did, however, retain the rights and obligations pertaining to these shares. The Government also agreed that, if any subsequent transfer of interest arose, in giving consent it would not attach more onerous conditions than were generally applicable to other licensees. Further, in giving such consents the Government would not attach a condition that the assignee had to concede participation in the assigned interest.

The second document dealt with the Oil Option. This provided that, in each of the fields, after five years of production BNOC would have the option at one year's notice, to buy at market price up to 23.2%[5] of Conoco and Gulf's oil, with smaller shares in years four and five. The third document was a letter stating that an option agreement for gas liquids and condensate similar to the Oil Option would be made if such liquids were produced in commercial quantities. But participation would not be sought in the Southern North Sea. The fourth document stated that BNOC would exercise its entitlement to oil in an even-handed manner in relation to other agreements. The last document stated that mutually acceptable changes to existing licence obligations, including reallocation of drilling obligations, was possible. The companies were informed verbally that their constructive attitude to participation would be given due consideration in the forthcoming Fifth Round.

Mr Lever announces agreement with Conoco/Gulf

The agreement was announced to Parliament by Mr Lever on 26th February 1976. Its importance was not only because it was the first to be signed, but because it was made with two substantial US companies who were under no special pressure to reach a settlement. The inherited NCB interest certainly facilitated the agreement, and the Government did not press for voting rights in excess of that interest. The proportion of oil covered by the option was much less than 51% because of the inherited NCB equity interest, and this also made agreement by Conoco and Gulf easier to accept. But the precedent of zero capital contribution by BNOC was useful in other negotiations.

Taxation and participation

Taxation did not feature as a prominent issue in the agreement but had certainly been discussed in the negotiations. Conoco had identified a number of circumstances in which participation could increase taxes or similar charges. These included capital gains on assignment of interests in the licence, gain on grant of an option to BNOC to purchase oil, and even a reduction in oil allowance for PRT. It was recognised by the Inland Revenue that the assignment by Conoco to BNOC was a chargeable occasion, but a chargeable gain required the presence of some consideration which would have to be valued. Items identified included the market value of the set of concessions requested by Conoco (such as those relating to licence obligations) in return for conceding participation. Conoco had requested a blanket covenant to the effect that the burden of taxation, duties and other levies would not be increased as a direct or indirect consequence of participation. The Inland Revenue was wary of giving such a blanket indemnity, but eventually agreed to confirm that the documents forming the final agreement would not give rise to capital gains chargeable to Conoco. The company had also been concerned about liability to Stamp Duty, but it was felt that only the 50 pence rate would apply to the assignment to BNOC given the limited nature of the benefits being transferred.

DEN pursues meaningful assignment

The subject of the value of the benefits featured in a further reappraisal of the participation objectives by DEN officials in early May. It was admitted that, while negotiators had to date felt it necessary to seek 51% title in the licence and/or the oil in order to demonstrate that majority state participation had been secured, in cases such as those with Conoco and Gulf, where the beneficial interests were retained by the companies, the term "title in the licence" had no real significance. Negotiators were now in some cases seeking to achieve a more meaningful assignment which would give more substance to BNOC's interest, and thus make it easier to obtain a presence on Operating Committees. The right of possession was also more secure with a fuller assignment as there were some doubts about whether the option agreements were enforceable in law. But there was considerable opposition among the companies to more meaningful assignments which arguably made them financially worse off, particularly by reducing their ability to raise finance based on the security of their economic interests in the fields. There were arguably severe practical limitations on the transfer of title approach, and these were greatly complicating the negotiations to such an extent that there were now doubts about whether the effort was justified.

Reappraisal of participation in pipelines/terminals

A second item requiring reappraisal was participation in pipelines and terminals. The NSRC had earlier decided that the Government would prefer not to do so when heavy costs were involved. But it was arguable that these facilities were integral parts of the process of exploitation, and many company partnerships had agreements covering all these assets. It was thus felt that BNOC should generally include pipelines and terminals where no capital contribution was made.

Reappraisal of how key objectives satisfied

DEN officials felt that key objectives would be satisfied with (1) an effective voice in Operating Committees with full access to information, and (2) access to 51% of the oil. The latter might not also require title in the licence. With respect to details capital contributions should be avoided, voting rights need not amount to 51% of the votes, access to oil should normally be in the form of options, secure access to 51% should come after five years of field production, no payment should be made for the option rights, and participation in whatever form should not reduce the oil company's ability to raise finance.

Mr Benn's intervention with BP negotiations

Meanwhile negotiations with BP were dragging on and eventually Mr Benn decided that dramatic intervention was required. He invited company representatives to a weekend negotiating session at Sunningdale starting on 27th June 1976 but without time limit. On the Government side along with Mr Benn were Mr Joel Barnett, Mr Lever, Lord Kearton, and a team of officials. The BP team included Mr Steel, Mr Pennell, Mr Laidlaw, Mr Walters, Mr Adam and Mr Milne. The Government's proposals reflected both the reappraisal of general objectives of participation and the special considerations raised by BP, including the Government's shareholding and downstream cooperation. Thus emphasis was put on the option rights to take oil from Forties and Ninian at up to 51% of production, full access to information, development of a joint downstream strategy, and consultations regarding how BP's overseas operations impacted on its North Sea activities. The Government representatives were aware that the volumes of North Sea oil likely to become available to BP in the near future were very large and thus access by BNOC to 51% had a major effect on the company. Thus the Government was prepared to provide that BNOC would not exercise its option to take 51% of Forties oil solely to advance its own commercial (as opposed to national) interest. It was also understood that BP had more refining capacity in the UK than prospective crude from the North Sea, but the company had already argued that it was economic to refine only about one-third of North Sea production in 1980. If BNOC exercised a 51% option the resulting obligation on BP would be to refine two-thirds of their 49%.

Agreement reached on principles

The negotiations continued well into the night but agreement on principles was reached. The key elements included (1) an option for BNOC to buy at market prices 51% of BP's oil production (net of royalty in kind) from Forties, Ninian and other commercial fields, (2) supply of oil by BNOC to BP at market prices in specified volumes in exchange for crude oil of the same value supplied by BP from the Middle East or elsewhere, (3) the assignment to BNOC by BP of 51% of its interests in commercial oil fields in the UKCS, with BP retaining its beneficial interests and obligations regarding exploration and other costs and the payment of royalties and taxes, (4) the provision of information which an equity participant might expect, (5) provision of a vote entitlement (but without controlling or veto rights) to BNOC on Operating Committees, and (6) provision of training by BP to BNOC on downstream activities, and general cooperation in this area. BP sought a clear reaffirmation from the Government that it would not interfere in the administration of the company as a commercial concern. Mr Benn felt that the proposed participation agreement was compatible with this. BP reaffirmed its view that the ex-Burmah shares should be sold as soon as practicable, but Mr Benn felt that it was inappropriate to link participation and the position of these shares.

Mr Benn announces agreement

Mr Benn immediately submitted a Minute to the Prime Minister hailing the agreement. The Prime Minister's advisers agreed that it was very satisfactory, and Mr Benn made an announcement to Parliament on 1st July, indicating that BP's commercial freedom was not adversely affected by the agreement. But much effort would be expended and much time would elapse before the full agreement was signed. Given the importance of BP in the North Sea it was clear, however, that the agreement on principles was a major landmark in the whole participation programme.

Continuing negotiations with Burmah

The first few months of 1976 also saw major developments in the negotiations with Burmah. By late 1975 it had become clear that the company's financial difficulties were such that it asked the Government for further support in the form of a rollover of the guarantee already given, an increase and extension to the standby credit, and interim guarantees of its North Sea expenditures. Help would facilitate the conclusion of a participation agreement. Officials, with the help of accountants Peat, Marwick, Mitchell, had spent much time unravelling the extremely complex financial affairs of the company. After detailed study of the possibilities officials concluded that there were three main options available namely (1) to refuse support which would result in the company going into immediate liquidation, (2) to help within the general framework of Burmah's request, or (3) to acquire Burmah's North Sea assets and organisation. There was general agreement that the company should not be allowed to go into liquidation, but also concern that continuing general support could cause liability for debt problems if the company did eventually go into liquidation. The preferred route was thus to inject funds into the company through the purchase of the company's North Sea interests by BNOC. It was hoped that this would provide Burmah with adequate funds to continue trading and repay the standby credit. Acquisition of the assets would give BNOC North Sea equity oil production projected to start in 1977 and rising to 5 million tonnes in 1981.

This proposal was accepted and further negotiations with Burmah ensued. An advance of £40 million was provided to the company to help it in its current difficulties. The negotiations were complex, particularly with respect to the issue of valuation. Burmah was also concerned about the tax position as it was clear that the disposal of its 20% share in Ninian would give rise to a substantial capital gain. To mitigate this it was agreed that BNOC would purchase the share capital of

Burmah's subsidiary company Burmah Oil North Sea Ltd (BONSL) which held the relevant licence, rather than buy the underlying Ninian and related assets directly. By effecting the transaction in this way the taxable gain was reduced through apportionment over a long period of time. A substantial gain would still be present, and Burmah proposed a complex depreciatory transaction to deal with the problem. This would involve the revaluation of the company's interest in Ninian to reflect the agreed purchase price, with the resulting capital reserve being distributed by BONSL to its holding company. But since BONSL would have insufficient funds to pay such a dividend, there would be a large debt from BONSL to Burmah at the time of the acquisition, which BNOC would satisfy by putting BONSL into possession of the necessary funds. This idea was received with much consternation especially by the Inland Revenue, and the company devised a much more complex scheme with the same objective. It was made clear that the Government could not be a party to the design of tax avoidance schemes. This could lead to Parliamentary criticism. Lord Kearton was also strongly against BNOC's involvement in what could be termed tax avoidance schemes. By mid-February 1976 BNOC was also unhappy about the protracted negotiations over Ninian and felt there was a danger that BNOC might eventually obtain an unprofitable investment while Burmah might be paid sufficient for it to reduce the pressure on it to sell its Thistle interests. The DEN view was that a fair market price was the objective, as criticism could occur if either more or less was paid.

Agreement with Burmah announced

To progress matters Mr Benn met with Mr Down of Burmah on 26th February. The subsequent negotiations led to a deal being agreed and announced to Parliament by Mr Benn on 10th March. The main elements were the purchase of the shares of BONSL for £83 million, with additional payments of approximately £8 million with respect to expenditure since 1st January 1976 (the effective date of the acquisition), plus interest. The only asset of BONSL was its share of the Ninian field in Block 3/3. The purchase was effected through a renounceable allotment letter which avoided the need to pay £1.8 million in Stamp Duty, but the scheme proposed by Burmah to avoid capital gains tax was rejected. Burmah would be able to have a 50% interest in any net benefit from the use of the Ninian pipeline by third parties.

At this time agreement was also reached in principle that BNOC should purchase 51% of Burmah Oil Development Ltd (BODL). This was the company which held Burmah's share of the Thistle field. Burmah was the operator of this field, and acquisition of BODL would be very significant as it opened the door to the possibility of BNOC becoming an operator. The arrangement was announced at this time before the details were agreed to ensure continuity of employment for the staff of BODL.

The negotiations were again difficult but a series of agreements was eventually made in July and August involving payment of £87 million for 65% of Burmah's interest in Thistle and 90% of BODL the field operators. The issue was complicated by Burmah's urgent need for a cash advance of £25 million. The BNOC Board felt the price paid was high and that it would be more satisfactory for BNOC to take 100% of BODL. The Board also asked that the Secretary of State issue a direction to BNOC to make the advance of £25 million. Eventually total payments of £103 million were paid to Burmah. The Government's relationship with Burmah on the company's need for financial support was to continue for some time involving further difficult negotiations. In these the DEN were concerned to ensure that Burmah did not go bankrupt and the developments of Ninian and Thistle were not delayed, as well as to promote the interests of BNOC.

Participation and financing become intertwined

In other cases where licensees had difficulties in financing their shares of field developments and Government assistance was sought, the two subjects of participation and financing became intertwined. The general approach of the Government was to make the provision of any assistance on financing dependent on the acceptance of participation by the licensees. The DEN had always been concerned to ensure that the development of viable projects was not held up through lack of finance. There was often some Government involvement, even in cases where the licensees were able to raise finance themselves. Thus, in the case of the large loan for the development of the Forties field, the Government agreed that the banks would be able to take over the rights under BP's licence if the company were to default. A link with participation arose when lenders sought assurances protecting the borrower's cash flow.[6] This included assurances relating to depletion controls.

Earlier, in late 1974, Burmah had approached the DEN to request financial guarantees to permit the further development of the Thistle field. Burmah was concerned that two members of the licence group – Tricentrol and United Canso – were likely to be unable to raise their share of development finance which might result in first production from the field being delayed by a year. DEN officials recommended that an assurance be given to Burmah that if United Canso or Tricentrol defaulted the Government would as a last resort meet their share of costs and take the corresponding share of the field. Mr Varley made an announcement in the House of Commons in December 1974 emphasising that the assurance was only a contingent guarantee relating to default.

In the same time period Tricentrol approached DEN requesting on its own behalf a Government guarantee to facilitate the raising of development finance. In essence the request was that the Government undertook to bear some of the risks of cost over-run and project completion, and in return would receive an overriding royalty in the 2.5%–5 % range. The company also submitted a participation scheme which included a buy-back provision for participation oil.

The National Westminster Bank was asked to advise the DEN on the matter, and proposed an alternative arrangement whereby any monies which the Government had at risk should be treated as an equity investment to be rewarded by a fee linked to the return on that investment. In addition, if the cost over-run exceeded a specified limit, the position would be reviewed with Government take-over being the likely result.

Ministers were asked whether they wished discussions to proceed on this basis or to let Tricentrol lose its position in the Thistle field. They felt that as the company was British and had a reasonable reputation as a licensee it should be helped but only on suitable terms. These were four-fold, namely (a) a Government loan guarantee up to a limit of £42.55 million, after which a review would be triggered with a Government takeover the likely outcome, (b) Government remuneration in the form of a royalty over the life of the field based on not less than 20% gross rate of return on the funds at risk, (c) acceptance by Tricentrol of 51% participation, and (d) the participation terms to reflect recognition that without Government help the company could not continue in the field.

Negotiations with Tricentrol

There then followed protracted negotiations between DEN officials and Tricentrol. Mr Varley announced details of an agreement at the end of April 1975, essentially on the lines suggested above. Thus the Government would guarantee the re-payment of loans up to £38.3 million, and in return it would receive a royalty though the life of the field at a minimum of five per cent. After a participation agreement for 51% was concluded the loan guarantee terms would relate to Tricentrol's 49% remaining interest.

The Parliamentary announcement was followed by further very long and complex negotiations. These were complicated by the need to unitise the field development (which resulted in Tricentrol's interest being increased from 8.4% to 9.1%), and continued cost escalation. This resulted in an increase in the bank loan guaranteed by the Government to £60 million, and the provision of further bridging finance. This was announced to Parliament by Mr Benn in March 1976. The royalty receivable by the Government would depend on the amount of guaranteed monies outstanding, but the minimum would be five per cent of the company's original production through the life of the field. At this time Tricentrol concluded a participation deal assigning 51% of its interest in Thistle to BNOC and giving the latter the option to buy 51% of Tricentrol's oil at market price at any time from first production.[7]

Negotiations with Ranger Oil

The Ranger Oil Company also sought Government help at this time in the form of bridging finance for a relatively short time pending availability of a larger loan package to cover its share of the Ninian field development costs. The background was again the cost escalation which was seriously affecting all of the North Sea. DEN officials were concerned that, if the company was unable to raise its share of capital and the Government did not help, the whole Ninian project would be delayed and confidence in the North Sea damaged. It was also recognised that, in return for help, fast progress could be made to conclude a participation agreement. Thus in August 1975 Ministers authorised officials to negotiate a guarantee to facilitate the financing of a shortfall in 49 per cent of the company's share of costs on the understanding that it made every effort to raise the monies itself. In late November 1975 Mr Benn announced to Parliament that a short-term loan guarantee for up to $20 million to cover Ranger's costs until the summer of 1976 had been given with security taken in the form of its share in Ninian.

There followed further negotiations with Ranger on participation and financing. These culminated in an agreement covering both in May 1976. Mr Benn gave his consent to a financing arrangement for Ranger's share of the development costs for Ninian involving a loan of $120 million from a syndicate of banks. The loan was guaranteed by Chevron, the field operator, and the Government guarantee of $20 million was discharged. The DEN took comfort from its involvement as a guarantor when the fee of over $800,000 was compared to the estimated cost of £125,000 for fees to their advisers and their own officials' time.

Discussions with Shell and Esso

Discussions with Shell and Esso had been slow in starting. Both companies had publicly declared their scepticism about the whole participation exercise. DEN officials felt that it was very important that they be included because of the large size of their reserves in the UKCS. The Permanent Secretary met with senior Shell executives in early March 1976 and explained the Government's objectives to them, emphasising the variety of schemes which could conform to the "no gain no loss" criterion, and indicating that the agreement with Conoco/Gulf through the "option route" was not the only acceptable method. Both companies explained how this route caused difficulties for them. They needed all the oil they had found in the North Sea for their UK markets. Exxon reckoned that they needed twice as much oil for their share of the UK market as their North Sea interests would provide. They felt that the Government should take into account the differences between companies which had large UK downstream interests and those which had little or none. The Government gained advantages from the former companies which provided a ready-made disposition route in times of emergency. Shell and Exxon also expressed concern about the roles of BNOC in providing information to Government given that the company planned to be on Operating Committees. This gave BNOC a competitive advantage. It was also regarded as particularly inequitable that BNOC could have a vote on an Operating Committee without putting up any capital for the development of the related field. The Permanent Secretary explained that in such circumstances BNOC might not have a blocking vote.

Progress was slow, but in June 1976 a short Press Release was issued by DEN and the two companies stating that preliminary discussions on participation were in progress and that any agreement, while meeting the Government's key objectives, would acknowledge the large downstream investments of the two companies. Following the agreement on principles reached with BP in early July Mr Benn invited Shell and Exxon to come forward with proposals. They did so at a meeting in early September in the form of a discussion draft which covered four areas, namely (1) title, (2) option oil, (3) upstream cooperation and (4) downstream cooperation. With respect to title the companies felt that participation should be restricted to delineated field areas rather than licence areas and thus sub-licences would be required. The companies made it clear that from their perspective transfer of title did not entail any transfer of the beneficial interests in the fields.

With respect to option oil the companies proposed that, given their large UK market requirements, the BNOC option should apply only to oil above these requirements. Lord Kearton pointed out that, given the refining capacity of the two companies at 35 million tonnes per year while their production could be in the 10–15 million tonnes range per year in the early 1980s from proven commercial fields, the proposed option was on non-existent oil. The companies would consider an option agreement if future discoveries created an excess of supplies over their own requirements. Such a situation was possible. Mr Benn indicated that the Government wanted access to 51% of North Sea oil in order to control its disposal in the national interest. He also felt that that the Government's ability to take royalty oil in kind should not be constrained by the market requirements of the companies.

In discussion of upstream cooperation Mr Benn insisted that BNOC should have a seat, voice, and vote in fields in which it participated, irrespective of its equity stake, with information exchange being on a continual basis. With respect to downstream cooperation the companies indicated that the BP scheme created difficulties for Shell and Exxon. They were willing to cooperate in non-proprietary, non-competitive areas, but US anti-trust legislation would forbid discussion of marketing arrangements with BNOC. This applied particularly to Exxon, but both companies were concerned that consultation would expose them to allegations of unfair marketing practices. They were also bothered about the confidentiality of their arrangements, as BNOC would acquire knowledge of the plans of several companies.

DEN proposals to Shell/Esso

At the end of the meeting it was acknowledged that, while there was a wide gap between the parties on the issues of options and downstream cooperation, there was a willingness to work towards an agreement, though the companies were prepared to accept the consequences of non-agreement. It was agreed that further work should proceed expeditiously. DEN officials then produced counterproposals highlighting BNOC's option to purchase up to 51% of the companies' production net of royalty oil taken in kind, but adding that, in support of their long-term commitments in supplying products to the UK market, each company would refine in the UK the balance of its production from the UKCS, and, within the limits of option oil taken up, BNOC would sell back to them oil required to sustain these UK activities. Information and voting rights equivalent to those of an equity participant were sought for BNOC.

Shell/Esso proposals

At a further meeting in September 1976 the companies indicated that, subject to satisfactory buy-back arrangements they were now prepared to accept the principle of granting BNOC an option to buy 51% of their North Sea production, but continued to stress their need for all their North Sea production to support their UK investments, and agreed that this was in any case its best use from the national viewpoint. In the light of these propositions both sides agreed to further consider their positions.

Government concession on buy-back arrangements

Mr Benn and Lord Kearton discussed the matter, recognised that there was some strength in the companies' arguments, and proposed a further discussion draft indicating that, provided they were satisfied that all the oil resold was to be used for their approved UK operations, the Government/BNOC would agree to sell back all the option oil. This was a significant departure from the stance taken in other negotiations and agreements. At a subsequent meeting the companies accepted that this went a long way towards accommodating their circumstances. They accepted the consultation requirement relating to the buy-back arrangement and were also amenable to BNOC having some voting rights.

Further negotiations ensued. From the Government's perspective there was clear recognition of the downstream needs of the companies, but a need to ensure that some control over their operations was obtained. Thus a sale-back of the 51% option oil had to be made conditional on the use of the oil in the companies' UK refineries. Agreement on how the conditions should be defined proved very difficult, with the companies being concerned about the ability of the Secretary of State to make judgements at his discretion. But the Government negotiators felt that, having conceded that all the option oil could be sold back, it had to have safeguards that the companies would use the oil in the national interest. To progress matters the Government requested that the most senior executives of the companies discuss the subject, and Mr Benn had meetings with Mr Pocock, Chairman of Shell Transport and Trading, and Mr Garvin, Chairman of the Exxon main board in November. By the end of that month there were four points deemed to be substantial remaining to be resolved. The first related to the insistence of the companies that participation be restricted to fields from existing licence areas which the Government found too restrictive, as it would exclude discoveries made in future licensing rounds. The second issue related to the sale-back of oil and the contingency conditions attached to this, with both parties wishing to have the right to make the ultimate judgement on the matter. The third issue related to title, with the companies arguing that the surrender of title would adversely affect their security and financing arrangements. While recognising its limitations the Government side was still keen to obtain title, but further possible problems relating to PRT and capital gains tax were emerging which were complicating the issue. The fourth area of disagreement related to BNOC's role in upstream operations. The companies were unwilling to accept that BNOC's rights should be equivalent to those available to co-licensees. They also had reservations about the extent to which information should be made available to BNOC which could give the company an advantage in relation to an adjoining vacant block.

Agreement reached on principles

Negotiations proceeded apace and on 23rd December 1976 Mr Benn was able to send a Minute to the Prime Minister indicating that a Memorandum of Principles had been agreed with the companies. The document was quite general on some of the issues which had been the subject of disagreement among the parties. The right of BNOC to purchase 51% of production (net of any royalty taken in kind) was clearly established, and provision was also made for buy-back arrangements. The companies then agreed to consult with the Government on all issues relating to their production from the UKCS and their refining and marketing activities. The consultation would include all planned future production and refining/marketing activities, the planned import of crude oil for refining, and exports of products and crude. All relevant information on these would be disclosed, so that the Government could assess the plans in relation to the requirements of UK markets. The companies would develop their refining programmes to optimise the use of North Sea oil production based on economic and operational considerations. Domestic and international trading arrangements would be conducted such that the benefits to the UK balance of payments would be maximised. The buy-back arrangements, particularly the volumes of oil, would be linked to these objectives.

This concept broke new ground among the agreements in the sense that participation was now for the first time linked to North Sea oil disposal and refining policy. The statement on the subject made by Mr Varley in December 1974 had no statutory backing, and, of course, the policy could be changed. A reasonable interpretation of the Memorandum would be that the licensees would observe that policy even when it was modified.

With respect to assignment and title it was agreed that BNOC would become a joint holder of the licence rights for each commercial field. This would require segregation of licences to separate the commercial fields from the rest of the licence area. The Memoranda of Principles were signed and published on 5th January 1977.

Link of participation to disposal/refining policy in conflict with Treaty of Rome?

The linking of participation to disposal and refining policy via the buy-back provisions caused a last-minute hitch to the Shell and Exxon agreements, and indeed threatened the whole participation exercise. This was a recognition that the linkage might be in conflict with the Treaty of Rome. DEN officials became concerned about this as negotiations with Shell and Exxon proceeded, and in early December 1976 urgently sought the legal advice of the Law Officers on the subject. They obtained an outside opinion from Professor Frances Jacobs who felt that the proposed arrangements would put the Government in breach of Articles 30 to 37 dealing with the free movement of goods, or BNOC and the other licensees in breach of Articles 85 to 90 dealing with cartels and monopolies. Changing the detailed provisions could alter the degree of risk, but there remained the basic problem of the limitation on crude oil exports. While having reservations on particular details of Professor Jacobs's opinion, lawyers from the Attorney General's Office, DEN, and FCO did not differ substantially from the main conclusions. It was thus recommended that, before full commitments were made, informal discussions should be held on the issue with the EEC Commission. It was also desirable that, because of its great importance, an Inter-Departmental Working Group be set up to examine the subject further and study the various options available to achieve the Government's objectives.

Working Group report

The Working Group immediately set to work. In an initial note to the Group on the policy aspects DEN officials noted that it was a misconception to suppose that the proposed Shell/Exxon arrangement was designed to prevent exports as such. Sale-back for export could take place. The purpose was to permit the Government to withhold sale-back for whatever reason of national interest warranted such a course. The dramatic opinions were given that a solution to the legal problem which denied the Secretary of State this ultimate discretion would be valueless, while a conclusion that the problem was insoluble could throw into the melting pot the whole Government policy towards North Sea oil.

The Working Group produced its report within a remarkably short time. It highlighted the rules of the Treaty of Rome relating to restrictions on exports and competition which made some aspects of participation potentially vulnerable. Specifically, conditional sale-back constituted an area of possible challenge. Because the companies were certain of sale-back only for oil to be refined in the UK, the structure of the agreement could be held to restrict exports. In that case the Government could be held to be in breach of Article 34 (export restrictions), and BNOC's role in conflict with Article 37 (discrimination based on nationality). BNOC and the oil companies would also be in breach of Article 85 which distorted competition. It was felt that there would not be a legal defence on the grounds that exports were permitted in a participation agreement, nor that the companies had no intention of exporting in a manner which could be frustrated by the agreement.

The report discussed the likelihood of a legal challenge being mounted. It was felt that it was most unlikely that the oil companies would take legal action because they would not wish to damage their relationship with the Government. It was just possible that if a sale-back was denied in circumstances which were felt to be unduly onerous a company might take legal action, but it was more likely that it might just retain possession of the oil and leave BNOC to take legal action to obtain it.

There was some risk that the Commission might take action, but interestingly the Working Group felt that there was more danger that this would occur under Article 85 (anti-competitive behaviour) because (1) such cases were less overtly political than those relating to export restrictions, and the Commission was less likely to be susceptible to political suasion, and (2) because the Competition Directorate was particularly active. The Group felt that other EEC Governments would take a pragmatic view of the subject, and would be more concerned with the total effect of participation and other UK oil policies on their own interests rather than with the legality of specific participation provisions.

Reducing legal risks

The Group considered how the risks of legal action could be reduced. Thus the competition aspect could be diminished by putting the potentially offensive actions in the hands of the Government rather than BNOC. A legally effective course would be to make no distinction between oil sold back for UK refining, and oil sold back for other purposes, and to make it clear that BNOC was obliged to sell back except when required not to do so by the Secretary of State, on the grounds that the companies had not established that the oil was required for agreed plans. Since the actions would be undertaken by the Secretary of State the competition issue would be eliminated. It was very doubtful whether this approach would be acceptable to the companies. Agreement with Shell and Exxon had been reached only by eliminating the Secretary of State's discretion over the part of the 51% sold back relating to UK refining. The companies would be most unlikely to agree to a more general discretion, but the Working Group felt that attempts should be made to amend the agreement in consultation with the companies. It could also be helpful to insert a clause to the effect that the agreements were intended to be implemented in a manner consistent with the legal obligations of all parties.

More fundamental changes in policy were also considered. But several Heads of Agreement and even full agreements had already been reached and the scope for a major change in policy was very limited. As Mr Liverman informed Mr Benn, it was ironic that the problem had arisen from the moderate nature of participation policy. Full nationalisation would have avoided any of the EEC problems. It was also clear that elimination of the conditions on sale-back would have removed all or most of the possible EEC difficulties. But at least a medium of control over the 49% as well as the 51% was the essence of the arrangement with Shell and Exxon. Any sale-back relating to the 51% alone and to UK refining/marketing requirements would result in automatic sale-back, and thus justify criticisms that agreements such as the Shell/Exxon one were meaningless facades.[8]

It was felt that no immediate approach should be made to the EEC Commission on the subject, but the UK Representative should attempt to discover if there was any interest in the subject. In terms of public presentation of participation the emphasis should be to restrict any statements implying that BNOC had a dominant position, or that oil exports would be restricted. Emphasis should rather be placed on other aspects of participation, namely that it (1) effected some measure of control over the oil giants, (2) established a form of sectoral planning, and (3) reinforced control for the purpose of effective taxation. An emphasis on non-discriminatory aspects was generally desirable.

Ministers deliberate

The subject was discussed at the NSRC in early February 1977 and the conclusions of the Working Group were broadly endorsed. The Attorney General attended the meeting and reiterated his concern regarding the agreements in their present form. The Cabinet Secretary felt that it was not entirely satisfactory that a decision which might lead to a clash with the EEC should be taken by the NSRC, and Mr Benn was asked to inform the Prime Minister of the Committee's views which, after further Ministerial consultation, were subsequently endorsed. Ministers took the view that other EEC Governments were unlikely to mount a challenge against a fundamental political objective of the UK Government. Subsequently, there were suspicions within DEN that oil companies were stirring up interest in the subject at the EEC Commission, but no firm evidence was found. Information had been received that Mobil had obtained legal opinion to the effect that participation policy was in conflict with the Treaty of Rome to such an extent that, before signing an agreement, the company should seek a negative clearance from the Commission. The Working Group met again later in the year and produced a report in early October. It was felt that the further negotiations with Shell and Esso and also the negotiations with other companies were achieving limited success in restructuring the terms in a less risky form. But there was still some risk attached to these restructured provisions. The Government should not approach the Commission on the matter as this could well be counterproductive. Ministers agreed with these suggestions. In fact the participation agreements despite their widespread publicity and controversy did not lead to any enquiries being received by the Government from the Commission.

Protracted negotiations with Shell/Esso lead to full agreement

Meanwhile the negotiations with Shell and Esso on a full agreement continued at a slow pace. In mid-May 1977 Mr Benn called a meeting with senior executives of Shell and Exxon (Mr Pocock and Mr Dean) to emphasise the need for speedier progress, particularly on four key items, namely (1) the build up of BNOC's option rights, (2) the use of statutory directions to BNOC to deny oil to the companies, (3) the companies' arguments that BNOC should not participate in pipelines and terminals, and (4) the companies' proposals for a sub-licence for BNOC. The company representatives emphasised the need for care in designing complex agreements which would commit the parties over the next 25–30 years. Some of the problems were due to understanding and educational gaps between the negotiating teams. They felt that speedy progress could be made on the outstanding items, though their understanding was that BNOC participation in pipelines and terminals had been excluded in the Memorandum of Principles. Eventually full agreements were signed in November 1977.

Negotiations with others and Amoco problem

The announcement of Heads of Agreement with BP, Shell, and Exxon gave an impetus to the negotiations with the many other companies now operating in the UKCS. They realised that there was little advantage in continued procrastination, and there was a possibility of a tangible disadvantage relating to the Fifth Licensing Round (See Chapter 10) where the Secretary of State had discretionary powers. This was illustrated in dramatic form in the case of Amoco which was excluded from the awards in the Fifth Round. The company had been negotiating for a long time, and the Government had hoped that an agreement could be reached in time for the Fifth Round awards. This did not happen, however, though the differences were not major ones. The company wanted more favourable terms on the sale-back of option oil than were in the Memorandum of Principles with Shell and Exxon. DEN negotiators also developed a lack of confidence in the tactics of their Amoco counterparts. Following the exclusion of the company from the Fifth Round awards changes in personnel were made and Amoco rapidly retrieved its good standing with the Government, and signed a participation agreement.

Restrictive Trade Practices Act, 1976

A further legal complication required attention in 1977 and 1978. This related to the Restrictive Trade Practices Act, 1976. Prior to this Act legal advice in the DEN was that the earlier Restrictive Trade Practices Acts (1956 and 1968) were unlikely to apply to an agreement between BNOC and another company, unless the parties accepted restrictions. If there were restrictions in an agreement they had to be registered with the Restrictive Practices Court, which could declare that restrictions were contrary to the public interest and thus void. But after the 1976 Act was passed the Office of Fair Trading advised the DEN that some features of the emerging agreements could cause them to be registerable. This would produce uncertainty and pose a threat to participation policy. On being informed Ministers decided that the doubts had to be removed. Accordingly primary legislation was introduced in the form of the Participation Agreements Bill which was designed to exempt all participation agreements from the 1976 Act. The legislation was passed in February 1978 and attracted very little interest. DEN officials were concerned that the Bill might attract the interest of the EEC Commission. During its passage care had to be taken to explain why the Bill was necessary in a domestic but not in a European context!

Agreement with ICI

The last agreement to be signed was with ICI. This had deliberately been left to the end, though negotiations had started at an early stage. It was felt that ICI had special circumstances, namely a major need for feedstocks, which justified generous buy-back provisions. But if these had been conceded at an early stage the precedent would have been unfortunate for other potential agreements, where generous buy-back arrangements were not so justifiable.

Agreements with sixty-two companies

The end result of the negotiations was agreements with the 62 companies (see Appendix 9.1) which held pre-1975 licences with actual or prospective fields. The only companies with whom negotiations commenced but were not successfully concluded were Total and Elf. But these companies did not have commercial oil discoveries under pre-1975 licences. The negotiations required a major input of DEN staff resources with 20–25 officials being employed in the task for over three years. In addition there was significant staff involvement from other Departments particularly the Treasury, Foreign Office and Inland Revenue. (In virtually all cases an understanding had to be reached with the Inland Revenue that the agreements by themselves would not have tax consequence.) The staff input from the oil companies was also very substantial. In addition there was much involvement of external advisers by all the parties, with the legal community being a substantial beneficiary from the whole exercise.

Reflections on agreements

From the Government's perspective the signing of agreements with 62 companies represented success. It was estimated that the oil options gave BNOC access to 2.8 million tonnes of oil in 1978 rising to 28 million tonnes in 1981, excluding royalty oil and sale-back oil, which, if added, would have produced an estimated total of 62 million tonnes in 1987. The acquisition of Burmah's North Sea interests gave BNOC some equity oil, and allowed it to become what Lord Kearton considered to be a "real" oil company, far more quickly than had been anticipated in the deliberations of DEN officials. Lord Kearton certainly galvanised matters with his energetic initiatives, though sometimes these had to be restrained as being counter-productive. His emphasis on obtaining downstream involvement for BNOC introduced a new and complicating element all to little effect in the event. But his insistence that BNOC required access to large volumes of oil did give a spur to the emphasis on oil options.

Lack of early clarity in Government objectives

The negotiations were prolonged in part because the Government objectives were not precisely specified at the outset, and because of the decision to be willing to consider alternative model proposals from the companies. The Government's own attitude to different participation models changed significantly over the period. A major factor here was the weakness of the economy (in turn partly due to an enormously increased import bill for oil), and the consequent need to seek assistance from the IMF. This led to the decision to drop the offset payments scheme and concentrate on models where no direct payments from the Exchequer were made.

The lack of clarity about the precise objectives of participation, the changes in approach, and the differences in emphasis between Ministers directly involved, may have been perplexing to the companies and perhaps strengthened their resolve to resist the Government's overtures. The Conservative Party encouraged them in this respect because of its opposition to the planned role of BNOC. The companies would certainly have preferred no participation. Only those few which were experiencing financial difficulties saw any benefit. They all used the so-called voluntary basis of the negotiations as an opportunity to dilute the terms as much as possible. In this they were generally successful, as the terms eventually agreed were hardly in accord with the expectations aroused at the beginning of the exercise. A turning point was, of course, the decision to produce a scheme with no gain and no loss to the investor. This was to encourage the dialogue between the parties, but it also greatly changed the substance of the debate and limited the Government's scope in negotiations. When the decision not to involve Exchequer contributions was added there was little left but agreements based on options. The emphasis on obtaining title was only presentational in its effect.

The participation agreements themselves thus did not add to the Government take from the North Sea. (The acquisition of Burmah's equity interests did do this but this was not strictly through a participation agreement.) State participation can, of course, add to the Government take as happens in many other countries, and it can do so on privileged terms through carried interest as was originally contemplated in the UK. While BNOC participation in the conventional sense was to be present in the Fifth and Sixth Rounds, it was absent in the agreements negotiated in the period 1975–1979.

National value of option agreements?

The question of the value to the nation of the option agreements thus arises. The options could only be exercised at market prices. Thus the only benefit could be to enhance security of supply to the UK market. There was already a landing obligation in force as part of normal licence obligations, but, of course, oil could subsequently readily be re-exported. There were unhappy memories of Mr Heath's attempts to secure favoured treatment for supplies to the UK market by British oil companies. BNOC would have secure access to substantial volumes of oil, and could readily supply the UK market with them. But to what extent would security of supply be enhanced? BNOC had no storage facilities or refineries, and trade in products within the EEC could not in general be restricted. As the life of the Labour Government drew to a close the issue of security of supply loomed large with the revolution in Iran and the consequent upheaval to the world oil market involving dramatic increases in price. The value of the participation arrangements would then be tested.

Appendix 9.1

Companies with whom participation agreements were signed.

AGIP (UK) Ltd
Allied Chemical (Great Britain) Ltd
Amerada Exploration Ltd
Amoco UK Petroleum Ltd
Ashland Oil (GB) Ltd
Blackfriars Oil Co. Ltd
Bow Valley Exploration (UK) Ltd
British Electric Traction Co. Ltd
British Petroleum Co. Ltd
Canadian Ashland Oil (UK) Ltd
CanDel Oil (UK) Ltd
CCP North Sea Associates Ltd
Century Power and Light Ltd
Charterhall Oil Ltd
Chevron Petroleum Co. Ltd
City Petroleum Co.
Conoco North Sea Ltd
Creslenn (UK) Ltd
Deminex Oil and Gas (UK) Ltd
Esso Petroleum Co. Ltd
Fina Exploration Ltd
Gas and Oil Acreage Ltd
Getty Oil International (UK) Ltd
Gulf Oil GB Ltd
Halkyn District United Mines Ltd
Hamilton Brothers Oil (GB) Ltd
Hunt Oil (UK) Ltd
ICI Petroleum Ltd
Kerr-McGee Oil (UK) Ltd
Lochiel Exploration (UK) Ltd
LL & E (GB) Ltd
London & Scottish Marine Oil Co. Ltd

Mesa (UK) Ltd
Mobil Production North Sea Ltd
Murphy Petroleum Ltd
Norwegian Oil Co DNO (UK) Ltd
Occidental Petroleum (UK) Ltd
Ocean Exploration Co. Ltd
Oil Exploration Ltd
Pan Ocean Oil (UK) Ltd
P & O Petroleum Ltd
Phillips Petroleum Exploration UK Ltd
Plascom Ltd
Ranger Oil (UK) Ltd
RTZ Oil & Gas Ltd
Saga Petroleum A/s. & Co.
St Joe Petroleum (UK) Corp
Santa Fe (UK) Ltd
Scottish Canadian Oil & Transportation
   Co. Ltd
Shell UK Ltd
Siebens Oil and Gas (UK) Ltd
Skelly Oil Exploration (UK) Ltd
Sunningdale Oils (UK) Ltd
Tenneco Great Britain Ltd
Texaco North Sea UK Ltd
Texas Eastern (UK) Ltd
Thomson North Sea Ltd
Trans-European Co. Ltd
Transworld Petroleum (UK) Ltd
Tricentrol Thistle Development
Ultramar Exploration Ltd
Unocal Exploration & Production Co.
   (UK) Ltd

10 The new policy in action: further licensing and related issues

Preparing for the Fifth Round

While the participation negotiations relating to pre-1975 licences were being negotiated preparatory work for further licensing was also under way. DEN officials had started to think about a Fifth Round as early as the summer of 1974. It was felt important to ensure that the momentum of activity in the UKCS was maintained in the medium-term, and this would require new licences to be issued in late 1976 or early 1977. But the policy reviews had not been completed, and, as these would affect licence terms, it was premature to determine the scope and nature of the Round, and further work was deferred until the key policies had been determined.

By late 1974 such work had been undertaken by DEN officials and a Round of around 150 blocks was the preliminary suggestion. The size of the Fifth and later Rounds should be tailored to depletion policy, and thus it was not until April 1975, when the Petroleum and Submarine Pipelines Bill was ready for introduction, that a fuller report was prepared and circulated by Mr Varley to his Ministerial colleagues. This suggested that there were around 700 blocks suitable for licensing in the next ten years and three or four Rounds could be conducted in that period with each involving 150–200 blocks. The report proposed that the Fifth Round be launched in the autumn of 1975 with awards to be made in mid-1976. It was noted that this timing would assist in the achievement of the participation objectives. The choice of blocks was limited by unresolved boundary disputes with the French and Irish Governments in the South Western Approaches and the Celtic and Irish Seas, and it would be necessary to include blocks in the Moray Firth and Cardigan Bay, where there were conflicts with the Ministry of Defence who had requirements for training and other military exercises.

Working Group studies Fifth Round options

Mr Varley's proposals were generally accepted, though the CPRS had a reservation about whether a Round with as many as 150–200 blocks was necessary. A DEN Working Party chaired by Lord Balogh the Minister of State subsequently decided that a study group be established to examine the most appropriate method of licensing for the Fifth Round. The Working Party felt that the objective of the chosen method should be to maximise British interests in the licenses (but to avoid challenges under the Treaty of Rome and by the USA), consistent with speedy and thorough exploration and depletion policy. The discretionary and auction systems were both considered, and it was concluded that, given the basic objectives, the discretionary system was to be preferred. By controlling the selection of licenses freedom and flexibility was provided to satisfy objectives, particularly with respect to the level of British and public participation. It was easier to encourage exploration on less prospective blocks, and it could more readily help to smooth out drilling activity through time via the negotiation of work programmes. It would also be easier to include or exclude small companies depending on perceptions of their financial capability. Lord Balogh was also keen to respond to the criticism of the Public Accounts Committee that the longevity of issued licences at 46 years without scope for revision was excessive. It was decided that this should be reduced by around ten years, and that a higher proportion of the acreage be surrendered after the initial period. But a major item, namely state participation in the new licences, remained to be settled.

What state participation in new licences?

This subject engendered much debate within the DEN and various options were considered. The first was very radical, namely involving BNOC as sole licensee. It would then decide on the nature of any relationships with the oil companies. This could range from (1) joint-licence agreements with them, (2) oil companies as contractors, and (3) BNOC acting totally independently. It was concluded that BNOC would be unable to carry out the whole operation on its own, and would have difficulty in negotiating the terms of its relationship with the companies.

The second was the possibility that BNOC would be a joint licensee from the very beginning of the licence. This would permit the Corporation to participate either on a par with the oil companies or on a carried interest basis at rates of participation which could vary according to geographic area or field production (as in Norway). The third option was that BNOC should automatically be given participation on a carried interest basis, with the rights being exercised when a field was declared commercial. Again the rate of participation could vary as with the second option. The fourth option was that licences be awarded with no participation obligations. This would help to maintain the interest of the oil companies.

DEN officials felt that only the first option should be excluded on the grounds that BNOC would not be ready to undertake the role of sole licensee in the relevant time period. It was felt that the Model Clause in the revised Regulations should be so framed that the Secretary of State would be able to announce the precise participation arrangements at the time of the announcement of any new Round. DEN officials also felt that the Government should have the right to issue licences solely to BNOC outside a Round as soon as its capabilities were demonstrated, and it was recommended that the Fifth Round announcement should explicitly refer to this, and state that blocks were being set aside for later award to BNOC.

Application of Treaty of Rome to UKCS

At this time (May 1975), when these matters involving licensing with associated privileges to BNOC were being discussed, the related issue of the application of the Treaty of Rome to the UKCS was the subject of inter-departmental discussion. The question of whether the EEC Treaties applied to the Continental Shelf was unresolved. The Commission felt that the Treaties should be applied, but the matter had not been formally discussed in Brussels, though it had been raised in other fora. Thus the other eight member states had supported a proposal that the effects of Treaty application should be studied in the context of the Law of the Sea Conference. It had also arisen in the Paris Convention dealing with marine pollution, where the Commission was arguing that the EEC should have control over pollution from offshore installations located in the Continental Shelf.

Inter-departmental paper for Ministers

An inter-departmental paper was prepared for Ministers on the subject to inform decisions relating to oil and gas. With respect to licensing it was felt that policy could be challenged only where discrimination against nationals of other countries was involved. This could apply to the nationality, incorporation, and central management and control requirements in the Petroleum Regulations, which required licence applicants to be either citizens of the UK and resident in the UK or bodies incorporated in the UK. One of the clauses empowered the Secretary of State to revoke a licence if these conditions ceased to apply. The Petroleum Bill currently being discussed in Parliament would remove the nationality and residence requirements, but retain the central management and control one.

This was necessary to permit effective taxation of licensees and to ensure that they behaved in accordance with laws and Regulations. The requirement and its enforcement were established in the UK, and thus licensing policy was effectively subject to the Treaties even though they might not apply to the UKCS. With respect to controls over oil and gas activities it was felt that the Treaties did not limit the rights of the UK Government to encourage, discourage or control the rate of development and depletion of oil and gas resources. The only area where there was room for debate was on possible discrimination against other EEC nationals. It was felt that a legal challenge would only be possible where specific controls were applied differentially across fields. Again this would be possible because the relevant controls were administered from the UK.

Landing requirement

The landing requirement was important as a device for ensuring that a high proportion of North Sea oil was refined in the UK and for ensuring that gas was readily available to the UK market. It was arguable that the provisions of the Treaty relating to trade barriers would not apply to North Sea oil and gas if the Treaty itself did not apply to the UKCS: there could be no export of a product which had never been within the EEC area. Of course, North Sea oil would become subject to the Treaties when landed in the UK.

Licensing criteria reassessed

These thoughts were available to the DEN Working Party in its consideration of factors to be taken into account in making awards. It was clear that the published criteria would have to be expressed in such a way that the risk of a successful EEC challenge was avoided. In drafting the criteria the Working Party considered that attention had to be given to several factors which had received inadequate attention in the past, including the financial capability of applicants. Recent experience had shown that it could no longer be assumed that funds would be available when a field was declared commercial. Despite this small companies could play a valuable role, but further thought was necessary on how this potential could be optimised.

The Working Party itemised a list of issues which should be considered when allocating Fifth Round licences. These included technical and financial competence, where the latter referred to exploration and development, the extent to which the applicant agreed to state participation in existing licences, and the extent to which he was prepared to offer such participation above the minimum specified by the Government. The extent of the British interest in an application group would be considered, as would its plans to purchase British equipment and employ UK nationals. Further contributions to the UK economy, including refining and other downstream activities would be considered, as was the degree of equitable treatment given to UK companies in countries of foreign applicants.

Royalty on landed value

With respect to financial provisions it was proposed that the royalty be based not on the wellhead value but on the landed value. This was primarily to remove complicated and time-consuming calculations and prolonged disputes with licensees on conveying and transport costs. It was also proposed that the current arrangement whereby licence fees could be offset against royalty be discontinued. Experience had been that there was no correlation between rent for territory held on licence and royalty paid on production from that territory. It was felt that it was not logical to relieve a licensee of rent because he had production, whereas a less fortunate licensee had to continue to pay in the absence of production.[1]

DEN officials produce proposals on financial terms

Officials prepared a paper on the more important financial terms for Lord Balogh. They felt that the objective should be to increase the overall Government take from royalty and licence rentals but only to the extent that, with participation and taxation, the package remained attractive to investors. With respect to participation officials considered flat rates lower than, equal to, and greater than 51%. In addition a sliding-scale of rates varying with production was considered. The last possibility was not recommended. The legal drafting of a clause to adjust the rate according to achieved production with the consequential adjustments to cost contributions would be extremely complex. The effect would in any case be muted because of the ensuing adjustments to tax. It was also agreed that a sliding-scale would not necessarily produce a corresponding enhancement to the profits received by the Government, because these were not necessarily a straight function of the level of production.[2] With respect to the level of flat rate participation it was felt that 51% gave the appropriate balance between control, contribution costs, and reaction by the companies. This was therefore recommended.

With respect to royalty rates, mindful of the decision to make the base the landed value, consideration was given to both lower and higher nominal rates. It was concluded that the 12.5% rate should be applied to the landed value which would equate to a rate of around 14% on the wellhead value. This was not out of line with recent practice in other countries. With respect to licence rental payments the up-to-date position in other countries was examined, particularly in Norway. It was recommended that the initial level be set at around £80 per sq.km. for the first six years, rising thereafter on an incremental scale to £3,000 per year per sq. km. These figures were somewhat higher than the current Norwegian terms. The idea of indexing the financial terms for inflation was considered but not recommended. It was argued, somewhat oddly, that, as a general practice, Government fees did not include provision for inflation. It was also felt that the prime objective of steeply increasing rentals, namely to dissuade licensees from retaining acreage without working it, could now be achieved more directly by employing the new powers over exploration and development included in the Petroleum Bill. It was also noted that the net gains in revenue would not be great because licence fees were tax deductible. With respect to application fees it was recommended that they be increased to £1,000 for production licences to reflect the processing costs involved.

Debate on form of BNOC participation

Much debate ensued on the form of state participation. In early August 1975 DEN officials favoured a carried interest scheme whereby BNOC would be a joint licensee from the outset in every new licence, but it would have no active role until a discovery had been made and declared commercial. At that point it would become an active participant and contribute to financing the development. This was felt to be preferable to the alternative where BNOC would have no initial involvement in the licence, but when a commercial discovery was made the Secretary of State would terminate the licence and issue a new one including the old licensees plus BNOC. When BNOC became an active participant DEN officials felt that it should immediately start contributing its share of costs on an ongoing basis. The Treasury saw some advantages in the cost contributions coming out of future production revenues rather than being paid on an ongoing basis. The Inland Revenue saw practical difficulties with this arrangement. As the legislation then stood in those circumstances the companies would pay 100% of the development costs in the early years but receive tax relief on only 49%. If interest were paid on the cost reimbursements it would be liable to corporation tax. It was even possible that, on one interpretation of the legislation, oil received by the companies to reimburse them for the field development costs would not fall within the PRT net.

Launch of round delayed

BNOC's participating terms were debated for several months, and helped to delay the launch of the Round. The issue of the selection of blocks to offer and the associated designation of further areas to be part of the UKCS involved substantial consultation. The DEN had originally chosen 267 blocks from which a selection would be made, but the Ministry of Defence, and the Marine Division of the DTI found problems generally relating to conflict of use with no less than 157 of them.

Boundary disputes with French and Irish Governments

Of the remaining 116 blocks, 53 had not yet been designated because of prolonged boundary disputes with the Irish and French Governments. In the latter case the issue had gone to arbitration. DEN officials felt that further designations were necessary to ensure the success of the Round. To expedite these, discussions were held with the FCO on what areas could safely be designated without exacerbating the disputes. It was agreed that the additional areas should be in the Western Approaches/Celtic Sea which offered good potential. The only remaining large areas currently undesignated were north of 62° North and in the Shetlands basin, both of which were very expensive in which to operate. There were also political advantages in avoiding the offer of too many blocks coyly described as being "from Scottish jurisdiction waters". Ideally the DEN would have preferred to designate up to the median lines with Ireland and France, giving full weight to islands (which had been an item of dispute), but, given the sensitivities of the disputes, the DEN proposed that only perceived prospective blocks be designated. On the Southern flank this entailed crossing the dividing line in one place suggested by the French Government in earlier negotiations, but in all other cases either standing back from it or coinciding with it. On the Western flank it was felt that at present there could be no designation up to the median line giving full weight to islands without appearing to prejudge the negotiations with the Irish. But it was also felt that if designation did not go beyond the line proposed by the Irish Government, credence would be given to their claim which was felt to be particularly specious as it disregarded all islands. DEN officials proposed that designation should follow a slipped line which crossed the dividing line proposed by the Irish in several places, but contained seven blocks regarded as very promising. The FCO felt, however, that such a decision should not be made at present, but should await the outcome of negotiations. The CPRS broadly supported the FCO view. Ministers agreed that proposals could be put to the French to accept a designated area which in places crossed their proposed dividing line. It was later agreed to confine the designation boundary to undisputed areas in order to secure acceptance by the French in time for the Fifth Round. No agreement was reached on the approach to the Irish Government which was deferred until a later date.

Concern about prospective downturn in activity

Meanwhile Mr Benn had been anxious to make a preliminary Parliamentary announcement which it was hoped would discourage the removal of drilling rigs from the UKCS and give a confidence boost to the offshore supplies industry. This issue was of particular importance in Scotland. The Scottish Office had set up a Working Party to consider the implications for Scotland of the proposed Fifth Round. It produced a detailed report indicating that, in the absence of this Round, there would be a marked rundown in oil-related economic activity after 1978. In fact there was a strong likelihood that some rundown would take place with the Round. Their conclusion was that, subject to some concern about the effects of oil activity on the fishing industry, as many as possible of the 267 blocks originally identified by DEN should be offered. From the viewpoint of the Scottish offshore supplies industry it was hoped that 150–160 blocks would then be licensed.

Mr Benn announces launch of Fifth Round

Mr Benn sent a Minute to the Prime Minister on 4th August indicating the progress which had been made and seeking approval for an early announcement. The problems with designation necessitated a postponement, however, but Mr Benn was not to be deterred, and in September sent a further Minute to the Prime Minister urging the case for an announcement. This was agreed and the announcement of the Round was made in the somewhat unlikely setting of the National Union of Mineworkers' Summer School at Ruskin College, Oxford on 23rd September 1975. It contained no details but emphasised the objectives of maintaining the momentum of activity and entrenching legitimate national interests, including majority state participation in commercial fields. The Chancellor of the Exchequer, burdened by problems of an escalating PSBR, requested that the word "all" not be linked to fields for which participation would be required.

Further debate on Fifth Round participation terms

The debate on the precise terms of participation in new licences dragged on and even involved the reopening of issues which had earlier been resolved. One such subject was whether BNOC should be (1) a co-licensee from the beginning of the licence, or (2) whether it would join a reformed licence only when a commercial discovery was made. The advantage of BNOC being involved at the outset was that there would be no break in the arrangements, but there were negative aspects. Thus the requirements on co-licensees to supply to BNOC full information gathered would amplify the concerns of the industry regarding confidentiality and unfair competitive advantages being given to the Corporation. BNOC would also be involved at an early stage with a burden of detailed negotiations with a large number of licensees. If, say, 150 licences were issued there would be a substantial strain on the Corporation's resources.

Timing of BNOC joining licence

The advantages of BNOC joining the licence at a later stage reflected the disadvantages of involvement from the start. There would be less partnership negotiations with co-licensees, and the information/confidentiality problem would be reduced. Relationships with the companies would be improved. It was acknowledged that a problem was the obligation of the Government to award a successor licence, which would be conditional on agreement between BNOC and the other licensees in circumstances where the Government did not have the necessary powers. The oil companies might also be discouraged by the obligation to reach agreement with BNOC before a successor licence would be granted. It was felt, however, that these doubts could be allayed if guidelines for the agreement were published at the time of the Fifth Round. DEN officials felt on balance that the second option was preferable. But Lord Balogh had reservations about this course, seeing the advantages of early BNOC involvement. As a result both options remained for discussion with other Departments. The Inland Revenue pointed out that if the second route were chosen the result would be a chargeable occasion for capital gains tax, and, regardless of whether cash passed between BNOC and the licensees, a large capital gain could arise. The only course which would guarantee BNOC participation without causing such a tax problem would be through BNOC's involvement from the outset, even though it was inactive.

Lord Kearton prefers participation from outset

The proposals of the DEN officials were sent to Lord Kearton who much preferred the first option under which BNOC would participate from the outset. The information it gathered from this date onwards would be very valuable, and the opportunity to participate fully in discussion with partners would ensure that BNOC understood the commercial philosophies involved. This would facilitate long-lasting harmonious partnerships to everyone's benefit. The work involved might be substantial but hopefully manageable. Lord Kearton also asked why, if the burden of detailed work on Operating Agreements proved onerous, relatively simple interim arrangements should not be agreed for the exploration phase, leaving the much more detailed provisions for the exploitation phase. This suggested a third possible model for participation in the Fifth Round, namely that BNOC might be given the option to participate at any stage. Lord Kearton also expressed the view that BNOC should be on an equal footing with its partners and should thus contribute to costs as they arose, and, if the Corporation did not participate from the outset, it would contribute towards any past exploration costs.

At a meeting with senior DEN and Treasury officials in late November 1975, Lord Kearton reiterated his views that BNOC should be a full partner in all licences from the time of their award. The Treasury expressed concern about the public expenditure implications of BNOC being a cost contributor from the start of the licence. The DEN was concerned that the workload on BNOC would be excessive, but Lord Kearton felt that this problem would not be insuperable.

Exploration prospects

At the meeting wider issues relating to the Fifth Round were discussed. Lord Kearton reported that the companies were rather lukewarm about the prospects. National Coal Board (Exploration) whose North Sea oil interests BNOC were to take over had reported this, based on discussions with their partners. Their views were based primarily on perceptions of the attractiveness of the blocks likely to be on offer. In the Northern North Sea there was a fear that, in order to obtain desirable blocks, they would have to accept unattractive ones on which they would have to do some drilling. In the Southern North Sea, while small fields could be discovered, there was no evidence that BGC was currently prepared to make meaningful offers for small reserves on which annual rentals were being paid, and thus there was no point in drilling to find more. With respect to the Western Approaches and the Celtic Sea their partners were very lukewarm about submitting any proposals. With reference to the Irish Sea the prospects were also not seen as attractive, and the company's partner (Gulf Oil) wanted to pull out. Prophetically NCB (Exploration) concluded that they would be happy to leave the Irish Sea to BGC.

The CPRS had also been warning the DEN that the terms of the Fifth Round being debated (including the new PRT) had been based on the assumption that fields discovered from new exploration might be unrealistically large. In a letter to Lord Balogh Sir Kenneth Berrill noted the views publicly expressed by the Vice-Chairman of BRINDEX (the Association of British Independent Oil Companies) that future fields would be relatively small. He queried the definition of a small field being employed by the DEN. This had recoverable reserves of 45 million tonnes (over 335 million barrels) which seemed too high in relation to the reserves indicated for the next set of possible commercial developments. Even then the prospective rate of return on such a field as calculated by DEN could arguably be regarded as low in relation to the risks involved.

By late 1975 it had become clear that the areas in the Western Approaches which could safely be designated contained very few promising blocks. Further, as the refreshingly open new Minister of State, Mr John Smith, indicated, for political reasons it was undesirable to have a large concentration of blocks "from Scottish jurisdiction waters". While it would still be possible to have a Round with 100–150 blocks it was desirable to include a reasonable proportion of promising ones to avoid any accusation of padding the list. Accordingly, he felt that a more gradual approach involving around fifty blocks per year over three years might be preferable.

Views of Mr John Smith on Round

In a letter to Mr Dell on the last day of 1975 Mr Smith intimated the above and also indicated his thoughts on other major issues. Thus he preferred the discretionary system in making awards, on the grounds that the new PRT meant that the auction system offered no serious prospect of greater revenue, and the discretionary mechanism enabled better control over the attribution of individual licences. With respect to criteria for judging applications he felt that, while those used in previous Rounds could be added to, in some cases it might be preferable to give informal indications of the Government's views to applicants as this could avoid the risks of causing what he coyly termed "international repercussions" from public statements. An example might be the issue of whether more favourable consideration would be given to applicants who had made a satisfactory response to the proposals for participation negotiations. On additional criteria he highlighted (1) the applicant's subscription to the Memorandum of Understanding and Code of Practice on Full and Fair Opportunity (FFO) for UK suppliers agreed with UKOOA, (2) the demonstration of applicants that they were doing something significant to train UK nationals in oil industry skills, (3) the demonstration that management decisions, technical and other, were being taken in the UK, and (4) plans to use UK drilling rigs.

Mr Smith followed this up with another letter to Mr Dell setting out his views on the form of participation in the Fifth Round. He expressed favour with the view that BNOC should be an active participant from the outset paying its share of all costs. Essentially he was supporting the arguments put forward by Lord Kearton. He reinforced the argument by noting the conclusions of two separate consultants which were that the proposed package of terms was likely to be viewed as only marginally attractive. If a softer line on participation terms were taken a tougher line could be taken on other parts of the package. Mr Smith acknowledged that at first sight this option might appear financially disadvantageous, but this was more apparent than real because, if the companies had to pay all the front-end costs, they would obtain tax relief on this greater sum. Thus the net cost to the Exchequer of BNOC being a full partner from the outset would be very much less than the gross cost.

Views of Treasury

The Treasury was broadly content with Mr Smith's proposals on the scale of the Round, and agreed that the discretionary method of assessment was acceptable if the other financial terms were set correctly. There was felt to be serious drawbacks about the participation proposals, particularly the public expenditure implications where the early outflow of funds would not be offset until a later date. The offset would in any case be incomplete as some companies would have unsuccessful exploration but had no discovery against which to set the costs. BNOC might end up spending substantial public funds for little return which would be imprudent when, through a carried interest provision, the risk could be avoided.[3] The Treasury was also concerned about the possibility that the DEN might want BNOC to be a sole licensee in some cases. One such circumstance might be in blocks where it was desired that drilling proceeded quickly to help establish claims in the boundary disputes with France and Ireland. Another might be in blocks where it was deemed appropriate to establish the existence of recoverable reserves but then to sterilise them for a few years in the interests of depletion policy. The Treasury discussed with DEN officials the idea that BNOC might actively partici- pate from the outset in a selected few licences only. This would involve BNOC having double options whereby it could (1) contribute to costs from the beginning, or (2) exercise its option to participate at the field commerciality stage, and do so either (a) by paying its share of past costs in a lump sum or (b) spreading these costs forward, enabling the co-licensees to recover the exploration costs out of BNOC's share of revenues. The Inland Revenue confirmed that, provided BNOC was a member of the licence group from the outset (even though a passive one) the capital gains tax problem would not arise. All these sentiments were conveyed to Mr Smith by Mr Dell. In subsequent discussions between them the issue remained unresolved.

Mr Benn's detailed proposals to colleagues

In March 1976 Mr Benn circulated a detailed paper on all aspects of the subject to his Ministerial colleagues. This contained many of the earlier proposals promoted by the DEN as discussed above, but also some fresh ones. The case for a smaller Round of 50–60 blocks was reiterated, with emphasis being put on the difficulties of offering more promising blocks outside Scottish jurisdiction waters. A problem had arisen in the Cardigan Bay area. There was pressure from Wales to have a Welsh dimension to the Fifth Round, and Cardigan Bay was sufficiently promising to justify exploration. But studies undertaken by MOD and DEN offi- cials had shown that, to make the whole of the Bay available for licensing, would entail the closure of the defence range and its transfer elsewhere. It would be possible to have limited exploration compatible with the existing defence activi- ties, but only if a maximum of five blocks were licensed. Unfortunately these were not geologically promising. Six more attractive blocks could be added, but only if special equipment were installed at an estimated cost of £0.75 million over four years to provide more sophisticated control over the testing of certain weapons. If the eleven blocks were offered there were hopes of a positive response from the industry, but the offer of only five indifferent blocks could lead to a negative response and the Bay could remain undeveloped. The clear licensing advantage was with the offer of eleven blocks involving the expenditure of £0.75 million.[4] It was proposed that the costs should be shared equally among the DEN, MOD, and Welsh Office. The MOD had agreed to this on the grounds that the new control equipment would produce some operational advantages, but the Welsh Office had not agreed to contribute, because matters of oil and defence were not within the field of responsibility of their Secretary of State. The DEN contribution could not be met from its existing allocation and it proposed that it be funded from the Contingency Reserve, but the Treasury had not agreed to this.

With respect to the method of licensing the exercise of Ministerial discretion was favoured on the grounds that the auction system offered no real prospect of enhancing Government revenues, and the discretionary system facilitated more control over the licensees. The criteria for judging applications should add to those of previous Rounds by including the performance of companies in the current participation negotiations and enhanced financial capability requirements. With respect to the former the options were to have an overt or hidden criterion. An overt one would signal the Government's determination to obtain participation agreements. A hidden one had less obvious impact but it would avoid the risk of criticism that the Government was unfairly influencing the course of voluntary negotiations. It also offered some protection against counteraction against British companies by the USA under its Mineral Leasing Act. It was possible, however, that hidden criteria might not remain hidden and disclosure could result in accusations of deviousness. On balance Mr Benn recommended that a final decision on this matter be deferred until the outcome of current participation negotiations, particularly those with Shell and Exxon, were known.

For the Fifth Round Mr Benn proposed that participation be at 51% in every licence and that the licences be issued only after the conclusion of a satisfactory Operating Agreement between BNOC and its partners. The paper noted the main two options regarding BNOC's contribution to costs, namely on a pay-as-you-go or carried interest basis, and itemised the pros and cons of each on the lines discussed above. Mr Benn acknowledged the major difference of view on this between Treasury Ministers and himself, with the former wanting to defer for as long as possible BNOC's cost contributions on the grounds that BNOC did not have to buy its way into licences, and that every commercial organisation naturally sought to defer making payments until there was revenue to cover them. Mr Benn argued that if BNOC contributed in the same way as its partners it would give credence to the claim that the Corporation would act in a commercial manner. He also argued that the proposed Fifth Round terms were among the most severe in the world, and carried interest could jeopardise its success.

With respect to licence conditions Mr Benn's proposals on royalty changes and licence fees were as discussed above. He also proposed that the Secretary of State should be able to award sole licences to BNOC or BGC in such a way as he saw fit at any time at his discretion. Relinquishment obligations were to have an initial period of four years after which one-third of the acreage would be surrendered. After a further three years another third should be relinquished, and the remaining one-third of the initial acreage could be retained for a further 30 years. Mr Benn also proposed that confidential consultations be arranged with the Trades Union Congress (TUC), Scottish TUC, Welsh TUC, UKOOA, and Confederation of British Industry (CBI) on his proposals.

Views of Chancellor

In advance of the Ministerial meeting Mr Healey, the Chancellor of the Exchequer, submitted a Minute to the Prime Minister clarifying his views on BNOC's cost contributions. He supported carried interest and saw no case for a Government contribution to exploration. He also felt that there should be no automatic contribution to development costs, and each case should be negotiated individually with a strong presumption that the Government would not contribute cash but would pay its share out of revenue. The co-licensee would be entitled to interest on the repayment of the contribution it made on behalf of BNOC. The Chancellor was, of course, most concerned about the growing PSBR. He did not think that disincentives would ensue. He thought that the borrowing capacity of investors would be enhanced by having BNOC as a partner, but, if the whole package was felt to be unattractive, the solution would be to adjust other elements such as licence rentals or royalties rather than have a Government capital contribution. Another possibility was to abandon a 1976 Round or drop the concept of a Round altogether. Companies could be invited to make bids for particular blocks within designated areas. Individual terms could be negotiated on a case by case basis, and the terms could be adjusted continuously to maintain the necessary flow of exploration.

Ministerial discussions without full agreement

The Ministerial meeting was held on 15th April 1976, and the major issues discussed on the lines indicated above. At the end there was general agreement that there should be a further Round of 50–60 blocks as proposed by Mr Benn. Some blocks in Cardigan Bay should be included and the three Departments with interests agreed to share the cost of the special weapons guidance equipment which would then be needed. No agreement was reached on the subject of cost contributions by BNOC, and it was agreed that further discussions be held among the Secretary of State for Energy, the Chief Secretary to the Treasury, the Chancellor of the Duchy of Lancaster and Lord Kearton.

Further Ministerial debate

Mr Benn then proceeded to prepare a draft consultative document with the main ideas being based on his submission to the Ministerial Committee plus its conclusions, and circulated it to his colleagues. The CPRS objected to part of a paragraph on criteria for judging applications which included the statement that one such criterion would be performance on the voluntary participation negotiations. Sir Kenneth Berrill felt that this should not be made overt. Mr Lever felt that the document was seriously incomplete by omitting reference to guidelines on BNOC's cost contributions, but felt that an overt reference to performance in participation negotiations was justifiable, and would not lead to retaliation in the USA if it was clear that American companies were not being discriminated against. Mr Barnett, the Chief Secretary, felt that the document should be deferred until agreement on BNOC's cost contributions had been reached. Mr Hattersley, the Minister of State at the FCO, expressed anxiety about the Full and Fair Opportunity (FFO) for the UK offshore supplies industry, which appeared both among the criteria for judging applications and the licensing conditions. The FCO was always lukewarm about the Memorandum of Understanding but took some comfort when it was described as voluntary. But what was being proposed for the Fifth Round weakened this important line of defence for it. The suggestion of a requirement to accept FFO contradicted the notion that it was voluntary, and it would be much more difficult to defend FFO in the EEC context. It was noteworthy that 43 out of the 44 major companies operating in the North Sea had accepted it on the understanding that it was voluntary. Given that remarkably high compliance there was no need to make it a requirement and open up the prospect of criticism from the EEC.

Agreement on consultation document

At the Ministerial meeting on 10th May these matters were discussed. The Committee generally favoured the incorporation of both criteria – performance in participation negotiations and in giving FFO opportunity to UK suppliers – in the consultation document. A note should be added stating clearly that there would be no discrimination in this respect between UK and foreign oil companies. On this basis the Committee approved the issue of the document. FFO was not mentioned as a licence condition but would be taken into account in judging applications.

Further debate on BNOC's cost contributions

But agreement had still not been reached on the issue of BNOC's cost contributions and a meeting involving Mr Benn, Mr John Smith, Mr Joel Barnett, Mr Lever, Lord Kearton, and senior civil servants (including the two who were Directors of BNOC) was held to resolve the issue. The familiar arguments were repeated, and it was concluded that neither general exclusion nor automatic acceptance of BNOC contributions was tenable. Cabinet should decide whether these should be the exception or the rule. One odd idea for consideration was whether BNOC should contribute to exploration but not to development costs.

In preparation for the Cabinet meeting the Treasury advised Mr Barnett that, in terms of BNOC's standing among the oil companies, contributions to exploration costs would not significantly enhance it, and once the idea had been agreed it would be difficult to refuse to contribute to the much larger development costs. It was preferable to have carried interest for both cost components.

Cabinet discussions

The subject was discussed in Cabinet on 13th May 1976. Mr Benn reiterated his earlier arguments for pay-as-you-go contributions by BNOC adding that the exploration costs involved might be only £50 million for the period 1977–1983 and the really large development expenditures would not commence until 1980. He was prepared to compromise and agree that contributions to development costs should be decided for each case on its merits. Mr Barnett agreed that the Fifth Round should be seen as successful, but did not feel that carried interest by BNOC would jeopardise this. It was unfortunate that overseas borrowing by BNOC counted as part of the PSBR. He was concerned that knowledge of the potentially huge obligations to contribute to development costs would create serious problems for Britain's credit abroad. He thus preferred the carried interest route. After discussion the conclusion was to support Mr Benn's compromise proposal.

Consultation document agreed and published

The DEN then produced a revised draft consultative document including a new appendix setting out the arrangements for BNOC's cost contributions. The Treasury was interested in two implications of the compromise. The first was that if BNOC decided that it did not want to participate in a development it would not be required to contribute to exploration costs. In such cases this would involve the oil companies refunding contributions already made by BNOC! The appendix indicted that capital contributions by BNOC would be at its option with the method of payment open for negotiation, and, where the contribution was deferred, interest would be payable at a commercial rate. The consultative document containing these curious provisions was then published on 27th May with an accompanying written Parliamentary Answer by Mr Benn and a fairly full Press Release.

A particular issue relating to BNOC's relationship with BGC was clarified in the consultative document. It had earlier been agreed that any BGC stake in a field would count towards 51% state participation. For the Fifth Round BGC would apply for licences on its own or in partnership with others, and it was agreed that such stakes would count towards the 51%. DEN officials suspected that BGC's partners might prefer to increase the share of BGC to 51% rather than have an involvement with BNOC.[5] The Government wanted BNOC to be in all Fifth Round licences. The matter was resolved at a meeting among Mr Smith and the chairmen of BNOC and BGC where BGC agreed not to increase its share beyond 35% so that BNOC would always have a minimum of 16%.

Reaction of UKOOA

Consultations proceeded immediately and DEN received representations from the bodies to whom the document was particularly directed. UKOOA submitted a long letter with several objections to the proposals. Unsurprisingly a key concern was BNOC's option to have its share of development costs carried. At a meeting on 15th June UKOOA indicated that the companies would need to know before applications closed whether co-licensees would be obligated to carry BNOC, and, if so, what the detailed arrangements were to be. The less than helpful response was that it was necessary to retain flexibility, and so it was not proposed to set down a standard pattern. The sums involved were very large and the Government could not commit itself irrevocably. The DEN suggestion was to defer the details until a discovery was made.

On the subject of the proposed relinquishment terms UKOOA felt that they were very stringent and would involve the surrender of productive areas. The somewhat novel four plus three years relinquishment proposal would in practice involve a negotiated seven-year work programme of which a specified part would be undertaken in the first four years. UKOOA also objected to the effective increase in the royalty burden which was defended on the somewhat curious grounds that BNOC would now contribute to exploration costs. UKOOA also expressed concern about other matters including conflicts of interest resulting from BNOC's involvement in all licences, and the small size of the Round which, given the wide geographic spread of the acreage, would reduce its attractiveness.

Reaction of STUC and TUC

The meeting with the Scottish Trades Union Congress (STUC) had a very different emphasis. The STUC welcomed the concept of small but frequent Rounds. There was much interest in the FFO provision and they would have preferred that this had been expressed more firmly. The international constraints in any overt reference to UK industry were acknowledged. The STUC wondered why BNOC should contribute to exploration and development costs.

At the meeting with the TUC on 23rd June 1976 the main issues raised were again FFO and participation, but also union access to offshore installations. It was explained that the OSO was able to monitor the performance of companies in providing FFO, and could advise Ministers on a ranking order of such perform-ances which would be taken into account in the award of licences. On progress with participation agreements the TUC were hoping that this would be fully taken into account in the award of Fifth Round licences. DEN officials pointed out that the small Round provided more leverage in this respect. The TUC also asked whether it would be made clear to applicants that their chances of obtaining licences would depend on their attitude to the provision of access to union repre-sentatives to offshore installations. DEN officials indicated that they expected that applicants would sign the proposed Memorandum of Understanding on access. It was hoped to send this Memorandum to operators in the near future, inviting their agreement on this matter.

Effects of carried interest on investment incentives

The debate with UKOOA continued and a further meeting was held on 8th July with Mr John Smith in the chair. UKOOA had now had time to analyse in detail the carried interest proposals and reported that it would reduce the internal rate of return on investment by 30%–40% which was a large disincentive. Mr George

Williams, the Director General, indicated that the only prudent assumption which operators could make was that BNOC would always exercise its option to be carried during the development phase. This meant that BNOC could not be regarded as a proper commercial partner. Mr Smith maintained that BNOC could always be relied upon to pay its full share of development costs. Mr Bill Bell the President of UKOOA emphasised that the key point was the time value of the carried costs. The offer that a normal commercial rate of interest would be paid was not fully satisfactory as it would not compensate for the project completion and reservoir risks. DEN officials maintained that a commercial lending rate was appropriate as repayment was guaranteed. Perhaps a schedule of repayment agreed with BNOC would reduce the uncertainty. UKOOA officers agreed that this would be an improvement. Mr Smith felt that a general form of assurance could be drawn up in a manner acceptable to both parties.

Effects of Limitation Notices

The subject of the implementation of powers to introduce production cuts through Limitation Notices as provided for in the Petroleum and Submarine Pipelines Act 1975 was also discussed at this meeting. DEN officials had suggested a dual formula whereby production cuts were limited to the lower of either a fixed tonnage or a percentage of agreed production. Mr Williams felt that this was unacceptable as it removed the guaranteed production floor implicit in the Varley Assurances. Their value was in their bankability in obtaining finance for field developments where production cuts would not exceed 20%. Under the scheme now proposed by the DEN higher than forecast production could be subject to cuts substantially exceeding 20%, while lower than forecast production would lose the bankable floor guarantee. UKOOA could, however, accept the dual approach to the issue if the choice was between the *higher* of either a percentage of agreed production or a fixed tonnage.

DEN officials argued that the Government required some protection against the possibility that its depletion powers were not negated by over-optimistic estimates by operators. This lay behind their proposals. Mr Bell's response was that, while UKOOA preferred the formula expressed by Mr Williams, a Limitation Notice based on the irrevocable choice of either a fixed tonnage or a percentage of production agreed at the time of development plan approval would be acceptable. The operator should be able to decide which route should be chosen. It was agreed that these matters should be considered further. DEN officials had also suggested a sliding scale of maximum cuts ranging from greater than 20% to less than 20% as field depletion progressed. It was explained that the sliding scale was intended to make the cuts less than 20% in the later years of field life but to keep the average at 20%. UKOOA was concerned that this was inconsistent with previous assurances and had a disproportionately negative effect on the present value of production. Mr Smith agreed to consider UKOOA's views further. DEN officials agreed that production cuts would be imposed in an equitable manner across fields. Mr Williams made the final comment that the flexibility which the

Government wished to maintain for itself on depletion issues equally meant greater uncertainty for the industry. Mr Smith promised to reflect further on this.

DEN views on UKOOA's suggestions

DEN officials advised Ministers generally to resist the UKOOA suggestions with the exception of those relating to relinquishment. It was agreed that they be modified such that, while the total share to be surrendered should remain at two-thirds, this should take effect in one operation after seven years instead of in two steps at four and seven years. UKOOA pursued the subject of BNOC's carried interest, and in a letter to Mr Benn in late June argued that his proposals, taken along with the new taxation and royalty régime would constitute a major deterrent to investment. The new Minister of State, Dr Dickson Mabon, reiterated to UKOOA that BNOC would ultimately pay its full share of costs with a commercial rate of interest, and promised to examine whether a general form of assurance on the matter could be provided. Various schemes were examined but UKOOA indicated in early August that it would not be realistic to expect the companies to lend to BNOC the large sums required, even at commercial interest rates. They argued that the only framework within which the carry would be workable and non-discriminatory would be where the banks were involved, which meant that the repayment terms would be those acceptable to them. They also proposed a scheme whereby BNOC would enter into legally binding agreements that any amounts advanced on its behalf towards its share of development costs would be repaid together with financing charges out of BNOC's net revenues (gross revenues minus operating costs and royalty) and, if all required payments had not been made by seven years after the date of the first advance, all outstanding amounts would then be repaid. All this would effectively have to be guaranteed by the Government. The DEN lawyers introduced another dimension to the problem with the revelation that any form of carried interest would count as a loan under the Petroleum and Submarine Pipelines Act unless BNOC's 51% share of a field development stayed in the ownership of the carrying company until BNOC began to pay. This would be difficult if not impossible to arrange. The carried interest would then count towards the PSBR. All this, of course, would defeat the purpose of carried interest, at least as seen by the Treasury.

Decision that BNOC should pay costs from start

Mr Benn then wrote to Mr Barnett outlining all these developments and requesting his approval for the employment of pay-as-you-go cost contributions by BNOC. The subject was discussed further within the Treasury and with Mr Lever, and in mid-September Mr Barnett replied. He reluctantly acquiesced to Mr Benn's request, making it clear that he had little enthusiasm for putting up Government money for financing North Sea developments when the alternative was for the oil companies to do it. He wondered whether it was necessary to agree that the Government should give any assurances on BNOC repayments to the companies, but noted that there was a lack of Government experience of the likely reaction of the companies to the type of terms being offered. His agreement to BNOC paying its costs on a pay-as-you-go basis was only with respect to the Fifth Round, and in subsequent Rounds the starting point should be carried interest until field revenues became available to pay for all BNOC's costs. Mr Benn immediately put out a Press Release indicating the decision, giving emphasis to the notion that, as development expenditures would not be significant until the early 1980s BNOC would by then be well placed to finance its share of these costs.

By this time much progress had been made on other aspects of the Round. Mr Benn sent a Minute to the Prime Minister on 13th July summarising the consultations with the Scottish TUC, TUC and UKOOA discussed above. He also reported that BRINDEX had expressed concern about the small size of the Round which would not favour the small companies. He also reported the results of the consultation with the Scottish Office and Welsh Office on the blocks to be offered. This had resulted in the selection of 71 full and part blocks for offer. These included several in areas not yet designated, a matter on which decisions were required, and which would then immediately lead to the publication of the details. Mr Benn also reported the results of the examination by Foreign Office lawyers of the worries expressed by Sir Kenneth Berrill at the CPRS on the subject of voluntary participation and possible retaliation by the USA. The legal advice was not conclusive but indicated that there might be scope for retaliatory action under US law. The Energy Counsellor in Washington confirmed the view in DEN that there was little likelihood of retaliation provided that there was no discrimination against US companies. After obtaining the agreement of his colleagues Mr Benn announced to Parliament the outcome of the consultations and the decision to modify the relinquishment terms. The licensing terms would thus be as in the consultation documentation plus this amendment.

Designation of new areas

The designation of new areas and the final selection of blocks were made by late July. The French Government had agreed to the proposals which in any case stopped short of their claim line. The proposals for acreage in dispute with the Irish Government extended beyond the line claimed by them. This issue had been debated at some length inter-departmentally. The CPRS had recommended designating up to the median line, and, after discussion, some designations were made beyond the Irish claim line with their Government being informed in advance. It was felt that it would not exacerbate the dispute which was then confidently expected to go to arbitration. The Designation Order was made on 27th July and a Press Release issued two days later.

Unusual features of launch of Round

The DEN was very anxious to progress the Round, the timetable for which had slipped considerably, but arcane Parliamentary procedures threatened to cause further delays. Invitations to apply for blocks were normally done via a Gazette Notice with Parliament being informed at the same time. The conditions of the Fifth Round were dependent on revised Regulations which would not become effective until 21 days after they were laid before Parliament. They were subject to negative resolution for 40 sitting days which, given the enormously long summer recess, would not expire until well into November. The Regulations and so the Round would remain at risk throughout this period. Given the Government's lack of an overall majority and the Opposition's lack of enthusiasm for several aspects of the proposal this risk was not insubstantial. While DEN Ministers fully appreciated these risks Mr Benn decided to lay the Regulations before Parliament on 29th July and lodged in the Library of the House of Commons a draft Gazette Notice which would be issued only when applications were invited. On this unusual basis the Fifth Round was launched and the closing date fixed at 5th October. Fortunately for the Government there was no prayer against the Regulations which thus came into force on 20th August on which day the Gazette Notice was published.

Assessment of applications

With successive licensing rounds the procedures for assessing applicants became more sophisticated and complex. Work on the weighting of the different criteria had actually started in the Autumn of 1975. This led to prolonged debate within the different Divisions of the DEN with each tending to argue for a "high" weighting to its own case interest. There were now more issues to consider, a main example being the FFO opportunity which became effective in November 1975. Eventually an agreed position was reached and proposals submitted to Mr Benn in September 1976. The procedure was initially to have a preliminary screening test which would eliminate applicants who failed to meet the requirements for FFO and trade union access or who failed to attain qualifying marks relating to technical and financial competence. Because of the problems which had arisen with licensees encountering financial difficulties the acceptable minimum financial threshold had been raised to £3 million to finance the applicant's share of exploration costs per block and £60 million for appraisal and development costs. Applicants who passed this initial screening were then assessed (awarded marks) under the broad headings of technical and financial competence. Other criteria were contributions to the UK economy (including downstream), FFO, and retention of profits in the UK (which put UK-owned companies at some advantage). It was noteworthy that attitude to participation was not included in the initial marking, but would be brought into play only at the final stage which would be after interviews with applicants had taken place. At the same time the blocks on offer would be given a merit ranking related to the response for each block, weighted by the perceived technical status of the applicants and the priorities accorded to the block by them. A computer programme was developed to match the applicants with the blocks, taking account of the marks and merit ranking, and thus produce a provisional ranking. The marks could be modified after the interviews.

The issue of attitude to participation was thus considered at a very late stage in the process. The attitude of some applicants were already known to DEN officials but others had not revealed their position. These were written to in October 1976 and asked to accept the principle of state participation in any commercial discoveries made under their existing licences. The responses were all in the affirmative but sometimes with qualifications.

There were 53 applicant groups and these were interviewed in October and November 1976 and a provisional allocation submitted to Ministers in late November. The only remaining major issue was the use of the leverage of the Fifth Round to further the participation negotiations. The award of licences could be held up for some weeks to permit at least Heads of Agreement on participation to be agreed, but longer delays would jeopardise the volume of drilling in 1977. This was becoming a major issue as a fall-off in drilling was now widely anticipated.

It was also decided to consult Lord Kearton on the provisional awards. He recommended that BNOC should become operator in a few blocks with strong technical and financial partners. But current practice was that the licensees determined the operator, though the Secretary of State had the power of approval. In announcing the Round nothing had been said about BNOC being operator of a licence group, and so it was decided that this could only be obtained by persuasion. Lord Kearton was asked to indicate the blocks which he wanted BNOC to operate. In late 1976 it was decided to allow more time for agreement to be reached on Heads of Agreement for participation. In January 1977 DEN officials could report that much progress had been made with a few applicants. Interestingly, by this time Lord Kearton had nominated three blocks for which BNOC would like operatorships. Two were the first preferences of BP and Shell/ Esso and, when they were approached, they agreed that BNOC could be the operator.

Amoco and participation

In late January Mr Benn submitted a Minute to the Prime Minister attaching his list of provisional awards. He highlighted the progress made in the participation negotiations and indicated that, of the big companies, only Amoco had not shown adequate progress. The company and its partners had provisionally been allocated some blocks, but Mr Benn proposed to give Amoco a final opportunity to reach an acceptable degree of progress, and if this was not forthcoming the company would be deleted from the list of awards. He reported that the allocations would involve 47 blocks and part blocks with 26 groups and 69 companies in total. Applicants who had performed well in the participation negotiations would be gratified because they were being awarded blocks to which they themselves had attached high priority. Nearly 70% of the acreage would accrue to BNOC and British companies, and about 25% to US ones. This contrasted with figures of 35% British and 44% US shares of existing acreage. Of course, the compulsory BNOC 51% share was the key reason for this dramatic difference.

EEC implications of participation

Mr Benn had to report one problem which threatened to delay the formal announcement. This was the EEC implications of participation, a subject on which an inter-departmental group was working at the Attorney-General's suggestion. The Prime Minister's response was cautious. He requested that the report of the inter-departmental group be considered before an announcement was made. He was also concerned about the presentational aspects of the high success rate for British-owned companies. Ministers agreed with the report of the group (see Chapter 9) that the EEC risks should be accepted. Mr Benn then reported to the Prime Minister that Amoco had not made satisfactory progress towards a participation agreement and should thus be excluded from Fifth Round awards. After deliberation among Ministers this recommendation was accepted on the condition that the announcement of awards should not highlight links with participation nor mention Amoco's exclusion. This required a last-minute adjustment to the offers. Two of the blocks intended for Amoco were awarded to BP.

Announcement of awards

Mr Benn made an announcement to Parliament on 9th February. A feature was the award of operatorship status to BNOC on six Blocks, two of which were priority ones for the Corporation. Interestingly on two of them the co-licensees (led by Canadian Industrial Gas) had proposed BNOC as the operator. The awards were provisional, depending as always on agreement on work programmes with the DEN, but on this occasion also on settling an Operating Agreement with BNOC.

Jurisdictional problem with Ireland

Work programme commitments were mostly settled by July 1977, but a problem arose with four blocks which had been awarded to BP in the West of Scotland region. These were in acreage which was in dispute with the Irish Government, and in June 1977 BP received a letter from the Irish Department of Foreign Affairs intimating that part of Blocks 132/15 and 133/11 fell within their jurisdiction. The company informed the DEN and a meeting including the FCO legal adviser was held in July 1977 to discuss the issue. BP sought the advice of the Government, pointing out that it had no previous knowledge of the Irish claim line, and that it had other contracts in the Republic of Ireland. The Legal Adviser at the FCO indicated that the Irish claim was without foundation in international law. It was based on a form of equidistance boundary but which ignored a list of named British islands located more than three miles from the mainland including, for example Islay and Jura.

The view of the Legal Adviser was that a judicial settlement would take several years, given that the parties had agreed in principle to submit the issue to an impartial tribunal. BP was concerned about the political repercussions of exploration (seismic or drilling) in the disputed areas, but no clear answer was available. DEN officials were concerned about a freeze on activities in the disputed areas which would affect other designated acreage. BP asked whether the Government could use its good offices with the Irish Government to ensure the continuation of its rights, but officials felt that this could prejudice the UK's case. The matter remained unresolved for a long time. BP adopted a cautious stance on the issue, preferring to leave the award in abeyance until the dispute was resolved, but the Government felt that this was undesirable as it suggested lack of confidence in the UK claim and might be unhelpful in any arbitration. Ministers therefore tried to persuade BP to accept the award, but the company still had misgivings. In March 1979 Ministers agreed that, if BP continued to be reticent, BNOC should be invited to be the sole licensee. Agreement was still not easy to reach. A further complication related to the work programme which BP felt should be favourable given the frontier location of the blocks (West of the Outer Hebrides). The licence was not confirmed until September 1979.[6]

BNOC and Joint Operating Agreements

Agreement of Joint Operating Agreements (JOAs) between BNOC and the companies also proved very time-consuming. The Corporation and UKOOA produced draft agreements in the autumn of 1976. These substantial documents revealed significant differences between the parties. BNOC's voting rights was a particularly divisive subject. UKOOA was also concerned about the degree of control retained by the Operating Committee rather than devolved to the operator. There was also concern about BNOC's privileged position, and UKOOA wanted provisions included which would protect the co-licensees against these privileges in case they were abused.

Broadly speaking the DEN supported BNOC's stance, but also expressed concern that the Corporation might be taking too tough a line which would prolong the negotiations and thus the commencement of work programmes under the Round. Eventually the DEN suggested that to obtain a speedier resolution, negotiations should take place between BNOC and individual licence groups. UKOOA then protested to Mr Benn about the apparent unwillingness of BNOC to negotiate a standard JOA with it. BNOC then submitted a draft JOA to all their prospective co-licensees and then engaged in the task of negotiating with no less than 22 separate groups. The discussions were hardly harmonious, and the first ones were not agreed until August 1977. Subsequently more agreements were made and the first set of licence awards was formally made on 23rd November, nearly nine months after the announcement of provisional awards.

Confirmation of Fifth Round awards and participation in old licences

The issue of confirmed awards could be used as a lever on the companies to agree to participation in existing licences. While most companies had signed Heads of

Agreement many full (and legally-binding) agreements remained to be agreed. The discussions on the details were quite protracted, and BNOC in particular was keen to ensure that the Government's power to confirm new licence awards was used to maximum effect in coaxing the companies to finalise participation agreements. Ministers decided that when Fifth Round work programmes had been agreed with the companies, progress with participation should be reviewed with them. It is likely that the companies understood the implications, but confirmation of further licence awards was still very slow with a further 13 blocks confirmed in February 1978, seven in April, and another six in the period up to August 1978. The original hope had been that Fifth Round drilling could commence in the later part of 1976. In the event on most of the blocks awarded drilling could only commence in 1978. In the meantime there had been a substantial decrease in exploration with the number of exploration wells started falling from 79 in 1975, to 58 in 1976, and 67 in 1977. This possibility and its damaging consequences had been foreseen by the Scottish Office in its submission on the Fifth Round plans back in 1975. The extensive consultation was one of the causes of the delay, but the evidence is that the keen desire of the Government to progress participation and to obtain JOAs with BNOC had a strong role in contributing substantially to the prolongation of the process.

Work on Sixth Round commences

Preliminary consideration of a Sixth Round commenced early in 1977 before the provisional Fifth Round awards were announced. There were internal discussions within the DEN which ranged over a variety of issues such as remaining prospectivity, role of BNOC, size of Round, and whether to offer licences in gas prone areas. Gas Division argued against offering licences in the Southern North Sea except to BGC. At the end of March Mr Liverman submitted a Minute to Mr Benn arguing that deferment of a Sixth Round for several months was desirable. The latest indications were that drilling activity in 1978 should increase to a satisfactory level, and the information from Lord Kearton was that the companies were fully occupied with their current activities. Deferring the announcement of a new Round would permit a more fundamental study to be made of licensing terms, and a forthcoming review of depletion policy could be taken into consideration.

Sole licensing to BNOC?

These suggestions were accepted and studies put in hand. Shortly afterwards Lord Kearton, ever the opportunist, suggested to the DEN that there were advantages if a number of blocks in the Moray Firth could be allocated to BNOC. The Corporation could then have discussions with the companies on the terms they were willing to offer to join the licence from a position of strength. Mr Liverman readily agreed that sole licensing to BNOC could be considered, but guarded against the allocation of blocks to BNOC followed by an immediate farm-out. This could raise the criticism that the Government was abrogating its licensing role to BNOC.

A meeting was held among DEN Ministers, Lord Kearton, and senior officials to discuss the possibilities on 20th June 1977. The meeting had received a report by Petroleum Studies Ltd which was used to inform the discussion. There was general agreement that the next step should be to award sole licences to BNOC and BGC. These might give the opportunity for the establishment of contractor relationships. This was an idea suggested by Petroleum Studies whereby BNOC would be the licensee but would contract out work to the oil companies. BNOC might take all the risks and rewards or alternatively might share them with the companies, for example via production sharing contracts.

While Lord Kearton felt there was no need to make an announcement covering both sole licensing and a Sixth Round, DEN Ministers were concerned with the political difficulty resulting from an announcement of only sole licences. Mr Benn accepted this argument, but added that it was necessary to exhibit confidence in BNOC, and the companies should have to approach BNOC rather than the other way round as at present.

It was agreed that there should be no major change to Fifth Round terms in designing those for the Sixth Round. There was support for the idea that BNOC should have an option to acquire some of its partners' oil, and that it should also have the option to be operator on specified blocks. Mr Benn felt that a higher equity share for BNOC should be considered as an alternative to the oil option. There was support for the benefits of encouraging small British companies. The smaller companies would readily accept oil option obligations. On the vexed question of how BNOC should contribute to costs there was agreement among Ministers and Lord Kearton that the pay-as-you-go scheme was optional. BNOC would have no difficulty in raising the necessary funds on advantageous terms.

Shortly after this meeting Mr Liverman wrote to Lord Kearton and Sir Denis Rooke confirming that an early award of sole licences to BNOC and BGC was being considered. The purposes would be (1) to underline the importance attached to the role the public sector should play in developing North Sea oil and gas, (2) to give the Corporations further experience and development of their capabilities, and (3) to maintain the momentum of drilling and to help provide work for UK exploration rigs which would soon become available for charter. A further possibility was that the two Corporations might explore on a sole basis to improve knowledge of the UKCS without necessarily immediately developing any discoveries made. The two Corporations were invited to nominate blocks for which they would like either sole exploration or production licences. No less than five or six blocks were recommended with a wide geographic spread.

A paper was prepared for Mr Benn to send to his Ministerial colleagues outlining these ideas and also giving his early recommendations on some aspects of the Sixth Round. He thought that a Round of between 30 and 50 blocks and part blocks would be appropriate. BNOC might have more than 51% of the equity, or it could have an option to purchase some of its partners' oil. He reiterated the arguments in favour of BNOC contributing costs on a pay-as-you-go basis.

Treasury views on enhanced roles for BNOC and BGC

The Treasury was concerned at these proposals on several counts. With respect to the sole right blocks it was not clear that the case had been made. BNOC would be busy enough with its existing workload relating to the ex-NCB and ex-Burmah interests, and was about to be given the operatorships of six blocks in the Fifth Round. This was a heavy load for an infant organisation. There were also public expenditure arguments against sole blocks. The notion that a major purpose of the Sixth Round was to provide BNOC with a larger role as licensee also caused concern. Had the effect on the willingness of the companies to invest in the smaller fields more likely to be discovered been adequately considered? With respect to the cost contributions of BNOC the Treasury felt that carried interest at least in part was preferable to pay-as-you-go on the exploration and development costs.

Assignments to BNOC

Mr Benn followed up his Minute on the Sixth Round with another to the Prime Minister on assignment policy. Recent practice had been to give permission for assignments on condition that the parties entered into meaningful negotiations on participation. To enhance the role of BNOC he now proposed that when he received requests for assignments he would ask the applicants to inform BNOC and give the Corporation the opportunity to express an interest. If an interest was expressed BNOC would be given the opportunity to enter into negotiations on a commercial basis. This would enable BNOC to extend its role in existing licences. It was understood that some other company might outbid BNOC.

BNOC and depletion policy issues

The issues were discussed by the appropriate Ministerial Committee in late July 1977. The Committee was sympathetic to the notion of awarding BNOC some sole licences, but had doubts about the practical details. The Committee requested that a fuller paper be prepared dealing with all the issues raised by Mr Benn plus depletion issues, taking into account the views of other interested Departments. The result was a substantial paper which incorporated the findings of the Working Group on Depletion Policy. This Group noted that only a small proportion of the total resources in the UK designated areas remained to be licensed, which reduced the importance of licensing as an instrument of depletion policy for the 1990s. Nevertheless a small Round with drilling commencing in 1979 was of value. It would provide new drilling rig requirements for the offshore supply industry which would otherwise suffer a decline in activity in 1979. The extra knowledge of remaining reserves would also be valuable. With respect to depletion control instruments production cutbacks of up to 20% constituted an effective method, but the Varley Assurances meant that they could not be used until 1982. No decisions on cutbacks need be taken now, but when they were taken a balance would have to be struck between the macro-economic case for extra production above self-sufficiency levels, and the energy policy case for depleting more slowly to provide additional supplies in later years when oil would become increasingly scarce. The Group also stated that, from the 1980s onwards, development delays would become an increasingly useful method of controlling production. It argued that BNOC should play an increasing role as sole licensee to enhance the Government's influence over the pace of exploitation and to explore virgin areas which would improve knowledge of reserves. With respect to gas the Group felt that new blocks in the Southern North Sea should be awarded to BGC as sole licensee. In the Sixth Round it might be desirable to include a few blocks in that area because of what were coyly termed international considerations. BGC might also be encouraged to procure interests through assignments in territory already licensed.

BNOC to have large oil disposal problem?

The DEN paper also discussed fears which had been expressed that BNOC's acquisition of sole licences plus a larger share in the Sixth Round would result in the Corporation being saddled with volumes of oil so large that they could only be disposed of with difficulty and perhaps at a loss. It was not easy to predict the future sales of BNOC, but it was recognised by the Corporation that a growing proportion of North Sea oil would have to be exported. By late 1978 exports could exceed one-third of availability. BNOC's lack of refinery capacity meant that a rising trend in crude exports was inevitable. But much of the oil becoming available to BNOC would be participation or option oil (perhaps 75% in 1980) and there was no obligation on BNOC to take all of it. The policy issue was perhaps not so much whether BNOC should add to its oil through sole licensing, but whether it should increase the proportion in the form of equity oil. The conclusion was that fears over future disposal of BNOC oil should not inhibit decisions on sole licensing in the Sixth Round.

Need for BNOC to have capability for exploration and development

The paper argued that it was important that BNOC developed an independent capability for exploration and development to lessen dependence on the international oil industry, to provide an informed source of advice to Government, and to influence the pattern of development and disposal of North Sea oil. This constituted the case for sole licensing by BNOC and BGC, for their participation in the Sixth Round, and for active involvement in any assignments. To be recognised as a respectable oil company BNOC would have to establish an expert staff and demonstrate that it could carry out major developments. The paper gave separate consideration to gas issues and the involvement of BGC in the forthcoming licensing. Better knowledge of gas reserves was desirable on the grounds of depletion policy and to avoid under-or over-investment in the other fuel industries. But if the expected gas reserves were to be used to best advantage, the UK was unlikely to require gas from dry gas fields not already contracted to BGC before the mid-1980s, or later if more associated gas became available. If dry gas were discovered there would be pressure from the licensees and the EEC to develop it, but there would be no such pressure from BGC. Thus sole licences awarded to the Corporation had national advantages.

Reaction of industry to discrimination in favour of BNOC and BGC?

The paper considered the possible reaction of the industry to the perceived discrimination in favour of BNOC and BGC. The judgement was that the Government's relationship with the companies would not be seriously disturbed, but they might be sensitive to the suggestion that their roles were diminishing whilst those of BNOC and BGC were growing. But there was no evidence to date that the companies were reluctant to invest in the UKCS, and the judgement was that the present régime was among the milder they encountered around the world. It was recognised that care would be needed in the presentation of the new measures to avoid upsetting EEC-based companies to the extent that they sought to raise some of the policies with the Commission. It was also important not to prejudice the chances of UK companies obtaining licences in overseas countries. But a modest programme of sole licensing should not have such an effect.

Cost of sole licensing to BNOC

The cost of the sole licensing of five blocks to BNOC could be around £35 million for exploration spread over five years from 1978. Development costs were more difficult to predict but were estimated at £50–£100 million for a small development and £300–£500 million for a medium-sized one. Such expenditures would not start before 1991. In a Sixth Round of the size envisaged BNOC's share of exploration costs would be around £100 million in the period 1979–1983 and its share of development costs could be in the range £150–£750 million from 1983 onwards. When all costs (including those relating to assignments) were considered the total over the next five years (excluding development costs) was unlikely to exceed £150 million. The DEN paper suggested that this could come from a wedge of uncommitted project finance funds agreed by Ministers as part of the Nationalised Industries Investment Review. On other issues it was proposed that the Sixth Round broadly follow those of the Fifth Round. This would apply to the financial terms (adjusted for inflation), relinquishment provisions, and consultation procedures, with the timing such that drilling could be effective in 1979 when it might otherwise dip substantially.

Sole licensing for BNOC approved

At the Ministerial meeting on 29th September 1978 the full report by DEN officials (in consultation with other Departments) was tabled, but Mr Benn sought approval only to prepare an announcement on sole licensing and to make preparations for it, and to instruct officials to prepare detailed plans for the Sixth Round. This was agreed and the more controversial issues such as BNOC's contribution to costs were not debated. At this time the Treasury had reluctantly come to the view that it would have to tolerate the pay-as-you-go method because it was by then planning to increase PRT and felt that this plus carried interest could introduce investment disincentives.

Soon afterwards DEN officials met with Lord Kearton and Mr Evans from BNOC. BNOC readily agreed to provide an order of preference for the blocks in which they were interested in having sole licences. Lord Kearton expressed interest in the South West Approaches and asked that, if possible, the awards should include two blocks located in as yet undesignated territory. To this end the DEN might arrange for designation up to the UK/French boundary as drawn on behalf of the Arbitration Tribunal.

More favourable terms for BNOC participation?

Many further discussions with BNOC ensued on Sixth Round terms. In general BNOC argued for more flexible arrangements whereby the Corporation hoped to negotiate favourable terms with individual companies. But DEN officials were concerned about the length of time likely to be involved, and this could delay the awards and thus drilling. In any case licensing terms were the responsibility of the Government. But the notions of the extent to which applicants might be prepared to *offer* to carry BNOC through the exploration phase, to *offer* the Corporation an equity share greater than 51%, and to accept a put option on BNOC's share of oil gained approval. The companies would be free to decline to offer anything under these headings. By the end of 1977 BNOC had also changed its mind about carried interest which it was now promoting for use at the exploration stage. Somewhat ironically the Treasury was now unenthusiastic because of the potential loss of tax revenues from the extra deductions by the companies for PRT.

At a meeting on 11th January 1978 involving DEN Ministers and officials, Lord Kearton and Mr Evans of BNOC it was eventually decided that, for sole licensing, BNOC should have eleven blocks and BGC one. Mr Benn wished to be assured that the case for the Sixth Round stood on its own merits and was not simply a counterbalance to sole licensing. Different views were expressed regarding prospective world oil supply and demand, but in any case production from Sixth Round fields would probably not commence until the late 1980s, and Ministers would have full control over depletion relating to any discoveries. The meeting agreed that BNOC should be carried through the exploration and appraisal stages, that companies could offer more than 51% to BNOC, and that the Corporation would have a put option for its oil. It was also agreed that BNOC should be the operator in six blocks from the outset of the awards through negotiation with co-licensees. A further conclusion of the meeting was that operators for the Sixth Round should be approved only for the exploration period. This was to maintain for the Secretary of State the option as to which company (public or private) should be approved as operator for the development phase.

Inter-departmental discussions

These proposals were discussed with other interested Departments on 25th January 1978. On timing the Scottish Office was concerned that the various proposed new arrangements risked delays to the completion of the Round and thus to new drilling activity. The Scottish Office would also have preferred a Round of 50 Blocks rather than 40 to enhance the activity generated. The FCO felt that if some European companies participated successfully it would aid acceptance of the UK's oil policies within the EEC. The proposed training requirement (full and fair opportunity for UK nationals) required sensitive presentation to avoid any suggestion of preferential treatment in the EEC context. Unsurprisingly there was much concern about the proposal that the Secretary of State could approve the operator for the exploration phase only, and would have discretion on whether or not that operator continued thereafter. This would certainly produce uncertainty and could deter applications. In defence of the proposal DEN officials argued that there was a limited pool of skilled labour available which constrained the ability of companies to undertake the work effectively. It was also necessary to safeguard the existence of the BNOC development team. The Treasury and Inland Revenue said that, although BNOC might benefit from carried interest, there were tax implications which could mean that there was little or no net benefit to the nation. Companies with large tax bills would be able to give spuriously attractive offers to carry BNOC. The biddable criterion would also favour some applicants over others just because of their tax position, and small companies could be particularly disadvantaged. It was agreed that this subject be examined further. A general concern was that the tightening up of terms in many areas (not just licensing) might deter applicants. It was agreed that further attention would be given to this issue, including requesting the advice of the UK Ambassador to the USA. His response was that the elements of the proposed package which would give most concern among the US oil companies would be those relating to BNOC's increase stake and role. In sum he felt that the whole package would be greeted with genuine alarm and would probably cause some diminution of interest.

Interaction of taxation and carried interest

The Treasury and Inland Revenue examined further the complex question of the interaction of taxation and the financing of carried interest. The carried expenditure was deductible to the companies involved, and on a full tax basis, if all the expenditure qualified for uplift, the net cost to the companies would be only around 10% of the related expenditure. If some of the expenditure did not qualify for uplift the net cost to the companies would be about 26% of the related expenditures. But if the fields obtained the benefit of the PRT safeguard the net cost of carrying £100 of BNOC expenditure would be negative to the companies (i.e. it would cost the Exchequer more than £100). The likelihood of the fields being in the safeguard and the time period over which this relief would apply were very difficult to foresee, but the open-endedness of the safeguard rules meant that there was a danger of serious budgetary repercussions. The proposal to carry BNOC was currently being proposed as a biddable item and it could be expected that those companies which expected to obtain the greatest tax relief would show more interest in carrying BNOC.

The Treasury considered the options in the light of these possibilities. Optional (biddable) carried interest without reimbursement could no longer be supported, because it would quite likely mean that the investor would recover more than 100% of the costs. Compulsory carried interest without reimbursement would be an improvement, but there could still be some cases where relief exceeded 100%. Compulsory carried interest with reimbursement only if the exploration was successful was more attractive, as the net cost to the companies of £100 of carried expenditure could be around £26. The Treasury saw no merit in a scheme of fully reimbursable carried interest whether on an optional or compulsory basis. This in effect involved BNOC borrowing from the licensees at a cost which could be greater than from their normal sources. These thoughts and the conclusion that the least unattractive method was compulsory carried interest with reimbursement if the exploration were successful were transmitted to the DEN.

Further inter-departmental discussions

Inter-departmental discussions continued on a range of Sixth Round issues. The Treasury expressed concern that the total package of terms facing investors was becoming tougher and that individual elements had to be viewed in this context. When various proposed measures were included there was a long list which included PRT changes, staged development consents, enhanced BNOC role, tougher participation terms, restrictions on long-term oil export contracts, restrictions on gas flaring, changes to the oil valuation rules, but no changes to the Varley Assurances. While a case could be made out for each of the measures the total represented a considerable tightening of the terms. They should also be seen in the context of the rampant cost inflation in the North Sea, and the view, as expressed by Lord Kearton, that the remaining prospects were less attractive than existing discoveries. It was thus suggested that DEN should consider further the overall picture.

Further paper from DEN

In the light of such discussions DEN officials proceeded to produce a further paper on the Sixth Round arrangements. While maintaining much of earlier thinking it incorporated at least some of the concerns expressed by other Departments. Thus the idea of requesting applicants to bid equity shares higher than 51% and to take at BNOC's option part of the Corporation's oil, were retained, but the offer to carry BNOC's costs was limited to the exploration phase. Repayment would be only where the development of a discovery ensued. It would be possible for applicants to offer not to carry any of BNOC's costs. The issue of whether BNOC's special position was inconsistent with the Treaty of Rome rules on competition was further considered, but Mr Benn felt that the arguments were inconclusive, sufficient hard evidence to support the accusation difficult to find, and thus the risk was acceptable. The criteria for judging applications included adherence to FFO for UK suppliers, access of trade union representatives to offshore installations, and the applicant's record of training for employment offshore (without reference to the nationality of the trainees). Other proposed features included provisions to (1) increase the weight of BNOC's vote in JOAs (though it would still be necessary for one other member of the Operating Agreement to support BNOC before an issue was decided), (2) allow BNOC first option on any assignment proposal, and (3) require the operator to agree with BNOC a training programme for some Corporation employees. It was also proposed that the announcement of the Round should indicate that BNOC would become the operator of six of the blocks awarded, and that operatorship would be initially approved only for the exploration phase. The justification for this was stated to be the limited pool of talent available, with the consequence that many separate operators would dissipate this pool to an undesirable degree. Other proposals were to adjust application and rental fees for the ongoing high inflation.

The paper was initially discussed inter-departmentally among senior officials. Some concern was expressed about the increasing toughness of the proposals when seen within the total package of terms. Particular concern was shown when it was revealed that Mr Benn planned to apply BNOC's first option on assignments not only to Sixth Round licences but to all other existing ones. Some worry was expressed about the legality of this.

A separate paper was prepared on sole licensing, proposing eleven blocks to BNOC and one to BGC (in the Irish Sea). No less than four of the BNOC blocks were located in the frontier West of Scotland, one in the Moray Firth, four in the Northern North Sea, and two in the South Western Approaches. BNOC had requested other blocks in the Moray Firth, but their first choices were not accepted because of conflicts with defence and fishing interests. Such conflicts were to be an ongoing issue in the Moray Firth over successive Rounds. DEN officials defined the blocks as covering a range of prospectivity, and Mr Benn argued that there could be no cause for any critic to accuse him of having awarded the prime prospects to BNOC.

Ministers consider proposals

The appropriate Ministerial Committee met in March 1978 and approved the Sixth Round and sole licensing proposals, but expressed concern with the assignment proposals. The issue of first offer to BNOC had been debated for some time within the DEN. Officials had envisaged that, when negotiations with BNOC failed, the licensee would be free to pursue other possibilities. But there was felt to be a need for protection against offers to BNOC which were not genuine followed by an agreement with another party on terms more favourable than those offered to BNOC. One possible remedy was for BNOC to be given the right to match any offer by others. The Secretary of State's right to approve assignments could be employed, but there was legal advice to the effect that such decisions could be challenged in the courts on the grounds of improper use of a discretionary power. Officials advised Mr Benn that an appropriate procedure would be for the licensee to negotiate with BNOC, and, if no agreement was reached, the company could negotiate with a third party, but on the understanding that the Secretary of State would consent to any resulting assignment only if BNOC was given the chance to take 50% of the assignment on a carried interest basis! At the Ministerial meeting there was strong opposition to Mr Benn's proposals on the grounds that they represented an unfair use of statutory powers. It was conceivable that BNOC would acquire a likely future profit without a prior payment while the licensee obtained less than the full market value for his asset. The powers of the Secretary of State to give consent to assignments were not designed to produce favourable terms for the state in a transaction. The Committee felt that there were two options namely (1) BNOC to be given the opportunity to make the first offer, or (2) the licensee to be given the full market value for his rights by referring the issue for independent determination.

Mr Benn makes preliminary announcement of Sixth Round and new assignment policy

Following this meeting Mr Benn submitted a Minute to the Prime Minister indicating his preference for the first option, noting that procuring independent valuations would be very expensive. He also submitted a draft statement implying that he expected that the negotiations with BNOC would normally result in an agreement. Mr Benn made his announcement to Parliament about the Sixth Round and the new assignment policy on 5th April 1978. The item on assignment was strongly attacked by the Opposition.

Following the Ministerial meeting the consultative document was finalised and published on 18th May. It clarified a few detailed points. Thus in the six Blocks where BNOC was to be operator it would pay its costs on a pay-as-you-go basis. This would encourage companies to choose BNOC as an operator. The guidelines for the JOAs stated that the Operating Committees would meet in Glasgow to relieve the strain on BNOC staff who, as a participant in all licences, had to attend many more committee meetings than other licensees! The unfortunate choice of Glasgow as BNOC's Head Office with the consequential increase in travelling times and costs for the whole industry had become a practical reality.

Response of UKOOA to consultation document

The most comprehensive response to the document came from UKOOA within a remarkably short time. They felt that the striking features were the discrimination in favour of BNOC, and the negation of assurances previously given by Ministers with the consequential undermining of the industry's confidence in Government. The size of the Round (c. 40 blocks) was too small to maintain a satisfactory momentum of exploration. The option bidding elements would produce even greater discrimination in favour of BNOC. On more specific issues UKOOA interpreted the document to mean that the Secretary of State could use his knowledge of all Sixth Round applications to award BNOC the operatorships for the six most prospective blocks. The blocks for which BNOC was to be operator should be announced in advance of any bids being received, as the fact of BNOC operatorship would influence applicants' attitude. UKOOA also argued that the identity of the operator for the development phase should be known at the outset. Otherwise the uncertainty would have a demoralising effect on the initial operator. UKOOA also suggested that BNOC's proposed voting rights were excessively generous. The Corporation should have no vote when it was being carried, and a 75% voting majority could be too low in some circumstances, notably in exploration drilling after the initial work obligation had been completed. UKOOA also expressed disagreement with the assignment proposals, and felt that they would lead to a serious decrease in exploration activity. There were also objections to the proposal that the Secretary of State could consult BNOC before making final decisions on licence awards. There was concern that confidential information would be made available to BNOC, and it would in practice be impossible for the Corporation to separate its role as Government adviser from that of its commercial interests. There were many other detailed objections and queries.

Discussions between DEN and UKOOA

A meeting was held between DEN officials and UKOOA representatives on 1st June 1978. On many of the points raised in UKOOA's letter officials indicated that they would draw them to the attention of Ministers. On some points raised assurances were given. Thus on the assessment of applications the Secretary of State would seek BNOC's advice on the method, but information on individual applications would not be disclosed. DEN officials encouraged licensees to make broad-based applications, as restrictive bids (one or two blocks) made the task of allocation extremely difficult. On the approval of operator in stages it was acknowledged that the split could help small companies which would have difficulty in being operator at the development stage, but UKOOA was bothered about the uncertainty caused to its members.

Comments from other parties

Comments were also received from BRINDEX, TUC, Scottish TUC, and CBI. While BRINDEX agreed with most of UKOOA's comments an interesting difference was their positive view on differentiating the operatorship between the exploration and development phases. This had attractions for their members. The trade union representatives were particularly concerned with access and recognition, and the STUC wanted access to apply to contractors as well as operators. The TUC requested that the record of applicants in recognising trade unions be taken into account. The CBI was primarily interested in continuity of business opportunities for the offshore supplies sector. Interestingly, they requested that the FFO opportunity mechanism be rigorously applied.

Views of DEN officials

DEN officials reported the responses to the consultation and their proposed replies to Mr Benn. They included mention of BNOC's response to the consultation document. Indicative of the fraught relationship between the Corporation and the companies, BNOC's initial thoughts were that the Government's response should be that the industry's comments were insulting, gratuitously offensive, and required an apology! Fortunately, wiser counsel prevailed and officials proposed a response which, while generally maintaining the thrust of the consultative document, included a few concessions. Thus (1) the Round might be of 45 blocks (rather than 40), (2) the blocks on which BNOC would be operator would be identified when applications were invited, (3) when an operator BNOC should pay its costs on pay-as-you-go basis, (4) when BNOC participated in a development after being carried it should pay interest on reimbursed costs, (5) BNOC should give 12 months notice when it wanted to exercise a put option, and (6) some guidance would be given on the relative weights of the factors employed in assessing applications. On the TUC's proposal that the record of applicants on trade union recognition should be taken into account in assessing applications DEN officials consulted the Department of Employment but were advised that this went beyond Government policy in this area.

Mr Benn's views on trade union recognition

Mr Benn was not convinced by this argument and wrote to Mr Booth, the Secretary of State for Employment, and Mr Millan, the Secretary of State for Scotland, on the issue. Agreement was not easy because Mr Benn's proposed wording implied a measure of coercion on employers to recognise unions without providing the opportunity for the workforce to express their views, but eventually a form of words was agreed which included reference to the wishes of the workforce and was thus consistent with Government policy in this area. On 23rd June Mr Benn sent a Minute to the Prime Minister summarising the main changes to the consultation document on the lines discussed above. It was proposed to offer 46 blocks and part blocks of which 24 would be off Scotland and 15 in the South Western Approaches. A new Designation Order had been prepared to extend the area in the latter region. Ministers agreed (1) to announce the final arrangements just before the Parliamentary recess, and (2) that the closing date should be 20th November 1978.

Ministers meet UKOOA

In the meantime DEN Ministers agreed to meet UKOOA. This occurred on 20th July. Dr Mabon, the Minister of State, essentially reaffirmed the Government's stance on the important issues, but assured UKOOA that the purpose of the new arrangements for approval of operators was not to advance the number of operatorships for BNOC. The criteria for approval would be the performance of the licensees and their demonstrated availability of resources to undertake the work. Nominations for operators at the development stage could be made well in advance to permit planning for the activity to proceed.

Mr Benn announces detailed proposals for Sixth Round

Following this Mr Benn made an announcement of the Round in early August 1978. The problem of Parliamentary procedures encountered in the Fifth Round again occurred, and so an advance text of the Gazette Notice was published listing the blocks on offer, the criteria and financial terms. The amendments to the Regulations and the Designation Order were also laid before Parliament. At the press conference Mr Benn gave details of the licensing proposals and was joined by Mr Barnett the Chief Secretary who announced proposals for increasing PRT (see Chapter 11).

Revisions to marking system

While awaiting the bids DEN officials were busy developing a revised marking system which reflected all the criteria for the new Round. This produced considerable debate, not only on precisely how to incorporate the unionisation and training criteria in ways which were not excessively judgemental, but on how to weight the substantially increased number of elements in the total. Thus the relative weights to be given to the four optional criteria (biddable items) in relation to those reflecting basic competence had to be determined for this Round. Another issue was how to weight criteria which clearly had major economic importance in relation to those which were politically significant but economically marginal. Problems arose with the assessment of individual criteria. For example, with FFO for UK suppliers there was a track record for existing operators. But there were newcomers and non-operators who could only be assessed on expected performance. On the new training criterion applicants were asked to produce a certificate from the Petroleum Industry Training Board with respect to existing training, but again newcomers could be assessed only on their plans. On unionisation assessment could take account of the records of applicants (and their operators), and, where this stage had not been reached, of their plans to ascertain the wishes of their workforce regarding trade union recognition. On the optional criteria marks and weights had to be given for each additional percentage equity share offered to BNOC above the minimum of 51%. Similarly weights had to be given for offers to carry exploration or appraisal costs.

Assessing role of smaller companies

Another issue concerned the role of the smaller companies and the extent to which the assessment criteria should acknowledge their position. Within DEN there were perceived positive and negative aspects with the positive ones dominating. It was felt that the smaller companies were more responsive to Government policies, they could be more adventurous at the exploration stage than the majors, and many of them were British. The OSO was supportive of an increased role for the smaller companies because it could lead to an increased British share of the supply/contracting business. Smaller companies were also more likely to be willing to dispose of their oil to BNOC. It was recognised that they would sometimes be unable to develop fields by themselves and often had limited in-house technical capabilities. Their enhanced involvement was likely to mean an increase in the number of farm-outs. To what extent these features should or could be reflected in the assessment criteria was not obvious, but one which was considered was to lower the relative weighting of the technical hurdle. When suggested weightings were submitted to Ministers some reassessment resulted. For example, Mr Benn was keen to increase the weighting given to the unionisation criterion. Eventually 30% was given for technical and financial competence, 20% for the optional criteria, and 50% for all the others, including 10% for unionisation.

Response of industry

There was much press speculation about the likely response of the industry against the background of the perceived tougher terms and the proposal to increase the rate of PRT from 45% to 60%. In the event 55 applications were received covering all 46 Blocks. This was emphasised in the Press Statement, and, at Mr Benn's suggestion, the full list of 94 applicant firms was also published. The Round was thus deemed to be very satisfactory, but a closer inspection revealed other features. Thus applicants were noticeably more selective than in earlier Rounds, but, as views differed as to which were the most attractive blocks, a wide spread of applications was still obtained. But four blocks attracted only one application each, and this was conditional on the company (Texaco) receiving a specific priority block. The number of companies applying was down by 25% compared to the Fifth Round. Some medium and small companies which had been active in earlier Rounds had not applied, while, of the large companies, Exxon did not respond at all, and Shell put in a very modest application (for three Blocks off the North West of Shetlands). This received substantial press comment and Exxon was quoted as deciding against applying having considered the geology of the blocks on offer and the economic and investment environment. Shell was quoted as saying that its decision resulted from an assessment of blocks and the overall fiscal conditions.[7]

   The debate on the success or otherwise of the Round continued, with UKOOA claiming that the uncertainty caused by the proposed increase in PRT was a major factor. DEN officials conducted further analysis, which, while somewhat inconclusive, did not indicate general lack of interest by the more established companies. It was noteworthy that nearly all applicants had included at least one optional offer. In the subsequent interviews with applicants a recurring suggestion was that the acreage on offer was less attractive than formerly which was at least one reason for the moderate response.

Interviews

An intensive series of interviews with applicants followed (54 in total). These led to some modifications to the provisional awards. Judgement was required in any case, because a feature of the bids had been the conditionality of a number of applications. A consequence of this was that not every block on offer could be licensed. The computer-based allocations were sometimes overruled. Examples were the overloading of operatorships to BGC beyond its perceived capacity, and the award of four blocks to Phillips which was felt to be beyond its capacity. Adjustments were sometimes made to increase the spread of awards in order to enhance the prospects for the attainment of thorough exploration. Texaco and Conoco would not receive awards because of their very limited applications and, particularly in Texaco's case, because of the high degree of conditionality attached to their bids. Officials termed this a self-imposed barrier. DEN officials felt that the optional elements of the criteria had been very successful because the varying levels of the (optional) offers had made a difference to the ranking as between companies of similar technical and financial competence. The offers proposed would reduce the public sector share of the exploration costs by some 25%, increase the public sector equity interest by an estimated 4% above the standard 51%, and offer BNOC significantly improved access to oil. The recommendations of DEN officials covered awards for 36 of the 46 blocks, and they proposed that BNOC and some of the companies who had made conditional offers be approached with a view to inquiring whether they were interested in the other ten. BNOC did not wish to take up any of these as sole licensee, but groups in which Amoco was a main participant agreed to interpret the terms of their bids such that a further six blocks for which no other companies had applied could be awarded to them.

Mr Benn announces awards

Mr Benn submitted a Minute to the Prime Minister on 25th March 1979 indicating the 42 proposed, conditional awards. The Northern North Sea had attracted the best response, but the interest shown in the frontier West of Shetlands was also encouraging. Unfortunately there was no interest in blocks off Wales which was a disappointment to the Welsh Office. The public sector would receive about 60% of the territory. The exclusion of Exxon, Texaco, and Conoco was not expected to have a serious effect. The Iranian crisis had emerged and promised to become even more serious, and so Mr Benn indicated that he would be seeking assurances from the companies with UK refining interests that they would not divert supplies which normally were destined for the UK market. He expected to receive satisfaction on this matter before announcing the awards. On receiving approval for his recommendations Mr Benn announced the awards in the House of Commons on 26th March 1979. These were provisional, and were conditional on the conclusion of JOAs with BNOC and the agreement of work programmes acceptable to the Secretary of state. Mr Benn estimated that this could be done within six months.

But the May general election intervened and a Conservative Government was elected. In opposition the Conservatives had been vociferously critical of the Government's policies towards North Sea oil and gas. The role of BNOC had come in for particular criticism, but so had the increasing level of Government intervention in the North Sea more widely. The Sixth Round terms and associated Regulations were certainly more radical than those in earlier Rounds. The issue of whether to confirm or modify them at a late stage in the cycle posed an interesting dilemma for an incoming Government which had a manifesto radical in the opposite direction from the inherited position (See Chapter 15).

Reflections on Fifth and Sixth Round terms

The evidence suggests that the muted response of the industry in the Sixth Round was at least in part due to the cumulative effect of the whole battery of Government policy measures progressively developed over the period since 1974. These included not only licensing and participation terms but depletion control measures, disposal and refining policy, and PRT, with the promise of a substantial increase in the rate from 45% to 60%. When added together these represented a fairly formidable toughening of the overall terms and the business environment.

Each of the individual elements on its own would not have made a major difference to the investment climate but the combined effects most probably did. The discretion available to the Government in the implementation of several measures increased the uncertainty of the operating environment, though, of course, this was viewed within Government as providing flexibility and thus a positive feature. It could be claimed that each of the measures was utilised in some other oil-producing countries and thus was not unfamiliar to an industry which had always been international in outlook. But in several overseas countries particularly in the Middle East the clear intention was to bring the industry under direct state control, whereas in the UK the stated objective was one of partnership which acknowledged the major continuing role of the oil companies.

Over the period since 1974 policy evolved in an ad hoc manner with individual new elements being continually added. Attention tended to focus on individual new measures and their possible effects to the neglect of a systematic assessment of the total package. The Treasury's concern on this matter was well-founded. Senior management within BNOC were determined to ensure that the Corporation made a substantial impact, and pursued opportunities in an aggressive manner, sometimes necessitating a restraining hand from the DEN.[8] It is clear that there was resentment among the companies at how BNOC was sometimes thrust upon them as an unwilling partner. There was little continuing overt opposition to the notion of a national oil company which was commonplace around the world, but resentment was certainly felt at forced marriages being paraded as voluntary in nature.

The debates over the Fifth and Sixth Round terms also highlighted the growing differences in perspective of the DEN and Treasury on policy measures. The DEN's prime interest lay in oil/gas and related energy policy, but the Treasury had key responsibilities for macroeconomic policy. The policy requirements of each did not always harmonise and could produce rather odd results. Thus it was clear that the original intention of participation policy was to procure substantial equity shares for the state in the original licences. But PSBR considerations resulted in this being modified generally to call options on oil for BNOC. Similarly, in the debates on participation terms for BNOC in the Fifth and Sixth Rounds the Treasury's attitude was largely determined by PSBR considerations rather than those of oil and energy policy. This problem was destined to loom even larger in subsequent years.

11 Increasing the Government take

Early concern about valuation in 1975 Act

The 1975 Oil Taxation Act had been in force for only a very short time when concerns began to be raised about the effectiveness of some of its terms. First oil production had come from the Argyll field in June 1975. The oil was landed in the UK but there was soon pressure from the licensees to permit the oil to be exported with the prospect of higher prices. One of the licensees was RTZ which had no refining capacity in the UK and had sold its oil at prices significantly below those applicable to the cost, insurance and freight (c.i.f). value of comparable imported crudes. This alarmed Lord Balogh, the Minister of State at the DEN, and he wrote to Mr Dell, the Paymaster General, on 8th October indicating his concern that, if small partners were not allowed to export and there was no fixed posted price for North Sea oil, there was a danger that North Sea prices would be established below imported parity prices and the result would be a reduced tax take. He suggested that the possible solutions could be either (1) a reversal of the earlier decision not to have a posted price, or (2) allow exports of North Sea oil beyond the levels indicated earlier by Mr Varley in his disposal and refining policy statement. If neither of these options were pursued there would be pressure for BNOC to become involved in downstream activities where it could secure what he felt were the excess profits accruing to the refining subsidiaries of the majors. His preference was for a posted price.

Inland Revenue views on valuation

Lord Balogh's letter was not well received in the Inland Revenue. The notion of an administered price had been discussed at length in the work on the Oil Taxation Bill, but it had been rejected, primarily because of the difficulty of reconciling it with the concept of a tax on profits and the resulting problems raised internationally. Where the administered price did not equate with that received in a genuine arm's length transaction there might well be difficulties in persuading the Internal Revenue in the USA that PRT and corporation tax qualified for credit there.

Under the 1975 Act, where the Inland Revenue was fully satisfied that a sale was genuinely at arm's length and unaffected by any other factor, the tax computation would be based on the price obtained. If the transaction did not conform to these conditions a calculated open market value would be employed. It was acknowledged that the existence of weak sellers had to be accepted as a fact of life, and if the transaction was genuine the price in question had to be accepted. But it was not intended that a low price accepted by a weak seller would be suitable as a criterion for the open market value generally and in particular in relation to strong sellers. In the current circumstances, for example, the Inland Revenue would rebut any argument by BP (which was buying Argyll oil from RTZ) that the same price could be used to determine the tax value of Forties oil. Thus where BP transferred Forties oil to its refining subsidiary the relevant price would be that which it could obtain in an arm's length sale to another refiner in a competitive market situation.

Inter-departmental discussions

An inter-departmental meeting was held to discuss Lord Balogh's letter. The DEN representatives were concerned that the relatively low price for Argyll oil might significantly affect tax valuations for many other transactions. It was pointed out that 30% of North Sea reserves were in the hands of non-majors who might be at some disadvantage in selling their oil. But it would be these very transactions which would give rise to the only arm's-length prices for North Sea oil. The solution favoured by DEN officials was to establish a norm price for North Sea oil based on Middle East prices with quality adjustments.

The Inland Revenue representatives pointed out that the current arrangements had been determined as a result of industry consultations which reflected objections to a posted price system. The industry would accuse the Government of bad faith if changes were made now. Further, if the posted price concept was introduced, it could jeopardise the current negotiations with the USA on the creditability of PRT. At the end of the meeting it was decided that the Steering Group on Valuation should examine the issues further.

In further reflections the Inland Revenue felt that the DEN's fears were exaggerated and that RTZ had made a particularly bad deal which hopefully would not be repeated as they had now appointed a selling agent with knowledge of the oil market. An administered price could produce a situation where the independent companies were not fully protected against the possibility of their facing additional tax on purely notional profits, but it could also mean that the price for the integrated producers was pushed downwards by the inclusion of relatively low prices for the independents in the calculation of the administered price. The DEN had suggested that there need be no right of appeal against any administered price. This would be unacceptable to the companies and was a departure from UK tax practice.

Options to protect Government revenues

The issue of how best to protect Government revenues from under-pricing of North Sea oil for tax purposes was given much attention in late 1975 and early

1976 by Inland Revenue and DEN officials with several schemes and formulae being scrutinised in detail. Thus the calculation of North Sea market values based on imported oil with quality adjustments, different credit terms, and estimates of freight costs based on Average Freight Rate Assessment (AFRA) and spot rates were examined, as were sales of North Sea oil under spot, contract, and different credit terms. It was felt that legal advice was necessary on the subject of strengthening the valuation rules by basing North Sea values on prices obtained for comparable quantities of imported oil. The Inland Revenue solicitor advised that the Government might not succeed with this argument before the Special Commissioners. The views of Counsel were sought, and his views were that a court would be unlikely to attach much weight to transactions in oil from other sources if direct price evidence for North Sea oil were available to it. He also advised that, for reasons of tax confidentiality, the Government could not adduce in evidence information involving transactions other than those involving the appellant company itself.

It was difficult to estimate the size of the revenue losses, but if the difference between arm's length prices of North Sea oil and the imported values of comparable Middle East oil was 50 cents per barrel the tax and royalty losses could be £130 million–£140 million per year in the early 1980s (or around 5% of the expected revenues). The other approaches which had been examined would be unlikely significantly to strengthen the Inland Revenue's hand, and it was felt that tinkering with the legislation in 1976 was undesirable. Emphasis should be given to continuation with negotiated settlements, and the experience gained could generate ideas for subsequent legislative change. A joint Inland Revenue/DEN Working Party on the subject was proposed.

Inland Revenue/DEN Working Party on valuation

This set to work in April 1976. Its remit was to examine not only the main alternatives of strengthening of the existing valuation rules by introducing an administered price arrangement, but to consider other approaches such as the establishment of a price fixing agency. Several papers were rapidly produced dealing with diverse subjects including (1) the operation of an administered price scheme in practice, (2) the Norwegian norm price system, (3) the role of BNOC as a buyer and its related future role in the downstream market, (4) the operation of the existing law, (5) the possible extent of the revenue loss, and (6) the exchange of relevant information between the DEN and Inland Revenue. It was recognised that there was a link with refining/disposal policy (which was also being reviewed) particularly as it affected the ability of independent producers to obtain the best price for their oil.

Precise nature of problem

One paper dealt with the details of the existing statutory rules and indicated the precise nature of the current problem. Thus in the Oil Taxation Act the market value of the oil was defined as the price at which the oil could have been sold to a willing buyer in an arm's length sale at that time, and the contract was for the sale of that oil and no other oil. This could be interpreted to mean that the valuation had to be geared to a spot valuation at the time in question, and it was understood that BP had interpreted the legislation in this manner.[1] The Working Party agreed that if the oil companies understood that the current legislation did not authorise the Oil Taxation Office (OTO) to insist on import parity values in the determination of market values there was a danger of revenue losses which were potentially so large that legislative changes might have to be made in 1977.

Administered price system

The DEN was pressed to produce a paper on how an administered price system might function in practice and did so in early July 1976. This suggested a formula based on a marker crude (which could be Nigeria or Middle East) with adjustments for freight costs, insurance, quality differences (compared to North Sea crudes), differences in refining costs, and differences in credit terms. The paper discussed in detail the complex calculations necessary to arrive at an import parity value. The Inland Revenue also produced a paper on the scope of an administered price emphasising the difficulties involved in implementing a scheme.

Report from Working Party

Eventually an agreed report from the Working Party was produced and delivered to the Secretary of State for Energy and the Chief Secretary. The report discussed at length the background to the valuation issue, the powers and procedures of the 1975 Act, and the problems recently encountered. On solutions the Working Party felt that the notion that BNOC as a buyer of last resort was not viable. It would not be able to assume this role without prejudicing its own financial position, and its membership of Operating Committees would not enable it to provide information on prices which were not available to the Inland Revenue. But its transactions could provide evidence of the market value of North Sea oil.

The report thus concentrated on (1) methods of reinforcing existing legislation, and (2) an administered price scheme. To reinforce the existing arrangements protection was felt to be necessary against possible undervaluation under the present definition of market value which gave undue weight to evidence of arm's length sales by weak sellers and to spot prices. The remedy was to revise the legislation to ensure that the courts attached more weight to parity values. In practice this meant that the legislation would provide that valuation would have regard to the c.i.f. Middle East prices adjusted for quality and yield differentials and credit terms. It was recognised that there was a problem in determining the weight to attach to parity values, and in the volatile oil market the relationship between the parity value and the arm's length price could differ. A definition which required the Special Commissioners and the Courts to take the *average* of spot prices and parity values should give a fair result over a period of time. The risk that the taxpayer might get the benefit of prices lower than the average could be reduced by producing detailed rules regarding the weight to be attached to different elements of evidence, but this would carry its own risks. It was felt that the only definition which would always produce reasonable valuations would be one based on the higher of spot or parity values, but this would be open to criticism by the companies.

Most promising approach

The most promising approach could be to define market value as that obtainable on the world market, defined as the parity value of imported crude or, if higher, the price actually obtained from selling North Sea oil. It was recognised that there were constraints on the Inland Revenue's ability to adduce as evidence in appeal proceedings all the evidence at its disposal, because of tax confidentiality rules preventing material in one company's returns being employed in proceedings against another company's. These restrictions could be modified by legislation, but this would be highly contentious. There was concern about the lengthy delays likely to be experienced in the current appeals machinery. To deal with this problem an ad hoc tribunal or perhaps an auxiliary panel of Special Commissioners could be established, but if appeals to the courts were still allowed there could be great delays. There were thus advantages in the establishment of a separate review body outside the normal tax appeal machinery.

The report considered that, if a satisfactory remedy to the problem could be found *within* the present scheme, a change of system would only be justified if it had clear advantages over the current one. It was felt unlikely that a new system would be acceptable to Parliament. A scheme whereby North Sea tax values were determined by the Inland Revenue or a Minister would have to allow the companies a right of appeal to an independent tribunal or the courts. But this would produce all the disadvantages of the current system.

Oil Valuation Board?

The alternative was an arrangement whereby an independent body would be responsible for determining or reviewing the determination of North Sea oil values. It would be entrusted with fact-finding duties, and would arrive at its decisions in an investigatory rather than an adversarial procedure. One value would be found and fixed for all of the oil from a field. The process would commence with the Inland Revenue's valuation, and the licensees would be given the opportunity to make representations to the new body which could be called the Oil Valuation Board (OVB) which would be responsible for determining the tax values. There would be no formal right of appeal against the decisions of the OVB. The details of the procedures relating to the OVB had still to be worked out, but the Working Party was satisfied that it would be administratively feasible. The Inland Revenue's confidentiality rules should be amended to permit the OVB to receive all relevant information. But the Inland Revenue should also be able to see all the representations made by the companies and to be able to comment on them. A problem could arise if a company were not permitted to see all the evidence submitted by the Inland Revenue because some information related to another company. It could then protest that it was at a disadvantage compared to the Inland Revenue. The OVB could be empowered to publish the valuations.

The Working Party argued that the OVB should not be responsible for determining the value of imported crude oil. The problems of defining a firm statutory base for the tax valuation of a vast range of foreign crudes would be quite intractable. The position with foreign crudes could change overnight, and a specified statutory framework could become obsolescent.

The next stage in the process would be to consult the Lord Chancellor's Office to see whether the removal of oil pricing from the jurisdiction of the Special Commissioners and the courts was possible. The Civil Service Department would also have to be consulted because the OVB would be a new body. Consultations with important overseas tax administrations would also be necessary. The industry would subsequently be consulted.

Reactions to Working Party report

This thought-provoking report was received favourably by Lord Balogh who had expressed much concern about the problem. The Oil Taxation Office (OTO) expressed some reservations about the Working Party's proposals. There was a worry that emphasis on making the OVB independent of the Government would leave the Government powerless. An arrangement was preferred whereby the OVB was given the functions of reviewing the facts and undertaking fact-finding in cases where the companies and the OTO could not reach agreement. The OVB would make determinations where its review was requested. The OTO was opposed to the recommendation that valuation should be determined by field rather than separately for each licensee, because it raised the real risk that a value would be superimposed on genuine arm's length transactions. More generally the OTO felt that its accumulated expertise in dealing with the industry on the full range of tax issues gave it a comparative advantage in terms of appropriate knowledge over an external body such as the proposed OVB.

Much debate ensued on all these issues. The advice of the Lord Chancellor's Office was sought on the legal aspects of the proposed OVB scheme. The result was hardly encouraging. The legal advice was that any acceptable scheme would have to provide for a right of appeal to the courts on any point of law emanating from the OVB's decisions. It would also be necessary for the oil companies to see and comment on all materials supplied by the Inland Revenue to the OVB and used by the OVB in arriving at its valuations. Insistence on the right of appeal to the courts affected (1) the Inland Revenue's ability to make effective use of all information at its disposal, (2) the Inland Revenue's confidentiality rules, and (3) the ability of the OVB to establish a consistent pattern of valuations. If the courts then decided to review the facts behind an OVB decision there was a danger that the result would be to nullify the perceived advantages of the investigatory (non-adversarial) procedure of the OVB.

The legal advice was also that the companies should see all the information supplied to the OVB. This meant that the Inland Revenue would have to consider a substantial relaxation of its confidentiality rules, or some restrictions on the information supplied to the OVB, or a different definition of market value. The implications of the legal advice were so far-reaching that, if they were acted upon, the question arose of whether there still was a strong case for the OVB. The Inland Revenue felt that, while some of the advantages foreseen by the Working Party would be lost, those relating to (1) the benefits of a body with more expertise than the Special Commissioners, (2) published field valuations, and (3) a consistent pattern of North Sea oil valuation would remain intact. But in the light of the legal advice the possible advantages of the current system could be reassessed. The only obvious advantage of the current system was regarding Inland Revenue confidentiality, and the balance of advantages lay in pursuing the OVB concept.

Parity formula

Meanwhile work on many other aspects of valuation was continuing. Thus a very detailed paper on the parity formula was produced. This was thought to be necessary if the concept was going to be employed in a major way. The paper dealt with many topics including the choice of appropriate market, namely UK, North West Europe, or US East Coast. While the UK seemed at first the obvious market this was questionable because it was peripheral in world market terms, offered no significant premium for low sulphur crude, and had no obvious centre on which to base a parity calculation. North West Europe was a more attractive choice because it was very substantial, oil offered for sale was free of any refining policy restrictions, and there was a substantial low sulphur premium. Rotterdam was an obvious focal point and for practical and presentational purposes it could be defined to include the UK.

Which marker crude?

The marker crude should be comparable to, and thus in competition with, typical North Sea crudes, and its free on board (f.o.b.) value should be readily ascertainable and clearly related to world prices. While Arabian light was an obvious choice the fact that it was the official OPEC marker made it responsive to political influences. Another possibility was Libyan Es Sider because of its close resemblance to North Sea crudes and its closer location to the North West Europe market. But the Libyan Government's pricing policy was unpredictable. Similar arguments applied to a less extent to Nigerian Bonny Light. Ekofisk crude had obvious attractions, but it did not have a uniform price at which it was available to all comers. If the marker had to be stipulated in legislation it would probably have to be Arabian Light. But if the main legislation were to authorise the use of a marker crude to be specified in regulations from time to time this would permit variations in line with changing market conditions.

In current circumstances the f.o.b. price of a marker crude should equate to the official Government selling price, but this might not survive indefinitely, and a better alternative would be to define it as the price at which the oil was made available to all comers. The relevant time period could be the mid-point of the month preceding that for the required valuation. The freight element could be based on AFRA or published spot rates. AFRA was preferable because of the wild fluctuations in spot rates, but it was not proposed to refer to AFRA in legislation. With respect to credit terms the suggestion was to prescribe a ready measure of credit which would then be applied to adjust the f.o.b. terms to a cash equivalent, and to further adjust the resulting parity value to normal North Sea credit terms (to be defined).

Problem of differentials

It was recognised that the most complex calculation related to fixing the differential between the value of North Sea crude and the marker on the basis of their product yields. Many permutations of products were possible from any one crude, and the data available on the different products was both limited and contentious. They also changed constantly in response to market behaviour. A range of representative products would have to be chosen, and then decisions were needed on the relative emphasis of each to obtain the overall product yield. This was not easy, with the two possibilities being (1) an assay of the crude in question, (perhaps by the Government chemist), or (2) an analysis on the basis of what products would normally be obtained if the crude was defined in a specified manner. The assay approach seemed easier at first sight, but assays could not simulate the secondary processes undertaken in refineries, and the fractions produced did not coincide with saleable products.

If product yields were to be determined by reference to refining processes it would probably be necessary to use a model refinery as all individual real ones would have their own peculiarities. Specification of the model refinery would be extremely complex, and could only be prescribed by regulation with scope for fine-tuning. Specification of the pattern of product yields would also be contentious. Putting values on the specified products would not be easy because of the difficulty in obtaining reliable data on markets which were typically volatile.

This paper was the source of much discussion and further extensive work, both conceptual and empirical, resulted. By the end of 1976 four different approaches to strengthening the definition of market value were being seriously considered. These ranged from minimum changes without an OVB, to a field basis with an OVB, and with the waiving of all the Inland Revenue's confidentiality rules. At the end of 1976 the OTO estimated that, on the basis of experience in 1975 and 1976, the tax and royalty revenues at risk for 1977–1978 would be £15.7 million and in 1980–1981 at around £36 million. If the undervaluation increased from 12 cents per barrel to 30 cents the figure for 1980–1981 could be £100 million. It was decided at the end of 1976 that legislation in 1977 would not be possible because of unresolved issues and the work overload of Parliamentary Counsel.

Use of parity valuation

Following further discussions and consideration of a report by Purvin and Gertz on the technical complexities in the calculation of parity values (confirming a range not a single value), a sub-group of the Working Party reported in early April 1977 that parity valuation should not be used to provide a mechanistic valuation for either the determination of market value or as a safety net below which the market value would not be allowed to fall. It was, however, recommended that the parity valuation method be recognised in legislation as one important item of evidence in market value determination. It was also recommended that provision be made in legislation that the market value did not fall below a parity valuation. But the detailed elements of parity calculation would not be set down in legislation.

Agreed report of Working Party

Eventually in late July 1977 an agreed report of the Working Party was produced. In the light of the studies undertaken a key recommendation was a new definition of market value which would require it to be based on evidence both of actual sales of North Sea crude and comparable crudes, but also on the parity values of such crudes in the various markets. This approach emphasised the notion of due regard being paid to all relevant factors which it was hoped would make the scheme flexible in response to changing market conditions.

The report confirmed support for the specialist OVB concept to replace the role of the Special Commissioners. A right of appeal would still be necessary on points of law, but it was hoped that, with the new definition of market value, such appeals would be rare, and provision would be made for such appeals to go straight to the Court of Appeal. The procedure would be that the Inland Revenue would issue its determination of market value of oil from a field to licensees who would then have one month to appeal to the OVB if they so desired. The OVB would investigate the matter, take written representations, and, if necessary call witnesses from the parties. The Inland Revenue's confidentiality rules would be relaxed so that in any appeal to the OVB information received from one company could be made available in a case concerning another company. The OVB's subsequent determination would be binding. It was envisaged that the panel would comprise a legally qualified chairman, two oil industry experts, and a support staff.

Ministers accept recommendations of Working Party

The recommendations of the Working Party were accepted by Treasury and DEN Ministers in September 1977. But consultation with the industry and preparation of legislation was then held up because of difficulties which arose with the proposed new double taxation treaty with the USA. Approval had been given by the House of Commons but in the US Senate there were difficulties, and advice had been given that any action which drew attention to PRT might put its creditability at risk. Thus while preparatory work was undertaken for legislation in 1978 no action was actually taken.

Relaxation of Inland Revenue confidentiality rules very controversial

The issue was considered further during 1978 and work was undertaken by officials with a view to introducing legislation in the 1979 Finance Bill. The problem of the double tax treaty was no longer an impediment, but other developments led officials to conclude in late 1978 that major legislation in 1979 was still not desirable. The Working Party had become convinced that the proposals for relaxation of the Inland Revenue's confidentiality rules would be very far-reaching and extremely controversial. Thus, in an appeal to the OVB by one company, if the Inland Revenue were to cite evidence of prices achieved by others, the Inland Revenue would also have to be authorised to release to the OVB information received by other companies on a confidential basis. Further, as a matter of natural justice the information released would have to be made available to all companies party to the appeal. All this would be greeted with alarm by the industry. A further aspect was the application of the proposals to BNOC and BGC. The latter's position with respect to new gas contracts would be very exposed because they were individually negotiated and prices were kept confidential because they varied considerably among contracts. With respect to BNOC the relaxation of the confidentiality rules would permit some companies to obtain better terms from BNOC by revealing the terms obtained by the strongest buyers or sellers. There was also a political argument in favour of deferring full legislation, namely the absence of a guaranteed Government majority for controversial legislation. Further factors were (1) recent experience where companies had frequently (but not always) accepted that term contracts were more relevant than spot prices, (2) that tax values should assume 30-day credit terms, and (3) that swap deals were not arm's length transactions. Differences remained on the question of the relative weight to be given to parity values of imported crudes.

Legislation postponed

Taking all the above into account officials advised Ministers not to proceed with major legislation in 1979. In early 1979 Ministers gave provisional agreements that limited legislation to close obvious loopholes be prepared. But even this proved to be very complex, with the prospect that it would occupy several pages in the Finance Bill. Meanwhile the oil market situation had changed quite dramatically. Following the Iranian revolution spot prices generally exceeded term prices, often by a considerable margin. There was thus no longer a threat to tax revenues from the valuation procedures, and officials advised that there was no great urgency to legislate in 1979. The issue was left to the incoming Conservative Government. But by this time the policy perspective was changing, with emphasis being put on moderating the pace of price increases. The basic issue remained unresolved.

Proposal to increase PRT

An additional reason for the reluctance to legislate on valuation was the proposal to increase PRT made in August 1978. This was the result of a long review of the operation of PRT. There was concern within the Inland Revenue and DEN regarding some aspects of the tax even before it was enacted. Some of the issues were technical ones, such as whether to allow foreign exchange losses, and the operation of the balancing charge mechanism, but two awkward problems which had been noticed related to the volume allowance. The decision to exempt BNOC meant that the company would not use its share of that allowance. This raised the prospect that this part could be used by co-licensees. Upon detailed examination it was found that in the participation agreements involving limited assignment this problem would not arise, but it would in cases where BNOC had a direct equity share in a field. This would apply to the ex-NCB interests which BNOC had acquired and to its 51% share in all Fifth Round licences. The OTO estimated in January 1976 that the potential long-term aggregate tax loss could be around £1 billion, though this was subject to great uncertainty. The OTO suggested that a scheme whereby BNOC was deemed to have received the allowance was the neatest way to deal with the problem, but other mechanisms were also examined.

The second problem with the volume allowance related to fields straddling the median line. The PRT legislation permitted licensees to claim the full allowance against revenues from the part of the field lying in the UK sector. This was because the field definition excluded areas lying outside the British sector. This was felt to be anomalous. Methods of dealing with the perceived problem would be to restrict the allowance to the recoverable reserves or production from the UK sector. But no action was taken at this time.

Investment environment

In the meantime from 1976 DEN officials were examining the economics of North Sea fields in the light of the rapid cost escalation affecting new developments, the growing shortage of orders for platform construction yards, as well as the new PRT. A DEN Working Group examined the impact of the 1975 tax package and considered the effects of modifications to the uplift, volume allowance, and safeguard, and to the definition of a field for PRT purposes. The anomalous position of the volume allowance when BNOC was a participant was noted and changes recommended. Royalty concessions were felt to be the most appropriate mechanism for encouraging marginal fields, but at this time (late 1976) licensees had not shown much interest in this.

Scope for increase in PRT

In April 1977 Mr Benn asked his officials to further examine the scope for an increase in PRT. He had been influenced by the promptings of Lord Balogh who was still an adviser to him as well as being Deputy Chairman of BNOC, and by the fact that the growing fields such as Forties and Piper were likely to be very profitable after payment of royalty and taxes. DEN economists conducted studies on the fields in production or under development and found that prospective returns were very attractive, depending on what future oil price was assumed. The Government take was around 73% of pre-tax cash flow and could rise to around 78% under very high oil prices. The DEN study examined the effects of increasing the PRT rate from 45% to 55% in one scenario and 75% in another and concluded that development activity would not be seriously discouraged. The study also examined the effects of abolishing the volume allowance which on its own would not have a serious effect on activity. But a combination of increased rate and abolition of oil allowance would probably reduce activity levels. At Lord Balogh's suggestion DEN officials also examined other permutations including a 60% PRT rate and reduction of volume allowance by 50%.

Joint Working Party examines options for PRT increase

In August 1977 a joint Working Party involving the Inland Revenue, Treasury and DEN was established to further examine the case for PRT changes. There was a complication of the yet-to-be-ratified Double Tax Treaty with the USA which incorporated the creditability of PRT. An increase in PRT might have a negative impact on attitudes in the US Senate in particular, and non-ratification would have a significant effect on the post-tax returns which US companies could expect.

The Working Party conducted detailed studies and found that there was some scope for increasing the Government's take but that this might deter some future investment which in the context of current thinking on depletion policy might not necessarily be a bad thing. It was also recognised that any tax increase would be highly controversial given the assurances on stability made during the passage of the Oil Taxation Bill. The Working Party considered three main options. These were (1) a straight increase in the PRT rate, (2) making PRT non-deductible for corporation tax, and (3) a multi-rate PRT related to profits or profitability. The Working Party ruled out the second option principally on the grounds that there was no clear justification for such a change. In principle the third option had some attractions, but the Working Party found some difficulties with it. The alternatives were to base the PRT rate on either the quantum of profits or the rate of return on capital employed. The Steering Group (the Deputy Secretaries of the three Departments) did not feel that some companies should be taxed at a higher rate simply because they made larger profits without regard to the capital invested. The scheme where the rate was based on return on capital provided a built-in indexation for oil price increases and would also produce an increased take from small but very profitable fields. However, the Steering Group surprisingly felt that it would be difficult to devise a workable scheme which would inevitably be very complex. The problem of inflation and return on capital in real terms was mentioned as a main complication.[2] It would take some time to devise such a scheme. The Steering Group also felt that this scheme would be less good in terms of revenue take than a straight increase in the PRT rate. This was, therefore, the favoured option with an accompanying reduction in the uplift allowance. To make any increase more palatable to the industry BNOC's exemption from PRT could be removed.

Ministers discuss report

Ministers discussed the report on 21st December 1977. Mr Barnett, the Chief Secretary, agreed with Mr Benn that there was a strong case for increasing PRT, but was very concerned that it might jeopardise the Double Tax Treaty with the USA whose terms he felt were advantageous to the UK. Ministers agreed that officials should prepare a simple PRT package on the lines already indicated so that it could be implemented in the 1978 Finance Bill if the Treaty were ratified in time. If it were not ratified in time the package could be introduced later.

Specific proposals from Working Party

Proposals from the Working Party were put to Ministers at the end of February 1978. An increase in the rate of PRT from 45% to 60% or 65% was proposed. The Treasury had a preference for 65%. The report suggested an uplift of 30% (compared to the existing 15%) with the 65% tax rate, though the Treasury felt that there was a case for 25% on the grounds that interest rates had fallen, and a lower uplift would reduce incentives to incur wasteful expenditure.[3] The report also suggested that the oil allowance be changed. Two methods were considered. One was simply to halve it. The second was to reduce it on the basis of a formula which reduced it gradually to zero when the cumulative profit from field production reached a certain multiple of cumulative capital expenditure. The second scheme protected small marginal fields more effectively and was preferred by the DEN, but the Treasury saw virtue in the simplicity of the first scheme.

The problem of ratification of the treaty with the USA remained, however, and when Mr Barnett and Mr Benn met on 8th March they agreed to defer any action until a further review in June. On 14th March the Chief Secretary sent a Minute to the Prime Minister indicating the intention to increase the PRT rate probably to 65% with a reduction in some allowances. He also alerted the Prime Minister to the problem of the Treaty with the USA and the proposal to reach decisions on the precise changes in June when the Treaty problem would hopefully be resolved.

Further report of Working Party

Officials made a further report in late June 1978. This reaffirmed the case for a 65% PRT rate and uplift allowance of 25%, but concluded that a single reduction in the volume allowance to 500,000 tonnes per year with a cumulative limit of 5 million tonnes was preferable to a discriminating allowance related to the ratio of cumulative net revenues to cumulative capital expenditure. The complexities of this scheme were not felt to be justified, though it would help marginal fields more effectively than the flat rate allowance. Officials also felt that BNOC's exemption from PRT should be removed. This was an irritant to the oil companies who thought that it encouraged the Corporation to act in a non-commercial manner. The original decision to exempt BNOC from PRT was taken when it was envisaged that the tax would not apply to companies accepting participation. This was no longer relevant and BNOC should become liable for the tax.

Ministerial discussions

Mr Barnett informed the Prime Minister of the PRT recommendations which he and Mr Benn had agreed, with the exception of BNOC's exemption from PRT which Mr Benn wanted to retain. The Prime Minister was also informed that progress had been made with the US Treaty but it had not yet been formally ratified. There were thus still risks with an early announcement of a PRT increase, and it was suggested that the US Treasury be informed of the proposals in strict confidence so that their reaction could be obtained. The Prime Minister's response was that Mr Healey should meet with other Ministers to discuss the issue. This occurred on two occasions in late July 1978. Mr Dell, now Secretary of State for Trade, sent a letter to Mr Healey expressing reservations about the proposals. He wondered whether the financial viability of some of the less profitable fields would become doubtful, and felt that if the proposed rates had been introduced from the outset in 1975 the development of some fields would have been seriously prejudiced. The tax system was not designed to slow down the pace of development. Mr Dell concluded that the increase in the tax rate and the reduction in the allowances went too far. He agreed with the proposal to withdraw BNOC's exemption from PRT. Mr Lever also expressed concern about the effects of the proposals on activity in the North Sea.

At the second meeting on 26th July Ministers had the benefit of the outcome of a meeting between officials and the US Treasury which indicated that an early announcement of a PRT increase would not damage relations with the US Administration. The US Senate might react negatively but not such as to have practical consequences for the Treaty. At the meeting Mr Dell and Mr Lever still felt that the proposals could inhibit the development of marginal fields. Mr Dell also felt that the large changes might be inconsistent with the assurances he had given during the passage of the Oil Taxation Bill. He felt that more modest increases in the rate would be more palatable and would reduce the need for royalty refunds. He felt that the Exchequer could benefit more by this route than from higher rates of tax offset by royalty remissions. Mr Benn and Mr Barnett supported the proposals. This was the majority view and the Chancellor thus concluded that the proposals be announced. The majority of Ministers also favoured the abolition of BNOC's exemption from PRT, but Mr Benn argued for its retention on the grounds that BNOC was obliged to show what PRT payments it would have made in its accounts, and that to reverse an earlier decision made against much opposition would be embarrassing.

Mr Callaghan's concerns

The Prime Minister was informed of the above. He was concerned that the 65% PRT rate might be too high, and requested that post-tax returns using a rate of 55% be indicated. He also asked what increase in tax take would be procured in (1) 1979–1980 and (2) the mid-1980s from a 55% rate. Further, he wanted to know how much of any increased take came from (1) higher rates and (2) reduced allowances. In posing these questions Mr Callaghan was influenced by newspaper reports of a new study which argued that increasing PRT would bring only a negligible increase in tax revenues.[4]

Mr Barnett's views and announcement of proposals

Mr Barnett responded to these queries. His views were not invalidated by the findings of the new published study which had employed hypothetical fields and costs which might not be typical. On the specific proposals he was still convinced that a reduction of the volume allowance by 50% was justified. In the light of the queries he and Mr Benn had then considered options of (1) 60% PRT rate with 35% uplift, and (2) 55% rate and 50% uplift. He was now prepared to accept the first of these options though his personal preference was still for the original proposals. Mr Barnett was still convinced that BNOC's PRT exemption should be withdrawn but Mr Benn was unconvinced. Mr Barnett's first revised proposal was accepted. Mr Benn's arguments for retaining BNOC's PRT exemption prevailed. The Chief Secretary had argued that the device of annotating BNOC's accounts to show what PRT would have been payable was not an adequate substitute, because this failed to distinguish between cash payments and charges to PRT in the accounts, and the latter would have had an effect on the 1977 accounts while no cash payments were actually made. The proposals for PRT rate of 60% and uplift of 35% were announced by Mr Barnett on 2nd August 1978 on the same day that Mr Benn announced the Sixth Licensing Round. Complex transitional arrangements to deal with the reduced uplift when contracts were in progress were also announced as was a statement of the Government's willingness to remit royalties on fields whose development was being impaired.

Reaction of oil companies

Protests were received from the oil companies. Common themes were that the tax increases were (1) excessive and unjustified, and (2) in breach of the assurances given in 1975. It was argued that the economics of the North Sea had not improved since 1975 which had exhibited decreases in oil prices in real terms and continuing development cost escalation. Overall returns were lower rather than higher than contemplated. Conoco informed the Government that the projected returns in the four fields in which it was investing were in the range 12.5%–14.3% under the existing PRT, but could decline to less than 10% under the Government's proposals. This was a matter of grave disquiet to the company. The increased tax would reduce the funds available for reinvestment and there would also be a consequential reduction in the company's borrowing capacity. The fiscal drag effect on returns in real terms was also a matter of concern given the continuing very high rates of inflation. Conoco also emphasised the need for stability in the tax system. This was also stressed by other companies including BP and Shell, both of whom suggested that PRT might remain unchanged for a specified number of years from the first production in a field.

PRT stability assurances?

An inter-departmental Working Group was established to examine this subject. The Group saw several arguments against giving PRT assurances. Thus the political risks were greater in many other countries, oil prices were likely to rise, the response to the Sixth Round had been reasonable, and the companies were being successful in raising finance for new field developments. Several arguments in favour of providing some stability were also recognised. Thus the Government had as part of its industrial strategy accepted the general need for a stable business environment. The investment costs and lead times in the North Sea were longer than in most other petroleum provinces. Looking ahead less profitable fields could be expected, and the response of Shell and Esso in the Sixth Round indicated that some companies were prepared to reduce their prospective activity. It would be highly undesirable if investment suffered through a lack of confidence.

The general conclusion was that it was desirable to give some assurance to the industry. But the form which that took presented problems. Thus no Government could bind itself or its successors indefinitely, and tax was one of the few areas of the total régime which could be altered without the risk of accusations of breaking contracts. Further, any pledges must leave open the possibility for technical changes to be made to remove anomalies or loopholes. Any assurance would also restrict the Government's future room to make changes in the event of changed circumstances (such as a major movement in oil prices).

One option was to reaffirm the Government's belief in the desirability of stability and repeat the promise made in 1975 that PRT would not be changed for short-term or demand management reasons. Further assurances might be given, such as those made by the Chief Secretary at a recent meeting of the Energy Commission, indicating that he did not anticipate further changes to be needed for some years, and there was no intention of employing tax as an instrument of depletion policy. This would leave the Government free to react to new circumstances, but the companies would not be reassured by the promise of stability for a period which in terms of North Sea investments could be regarded as quite short.

This raised the idea that a promise might be given that PRT would not be changed for a fixed period of years. This would be an obvious advantage to the companies, but if the period was short, say no more than five years, it would still not be of much help in facilitating new long term investment decisions. But if the period was, say ten years, this would greatly constrain the Government in a time period when major changes in circumstances could occur.

The third option considered was to list the circumstances in which PRT could be changed. Specifying circumstances had advantages to both parties, but designing the list would be difficult: it could be quite long, and if comprehensive would have to include technical changes as well as general ones. One idea would be to limit the conditions to changes in oil prices, as the Government would not want to encourage the thought that if the industry reduced costs the resulting benefits would be clawed back in higher tax. But it was felt that in practice the change in circumstances would only be specified in qualitative terms which would mean the issue would remain open to argument. Oddly, it was felt that changes in price could not be specified for this purpose. There was also a fear that important considerations would in the event turn out to have been omitted. This suggested that a caveat could be added stating that the Government would change the régime in unforeseen circumstances.

Conclusion of Working Group

The conclusion of the report was that the second and third options involved too many difficulties. The recommendation was that the first option was the best available. Thus the Government should reaffirm its belief in the general desirability of stability, and should repeat the promise made in 1975 that it would not change PRT for short-term or demand management reasons.

Royalty refunds for marginal fields

Officials in the DEN gave particular attention to the suggestion of Dr Dickson Mabon, the Minister of State, that marginal fields could be more effectively helped by royalty refunds. The Working Group had found that the royalty refund was a powerful weapon which could offset the impact of the proposed changes. At late 1978 only two requests had been made for refunds. In the first case the applicant was in effect attempting to use the concept like a negative income tax to guarantee a minimum return on investment. This was unacceptable to the Government. The industry was unanimously of the view that discretionary royalty remission was unhelpful in making investment decisions because of lack of knowledge of how it would be used. But the legal opinion in the DEN was that a commitment that the Secretary of State's discretion would be exercised in a particular way was unlawful as a fetter on his discretion. This was so because it represented a decision by the Minister on the exercise of his discretion at a time when it was impossible for him to take into account all the factors which were relevant to the exercise of that discretion.

The Working Party's deliberations continued into 1979. The evidence provided by the oil companies that the operating environment had changed adversely since the announcement of the proposals in August 1978, principally through cost escalation was generally accepted. The conclusion reached in February 1979 was that these proposals were still justifiable but that if Ministers wished to be risk averse the proposal to halve the oil allowance could be withdrawn.

Meeting with UKOOA

Shortly afterwards Mr Barnett, Dr Mabon, and officials met with senior UKOOA representatives. UKOOA argued that the proposals were in breach of the stability assurances given in 1975 and that investment uncertainty was enhanced by the proposals. Mr Williams, the Director General, described the industry's response to the Sixth Round as weak. UKOOA was looking for a reduction in the August 1978 PRT proposals to restore confidence. Calculations based on Wood Mackenzie's analysis of nineteen existing fields were produced indicating a prospective average rate of return of 11.8% which was very low for a high risk business. UKOOA also argued that most future fields would have reserves below 300 million barrels and produced data indicating a sharp drop in rates of return on such smaller fields. UKOOA's view was that there should be no increase in PRT, and incentives to develop small fields through automatic (non-discretionary) royalty remission made known at the exploration stage were desirable. In response to questioning by Mr Barnett, UKOOA representatives agreed that the various PRT allowances meant that PRT itself was not a major disincentive on small fields, but substantial returns on some fields were required to maintain incentives for continued exploration and development.

Rapidly rising oil prices

By March 1979 the repercussions of the Iranian revolution on the world oil market were such that oil prices were rising strongly and the UKCS was becoming an increasingly attractive investment province. Ministers readily agreed that there was no need to modify the original proposals and a draft Finance Bill was prepared. The General Election then intervened and a stop-gap Finance Bill was introduced. The issue had thus to be examined by the new Conservative Government after the May election. Very soon after the election the Inland Revenue prepared a submission to Sir Geoffrey Howe, the new Chancellor, explaining the background to the August 1978 proposals, the work of the Inter-Departmental Working Party, including its reassessment of the position in the light of representations from the oil companies, and recommended that the proposed increases should be enacted. The expectation was that the package would increase tax revenues by £0.13 billion in 1979–80 and by £2.3 billion in the total period to 1985 (at 1978 prices). Detailed calculations of field investments using a 15% real discount rate for cut-off purposes accompanied the submission. The proposed 35% uplift was not very different in effect to a proxy for loan interest, but the inducement to greater cost consciousness was an important motive for the change. It was also argued that BNOC's exemption from PRT which was an irritant to the companies be withdrawn. A technical concession could be given which would make the point at which the oil was valued coincide with the cut-off point for allowable expenditure. The PRT expenditure rules were narrowly drawn and could well mean that some expenditures required to deliver the oil to buyers were ineligible for relief. It was also explained that it would not be possible to prepare very different proposals in time for a June 1979 budget.

DEN/Treasury discussions

A meeting between the Minister of State at the Treasury (Mr Peter Rees), the Minister of State at the DEN (Mr Hamish Gray) and senior Treasury, Inland Revenue and DEN officials was held on 17th May to discuss the subject. There was ready agreement that a PRT package should be included in the forthcoming Budget. On the content Mr Rees indicated that the primary consideration from his perspective was to maximise revenue in the current year given the large PSBR problem. This pointed to acceptance of the proposals which would not come as a shock to the companies. He was happy with the proposed increase in the PRT rate, but before coming to a final view on the changes to the allowances he wanted more information on the impact of the proposals on marginal fields. Mr Gray felt that the recent price increases had dispelled any reservations regarding the August 1978 proposals. The only point requiring further consideration was the reduction in the oil allowance. He also wanted consultations with the industry on the effect of the package on marginal fields. It was agreed that the concession on coincidence of tax valuation and the cut-off point for allowable expenditures was desirable. Making BNOC liable to PRT was also desirable but work on some technical aspects was needed. It was also agreed that, in view of the revenue implications, the effective date for the changes should be 1st January 1979, even though this was open to the objection of retrospective legislation.

Inland Revenue response

The Inland Revenue rapidly produced a note on marginal fields employing the studies and information conducted over the previous months. The conclusions were that there were already several tax and royalty incentives for those fields and the proposed PRT increases did not especially damage the returns to them. With respect to removal of BNOC's PRT exemption the technical problem arose because expenditure whenever incurred was allowed on a claim before an assessment was made. Thus, if BNOC's exemption were removed from 1st July 1979, it would be entitled to claim all expenditure so far incurred. The problem could be solved by withdrawing BNOC's exemption from the start of PRT, but this would involve retrospection for four years. The preferred method of dealing with the problem was to withdraw BNOC's exemption from 1st July 1979 and to limit the expenditure available for carry forward to July 1979 by the price or value of the oil delivered by BNOC in the exemption periods. The Secretary of State for Energy, Mr David Howell, proposed that the volume allowance be reduced by one quarter rather than one half. Sir Geoffrey Howe did not agree with the moderation to the reduction in the oil allowance, but did agree to a review of marginal fields.

Response of industry to PRT proposals

The PRT proposals were announced in the Budget on 12th June 1979 and on 21st June Mr Gray announced the review of marginal fields. The oil companies objected to the proposals. Conoco emphasised what were perceived to be structural defects in the system with a marginal PRT rate of 80% when the field was in the safeguard, and an overall marginal rate in these circumstances exceeding 91%. The company favoured a progressive PRT system. The Inland Revenue felt that the average rate was more important and, as in 1975, did not favour a system progressively related to profitability. Other companies including Shell and Esso emphasised the need for stability and sought assurances to this effect. A suggestion that the oil allowance could be utilised in priority to expenditure relief would give a timing advantage to the companies which the Inland Revenue felt could not be justified because of the substantial near term loss of revenue. The suggestion that the uplift should not be reduced below 50% was also felt to be unduly generous. The proposed uplift was a reasonable proxy for interest and the combination of 35% uplift with 60% PRT rate provided more investment relief than 75% uplift with 45% rate. The decision was made to proceed with the original proposals, and these, including the ending of BNOC's exemption, were implemented in the Finance (No. 2) Act 1979. The Opposition argued that the increases did not go far enough given the substantial recent increases in oil prices.

PSBR problem becomes dominant

As 1979 progressed the problem of the PSBR loomed ever larger and the Government examined various ways by which it could be reduced in the near term. In June Mrs Thatcher wrote to Sir Geoffrey Howe asking whether part of the substantial PRT receipts due in 1980/81 could be brought forward to 1979/80. The Inland Revenue indicated that this could be done in one of two ways. The chargeable periods for PRT ended on 30th June and 31st December. These could be changed to 30th April and 31st October which would mean that tax payable for both chargeable periods would be paid in that financial year.[5] The result would be an extra £400 million in 1979/80.

The second method would be to retain the chargeable periods as they were, but to reduce the length of the interval between the end of a period and the actual receipt of the payment. This was the preferred option on cash flow grounds. The two month period allowed to the companies to complete returns could be reduced. Other elements in the existing total four-month period could not be reduced. The companies would certainly protest strongly as the four-month period had been determined as the minimum necessary, and it compared unfavourably with the nine months allowed for corporation tax. At the summer of 1979 the Inland

Revenue felt that the issue might be better dealt with in year 1980/81 when the PSBR problem was expected to be more difficult. In the event the Chancellor announced that legislation would be introduced before the end of the year, and on 5th December 1979 the short Petroleum Revenue Tax Bill was introduced. It became effective from 31st January 1980 and the first payment on account was received on 1st March 1980.

Studies on further tax increases

But the Government's needs for further revenues from North Sea oil were by no means fully satisfied and as the year 1979 progressed ways were being examined to further increase the take. Oil prices continued to rise strongly in the light of the Iranian revolution, the associated disruption to that country's oil exports, and the panic reaction of buyers. In making a submission to Mr Rees in November 1979 officials discussed the case for further tax increases, the details of which would be clarified after the consequences of the December OPEC meeting had been ascertained. But increases in the PRT rate to 65% or 70% were already being contemplated. The latter rate was regarded as the maximum which, given the uplift, was consistent with tax relief not exceeding 100% of the associated investment. An increase in the rate would not be a breach of the stability assurances which had acknowledged that changes could be made in the light of major oil price movements. It was expected that oil company profits for 1979 would show a major increase which would be announced about budget time. This would therefore be the appropriate time to announce a tax increase. The effect of the increased rate to 65% or 70% on overall yield was expected to be very considerable, at £1.4 billion–£2.5 billion in the period 1980–1985. This would significantly impact on the PSBR.

PRT and gas banking

But officials also had in mind some concessions to the industry to remove what were perceived to be anomalies or distortions. Some of these related to the exploitation of associated gas where the rate of production was inextricably linked to the oil production from a field. This was a complex problem which had been debated with the industry for some time and several anomalies had become apparent. One of these related to gas banking schemes. The Government was keen to reduce gas flaring (see Chapter 12) and gas banking was an alternative to this. Gas banking schemes related to situations where associated gas was produced in one field but stored in another (often involving a different licensee) for some time (perhaps several years) before the gas was sold to BGC. But in the meantime PRT was charged to the licensee (or depositor) in the period when the gas was produced. This also determined the corporation tax position of the licensee storing the gas (the banker). All this was regarded as arbitrary and capricious by the industry and requests had been made to change the legislation. A related issue was the valuation of associated gas. Gas was normally fractionated into its component streams such as methane, propane, and butane, before being sold, but the then current law required the gas to be valued in its unfractionated state with no relief being given for the costs of fractionation. A further anomaly was that, although the process of separating the methane and fractionating the remaining gas could well be performed in the same plant, a cost attributable to separating the methane had to be calculated because only this cost was allowed for tax purposes.

Detailed paper from BNOC

Following representations from the industry an Inter-Departmental Working Party was set up to examine the issue. Among representations made was a paper prepared by the taxation manager of BNOC, Mr David Underdown, who, as a former official in the OTO, was well-placed to analyse the issue in a dispassionate manner. The paper argued that associated gas was becoming increasingly important, and the industry was faced with very substantial investment without having assurance of proper tax reliefs for the expenditures. This was now constituting an impediment to effective national gas conservation and an inhibiting factor in the development of fields where associated gas and condensates constituted a major part of the reserves. On the valuation question it was argued that the market for associated gas was distorted, resulting in problems over transport, treatment, and security of supply, and, because of the influence of BGC as the monopsony buyer of methane, at artificially low prices.

Most associated gas apart from methane had to be sold on terms other than arm's length transactions, and it was felt that the valuation formula in the 1975 Act did not cater for the complexities of associated gas exploitation. The possible range of values was extremely wide varying from oil when the gas would otherwise be flared, through a middle value applicable to fuel gas, to a premium value which might be obtained in the case of gas used in petrochemicals. Even in circumstances where the physical use of the gas had been established its value could be clouded by the restricted market if, for example, the buyer had to invest in elaborate facilities. The extent to which the gas had been fractionated also determined its value. All these uncertainties precluded any accurate analysis of post-tax returns on the projects. An additional point was that the valuation of associated gas impacted on the gas value of the oil allowance where the conversion formula in the 1975 Act already produced a rough and ready result.

With respect to the incidence of taxation the BNOC paper felt that the treatment of gas used for production purposes, gas flaring, and gas reinjection was appropriate (in effect being exempt), but there were problems with regard to disposal and subsequent buy-back, especially when gas reinjection in a field was impracticable and it was sent to another field for reinjection, but subsequently sent back to the original field when it became gas deficient. The tax position was obscure, but there was a danger that, when the gas was first produced, there was a disposal for tax purposes and a tax charge would ensue even though no disposal proceeds were received. The paper also discussed the tax problems of gas banking schemes as outlined above. The normal arrangement was that the producer of associated gas (the depositor of the excess gas) had to accept a deferral of his sales proceeds so as to leave the financial position of the receiving licensee field (the banker) unimpaired. For taxation purposes there was a concern that there was a disposal at market value when the associated gas was initially produced.

The paper also discussed the problem of the allocation of expenditures between oil and gas in a field where the gas was exempt from PRT. A major example was Brent. There was no statutory guidance on the basis for allocation which might be volume, mass, or market values. A further issue raised related to the joint use of facilities such as pipelines and terminals by licensees in different fields. This was being encouraged by the Government, but there were tax problems emanating from the disallowance of reliefs to the owner of a pipeline when it was being used in part by a third party. This had consequences for the user party in terms of tariffs which would be charged to him. The problem was wider, involving gas banking and gas gathering schemes. It was argued that the current system militated against any third party which might plan to construct and operate a gas gathering pipeline, something which the Government was generally keen to encourage.

BNOC's proposals

BNOC concluded that in all the circumstances the only equitable tax treatment was that taxable receipts should only arise when sales proceeds from the gas had been received. BNOC also felt that facilities employed for producing and disposing of associated gas should be seen as a necessary incidental cost of oil production and should be fully allowable for tax and royalty purposes. This would remove the allocation problem (but would be quite controversial if the income from associated gas was not subject to PRT). The BNOC paper further concluded that the costs of fractionation plants installed at oil terminals should be allowed for PRT and corporation tax.

Report of Working Party

Other companies, notably Texaco, Total, and Occidental, had also written to the Government on the gas banking problem in particular and on the other perceived problems regarding associated gas as discussed in the BNOC report. The Working Party had several meetings on the subject both within Government and also with UKOITC. It produced its report in November 1979. This had five key findings. The first was that there were examples of cases where the returns to the companies from associated gas were low, but, as the effect on overall profitability (including oil) was low, there would be little adverse effect on exploration and production if the tax rules were not changed. The second finding acknowledged the anomalies relating to gas banking schemes as discussed above, including the timing problem in particular. The third finding related to valuation. The current law required the associated gas to be valued as if it were delivered to a willing buyer onshore (that is as sold to BGC). But when gas was deposited in an offshore bank it was still valued at the price which BGC would pay for an even flow of gas delivered onshore. This was anomalous, but the Government was concerned that if the rule was changed and banked gas was valued at its (much lower) offshore value tax avoidance could result. On the other hand the present rules positively discouraged gas banking schemes.

Third party use of pipelines

The Working Party also accepted the argument that the whole basis of valuation of associated gas did not conform with commercial reality as gas was not generally sold in crude form, but was first fractionated. A further key finding related to a technical issue on third party use of pipelines. It was accepted as anomalous that there was different PRT treatment between tariffs received under a hire contract (where the owner of the pipeline obtained relief for the cost of the pipeline and paid tax on the tariffs received), and tariffs received under a throughput arrangement (where relief for the costs was restricted and the tariffs received were ignored for PRT).

Tax system should be neutral in effect on gas banking

The Working Party recommended that the tax system should be broadly neutral in its impact on gas banking schemes. This could be procured in a number of ways including a change from production to receipts basis as requested by the industry, or by leaving the production basis but postponing collection until payment had been received. A modified form of the receipts basis was the preferred solution. Tax and royalties would then follow conventional commercial practice. A restriction to the operation of the PRT safeguard was proposed to minimise the effect on Government revenues. On valuation the Working Party again recommended that commercial practice be followed. Thus associated gas would be valued in the fractionated state at which it was sold and the fractionation costs would be allowed. On shared pipelines the Working Party recommended that the tax treatment given to hire tariffs be extended to throughput tariffs.

PRT in kind?

During this period other specific taxation issues were also debated within Government. As 1979 progressed security of supply became an ever-growing concern. The Government already had powers to take royalty oil in kind but the DEN considered whether PRT could also be taken in kind. The Inland Revenue was quite unenthusiastic for technical tax reasons. The complications would be much greater than those caused by taking royalty in kind. Unlike the case with royalty the taking of PRT in kind would not reduce the equity interest or profit base. The oil diverted to tax payments would not fall out of the tax computation. Taking PRT in kind would introduce an additional purpose for valuing the oil. This would cause extra work and complications, and the Inland Revenue strongly advised the DEN against the pursuit of this method of increasing supplies to the UK market. Mr Howell also asked officials in late 1979 to consider whether PRT should be based on spot values (which were then exceeding term prices by a considerable margin). The strong advice was against this idea. Spot transactions still constituted a very small element of total oil sales from the UKCS, the oil companies would protest vigorously with some justification, and the creditability of PRT in the USA would be endangered. The correct way to increase Government take from the UKCS was to increase PRT.

Inland Revenue proposes further increase in PRT rate

At the end of January 1980 Inland Revenue officials made a submission to the Chancellor, Mr Howe, on the scope for increasing PRT. Their conclusion was that a rate increase from 60% to 70% would be tolerated without harming the viability of existing fields and those whose development was imminent. The all-important increases in take were £240 million in 1980/81 and £1.56 billion in the period to 1985/86 (all at 1978 prices). Rates higher than 70% did not bring much extra because the fields received more protection from the safeguard provision.[6] The effects of the increase had been tested on a suite of fields (real and proxy), and with a 70% PRT rate most fields achieved real post-tax returns of 15% or above. Increasing the PRT rate further also increased the possibility that companies would incur wasteful expenditure, because, in circumstances shortly before a field was expected to benefit from the safeguard, expenditure of £100 could well produce post-tax benefits exceeding £100. To date there was no evidence that this was actually happening.

The Chancellor was warned that the industry reaction would be hostile, but he should not be perturbed. The work to date of the Working Party on Marginal Fields had found that, compared to royalties, PRT had only a slight impact on the returns to these fields. Consultation with the industry was necessary if only for cosmetic purposes. Although this would be the third tightening of the fiscal régime within a year it was felt that it was consistent with the stability assurances in the light of the continuing oil price increases.

Yet more short-term revenues required

But the Treasury was searching for still further near-term revenues from North Sea oil to ameliorate the ever-pressing PSBR problem. On 7th March 1980 a meeting involving the Chancellor, Chief Secretary, Minister of State, and senior Treasury and Inland Revenue officials was held to consider the options. One possibility raised by the Chancellor was a straight surcharge to raise £500 million in 1980/81. Inland Revenue officials advised against such a non-repayable one-year surcharge which would be arbitrary, and would involve overriding the uplift and safeguard provisions, and would be contrary to the assurances given in 1975. But these arguments could not be levelled against an advance refundable payment. An advance payment of 15% along with the proposed 70% PRT rate would be plausible. In terms of the macroeconomic aspects the argument for the increase could be developed in terms of the growing imbalance between the oil and non-oil sectors and the rapid increase in oil prices. The Chancellor agreed with this. The Chief Secretary noted that the harmful effects of North Sea oil on the rest of the economy through the high exchange rate and the loss of competitiveness in export markets were already noticeable, and it was important to maximise the tax revenues from the North Sea over the next two years.

Inland Revenue officials estimated that the combined effect of the rate increase and 15% advance payment would be to produce around £500 million of additional revenues in 1980/81. This was on the assumption that the scheme would begin with the chargeable period July-December 1980 with the first advance payment becoming due on 1st March 1981.[7] The Chancellor then submitted his proposals to Mr Howell who, while agreeing with the Chancellor's proposals, indicated his concern at the effect on the confidence of the industry, and commented that the Government's behaviour was teetering on the edge of gangsterism.

Correspondence with industry

Mr Rees had met with UKOOA and discussed the subjects of oil prices and possible increased taxes. This led to the receipt of letters and reports from several oil companies. The emphasis in each was different with some arguing for no increase, but others argued for a major restructuring with PRT being replaced by a progressive tax, and some requesting particular reliefs (such as for marginal fields and gas banking schemes). Most favoured some stability assurance. Inland Revenue officials advised Mr Rees that, given the huge increase in oil prices since the 1979 budget from $20.70 per barrel to $33.74 at mid-March 1980, Ministers should guard against giving further stability assurances, but could indicate that because of the extreme market volatility any assurance would not be very meaningful.

Sir Geoffrey presents budget proposals

The Chancellor presented his budget proposals on 26th March 1980. It contained all the provisions on PRT discussed above including the rate increases and advance payments, allowance for costs of separating gases, valuation of gas in its separated state, and an option that in gas banking schemes tax became applicable when sales proceeds were received. No assurances on stability were given. The Chancellor was keen to ensure that the 15% rate of advance payment could be modified by an Order in Council rather than via further primary legislation.

Working Party examines scope for yet further tax increases

Well before the 1980 budget proposals were enacted consideration was being given by officials to how the Government take from the North Sea could be increased yet again. The Inter-Departmental North Sea Fiscal Régime Working

Party was reconvened with this in mind in February. Its remit included examination of the uplift and safeguard allowances with a view to eliminating incentives to wasteful expenditures. An initial paper was quickly produced by the Inland Revenue which (a) reviewed the published work of various academics (including the present author), and (b) considered the case for a multi-rate PRT system. The paper noted that the advantages of such a scheme were threefold. Firstly, it would allow investors to obtain a certain rate of return before PRT became payable. The rather crude devices of oil allowance and safeguard would become unnecessary. Secondly, by graduating the tax according to profitability it would be possible to obtain a higher take from the really profitable fields. Thirdly, it would provide an automatic means for the Government to increase its take when oil prices increased and lower it when they fell.

But the report found several disadvantages with such a scheme, especially regarding the changes from an established tax system to a new one. Firstly, a change to a multi-rate system would represent a major change in the tax structure which would be unwelcome to the companies and which could hold up investment while the new system was being appraised. Secondly, a radical change would reopen the issue of creditability of PRT because the multi-rate PRT would be different from the current one. Thirdly, the Inland Revenue had earlier experience of taxes graduated according to return on capital such as the Excess Profits Tax and Excess Profits Levy. They were very difficult to administer and encouraged waste. In amplification the paper indicated that the most difficult problem related to the choice of the rate of depreciation which it was felt was necessary, as it would form the basis of calculating the rate of return which determined the tax rate. Further problems would relate to the appropriate definition of investment. Finally, there would be problems in determining the appropriate tax rates.[8]

By June 1980 the Treasury was looking urgently at the scope for obtaining extra tax receipts from the North Sea. Within the existing régime royalties and corporation tax could not be changed. A discriminatory corporation tax would prejudice its creditability. PRT receipts were now coming in but the front-end reliefs were constraining the amounts. Three options were considered namely (1) an increase in the PRT rate, (2) an increase in the rate of advance payment, and (3) the introduction of an entirely new charge. It was acknowledged that in the short-run there was no point in increasing the PRT rate because the extra yield would be negligible and it could lead to wasteful expenditures. The rate of advance payment could be increased either by amending the current Finance Bill before the end of June or later by invoking the order-making power provided for in the Bill. An increase from 15% to 25% would yield a further £160 million during the financial year. Because it advanced payments by only six months it would not hit companies still some way from paying PRT. There was a need to advance PRT expected to accrue in 1981 and 1982. But the Inland Revenue had advised that there was no way by which future profits could be assessed (even for one year ahead) on a basis firm enough to substantiate such a system of advance payment. The question then arose of whether some arbitrary basis of assessment could be devised. This pointed to the possibility of a new tax.

Barrelage tax?

The Treasury thus started considering the idea of a barrelage tax. The tax base might be the value of physical quantities like an excise tax on the lines of the US Windfall Profits Tax. Alternatively it could be related to the increase in values reflecting oil prices. There were two ways of approaching the issue namely (1) a new tax deductible for PRT, or (2) an advance payment of PRT calculated by reference to barrelage which would then reduce regular PRT payments as they became due or be repayable if no regular PRT occurred.

The Chancellor was advised of the thrust of the above thinking very early in June, 1980. The idea of introducing new measures through a late amendment to the Finance Bill was also raised. The Minister of State, Mr Rees, reacted by saying that to introduce a fundamental tax charge such as a barrelage tax without consultation smacked of the kind of instant and ill-thought out Government which he and his colleagues had deplored under the Labour Government. But Sir Geoffrey welcomed the thinking of officials and his initial thought was that a new barrelage tax could replace the new advance payment scheme.

A more detailed paper was prepared by the Treasury and Inland Revenue and submitted to the Chancellor on 13th June. The purpose was to explore further means by which the Government's share of revenues from the North Sea could be increased over the next 18 months. The context (as seen by the Treasury) was the major increase in oil prices which had increased inflation and, through its effect on the exchange rate, disadvantaged the export-based industries. This could be offset at least partly by lower interest rates, which in turn required a reduced PSBR and thus increased tax revenues. It was expected that 1981/82 would be the most difficult year as far as the consistency of the PSBR with the Medium Term Financial Strategy was concerned.

Increase rate of advance payment?

The paper then discussed the structural aspects of the present tax system on the lines noted above. To solve the problem of short-term revenues to alleviate the PSBR the rate of advance payment could be increased from 15%, and there was already an Opposition amendment to raise it to 25%. The maximum would be around 40% which could procure an extra £330 million in 1980/81. But if still further revenues were required the advance payment scheme as currently designed could not cope very well. Though the rate of advance payment could be increased for subsequent periods PRT was only being paid on a handful of fields, and the cash flows of the relevant licensees would be very adversely affected.

Perceived advantages of barrelage tax

A wider effective tax base over the next two years was thus required, and this suggested an approach based on barrelage. This might be a flat rate charge on output, perhaps £x per barrel or x% of sales. This would immediately bring into liability many more fields and companies. A barrelage tax could operate as a new form of advance payment, replacing the existing 15% one and being set off against future PRT liability. Because it impacted on a broader tax base it would procure substantially more revenue and had the advantage of being more highly geared to the oil price. It could be introduced at the Report Stage in the current Finance Bill. Because it was a payment on account and offsettable against future PRT, problems of international law were unlikely to arise.

The paper then considered a second possibility namely that the barrelage charge become an additional permanent tax in the North Sea which would produce an overall increase in the tax payable over the life of a field. An advantage was that it would not be offsettable against PRT. It was recognised, however, that arguments would be produced against the notion that tax would be payable on fields where no PRT profit ever emerged. There would also be international complications as such a tax would not be creditable in the USA because it was unrelated to profits. It might even be argued that a permanent barrelage tax broke contractual arrangements because of its similarity to a royalty, and might even be in breach of international law if held to be confiscatory or penal. Consultation with the industry would be required for a new tax and thus it could not be included in the current Finance Bill.

A hostile reaction from the industry to any significant new tax was guaranteed. The Treasury had estimated that the net cash flow for the industry for 1980/81 was quite limited and on some new fields the net cash flows would turn from positive to negative with consequential increase in their borrowing requirements. A new tax might damage investment in new projects. The Secretary of State for Energy could be expected to show concern at any new tax proposal.

Treasury Ministers request further work on new tax

The paper was discussed with the Chancellor and other Treasury Ministers at the beginning of July. The issues were debated on the lines noted above, and the Chancellor indicated that further work should be undertaken with a view to increasing the tax take for 1981/82 by £500 million-£1 billion. The Inter-Departmental Working Party subsequently met to discuss this, and given the need to raise up to £1 billion extra in the short-term, the emphasis was on a new tax. There was discussion of various options, namely (1) a straight barrelage tax, (2) a turnover tax, (3) a tax on operating profits, (4) a tax on profits including a deduction for investment expenditure, and (5) a tax on the difference between a base price and the actual selling price. All options had negative and positive features and further studies were necessary. It was, however, felt that a new tax could be designed to raise £1 billion in 1981/82. The danger of being locked into a régime tailored to short-term requirements was noticed, particularly with respect to its effects on marginal fields. Scheme (4) was most appropriate from this viewpoint.

Further studies by Working Party

The Working Party then conducted a large amount of further work on how the take could be increased, particularly in the short-term. At the beginning of October a substantial report was produced. It reiterated the issues discussed above, and somewhat surprisingly included the statement that PRT lacked oil price progressivity because of the single marginal rate.[9] In the past investment threshold rates of return of 15% in post-tax real terms had been employed, but there was now some evidence that lower cut-off rates were acceptable, and so economic tests were undertaken using 10% real discount rates. There were many uncertainties surrounding investment decisions including future oil prices. The central assumptions in the modelling were £86.3 per tonne in 1980 falling to £77.5 in 1983 and rising gradually to £99.2 per tonne in 1990 (all at 1987 prices). The central finding was that there was scope for increasing taxation. Some fall-off in activity would be expected but not in proportion to the revenue gains achieved. The effect would depend on the distribution of the increased tax burden across fields.

The report considered four main ways by which the revenues could be augmented. The first was raising the rate of advance payment, but this would discriminate against companies already paying substantial amounts of PRT. It would hit BP very hard and could remove all the company's cash flow from the North Sea for 1980/81. This method was not recommended. The second method, raising the PRT rate, would be ineffective because the allowances, including the safeguard, would protect many of the fields. Abolishing the safeguard would permit a significant further increase (£420 million) for 1981/82, but fields of modest profitability would be hit hardest. To prevent incentives to wasteful expenditure if the PRT rate was increased to, say, 80% the uplift would also have to be reduced. But significant short-term increases in revenues could only be obtained by reducing the uplift on fields where expenditure contracts had already been signed, and this would raise the problem of retrospective legislation.

Modified advance payments scheme

The report then considered a modified advance payments scheme which would require payments from fields which had not started to pay PRT in 1980/81 or 1981/82. It would bring forward PRT revenues from later years rather than permanently increase the take. The advance payments would have to be repaid, but this might not be for several years on some fields depending on the detailed terms. A specific case examined was where the taxable base would be calculated as for PRT except that there would be no uplift, oil allowance, or safeguard. A rate of 30% was used. The advance payment would be set against the payment due on account six months later for that same period and would be repaid to the extent that it exceeded the liability then due. The scheme would yield £600 million in 1980/81 and the same in 1981/82. The perceived disadvantages were that it would not accurately shadow the eventual PRT liability, and, because of the front-end reliefs for normal PRT, would not procure an increase in yield from newly-producing fields. While it had some advantages it was clearly a makeshift proposal, would require complex legislation, and would be difficult to administer.

Multi-rate PRT related to profitability

The report then considered the case for a multi-rate PRT geared to field profitability. The Working Party examined this scheme and found that, while it could procure more revenues than the current PRT and would be inherently more flexible in the event of oil price increases, it would have inherent problems relating to wasteful expenditure, definition of capital expenditure base, and very high marginal rates.[10] It would also cause transitional problems and possibly prejudice the creditability of PRT in the USA.

Structure of new tax

The fourth option was a new tax. The revenue requirement of £1 billion for 1981/82 ruled out a windfall profits tax such as that recently introduced in the USA where the base of the tax was much lower than the current market value in the UK. The large differences in costs across fields in the UKCS also made such a tax inappropriate. It also ruled out a straight barrelage tax based on turnover. This suggested a tax based on sales less some deductions, termed by the Working Party a Petroleum Production Tax. The allowance could be flat-rate or one based on expenditure. At 20% rate the new tax, if deductible for PRT and corporation tax, would increase the top marginal rate to over 90% (and 93.5% under the safeguard). It would also impact on marginal fields. This was awkward because the conclusion of the review of this subject was that PRT had little effect on these fields on which royalty impacted more severely. A new production tax could have a similar effect. The Government had also encouraged small British companies to apply for licences in the Seventh Round. Some would have little corporation tax payments against which to obtain reliefs, and the new tax would make their prospects worse.

Volume allowance for new tax

The Working Party felt that the most appropriate allowance for the new tax would be related to volume with a million tonnes per year being favoured. This was rather surprising given that the value of this allowance varied directly with the oil price and so was more valuable at high prices when less relief was necessary. Operationally the volume allowance would be more straightforward than an expenditure relief because there would be no need to claim and agree allowable expenditures. Legal advice was required on whether the resulting tax package with its very high rates could be regarded as penal and confiscatory. There was also a risk that it was akin to a retrospective amendment to the licence royalty obligations.

Legal advice was somewhat comforting. The proposed tax should be defensible against the charge that it was a disguised royalty despite its similarity to a severance tax (which legal opinion in 1973 held was probably contrary to international law). The fact that there was to be an allowance for the tax increased the likelihood that it would be regarded as a genuine tax. That likelihood would increase the greater the allowances and the closer the base of the tax came to net profits. Expenditure-related allowances would be more appropriate from this viewpoint. It would be better not to refer to the new tax as being based on production. On the issue of confiscation the interesting opinion was that there was a tolerable defence where the top marginal rate was in the lower nineties, especially if the increase over the existing situation was no more than two or three percentage points. But a top marginal rate in the middle to upper nineties would be open to challenge.

Extra revenues from UKCS needed

At a meeting among the Chancellor, other Treasury Ministers, and senior Treasury and Inland Revenue officials in late October the subject was discussed further. The background was the need to contain the PSBR. Increasing the take from the North Sea would help the sectoral balance of the economy (oil compared to non-oil) as well as reducing the PSBR. Increasing the take by £1 billion in 1981/82 would still leave the companies with a real rate of return of at least 10% which was significantly more than was being achieved elsewhere in the economy.

Increased advance payments or new tax?

The meeting considered the options for increasing the take on the lines discussed by the Working Party. At the end the Chancellor asked officials to prepare a further paper outlining the advantages and disadvantages of an enhanced advance payment scheme and a new petroleum production tax, and to show the extra revenues on a quarterly basis indicating their effects on the PSBR profile. The response was that in the short-term there was little to choose between increased advance payments and a new production tax. The advantage of the latter was that it also offered the prospect of longer term flexibility. As a separate exercise the current PRT reliefs needed overhauling for anti-avoidance reasons. Sir Geoffrey Howe was also informed by the Permanent Secretary in his capacity as the custodian of the Government's shareholding in BP that implementation of the options would reduce the company's net cash flow from its North Sea operations in 1981/82 to negligible or even negative amounts. Other Treasury officials felt that this might be tolerable at a time of high investment.

Chancellor favours new tax and announces proposals

The Chancellor, Treasury Ministers and their senior officials held a further meeting on 10th November to discuss the options. The new production tax found favour, though Mr Rees was very concerned about its inconsistency with the stability assurances he had given. To gauge its effect on North Sea activity one possibility would be to announce the tax as a proposal and then examine the industry's reaction. The Chancellor indicated that he would discuss the tax with Mr Howell. This occurred the following day and the Chancellor emphasised the increased flexibility which the new tax would give in the years ahead to respond to further oil price increases. Mr Howell questioned whether a fourth tax was the right approach. He felt that other routes to increase tax revenues should be explored including further impositions on consumers. He was concerned about the effect on activity levels. Raising £1 billion through the advance payments scheme would be politically less damaging than a new tax. At the end the Chancellor felt that the arguments pointed strongly in the direction of the new tax and he proposed to inform the Prime Minister accordingly. An announcement would be made indicating the Government's intention but only a provisional rate would be given. Mr Howell argued that further consultation would be needed to ensure that marginal fields were protected.

In his Minute to the Prime Minister the Chancellor emphasised the PSBR problem, the large increases in oil prices (though noting that the sterling price had fallen recently), and the prospective medium-term substantial further increase. He outlined the options for procuring an extra £1 billion for 1981/82 on the familiar lines discussed above and why he favoured the new tax. It had the advantages of being able to procure extra revenues quickly, but it could also continue to raise substantial funds in subsequent years. Mr Howell also submitted a Minute indicating his reservations. The Prime Minister indicated her agreement with the Chancellor's proposals and he made a statement in the House of Commons on 24th November. The new tax would be charged on the gross revenues on a field basis less a volume allowance of one million tonnes per year and would be deductible for PRT and corporation tax. It would take effect from 1st January 1981 and should raise the net yield from the North Sea by £1 billion in 1981/82 at an illustrative rate of 20%. The precise rate would be announced in the 1981 budget after discussions with the industry. The various PRT allowances would also be re-examined and changes would be introduced in the 1981 budget after discussions with the industry. The new tax was justified on its own merits in the light of the profitability of the North Sea. The increased yield would help the PSBR and promote lower interest rates. An underlying assumption was that *real* oil prices would remain constant for 1982 and rise by one per cent per year thereafter (much higher in MOD terms).

Hostile reaction of industry

The reaction of the industry was predictably hostile. George Williams, the Director General of UKOOA, said he was horrified and wondered when it (the tax increases) would stop. There followed a series of letters to the Treasury from many licensees. While the emphasis was different there were some common features in the points made. Shell perceptively noted that, while the current economic difficulties of the Government were appreciated, the response to what should be a short-term situation was to introduce fundamental changes to North Sea taxation which imposed a permanent additional burden on the industry. The confidence of the company had been severely shaken by the very drastic form and extent of the proposed new taxation. In the meantime the company would have to review its current investments and plans in the light of the new burden placed upon it. It was already clear that either borrowing would have to be increased or capital expenditure restricted. Esso emphasised the point that it had six undeveloped discoveries which offered marginally attractive returns under the existing tax terms. They would be particularly hard hit by the proposed new tax. Both Shell and Esso noted that the application of the new tax to gas would be particularly onerous as the gas was sold to a monopsony buyer at prices far below free market values. At a meeting with Treasury officials on 8th December Shell representatives indicated that the new supplementary tax would significantly increase the size of marginal fields which the company would be prepared to develop. This would seriously jeopardise the prolongation of UK oil self-sufficiency into the 1990s. On related issues Shell felt that the benefits of North Sea oil had largely gone into consumption, and the Government appeared to be preoccupied with the short-term.

The Chancellor replied in writing to the chairman of Shell emphasising that his proposals were not simply a short-term reaction to short-term difficulties but a permanent increase in the Government's share of North Sea revenues justified on its own merits. He had no intention of engaging in attempts at fine tuning! He recognised that the treatment of gas deserved special examination. This was put forcefully by Sir Denis Rooke, the Chairman of BGC. He was concerned that under the terms of existing contracts BGC could be required to reimburse the new tax to the producers. The announcement also had a profound effect on negotiations in progress, with some being stopped dead. In another case of renegotiation (Hewett field) there was a hardship clause which BGC were hoping to have abolished, but the deal could not now be completed and there was a possibility of the contract going to arbitration which revived most expensive and unhappy memories of an earlier arbitration case.

Inland Revenue publishes paper on PRT reliefs

The debate with the industry was extended on 24th December with the publication of the Background Paper on PRT Reliefs by the Inland Revenue. With respect to uplift the paper emphasised that it was intended as a substitute for loan interest but was given at the same rate irrespective of whether the investment expenditure was incurred early in the development phase or was incurred later when it could be financed from cash flow.[11] The result was that in current circumstances about 95% of post-development expenditures were relieved shortly after incurring them. The expenditure also added to the safeguard base, and, if safeguard benefits were obtained, there would be a further relief of 11.5% of the expenditure (after corporation tax consequences) for as long as the safeguard benefits were received. The overall effect was that total relief could exceed the expenditure incurred and could encourage wasteful expenditure (or gold plating as it became generally called).

Uplift and contractor financing

Uplift was also relevant to contractor financing, a subject which had been of much concern to the Inland Revenue for some time. Thus by paying for a contract in a lump sum on completion rather than by staged payments companies could roll up financing costs into a higher contract price and obtain full expenditure relief with uplift as well. Consultations were under way on this issue, but it added to the case for structural reform. The paper suggested that uplift might be removed after field pay-back had been attained. Pay-back could be defined in various ways, including not only the financial measure of pay-back but a specified date after field production commenced.

Value of volume allowance better fixed?

The current oil allowance was specified in volume terms and its value increased with the oil price thus sheltering from PRT quite profitable fields. The paper suggested that the value of the allowance could be fixed at a specified date such as January 1981 or at the period of commencement of production.[12]

Safeguard protects profitable fields

With respect to the safeguard provision, because of the successive increases in the PRT rate, it was now protecting quite profitable fields, sometimes for all their expected lives. There was a widening of the band of profits attracting this relief, and this band was now charged at a marginal rate of 91.6% which would be increased to 93.5% if the new tax was introduced at 20%. To increase the taper rate to 90% would postpone the time at which the relief became operative, but this could run counter to the original intention of providing assistance to fields of modest profitability in the early years of their lives, and would increase the marginal rate to 96.8%. This would further reduce incentives to control costs. The paper discussed various ways by which this problem could be remedied, putting emphasis on the notion that entitlement to the relief could be cut off after a period fixed either in terms of years, or as a formula determined by the ratio of cumulative adjusted profits to cumulative capital expenditure. This would in effect return safeguard to its original purpose, namely to protect fields during the early part of their lives.

Variations of PRT allowances

The paper was the outcome of many detailed studies on the PRT allowances undertaken by the Working Party over the previous several months. These studies considered several permutations of allowances. For example, the idea that safeguard could simply be abolished was considered. This would permit higher rates of PRT to be more effective in raising revenues, and the incentive to incur wasteful expenditure would be reduced. But marginal fields still required protection, and the case for a variable oil allowance to replace the existing flat-rate one was examined. The flat-rate allowance was not well-related to profitability, and studies were undertaken which examined the idea that it be replaced by one which was calculated by reference to the return on capital. This would make it more discriminating than the current one. It could be inversely related to profitability, and in practice could be based on the ratio of cumulative profits to cumulative investment. Several variants were examined most of which exhibited extraordinary complexity, but which produced results that were deemed to be less than satisfactory.

Further correspondence with companies

The publication of the consultation document increased the flow of correspondence from the oil companies. Many issues were raised with some common themes, while others reflected the particular problems of individual companies. Thus companies which had substantial gas interests in "old" PRT-exempt fields, including Elf, Total, Shell, and Esso argued strongly that, because of the relatively low prices obtained, such gas should be exempt from the new supplementary tax. Interestingly, two companies which were producing gas from PRT-paying fields felt that the supplementary tax should apply to old gas fields on the grounds that, if the Government required £1 billion extra in 1981/82, exemption of those fields would result in a bigger burden on oil and PRT-paying gas fields. Texaco produced the interesting argument that exemption would increase the distortion in the market between gas and oil, and would arrest the trend towards pricing gas on an energy equivalent basis.

Supplementary tax and "old" gas contracts

DEN and Inland Revenue officials examined the gas issue. It was clear that under the "old" gas contracts the producers would be able to reclaim the supplementary tax under the repayable gas tax clause, given that it was not a profits tax. In the case of the Frigg field there was such a clause, but whether it would be activated was open to doubt as it depended on whether the intention was to tax the producer's profits or not. In the case of the Brent field there was no repayable gas tax clause and so the new tax would be borne by the companies.

Officials estimated the amounts of revenue at stake and the effect on BGC if it had to reimburse the companies. The Corporation's profits would be reduced (unless prices to consumers were raised), and the further consequences would be that the proposed Gas Levy on BGC (see below) would have to be reduced or there would be a reduction in BGC's external financing limit (EFL). No net gain to the PSBR would ensue. If the tax on Frigg (UK) gas was borne by the companies the real rate of return would fall to under 8% on favourable assumptions and around 4% on unfavourable ones, well below the cut-off point which companies would employ for North Sea investments. The companies might request a renegotiation of the contract. In turn this could have repercussions for the Norwegian Frigg contract which could be costly to the UK. In the case of Brent the effect on profitability would be less, but the field as a whole did not have a large rate of return. Exempting all gas fields from the new tax was not an attractive option. New purchases of gas by BGC should pay the full market price and thus the full North Sea tax system should be imposed. The conclusion was to recommend that gas sold to BGC under contracts before July 1975 should be exempt from the supplementary tax.

UKOOA's views on tax proposals

In January 1981 UKOOA submitted its detailed views on the proposed supplementary tax and the changes to the PRT allowances. This emphasised the dramatic increase in costs which had taken place along with the rise in oil prices. Given the increases in PRT which had already taken place there was no justification for further increases. These would restrain investment at a time when it was desired to extend UK oil self-sufficiency into the 1990s and beyond. Investment uncertainty had already been greatly increased and further increases contributed to more instability. The new supplementary tax plus the existing royalty meant that a very high proportion of the tax take was unrelated to profits. This was particularly inappropriate to a risk-taking activity such as oil. The new tax would slow down the recovery of investment, prolong the period of negative cash flows, and make new projects more difficult to justify.

UKOOA was concerned at the very short time permitted for consultation and urged that no permanent changes be made to the tax system until the total effect of the proposals had been fully evaluated by the industry. Further, any additional revenues obtained in 1981/82 should be effected via a temporary provision which would accelerate but not permanently increase total tax payments. For the longer term the Government and the industry should jointly examine the possible alternatives which would provide the basis for a more stable and predictable régime.

These points were reiterated by UKOOA representatives at a meeting with Government officials in late January 1981. Officials pressed UKOOA for details of any realistic alternatives, but the organisation had difficulty in coming to an agreed view on a major matter within such a short time period. Individual companies wrote with their own proposals. These varied greatly but had some common features. Thus many emphasised the need for the new tax to be creditable in the USA, and that it should be replaced by a temporary levy for 1981/82 only. Shell produced a detailed and well-articulated paper on an alternative in the form of an advance PRT which would be creditable against future PRT. BRINDEX and some individual companies argued that actual costs should be allowed as deductions for the new tax. Several companies argued strongly that PRT-exempt gas should also be exempt from the new tax. Some argued that a reduction in uplift and safeguard relief would particularly hit incremental investments and effectively shorten field life. BRINDEX and some companies argued that a multi-rate PRT should be introduced. Several companies proposed that actual interest be allowed for PRT instead of the uplift, and some argued that the oil allowance should be increased in annual size and extended through field life. Many technical changes were proposed by UKOITC.

Further report of Working Party

The Working Party considered the proposals from the industry and produced a further report. The report rejected the notion of a temporary levy instead of the new tax, arguing that this only delayed the time for the desired permanent change which was still felt to be necessary. Its postponement for a year was undesirable. It was now proposed to call the new tax Supplementary Petroleum Duty (SPD). The further economic modelling undertaken had left intact the earlier view that a 20% rate and 1 million tonnes per year allowance along with substantial reductions in the PRT allowances would still leave the companies with acceptable returns based on 10% real cut-off rates. Amazingly, consideration was also given to raising the SPD rate to 22.5% which would have raised a further £120 million in 1981/82, but as this would have raised more than the £1 billion highlighted in the Chancellor's November statement the recommendation was made to retain the 20% rate. The simple but crude volume allowance was also recommended as none of the industry's proposals were felt to be superior.

Safeguard necessary?

With respect to reform of the allowances the report argued that safeguard was the main cause of the encouragement to wasteful expenditure, and the tapering relief put a ceiling on the effective rate of PRT. Safeguard had been introduced to provide security against a collapse in oil prices, but this was no longer a realistic long-term scenario and thus the allowance was no longer necessary. The Working Party had considered ways of mitigating its complete abolition, including adding another volume allowance for large but not very profitable fields (such as Ninian), by retaining it for a few years only, or by relating it more closely to the rate of return. But the assistance provided could only be worthwhile at the price of retaining incentives for wasteful expenditure. Abolition of the safeguard would restore incentives to cost control, reduce the top marginal rate and remove constraints on future increases in taxation. This was therefore one option. But if further large but marginal fields were discovered and it was felt necessary to protect them the alternative of retaining safeguard for a specified limited period should be considered. With respect to oil allowance the Working Party had found it impossible to devise a more discriminating mechanism without introducing incentives to wasteful expenditures.[13] Future fields were expected to be small and thus very dependent on the volume allowance. No change was thus recommended.

Lower volume allowance for Southern North Sea?

But the Working Party were aware that in the Southern North Sea the water was shallow, and thus there was a case for reducing the allowance just for the fields there (despite their expected small sizes). If BGC's monopsony powers were removed the adequacy of the tax system required further examination and the size of the volume allowance was an obvious consideration. If action were taken on such fields because the water was shallow the same consideration applied to onshore fields. Further, if the sale of the BGC share of the Wytch Farm field was to proceed there was an urgent need to study the onshore situation.

Remove uplift after field payback?

The Working Party felt that the uplift allowance (a substitute for loan interest) required modification because, as it did not vary with the time required for a return on investment to be achieved, it was sometimes excessive. This plus the high rates of tax contributed to the wasteful expenditure problem. The solution was to withdraw uplift relief after the period of field payback or, if that proved unworkable in practice, from a specified number of years after field production commenced.

Contractor financing

The Working Party considered three approaches to the contractor financing problem. The first would specify rules for the normal timing of payments and adjust the tax relief (strip out the interest element) on contracts which diverged from the specified norm. The second approach was to vary the uplift according to the length of time before a field came on stream, and the third was to deny uplift to those payments which deviated markedly from the norm. Discussions had been held with the industry, and the Working Party had concluded that the third option was to be recommended. The first two would be very complex to operate for both the Inland Revenue and the companies, but the third approach would not penalise present normal contract practice.

Smoothing tax receipts

The Working Party also considered the separate issue of how the tax receipts could be spread more evenly over the year to help smooth the PSBR. Currently North Sea tax payments were very peaked but spreading based on the final liabilities of the licensees would involve a loss of revenues from 1981/82 into 1982/83. This suggested the collection of advance payments based on the previous year's liability. Proposals for collecting SPD on this basis had been put to the companies, but had been met with strong protests, especially from the integrated companies who argued that they did not receive cash for their oil until they sold refined products which occurred some months after production. The Working Party was not persuaded by this argument and felt that the smoothing proposals for SPD should remain.

Some concessions to industry?

The proposed package was regarded as being tough and the Working Party wondered whether other concessions were appropriate. There was a logical case for abolishing advance PRT, but this was not recommended as the cost would be

£120 million in 1981/82. The concept of advance PRT could also be employed to develop a smoother pattern of PRT receipts in the future. The US companies' had asked for spreading elections for the PRT allowances because currently there were differences in the timing of reliefs in the USA and UK which meant that US companies' could pay US corporation tax on North Sea profits before they had a PRT liability in the UK to credit against the US tax. To give this concession had no cost to the UK Exchequer, and it was recommended that it be given. The effect of the total recommended package would be to increase Government take by just over £1 billion in 1981/82 and by £4.4–£4.5 billion up to 1986.

Continued dialogue with companies

The debate with the companies continued through this period when 1981 Budget decisions were being finalised. Many submissions were received generally raising the issues noted above. An additional subject was the proposal that some downstream costs, notably those relating to petrochemical investments should be allowed as a deduction against North Sea upstream income. While the Government was keen to promote petrochemical developments the Inland Revenue calculated that the loss of tax revenues could be substantial and could lead to other requests for breaches of the ring fence. No encouragement could be given to such proposals. The Chancellor and senior officials met with UKOOA representatives on 6th February to discuss the major proposals. UKOOA argued that the existing level of tax take was justified, but that the proposals would increase it to an unreasonable level. Sir Geoffrey Howe did not agree, but the Director General of UKOOA pointed to the reality of the current level of exploration and development which he described as abysmally low. It needed encouragement and the proposals did not recognise the increasing risks in the North Sea which pointed to the need for a tax reduction. The proposals did not relate taxation to profitability which was particularly unsatisfactory. The Government could raise additional revenues from advance payments of PRT. Sir Geoffrey Howe felt that the changes in oil prices justified an increase in take not just an acceleration in payments. For UKOOA Mr Williams asked whether the Government would reduce taxation if the oil price fell. The Chancellor's response was that this could only be answered at the time of any fall. UKOOA also queried the changes to the PRT allowances. They denied that the lower than expected tax take to date was due to wasteful expenditure (commonly referred to as gold plating), but was due to production to date being lower than envisaged. UKOOA felt that the accusation of deliberate wasteful expenditure indicated a lack of understanding of the industry's behaviour. UKOOA wanted a detailed discussion with the Inland Revenue such as had occurred in 1974–75, in order to minimise damages to investment and confidence. The Chancellor indicated that budgetary considerations required him to make changes in the 1981 Budget, but was content that the companies continue detailed discussions with the Inland Revenue to see whether improvements to the proposals could be made.

Further discussions among Ministers and senior officials

On 11th February the Chancellor, Mr Rees, Mr Howell, and senior officials from Inland Revenue, Treasury, and DEN met to discuss the key issues. Sir Geoffrey felt that SPD should be introduced on the proposed lines, but he proposed that the legislation might be for one year, at least in the first instance. Mr Howell agreed with this, and suggested that an explicit invitation be extended to the oil companies to submit their further views. The phasing of the payments (namely ten monthly payments (avoiding payments in the months where PRT was due) had been designed to smooth the contributions to the PSBR, but had been criticised by the companies. The Chancellor thought that the Inland Revenue should be prepared to consider hardship cases, particularly if, as Mr Howell said, companies might be required to pay the tax before they had actually received the related income.

A particular but important issue was whether the proposed changes to the PRT allowances would jeopardise its creditability in the USA. At this point the Inland Revenue, while sympathetic to the issue, could give no assurance as this depended on the US Internal Revenue (IRS). It was acknowledged that non-creditability would substantially harm the net returns to US companies. One fear was that in coming to a view on the issue the IRS might aggregate all the changes made to PRT since 1975 when the Double Taxation Treaty with the USA was signed. If PRT creditability was denied steps would be taken to restore it as quickly as possible, though all this would have undesirable wider political consequences.

Strong pound and its effects on manufacturing industry

A further particular effect relating to North Sea gas was discussed at this meeting. Sterling was now very strong in the foreign exchange market, due to the tight monetary stance of the Government and to the positive effects of rapidly growing North Sea production and revenues on the balance of trade. From initial oil production in 1975 output had grown at an extraordinarily fast pace by international standards such that self-sufficiency had been achieved in 1980. The strong pound was a mixed blessing, and manufacturing industry was suffering from this, particularly in export markets. Energy prices paid by industrial consumers were now the second highest in Western Europe, and the Chancellor acknowledged that there was a strong case for alleviating the problem by reducing the Heavy Fuel Oil Duty. This had been pressed by major energy users. A big problem was the effect of doing so on the terms of the Frigg gas contract. The operation of the complex indexation formula (see Chapter 6) was to double the cost of any reduction in the Duty, with much of the benefit accruing to the licensees in the Norwegian sector. DEN lawyers and BGC had examined the contract, but there was no break clause and it would run until contract expiry. It was also noteworthy that, even if the contract could be broken, gas purchased under a revised one would be more expensive than under the existing terms. The Chancellor asked that the contract be further reviewed.

Concessions in light of imposition of SPD?

Following the decision to impose SPD consideration was given to the details and whether any concessions should be included in the forthcoming Budget in the light of the criticisms received from the industry. The notion that in the first instance it should be temporary while talks continued with the companies was considered sympathetically and Inland Revenue officials recommended that it be initially imposed for eighteen months. This period would ensure that instalments for the first chargeable period of 1982 would be collected. Consideration was also given as to whether, given the decision not to have any allowance for costs, a safety net should be provided to ensure that developments were not rendered unprofitable by SPD. Experience with the safeguard for PRT was not a reassuring precedent for its further use, and the discretionary royalty remission scheme was not attractive to the investors because of the uncertainty regarding its use. The licensees of the Buchan field had, however, proposed a limited safety net which was worthy of serious examination. Buchan was a small field where the reserves were subject to much uncertainty, and production might even cease before investment costs had been recovered. But the profile offered the prospect of high production for a short period during which substantial SPD would be paid. The licensees had suggested that if a field ceased production before its investment costs were recovered it ought to be able to reclaim any SPD to the extent that the payments contributed to the failure to recover costs. Interest on this element should not be allowed, but uplift could be given instead. Officials felt that this concession was justified. They were not convinced by the arguments of the industry against the proposed instalment provisions for SPD. Similarly, they were unconvinced that SPD would introduce distortions to decisions in late field life.

Restrictions to uplift and safeguard

Meanwhile the details of the modifications to the uplift and safeguard allowances for PRT had to be finalised. The main objectives were to increase the tax base and to reduce the incentives to incur wasteful expenditures. Restrictions to the availability of uplift could readily be expressed in relation to a number of years from first production, but a more meaningful formulation would be in relation to the field payback period. This would protect fields which took a long time to recover their investment costs from production revenues, and this was eventually agreed to be the most sensible definition, even though it was legislatively complex and could involve some future revenue losses compared to a tougher restriction. It would also be consistent with the definition of a tax which would remain creditable under the US Treaty, a subject which was still not resolved. Given the preference for a definition for uplift based on payback it was logical that the length of the safeguard period should also be expressed in relation to payback. Experiments were conducted with different percentages of the payback period to highlight the effects on tax revenues, and eventually a formula was agreed which stated that the safeguard period would be 1.5 times the payback period. In calculating the field payback period the definition of outgoings would include all allowable expenditures plus uplift, royalties and the new SPD.

BNOC stops proposal to develop satellite of Thistle field

At this late stage in the Budget process consideration had to be given to a letter received from BNOC stating that the company was now withdrawing its proposal to develop a satellite of the Thistle field at least in part due to the SPD and PRT tax proposals. Mr Rees was advised by the Inland Revenue that this project was probably sub-economic on a pre-tax basis, that it would have been subsidised by the tax reliefs, and Ministers should lose no sleep if it was abandoned. In any case increases in oil prices should rescue the project.[14]

Sir Geoffrey's budget proposals

The Chancellor then submitted a Minute to the Prime Minister on his oil taxation proposals. The SPD would initially be imposed for a temporary period to allow further consultation, but the Chancellor expected it to become permanent. In his Minute Sir Geoffrey gave his view that the industry had generally accepted the view that his proposals were justified by current North Sea economics. This was disputed by Mr Howell who felt that the industry had only accepted a temporary levy, and not the case that there was longer term scope for collecting more economic rent from the North Sea. Mr Howell was also unhappy about the new tax starting off on a monthly payments basis, which, while convenient for smoothing the PSBR, could have serious effects on the industry's cash flows. He was also concerned that the introduction of the PRT changes at the initial stage of the Finance Bill before creditability under the US Treaty had been established carried substantial risks. It would be less risky to continue discussions with the US authorities and introduce the PRT changes later, perhaps at the Committee stage. In the event the Prime Minister expressed agreement with the Chancellor's proposals and these were announced in the Budget on 10th March 1981. It contained all the main measures discussed above.

Debate with industry during Finance Bill

The debate with the industry continued with much correspondence especially during the passage of the Finance Bill. The industry expressed continued concern with both the SPD and PRT proposals. With respect to SPD UKOITC requested some technical amendments, including a substantial one that any SPD allowance unused in one year be carried forward or backwards. Officials advised Mr Rees not to allow this as it would be expensive in terms of revenues lost, and it was not clear that the resulting redistribution of tax among fields would be more satisfactory. A more positive response was given to representations that the advance payment arrangements could in some circumstances result in hardship. In the early years of field life with rising production, and thus also SPD liability, the advance payments being related to payments in the previous period would lag behind the likely eventual liability, while with falling production the opposite would be the case. It was recognised that occasionally short-run cash flow problems could arise where field production dropped sharply from one period to another (perhaps because of a problem with the field). It was decided that a concession could be given in such a case to the effect that, if in a calendar month no production took place, one instalment of advance payment could be withheld. This would deal with the problems of interrupted production and cases where production declines were steep.

Several PRT issues were raised by the industry. Thus UKOITC argued that the restriction of uplift to investment incurred before field payback on the grounds that later expenditures could be financed from cash flows was unduly restrictive, and that investment in satellite developments and enhanced oil recovery should qualify. They could well require borrowing to finance the expenditures. Uplift should also apply when a field slipped into the red after payback. Further, the payback computation should include abortive exploration costs and exempt gas expenditures and revenues. UKOITC also argued that incremental expenditure on satellite developments would attract tax relief at a lower rate than the tax on the related income. Officials felt that a concession could be given for a situation where payback was temporarily achieved, by allowing the PRT loss provision to operate for the (hopefully temporary) period. They were not persuaded that abortive exploration costs should be included in the payback calculation on the grounds that they were not field costs, and in any case could be relieved against the income from other fields. They were also not persuaded that exempt gas costs and revenues should be included in the payback calculation. The argument of the companies was that positive net cash flow was not attained until *all* revenues started to exceed *all* costs, but the point was felt to be too esoteric to justify the necessary complex legislation.

Uplift and phasing of committed investment in Beryl field

The companies continued with their lobbying. An interesting case was the representation by Mobil on behalf of the Beryl field licensees that, prior to the Budget, they had committed to investment in a second platform (Beryl B) on the understanding that uplift would be available for the expenditure. But this would take place after the field had attained payback and so it would no longer be available. If they had known that uplift would be withdrawn the investment would not have been sanctioned. The transitional provisions in the Finance Bill that protected expenditure incurred before 1983 under contracts entered into before 1981 provided some, but not enough, help. It was acknowledged that the licensees had made a noteworthy point but, it was also felt that the combined set of tax increases did not hit the Beryl field unduly harshly, and no concession was felt to be necessary.

Contractor financing and milestone contracts

Another issue on which continued representation was made concerned contractor financing. The Finance Bill contained a clause which denied PRT relief on contracts lasting more than six months under which payments were made later than on a prescribed minimum pattern. This was to prevent interest relief being given in a disguised form. The minimum period proposed in the Bill was three months in proportion to work performed or expenditure incurred by the contractor. This was designed to conform with normal commercial practice. While the oil companies did not dispute the approach they were unhappy about the detailed provisions, which they felt would catch *bona fide* contracts. UKOITC was concerned about milestone contracts, where it was not possible at the start of a contract's life to determine how long the intervals would be between milestone payments. UKOITC was also concerned about small contracts and recommended exemption of those whose value was less than £10 million. These and several other proposed technical changes were considered by the Inland Revenue, and eventually it was agreed that (1) contracts with total considerations of less than £10 million would be exempt, (2) the overall limit noted above would be changed to nine months and the limit for individual instalments to six months, and (3) the test on the reasonableness of the timing of payments would be made when the contract was made disregarding subsequent variations due to slippage or disputes.

Overriding royalty and liability for SPD

A quite different submission was made by Ranger Oil. This related to an 8% over-riding (tax free) royalty which the company had given in 1976 in order to facilitate its share of project finance for the Ninian field. Ranger argued that the new SPD should fall on the royalty owner rather than itself because SPD was fundamentally different from PRT and thus a different treatment of overriding royalty was required. It was recognised that the company had a problem but no concession was given. In a letter to the chairman of Ranger Oil Mr Rees argued that the PRT rules established in 1975 with respect to overriding royalties should continue to apply with SPD, and produced the remarkable argument that the new tax was not sufficiently distinct from PRT to justify changing the precedent established for that tax. Making a change as suggested by Ranger would also involve complex legislation.

  The controversial Bill was subsequently enacted on the lines discussed above. The result was a tax régime involving the highest level of prospective take ever seen in the UKCS. Oil prices had also reached their highest level at the beginning of the year. But by the time the new measures were enacted oil prices were falling and many of the assumptions underlying the case for the SPD were open to question.

Gas Levy

This period also saw the introduction of another new imposition in the form of the Gas Levy. It originated from the growing realisation in 1979 that, with the sharp increase in oil prices, gas prices were becoming increasingly out of line with their market values. By late 1979 the Government had decided that substantial increases in gas prices to consumers were appropriate. On 16th January 1980 Mr Howell announced that domestic tariffs would increase by 10% per year over and above the (considerable) rate of inflation for the three years commencing 1980/81. At the same time the Government set BGC a financial target for the same three years of securing an average return before tax of 9% on net assets valued at current cost. BGC would then receive large windfall profits, and studies were undertaken on the most appropriate way to ensure that the nation as a whole captured the benefits. In February 1980, a joint DEN/Treasury paper was prepared on the subject. The source of the excess profits was the access by the Corporation to large supplies of gas exempt from PRT at prices well below their market value. Currently not all the economic rent was collected by BGC with a considerable element going to consumers. The proposed price increases would gradually remove this, and any new tax should be related to the share of the resulting economic rent which the Government wished to collect. BGC's pricing and financial targets had already been determined resulting in its expected profits rising from £654 million in 1980/81 to £1,511 million in 1982/83.

Any tax should not undermine BGC's efficiency, which involved continued keen purchasing of gas and exploration and production in the UKCS. Thus the tax should be related only to PRT-exempt gas which was where the economic rent arose. Four taxes were considered. The first was to remove the PRT exemption. But it would not be practicable to impose PRT on these fields without renegotiation of the contracts between BGC and the oil companies. The gas prices would have to rise to something like the Frigg market price which was expected to be around 17 pence per therm in 1980/81. But the negotiations with the companies would be difficult, and complex legislation on allowable cost offsets for taxation would be required. It was unlikely that the tax could appropriate to the state all the increase in the companies' revenues and thus there would be some loss to the PSBR. A large part of such losses would accrue to non-UK companies. The renegotiated prices could result in BGC making substantial losses. This approach was therefore not recommended.

The second possibility was to introduce a new tax on gas production. It was likely that the tax could be passed on to BGC and would thus reduce its profits. The tax could be expressed in terms of pence per therm of PRT-exempt gas and the level could be such as not to cause a loss to BGC nor disturb the pricing decisions already taken, though BGC's financial target would have to be adjusted. An advantage of the tax was that it would appear as a cost in BGC's accounts, and would reduce its profits which had presentational advantages. But complex primary legislation and administration would be involved, and it would be seen by the oil companies as another destabilising element in the North Sea tax system and would probably be opposed by them. A gas production tax was thus not recommended.

The third possibility was to set a levy on BGC's purchases of PRT-exempt gas. This gave most of the advantages of a production tax with fewer of the disadvantages. It would appear as a cost, reduce BGC's profits, and thus reduce public interest in the size of the Corporation's profits. BGC's financial target would require amendment. But it would affect BGC only and not the rest of the industry. It could be expressed in pence per therm on BGC's purchases of PRT-exempt gas. There was merit in this approach.

The fourth possibility was to set a lump sum levy, calculated by reference to the economic rent arising from PRT-exempt gas, against BGC's profits. It would be administratively more simple, but would have fewer presentational advantages. It could have a disincentive effect on BGC's purchasing and investment decisions. It was not recommended.

Determining size of levy

Officials had calculated that the prospective economic rent available from PRT-exempt gas could be around £2 billion per year which would involve a levy of 10–12 pence per therm. But with BGC's profits estimated to rise from £654 million to £1,511 million over the target period such rates of levy would result in BGC making losses or the need to impose further increases in domestic gas prices. The objective should be to set the levy at a rate which would remove from BGC as much of the economic rent as possible while leaving its profits at a commercially justifiable level, and which would avoid a major public disagreement with the Corporation. As an indication of the possibilities it was estimated that a levy rate of 1 pence per therm in 1980/81, 2.5 pence in 1981/82 and 5 pence in 1982/83 would leave BGC with an average return of around 5% per year on current cost assets over the target period. This would collect around half the expected rent in the period.

Effect of Gas Levy on PSBR and public expenditure

The complex effects of the levy on the PSBR and public expenditure had also to be considered. The effect on the PSBR would be neutral because the levy would replace corporation tax and deposits into the National Loans Fund (NLF) which BGC would otherwise have made. The effect on public expenditure was more difficult to estimate, because BGC's NLF deposits reduced public expenditure whereas corporation tax and the levy were receipts. The net effect would be to increase public expenditure by the amount by which BGC's NLF deposits were reduced. This was an inconvenient effect of converting a large element of BGC's profits from NLF deposits (which reduced total net new borrowing) into a tax receipt (which increased Government revenues). The prospective increase above planned public expenditure levels was very large, and, while this had little significance for the economy, there were presentational implications.

Ministers concerned about presentational aspects

The paper was discussed at a Ministerial meeting chaired by the Prime Minister on 26th February 1980. The key recommendations were readily agreed, but Ministers were concerned about the presentational aspects. Thus to call the new imposition a tax and announce it in the Budget could be misunderstood as a new burden on gas consumers. The announcement should thus be made separately and legislation could be held over until the next session of Parliament. The title of the levy should associate it explicitly with the North Sea, and the concept of a rent could be incorporated with some such title as North Sea Gas Rental Levy.[15]

Officials advised that a technical issue also pointed towards separate legislation. This was the danger that the clauses dealing with the issue would make the Bill hybrid because there was at least one purchaser of PRT-exempt gas other than BGC. If the levy were to apply to *all* gas purchases by BGC the danger of hybridity was increased, but the Corporation was also purchasing gas subject to PRT. A further complication was the precise definition of gas for purposes of deciding whether the clauses would be hybrid. Given the doubts it was agreed that separate legislation was appropriate.

Inland Revenue notes limitations of flat-rate levy

While Ministers had readily agreed to a flat-rate levy, perceptive comments were made by Inland Revenue officials on its limitations. Thus the prices paid by BGC for PRT-exempt gas varied considerably from around 3 pence per therm to around 11 pence. A flat-rate levy would thus impact differently on the total gas acquisition costs. It was even conceivable that the impact of the levy could result in BGC paying more for PRT-exempt gas than for PRT-paying gas. There might be a temptation for BGC to renegotiate their gas purchase contracts such that the PRT exempt status was lost. This would produce the possibility of a choice between the levy route and the PRT route. If the basic aim of the levy was to secure as much as possible of the economic rent without adding to distortions, it would be more logical to relate the amount of levy payable to the price BGC was paying, with lower-priced gas having a higher rate of levy. A multi-rate levy would have some additional administrative problems, but would be conceptually sounder and more easily justified. However, the argument of simplicity with the flat rate levy was felt to be decisive.

Studies on details of levy

Mr Howell announced to Parliament on 8th May 1980 that the Government had agreed in principle to impose a levy on BGC's purchases of PRT-exempt gas. The details were not yet determined but the Corporation's financial targets would be adjusted accordingly, and no further increase in gas prices would ensue. Thereafter further work was undertaken, by the DEN, Treasury and Inland Revenue on the form and amount of the levy and how negotiations with BGC should be handled. Estimates (inevitably subject to large assumptions) were made of the economic rent likely to accrue to BGC. It was found that some economic rents were obtained from non-exempt fields including Norwegian Frigg gas, but it was decided that any attempt to include this would be opposed by the Norwegians, and inclusion of non-exempt gas generally could distort BGC's purchasing decisions. The calculations were thus restricted to PRT-exempt gas.

It was found that if the levy were set at a level which removed *all* the economic rent from BGC the Corporation would at best make only a small profit. This would be strongly resisted by the Corporation, but would also be difficult to justify because (1) the calculations were the subject of much uncertainty, and BGC could certainly challenge DEN's employment of marginal costs rather than full costs, (2) setting the levy at 100% of the economic rent would have a disincentive effect on BGC, and could reduce its incentive to negotiate for and exploit cheap gas, and (3) the overall system would be more penal than the PRT plus royalty scheme.

The setting of the amount of the levy needed to take all these factors into account. BGC had to make provision for capital expenditures and working capital requirements. One approach would be to relate the levy to PRT and royalties. This would mean that BGC should lose around 74% of their share of the economic rent. Arguably this would constitute generous treatment of BGC as it had not been exposed to the degree of risk experienced by the oil companies. The calculation also ignored the economic rent obtained on non-exempt gas. Employing these assumptions would produce a levy per therm of 2.5 pence in 1980/81, 4.5 pence in 1981/82 and 7.5 pence in 1982/83. Because the assumptions on which the calculations were based were subject to much uncertainty, it was important to provide that the primary legislation should permit the rates to be changed by Order in Council. In negotiations with BGC the opening position could be that the full economic rent should be removed by the levy, and the Corporation would have the opportunity to argue for lower rates. It was agreed that the DEN should have responsibility for the administration of the levy on the grounds that (1) it was closely connected with gas industry economics for which DEN had responsibility, and (2) the further it was removed from the Treasury the less it looked like a tax. It was decided that the imposition be called the Gas Levy.

Announcement of rates of Gas Levy

Much discussion and negotiations ensued, particularly on the appropriate amounts of levy. Eventually it was agreed that the rates of levy for the years 1980/81 to 1982/83 should be 1 pence, 3 pence and 5 pence per therm respectively. The Secretary of State for Energy revealed these in mid-February 1981 in his speech on the Second Reading of the Gas Levy Bill. It was emphasised that the rates were consistent with the gas pricing policy announced earlier. The arguments for the

Levy were on the lines discussed above. BGC's financial target was revised for the three-year period to an annual return of 3.5% on net assets valued in current cost terms, reflecting the announced rates of Gas Levy. One clause dealt with a particular issue relating to gas banking, stipulating that where gas was stored in a partially depleted gas field it should not be double-charged to the Gas Levy. This issue was later to prove troublesome. The Bill was quickly passed and the Gas Levy Act became effective in March 1981.

Reflections on tax increases

The passing of the Gas Levy Act and Finance Act of 1981 saw the (prospective) share of North Sea oil and gas revenues taken in tax and royalties at its highest. It coincided with the time of the highest oil prices in real terms in the 20th century which was a main justification for the remarkably high marginal rates. It was also the culmination of a series of substantial changes since the 1975 Act which established the basic package of North Sea taxation. The obvious questions are the justification for all the changes and their consequences. Oil prices rose from an average of just under $12 per barrel in 1975 to an average of nearly $37 in 1980 and $36 in 1981, with a brief spot market peak of around $40 at the beginning of the latter year. These prices were certainly not anticipated by the Government, nor indeed by anyone else, when the 1975 package was designed. The expected economic rents as seen at the end of the 1970s were substantially greater than when perceived in 1975. That could justify some discretionary changes to the tax system. Whether it justified so many modifications is much more debatable. One change sometimes led to the need to make further changes. Thus the increases in the PRT rate to 60% and then 70% highlighted and exacerbated the issue of incentives to incur wasteful expenditures, which in turn led to the modifications to the uplift and safeguard provisions.

The discretionary changes to PRT also reflected the decision in 1975 not to have a tax system where the rate was directly and progressively related to the profitability of investments. This would have required a scheme with more than one rate of tax and the opposition to this notion in 1975 remained through the period of reassessment in 1980 despite its growing acceptance elsewhere. The only perceived alternative was to make discretionary changes but with the retention of a single PRT rate.

The most controversial change was certainly the addition of SPD as a fourth element in the tax package. A tax based on gross revenues minus a volume allowance was clearly inconsistent with the philosophy of the 1975 package which emphasised the profit-related nature of any special taxation on North Sea oil. It was payable before investment costs were recovered, whereas a key feature of PRT was to permit prior recovery of investment costs. The choice of SPD was essentially dictated by considerations of short-term macroeconomic management. Had there not been a major PSBR problem in the early 1980s the SPD would not have been introduced at all. It was an example, but by no means the last one, of the needs of macroeconomic policy taking precedence over energy policy. There was a certain irony in these needs leading a Government elected on a tax reduction manifesto increasing marginal rates to over 90%.

The question of the effects of the evolving tax increases on North Sea activity levels has no easy general answer. The 1979 increase was almost certainly absorbed by the companies without noticeable negative effects on exploration or development. The 1981 increases almost certainly had negative effects. Through that year of very high oil prices no new field development approvals occurred. This was a unique experience. At least three new developments – Andrew, Tern, and Eider – were postponed with the tax increase being mentioned as a factor. The system was designed for a situation of continually rising oil prices, and by the time the 1981 Finance Bill was enacted the price was falling from its high point. The four-tier scheme was already becoming unsustainable.

With respect to gas the decision to raise gas prices to their market values and to ensure that the ensuing economic rents were collected to the nation as a whole rather than being received by BGC and gas consumers was conceptually correct. The Gas Levy was clearly a very blunt instrument. A fixed amount per therm has different effects depending on the wholesale field gas price. Further, it would impact differentially on the incentives facing BGC in buying incremental gas (requiring incremental investment) from different fields. BGC would certainly take into account the effect of the Levy in determining the price it would offer to the producer. In a high cost field with a relatively high price reflecting costs, the addition of the Levy could result in contracts otherwise satisfactory to the two parties being impossible to conclude. A scheme whereby the size of the Levy was inversely related to the wholesale price would have been more efficient. Given the small number of fields and contracts involved this more sensitive scheme could have been introduced with advantage.

12 Depletion and conservation policies

Government's wide-ranging powers

The 1975 PSP Act gave the Government wide-ranging controls over field developments, depletion, and conservation of production. Field development plans had to be approved by the DEN, and, where production had already commenced, temporary consents were given until plans were submitted and approved. Limitation Notices were to be issued at the same time indicating the maximum cuts (or increases) which the Secretary of State could require. Twelve fields were covered by the temporary consents, and in the event ten of them, including large ones such as Forties, Leman, Indefatigable, and Hewett, were subject to six-monthly consents. It was recognised that it would be very difficult to enforce major changes to the development plans for these fields, and the DEN concentrated its efforts on assessing the plans for new fields. For fields which were commercial in 1976 the Limitation Notices specified the maximum cut at 22% in the first year permitted by the Varley Assurances with a reducing percentage through field life. Exceptions were made for three fields (Piper, Claymore and Thistle) where undertakings had been made by the DEN to the banks which financed their development to limit any cuts to no more than 20%.

Staged approval for new fields

DEN officials suggested to their Ministers that for new fields a scheme of staged approval should be introduced. For fields already under development it had been agreed that plans would be approved for the lifetime of the field, but officials felt that greater flexibility was desirable for new ones in order to accommodate any requirement of depletion policy. It was argued that life of field approval was not of great value because the operator could not really predict the behaviour of production at the outset, and in practice plans were subject to revision. DEN officials thus felt that there was a case for establishing review points over the life of the field. It was suggested that initial approval might be for, say, two years, followed by a second stage covering the production plateau. This would be adjusted to conform to national depletion policy. The third phase would be aimed at the maximisation of economic recovery. There might be a need to have an overriding minimum profile to safeguard the viability of the field.

UKOOA's objections to staged approvals

In April 1977 UKOOA was informed of the intention of DEN to advise their Ministers not to provide field lifetime approvals for new fields. UKOOA was predictably against the whole concept of staged approvals and persistently protested against the whole notion. If the idea were to be implemented a minimum ten-year initial period was required to enable finance to be raised for a development. DEN officials concluded that further discussions with UKOOA were unlikely to be fruitful, and recommended that staged approvals be discussed with individual licensees when they approached the DEN with a development plan.

Three-stage system

DEN Ministers agreed to this and subsequently a system evolved which generally contained three stages, all of which were agreed from the outset. The first involved approval of the field development and base production plan. The second provided that specified production cuts could be imposed if required for depletion policy. These would take the Varley Assurances into account. The third element involved a side letter giving the licensee some assurances. The first two stages were intended to cover a production period sufficiently long to ensure cost recovery plus a significant profit to the licensee. In practice the periods were often around four years for each stage. During the first stage a review of the field's performance would be made by the DEN with a view to the production of a plan for the remainder of field life. The purpose of the side letter was to provide some assurances regarding extension of the first stage if first field production was delayed. (This was a common phenomenon at the time.) The letter also assured the licensee that production could continue after expiry of a consent, and indicated that the DEN would not require uneconomic investment as a condition of third stage approval. By 1980 ten fields had been developed under this system.

Beatrice field development plans

A specific case involving much publicity where the DEN invoked its development consent powers to the full occurred with the Beatrice field which was discovered by Mesa Petroleum in 1976 in the Moray Firth (Block 11/30) only twelve miles from shore. The oil was very waxy, and from an environmental viewpoint there was a concern that if a spill occurred the oil would soon reach the shore. The Moray Firth was a rich fishing ground and the fishermen's organisation was unenthusiastic about the development. Mesa Petroleum favoured a development plan based on offshore tanker loading via a 250,000 dwt tanker which could store more than one million barrels in heated conditions (because of the waxy nature of the oil). The company preferred this system because of the perceived difficulties in transporting the waxy crude by pipeline.

Pipeline or offshore tanker loading and environment

The DEN was not satisfied with this proposal because of the environmental risks and a concern that the pipeline option had not been comprehensively examined. Mesa's consultants had argued that the risk of a spill was no higher with offshore tanker loading than with a pipeline. The DEN appointed two engineering consultants, one to advise on the offshore loading system and the other to study the pipeline scheme followed by tanker loading from a terminal. The first study expressed doubts about the offshore loading option, especially the tanker mooring arrangement, and the other reported favourably on the use of an insulated pipeline to shore. The company was then advised that an offshore loading scheme would not be approved.

Development plan and depletion policy

Mesa subsequently prepared a new development plan based on a pipeline to Nigg Bay where the company actually had the luxury of a choice between two possible terminal locations. This scheme involved both higher cost and delay to first oil compared to the tanker loading scheme. Before the (staged) development could be approved the DEN pressed the company to make faster progress with the participation negotiations. The DEN also considered whether the development of the field should be delayed as part of depletion policy. (As the field had been discovered after 1975 it was not protected by the Varley Assurances.) DEN officials saw that the field's plateau production, while small in absolute terms, could well coincide with the period when aggregate UK production would be at around its peak. But there were arguments against development delays. No intimation of the possibility had been given to Mesa throughout the protracted discussions over their development plan (which itself caused a substantial delay). The Scottish Office was concerned about the dearth of orders for the offshore construction industry at this time (1978) and favoured no further delays. The Treasury was also against delay on the grounds that earlier oil production was advantageous on macroeconomic grounds. Ministers wisely decided against further delay and development approval was given in August 1978.

Gas flaring and reinjection

The 1975 PSP Act also gave the Government powers to control gas flaring and reinjection. The issue applied particularly to associated gas, and the DEN had concluded that flaring should not be permitted unless a strong case was made that there was no sensible alternative. It was appreciated that this would often be the case, especially when the volumes of gas were small and the transportation cost very large. Of the very early oilfields both Argyll and Auk clearly qualified, and were given flaring consents for entire field life. It was also appreciated that temporary flaring would be necessary in the early years of a field's life when gas pipelines or terminals were not ready until some time after early oil production. In these circumstances gas reinjection was desirable, but, in practice, if the necessary equipment (such as for compression) had not yet been installed, requests would be made for temporary flaring. In other cases it was possible that the DEN's assessment of the economic viability of a gas collection scheme might differ from that of the licensee. The DEN was also expected to take a wider national view of the matter, including the gathering of gas from a group of fields, perhaps even via a communal pipeline.

Problem of gas flaring on pre-1975 Act fields

Thus when field development plans were examined the DEN sought to ensure that alternatives to flaring were fully examined, and in any case flaring minimised (within an economic framework). But while this could readily be undertaken for new fields under the 1975 Act there were serious constraints for fields where developments had already taken place. For example, if gas processing equipment had not been installed in a platform, retrospective installation could be extremely expensive and could also be constrained by lack of space. A further dilemma for the Government was the possible conflict of gas flaring restrictions with the need to encourage oil production. The Parliamentary and wider interest at this time was primarily in the waste of a useful fuel rather than a concern over the potentially harmful atmospheric emissions. Consents were normally given for three-month or six-month periods to permit examination of changes in circumstances.

Case of Forties field

The DEN had to deal with some difficult cases in the second half of the 1970s. One was the Forties field which in 1978 accounted for around 25% of gas flared in the UKCS. The original development plan had made no provision for gas collection above that required for fuel on the platforms and the Natural Gas Liquids (NGLs) which could be transported with the oil in the pipeline to Grangemouth. BP, in conjunction with the DEN, had considered several options for collecting the gas, including methanol production, participation in a gas gathering scheme and power production, but all had been found to be uneconomic. The volumes flared were substantial because the field was very large, but the gas: oil ratio was quite low.

When the DEN obtained powers to control flaring BP was given a consent for two years, but in early 1977 the company found that it was unable to keep under its consent limit because hydrocarbon production and the gas: oil ratio were both higher than anticipated. The DEN agreed that flaring could be increased from 35 mmcf/d in 1976 to around 100 mmcf/d in 1977. Oil production was increasing from 400,000 b/d to around 500,000 b/d which, of course, was welcome on other grounds.

But the large gas flaring was disconcerting, and consents were then given for shorter periods, and the company was asked to re-examine schemes for conserving the gas. BP appointed consultants to examine various schemes including bringing the gas onshore with a new pipeline or building a pipeline to the Piper platform from whence it would go to the Frigg pipeline. Unfortunately the conclusions of the studies were that neither of these schemes were economic. This was accepted by the DEN and limited consents with regular reviews with the company resulted.[1]

Case of Brent field

The second major case was with the Brent field. It was also extremely large and had a high gas: oil ratio. The field development plan produced by Shell in April 1974 foresaw oil production commencing in 1976 and gas sales in October 1977. There was thus no justification for the installation of expensive compression facilities to reinject the gas for this short period. Unfortunately several slippages occurred in the development programme, and in June 1976 it was estimated that gas sales would commence in October 1978 at the earliest. Thus plans were made to install compression facilities on two of the platforms by October 1976 and on the other two by October 1977. These would permit gas reinjection, and the DEN accordingly gave (temporary) flaring consents for the Brent Bravo platform where oil production commenced in 1976.

But in 1977 the company reported delays in the delivery and commissioning of the compressors. The DEN's calculations now found that wasting the gas through further flaring was unjustified, and that oil production from Brent Bravo should be deferred. The platform was shut down for a time. Unfortunately delays continued and flaring consent at the platform was again refused in June 1978. DEN Ministers indicated that this would continue until the reinjection equipment became operative. These dramatic decisions highlighted the seriousness of the Government's attitude to gas conservation. During 1978 further problems involving delays occurred on the field, but on this occasion Mr Benn decided that no further reductions in oil production for 1978 would be required, and that for 1979 the flaring consents would be such as to reduce oil production by only a modest amount. The Chief Secretary to the Treasury, with anxieties about the balance of payments and the PSBR being uppermost in his mind, readily supported Mr Benn. Flaring was closely monitored in 1979 with Shell being given strong incentives to progress the reinjection programme. When the Iranian crisis developed and the world oil market became very tight it was felt appropriate to permit more flaring. But conditions were attached, with Shell and Esso having to promise that the extra oil produced would be destined for the UK market. After the Iranian crisis subsided stricter controls were reimposed. The volumes of gas flaring in this period are seen in their historic context in Appendix 12.1.

Case of Piper field

Another example of Government pressure to reduce gas flaring related to the Piper field. In this case the DEN prompted Occidental, the operator, to progress negotiations with (a) BGC for the purchase of the gas, and (b) Total for third party access to the Frigg pipeline to transport the gas to St. Fergus, and also to build a pipeline from the field to link into the Frigg pipeline. The DEN felt that these pressures led to the conservation of gas from an earlier date than would otherwise have been the case.

Working Group on Depletion Policy

Several detailed reviews of the wider aspects of depletion policy were undertaken in the period from the mid-1970s to the early 1980s. In September 1975 an Inter-Departmental Working Group on Depletion Policy (WGDP) was set up. It was chaired by the DEN and included representatives from the Treasury, FCO, CPRS, and the Scottish Economic Planning Department (SEPD). Much work was undertaken in a relatively short time and a substantial, thought-provoking report was produced in January 1976. It considered the long-term potential of the UKCS, the Government's existing depletion control powers, and the related legal and international constraints, but the meat of the report was concerned with a discussion of the case for a restrictive depletion policy. Estimating the ultimate potential of the UKCS clearly involved major uncertainties, and for oil the central case was 3.5 billion tonnes with an upper figure of 4.5 billion tonnes.[2] This potential was clearly very substantial, but the report did note that a new UK energy supply situation would be encountered by the end of the century when reserves would be diminishing.

Four aspects of depletion policy

The case for and against a restrictive depletion policy was considered under four headings. The first was the microeconomic aspect which centred on the argument about whether oil would be more valuable to the nation if taken later or sooner. The second was the macroeconomic aspect which considered whether a restrictive depletion policy would ease the nation's macroeconomic problems of absorbing the new-found wealth and then doing without it. The third issue related to energy strategy and security, where the question was whether a restrictive depletion policy would assist the UK in adjusting to the new energy situation by the turn of the century with diminishing reserves and increasing import requirements. The fourth issue related to the offshore supplies industry where the consideration was whether a restrictive depletion policy would damage its prospects.

Microeconomic aspects

The microeconomic issue was how to optimise the benefits from North Sea over time which the Working Group interpreted as maximising the expected returns on the stock of wealth offered by the oil and gas. This involved a comparison of the returns from (1) leaving some of the oil in the ground with (2) the resources made available by depleting the oil. The return from leaving the oil under the sea was linked to the expected real oil price increase. Several long-term scenarios on what was termed the planning price for oil had been developed by the CPRS, and a central case was one where the *real* oil price grew at 3.5% per year between 1980 and 2000. The report noted that, if exploitation costs were to grow at the same pace, the profits would also grow at 3.5% per year in real terms, and this represented the return from leaving the oil in the ground. It was fully understood that the future oil price could be very different from the central CPRS projection and the report did undertake price sensitivity analysis (including a low probability case where a price crash did occur).

The expected returns resulting from oil production were also difficult to calculate. In principle they would reflect the uses made of the extra resources and the rates of return subsequently obtained. But what these might be was by no means clear, and the Working Group employed discount rates from 5% to 7% for this purpose. The maximisation of the net benefits from North Sea oil exploitation in relation to the timing of depletion then depended on (1) the level of costs in relation to prices, (2) the expected behaviour of oil prices, and (3) the discount rate employed. Several permutations of the relationships among these three variables were possible, and the report produced an illustrative range of results for fields with different ratios of unit cost to price. It was found that the higher the unit cost as a percentage of price, and the higher the growth rate in the expected oil price in relation to the discount rate, the longer was the optimal period of delay in the development of fields.[3] The report pointed out that an implication of the analysis was that it would be most unlikely to curtail output from producing fields where development costs had already been incurred and only the relatively small operating costs remained. A detailed analysis was undertaken to show how sensitive the period of optimal delay was to different combinations of oil prices, unit cost/price ratios, and discount rates. There were many permutations in the results, but the general conclusion was that on most assumptions employed, while delay did involve some modest cost, the difference in net benefits between early and late development for typical fields was not great. It would, however, be costly to delay production from fields already developed.

Macroeconomic aspects

With respect to the macroeconomic aspects of the subject the approach taken was to examine what difference the existence of North Sea oil and its rate of depletion made to a hypothetical underlying situation in which the UK had no oil. The oil was thus a bonus. The possible problems arose because of the potential scale of the finite oil resources and their possible effect on the balance of payments and exchange rate. By the mid 1980s oil production could yield resource benefits of around 4% of GDP. This was relative to the situation in which the UK would have had to import the oil and pay for it by expanding resources of equivalent value to the world price, whereas the North Sea permitted oil to be obtained at a resource cost equivalent to less than half the world price. The indirect benefit to the balance of payments was a valuable extra. Some appreciation of sterling would be expected which would penalise non-oil exports and give extra competition to home production from imports. There would be a shift of resources among markets. The extra resource benefits would initially accrue in the form of traded goods, but if this was not the national preference and other goods and services (such as infrastructure improvements) were deemed of higher priority, these shifts in resource allocation would become necessary. If North Sea oil was depleted quickly and production tailed off in the 1990s resource shifts might not take place quickly enough. The Working Party undertook simulation work indicating that, if depletion was very fast, the real exchange rate could appreciate by 10% by the end of the 1980s and would subsequently depreciate to the same extent over the next decade as resources were shifted back into the balance of payments. This was termed the re-entry period, and it was estimated that substantial resources, perhaps about 0.75% of GDP would have to be shifted into the balance of payments each year during the 1990s. This was a substantial claim on national resources.

It was estimated that the 10% real appreciation of sterling would reduce the growth of demand for traditional exports by about 2% per year in the 1980s, which would mean that by the end of that decade exports could be around 20% less than they otherwise would have been. If the UK market did not absorb any of the production lost to overseas competitors total domestic production of traded goods might fall by some 20%, which was the full amount of the resource gain from North Sea oil. It was anticipated that the effects would be smaller, as a complete mismatch between the sectors was very unlikely.

It was obviously very difficult to estimate how serious the problems of adjustment and re-entry would be. But they could be reduced by an interventionist depletion policy. It was also felt that, no matter how strict the conservationist policy, there would be some upward pressure on sterling and consequential loss of competitiveness. It was also recognised that the upward pressure on sterling could be mitigated by running current account surpluses in the 1980s and using the surplus to accumulate overseas assets (or add to reserves). Any excess assets could be utilised later when the oil started to run out.

Utilisation of benefits and depletion rate

The report also raised a further issue emanating from its analysis of the micro and macroeconomic aspects of oil depletion discussed above. This was the question of how the benefits of the North Sea oil resources should be used. Essentially this depended on how the nation wanted to spread the benefits over time and how closely this dictated the depletion rate. The Working Group emphasised the idea that North Sea oil made the nation better off only in comparison to a situation in which oil was expensive and the UK had none of its own. North Sea oil did not make the nation better off than in the days of cheap oil, and was in essence best regarded as a partial offset to the huge increase in price which had occurred in 1973–74.

But there was a choice of depleting the reserves slowly or quickly and of spreading the benefits over a longer or shorter period. In turn this would to a large extent depend on views about living standards in the 1980s compared to the

1990s and beyond. There was a presumption that all the oil revenues should not be used to increase immediate consumption and leave nothing to future generations. On the assumption that the benefits should be spread over a long period the question that then arose was whether it was better to bequeath to future generations wealth in the form of oil in the ground or in the form of more industrial plant, infrastructure, or public goods such as hospitals. Fast depletion would provide extra resources for investment in the 1980s without reducing consumption, and this would constitute one way of transmitting the oil benefits to the future.

Absorptive capacity of economy and investment opportunities

But whether this was the optimal way to spread the benefits depended on several factors. The first was whether profitable investment opportunities existed. The second was whether the economy had the capacity to absorb revenues on the likely scale. To illustrate this point it was noted that the difference between a rapid depletion policy and a self-sufficiency one could amount to around 100 million tonnes[1] per year during at least part of the 1980s, which could be translated into perhaps £3 billion per year in resource terms. If this was to be absorbed the level of national productive investment would have to be raised by around 20%. The third factor was the need to ensure that the proceeds actually were invested. This might require further investment incentives or novel policy instruments. It was felt that if all these conditions were not going to be met conservation would be a better way of spreading the benefits intergenerationally. The Working Group felt that the question of the use to which the resources released by North Sea oil should be put was so important that it should be considered further as a separate issue perhaps by another Working Group. Unless plans were made for making use of the opportunities they could all too easily be frittered away.

Advantages of no further depletion assurances and small licence rounds

The Working Group felt that on the basis of the results of the studies referred to above no further assurances should be provided beyond those given in December 1974 by Mr Varley regarding the Government's rights to require production cutbacks and delay the development of new fields. The Working Group also examined the implications of its findings for new licensing. Given the impending large excess of production over UK oil demand from fields developed under existing licences, a large new licensing round would involve the possibility of larger surpluses of production over demand. Small rounds would permit greater control and flexibility to be held by the Government. A series of small rounds would also smooth the rate at which orders flowed to the offshore supplies industry. Thus, with regard to the forthcoming Fifth Round, around 50 blocks would provide a reasonable momentum to the supplies industry, though it might not fully compensate for the peak caused by earlier licensing. The SEPD had also emphasised the need to think in terms of further small rounds following reasonably quickly after the Fifth Round. The Working Group concluded this part of its analysis by stating that the size and frequency of licensing rounds should be used as the main instruments for adjusting longer term potential oil supply.

Special issues affecting gas depletion

It was felt that there were some special features affecting gas depletion. The cost structure was different from that of oil with the transport element being a far larger component. Producing and transportation facilities generally had to be built to accommodate peak demand requirements. Marginal gas supplies could not be procured in the short-term as quickly as marginal oil. The remaining reserves (including future discoveries) were very substantial, with an estimated 32 tcf under contract, 46 tcf uncontracted dry gas (including future discoveries), and 17.5 tcf uncontracted associated gas (again including future discoveries).

BGC's depletion strategies to depend on size of reserves

BGC had considered two strategies in its 1975 Corporate Plan. The first was to take gas in line with the normal commercial rates of gas development and production. The second was to match the take of gas after 1980 to the requirements of the premium market only. BGC had also calculated that, following the microeconomic analysis discussed above for oil, if the discount rate were below 8% it would pay to rephase the gas depletion profile to a more conservationist one, with substantially less production in the 1980s and correspondingly more in the 1990s. The report also noted that the BGC calculations involved an expansion of interruptible gas sales. The Working Group's view was that in the period from 1980 onwards BGC should concentrate on the premium market only, unless discovered reserves exceeded 50–60 tcf. Further, it should consider reducing interruptible sales, avoiding any significant displacement of low-value coal or oil from the bulk heat market. Future proposals to purchase foreign gas should be tested against the uses to which the gas was likely to be put. If discovered reserves turned out to be much greater (say around 100 tcf),[5] it was by no means clear that a conservationist policy would be preferable to either exports or deep penetration into the bulk fuel market. The conclusion of the Working Group was thus that if substantial additional reserves were discovered a further study of the relative advantages of conserving them or exporting gas or selling more in the bulk fuel market should be undertaken. To put all this in perspective the actual behaviour of remaining gas reserves since 1974 is shown in Appendix 12.2 and actual production and consumption in Appendix 12.3.

Methods of implementing gas depletion policy

Because BGC had very substantial monopsony powers there were more methods available for implementing an interventionist depletion policy. Thus BGC could defer contracting for gas from a particular field or buy it on terms which permitted such a deferral. The Corporation had been doing this in its negotiations with Allied Chemicals for gas from a field in the Southern North Sea. BGC could also defer its need for UK gas by importing other gas. It could also buy a complete field and then deplete it at whatever rate was felt to be appropriate. There were, of course, constraints to these methods, especially where the gas was associated with oil. Even with dry gas the contracts were on a take-or-pay basis which involved obligations by the Corporation. The Working Group was clear that the cheapest way to match the flow of gas to the preferred depletion profile was to delay field developments. Thus the recommendation was that, if further finds of dry gas were made, BGC should be encouraged to contract for supplies in terms which gave the Corporation the right to remove the gas for future use, even though this was more expensive than a straightforward contract for more immediate supplies. It was recognised that this could not apply to associated gas, and thus it might be necessary to reduce the take from the dry gas fields to compensate for the additional flow of associated gas. BGC should be encouraged to extend its options to do this in its contracts in Southern North Sea fields. Finally, it was recommended that BGC should receive a proportion of future licences as sole or dominant licensee in gas prone areas to increase the future scope to determine depletion rates.

Energy strategy and oil/gas depletion

With respect to energy strategy the Working Group was clear that North Sea oil supplies would be diminishing by 2000 when the world was likely to be moving into oil scarcity. Increased reliance would be placed on coal and nuclear power, and, although postponing oil production could not solve the problems of adjustment to a new energy supply situation, it would buy extra time for making the necessary adjustments. The Working Group concluded that, while the difference between slower and faster depletion policies did not greatly affect the nature of the necessary adjustment, slower depletion would offer greater security of supply over a longer period as well as providing more adjustment time.

Depletion rate and offshore supplies industry

With respect to the offshore supplies industry it was clear that the rapid development in the early 1970s had produced a bunching of orders and an expansion of the offshore supplies sector which was likely to peak in 1977 or 1978. The industry needed a steady flow of orders from the home market, and from 1978 onwards depletion policy would have an important influence on its fortunes. The Working Group concluded that, with the exception of production cutbacks, restrictive depletion policies would reduce employment in the offshore supplies industry, and would damage its future prospects. But several other factors were relevant to depletion policy decisions.

Need to preserve flexibility to operate restrictive policy

The overall conclusions of the Working Group were that it was desirable to hold output below the sharp peak which would result from a policy of rapid depletion. It was not possible to establish a precise, optimal profile at present. In the meantime the Government should preserve as much flexibility as possible to operate a restrictive policy should developing circumstances show this to be in the nation's best interests. No further commitments should be made which would restrict the Government's ability to intervene. Further reviews should be undertaken.

Varied views within Treasury and DEN

Unsurprisingly, given the nature of the subject, the report was a compromise and individual views within the Treasury and DEN varied considerably. One queried the employment of the discounting process and calculation of net present values from fields on the grounds that this could only relate to the welfare of the present population. Future UK populations might not be impressed to know that the oil revenues had mostly been enjoyed in the 1980s. Intergenerational equity demanded that the resources released by North Sea oil should be converted into real assets of at least equivalent expected return. This could slow down depletion considerably. Another view favoured fast depletion on the grounds that it would significantly ease the balance of payments constraints which had reduced the UK's ability to achieve adequate investment and growth.

Ministers request further reviews and study of utilisation of benefits

The report was considered by a Ministerial Committee under the chairmanship of the Prime Minister on 13th April 1976. The key elements of the Working Group's report were endorsed, and officials were requested to prepare further reviews and to commence work on a separate study on how the additional resources generated by North Sea oil could be best used.

Review of December 1976

Accordingly, the Working Group was reconvened some months later in October 1976. It undertook the first review of depletion policy and produced its report in December of that year. This was much shorter than the original review and did not add much of substance. The estimates of ultimately recoverable oil reserves were unchanged, though the proportions in the probable and possible categories were increased. Production was coming on stream more slowly than anticipated earlier due to technical, design, weather, and procurement problems. Consequently the expected production profile was now projected to rise less steeply to a lower peak and flatten out during the 1980s at around 130 million tonnes per year. Production for 1980 and 1981 was now expected to be 15–20 million tonnes per year below earlier forecasts. UK oil demand forecasts had not been significantly changed, and still showed a rising trend from 1980 onwards to 135 million tonnes in 1990.[6] The behaviour of UK oil production and consumption since 1974 is shown in Appendix 12.4 and, for completeness, remaining oil reserves are shown in Appendix 12.5

Since the first report a full Energy Policy Review had been undertaken by the DEN.[7] This had highlighted the potential benefits that an active depletion policy could make to the problem of adjusting the UK energy economy around the end of the century to a situation when oil production was running down, coal and nuclear might be difficult to expand at the necessary pace, and imported energy might be costly. Depletion policy could help by providing more time for the necessary adjustment by ensuring a slower oil decline rate.

Depletion policy instruments

With respect to policy instruments licensing arrangements were the most appropriate for determining the broad area within which future production should lie. The report then discussed how the powers obtained under the 1975 PSP Act should be implemented. Of the fields discovered prior to the end of 1975 and now declared commercial fourteen were operating under temporary consents. The Limitation Notice arrangements now in force should incorporate the full extent of cutback provisions[8] unless there were strong arguments for relaxation. Cutbacks could not be implemented until 1982 at the earliest, but there was a potential to defer around 70 million tonnes from 1982–1988 to later years. For fields discovered before the end of 1975 but not yet declared commercial the same maximum discretionary Government scope was recommended. There was a potential to defer 30 million tonnes to the 1990s. The general idea was that the Government should retain maximum flexibility to react to the evolving conditions.

Second review, September 1977

A second review was produced in September 1977. The tenor was somewhat different from the first review, with doubts on the macroeconomic benefits of a more conservationist policy given more emphasis. There was a small downward shift in the estimates of oil reserves. The oil production forecasts were increased for 1980, but significantly reduced for the period 1982–1990, with a maximum of 125 million tonnes being attained in 1982. But the estimates of UK oil demand were also reduced somewhat. The Working Group had now taken a more pessimistic view of long-term oil price prospects indicating that it would rise even more steeply, at least doubling and perhaps trebling in real terms by 2000. This would, of course, reinforce the case for a more conservationist policy. Despite this, however, further macroeconomic considerations pointed to the need for faster depletion. Thus the domestic resources of the UK were underemployed and this could continue even until the mid-1980s. Increasing North Sea oil production would make it easier to achieve full employment and a satisfactory balance of payments. Even if oil output were unrestricted in the period to, say, 1985, the balance of payments might not be strong enough to permit the attainment of full employment of resources. Extra North Sea oil output would make it possible to put to use resources which otherwise would have remained idle. It was acknowledged that the advantages of early depletion would depend on the uses to which the resources derived from North Sea oil were put.

Effects of depletion restrictions on returns on investment

The Working Group had carried out an analysis of the effects of production cutbacks and development delays on the returns to field investments. Cutbacks imposed after an investment had been made would certainly be unpalatable to the companies involved, though production from the affected fields would continue. Development delays were likely to be more acceptable, and the Working Group felt that, having examined the effects of three and six year delays on the returns to investment (internal rate of return and net present value), the delays were unlikely to deter the undertaking of the projects.

Effects on offshore supplies industry

With respect to the effects on the offshore supplies industry it was noted that employment in the sector was now over 100,000, with a large proportion being located in Scotland. The Working Group surprisingly felt that employment had now passed its peak and would decline as the high level of exploration and development activity was now over! It was felt that a two-year development delay on post-1975 discoveries would depress platform orders from 1979 onwards and virtually eliminate new ordering by 1982. This would threaten the survival of the construction yards. In general in the debates on depletion policy the fluctuating fortunes of the offshore suppliers industry were acknowledged but not given a high weighting in decisions. The extent of the large variations in activity can be seen from Appendix 8.5 showing the expenditures of the oil companies and in Appendix 12.6 showing the numbers of wells drilled.

Gas depletion and exports

With respect to gas the DEN's estimates of reserves (55 tcf) were lower than those of BGC, but were regarded as being more prudent for planning purposes. In any case it was felt that if they were, say, 75 tcf the effect would be to prolong the plateau rather than increase the peak, because the additional reserves were unlikely to be exploited before the late 1980s. The report briefly considered the possibility of exporting any surplus gas, but argued that the opportunity for exporting surpluses above UK needs was likely to be limited, and it was certainly not desirable to commit gas for export over an extended period when it could be retained for consumption later. The Working Group was aware of the rigidity in the supply of associated gas, and felt that the response should be to defer new Southern Basin gas to 1990 or later. The licensees might well be unhappy at this and might request compensation. The Government had no obligation to do so, but the Working Group suggested that BGC could purchase a lien on the gas, with the timing of its production at its own option. This possibility should be explored with BGC.

The Working Group was unconvinced that the macroeconomic arguments for early oil depletion outlined above were applicable to gas. Extra quantities of UK gas production could only be sold at reduced prices in low value, non-premium markets. Any macroeconomic benefits from earlier depletion were unlikely to outweigh the losses from selling gas in low value markets which could later be sold in premium markets. The Working Group felt that BGC should be awarded sole licences in gas prone areas to increase the Government's flexibility over the rate of depletion.

Review of May 1978 highlights sharp peak in oil production

Ministers were generally content with the report and requested further studies to be undertaken at intervals of twelve months. A third review thus commenced in May 1978. Updated studies on the production prospects were produced. In comparison to the previous study the new profile had a prospective uncomfortably high peak on oil production in the period 1983–85 with figures for earlier and later years being reduced. The main explanation was slippage from earlier years which pushed the peak back. A significant policy implication of the new projections was that there now appeared to be little scope for using development delays to flatten the profile and the main weapon would have to be production cutbacks.

BNOC suggests deferral of royalty as depletion policy instrument

A further element was injected into the debate by BNOC who suggested that a depletion policy instrument could be the exercise of the Government's right to take royalty oil in kind but to defer taking it. In the interim the licensees would reduce their production by that amount but would pay no royalty. A new production profile would be worked out accordingly, and later when the royalty oil was to be delivered the produced oil would notionally consist of two categories, namely royalty in kind, and production subject to tax and royalty. In principle the cash flow of the licensees should be the same as in the original profile. BNOC argued that the attraction of the scheme was its offer of a way round the Varley Assurances and so would permit production cutbacks before 1982 or from fields in what would otherwise be their initial protected periods. The device would also permit cutbacks to exceed the 20% which was the expected maximum under the Varley Assurances.

DEN officials unconvinced of merits of royalty deferral

DEN officials considered the idea at some length. It was recognised that in any revised production profile the timing of the deferral and subsequent delivery of royalty oil would require detailed specification. There would also need to be provisions dealing with the eventuality that deferred royalty oil proved not to be available because the reserves had run out faster than anticipated because of reservoir problems. It was felt that this risk would have to be imposed on the licensee. All the provisions necessary for the operation of the scheme could be devised but new legislation would be required. It would also become apparent that the purpose of the new power would be to circumvent the Varley Assurances. It was also felt that it would be very rash to defer production except on the basis of careful consideration of the characteristics of individual reservoirs. The conclusion was that, while the scheme was possible, it was not clear that it offered advantages over the other available methods.

Further review, late 1978

The third review was completed in late 1978. The central estimate of recoverable oil reserves was reduced to 3.32 billion tonnes and peak production was now anticipated to be 135 million tonnes in 1983. Slippage had occurred but self-sufficiency would still be obtained in 1980. Production was now expected to fall away more rapidly from 1987. Because the UK oil demand forecasts had been reduced the net exportable surplus in the period 1980–87 had actually increased by 40 million tonnes compared to the position with the second review.

Energy policy and macroeconomic policy have conflicting implications for depletion rate

The coincidence of the substantial fall in production from 1987 and the (revised) expectation that real oil prices could even treble by the year 2000 enhanced the energy policy argument in favour of depleting the oil resources more slowly to ensure secure supplies for energy users where oil was not easily substitutable and thus ease the transition to an energy economy where indigenous oil production would be small. The macroeconomic arguments favouring more rapid depletion remained, and one view considered was that in the early 1980s the balance of payments would continue to remain a constraint on expanding national output. It followed that currency earned from additional oil production would be regarded as having a *higher* value to the nation than its market price. But there was uncertainty about the scale of this premium attributable to increased foreign exchange earnings. Any near term benefits would also have to be set against the disadvantages of having less indigenous oil in later years when the so called re-entry problem could be very demanding.

Depletion rates and tax receipts

The Working Group raised a new issue in its third review. This was the effect of variations in the production profile on tax receipts. Development delays deferred both tax reliefs and receipts. Production cutbacks could defer substantial tax receipts, and for the period 1982–87 these were provisionally estimated at around £600 million per year.

It was acknowledged that the offshore supplies industry would suffer from development delays, and discontinuity in orders could cause severe local unemployment, and could even imperil the maintenance of an efficient, competitive industry, but no easy solutions to the problem were evident.

BGC has enhanced flexibility in contracts

With respect to gas the Working Group now felt that the estimate of the remaining potential could be increased from 55 tcf to 70 tcf. A noteworthy development had been the renegotiation of the large Leman and Indefatigable contracts which gave BGC substantially greater flexibility. Thus the amount of gas which the Corporation was obliged to take in the summer months was reduced from 33% of the daily contract quantity to zero. Further, the period in which BGC could make up any shortfall in take was lengthened to the life of the contracts which were now extended from 1993 to 2010. With respect to the suggestion made in the first report that BGC should be encouraged to enter into contracts for dry gas on terms which would permit it to reserve the supplies for future use, discussions had taken place between BGC and BNOC on such a possibility with a small discovery in the Southern Basin.

Case for slower depletion now stronger

The Working Group's overall conclusion was that the changes which had occurred in the period since the last review indicated a more positive case for favouring slower rather than more rapid depletion. Major changes in policy were not advocated, however. The Working Group did consider whether modifications to the Varley Assurances should be made. It was concluded that any changes which were adverse to the licensees would seriously undermine investor confidence. A further idea considered was to negotiate development delays on fields protected by the Varley Assurances in return for undertakings to mitigate cutbacks from these or other fields being produced by the same companies. A similar idea was to negotiate production cutbacks on fields protected by the Varley Assurances. Both ideas required further study. A further new idea was for BNOC to defer taking its participation oil. The perceived problem was that the companies would seek full compensation for the cash flow disadvantages to them.

Comments from Dr Owen

The report was circulated to Ministers and, perhaps surprisingly, Dr David Owen the Foreign Secretary took a keen interest and sent a detailed response to Mr Benn. His key point was that the projections of UK oil demand were very likely to be too high. He noted that they were based on economic growth rates of 3%, but recent estimates had indicated that a growth rate of 2% was more likely in the period to 1985. The consequence would be a substantially lower growth in oil demand, and the result could be an excess of UK production over UK demand of around 175 million tonnes in the period 1980–87 rather than the 145 million tonnes indicated in the report. His conclusion was that the Government should now take steps to cut the expected hump of surplus production to the maximum extent possible.

Ministers favour slower depletion rate

The report was considered at a Ministerial meeting on 14th March 1979. Mr Benn supported the views of the Working Group, though he also expressed sympathy with Dr Owen's sentiments. In discussion there was some strong support for the view that all measures short of revoking the Varley Assurances should be taken to reduce the peak in oil production in the first half of the 1980s. It was also recognised, however, that there was little scope for changing the UK's public posture at the present time, given the Iranian revolution and the consequent upsurge in world oil prices. But all this emphasised the point that the UK was fortunate to have substantial oil reserves. The conclusion of the meeting was that Ministers favoured a more conservationist policy than that recommended by officials, and, while the Varley Assurances should be upheld, the Secretary of State for Energy should arrange for officials to examine the possibilities for slowing down output growth in the first half of the 1980s. A further report should be produced later in the year.

Report to Conservative Government, September 1979

Work proceeded on this study before and after the change of Government in May 1979 and a report was completed in September. The central estimate of oil reserves was 3.3 billion tonnes. Peak production was forecast to be 131 million tonnes in 1984 followed by a rapid decline from the later 1980s onwards. Oil demand forecasts had been adjusted downwards but still exceeded 100 million tonnes per year from 1983 onwards. The aggregate exportable surplus between 1981 and 1988 was in the 140–190 million tonnes range. With oil expected to become increasingly more expensive during the rest of the century and beyond, the energy policy argument strongly favoured deferring the oil production from the peak years to the 1990s and beyond. In these calculations the central oil price assumption was a real annual growth of around 4.5%, and the discount rate 5% in real terms.

Major change in assessment of macroeconomic aspects

In this fourth review there was a very substantial change in emphasis on the assessment of the macroeconomic aspects. Thus, while North Sea oil increased the UK national income, its impact on the balance of payments was likely to cause a rise in the real exchange rate with a consequential loss of industrial competitiveness. Much of the improvement in the oil account would be offset by a deterioration in the non-oil trade account. Some loss of competitiveness would ensue and the profitability of the open sectors of the economy would suffer. In due course when oil production fell these effects on competitiveness would be reversed. The scale of the appreciation in the exchange rate would depend on how the additional North Sea income was used, in particular whether it was spent, or saved and invested overseas. There could be no precise link between the oil production profile and the real exchange rate. Much depended on the monetary and exchange rate policies adopted by the Government. The prospective peak in oil production increased the risks that the exchange rate profile would be similarly humped. While depletion policy could not eliminate the appreciation of the exchange rate it could smooth out the production profile and hence might help to smooth out the movements in the real exchange rate. On balance there was thus a case on macroeconomic grounds for a policy of slower depletion. The macroeconomic effects were, however, somewhat unpredictable, and the case for slower depletion rested more on the elimination of avoidable shocks.

Merit in increasing size of licence rounds to influence long term depletion

It was acknowledged that varying the size and timing of licence rounds offered no scope for influencing the production profile during its expected peak period. But it could play a useful role in moderating the rate of decrease projected for the 1990s. There was thus merit in increasing the size of rounds above those of the Fifth and Sixth Rounds. With respect to the offshore supplies industry it was anticipated that after 1981 the demand for platforms would turn down to such an extent that there would be work for no more than three of the five construction yards. By the late 1980s more field developments could come forward, but many of these would probably not require large platforms.

EEC interest in depletion policy

Depletion policy raised some international considerations especially with the EEC. The Commission had shown keen and continuing interest in the UK's policy to date. The issue of sovereignty over the resources was not in doubt, and EEC energy policy did not diminish the control exercised by individual member states over their rate of exploitation. But, following the Iranian crisis, there was pressure to remove restrictions on all indigenous energy production. A more conservationist approach could also cause difficulties if OPEC countries cited UK depletion policy as a justification for their own production restrictions.

Tougher views on gas flaring and upward profile variations

The fourth review discussed the various policy instruments on the lines of previous reports but added two more. It was argued that permission to flare associated gas had been too liberal in the past and a tougher policy was advocated. This would affect the oil depletion rate and had the advantage that it could be implemented without delay. Holding operators to their recent forecasts of gas to be flared could result in significant reductions in oil production in many fields including Brent, Forties, Ninian, and Piper. The second instrument related to upward profile variations requested by companies on fields which were performing better than anticipated when their field development plans were approved. The Government could exercise its powers to refuse requests for upward profile variations. Use of this power could be immediate and the Working Group estimated that between 1981 and 1986 some five million tonnes per year could be deferred by the use of this mechanism.

Implementation of depletion policy decisions

The report also considered when decisions should be made with the different measures and what the consequential effects would be. The licensees would have to be given reasonable warning with respect to development delays and production cutbacks. Thus the report indicated that gas flaring restrictions could be made in 1979–80. In 1984 these could achieve a maximum reduction in oil production of five million tonnes. Decisions to refuse upward profile variations should be made in 1980 and could result in a reduction in production of five million tonnes in 1984. Decisions on development delays should be made in 1979–80 and could result in a production decrease of seven million tonnes in 1984. Decisions on production cutbacks need not be made until 1981, and these could produce production decreases of sixteen million tonnes in 1984.

Report endorsed but rethink on macroeconomic aspects in Treasury

There was some delay before the report was considered by Ministers but on 11th March its general conclusions were endorsed. The detailed implementation of the recommendations needed to be worked out and DEN officials started an examination of the pros and cons of deferring the development of various fields. In the meantime, however, some rethinking on the issues was being conducted within the Treasury. The Financial Secretary, Mr Lawson, expressed scepticism regarding some of the policy instruments discussed in the Working Group's report, and felt generally that a high rate of development in the North Sea was the best way to ensure security of supply. He also expressed some scepticism regarding the effect of a fast depletion rate on the exchange rate and requested that this subject be studied further. The advice at late April 1980 was that, while North Sea oil was probably the most important single factor behind the strength of sterling the main effect operated via expectations rather than the current account. Market operators were more influenced by the fact of possession of oil rather than its rate of depletion. Scepticism was expressed on the value of depletion policy as an instrument for influencing the exchange rate, at least in the short-term. But over the medium to longer term the real exchange rate was likely to be lower with a slower rate of depletion.

Oil depletion, exchange rate, and balance of payments

The growing conventional view was that the mechanism for any sterling appreciation from North Sea oil production started from the positive effect on the trading account. The improvement would be offset by a deterioration elsewhere which could be the non-oil current account or the capital account. If the offset was via the capital account there should be no effect on the real exchange rate, but this would occur only if the North Sea income were invested in foreign assets. As this income approached in value to the North Sea take, this would probably mean that the tax revenues should be used to reduce the PSBR. The Government could then acquire foreign assets directly by intervention or induce the private sector to do so by reducing the supply of Government securities to the market.

In the absence of a long-term change in the capital account the adjustments would come via the rest of the current account. This would happen if the oil revenues were distributed to the private sector. There would be an increase in demand for non-traded goods, but an increase in the real exchange rate would be required to divert some demand to traded goods. The size of the effect on the exchange rate would depend on the value of the oil production and thus both volume and price. Thus a lower rate of production over the next few years would reduce the upward pressure on the exchange rate. To date, however, the effect of North Sea oil on expectations had been all important in causing this upward pressure. There was a substantial and growing current account deficit but massive capital inflows reflecting expectations. In the short run changes in expectations could swamp the direct balance of trade effect of changes in oil production on the exchange rate.

Industry views on depletion policy

Meanwhile the oil companies were making their contributions to the debate. UKOOA wrote to Mr Howell, the Secretary of State for Energy, arguing that, given the objective of ensuring self-sufficiency in oil and gas for as long as possible, the emphasis should be on stimulating exploration and providing incentives to develop the smaller fields. UKOOA expressed concern about the negative effects of any depletion control measures on the incentives to undertake exploration and development. BP made a detailed presentation on the subject to DEN Ministers on 17th March 1980. The company's projections of North Sea production and UK demand differed from those of the DEN, with a smoother production profile and much less sharp decline in the 1990s. Like UKOOA, BP felt that the priority should be to encourage vigorous exploration, and argued against production cutbacks, emphasising the resulting reductions in GDP. Delaying new field developments from the 1980s to the 1990s might be justified, but only if the oil price were confidently expected to increase faster than the general inflation rate. Oil exports in the 1980s were justified because of the additions to GDP thereby produced.

Chancellor's growing concern about negative effect of slower depletion on tax take

Meanwhile the Chancellor, Sir Geoffrey Howe, had become increasingly concerned about the effects of lower than expected oil production on the Government's tax take. He had become aware that the estimate for 1981 had been reduced from 100 million tonnes to 91 million with smaller reductions for 1982, 1983, and 1984, and a larger one in 1985 from 126 million tonnes to 115 million.[9] The Inland Revenue had estimated that the negative effect on Government take would be £0.4 billion in 1981/82, £0.7 billion in 1982/83, and £3.5 billion in 1983/84. This would make it more difficult to reduce the burden of taxation generally. In the circumstances the Chancellor felt that the decisions on depletion policy taken on 11th March should be reconsidered. Further reductions in production through interventionist policy would make it yet harder to meet the Medium Term Financial Strategy. In any case the reductions in the forecasts had gone a long way to reduce the prospective hump in production. The Chancellor wrote to Mr Howell on the above lines, and suggested that officials should prepare a study which would show the effects of the various depletion decisions on Government take. This should be considered before any announcement was made on depletion policy.

Further studies by Treasury on macroeconomic aspects

Discussions on the effects of North Sea oil within a macroeconomic framework continued within the Treasury. The growing concern about the PSBR was such that for 1981/82 increases in taxation (generally, not specifically on North Sea oil itself) or expenditure cuts would be required. The problems of the non-oil traded sector were now very urgent. It was felt, however, that there was unlikely to be any significant impact on the exchange rate if the rate of production growth was slowed down. The existence of oil in the ground would maintain a relatively high real exchange rate whatever the rate of production. This suggested that it would be better for manufacturing industry if North Sea oil output was relatively high in the short and medium-term as this would produce more tax revenues from the oil sector, and thus help to reduce the PSBR and interest rates which would be helpful for the non-oil sectors.

Inter-Departmental study of depletion policy measures and tax take

Following the Chancellor's letter to Mr Howell a quick study was conducted by officials from the DEN, Treasury, FCO, and CPRS on the tax revenue implications of the various depletion measures. The study did not consider production cutbacks as they could not be implemented until 1982 at the earliest. It considered the effects of gas flaring restrictions, refusal of upward profile variations, and development delays in the period to 1985. The combined loss of revenue averaged just under £150 million annually with the largest reduction being in 1982/83. By far the largest contribution to the total loss came from gas flaring restrictions. The projected loss from upward profile variations at this time (June 1980) was less than anticipated in 1979, because BP was not now expected to request an increase on the Forties field.

Mr Howell continues to favour slower depletion

Mr Howell wrote to Sir Geoffrey Howe at the beginning of July arguing that the results of the study had not changed the strategic arguments for implementing depletion policy as discussed by Ministers on 11th March. Although oil production forecasts had been reduced UK oil demand projections had also been reduced. There was therefore still a very large net exportable surplus in the mid-1980s. Mr Howell felt that it was essential on strategic and economic grounds to roll forward some of this surplus to the late 1980s and 1990s, to reduce dependence on OPEC oil which promised to be less secure then than now. The three depletion measures (excluding production cutbacks) would only roll forward a limited proportion of the net exportable surplus. The reduction in tax revenues at around £150 million per year was relatively small. They were within the margin of error in calculating the tax take. To substantially reduce the figure would involve allowing more gas flaring which was unjustifiable on conservation and energy policy grounds and could certainly not be justified to Parliament or the electorate. Development delays would, of course, increase the tax take in the period to 1985. Mr Howell's conclusions were thus that the decisions taken in March should not be reopened. If decisions on development delays and gas flaring were not taken in 1980 some of the options would be permanently foreclosed.

Treasury Minister opposes production cutbacks but favours development delays

At the Treasury Mr Howell's letter was received with concern. Mr Lawson was particularly bothered about production cutbacks which he felt were potentially dangerous. He was also worried about forbidding upward profile variations. The Chancellor replied to Mr Howell on 15th July. He accepted the need for gas flaring restrictions, but could not agree to refusal of upward profile variations and asked that reference to these be omitted in the forthcoming statement on depletion policy. He felt that consents to such requests should be approved given the pressure on the PSBR. Sir Geoffrey favoured delays to development because of their positive effect on the PSBR. He expressed particular interest in the Clyde field which was operated by BNOC, and postponement of its development would produce useful savings to the Corporation's external financing requirements and thus in public expenditure. The Chancellor then expressed great concern about the imposition of production cuts which would cause him serious difficulties through the reduced tax take. He had asked for a detailed review to be made of the taxable capacity of the North Sea to see whether there was scope for additional revenues from that source. The results of this study would have a bearing on his attitude to production cuts.

Mr Howell's statement on depletion policy

Eventually it was agreed that, while no reference would be made to restriction on upward profile variations in the forthcoming statement, this should not be taken to mean that the whole policy had been reversed. The statement was made by Mr Howell on 23rd July 1980. It emphasised the need to encourage exploration for the long-term, but also to defer some oil production from the 1980s. Given all the uncertainties there could be no rigid plan, there was a need for flexibility, and decisions on field developments would be taken on a case-by-case basis, bearing in mind the need to limit the sharpness of peak production. The Varley Assurance would be upheld. There would be tighter control on gas production. No decisions had been made on whether to impose production cuts.

Ministers discuss Clyde field development delay

The issue of the delay to the Clyde field development was discussed by Ministers in mid-September 1980. Mr Howell proposed that the development be delayed by two years on depletion policy grounds. A delay beyond five years could be held to frustrate the purposes for which the licence had been awarded. He had considered a five-year delay which would bring some gains to the PSBR over the total period of around £140 million from deferred spending by BNOC and a possible further £60 million from deferred tax relief by their partners (Shell and Esso). There were strong arguments for a shorter deferral. Thus the five platform construction yards currently had some orders, but they would be completed by late 1981 or early 1982. Further major orders were needed, and Clyde represented a clear prospect for a major steel platform order to commence in 1982. BNOC, the field operator, was currently undertaking the Beatrice field development, but, unless it was able to start the Clyde development by mid-1981, it would lose the majority of its staff which dealt with field development issues when the Beatrice project was completed. It could take the Corporation several years to recover from such a setback. Shell and Esso were fully supportive of BNOC's plans and wanted the development to proceed as soon as possible. They also felt that from a national viewpoint the contribution of the field to total production was insignificant. A two-year, but not five-year delay, was desirable on depletion policy grounds. But the Treasury argued for a five-year delay on the grounds of depletion policy but also because of the additional benefits to the PSBR. The Ministerial group found in favour of the five-year delay, but gave Mr Howell the opportunity to reopen the issue.

Representations of BNOC and reopening of issue

Following this decision Mr Shelbourne, the Chairman of BNOC, made representations about the damaging effects which the five-year delay would have on the Corporation. Without the operatorship of a development project for five years great damage would be done to its capacity as an upstream company, and the other companies might become reluctant to have BNOC as a partner. Mr Raisman, the Chairman of Shell UK, also made strong representation against the deferral of the development for five years. The issue was then reopened by Mr Howell and at a Ministerial meeting later in the year it was debated again. Mr Howell reiterated his earlier arguments, but the CPRS continued to argue for a five-year delay, emphasising the idea that, because oil prices were expected to increase at a higher rate than the field development costs, deferral would produce a substantial economic gain. Early development was an expensive way to provide employment, and BNOC should recognise the need on occasions to sacrifice short-term gains for longer-term objectives. After discussion it was agreed that the development should be delayed for two years, but on the understanding that BNOC would undertake sales of oil for advance payments such that the effect on the PSBR of a two-year delay would be the same as for a five-year delay.

Upward profile variation on Forties

Meanwhile in November 1980 BP had submitted their plans for further production from the UKCS which included a proposal for an upward profile variation from the Forties field. This led to a debate between the Treasury and DEN. The former was wholeheartedly in favour of permitting increases in near term production so long as the reservoir was not damaged with possible adverse consequences for maximisation of long-term economic recovery from the field. The sums involved were substantial. The Treasury calculated that for the first half year alone the Government take would be increased by £45 million if BP's request were granted. The DEN was concerned about the consequences of short-term increases in production later in the 1980s when aggregate North Sea output would be falling. It was also argued that deferral of some production to the late 1980s would result in a higher overall Government take on the assumption that the oil price continued to rise in real terms. Just before Christmas 1980 it was agreed that BP could increase production for the first quarter of 1981 without prejudice to decisions for subsequent periods. The Treasury calculated that BP's proposed production for all of 1981 would produce extra tax revenues of around £150 million compared to their original profile. Thus they continued to argue for the proposed increase. They were encouraged in this view by the news that production prospects for some other fields had deteriorated. Eventually on 17th February 1981 Mr Howell agreed that only considerations of good oilfield practice, but not those of depletion policy, should determine production from Forties in 1981. This concession would not prejudice decisions on production in future years.

Production cutbacks from 1982 onwards?

The debate then concentrated on the question of whether there should be production cutbacks from 1982 onwards. The Working Group on depletion policy examined this in some detail and produced a report in May 1981. There were three main considerations which affected the issue namely (1) security of supply, (2) macroeconomic factors, and (3) microeconomic factors. The latest projections indicated that UK production would exceed consumption by over 20 million tonnes in 1982. The longer term projections indicated that both production and consumption would be lower than in earlier reports with consumption in particular being greatly reduced. Thus for the period 1981–1993 there could be a net surplus of production over consumption of 236 million tonnes. Imports would grow in the 1990s. It was expected that the oil price would increase substantially in the long-term with the average annual increase possibly being around 4% in real terms. Prolonging self-sufficiency would enhance security of supply.

Microeconomic arguments favour deferral of production

The report argued that on microeconomic grounds there would be national gains from deferring production in the form of increased net value of the output even after taking into account the time value of money. The central case was based on the assumption that the dollar price of oil would increase in real terms by 4% per year and the sterling price by 5% annually. The discount rate employed was 5% which was then the standard rate for assessing public investments.

Macroeconomic arguments against production cuts

The macroeconomic arguments presented in the report were now against production cuts. There were three main reasons for this. Firstly, the expected hump in production was now flatter than envisaged in earlier studies. If future production forecasts were to follow the past pattern there would be less need to postpone production beyond the 1980s. Secondly, there was much uncertainty surrounding the relationship between oil production and the real exchange rate. The effect depended on the value of oil production not the physical quantity. The prospective profile of the gross value was much less humped than that for the volume. Further, the net exportable surplus was not felt to be very relevant for this purpose as oil consumption in the UK was not particularly affected by the existence of North Sea oil.

Complex effect of North Sea oil on exchange rate

North Sea oil had certainly improved the current account of the balance of payments though this was substantially offset by outflows of interest, dividends and capital. The effect on the exchange rate was complex. The Treasury model suggested that the net *ex ante* effect between 1979 and 1980 would be around 5%, whereas it appeared in practice that perhaps 15%–20% of the 45%–50% rise in the real rate since early 1979 was due to oil-related factors. The difference was explained by the effect of North Sea oil on expectations. Thus the upward movement of sterling came from large capital inflows inspired by a view of sterling as a petro-currency, rather than from the direct effects of North Sea production on the balance of payments. Thus the effect depended more on the possession of oil reserves than the rate of their depletion. It was not clear how relatively small changes in production rates would affect expectations and thus the exchange rate. Depletion policy was thus a highly uncertain instrument for influencing the exchange rate.

Greater need for tax revenues from UKCS

The current prospects for future total tax receipts and public expenditure had deteriorated such that the perceived need for revenues from the North Sea was noticeably greater. A slower rate of depletion in 1982 and later years would mean lower North Sea tax revenues. In the context of the Medium Term Financial Strategy (MTFS), with unchanged monetary aggregates the PSBR would increase, and there would be upward pressure on interest rates. If it were felt necessary to hold down interest rates other taxes would have to be raised or public expenditure cut. It was arguable that delaying production would do little to alter the real exchange rate but could prolong the recession. On these grounds there was a case for faster depletion because this would reduce the interval between discovery and exploitation, thus minimising the adverse impact of a deterioration in competitiveness on the economy.

Production cuts unpopular with companies

The report acknowledged that production cuts would be unpopular with the industry, but argued that such considerations were not decisive if the implementation of the cuts was done on a field-by-field basis in consultation with the companies. Similarly there might be international reaction within the IEA and the EEC but again it was felt that any problems could be overcome by consultation with the relevant bodies.

Ministers discuss production cuts

The report did not make firm recommendations to Ministers on the principle of production cuts in 1982 and beyond but invited them to make the fundamental decision. Upon receipt of the report Mr Howell submitted a Minute to the Prime Minister on 12th May briefly summarising the issue and recommended that a decision be deferred to the autumn when hopefully the wider economic uncertainties might be less. Given the need for consultation with the oil companies this meant that there could be no production cuts in the first half of 1982, but these could still be made for the second half when the net exportable surplus would be larger. On the same day Mr Hamish Gray announced in Parliament that no decisions had been made on production cuts.

The Chancellor in his Minute to the Prime Minister expressed his agreement to this postponement, but added that he saw no scope for production cuts in the life of the present Parliament. If they were made offsetting tax increases or reductions in public expenditure would be required to keep the PSBR consistent with the MTFS. The Minute from the CPRS argued in favour of production cuts despite the acknowledged macroeconomic difficulties. The enhanced security of supply and the attractive prospective return to oil as an investment in the ground outweighed the benefits of early depletion. The difficulty of finding near-term taxation revenues from other sources should be faced. Deferring a decision was not the answer and had the unfortunate consequence that no cuts could be made on the first half of 1982. Alan Walters, the Special Adviser to the Prime Minister, also submitted a Minute supporting the view that there should be no cutbacks in production. He felt that in the longer term the price of oil was just as likely to go down as to increase and so investment in oil in the ground might not bring an attractive return. Long-term security of supply could probably be better enhanced by the holding of adequate stocks of oil rather than by slower depletion.

Decision deferred and further studies undertaken

It was agreed that the decision should be deferred to the autumn and an announcement was made by Mr Gray that the position on production cuts would be reviewed then. In the meantime studies continued on the subject. The subject had also attracted the attention of the House of Commons Select Committee on Energy which launched a long-lasting inquiry into Oil Depletion Policy. It received evidence not only from the DEN and Treasury, but various companies including Shell, BP, Esso, Mobil, BNOC, BGC, and Brindex, and several academics. There were no less than eleven oral evidence sessions terminating with that of Mr Gray on 17th December 1981. The oil companies generally argued against any interventionist depletion policy. Production cuts were felt to be particularly inappropriate as they did not permit optimal use of existing capital equipment, resulting in capacity underutilisation and a misallocation of resources. Development delays were generally a lesser evil, but, given the lack of advance knowledge about the duration of the delays, they increased the uncertainty of the investment environment with possible negative consequences. Some of the companies argued that if depletion rates had to be reduced royalty banking should be employed. This put the cost on to the Government and was thus strongly resisted by the Treasury. The emphasis of much of the company evidence was on the need to encourage exploration and development, particularly by relaxing what was perceived to be an excessively tough régime. Such relaxation would facilitate longer term production which would prevent the aggregate profile from falling steeply. This idea was enthusiastically promoted by the Chairman of BNOC who argued that what was required was a *repletion* rather than a depletion policy to deal with the greater problem of a sharp decline in production from the later 1980s onwards.

Mr Lawson's views

Meanwhile studies continued within Government on lines similar to those in the earlier part of the year. The appointment of Mr Nigel Lawson as Secretary of State for Energy had a major impact on thinking within DEN. He quickly made known his views on depletion policy generally in a speech to the Norwegian Petroleum Institute on 22nd October. His starting point was the impossibility of a detailed North Sea Oil Master Plan because of the inherent uncertainties. The idea of deferring some of the prospective surplus of production over consumption to the 1990s and beyond seemed straightforward but concealed a host of uncertainties. He had considered the arguments that (1) the price of oil was likely to rise in real terms, which could make investment in oil in the ground attractive, and (2) the oil companies were primarily concerned with the high front-end investments involved and thus the need for early production, with long-term income prospects being heavily discounted. But all this depended on the assumptions of continuing rising real oil prices and the view that the oil companies would not take a long-term view if price expectations indicated that this was the more profitable option. These assumptions might be incorrect. Equally doubtful was the ability of Governments to weight all the uncertainties more accurately and come to better conclusions about the future than the market. There were many uncertainties regarding future UK oil supply and demand and the range of possible outcomes was very wide. Thus the Government had to tread very carefully. It had to consider both the long-term health of the North Sea industry while not damaging the near-term prospects for economic recovery.

Working Group reports again

Meanwhile the Working Group was updating the May report. DEN officials examined the changes which had occurred since then and noted the fall in oil prices. The production projections for 1982 had changed little since May, but the oil demand figures were substantially down to date in 1981. This was expected to continue and so the net exportable surplus was expected to be greater. The conclusion was that the argument for production cuts in 1982 had become stronger. The value of sterling had fallen substantially since May but the DEN view was that the real effective exchange rate against a basket of currencies had not much changed. The only general economic factor which had changed was the oil market outlook which was now for falling short-term oil prices. But the conclusion drawn was that this improved the case for production cuts beyond 1982. A revision to the May report was produced in November 1981. There were no major changes. Production cuts of 5 million tonnes in 1982 and 10 million tonnes in 1983 were proposed.

Mr Lawson opposes production cuts

Mr Lawson had his own views, however, and on 20th January 1982 he submitted them in a Minute to the Prime Minister. He acknowledged that in the period 1982–85 there could be a cumulative surplus of production over consumption ranging between 70 and 180 million tonnes. The scope for production cuts was 5 million tonnes in the second half of 1982 and 13 million tonnes in 1983. He acknowledged the well known arguments for imposing production cuts namely (1) that they were the only means by which there could be a significant reduction in the hump of production in the 1980s in the interests of long-term security of supply, and (2) the present was the most propitious time to cut production given the slackness in the world oil market. But he was also aware that cuts of 5 million tonnes in 1982 and 10 million in 1983 would increase the PSBR by £600 million in 1982/83 and £1.7 billion in 1983/84. Further, any receipts from the privatisation of BNOC's and BGC's oil interests would be depressed and further investment in the North Sea could be discouraged. Mr Lawson concluded that there should be no imposed production cuts. This should be announced positively in terms of depletion policy, stressing the need to encourage sustained high production, and the announcement should cover the lifetime of the present Parliament.

Ministers decide but announcement delayed

The Chancellor was very supportive of Mr Lawson's conclusions and sent a Minute to the Prime Minister indicating this, adding that it was no part of the Government's philosophy to engage in commodity speculation which he felt was entailed by dictating that there should be investment in oil in the ground. The CPRS expressed its reservations, but the Prime Minister agreed with Mr Lawson, querying only the period of no cuts. She felt that a period of two or three years might be preferable. Mr Lawson was content to avoid linking the decision to the life of the current Parliament and proposed the end of 1984. He wanted to make an early announcement, but the Chancellor felt that it should be made at the same time as the Budget when North Sea tax changes would also be announced. In the event Mr Lawson wanted to postpone his announcement because of the growing weakness in the oil market. The context was BNOC's view that its bargaining position on oil prices was very weak, because the oil companies were aware of the Government's wish to maintain oil production at high levels to maximise the tax take. The DEN felt that this weak bargaining position would be further eroded if an announcement of no production cuts were made. The announcement in Parliament was thus not made until 8th June 1982.

Report of Select Committee against restrictive depletion policy

By that time the report of the Select Committee had been published. The Committee had not been persuaded that an interventionist, restrictive depletion policy was justified. It felt that, because of the magnitude and diversity of the uncertainties relating both to production from the North Sea and to UK oil demand, there was no convincing means by which the Government could decide when and by how much the depletion rate determined by the producers was non-optimal. The Committee was also unconvinced that in practice the Government was consistently taking a longer view than the oil companies.

Response of Government to Select Committee

In its reply to the Select Committee's report in July 1982 the Government said that before a restrictive depletion policy could be justified there had to be clear economic advantages. But such clear advantages could not be demonstrated and the uncertainties were too great to justify Government action in the foreseeable future to delay UK oil production. Somewhat more surprisingly the memorandum went on to say that there was no case in the foreseeable future for deferring new field developments. This reflected Mr Lawson's view that there had already been delays in bringing projects forward for other reasons, and that the imposition of further delays would damage the confidence of the industry. There had been no field development approvals in 1981 and investor confidence had certainly been shaken by the tax increases in that year. The memorandum also stated that the Government would retain reserve powers of intervention against the possibility of a major shift in the market which threatened to produce a significant divergence between the national interest and the depletion rate produced by market forces. But it was emphasised that these powers would not be used lightly.

Interest in restrictive depletion policy subsides

The change in thinking within the DEN clearly reflected the views of Mr Lawson. It was a happy coincidence that there was much agreement with the Select Committee's views. Thereafter interest in an interventionist depletion policy for oil subsided. Attention was concentrated on the need to encourage exploration and maintain activity levels in the North Sea given the prospective decline in production. DEN officials were aware of the expiry of the Lawson Assurance on production cuts at the end of 1984, and in December of that year consideration was given as to whether any statement needed to be made regarding policy thereafter. It was decided that no announcement was needed on the grounds that (1) there had been no request by the industry for a statement, (2) Government policy had been clearly stated in the 1982 memorandum to the Select Committee, and (3) a statement confirming the policy of maximum economic production at a time when the oil price was falling could provoke pressure from OPEC countries to alter policy. If questions on depletion policy were asked reference should simply be made to the 1982 memorandum.

Reflections on oil depletion policy debate

From 1975 to 1983 much thought was clearly given to oil depletion within Government. The first report of the Working Group raised the pertinent issues in a thought-provoking manner with the microeconomic, macroeconomic and security of supply issues being clearly identified. There was an understandable difficulty in arriving at a final decision on whether intervention was justified when the macroeconomic and microeconomic arguments pointed in different directions. The long term security of supply issue was very difficult to handle analytically. The question of what premium to put on extra security of supply was not easy to answer and made objective decision-making more difficult. While the welfare of the offshore supplies industry was acknowledged as being relevant it was never given much weight.

The macroeconomic arguments changed in character in the period reflecting the corresponding changes in the perceived key UK macroeconomic problems. The arguments presented initially favoured a moderation to the depletion rate in a rather lukewarm manner, but as the problem of the PSBR became increasingly pressing the near-term taxable capacity of the industry assumed ever-increasing importance and the perceived macroeconomic case for fast depletion stronger. This was despite the acknowledged upward effect on the exchange rate which the growing revenues were having. The microeconomic arguments presented over the years continued to favour slower depletion, but at the end of the day the macroeconomic arguments prevailed. This was another example of macroeconomic considerations dominating energy policy ones.

With the benefit of hindsight the microeconomic argument that oil left in the ground would have been a sound investment was surely not upheld by later events. The oil price fell dramatically to $10 in 1986, and in real terms had not recovered to the levels seen in 1980 and 1981 by 2005. Broadly speaking extra oil in the ground would not have proved a good investment in that period. Similarly, security of supply in the period to the end of the century was not an issue. Oil and gas supplies were generally ample. The projections of oil (and gas) production from the UKCS for the 1990s made in the period of the depletion debate also turned out to be spectacularly pessimistic, with oil production climbing in the 1990s to a new peak in 1999.[10] If post-2005 oil price conditions are also considered the discount rate necessary to support depletion policy delays in the 1970s and early 1980s would have been very low indeed.

The issue of the extraction rate of North Sea oil can be linked to the question of how the benefits from its depletion are maximised. This was clearly understood by the Working Group in its first report on depletion and led to the recommendation that a separate working party examine the issue of how the benefits should best be utilised. This is the subject of the next chapter.

Appendix 12.1

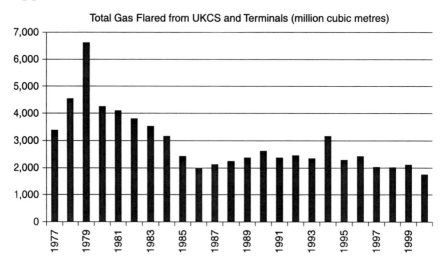

Appendix 12.2

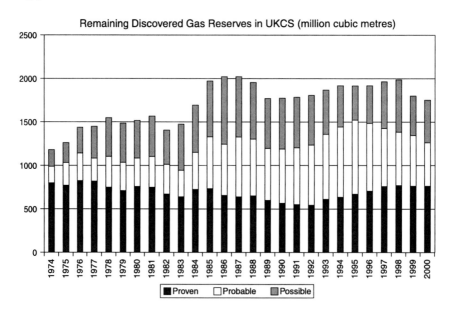

Appendix 12.3

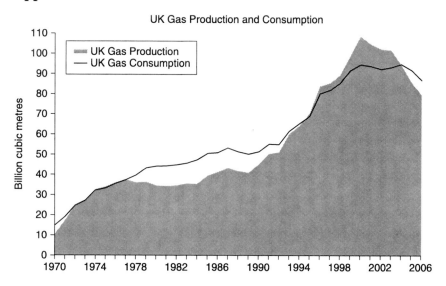

Appendix 12.4

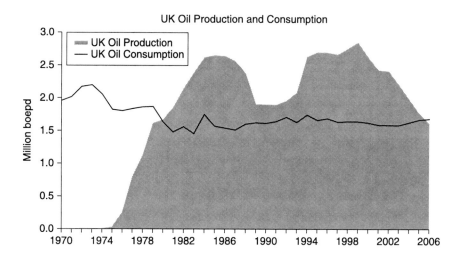

Appendix 12.5

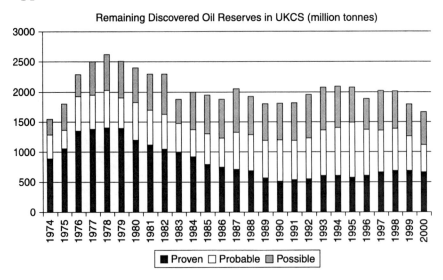

Appendix 12.6

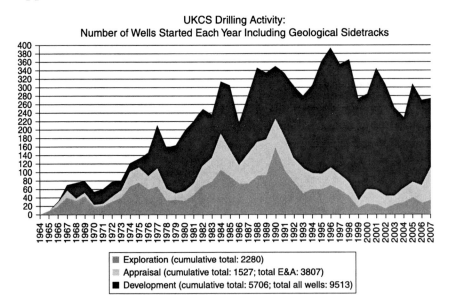

13 Utilising the benefits

Scale and volatility of benefits

The direct benefit of North Sea oil and Gas is most obviously expressed as its contribution to national output. This grew dramatically from 1975 to reach a peak of around 6.9% of gross value added (GVA) in 1984, followed by an equally dramatic fall in subsequent years (see Appendix 13.1). The collapse of oil prices to a low of $10 in 1986 was a major contributory factor (see Appendix 13.2), but oil production also fell significantly to 1990 (see Appendix 12.4). As noted in Chapter 8 investment in the North Sea grew dramatically in the 1970s (see Appendix 8.5), and constituted a major element in total UK industrial investment (see Appendix 22.1). The historic behaviour of gross and post-tax net industry income (at 2006 prices) is shown in Appendix 13.3. Total Government revenues (also at 2006 prices) are shown in Appendix 13.4. These revenues (in real terms) attained very high levels in the first half of the 1980s, reaching £17 billion in 1981/82, £19 billion in 1982/83, over £20 billion in 1983/84, and peaking at nearly £27 billion in 1984/85. Thereafter they declined dramatically to just over £10 billion in 1986/87 and £2 billion in 1991/92.

For whose benefit?

Chronologically the aspect of the optimisation of the benefits of North Sea oil which first received detailed attention within Government related not on how they should be utilised but who should receive them. In the two 1974 elections the SNP made substantial gains at the polls on a platform which put considerable emphasis on "Scotland's Oil". For many voters in Scotland the most vivid impact was the election poster showing a picture of an old woman pulling her shawl closely around her in front of a dying fire while the accompanying caption stated "And it's her oil too".

Working Group on response to Kilbrandon Report

The SNP electoral success was greeted with some alarm within Government. It occurred at a time when consideration was being given to the response to the

Kilbrandon Report[1] for which a Constitution Unit had been established within the Cabinet Office. This Unit along with the Treasury, Inland Revenue, DEN and Scottish Office all involved themselves in the response to the perceived threat. Work on the response to the Kilbrandon Report was under way by early 1974. An inter-departmental Working Group chaired by the Treasury examined the economic and financial issues. These included the question of tax-raising powers to devolved tiers of Government. It produced a report in February 1974 which generally supported the centralisation of tax-raising powers. In a short section on North Sea oil it was argued that the conclusive argument was that all UK taxes should go into a common pool for the benefit of what was a single economy, and to do otherwise would be to deny the sovereignty of Parliament and the economic unity of the United Kingdom. These assertions, unsupported by detailed argument, were followed by the further curious assertion that there was no point in allowing Scotland or Wales a proportion of oil revenues unless it improved standards relative to England. There was no mention of the fact that licence fees and royalties from the UKCS had been shared with the Governments of the Isle of Man and Northern Ireland since 1968.

DEN against devolution of responsibility for petroleum exploitation

DEN produced a paper on the possibility of devolving responsibility for petroleum exploitation to the proposed Scottish and Welsh Assemblies and found that, although there were no legal objections, there were overwhelming grounds against it. Energy policy must be planned on a national basis. The interests of Scotland would not necessarily coincide with those of the UK. With an oil demand only one-tenth of the UK's Scotland alone might feel it appropriate to cut back oil production from the levels necessary to satisfy UK demand. It was concluded that it would be inconsistent with the political and economic unity of the UK to devolve responsibility for exploitation to the regions. No mention was made of the fact that petroleum licensing for onshore exploitation was already devolved in the case of Northern Ireland!

Working Group searches for arguments against devolution of oil revenues

The subsequent work of the Working Group as far as North Sea oil was concerned consisted of a search for additional arguments against the devolution of oil revenues, or indeed any other significant extra powers relating to oil developments. To assert that North Sea oil revenues should in some sense belong to Scotland was to deny the sovereignty of Parliament, and to assert that one area had claims over a certain tax revenue because that revenue was derived from that area regardless of other national needs had no foundation in law, as rights over the UKCS belonged to the UK as a whole and not to particular parts of it. It was also argued that, even if it was accepted that a region had a reasonable and equitable right to a share there would be great difficulties in determining and collecting the attributable amounts.[2]

Other arguments were subsequently produced against devolution of oil revenues. Thus, so long as Scotland remained an integral part of the UK with limited autonomy, the wider UK interest demanded central not local control over the Government take. The prospective oil revenues were an almost accidental addition to total national wealth, they greatly exceeded Scottish needs, and they bore no relation to the strength of the local economy. Further, they were not inexhaustible, and so it would be quite wrong to base the fiscal autonomy of Scotland on a temporary plateau in the size of its tax base. Finally, since the rest of the UK had effectively subsidised the Scottish economy for many years it was unjust to penalise England just when the tide was turning.

Other views

Other views were also expressed in the debate. Thus some felt that it would be a mistake to rely too much on the truism that it was the UK which had sovereignty over the oil because the reality was that Scotland's membership of the UK was a matter of consent. It was also felt that the argument that it was an accident that the oil lay off the Scottish coast should be avoided as it was equally an accident that it lay off the UK coast. The argument that the oil likely to be available greatly exceeded Scottish needs was also not compelling given that this happened with other producing countries such as Kuwait. When this argument was coupled with the proposition that it would be wrong to base the fiscal economy of Scotland on the basis of revenues which were exhaustible and thus temporary it invited the response that an independent Scotland could make it last longer. But a recurring view was that the oil revenues were much too big to leave to a regional or intermediate-level Government.

Views of Scottish Office

In late May 1974 the Scottish Office made a contribution to the debate which was to some extent separate from the discussions on the Kilbrandon Report. Mr Willie Ross, the Secretary of State, felt that there was now a need to devise a means whereby oil revenues were brought to bear on the long-standing economic problems of the country. He had formed the view that some form of development agency should be established which could be financed partly from oil revenues. If nothing were done about Kilbrandon it would be imperative to demonstrate that Scotland was benefiting from oil revenues. Scottish Office Ministers were anxious to make rapid progress on the issue even before the Kilbrandon consultations were completed.

The Scottish Office paper argued that, to meet the commitment made in the Queen's Speech, additional expenditure based on North Sea oil should be linked to specific projects of limited duration, rather than to provide support for items of indefinitely continuing public expenditure which were more suitably financed from general taxation. General benefits to the UK balance of payments would improve economic conditions in Scotland, but would not be regarded as fulfilling the Government's pledge, and thus additional measures were needed. It was acknowledged that any special arrangements could be applied not only to Scotland but also to all other areas classified for regional development support. The result would be a great dilution in the impact of any extra expenditure. This problem would not arise if the expenditure was limited to Development Areas or even Special Development Areas. But from the Scottish viewpoint there was a case for using oil revenues to help provide the necessary North Sea infrastructure, and to assist reclamation and recovery in those parts of Scotland which experienced the greatest dislocation and disturbance as a result of North Sea developments.

Case for Scottish Development Agency (SDA)

The Scottish Office paper then suggested that there was a case for establishing a separate institution with its own powers of initiative, assessment, and execution to channel resources made available by North Sea oil to the greatest advantage. It might be called a Scottish Development Agency. An institution of this kind had already been proposed to deal with the deep-seated problems of West Central Scotland, but it seemed desirable to set up the Agency for Scotland as a whole. It could be financed at least in part by revenues from North Sea oil. It was felt that the extra expenditures could be concentrated on (1) the strengthening and development of selective assistance to industry, (2) environmental recovery in the oldest industrial areas, and (3) infrastructure, particularly the preparation of industrial sites. The funds might also be used to finance North Sea oil infrastructure.

Treasury against hypothecation of oil revenues

The Treasury's reaction to the paper at the end of May 1974 was to assert that the correct and logical use of North Sea oil revenues would involve (1) no hypothecation, and (2) no extra expenditure on regional or other developments just because of oil discoveries. The commitment in the Queen's Speech to assisting Scotland and the regions in need of development did not get round the illogicality of the ideas. Establishing a Scottish Development Agency (SDA) would highlight the favourable treatment of Scotland compared to the rest of the UK.

Decision to establish SDA

Ministers were well aware of the political importance and implications of policies relating to North Sea oil revenues, and in the July 1974 White Paper (Cmnd. 5696) the notion that the oil resources should confer maximum benefit to the community, particularly in Scotland and other regions in need of development, was reiterated. The decision to establish a Scottish Development Agency was announced, but it was made clear that it would be financed from the UK Exchequer and not from the oil revenues. It was added that as oil exploration developed in the Celtic Sea similar arrangements would be made for Wales.

Response to Kilbrandon favours devolved assemblies

The debate on the issue of North Sea revenues in the context of devolution continued within Government with the Constitution Unit and the Treasury playing the major roles. By September 1974 the Government had decided to accept the main conclusion of the Kilbrandon Report that there should be some devolution to Scotland and Wales and announced the intention to create assemblies for these countries in the White Paper, *Democracy and Devolution Proposals for Scotland and Wales* (Cmnd. 5732). In late March, 1975 the Unit requested the views of other Departments on the issue and put full Scottish independence with the implications for North Sea oil into the debate. The impressive performance of the SNP in the October, 1974 general election when it obtained 30% of the Scottish vote with eleven seats in Parliament concentrated attention on the issue. There was concern that a devolved Scottish Government could slow up the pace of oil developments by delaying planning permissions and local infrastructure provision. All this could lead to a reduced rate of production and damage to the balance of payments. To persuade the devolved Government to behave more cooperatively there was a concern that a Scottish Government would ask for a specific share of the oil revenues or alternatively an increased block grant.

The UK Government could respond in various ways, and the Constitution Unit raised many for discussion, including several designed to highlight the view that Scotland's future lay within a unified UK economy. Possible tariff barriers against Scottish exports and the vulnerability of the economy to fluctuating oil prices were examples.

Detailed Scottish Office paper

A Scottish Office paper prepared by Dr Gavin McCrone, the Under Secretary, on the Economics of Scottish Nationalism was submitted to the Working Group. This was fairly detailed and demonstrated that the advent of North Sea oil had completely overturned the traditional economic arguments used against Scottish independence. It was argued that an independent Scotland could expect to have large budget and balance of payments surpluses, and with an appropriate depletion policy this situation could be maintained for a very long time into the future. Further, provided sensible policies were pursued, it was possible to see how this situation could be used to re-equip Scottish industry and renew outworn social capital, with beneficial consequences for employment and productivity. For the first time since the Act of Union in 1707 it was possible to argue that Scotland's economic advantage lay in its repeal.

External financing considerations

In further deliberations the Treasury unveiled a further argument in favour of the continued centralisation of UK oil revenues. This related to external financing with the key issue being the perception among external UK creditors that the prospective self-sufficiency in oil by 1980, with a net export surplus to follow, provided the key underpinning for the servicing and repayment of the debt currently being accumulated. There was a risk that the publicity surrounding the path to devolution would call into question the viability of the UK as a debtor. If the new assembly in Scotland had a nationalist–dominated Government external creditors of the UK could take fright. The remarkable conclusion drawn was that progress towards devolution should be delayed for as long as possible. The longer the delay the better the prospect that the external deficit would have narrowed.

The above line of argument was enthusiastically developed within the Treasury. Thus if a Scottish Government threatened or sought to implement a restrictive depletion policy it would have a negative effect on the UK's credibility as an overseas borrower. The fears of creditors would be compounded the greater the perceived likelihood that independence was in prospect.

The subject continued to be discussed within Government along with the debate on devolution, Scottish independence, and the size and use of North Sea oil revenues. Considerable attention was given to how the growing claims of the SNP could be discredited. For example, the Foreign Secretary, Anthony Crosland was concerned that the UK's creditworthiness was being weakened by the SNP claims and in January 1977 suggested that these could best be countered by discreet briefing of the media and other opinion formers. The Director of Information at the DEN indicated that his Division had for a long time in briefing sought to undermine SNP claims to North Sea oil, and had, for example raised doubts about the angle of any dividing line between England and Scotland following that currently in use or even one based on median line principles. The uncertainty about whether Shetland or even Orkney would wish to be part of an independent Scotland with all the consequences for oil revenues had also been intimated.

North Sea oil and Regional Accounts

Another indication of Government sensitivity to North Sea oil and the relationship with Scotland arose over the apparently technical question of the compilation of the Regional Accounts of the United Kingdom. The question arose of the treatment of North Sea profits in these accounts. It was discussed at a meeting of the Statistical Policy Committee in March 1977 chaired by Mr Dell, the Secretary of State for Trade. The Director of the Central Statistical Office (CSO) indicated that North Sea profits would become very large and how they were treated in the accounts would become important. Two approaches were possible. The first was to apportion the activities to the regions adjacent to the North Sea. But it was stated that there was no agreed way to allocate the North Sea area to the regions, and it was further argued that to do so would distort the regional accounts. The great majority of the profits would accrue to Scotland, and in due course would represent nearly a doubling of Scottish GDP. The Government had already agreed that the resources of the North Sea were attributable to the UK as a whole and not to individual parts of it.

Separate region for North Sea oil and gas

The second approach was to allocate the oil and gas activity to a new (twelfth) region. This avoided the disadvantages of the first approach, was consistent with international accounting concepts for statistics of this kind, and was thus the recommended approach. The proportion of profits arising from North Sea onshore installations would still be attributed to the existing regions in which they were located. Income from employment would not be treated in this way but the total amounts were relatively small, and it would be possible to make a judgement of the amount which was appropriate to the offshore region to provide an estimate of the GDP arising in the proposed offshore region.

The Committee generally supported the proposal despite its dubious logic. The idea that other activities which took place largely outside the territorial area of the UK such as fishing, aviation, and shipping might also be included in the accounts for an offshore region was discussed on the grounds of logic and in diluting the impact of petroleum profits on their own. It was noted that under current practice profits from overseas insurance were attributed to the "centre of interest" which meant the GDP of the South East of England, and critics of the proposal for an offshore region for petroleum could argue that it was inconsistent with that for overseas insurance. Eventually a separate sector for offshore petroleum activity was established in the Regional Accounts.

North Sea revenues and Shetland Islands

In 1974 there was another case regarding the extent to which North Sea oil revenues should be centralised. This related to the Shetland Islands. It had become clear that very large volumes of oil from the East Shetland Basin would be most economically landed in Shetland from whence it would be transhipped elsewhere. The Zetland County Council considered that the terminal facilities should be concentrated at Sullom Voe. The Council was also keen to ensure that it controlled the related developments. To this end a Private Bill, the Zetland County Council Bill, had been promoted. This was enacted in April 1974, and gave the Council wide-ranging powers on the acquisition of land and the provision of services in the Sullom Voe area. Lengthy negotiations took place between the Council and the operating companies for the fields in question (Shell, BP, Conoco and Total). The result was the establishment of an executive body, the Sullom Voe Association, owned jointly by the Council and the pipeline operating companies. This was a non-profit making limited company whose functions were the detailed design, construction and operation of the terminal facilities.

Request by Council for disruption payments

In the negotiations the Council requested that the oil companies using the terminal make a payment related to the amount of oil passing through the terminal. This was to be separate from the harbour dues which the Council would impose in its role as harbour authority for Sullom Voe. The payment was regarded as a compensation for the serious intrusion and disturbance which the industry would cause to the environment and social/economic life of the islands. The money would be put into a fund for which provision had been made in the Zetland County Council Act. It was anticipated that the monies would be used for environmental rehabilitation, and to ease the transition when oil-related employment passed its peak.

By the time the Zetland Act came into force no agreement had been reached between the parties on the amount of the payment. The Council's original request was a payment of 0.5%–1% of the landed value of the oil. This was a straightforward royalty which the Scottish Office estimated in April 1974 could bring in £7.6 million in 1980 and £13.9 million at peak production. The companies' initial offer was 1p per ton which they would be prepared to raise to 2p per ton. At April 1974 these were estimated to bring in £0.76 million in 1980 and £1.4 million at peak production. The Council then put forward an alternative proposal involving a fixed annual sum for each pipeline coming ashore. The suggested amounts were £3 million for the first one, £2 million for the second one, and £1 million for each additional one.

Concerns of Government departments over disruption payments

The Scottish Office, Treasury and DEN were concerned at these developments. It was discovered that the Council had no legal powers to require the companies to make such payments. But they had the right to receive them if they were voluntarily paid as gifts! If this happened the Government had no powers under existing legislation to prevent the Council receiving them or to control how the money was spent. Further, the receipt of the monies would affect the Council's entitlement to Rate Support Grant only to the extent that it was used to pay for rate-borne services. Equally there was nothing to prevent the oil companies from making such gifts.

Within Government the implications of any agreement between the parties were felt to be three-fold namely, (1) the effect on the Government's own take, (2) the precedent set for other areas, and (3) its bearing on the arguments about the hypothecation of oil revenues to Scotland. If the payment was in the form of a royalty it might be inconsistent with the Continental Shelf Act 1964 which specified the Government's right to levy royalties. If the payment were in the form of a fixed sum per ton this concern was much reduced. It was also noted that to some extent there was a precedent in an agreement made between Shell and Anglesey County Council under the Anglesey Marine Terminal Act 1972. This provided for a payment of 1p per ton of oil passing through the terminal in favour of the Anglesey County Council. There was a difference from the Shetland situation in that the payment was regarded as a harbour due and subject to the oversight of the National Ports Council.

There was concern that if a disturbance payment were made in Shetland it would almost certainly lead to similar arrangements being sought by other local authorities. It had already become clear that the Orkney County Council was negotiating a similar arrangement with Occidental for oil landed from the Piper field at Scapa Flow. But the Government was concerned that other local authorities where different, but nevertheless intrusive, oil-related developments would occur, might feel that they should receive similar payments. The likely impact of these considerations would depend on the size of the payments. Small sums could be defended as reasonable recompense but very large sums could raise acute difficulties. A worry was that protracted negotiations would delay the landing of oil from the Brent field.

Options for Government

An inter-departmental meeting chaired by the Treasury considered the issues noted above in April 1974. It was felt that there were four options. The first was to stand aside and leave the companies to reach agreement with the Council. The worry was that, because of the need to obtain early production, the companies might settle quickly and agree to make large payments. The second option was to discreetly encourage the companies to hold out for a settlement on the lines of their existing proposals. But this might well cause delay, and there was a danger to Government popularity if it became public knowledge that it was supporting the large oil companies against a small local authority. The third option was to intervene overtly as a broker and try to persuade the parties to agree an amount which was acceptable from a Government perspective. The fourth option was to introduce legislation which might provide for local authority schemes financed by the Government designed to offset the adverse effects of North Sea oil developments. As an alternative the Government could compulsorily acquire the land needed for the oil developments. This would certainly antagonise the Zetland Council.

It was concluded that the third option was the preferred one. Ministers should be advised to talk to the Council with a view to agreeing a level and mechanism of payment which was tolerable to the Government. The question of the use to which the monies should be put should also be examined. If an acceptable agreement could not be reached further action including legislation should not be ruled out. Given the seriousness of the issue the Secretary of State for Scotland should send a Minute to the Prime Minister explaining the situation.

Mr Ross briefs Prime Minister

Mr Ross sent a Minute to the Prime Minister on 11th April. He briefly outlined the background to the issue, but also noted that the Sullom Voe development would involve capital expenditure by the Zetland Council exceeding £100 million. The Government thus had an important direct stake in the developments and were discussing the means of financing it with the Council. On the disturbance payment Mr Ross gave an estimate of the offer by the companies over the next ten years at £15 million while the Council had requested an estimated total of £46 million. The companies urgently needed to commence work at the site, but the

Council had indicated that this could not happen until agreement on the disturbance payment had been reached. The oil companies had asked for the Government's views on their offer. Mr Ross summarised the Government's concerns on the lines discussed above. He then proposed that he should meet the Council where he would express concern about the impasse, and hope to persuade the Council to agree to a level and mechanism of payment which would avoid the difficulties of precedent. If it appeared that an acceptable agreement could not be reached the possibility of legislation to bring the matter under the Government's control would have to be considered, and legislation could stipulate that any disturbance payments had to have Government approval. The Minute added that the Paymaster General agreed with his suggestions. The Paymaster felt that it was unacceptable that such large sums as were in prospect should escape all control and taxation, and that legislation might therefore ultimately be required. But this should be a last resort, a sentiment which was echoed by the Lord President.

Scottish Office discussions with Council

Mr Ross and Scottish Office officials met with the Council Convener, Chairman of the Landward Committee, and Mr Iain Clark, the County Clerk on 14th May. Mr Ross indicated general support for the Council in its wish to control oil developments in the wider interests of Shetland and the UK as a whole. He welcomed suggestions that the oil companies might be encouraged to make financial contributions towards the direct expenditure incurred on their behalf by Government authorities, and was interested to hear about the current negotiations between the Council and the companies. The Council representatives emphasised that they had anticipated the problems which oil developments would bring, and were now carrying out their statutory duties to reduce the adverse effect on the Shetland way of life. Perhaps uniquely among oil producing areas the advent of oil was not unreservedly welcome and there was a danger that it would destroy the existing economic and cultural life. They had made it clear to the companies that further developments could not take place until the companies had offered suitable financial terms for the landing of oil in Shetland. They also expected the companies to make adequate provision for workers' hostels, though the Council had itself offered to build hostels. On the financial arrangements the Council representatives felt that the oil companies were dragging their feet, though they had just heard that an offer would soon be made.

Concerns of Mr Ross

Mr Ross emphasised his support for the idea that the companies should contribute towards the direct costs falling on the local authorities resulting from oil developments. He was, however, concerned that the Council might exact high payments unrelated to direct expenditures on the necessary infrastructure. This might encourage other local authorities to introduce similar schemes. It would also reduce central Government revenues which would impact on the welfare of the whole nation. Mr Ross wanted to know what the Council proposed to do with the revenues collected into the Reserve Fund, given that site rehabilitation costs could be borne directly by the companies as a planning consent requirement. He added that, through the Rate Support Grant and other specific grants, central Government was contributing 80%-90% of the local authority expenditure, and in future such grants would have to pay regard to all the Council's resources, including revenues from any special deal concluded with the oil companies. Mr Ross reminded the Council that it would still need his consent to borrow for major developments and his approval for compulsory purchase procedures.

The Council's position

The Council representatives responded that they did not really want the oil, and thus it was morally justified for them to expect the companies to make a contribution for the disservice they were causing. The purpose of the fund was to accumulate sufficient monies to be used in the long-term to offset the adverse effect of the inevitable decline in the oil industry. The oil companies had also accepted the principle that they should make payments unrelated to the supply of specific services to them by the local authority. In summing up at the end of the meeting Mr Ross reiterated his earlier views, adding that he would like to see details of the companies' new offer and hear from the Council how they proposed to use the revenues.

Revised offer and counter offer

Shortly afterwards the oil companies made their revised offer. It comprised a combination of initial fees followed by a rate (pence) per ton of oil received in Sullom Voe, with the rate being indexed for inflation. The Council replied very quickly with a counter offer also incorporating initial fees and higher rates per ton. The DEN was in close touch with the companies and quickly made some estimates of the likely size of the receipts. This involved many assumptions regarding throughput and inflation, but for the period 1974-1984 the cumulative payment under the companies offer was £24.7 million while under the Council's proposal it was over £39 million. To 1990 the cumulative offers were respectively £53 million and over £94 million.

Agreement reached, June 1974

There then followed a long negotiating session in June 1974 which ended in an agreement. The package had several components. The first was a series of early payments of £250,000 each, relating to signature of the agreement, access to the site, and access for construction commencement. The second component related to pre-payment charges which were set at 60p per barrel (with escalation) of maximum pipeline capacity for each pipeline, payable from the date which application for each pipeline was made. The third element was the throughput charge which was set at 2p per ton (with escalation) from the date of first oil flow through each pipeline. The fourth element set an absolute limit on escalation to the tonnage rate twelve years after the oil started to flow. The early estimates of DEN officials were that for the period 1974-1984 the cumulative payments could be £32 million, and in the period to 1990 about £74 million.[3]

The offer was accepted by the full Zetland Council on 18th June. The Convener added that the agreement did not compromise the Council's position regarding the fixing of reasonable charges for rent, rates, port dues, and other services. The agreement was formally signed on 12th July. Within Government the whole episode was greeted with mixed feelings. There was relief that work could now proceed with the enormous construction work involved at Sullom Voe. But the dominant feeling was one of concern that the agreement would encourage other local authorities to attempt to produce similar schemes. No one in central Government felt like congratulating the Council on making an agreement for the substantial benefit of current and future generations of Shetlanders! A primary concern of no dilution of central control of North Sea revenues remained.

Agreement with Orkney Council

The Orkney County Council had in the meantime been promoting its own Bill in Parliament broadly to acquire similar powers to those held by the Zetland Council. The Scottish Office generally supported the Bill. Other Departments expressed some concern about the Reserve Fund which was also a feature of the Bill, but Occidental had agreed to the concept of a throughput charge. The Bill was enacted and an agreement made with Occidental with far less fuss than in the Zetland case.

Valuation of North Sea oil installations for rating

The Government was quick to intervene in another issue where the centralisation of North Sea oil revenues was felt to be at risk. Somewhat fortuitously this also related to Scotland. In early 1976 concern arose in the Scottish Office after two local authority assessors responsible for valuation for rating purposes put some North Sea platforms on their valuation roles. Specifically, the assessor for Fife region had put the platforms in the Auk and Argyll fields in the roll with a rateable value of £3 million each. The assessor for Grampian Region had done likewise with the Forties platforms and pipeline at a value of £8.8 million. The assessor for Fife and the oil companies involved were planning to put forward a stated case for the Opinion of the Court of Session on whether the action of the assessor was *ultra vires*.

Mr Ross opposes offshore rating rights of local authorities

The Secretary of State, Mr Ross, submitted a memorandum on the issue to the Ministerial Committee on Economic and Industrial Policy in early April 1976.

After reviewing the background Mr Ross reiterated the basic policy position that central Government should be the sole recipient of taxation arising from the exploitation of North Sea oil. He felt that if the courts were to decide in favour of the assessor the decision should not be allowed to stand. His argument had a familiar ring. Large sums would be involved. They would distort the arrangements which had been devised for North Sea taxation, and they would adversely affect relations with the oil companies. Additional revenues on the scale envisaged would grossly distort the basis on which rate support grant was distributed. There would be additional complications if the basis of valuation was related to throughput and could vary over the years.

Mr Ross felt that the thrust of existing policy should be maintained. As far as valuation was concerned his proposal was that a distinction should be drawn between oil installations above the low water mark (which should continue to be rateable), and those beyond the low water mark which should not be rateable. The memorandum did acknowledge that some subjects which extended beyond the low water mark (such as coal mines) were rateable. It was also acknowledged that on occasion local authorities had responsibilities below the low water mark. Mr Ross concluded by requesting the Committee to agree that oil installations below the low water mark should not be rateable, and that early legislation should be introduced to put the position beyond doubt.

Legislation enacted

The Ministerial Committee agreed and legislation was rushed through Parliament in the form of the Valuation and Rating (Exempted Classes) (Scotland) Act 1976. The notions that the benefits of North Sea oil exploitation should accrue nationally and a charge to rates would reduce the yield of PRT and corporation tax were emphasised. The Government felt that some local authorities should not benefit from an uncovenanted increase in rateable value, and so provision was made for the exemption of oil and gas fields with their associated installations to the extent that they were located seaward of the low water mark of ordinary spring tides.

Dubious logic of legislation

The logic behind this legislation can certainly be queried. It is arguable that the distinction made between installations and pipelines below and above the low water mark is quite artificial and in any case irrelevant. Thus installations such as the terminals at St. Fergus, Sullom Voe, and Flotta are part of the North Sea infrastructure and are subject to rating. Onshore oil production facilities are also rated. The fact that other installations and pipelines are located below the low water mark does not make them different from this viewpoint. The odd situation is produced where an offshore pipeline is not rated but an onshore one carrying the same oil is rated. The concept of an uncovenanted increase (or decrease) in rateable value occurs in plenty other circumstances such as the opening (or closure) of new factories.

The memorandum of Mr Ross also did not discuss the basic fact that local authorities have to provide services for offshore oil activities. Thus, for example, the Grampian Health Board and Grampian Police provide services on an ongoing basis to the North Sea industry. The cost of offshore policing is consistently one of the larger items in the expenditure of Grampian Police. The desire to centralise North Sea revenues was clearly felt to be more important than the anomalies created.

Debate narrow, ignoring wider but relevant financial issues

The debate within Government on the issue of whether oil revenues could be shared with devolved Governments whether at Scottish or local level was generally blinkered and one-sided. It was taken for granted that they should accrue to central Government, and the debate essentially consisted of attempts to build up arguments in favour of this and in rebutting any contrary arguments. There was no examination of practice and ideas in other countries. By the 1970s the issue had been debated in several other countries, and some of the concepts raised were worthy of consideration in the UK.

In the literature the issue of which tier(s) of Government should receive the economic rents from petroleum exploitation had received attention.[1] The starting point is usually the legal one of the ownership of the mineral rights which produce a *prima facie* case that the host Government (in this case the UK Government) can legitimately claim at least a substantial share of any economic rents collected. But there are several other pertinent arguments, the first of which relates to the benefit received by the oil producers from the provision of services necessary for the oil exploitation. These are generally provided by the relevant local authorities, and the beneficiaries (the oil producers) generally pay for these at the local level through business rates. In the case of the UK the central Government did provide extra financial support to local authorities (such as the Zetland (later Shetland) Council) to enable them to finance the infrastructure. This was by no means always smoothly executed. Thus in the 1970s the local authorities in the Grampian Region were under severe pressure to enhance the infrastructure at a fast pace and on a (relatively) huge scale. The extra expenditures involved were unprecedented, and well beyond the budgets of the councils. The reaction of the Scottish Office to requests for special help was generally sympathetic, and in 1973 it submitted a proposal to the Treasury for specific oil-related grants to cover the extra expenditures. The request was for a special grant of 75% of the extra oil-related costs.

The response of the Treasury was quite discouraging, claiming that the extra costs should be met from the rates and rate support grant. Special direct grants raised very difficult issues of precedent. There was little comprehension of the urgency or scale of the problem. This only changed gradually when it appeared that the inevitable delays in the provision of infrastructure would lead to postponement of oil production and thus royalties and tax receipts. Eventually an oil-related element was provided in the rate support grant in 1975–1976 but only for specific, approved capital projects. The Scottish Office and the local authorities still had to provide very substantial contributions themselves. The sums provided through the oil-related grants were relatively small in the 1970s (when they were most required) but grew in the early 1980s. It is also noteworthy that any increase in rateable values resulting from the oil developments resulted in the council losing grant on a pound for pound basis through the operation of the rate resources equalisation grant scheme.[5]

Government grants appropriate for special infrastructure

Returning to the conceptual issue of whether local authorities should directly share in oil revenues from the need to provide extra and special infrastructure, it is clear that there is likely to be a serious mismatch between the timing of the revenue receipts and the infrastructure provision. It is arguable that the necessary revenues should be related to these costs (rather than the economic rents from oil production). Central Government grants are thus conceptually sensible. In the case of the UK these were provided in a curmudgeonly manner, and probably contributed to the delays, including the achievement of early oil production.

Compensation for disruption costs

The second argument that has been deployed in favour of local governments obtaining a share of the oil revenues relates to the disruption and related costs (including external costs) imposed on local economies and communities. These were undoubtedly present in localities such as the Sullom Voe area with respect to the terminal, harbour and pipeline activities, and in Easter Ross and Wester Ross with respect to construction yards. Even in the Aberdeen and Peterhead areas in the 1970s concern was sometimes expressed about the negative social and even economic effects of oil developments, particularly in sectors which were suffering from very high house prices and labour shortages. It was sometimes argued that the coming of the oil industry accelerated the decline of indigenous traditional industries. There have, of course, been major benefits, particularly in the Aberdeen area, which have greatly outweighed the disruption and other social costs, but in various parts of the Highlands and Islands the disruption and other social costs were clearly very substantial, particularly in the 1970s and early 1980s.

For communities such as the Shetland Islands which were severely disrupted by the scale of the oil developments there was a case for compensation, the size of any payments being related to the value of the costs involved. These costs were undoubtedly increased by the perceived imperative within central Government and the oil industry for a very fast pace of development. The Zetland Council would have preferred a slower pace of development to reduce the disruption costs involved. In 1970 the population of the Shetland Islands was around 17,000.

When the terminal and other facilities at Sullom Voe were being constructed around 7,000 workers, mostly from outside the Islands, were engaged in the work. They were housed in two accommodation camps at Toft and Firth in the country near Sullom Voe, and for a time also in two accommodation ships moored in the Voe. Over 300 daily bus trips to the terminal were required. This gives an indication of the scale of the activity in relation to the local economy and wider community.

Priorities of central Government

While the Scottish Office was generally well aware of these matters the priorities of other Government Departments in London were different. The main concern was the attainment of early production, and there was continued fretting about the delays to the completion of the terminal and the development of the related fields. Compensation for disruption and other external costs was not a significant consideration, and would certainly not have occurred if the Council had not made its own initiatives. Generally, however, compensation payments should be directly related to the value of the loss incurred, and it is by no means obvious that the Shetland scheme itself and the scale of payments negotiated by the Council were appropriate for this purpose.

North Sea oil a non-renewable resource

A third argument regarding sharing of oil revenues relates to the exhaustibility of the non-renewable resource. The inevitable depletion of the oil reserves means that the regions in which the oil activity is located will sooner or later suffer from the consequences of its economic exhaustion. The greater the reliance of a community on oil-related activities the more keenly will this phenomenon be felt. For local or regional Governments there is likely to be a consequential need to maintain or enhance the infrastructure and take steps to revitalise the economy. It can be argued that obtaining a share of the oil revenues enables these Governments to meet these eventualities. The issue has certainly been a real one for the Highlands and Islands in particular. Most of the construction yards developed in the 1970s are now closed or without orders. Oil-related employment at Sullom Voe has fallen substantially since its peak, and a substantial number of houses in the vicinity are now empty. The rateable values have suffered accordingly.

Reserve fund and long term decline of oil activities

A share of oil revenues invested in a fund can obviously help to deal with the problems from the subsequent decline in oil-related activities. This was actually one of the reasons given by Zetland Council in response to repeated questions from central Government Departments about the use to which the monies in the fund would be put. The Council was in this sense more farsighted than central Government which eventually did not feel that a national fund was justified. The dissatisfaction felt at the Council's response to this question in 1974 is generally unwarranted, and the Council's decision to maintain funds for the time when oil activity declined has been vindicated. Of course, funds could in principle be provided through a benign and understanding central Government to deal with the problem, and a fund of the type established in Shetland is not essential for this purpose.

Greater risk-bearing capability of central Government

There are several other issues concerning the allocation of oil revenues to different tiers of Government. One concerns risk-bearing capabilities. Oil revenues fluctuate very substantially due in large part to the major fluctuations in oil prices. A Government which is very dependent on oil revenues will thus face the likelihood of major fluctuations in its revenues. Governments which have well-diversified sources of revenues are better able to bear this risk. Central Governments will also generally have better access to capital markets to deal with this problem. Of course, the availability of reserves in an oil fund can also be used to provide a cushion in the event of a sudden fall in oil revenues. Another argument which has become common in more recent years states that the sharing of oil revenues contributes to alienation reduction. Such alienation arises when the known (large) oil revenues are seen to accrue to central Government, while only the crumbs from the activity accrue to the regions where production occurs. Revenue sharing arrangements would reduce this undoubted perceived problem.

Reflections on revenue-sharing schemes

In sum there was a case for the sharing of North Sea oil revenues among different tiers of Government. There could have been both economic and political benefits. The determination of the Treasury, supported by other Departments, to receive all the revenues centrally plus the minimalist approach to devolution adopted by the somewhat unimaginative Constitution Unit determined the outcome. The attitude of the Zetland Council was widely regarded as controversial at the time not so much with respect to the conceptual basis of their scheme, but for the size of the payments requested. History surely vindicates the concept of the fund with the accompanying decision to reserve a large element for the time when oil activity declined. The issue of the size of the payments remains controversial.

Working Group on Long Term Benefits of North Sea Oil

Meanwhile the Inter-Departmental Working Group on the Long Run Use of the Benefits of North Sea Oil met several times under Treasury chairmanship in 1976. By August it had been agreed to stress the dangers of doing nothing and allowing the benefits to flow into consumption as had happened with North Sea gas. Three main ways by which the benefits could be used had been identified, namely (1) repayment of overseas debt, (2) investment in energy generation, and (3) improvements in the

UK's industrial base with special reference to the problems of the UK economy. No matter which was to be emphasised there was a need to take action soon to ensure that the benefits were actually directed towards defined goals.

At a meeting of the Group in August the Department of Industry produced a wide-ranging preliminary list of options with emphasis on instruments under their control. The list even included a reduction in the higher rates of personal taxation, which was justified on the grounds of the perceived lack of managerial incentives. This proposal was queried on the grounds that it would encourage personal consumption rather than assist industry. The problem of fully evaluating the relative merits of the various options was noted. The Scottish Office representative emphasised the potentially explosive situation which could develop in Scotland as oil-related employment began to decline, whilst oil revenues increased rapidly and a Scottish Assembly was brought into being with little or no revenue of its own. The Scottish Office was well aware of the opposition in the Treasury to sharing or hypothecation of revenues, but felt that there was a case for an oil fund, so that there was a clearly defined sum available which would not be used for normal budgetary purposes. The Working Group accepted that some of the North Sea revenues should be seen to be helping Scotland, but were concerned about the presentational aspects of achieving this without actual hypothecation.

The meeting also considered the idea from the DEN that oil revenues be reinvested in the energy sector. The context was the perceived energy gap which could emerge in the UK by around 2000. There would need to be new investment in domestic sources of energy, but also in building up the UK's industrial capability to enhance the ability to import expensive energy. The Treasury reported that the latest figures indicated enormous prospective payments of interest on overseas debt. Thus one way of looking at the issue was to regard the benefits as having already been consumed through borrowing which would then have to be repaid in effect from North Sea oil resources.

Report of Working Party

Much further work was undertaken and a full draft report was completed for discussion by the Working Party in early 1977. The report began by reiterating the concern that, if no positive action was taken, the benefits would flow into consumption, and the opportunity to strengthen the UK's industrial base would be lost. It would also be necessary to prepare for the time when large scale oil imports would again be required. The report then showed estimates of the addition to national resources from North Sea oil to 1995. This was subject to the uncertainties regarding production levels, oil prices and exploitation costs which were all necessary to calculate the net addition to national resources. The net addition was defined as the Government take in royalties and taxes, plus the gross profits of the companies less royalties/taxes paid and capital expenditures. The annual values for oil alone were estimated to increase at a steady pace from less than £1 billion in 1977 to £3.8–£7.8 billion (at 1976 prices) by the mid-1990s. The calculation was undertaken separately for gas where there was the additional perceived uncertainty of the depletion rate. The prospective range of net additional resources rose annually from £0.3–£1.2 billion in 1977 to £1.3–£5.6 billion in 1995 (at 1976 prices). The benefits to the current account of the balance of payments were very substantial even after accounting for overseas remittances of dividends and interest. The PSBR would also benefit substantially. A further calculation produced estimates of uncommitted additions to national resources from North Sea oil averaging annually £1.0–£3.5 billion in the period 1981–1985 (perhaps 0.8%–2.7% of GNP), and £1.6–£5.6 billion in the period 1991–1995 (perhaps 1%–3.5% of GNP).

External debt

The report then considered in some detail the issue relating to the use of the North Sea resources to improve the external debt situation. If a conscious decision was made to do this substantial current account surpluses had to be planned for by deliberate policy initiatives. It was noted that large principal repayments were falling due in the period 1979–1984 as well as ongoing interest. Even with further borrowing repayments in 1982 alone could amount to $6.5 billion. On the assumption that the external accounts took priority in policy in the first half of the 1980s the required average annual current account surplus could be as much as 2.5% of GNP, comprising 1.5% for debt repayment and 0.5% to cover the capital account deficit. In the period 1985–1990 the total requirement might be 1.5% of GNP.

Reinvestment in energy sector

The report then considered the notion of reinvesting the additional resources in the energy sector. In a worst case scenario after the year 2000 energy import requirements could amount to 7.5%–10% of GNP per year. This could be reduced by the development of further indigenous energy. There were many uncertainties regarding further long-term investments in coal and nuclear power, but there was a case for believing that this would be a preferable alternative to substantial reliance on imported energy. It was foreseen that substantial public sector investment would be required.

Strengthen industrial base

The oil revenues could also be used to strengthen the UK's industrial base. The adoption of the most appropriate macroeconomic policy was perhaps the most important ingredient to achieve this. The help to the balance of payments from North Sea oil should produce a more stable macroeconomic environment. Taxation policies should not inhibit enterprise and motivations to work. Supply-side measures could help in various ways. The skill, composition, and mobility of the work force could be enhanced. The road system could be improved to reduce congestion. Technical training at all levels could be augmented. More specifically additional resources could be channelled into selective assistance to industry through the NEB and the Scottish and Welsh Development Agencies. Particular sectors could be promoted, particularly the newer industries and technologies. Declining industrial and urban areas could be regenerated. A North Sea Oil Investment Fund could be set up to allocate the oil resources. It would have presentational advantages, and the allocation of revenues into the Fund would make it easier for Government to resist pressure to dissipate the oil revenues on increased consumption, or divert them into financing general public expenditure which would in any case have been undertaken.

Macroeconomic framework

The report also had a section on the macroeconomic framework. This reaffirmed the priority to be given to generate a substantial balance of payments surplus in the early years of oil revenues. The need to avoid undue appreciation of sterling was recognised. Consumption growth should be restrained. Corporate and personal taxation measures should encourage investment, enterprise, and work. It had to be recognised that, if some of the oil-related revenues were used to reduce foreign debt and build up foreign exchange reserves, they could not be channelled into domestic investment. The perceived need to invest more in the energy sector would also reduce the resources available for other industrial investment, though the opportunities would be greater in the period before the 1990s when additional energy investment would become necessary.

With respect to the practical implementation of the use of the extra resources the royalty and tax revenues could be directed to obtain the industrial benefits noted above or to reduce the PSBR. The Government had little control over the resources accruing to the oil companies beyond creating a favourable climate for investment in the UK. It was also noted that, while a North Sea Fund could be established, money could be creamed off from the existing National Oil Account for specified purposes.

Conclusions of report

The conclusions were that, in the period to 1984, the bulk of the additional resources should be used to reduce indebtedness, cover capital account deficits, and build up reserves. After 1984 a growing proportion should be channelled into strengthening the industrial base, and in the 1990s a growing priority would be public sector investment in the energy sector to reduce dependence on energy imports.

North Sea Development Fund?

The report was discussed by the full Working Party and much further debate and redrafting ensued. The notion of a North Sea Development Fund continued to cause controversy and Ministers became involved. John Smith, Minister of State at the DEN, took exception to the astonishing comment recorded at a meeting of the Ministerial Committee on Economic and Industrial Policy that such a fund would be a red rag to Scottish opinion, and wrote to the Chief Secretary at the Treasury urging that the idea of a UK-wide capital Fund financed by some of the oil revenues as a source for employment-generating investment in parts of the UK with special economic problems be studied in more depth. Following a meeting between the Chief Secretary and the Minister of State at the Privy Council Office on 27th June, it was agreed that this should be done, and an inter-departmental committee, chaired by the Treasury, was formed with representatives from DOI, DEN, Department of Employment, Inland Revenue, Bank of England, Constitution Unit, and CPRS.

Inter-departmental report on oil Fund

A report was produced in September 1977. It considered the possible objectives of a Fund, and saw them in terms of demonstrating how the extra resources from the North Sea were being used in the economy, such as strengthening the industrial base, rather than being dissipated in financing unproductive consumption. On the possible form of the Fund it was felt that decisions would have to be made regarding what revenues should be paid into it, and what categories of development expenditure would be financed from it. The report noted that in theory there could be an independent board which would allocate the funds in accordance with prescribed objectives. But this was immediately dismissed as being out of the question, on the grounds that the allocation of resources in the economy was a matter for the Government. It was felt that a separate institution would have no clear role given the existing number of institutions dealing with regional development and industrial finance. It was taken as axiomatic that Government would remain responsible for disbursements from the Fund.

Fund expenditure-revenue-determined?

The most plausible arrangement was thus a Fund into which specified North Sea revenues would be paid, and from which specified public expenditure would be financed. The Fund could be expenditure-determined in the sense that the amount of revenues paid in would be limited to the expenditure from the fund. An alternative would be a revenue-determined Fund whereby a specified source of revenues would be assigned to it for the purpose of financing defined categories of expenditure. Many categories of expenditure were possible including programmes already functioning, such as regional development grants (a very large item), selective assistance to industry, the Scottish and Welsh Development Agencies and Northern Ireland industry and employment (a large item). There were plenty other possibilities including infrastructure (such as ports, roads and railways). The commitment of Government to help the regions in greatest need was noted here. At this stage the report also highlighted the statement in the 1977 White Paper on Financing the Devolved Services which emphasised that North Sea oil revenues accrued to the UK as a whole and formed part of the national pool of resources from which funding for the devolved administrations would be drawn. The White Paper continued by stating that there could be no question of making any part of these revenues available directly to the devolved administrations. In any case it might not be easy to find sensible ways of increasing expenditure further given that the main determinant of assistance was the level of business activity.

The report also considered the idea that monies from the Fund could be used to strengthen the industrial base, which in practice related to the programmes currently covered by the National Enterprise Board (NEB), and selective assistance, plus possible expenditures on energy, including not only further long-term supplies but energy conservation. Yet another possibility was industrial training and retraining. The majority of these programmes were capital ones and the report felt that expenditures should be restricted to this category to be consistent with the need to produce lasting benefits.

The report then considered how, if the Fund expenditures were concentrated on anticipated regional industrial programmes, these would compare to anticipated North Sea revenues. There were many uncertainties, but it was unlikely that regional industry expenditures would approach the likely revenues to 1985. But the revenues would be considerably reduced if deductions were made for overseas debt repayments. If this happened the income in the fund would be very small in the years of highest debt repayments.

Working Party's views on conceptual basis of Fund

The report then considered what it called the analytical basis of the concept. It argued that a Fund would not reveal anything new about the use to which North Sea revenues were put. It would not be possible to isolate additional expenditures or tax reductions in the Fund, which it was felt would be the question of real interest. It could be positively misleading, as it could concentrate attention on the wrong features, namely items of expenditure much of which would have occurred anyway. If attention were required to be drawn to the use of North Sea revenues it would be more appropriate to publish papers on general economic strategy and the choices to be made. There was a further concern that, if the Fund were revenue-determined, the related expenditures would be made contrary to current public expenditure doctrine, and would also contradict the statement in the 1977 White Paper noted above. Hypothecation of the revenues to specific purposes would reduce the scope of the Government to weigh the proposed use of the monies from the Fund against alternative uses. A Fund could give the misleading impression that the revenues were extra and could safely be spent. An expenditure-determined Fund was also open to serious objections. The report felt that it would generate pressure for additional expenditure which could be anticipated as a result of its establishment. The conclusion was that a North Sea Fund was bogus as an analytical instrument, and would have undesirable economic consequences. If it had a real effect on expenditure decisions this would be undesirable, and, if it were a presentational device, it would be seen as such and open to attack.

Scottish Office sympathetic to Fund concept

The Scottish Office felt that most of the perceived difficulties noted above would be avoided if the Fund were to be relatively small, with a fixed sum allocated to it annually and the expenditures devoted to additional initiatives in the regions (perhaps development areas and Northern Ireland). There would be no direct hypothecation of North Sea revenues. The expenditures could be devoted to modernising industry and encouraging investment in the regions, and further modernisation of the infrastructure and environment. The expenditures should be clearly seen as additional. Applications from public and private bodies for funding would be considered by the Government under one model, while under an alternative model Departmental Ministers would make the allocation of funds.

Rest of Committee against Fund

The rest of the Committee did not agree with this version of a Fund. They felt that a small Fund would provoke damaging contrasts with North Sea revenues. They also felt that expenditure decisions should be taken through the normal mechanisms for allocating resources among competing claims. There was no satisfactory way of identifying additional desirable projects which would not have been undertaken in the absence of North Sea oil revenues.

The conclusions of the report thus emphasised the perceived formidable objections to the Fund proposal. The question of how this could be presented in the context of the promised Green Paper on the Benefits of North Sea Oil was awkward. Uncommitted reference could be made to the idea while bringing out the substantial objections (particularly diversion of resources and loss of Government control), but most members preferred to omit any reference to the Fund at all in the paper.

Reflections on Working Party report

The report was submitted to Ministers and fed into the Working Party on the Benefits of North Sea Oil. It clearly had a substantial effect, and it is unfortunate that the analysis of the concept was narrow and incomplete. Both in the literature and in practice the idea of an oil Fund has developed in relation to the concept of sustainable development. The starting point is the notion that the present generation should ensure that future generations are at the very least made no worse off by its actions. This is interpreted to mean that future generations should inherit a total capital stock no less than the current one. The nation's capital stock includes natural as well as man-made capital. The depletion of oil and gas involves a diminution in the national capital stock akin to depreciation of man-made capital. The tax revenues from North Sea oil are thus fundamentally different from, say, income tax or VAT. Under the sustainability approach to the issue a sufficient proportion of the economic rents from the North Sea should be invested to ensure that the diminution in the nation's capital stock from depletion is at least counterbalanced by new investment.[6] Because a high proportion of the economic rents are collected in royalties and taxes the Government is necessarily much involved. The inter-generational aspect of the depletion of the stock of oil reserves was not discussed by the Working Party.

Example of Alaska Permanent Fund

The above does not require a Fund, but it is a device which can ensure that any required distribution of the revenues between investment and consumption is maintained. It can also ensure that the monies are not used for "normal" budget purposes which was a consideration of the Committee which examined the subject. It can do this via the definition of the rules of the Fund and by separating its management from those responsible for the Government's normal budget. There are several examples of petroleum funds around the world which illustrate the possibilities. In Alaska a so-called Permanent Fund was established in 1976 following advice from two Nobel prize-winning economists Kenneth Arrow and Milton Friedman. The Fund is clearly separate from normal Government budgeting, and receives 25% of the annual monies from oil and gas bonus bids and royalties. These monies constitute the principal of the Fund and cannot be withdrawn under the current constitution, thus justifying the title of the Fund. Very broadly the size of the Fund has grown to compensate for the long-term decline in the state's discretionary tax receipts from oil production as oil reserves have depleted.[7] The monies are invested by managers (not by the State) in a portfolio of stocks and shares. The income from these have been distributed to the extent of around 50% in dividends to Alaska residents, while the remainder has in practice been added to the principal (though it could be appropriated by the State if it so chose).

The Alaska Permanent Fund is an example of how a scheme can be devised to ensure that (1) a specified share of the revenues is invested (thus dealing with the sustainability issue), and (2) the Government does not have to become involved in "picking winners" which is generally not a sensible function of Government. The separation of the Fund from normal Government functions also helps to meet the accusation that it duplicates the existing and normal functions of Government. There are several other long-established examples including the Alberta Heritage Fund, the Norwegian Petroleum Fund, and in Kuwait the Reserve Fund for Future Generations. Each has its own distinct constitutional arrangements. While the growth in interest in such funds in other countries such as Azerbaijan does not prove that one was necessary to optimise the benefits from North Sea oil, a well-designed Fund could have avoided some of the problems which dogged the debate in the UK. This did not fully address the sustainability and inter-generational issues and how the nation's total capital stock could be maintained as the oil was depleted. The Committee did not appreciate the potential role of the Fund in this respect, but in effect assumed that it would spend all the monies as soon as they were received. That should not be the purpose of a Fund, a point which has been well recognised by the Shetland Islands Council.

Draft Green Paper on Benefits of North Sea Oil

In late September 1977 a substantial final draft Green Paper on the *Benefits of North Sea Oil* was produced. Despite a warning that North Sea oil revenues would produce extra resources which at their peak would represent the equivalent of only two years' normal growth of GDP the draft paper emphasised the wide range of benefits which they could bring. These were perceived to involve contributions to the solution of a substantial list of both current macro and microeconomic problems, namely the need to (1) control inflation, (2) meet overseas debt repayment obligations, (3) make manufacturing industry stronger and more competitive and to improve the position of the regions, (4) provide for energy requirements when North Sea oil became exhausted, and (5) reduce unemployment and raise real living standards. A contribution to the reduction of inflation could be made through lower taxation and thus moderation of pay settlements. The overseas debt problem could be reduced through producing a significant surplus on current account. The investment overseas of some oil revenues had also been mooted, but the Working Group felt that investment in the UK was likely to produce a substantially greater return. With respect to the regeneration of industry reducing personal taxation could improve work incentives, while extra incentives to the company sector could be given through corporation tax incentives and regional development grants. The public sector could ensure that the infrastructure was improved. With respect to particular sectors encouragement should be given to the use of oil and gas as industrial feedstocks such as in petrochemicals. The Scottish and Welsh Development Agencies and the NEB should be helped in their activities in the areas where economic performance was weak. Oil revenues could also help in the development of a comprehensive manpower policy. In the energy sector the revenues could help in the development of unconventional energy sources, energy conservation, and nuclear power to meet the UK's needs when the oil and gas were exhausted. It was important to ensure that the revenues should not be dissipated in a consumption boom.

Views of Ministers

The draft Green Paper was then circulated to Ministers who eagerly expressed their views. A substantial difference emerged between the Chancellor, Mr Healey, and Mr Benn, the Secretary of State for Energy. Mr Healey broadly supported the draft Green Paper, while Mr Benn's priorities were different. He felt that there should be immediate tax cuts and a reversal of the public expenditure cuts, even before the oil revenues became large, to ease the rise in unemployment. The oil revenues were likely to be relatively small and could decline rapidly after 1990. As oil revenues increased the economy could be expanded through a major extension of planning agreements. Pouring the revenues into a stagnant economy in tax cuts would produce a brief illusion of recovery. The notion of dividing the uses of the oil revenues among (1) debt repayment, (2) sustained tax cuts, and (3) industrial and public investment would not be effective, because the monies available were not large enough to make a worthwhile impact in all three categories. In order that the oil revenues should be visibly and accountably allocated a special Fund should be established, and its accounts should be presented to Parliament. In deciding how the monies should be utilised the overriding objectives should be (1) the rebuilding of the national economy to ensure that it could survive in the 1990s when the oil began to run out, (2) the reindustrialisation of Scotland, Wales, Northern Ireland and the English regions, and (3) the restoration of full employment. Mr Benn disagreed with the view that the revenues should be invested abroad, because this would perpetuate unemployment and there could be no guarantee that the sums invested overseas would return to the UK. Also, he did not favour rapid repayment of debt. This could be rolled over. Rapid and major debt repayment would mean that there could be little stimulus to the UK economy. Using the revenues for a sustained and major tax reduction would create a consumer boom, do little for declining regions, and would entail a further deterioration in the public services. The priorities should be to reconstruct the economy based on the re-equipment of manufacturing industries and improvement of the public services. The planned reconstruction could not be left to the market mechanism or generalised incentives but had to be led by investment of public funds. The NEB and the Development Agencies had major roles to play.

Ministers continued to submit their views on the subject to each other. In mid-November 1977 Mr Healey sent to the Prime Minister the recommendations of the Industrial Strategy Team, an inter-departmental group under the chairmanship of the Department of Industry. These emphasised support for micro-electronics, the encouragement of the chemicals and petro-chemicals industries, and further assistance through the Selective Investment Scheme. Mr Healey endorsed these recommendations, but added that in his view the most important benefit which North Sea oil offered was to improve the macro-economic climate. He emphasised the improvement to the balance of payments and tax reductions.

Cabinet discusses draft paper

Much effort was then exerted to produce an agreed paper between the Chancellor and Mr Benn. The political sensitivities were highlighted by the substantial involvement of their and the Prime Minister's special advisers. Eventually an agreed paper was produced and submitted for cabinet discussion on 15th December 1977. The paper discussed the various options for the use of the North Sea resources along the lines of the official report and Mr Benn's paper discussed above. The pros and cons of the options were discussed, but no firm recommendations on priorities were made. The arguments for and against an Oil Fund were presented. At the meeting a wide variety of views was expressed, largely reflecting those of Mr Healey and Mr Benn. At the end it was decided that the document should start with a statement of the political background and then state the Government's objectives such as the need to (1) invest in new energy resources and conservation in preparation for the time when North Sea oil would run down, and (2) achieve a basis for permanent economic growth and full employment. The question of the desirability of an Oil Fund would be considered further by the Cabinet on the basis of alternative drafts. The Prime Minister would oversee the preparation of a further draft to be produced by the Secretary of the Cabinet. The published paper would be a White Paper indicating the Government's intentions, rather than a Green Paper.

Ministers indicate views

Cabinet members were invited to circulate their own ideas, and this led to substantial correspondence. Mr Bruce Millan, the Secretary of State for Scotland, submitted a draft White Paper in which he highlighted several of the areas of desirable investment already acknowledged by his Cabinet colleagues, but emphasised the need for a special Fund which he felt was necessary to demonstrate how the oil revenues would bring lasting benefits to Scotland and other development areas. Mr Stan Orme, the Minister of State for Social Security, supported the concept of an Oil Development Fund which should ensure that a substantial part of the oil revenues was invested in the public and private sectors. He supported the conclusions of the Industrial Strategy Team, and emphasised the need for investment in newer sectors such as medical equipment. The oil revenues would also permit the economy to grow at a higher rate. It was important to ensure that sterling should not appreciate substantially.

Mrs Shirley Williams, the Secretary of State for Education, emphasised the need for firm commitment to research at the Universities and elsewhere on new energy sources, energy conservation, and industrial regeneration. There was a need for further investment in education in the schools, but also in expanding training in the 16–18 age group to enhance the skills of technicians. Mr Ennals, the Secretary of State for Health and Social Security, emphasised the need for further investment in health and personal social services, especially for the elderly and handicapped. Mr Healey sent his comments on Mr Millan's outline White Paper. He queried the danger of a substantial appreciation in sterling which Mr Millan had felt was a main risk. But his main point was to query the notion of an Oil Fund, whether large or small. A large Fund would introduce the risk of misallocating resources, and would pre-empt possibilities of tax reductions which some colleagues had regarded as a priority. A small Fund would not be helpful in showing how the totality of oil revenues was being spent and would attract criticism because it was small.

Dr David Owen, the Secretary of State for Foreign affairs, was not in favour of a heavy utilisation of the oil revenues to pay off foreign debts which he felt could be rolled over at relatively low cost. The return from investing North Sea revenues elsewhere should be higher. But debt repayment should be used to influence the exchange rate as required. He was not personally endeared to the concept of an Oil Fund, but the political arguments in favour of it were strong, and so he accepted the need for it. The Fund should be used, firstly, to finance public sector projects to strengthen the industrial base which in practice included many of the schemes discussed in the Cabinet paper. Secondly, the Fund should be used to help finance investment in the private sector, and he saw virtue in concentrating assistance on firms which were willing to form planning agreements with the Government. A new Industrial Investment Fund financed by North Sea oil could persuade companies to cooperate. The Secretary of State for Industry emphasised the need to invest in manufacturing industry. He highlighted the importance of the selective assistance scheme, industrial investment financed through the NEB and the Development Agencies, and investment in infrastructure to attract further investment. Finally, Mrs Judith Hart and Mr Frank Judd requested higher foreign aid commitments.

In January 1978 Sir John Hunt, the Secretary of the Cabinet, drafted a White Paper which took into account the suggestions of individual Ministers. He felt that the Paper should concentrate on a few major priorities namely, that North Sea oil revenues would permit (1) the economy to operate at a higher level of demand, (2) higher industrial investment, (3) investment in long-term energy sources, and (4) investment in the social and economic infrastructure. He felt that the suggestions by Ministers for further expenditures on their own Departmental programmes should be resisted. The White Paper would lose credibility if there was "something for everyone" and it would not make the right impact.

The draft White Paper indicated the potential size of the benefits to 1985 highlighting the modest addition to total national resources, but the sizeable addition to Government revenues and the major improvement to the balance of payments. The revenues were not a panacea, but provided an opportunity to enhance the long-term performance of the economy on a sustainable basis and to develop alternative energy sources. The general priorities which would be pursued with North Sea oil revenues were the four summarised above and the paper discussed these further. The need to reduce inflation and promote a new approach to industrial relations were emphasised. As the Prime Minister had requested there was a substantial political tone to the paper. Alternatives for and against an Oil Fund were presented. The case for the Fund was put very weakly, however, stating that it would be somewhat artificial, as its purposes would also be financed through the Government's normal public expenditure programmes, and the distinction between ordinary and additional expenditures would be somewhat arbitrary. The advantages were thus presentational. The inter-generational and sustainability issues which, as discussed above, are central to the case for a Fund were not even mentioned! The case against the Fund emphasised the idea that the intention was to use the benefits of North Sea oil as one element in a much wider economic strategy. It was then argued that this meant that there would be no way of showing clearly which expenditures were additional as a consequence of North Sea oil.

The Prime Minister was pleased with the substance of the paper but felt that its political presentation could be improved. Dr Bernard Donoughue of the Prime Minister's Policy Unit was asked to attend to this. Shortly afterwards the Prime Minister met with senior office-bearers of the Scottish Council (Development and Industry). He asked them about the merits of an Oil Fund. Lord Clydesmuir felt that a Fund would give a sense of discipline in the use of the revenues, and Dr Robertson felt that a Fund would be a visible expression of the benefits of

North Sea oil, and would help to boost regional policy measures which in Scotland were decreasing in effectiveness. A Fund would also help to preserve the unity of the UK which was felt by the Prime Minister to be the ultimate need.

Cabinet discusses draft White Paper

The draft White Paper was discussed in Cabinet on 26th January 1978. This produced requests for some redrafting. Thus the sections on the regions should specifically mention Northern Ireland as one of the beneficiaries. A small majority of the Cabinet were in favour of a Fund. Mr Millan felt that the case for it had not been adequately presented, and submitted a revised paragraph which stated that an Oil Fund was more likely to safeguard the oil revenues coming into the budget from the competing claims of other needs which might be desirable but which were of less long-term value. Several other Ministers sent Minutes with suggested revisions. The Chancellor emphasised the importance of North Sea revenues for facilitating debt repayment. On the very day when the Cabinet discussed the draft White Paper he had announced in the House of Commons that the Government would shortly be repaying debt of $1 billion to the IMF.

Paper on operation of Oil Fund

At the Cabinet meeting it was decided that a paper should be prepared showing how an Oil Fund would operate. This was duly prepared by officials led by the Treasury, but including Scottish Office and Cabinet Office representatives, and was submitted to a further Cabinet meeting in February. The paper was narrow in scope and negative in tone, emphasising the perceived technical problems of three possible forms of funds examined namely (1) large/presentational, (2) large/ additional expenditures, and (3) small/additional expenditures. There was no discussion of the type of arrangement designed for the Alaska Permanent Fund. One perceived technical problem was the likely fluctuations in the annual revenues around a rising trend. There could be a problem in ensuring that the revenues matched the expenditures which would require flexibility in the amounts spent. The alternative could be unspent balances which was felt to be a problem requiring major changes in Government accounting and risking the disapproval of the Public Accounts Committee! The inter-generational issue and the notion that the Fund could deliberately have a permanent capital to ensure sustainability with only the income from it being spent, was not even mentioned.

The memorandum also stated that there would be major problems in identifying additional expenditure from the Fund and in coordinating activities financed by the Fund with those financed by normal Government programmes. With respect to the idea that a share of the revenues from the Fund could be made available to the devolved administrations the memorandum stated that this would run counter to the general approach of the Scotland and Wales Bills by which, within the limits approved by the House of Commons, the devolved administrations would determine their own priorities.

The report was thus very one-sided in its assessment of the operation of a Fund, making no reference to other models such as the Alaskan Permanent Fund. The underlying general assumption was that all the revenues would normally be spent as soon as they were received and any difference between the two sums was a problem! Unfortunately the document had a substantial influence. Sir John Hunt, the Secretary to the Cabinet, in his Minute to the Prime Minister on the subject indicated that he had started with a presumption in favour of a Fund on the grounds that it would impose a discipline on the Cabinet to prevent it from treating North Sea revenues as an extended contingency reserve. He had now concluded, however, that a Fund would be unworkable. A Fund which was essentially cosmetic would be seen through by commentators, and it would not serve its main purpose which was to check on Ministers' spending propensities. Variants of a Fund could be designed to avoid this, but the costs would be high. Thus legislation would be required and there could be difficulties in getting this passed. There could be pressure to hand over large parts of the Fund to the Scots. Further, the administrative arrangements for running the Fund could be inordinately compli-cated. Ministers might be excluded from the decision-making process regarding the use of the Fund monies by the establishment of an independent board, or alternatively several Ministers might be involved in spending money from the same Fund with terrible arguments ensuing. Dangerous rigidity could be intro-duced into spending programmes if these were laid down in the rules for the oper-ation of the Fund. Accounting for the Fund to the PAC would involve half a dozen Departments, and if some of the monies were handed over to the Scottish and Welsh Assemblies there would be further complications regarding the proposed block grants. While none of these objections were individually insoluble taken together they would constitute an administrative nightmare. His conclusion was to back the idea of an annual report to Parliament which would indicate not only the use made of the resources but the revenues as well.

The Cabinet Secretary's Minute did not follow through all the implications of the comments made. Thus the notion that the Fund could be administered by inde-pendent but accountable fund managers would have removed many of the prob-lems identified such as the involvement of squabbling Ministers.[8] It would have ensured that its activities were separate from the Departments' normal programmes. Many of the practical problems of accountability would also have been overcome.

Further Cabinet discussion on fund

The issue was discussed at Cabinet on 9th February 1978 and the Prime Minister expressed his own view that while he had originally been in favour of a Fund he now believed that the practical arguments against it were decisive. The meeting discussed the familiar arguments for the Fund, including the existence of bodies such as the NEB and the Development Agencies which were free of direct Ministerial control. The idea of the establishment of an investment bank charged with using a proportion of North Sea revenues was also mooted. The familiar arguments on the lines discussed above against the Fund were also presented.

Pro-Fund Ministers state their case

The Prime Minister in summing up the discussion indicated that before a final decision was made Ministers in favour of it should prepare a paper indicating how a practical scheme could be devised. Accordingly, the Secretaries of State for Energy, Environment, and Scotland prepared a paper on a North Sea Oil Development Fund. This stated that a non-statutory development Fund could be established without the need for legislation and without administrative complications. An illustrative proposal was that the Fund would secure reinvestment of a substantial part of the North Sea revenues in new industrial and social infrastructure projects with emphasis on regional development in Scotland, Wales, Northern Ireland, and the Development Areas in England. A Ministerial Committee would authorise projects, and the expenditures would be covered by normal Public Expenditure Survey Committee (PESC) arrangements. It was felt that such an arrangement under Ministerial control was preferable, rather than transfer of responsibility to an independent board which could not be relied on to meet the Government's priorities. Ministers would thus retain responsibility for deciding between competing claims on the Fund. The monies would be used to provide additional resources to the NEB and the established Development Agencies. There would also be expenditures on the social infrastructure in the assisted areas.

The establishment of a Fund could constitute a political commitment not to spend all the revenues on consumption, but to earmark a substantial proportion for investment. Without the Fund a generalised statement of commitment would lack credibility and could fail to achieve further investment. The existence of the Fund at least increased the likelihood that investment would be increased in an environment of competing claims. The Ministers were in favour of allocating a large share of the oil revenues to the Fund.

Cabinet Secretary unconvinced

The Cabinet Secretary did not find the paper persuasive and reported accordingly to the Prime Minister. He emphasised practical difficulties, such as how the suggestion for additional expenditures would sit alongside the figures in the Public Expenditure White Paper which already reflected the additional resources from the North Sea. He then came to the conclusion that a Fund would entail the diversion of resources from other published public expenditure programmes, or additional tax or additional borrowing! He also felt that Cabinet would want a fully worked out list of projects in which the Fund monies would be invested. The phrase "industrial investment and infrastructure" was too vague. The Cabinet Secretary's advice was against the Fund. To announce the establishment of a Fund in general terms would mean either pre-empting a decision on public expenditure or a commitment to a paper Fund which would simply reallocate expenditures within an existing total. Both were undesirable.

Cabinet decides against Fund

The paper by the three Secretaries of State was discussed in Cabinet on 16th February. Mr Benn led the argument for the Fund on the lines noted above. The Chief Secretary to the Treasury argued that he also wished to avoid frittering away the revenues, but that a separate Fund would encourage such waste. The key issue was additionality, but it was likely that, almost by definition, industrial projects supported by the Fund would be of lower priority than others in existing programmes. In discussion the familiar arguments for and against the Fund were repeated. These included the criticisms indicated by the Cabinet Secretary in his Minute to the Prime Minister. An interesting point was made to the effect that if there was not to be a Fund was there really any point in having a White Paper at all?

At the end of the discussion it was clear that a substantial majority of the Cabinet now opposed the creation of a separate Fund and the Prime Minister requested that the paper be redrafted accordingly, stating the arguments for and against it, and explaining why it was not practicable. The redrafting should include a statement that an annual report would be made to Parliament indicating progress on how the objectives set out in the White Paper were being met. Even this caused problems, with the Scottish Office arguing that an account of how the revenues were being used should include a list of additional expenditures made possible by North Sea oil. The Treasury on the other hand felt that to segregate these expenditures would be very difficult, and the report should simply be a general economic one, indicating what had been done to expand the economy and in increasing public expenditure without itemising any projects.

White Paper is published

Eventually after still further debate on the details the White Paper was published on 21st March 1978 (Cmnd. 7143). In some ways it reads like a detailed manifesto, due at least in part to the intervention of the Prime Minister who was personally involved in the final drafting and saw it in the context of a future election. Thus the opportunity provided by North Sea revenues was clearly to be viewed in the context of broader economic policies. Economic growth could be enhanced and unemployment reduced, investment in industry could be increased, regional policies could be made more effective, investment in future energy sources and conservation could be enhanced, taxes could be reduced, and public investment on infrastructure and training could be increased. In short, North Sea revenues could contribute to the solution of all the nation's economic ills!

No analysis of inter-generational/sustainability issues

While it was acknowledged that the revenues were finite there was no direct discussion of the implications of this, particularly the sustainability issue and how the benefits should best be shared intergenerationally. The benefits would accrue from their use as an ingredient of macroeconomic and other general economic policies. The whole debate was thus narrow and incomplete. There was excessive emphasis on how the monies should be spent, and a clear implication that they should be spent as soon as they became available. The notion that rules could be established which would ensure that future generations were guaranteed to receive some of the benefits by maintaining capital in the Fund and consuming the income from it was not given serious consideration. The underlying assumption was simply that investment of some of the revenues in projects and/or infrastructure in the current period would ensure that the intergenerational benefits were optimised.

Political atmosphere in later 1970s

The political atmosphere in the mid-and later 1970s encouraged this line of thinking. The newspapers contained discussions on how the revenues should be spent. Politicians thus felt obliged to enter the debate in the same vein. This produced the undesirable result that several Ministers simply argued for enhanced expenditures relating to their own Departments' functions. The case for the capital in the Fund being built up for some years was not seriously considered either by officials or by the small group of Ministers promoting the idea. The full range of options was certainly not put before the Cabinet, and it is interesting to speculate on the outcome of their deliberations had this been done.

Emphasis on oil revenues as part of macroeconomic policy under Conservative Government

Interest in the subject of the utilisation of the benefits continued within Government after the White Paper, though in a somewhat less intense form. Following the election of the Conservative Government in 1979 attention was increasingly given to the use of the revenues as part of macroeconomic policy with their potential contribution to overall tax revenues and the reduction of the growing PSBR being of central importance. The continued appreciation of sterling brought substantial difficulties for the non-oil trading sectors and prompted the memorable intervention by Sir Michael Edwardes, the Chief Executive of British Leyland at the 1980 CBI Annual Conference when he stated that "if they [the UK Government] cannot cope with North Sea oil then leave the bloody stuff in the ground".

Macroeconomic effects of North Sea oil

At this time there was much interest in the relative effects of North Sea oil and other policy measures, particularly the tight monetary stance, on the exchange rate and the economy generally.[9] Most of these studies concentrated on the extent to which the exchange rate and the manufacturing sector were affected by North Sea oil. An interesting and slightly different perspective was given by the Governor of the Bank of England in The Ashridge Lecture for 1980.[10] This argued that the North Sea had made the UK better off only in the relative sense that developing the North Sea was less costly in resource terms than importing the necessary oil. But this was more expensive than the cost of importing oil at the much lower prices ruling in, say, 1970 when the cost was around $2.20 per barrel compared to an average resource cost of around $10 per barrel to produce it from the North Sea in 1980 (within a large range of, say, $5 to $25). The UK was clearly better off now (self-sufficient in oil) than her industrial competitors who had little or no oil, but the coming of North Sea oil was better viewed as the avoidance of a large windfall loss (which competitors in Europe were suffering), rather than the receipt of a large windfall gain. The Governor felt that oil self-sufficiency should be viewed as a reprieve rather than a bonanza. He thus queried the appropriateness of the growing and fairly-widely held view that, because of North Sea oil, it was inevitable or even desirable that industry, particularly the manufacturing elements, should contract or grow less fast. While adaptations to the higher cost of energy were needed these should take place within the industrial sector (including responding to the North Sea opportunity), and in the non-oil economy more widely. New areas of industrial and other activity should be developed to replace those that would fall out. It was necessary to maintain a strong industrial presence during the years of plentiful North Sea oil to moderate what would otherwise be very costly re-entry problems when oil production dwindled.

North Sea oil was a capital asset but a wasting one, and so it was necessary to ensure that a considerable portion of the revenues was devoted to investment. The Governor added that using North Sea oil to maintain living standards might even be held to involve an inadequate allocation of the resources made available to investment and an excessive amount to consumption.

Need to ensure investment of oil revenues?

This thought-provoking assessment ensured that the subject of the wider benefits of North Sea oil continued to receive attention within Government as well as elsewhere. There was some unease within the Treasury by 1981 that more direct use of North Sea revenues to finance investment should at least be considered. There was a feeling in some parts of the Treasury that the Medium Term Financial Strategy (MTFS) was boxing in the Government, and that there might after all be some merit in the ideas associated with a North Sea oil Fund. There had been little or no discussion of the idea since the Conservative Government took office but others, including the Social Democratic Party, the TUC, and even the CBI had been discussing the notion of using North Sea oil revenues for specific purposes rather than as simply an element of macroeconomic policy. Further, there was concern that there was little sign of the hoped for structural changes in the economy which were widely believed to be necessary. Much time and money was being spent on propping up declining sectors and, worryingly, current public expenditure was continuing to rise and capital expenditure to fall. Company profitability and rates of return excluding North Sea oil were consistently falling and were at the lowest ever recorded.

Reconsideration of oil Fund

All these developments prompted some reconsideration of a Fund. Some of the issues debated in 1977 were aired again, with some new elements added such as projects being financed jointly with private sector sources. But the perceived familiar strong arguments discussed earlier against a Fund were still acknowledged. North Sea revenues were already taken into account in the MTFS, and consistency could only be maintained if offsetting savings were made in other public expenditure programmes. But a new element in thinking compared to 1977–78 was that no additional public expenditure would be involved, but rather a change in priority which could be easier to obtain if there were a North Sea Fund. It was acknowledged that some of the earlier arguments against a Fund were misconceived, but it was still arguable, that, if the Government wanted to change its plans to increase investment, a Fund was not necessary to achieve this.

Need for structural change

In discussion within the Treasury it was recognised that structural change was required, partly as a result of North Sea oil, but the question of whether or not the private sector was changing and behaving accordingly was raised. Only if there was no appropriate response due to market imperfections would there be a case for setting up a Fund. There was perhaps a lack of finance available on terms which investors found reasonable, possibly because the banks were very risk-averse, though the Wilson Committee had not found any general problems in this area. On the issue of choice of investment projects there was a concern that civil servants or other bodies such as the National Economic Development Office (NEDO) were not especially perceptive in seeing profitable opportunities. There was in effect a choice between using North Sea revenues to keep down the PSBR and thus interest rates with a given money supply, or allocate them to a Fund for investment. The main potential benefits of the Fund would be to boost the share of investment in total output, and to help to overcome capital market imperfections. The scheme should be market-based whereby the private sector decided on a project, and sought finance from the private sector bank which in turn sought resources from the North Sea Oil Fund. One idea was to build on the loan guarantee scheme which would allow the banks to lay off part of their lending risk while retaining a proportion of it. The North Sea Oil Fund would be a Guarantee Fund. Because the need for structural change was partly due to North Sea oil, hypothecation of the tax revenues to a Fund had some attractions.

Temporary nature of oil resources acknowledged

In further discussion within the Treasury the temporary nature of the extra resources from the North Sea, and thus the need for increased investment, was contrasted with the current (1981) situation when investment was falling and the

North Sea resource was effectively being used to keep other resources in the economy idle. If domestic investment could not be increased the depletion of the resource should be accompanied by an increase in external assets including gold as well as foreign assets. This could relieve the troublesome upward pressure of the exchange rate. The key question was what would the present generation pass on to its successor as an inheritance in substitution for oil. It had to be investment in some form, and if UK domestic investment could not be increased then the North Sea wealth could be stored by investing abroad, which could be done by the Government itself.

Ranking options for utilisation of oil revenues

Another view was that investment abroad, while providing a store of value for later use, would in the interim have no dynamic effects on the UK economy but could be beneficial to other economies. This suggested that the ranking of the order for the utilisation of the North Sea revenues should be (1) domestic investment (public and/or private), (2) external investment (private and/or public), and (3) consumption. But to date (late 1981) the North Sea revenues had been overwhelmingly devoted to consumption. North Sea output had effectively replaced manufacturing output which would otherwise have occurred. The North Sea revenues had been used via taxation and current public expenditures to maintain in idleness the people who would have produced that manufacturing output. Hopefully this would be a temporary phenomenon, and the question was for how long should the North Sea revenues be used for keeping people out of poverty. Increasing the level of investment should be given a higher priority, but it was still not clear that a Fund was necessary for this purpose.

Bank of England's views on impact of North Sea oil revenues on economy

While the debate within Government on how the benefits of North Sea oil should best be utilised continued apace, interest in a Fund declined. But considerable further effort was expended on understanding how the oil revenues were impacting on the economy, and in March 1982 two separate substantial papers were published by (1) a group of senior Treasury officials, and (2) the Bank of England. The Bank's paper[11] was a substantial elaboration of the Governor's Ashridge Lecture with much empirical data added. These included estimates of the large anticipated economic rents from oil production (with an interesting aside showing how measured sales revenues from the Southern North Sea greatly underestimated the true economic value to the nation of the gas output). The benefit of the economic rents accrued in large measure to the Government, and in 1980 these accounted for 4% of total tax receipts. This figure was expected to more than double by 1985. The aggregate present value of the total economic rents from the group of fields outside the Southern North Sea could be around 45% of the GNP of 1980.

The Bank calculated, however, that the two oil price shocks of 1973–74 and 1979–80 resulted in UK real disposable income being reduced more than it was increased by the discovery and development of the North Sea. Thus in 1970–72 less than 2% of GDP was required to produce goods for export in exchange for imported oil, while in 1980 resources equal to 3% of GDP were required to produce North Sea oil and gas. The real resource cost of oil produced in the North Sea was around £23 per tonne before 1973 and £35 per tonne in 1980 (both at 1980 prices). But the Bank emphasised how such calculations overestimated the annual value of North Sea output because no recognition was given to what was termed a wasting asset. Because North Sea oil was a finite asset some allowance needed to be made for this in determining how much production in any year should be reflected in living standards. The Bank calculated that if a 5% real rate of return could be obtained on the present value of the economic rents a significant increase in private plus public consumption of 3%–6% of current GNP would be sustainable, but any excess of net production revenues above this contribution to permanent income, would have to be invested to maintain the real value of capital from the North Sea.

Effect of North Sea oil on exchange rate

The paper discussed at some length the possible effect of North Sea oil revenues on the exchange rate and concluded that the strength of sterling was largely due to factors other than North Sea oil, such as the asset preference of the world's major oil exporters and the high UK interest rates. It was concluded that no large degree of structural change was desirable or inevitable because of North Sea oil. It was other consuming, non-producing countries who had to expand their industrial sectors to pay for higher cost oil. North Sea oil made the nation better off compared to a situation of no oil to the extent of the permanent increase in consumption made possible from the North Sea. This could be around 3%-6% of GNP, while, at least to 1985, the sales revenues net of current costs could be around 5%–7% of GNP. Any excess of the latter over the former should be invested to procure income for the years when net oil imports would again be required.

Treasury views on effect of North Sea oil revenues on economy

The emphasis in the paper by the five Treasury economists[12] stressed the fact that the coming of North Sea oil had coincided with a period of a huge increase in real oil prices. This would have had major implications for the structure of the UK economy if North Sea oil had *not* been discovered, and, to assess the effects of oil relative to past trends, it was necessary to look at the two features (increased UK oil production and oil prices) together.

In a situation of oil self-sufficiency and unchanged oil production there would be no change in the nation's real income following a rise in oil prices, but a redistribution from oil consumers to the producing companies and the Government. The sterling exchange rate could have increased by as much as 10%–15% compared to what otherwise would have happened due to the savings to the balance of trade and capital inflows from the OPEC countries with large surpluses. The rise in the sterling exchange rate would lead to a contraction in the relative size of the manufacturing sector.[13] At this time several independent studies were published on the effects of North Sea oil on the exchange rate and the wider economy. The Treasury estimates were unexceptional, with some other studies on the size of the exchange rate effect being less and others much greater.

Benefits employed as part of macroeconomic policy

Thereafter within Government the continuing pressures of the PSBR ensured that the benefits of the revenues were employed as part of macroeconomic policy. Investment as a share of GDP remained stubbornly low for some years. The incentives from North Sea oil highlighted by Ministers were through the reduced PSBR and thus lower interest rates, and to some extent from lower personal taxation. But it is arguable that the revenues were essentially employed for normal budget purposes, and not enough was done to deal with the sustainability aspect of the depletion of the North Sea reserves. While a Fund was not necessary to achieve this, with the proper constitutional terms it could have ensured that the revenues were deployed to maintain the nation's total capital stock through time and still allow some of the benefits to be taken in ongoing consumption.

North Sea Oil Bond

In the early 1980s a rather different approach to the sharing of North Sea revenues was discussed within Government. In October 1980 Mr Howell, the Secretary of State for Energy, announced the Government's intention to offer to the public a share in North Sea oil through the creation of a revenue bond scheme linked to the fortunes of BNOC's fields. A new personal savings bond would be issued by the Government and the return on it would be related to the revenues from BNOC's North Sea fields. The Government would be committed to redeem it on demand at its accumulated value. It would represent an opportunity to the general public to share directly in the benefits from North Sea oil. At the same time it was announced that (separately) the Government would introduce a Bill to obtain powers to sell to the public equity shares in BNOC.

A considerable amount of work was then undertaken within Government on the details of the bond. The Treasury played a major role here with the Department for National Savings also being involved. By mid-1981 it was agreed that it would be a National Savings Certificate to be named the North Sea Oil Bond with a maturity of five years. The coupon, not the capital, would be indexed, and bond-holders would be protected by a minimum rate of return and be able readily to encash their holdings. The oil index would reflect the sterling value of oil sold by BNOC. These features were the outcome of considerable debate. Initially a marketable instrument providing for a more direct stake in North Sea oil had been contemplated, but it was concluded that the bond as outlined above would ensure protection against offering the investor what could be a bonanza at the taxpayer's expense. The bond would also be appropriate to the small saver to whom it was targeted.

The Working Group developing the bond proposed that the remuneration should comprise (1) a guaranteed amount of interest, (2) a terminal bonus, and (3) an oil bonus. The details were quite complex and are not fully itemised here, but the oil bonus was to reflect the sterling value of North Sea oil sold by BNOC including both equity and participation oil. Because a prospectus had to be issued which included illustrative examples of how the value of the oil bonus might evolve over the five-year period, projections of both volumes and oil price were required. These were always difficult to make, but, at a meeting in July 1981, the recent reduction in the oil price of $4 per barrel had introduced much uncertainty, and the Financial Secretary indicated that he would not wish to proceed with the launch of the bond later in the year if there was a probability of it turning out to be a flop. Investors might hold back from purchasing the bond if oil prices were falling.

Complications from BNOC privatisation proposal

Complications had also arisen with the proposal to privatise BNOC. This raised the prospect of confusion in the public's mind. It might even be felt by bond-holders that the Government was selling off the oil on which the value of their bonds was based! Accordingly, the idea that the bonds should be linked to the value of total North Sea oil production gained favour. Mr Howell felt that the plans for privatisation of BNOC should be announced before the launch of the bond, so that the context could be clearly seen by potential investors.

Draft prospectus

The need to incorporate in the prospectus projections of gross revenues and taxation as well as production for five years ahead caused some consternation within the Treasury, Inland Revenue and DEN, but eventually in October 1981 a draft prospectus was prepared along with a point of sale leaflet. Much work had been done on the guaranteed rate of interest, but this had to be seen in relation to the likely value of the oil index in order to estimate the total expected return. There was some reluctance to publish projections of revenues and taxes in more detail than was already being done, but it was understood that any such material should be made available prior to the launch of the bond.

Abandon North Sea Bond?

Following further deliberations in late November, Treasury officials submitted a Minute to the Economic Secretary recommending strongly that the bond should not be launched before the 1982 Budget, and inviting consideration of the idea that it be abandoned altogether. There were conflicting considerations, namely marketing and adequate disclosure on the one hand, and on the other the need to avoid either the risk of criticism for misleading investors, or tying the Government's hand on major policy issues regarding, for example, taxation and depletion policies. The cost of the scheme to the Government (in terms of expected returns to investors) could be higher than other National Savings Certificates, and would have to be justified as a limited way of spreading the benefits of North Sea oil, rather than as a Government funding scheme. There were serious problems of disclosing all oil policy decisions (which could affect the value of the bonds) when the interests involved went far beyond those of some investors in National Savings Certificates. A delay in the launch beyond the 1982 Budget would be helpful, as taxation and depletion policy decisions relevant to the value of the bond would have been made. But the supply of information problem would reappear for the lifetime of the bond.

The Economic Secretary responded promptly by agreeing that the bond could be postponed until after the budget, and added that his strong preference was for abandoning it. It was a gimmick designed to give respectability to the earlier decision not to privatise BNOC. This was no longer relevant. Further, the oil price had fallen recently and there was a danger that the launch would be a flop. Lastly the possible embarrassment regarding publication of information would remain. Mr Lawson, now Secretary of State for Energy, felt that, while there were political advantages in going ahead with the bond, he was content that the whole project be abandoned. Presentationally there were advantages in announcing this at the same time as the measures to privatise BNOC. Thus the North Sea Oil Bond died before its official birth.

Reflections on utilisation of benefits

It is clear from the discussion in this chapter that successive British Governments were well aware that the benefits from North Sea oil were to be temporary, albeit with much uncertainty about what the time period might be. There was a general understanding that these benefits should not all be consumed by the current generation, but much uncertainty about how they should be optimised through time. The concept of sustainability, now very much in vogue, was known at the time, but how it could best be applied to the inter-temporal allocation of North Sea revenues was not widely appreciated. The appropriate underlying concepts were clearly enunciated in the Bank of England article in March 1982, but the policy applications were not followed through.

While an Oil Fund was not strictly necessary to ensure that the monies were invested on the scale necessary to procure sustainability, if properly designed it could have ensured such a result. Unfortunately the specific schemes considered by Ministers were not designed to procure sustainable development: they were all predicated on the notion that the revenues should be spent as they accrued. The debate was thus not fully informed of all the possibilities. The Shetland Islands Council, while not aware of all the subtleties, did have an understanding of the importance of sustainability.

Nationally North Sea oil revenues have been used as part of macroeconomic policy. In real terms they were largest in the first half of the 1980s when they were used to keep down the PSBR. They were used as components of the normal budget in a period when unemployment was generally increasing to very high levels. The facilitation of long-term investment was in principle via the reduced PSBR and thus lower interest rates. The share of total national investment in GDP remained relatively low, though, of course, it might have been lower still in the absence of North Sea oil revenues. In sum it is difficult to refute the accusation that the revenues were substantially consumed and that insufficient was set aside to maintain the nation's capital stock. The need to sustain consumption from the oil revenues during a period of high unemployment is, of course, perfectly understandable, but, if the claim made at the time by Charles Bean, namely that consumers are "unduly myopic or do not care sufficiently about future generations and are thus unlikely to save as much of the proceeds from oil as is socially desirable",[11] is valid, the accusation is reinforced.

Appendix 13.1

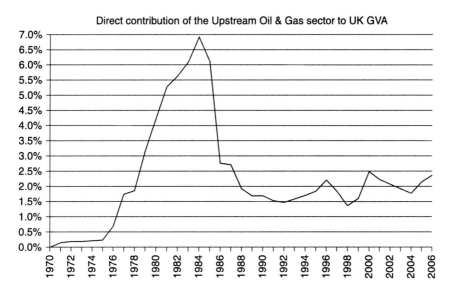

Direct contribution of the Upstream Oil & Gas sector to UK GVA

Appendix 13.2

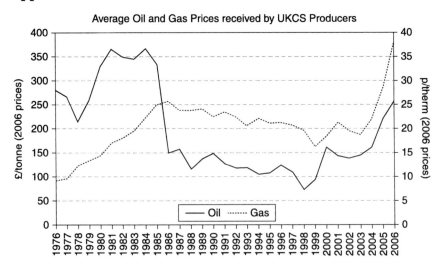

Average Oil and Gas Prices received by UKCS Producers

Appendix 13.3

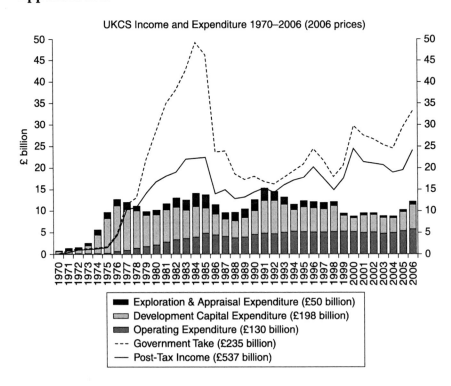

UKCS Income and Expenditure 1970–2006 (2006 prices)

- ■ Exploration & Appraisal Expenditure (£50 billion)
- ▨ Development Capital Expenditure (£198 billion)
- ▨ Operating Expenditure (£130 billion)
- --- Government Take (£235 billion)
- — Post-Tax Income (£537 billion)

Appendix 13.4

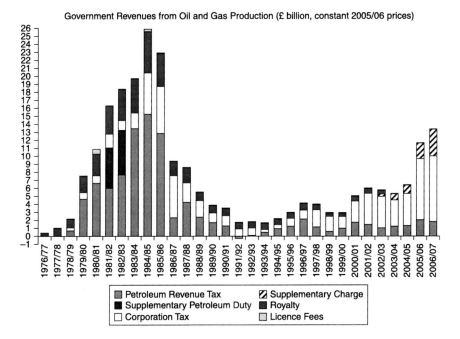

Government Revenues from Oil and Gas Production (£ billion, constant 2005/06 prices)

Conclusions to volume I and preface to volume II

There can be no doubt that the discovery and exploitation of oil and gas in the North Sea was a major event in the post-war economic history of the UK. The size of the reserves discovered in the 1960s and first half of the 1970s greatly exceeded early expectations. The perceived high exploration risks account for the liberal terms of the early licence Rounds. As the scale of the discoveries became clearer and oil prices increased the terms were toughened, particularly with respect to taxation.

The appropriate role of the state was the dominant public policy question throughout the period examined. In the 1960s there was a political consensus that the state should have control over the utilisation of North Sea gas and that producer prices should be cost-related with the benefits being shared between gas consumers and the Gas Council/BGC. A long time was to elapse before the contradictions and distortions in the energy market caused by gas prices being regulated on a cost-related basis while oil prices were freely determined were fully appreciated and reflected in consistent policies.

Increased state control over oil exploitation was the dominant policy theme of the 1970s. This was prevalent in many other oil-producing countries where more draconian state intervention than occurred in the UK was common. In all cases the motives were mixed and not always clear. While security of supply and control over depletion rates were often mentioned in the UK debates enhanced state control for its own sake sometimes emerged as an underlying goal. Individual measures related to a variety of issues, including the extent of state oil company participation, refining and disposal, and opportunities for British industry, as well as a continual tightening of licensing and taxation. Each was justified as being necessary to ensure that the UK received maximum benefit from the gift of this increasingly valuable natural resource. The result was that North Sea oil became the subject of far more state intervention than British industry generally.

While the wisdom of some of the specific policies was the subject of dispute between Government and Opposition there was less disagreement about the need for substantial intervention. This largely reflected the reactions to the disruptions and continued uncertainties in the international oil market in the 1970s into the beginning of the 1980s.

The macroeconomic problems relating to the balance of payments in the 1960s and much of the 1970s clearly played a major role in the policy stance taken towards North Sea oil and gas. The need to maximise benefits to the balance of payments was the underlying justification for many of the policy measures though they were often expressed in terms of energy policy. Similarly, the influence of the PSBR problem played an increasingly dominant role in determining the many changes to both the level and structure of petroleum taxation in the period covered in this volume.

As the 1980s progressed the nature of both the key macroeconomic and energy issues changed. In particular the international oil market exhibited a dramatic change from being tight to very fully supplied. In turn this caused a rethink of oil and gas policies and made possible a major reduction in state intervention without encountering the problems which that intervention was designed earlier to counter. These issues form the subject of Volume 2 of this history, the chapters of which are shown below.

The Official History of North Sea Oil and Gas
Volume II: Moderating the State's Role

Chapter 1 – Natural gas in the new market environment
Chapter 2 – Oil policies in the new market environment
Chapter 3 – Taxation for changing market conditions
Chapter 4 – Licensing in changing market conditions
Chapter 5 – The demise of state intervention
Chapter 6 – Further taxation developments
Chapter 7 – The onshore impact and policies
Chapter 8 – Licensing and related issues into the 1990s
Chapter 9 – Health and safety
Chapter 10 – Decommissioning and environment
Chapter 11 – Concluding reflections

Notes

Preface

1 Excluding Gas Levy.
2 Notable examples of files which have been destroyed are all those of BNOC and those of the Offshore Supplies Office relating to the period from 1982 onwards.

1 Initial legislation and licensing

1 The results of the conference are conveniently summarised in *Report of the First United Nations Conference on the Law of the Sea*, Cmnd. 584, HMSO, November, 1958. This document contains the text of the Four Conventions.
2 *ibid..* p.40
3 *ibid..* p. 11
4 *ibid..* p. 40
5 *ibid..* pp. 11, 12
6 *ibid..* p. 41
7 *ibid..* p. 12
8 This summary of the pre-1964 legislation draws on the admirable discussion by M. Lynch-Bell and I. J. Robbie "Licences, their Economics and Royalties" in *United Kingdom Oil and Gas Accounting*, Chiltern Publishing, 1991, Chapter D.
9 M. Lynch-Bell and I. J. Robbie, *ibid..* p. D1/4.
10 See D. J. Payton-Smith, *Oil: A Study of Wartime Policy and Administration*, HMSO, London, 1971.
11 U. R. Vass, "A Comparison of American and British Offshore Oil Development During the Reagan and Thatcher Administrations: Part II", *Tulsa Law Journal*, Vol. 21, No.2. 1985, pp. 225-316.
12 U. R. Vass *ibid.* p. 229.
13 T. Daintith and G. D. M. Willoughby, *A Manual of United Kingdom Oil and Gas Law*, Oyez Publishing Ltd, London, 1977 p. 236.
14 *The Guardian*, 5th August 1964.

2 The early North Sea boundary issues

1 The Gnomonic projection also has several flaws. It is not conformal, and the radial scale (from the poles) increases rapidly, and thus distance measurement may be unreliable. The Hydrographic Department of the Ministry of Defence were aware of the limitations of the technique but "considered it sufficiently accurate for the present purpose".
2 T. Daintith and G. D. M. Willoughby, *ibid..* p.5.
3 International Court of Justice *North Sea Continental Shelf Case*, 1969, p.32.

4   *ibid.* p.31.

5   Daintith and Willoughby, *ibid.* p.7

6   The dispute between Denmark and West Germany had substantial implications. In 1963 the Danish Underground Consortium (DUC) led by the A. P. Møller group was awarded an exclusive licence for the whole of the Danish Continental Shelf. The boundaries with neighbouring countries were not yet determined. The DUC subsequently undertook exploration and made a discovery in an area which, though in the Danish sector according to median line principles, was claimed by West Germany. For a discussion of this from the investor's viewpoint see M. Hahn-Pedersen, *A. P. Møller and the Danish Oil*, Schultz, 1999. The International Court made its judgement that the boundary should be determined on the basis of the natural extension of the countries into the sea, rather than on median line principles. This led to further negotiations between the two countries and an eventual agreement which put the discovery in the Danish sector.

4   The early gas contracts

1   The White Paper, *Fuel Policy*, (Cmnd. 3438) had just been published (on a pre-devaluation basis). It projected a natural gas market of 4,000 mmcf/d by 1975.

2   The National Board for Prices and Incomes had just produced a report on gas price increases which was proving politically very controversial.

3   There had been direct cost-related contracts between these companies and Government Departments which became very controversial on the issue of "excessive" profits. The North Sea gas contracts were conceptually quite different.

4   This refers to the extent to which the base is above the initial price. In the Phillips contract it was 10%.

5   G. Polanyi, *What Price North Sea Gas?* Hobart Paper No. 38, Institute for Economic Affairs, January, 1967.

5   The coming of oil, the Fourth Round controversy and its consequences

1   Flow rate of 1,000 b/d or more from a test well for oil and 15 mmcf/d or more for gas.

2   See J. Bamberg, *British Petroleum and Global Oil 1950–1975: the Challenge of Nationalism*, Cambridge University Press, 2000, pp. 202-203. Another indicator of the initial scepticism of the company regarding the prospect for oil was the offer made by a well-known BP geologist to drink every barrel of oil found in the North Sea. See Petroleum Exploration Society of Great Britain, *Newsletter*, July, 1999.

3   For details of the situation at the time as perceived by Shell see R. Moreton (ed.) *Tales from Early UK Exploration 1960–1969*, Petroleum Exploration Society of Great Britain, 1995, ch. 6.

4   *North Sea Oil and Gas*, First Report from the Committee of Public Accounts Session 1972–73, HC. 122, February, 1973.

5   While this may be correct with respect to the Excess Revenue Tax it is generally incorrect with respect to a severance tax, payments of which occur from early in field life.

6   Further gas developments and the Frigg contracts

1   This point is generally misconceived. It is the provision of pipelines which can be regarded as a natural monopoly. The supply of gas through them can be organised competitively. Use of the gas industry's pipelines on behalf of third parties was already recognised. A then current example was the proposal that BP send gas from the West Sole field through a gas industry pipeline to its works at Saltend on the Humber.

2 The Price Commission had just refused to allow price increases on the scale requested by BGC.

7 Designing the tax package

1 This was a misconception. The Government would have a share in the licence but not in the ownership of the investor.
2 The concept is also consistent with later thinking on the issue. See for example, A. G. Kemp, "Petroleum Exploitation and Contract Terms in Developing Counties after the Oil Price Collapse", *Natural Resources Forum*, May, 1989 and D. Lund "Petroleum Tax Reform Proposals in Norway and Denmark, *The Energy Journal*, Vol. 23, No. 4, 2002. In the latter paper an alternative mechanism to procure earlier revenues is proposed through the allowances for field investment not being given on 100% first year basis but spread over a longer time period, with the allowed margin expressed as a percentage of the reducing balance of the investment.
3 Edmund Dell, "The Origins of Petroleum Revenue Tax", *Contemporary Record*, Vol. 7, No. 2, Autumn 1993, pp. 215–252.
4 R. G. Garnaut and A. I. Clunies-Ross, "Uncertainty, Risk Aversion and the Taxation of Natural Resource Projects", *Economic Journal*, June, 1975. pp. 272-287. The tax was first introduced in Papua New Guinea in 1974.

8 Providing for BNOC and enhanced state control

1 To put this in perspective by the end of 2004 a cumulative total of 3 billion tonnes had been produced and the DTI estimated that the remaining potential (including substantial undiscovered resources) was in the 1–1.9–3.6 billion tonnes range with 1.9 billion tonnes being the central estimate.
2 Like all such longer term projections these made in 1974 turned out to be quite inaccurate. Actual production in 1980 was 80 million tonnes and in 1990 91.6 million tonnes (including onshore and condensate). In the latter year oil consumption was 71.6 million tonnes.
3 This was before the concept of approval of field development plans (later widely termed Annex B approval) had been introduced in legislation.
4 In fact UK refinery throughput peaked at 114.3 million tonnes in 1973 and became 86.3 million tonnes in 1980 and 78.4 million tonnes in 1985.
5 *The Press and Journal*, editorial, 15th July 1974.
6 Alistair Gibson, "BNOC in Glasgow – Political or Practical", *The Oilman*, 17th May 1975.

9 The new policy in action: State participation

1 It actually fell substantially over the period 1975–1985.
2 The undertakings and the main support measures were announced by Mr Varley in January 1975. See *Hansard* 25th January 1975 cols. 448–449.
3 It is noteworthy that DEN had no formal powers in the approval of operators until the Fifth Licence Round.
4 *Nationalised Industries and the Exploitation of North Sea Oil and Gas*, First Report from the Select Committee on Nationalised Industries, Session 1974–1975, HC. 345
5 The difference between this figure and the 26.5% in the Assignment is explained by the company's continued responsibility for the royalty obligation of 12.5% on the assigned interest.
6 They also sought assurances on other matters such as continuity of security in the event of revocation of a licence in circumstances where the field was the key source of repayment of the loan.

7 The saga of Tricentrol's loan guarantees was to continue for a long time afterwards. In December 1976 the company asked DEN to extend the size of the loan guarantee from £60 million to £75 million to meet their investment commitments in the Thistle field. The Government agreed to an extra £10 million but on tougher terms, including the payment of management and reservation fees. Eventually the company was able to replace the Government-guaranteed loan with a conventional commercial one from the banks as production from Thistle grew. In August 1979 the company was permitted to commute and pre-pay the special royalty, and in June 1980 it repaid the last of the debts guaranteed by the Government. DEN obtained fees of £17.39 million for provision of the loan guarantees.

8 There had been press criticisms to this effect when the Memorandum of Principles was published.

10 The new policy in action: Further licensing and related issues

1 The issue arose because royalties were payable on the whole of a licence area which could extend to several blocks, and area fees could be offset against royalties on any of the licence blocks.

2 It is noteworthy that Norway introduced sliding-scale participation at this time.

3 This argument implies that the exploration effort would remain unchanged whether BNOC participated as a full risk taker or on a carried interest basis. But the expected return (expected monetary value) facing the oil company will be less with carried interest and at 51% the result could then be that less exploration would be undertaken.

4 The paper notes that licence fees over a four-year period could produce £0.2 million in receipts but does not discuss the much larger sums that would ensue from the exploitation of one or more discoveries.

5 The incentive to do so was increased because BGC paid its share of all costs on a pay-as-you-go basis.

6 There was a further irony in relation to the disputed Blocks 132/15 and 133/11. The original intention had been to award them to Amoco!

7 "The Times", 21st November 1978.

8 The sometimes aggressive attitude of BNOC management is evident from correspondence with the DEN. Unfortunately BNOC's own files have been destroyed.

11 Increasing the Government take

1 At this time spot prices were noticeably below long-term contract values.

2 At this time inflation was very high in the UK generally and in the UKCS in particular. But the concept of indexing for inflation in such a tax system was reasonably well known as it was for gas contracts.

3 Officials had become concerned that the interaction of the uplift with the safeguard for PRT could in certain circumstances produce a situation where an incremental investment resulted in more than 100% tax relief.

4 C. Robinson and J. Morgan, *North Sea Oil in the Future*, Trade Policy Research Centre, 1978. The authors argued that increases in the rate of PRT would not bring significant extra revenues because, in the shorter term at least, the various allowances removed much of the effective liability.

5 Thus the sixth month chargeable period ending 31st December 1979 would become one for the four months from 1st July to 31st October and the PRT in respect of it would become payable on 1st March 1980.

6 This was an unintended consequence of the clumsy safeguard provision which was designed to assist fields of low profitability

7 The details of the scheme were quite complex. Thus at 1st March 1981, when the companies made their payments on account for the chargeable period ending 31st December 1980, the advance payment would be the larger of (a) 15% of the assessed liability for the previous but one chargeable period (January-June 1980), or (b) 15% of the payment on account for the previous chargeable period (July-December 1980). In papers before the Budget decision figures much higher than 15% were considered.

8 These criticisms are unconvincing. In the conventional resource rent tax (by this time well-established in the literature) no depreciation calculation is required. The return on the investment is found by compounding forward the net cash flows relating to the defined investment which could be field-based (as for PRT) or block-based. The question of choice of tax rates is no more difficult with a resource rent tax than with PRT or other comparable tax.

9 The average or effective rate is certainly progressive as the allowances shelter a smaller proportion of the field income as oil prices rise.

10 These are not inherent problems of the scheme but emanate from the choice of specific threshold and tax rates. For a detailed exposition see R. Garnaut and A. Clunies Ross, *Taxation of Mineral Rents*, Oxford University Press, 1983.

11 In fact it was available irrespective or whether any loan finance was employed at all.

12 It is ironic that this defect in the oil allowance was pointed out at the very time when it was being proposed for the new supplementary tax.

13 This was because the alternative schemes examined were based on returns on investment, which, in conjunction with the chosen high rates of tax, produced incentives to wasteful expenditures. But threshold and tax rates can be designed to avoid this problem.

14 Most analysts at this time felt that oil prices would continue to rise. The 1981 budget was eventually prepared on the basis of oil prices increasing in *real* terms by 2% per year (and thus at much higher rates in money-of-the day terms). In fact they peaked in early 1981 and subsequently fell to $10 in July 1986.

15 Through a curiosity of Government accounting the Gas Levy is not formally shown as a North Sea tax or royalty because it is regarded as a tax on expenditure (by BGC).

12 Depletion and conservation policies

1 An interesting speculative question is whether the pricing of natural gas at well below its market value along with earlier underestimation of the reserves of gas produced the result that a gas collection scheme was uneconomic.

2 To put this in perspective at July, 2005 the DTI central estimate of the ultimate oil potential was 4.88 billion tonnes with a low value of 4 billion tonnes.

3 The framework for the modelling is broadly consistent with the famous Hotelling model and is subject to the same limitations as that model. See. H. Hotelling "The Economics of Exhaustible Resources", *Journal of Political Economy*, Vol. 72, No. 1, 1931.

4 This turned out to be a substantial exaggeration.

5 To put this into perspective by the end of 2005 around 71.6 tcf had been produced from the UKCS. Remaining potential (including undiscovered) was estimated by the DTI at July 2005 at 55 tcf (central case) and 33 tcf (low case).

6 The production projections for the mid-1980s accorded well with the outcome of 127 million tonnes in 1985. The oil demand projection for 1990 was much higher than the outcome of 80 million tonnes.

7 This was later published as *Energy Policy: a Consultative Document*, Cmnd. 7101, HMSO, February, 1978.

8 The maximum cutback compatible with the Varley Assurances was 22% in the first year reducing by 1 percentage point per year thereafter.

9 In the event the earlier estimate was very close to the outturn.

10 It should be emphasised that DEN long-term projections of oil production made in the period 1975–1983 were *higher* than those made by most other analysts.

13 Utilising the benefits

1 Royal Commission on The Constitution, 1969–1973, Cmnd. 5460, HMSO, October, 1973.

2 It is again noteworthy that no mention was made of the sharing of licence fees and royalties with the Isle of Man and Northern Ireland Governments. This issue remained live. Thus when PRT was introduced the Isle of Man Government requested that the revenues be shared on the same basis as royalties. The UK Government refused on the legalistic grounds that PRT was not a licence consideration. When SPD was introduced the Isle of Man Government received the same response to its request for a share of these revenues.

3 The figures were always highlighted in this cumulative form, probably to dramatise them. On an annual average basis the estimates were £2.9 million to 1984 and £4.35 million to 1990.

4 A good example is A. Scott (ed.), *Natural Resource Revenues: a Test of Federalism*, University of British Colombia Press, Vancouver, 1976.

5 A more detailed account of these issues is to be found in W. Mackie, *The Impact of North Sea Oil on North East Scotland, 1969–2000*, Ph.D. Thesis, University of Aberdeen, 2001

6 The issue as discussed in the literature is substantially more complex depending on whether weak or strong sustainability is involved. There are also different approaches to the valuation of the depletion of reserves including not only the depreciation method but the user cost or permanent income approach. The Central Statistical Office took a commendable interest in the issue. For a good discussion see C. Bryant and P. Cook, "Environmental Issues and the National Accounts", *Economic Trends*, No. 469, November, 1992, pp. 99–122, and P. Vaze "Environmental Accounts – Valuing the Depletion of Oil and Gas Reserves" ' in P. Vaze (ed.), *UK Environmental Accounts 1998*, SO, 1998. On the wider issues see D. W. Pearce, *et al. Blueprint 3: Measuring Sustainable Development*, Earthscan Publications, 1993, S. G. Hall and F. Atkinson, *Oil and the British Economy*, Croom Helm, 1983, and T. Tietenberg, *Environmental and Natural Resource Economics*, Pearson Educational, 2006, Chapter 5.

7 See R. Hannesson, *Investing for Sustainability: the Management of Mineral Wealth*, Kluwer, 2001, Chapter 5.

8 This is a feature of the Alaska Permanent Fund.

9 See, for example, P. J. Forsyth and J. A. Kay, "The Economic Implications of North Sea Oil Revenues", *Fiscal Studies*, Vol. No. 3, July 1980, T. Barker and V. Brailovsky (eds.), *Oil or Industry?*, Academic Press, 1981, and G. D. N. Warwick, " North Sea Oil and the Decline of Manufacturing", *National Institute Economic Review*, No. 94, 1980.

10 See "The North Sea and the United Kingdom economy: some longer term perspectives and implications", *Bank of England Quarterly Bulletin*, Vol. 20, 1980.

11 "North Sea Oil and Gas – Costs and Benefits", *Bank of England Quarterly Bulletin*, Vol. 22 No. 1, March, 1982.

12 I. Byatt, N. Hartley, R. Lomax, S. Powell and P. Spencer, *North Sea Oil and Structural Adjustment*, Treasury Working Paper No. 22, March, 1982.

13 The Chancellor had seen a draft of the Treasury paper and commented on one of its assumptions, namely that world oil prices were likely to rise in real terms between the mid-1980s and 2000. Prophetically, he felt that a falling real oil price was much more plausible.

14 C. Bean, *The Macroeconomic Consequences of North Sea Oil*, London School of Economics, Centre for Labour Economics, Discussion Paper No. 262, November, 1986.

Index